# A History of Religion

# A History of Religion

By

HERBERT H. GOWEN, D.D., F.R.As.S.

*Professor of Oriental Studies in the University of Washington*
*Hon. Fellow St. Augustine's Coll., Canterbury*
*Author of "The Universal Faith," "Asia, a Short History," "An Outline History of Japan," "A History of Indian Literature," &c.*

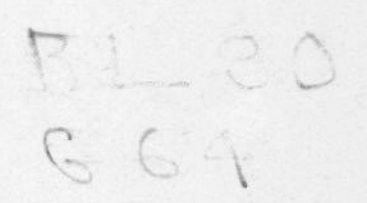

THE MOREHOUSE PUBLISHING CO.
MILWAUKEE, WIS.

*First published* 1934

PRINTED IN GREAT BRITAIN BY THE EDINBURGH PRESS, EDINBURGH

## FOREWORD

THE present volume follows on the general lines of a smaller book, entitled *The Universal Faith*, I published some years ago.[1] It also uses some of the material there assembled. But I have attempted here something much more ambitious. It is indeed a survey so comprehensive in its scope that a few of my friends tell me it is the attempting of the impossible, namely, the relating of the entire religious story of mankind, from as near as we can get to the beginning up to the present stage of its unfolding.

No one can be more sensible of the difficulties to be expected in the effort to treat such a subject, or of the many ways in which I was bound to fall short in fulfilling my heart's desire. In many respects defects have been corrected by the kind advice of colleagues and associates in many parts of the world. I am sorry that, through the exigencies of travel, in some cases suggestions reached me too late for use in the text. For example, the chapter on Egyptian Religion would be much less faulty had I been able to use help which came too late from Dr. S. A. B. Mercer, of Trinity College, Toronto. To all my friends, however, too numerous to be separately mentioned, I offer sincere acknowledgment. I wish, however, specially to acknowledge the sympathetic patience of Dr. W. K. Lowther Clarke, of the *Society for Promoting Christian Knowledge*, whose help has followed me over many thousand miles of sea and land. If any errors still remain (as in all human probability is the case), I must ask the consideration of the critical. I should be ungrateful indeed, again, if I did not express gratitude to my wife for assistance in the arduous task of compiling the Index.

[1] Morehouse Publishing Company, Milwaukee, 1926. Third Edition, 1929.

My main hope now is that, through all the labyrinthine ways of the human story, which I have endeavoured to trace, there may be made plainer to the eyes of my readers the vision of a divine purpose slowly but surely being realized, through which the human spirit is being led towards the goal set forth from all eternity.

HERBERT H. GOWEN.

TOKYO
Feast of all Saints
1933

# CONTENTS

## BOOK III.

## THE STATE RELIGIONS OF ANTIQUITY



## BOOK IV.

## THE RELIGIONS OF THE ORIENT



## BOOK V.

## THROUGH JUDAISM TO THE CHRIST

## SECTION II.—CHRISTIANITY TO THE RISE OF ISLAM



## SECTION III.—THE STORY OF ISLAM



## SECTION IV.—THE SECOND MILLENNIUM OF THE CHRISTIAN CHURCH

# A History of Religion

## INTRODUCTION

MANY books have been written on the history of religion; more still on the history of religions. Of these, too, many have been written in a spirit of supposedly scientific detachment from any particular conviction as to religion itself. Hence, to avoid misunderstanding, I wish to confess here and now that the present volume is conceived unashamedly from the Christian point of view.

At the same time, lest so naïve a confession should seem from the first to invalidate my attempt, let me add that I do not thereby adjudge myself disqualified from showing respect to the facts which a survey of such a subject must necessarily involve. On the contrary, such a standpoint for me seems to unify the survey in a manner which otherwise would appear unthinkable. I make here no criticism of those who write histories of religions as though these were separate developments of the human spirit, unrelated to one another, and unrelated to any general scheme of cosmogony. My reasons for rejecting such a method will appear as I proceed. For me religion can mean little at all unless it represent a biological necessity, implanted in mankind by the author of life, going back beyond the dawn of human consciousness, and extending onward beyond our term of existence upon this planet, even to the ultimate goal of human evolution. To use the words of John Dewey: "Religion is a universal tendency of human nature." Such an approach forces me to conceive of religion as vitally and continuously associated with life, as it has been through the indefinite past, as it is to-day, and as it is to be throughout the ages of the future. There is no religious interest of the past which is without survival value for the present, and which is not predictive of completer expression and experience in the future.

A general sympathy for, and appreciation of, all forms of religious belief and practice seems to demand that these should find inclusion within the bounds of an all-comprehensive scheme which is purposeful from the beginning and which represents an advolution as well as an evolution. To study a number of religious systems, embodying human ideals which have been fertilized with the contributions of great personalities (unknown as well as known), only to arrive at the conclusion that they are all equally true or equally false, would be ruinously disastrous to our spiritual life. Or to study the subject merely in order to reach the conclusion of Auguste Comte that religion represents an attitude towards the problems of life which must be presently superseded and pass away, would make a history of religion only of archæological interest, a story ending in futility, like a stream such as promised to be the river of the water of life in the City of God ending in a desert.

If I may make my own conviction clear once for all, it is that the Christian religion supplies just that unifying principle for the religion of the past and of the future which we need to render the entire subject intelligible. It assures us as to the ultimate significance of the end, even as it postulates an initial purpose, all within the bounds of a creative process. Others may find some other kind of unifying principle; for myself I can only see the history of religion against the background of a Christian philosophy. And I love to think that the old Keltic Christians had some such idea when they built their churches (as in Brittany and Wales) within the great stone circles of their pagan ancestors. Even if only half conscious of what they did, their action pointed to the proper synthesizing of religious systems and experiences.

Perhaps I may put the substance of what I have in mind in the form, as it were, of a diagram. It was Lord Salisbury's advice to those engaged upon big questions of foreign policy that they should learn to use large maps. To judge rightly of a subject so vast that it includes the consideration of all past human history and the forecast of

ll that is to come, nothing may suffice except the largest
nap of all, namely, the entire scheme of cosmic purpose
uch as embraces all history and at the same time starts
nd closes with some vision of the eternal. Such a plan
nay present itself in the form of a double triangle (in shape
ot unlike an hour-glass), with the apices of the two
riangles in contact. The apices are supposed to be in
istory, but the two base lines represent the eternity of the
ast and the eternity of the future. In the first of these
wo triangles we may think of God as revealed in relation
o a plan to be unfolded which includes nothing less than
ll heaven and earth, that is, the universe. The base line
ives a starting-point from which is seen the working out
f a process which by successive siftings and selections
rings us to our first apex, a single point at which (for
hristians) is concentrated in Christ the full revelation of
od, the first-fruits of the ideal creation. From this point,
n history, as from a second apex coincident with the first,
tarts our second triangle, revealing the process by which
he ideal realized in the first-fruits is reproduced in the
nass. By a succession of expansions and inclusions, the
ffects of the divine revelation are seen broadening out
owards that ultimate base line which represents—in contact
vith eternity—the purpose of creation realized, as a new
eaven and a new earth, that is, a new universe.

Now as to the ideal completeness of the former triangle
here will be—for Christians—little or no question. All
hings here are seen climbing out of nothingness to set
heir feet upon the way (which is Christ) towards the goal
which is also Christ). From atom to cell, from cell to
iving organisms of every kind, from these again upward to
nan, the way is continuous. With man appears that
" sense of the numinous " which is the history of religion
tself in germ. Man's " august anticipations, hopes and
ears " contain within themselves the prophecy of his
lestiny. His aspirations shape themselves as a quest for
od; his failures to realize fellowship with God beget the
ense of sin; his efforts to remedy these failures become
reeds and cults, institutions and disciplines. As time
oes on, the moral earnestness of mankind digs and deepens

channels into which the currents of religious history are seen to flow. Into one of these channels, dug by an otherwise insignificant branch of the Semitic family, flow not only the clarified feeling, reasoning and activity of the primitive religions, but also the accumulated gains of the great world religions of Babylon, Egypt, Persia, Greece and Rome. Finally, as I have already suggested, our triangle finds its apical point in the Christ, the full revelation of God, as at once transcendent, immanent and human, the revelation, moreover, of human life present and to come, a microcosm of the perfect society which is by and by to be realized in the City of God.

May I not find in the symmetry of such a cosmic plan (no longer to be regarded, since Sir James Jeans' *Mysterious Universe*, as the mere figment of a pious imagination) the fitting background against which we may set the slow unfolding of religious ideas from prehistoric times to the present and against which we may forecast the possibilities of religious development in the centuries to come?

Moreover, may I not here set forth what I conceive to be the method by which religious advance has been made in the past and by which religious unity is to be secured in the future?

There would appear to be three possible conceptions of the road to be followed toward the realization of a universal religion.

The first is what we may call the *exclusive* way, by which I mean the method of securing universality through the repression and exclusion of all but one of a number of competing systems. On this theory we must deal with religions as the Masoretic editors of the Old Testament dealt with the various readings of the then existing Hebrew MSS., or as the "Companions" of the Prophet dealt with the varying copies of the Quran—with the result that the present uniform texts are more confusing and, of course, less accurate than would have been the perpetuation of the many textual differences. Similarly men have argued that if all religions but one are eliminated, the victorious creed and cult would have an indisputable title to universality. Missionaries of all faiths have occasionally taken this view

I have a copy of an old Indian missionary's account of the *Gods of South India* which was refused publication by the Society to which he was accredited because he "was sent to India to destroy the gods and not to write about them." Far be it for me to deny that he who would promote the cause of universal religion must at times be a good and courageous iconoclast. "When the gods arrive the half gods must go." Doubtless men like Boniface had ample warrant for smashing the images which held back the Frisians from giving up their paganism. But we must be careful lest in smiting at the religion of primitive people we smite where God has left some witness to Himself, rather than at what is literally a *superstitio*, that is, a "hold-over"—something which has outlived its use. The story of Paphnutius, casting a stone at the Sphinx and hearing from the smitten lips of limestone the gently breathed name of Christ, is a warning to those who would heedlessly destroy all outside of their own (often narrow) conception of a creed.

The second path is that which we may name the *eclectic* or *syncretistic*, that is, the picking out of elements here and there from various creeds to make a kind of cosmopolitan patchwork with appeal to everybody. Of course, all religions borrow, more or less unconsciously, from one another, but I am speaking not so much of the subtle osmosis which is a part of every vital process as of the deliberate attempt to build a system out of discongruous elements. It has been a method with special attraction for some, especially in lands which have a syncretistic culture. It was pre-eminently the Persian way, from the days of Mani and Mazdak down to the time of Babism and the eclectic systems which have from thence made their way to the United States. It may prove the American way unless we perceive the futility of the method and stop cluttering up our religious life with the wrecks of short-lived systems of this type. For, even though men doubt the wisdom of Horace, who taught the folly of so combining diverse parts that "turpiter atrum desinat in piscem mulier formosa superne," we might learn from science that such is not the organic and natural way to make anything that is to live.

The third and only possible path is that which we call the *evolutionary*. It may seem strange at this date to confess the necessity of having to guard oneself from the implication that an evolutionary method of reaching universal religion has to be a method deprived of the purposeful and directive power of God. No study of process, however deep or high, can be effective which does not feel continuously the mystery that lies in and beyond the process. As a little child, gazing at eventide upon the sun-suffused sky, expressed the thought that "God is shining through," so it must be with the student in any department of knowledge. To use familiar words:

> A fire-mist and a planet,
> A crystal and a cell,
> A jelly-fish and a saurian,
> And caves where cave-men dwell;
> Then a sense of love and duty,
> And a face turned from the clod;
> Some call it Evolution,
> And others call it God.[1]

In forming an evolutionary conception of religion we do not thereby represent the universe as hurtling through time and space uncontrolled, like some train with a dead engineer at the throttle, but as something which needs God in it and with it all the way from the first impulse of "the love that moves the sun and all the stars." It is God, faithful to Himself throughout, exhaustless energy harnessed to an infinite idea, in the animal which "climbs up its own genealogical tree," as well as in the spirit which seeks to rise to closer co-operation with a divinity whose kinship is felt and understood.

It is obvious that such a conception of religion supplies us with adequate reasons for regarding history as "a novel with a plot"—all the past as the sphere for the operation of "that Holy Spirit of assimilation" which we call Revelation; all the present, with its apparent tragedy and waste, as part of that act of creation which is itself limitation and Passion; all the future as the assured triumph of Him who sees from the beginning to the end the travail of His

[1] Professor Carruth, quoted by R. F. Horton, in *Great Issues*.

soul and its reward. The story of the universe is one story whether, from above, we regard it as the revelation of a transcendent God, or, from below, as the evolution of a creation in which the divine element is necessarily immanent. Not only is the moral advance of man a divine unfolding and growth, but the physical, too, God's secret working at the web and woof of the flesh, that our bodies may become at length the shrine of the All-holy.[1]

Is it not essential for the unity of religion that Christianity should not merely fit into but actually itself comprise such an evolutionary scheme? It is certain that a Christianity which is simply regarded as one religion among a number of competing systems, perhaps mainly true where others are mainly false, or a Christianity regarded as a kind of medley, made up of the shreds and patches of Judaism and the mystery cults, must be a very different thing from the Christianity which claims to be coextensive with the entire divine purpose, something, in fact, which may be fitly called a cosmic epic, in the sense intended by Dante in his *Divina Commedia*.

There have, of course, been dark ages in Christian history when the more limited conception of religion was common, if not general. Perhaps there are still to-day those to whom the gods of other religions are nought but devils and all earlier forms of ministry or sacrament but the blasphemous parodies of Satan. There are, again, those to-day for whom Christianity is sufficiently explained as a complex eclecticism, with elements borrowed from Jew and Greek, from Persian and Buddhist. Yet, if we ask what is Christianity's own claim, in the light of its hope to be the answer to all men's prayers and the supply of all men's needs, the reply will be no uncertain one.

In one of the old Mystery Plays a figure crosses the stage at the beginning of the performance which is explained as "Adam on his way to be born." Similarly, long before the curtain of the New Testament lifts, we are made aware that if the light of the Cross is to stream infinitely forward,

[1] Psalm cxxxix. 15.

it must also illuminate the way back to the very beginning.[1] The very fact that the New Testament is preceded by an Old Testament which has for its opening words: "In the beginning God created the heaven and the earth," will suggest this thought. Henry Adams has told us of that window in the Cathedral at Chartres in which are depicted, somewhat grotesquely, the four Evangelists riding pig-a-back upon the shoulders of the Old Testament prophets, St. Matthew on Jeremiah, St. Mark on Daniel, St. Luke on Isaiah, and St. John on Ezekiel. The grotesqueness conceals the truth attested by Christ Himself when He expounded to His disciples the fact that the Law, the Prophets and the Psalms were full of things "concerning Himself."[2]

But the Old Testament must go back farther than to the history of the Jew. The real scope of the Christian revelation is best summarized in that wonderfully comprehensive statement with which the *Epistle to the Hebrews* opens: "God, having of old time spoken unto the fathers in the prophets by divers portions and in divers manners, hath at the end of these days spoken unto us in His Son, whom He appointed heir of all things, through whom also He made the worlds." Such a comprehensiveness is the basis of the claim: "Other sheep I have which are not of this fold," and of the commission (a true tradition, even if a faulty text): "Go ye into all the world and make disciples of all the nations."[3] It is the basis also for the missionary strategy of the greatest of all the apostles. For when St. Paul testified to the Jews, as in the synagogue at Antioch,[4] it was to the past history of the Jew that he appealed to establish reasons for their acceptance of his Gospel. But when the Apostle preached among the heathen of Lycaonia, he appealed to their experience of a God "who gave them rain from heaven and fruitful seasons, filling their hearts with food and gladness," since for them there was no need to recite the experience of the Jew.[5]

[1] It is interesting to note that in the early Christian work known as *The Shepherd of Hermas*, the Church is represented as an aged woman with many wrinkles, because her age is the age of the world.

[2] Luke xxiv. 27.

[3] Matthew xxviii. 19.

[4] Acts xiii. 16 ff.

[5] Acts xiv. 15 ff.

Again, when speaking to the Athenians, with inspired common sense as well as out of a complete grasp of what his faith implied, the Apostle, preaching neither the lessons of Hebrew history nor the witness of natural religion, found in "your own poets" the testimony to the truths he desired to present.[1] And, once again, it is the basis for the claim made by many of the wisest and most far-seeing of the Christian fathers. I quote but one passage, from St. Clement of Alexandria, as follows: "It is clear that the same God to whom we owe the Old and New Testament gave also to the Greeks their Greek philosophy by which the Almighty is glorified among the Greeks."[2]

What an ancestry then for Christianity and for Christ! When the Prophet asks his question, "Who shall declare His generation?" may we not, for our part, answer, with a conviction no preceding age has known, that we trace it, not merely, with St. Matthew, to Abraham, or, with St. Luke, to Adam? Rather we trace it still farther back, if you will, to Caliban or to the Heidelberg man; yea, still farther to that first dawn of consciousness; we trace it back to the birth of the cell; to the appearance of the atom; yes, still farther back to the birth of the elements among the stars and nebulæ. At this point, or at any other along the way, we have still to clinch our genealogy with the affirmation of its ultimate term, in the words used by the evangelist to close his own: "Which was the Son of God." In such a generation there is no break, no missing link. The chain holds all the way from God the Eternal to the Christ of history, and from Christ to the humblest of those who through Him are partakers of the divine life.

It will be plain, I hope, moreover, that the genealogy I am claiming for the religion of Christ necessarily draws into it all religion, from the crudest and most primitive

[1] Acts xvii. 22 ff.

[2] *Stromata,* VI. v. 42. Cf. also *Strom.*, I. v. 28; Justin Martyr, *Apol.*, i. 46; and St. Augustine, *Retractationes*, i. 13: "Res ipsa, quae nunc religio Christiana nuncupatur, erat apud antiquos, nec defuit ab initio generis humani, quousque Christus venerit in carnem, unde vera religio, quae jam erat, coepit appellari Christiana."

to the most advanced which may demand the homage of the human heart.

Having now, I trust, made clear my way of approach to the subject, let me from henceforth sink the theologian in the historian.

# BOOK I

## THE PRINCIPLES OF PRIMITIVE RELIGION

## CHAPTER I

### *The Meaning and Scope of Religion*

MANY various interpretations have been given of religion and many definitions attempted. Most of them have erred either from excess of precision or through some defect in comprehensiveness. It is natural to approach the subject first by way of etymology and derivation rather than directly by definition. But unfortunately such a method does not take us very far. We have, for instance, the two Latin verbs which have been suggested as the derivation of the word "*religion*" itself. But, while these give us ideas as to what religion might have been for the Romans, neither points the way to a satisfactory definition for ourselves. *Religo* (Inf. *religare*), to tie, or bind back, is the word suggested by Lactantius in the sentence: "Hoc vinculo pietatis obstricti deo et religati sumus, unde ipsa religio nomen accepit." On the other hand, Cicero uses the word *relego* (Inf. *relegere*), to re-read, select, or care for (the opposite to *negligere*), and implies that, so considered, religion is a careful knowledge of the needs of the gods. In the treatise *De Natura Deorum* he says: "Qui autem omnia quae ad cultum deorum pertinerent, diligenter retractarent, et tanquam relegerent, sunt dicti religiosi." And again, contrasting the idea of religion with that of superstition, he says: "Religentem esse oportet, religiosum nefas." But, putting both these ideas together, we feel that the Romans had an utterly inadequate conception of religion.

Nor are we much more fortunate in the vocabularies of other peoples. The Hebrew words *yir'ah* (fear) and *ḥesed* (piety) stress only particular aspects of religion. The Greek εὐσέβεια (cf. Acts iii. 12; 2 Tim. iii. 5) corresponds only to the Latin *reverentia*, while δεισιδαιμονία (Acts xxv. 19) implies rather what we mean by *superstition*. Or, to go much farther afield for a term, we do not fare better in borrowing the word *chiao* from the Chinese, or the word *matsuri* from Japan. The former word is written with the pictographic symbols *to beat* and *filial*, forming the ideograph with the signification of *to teach*. "Only indifferently," says Soothill, "does it connote our idea of religion." The Japanese *matsuri* is really concerned with something official and expresses religion only in a secondary way.

Altogether, an attempt to find a satisfactory explanation of religion in the terms used to express it is disappointing. Perhaps we shall do better to recall the definitions which have been put forward by writers on the subject. Alas, even here we fall short of success. It is plain that for the most part the makers of definitions have had in mind a particular aspect of religion rather than religion itself. Here are a few examples:

In Plato we have *Euthyphro* asking the question, "Is not religion perhaps merely a science of begging and getting?" We need not suppose this was Plato's own view, but many to-day unconsciously or consciously entertain it. Otherwise we should not have so many staking their religion on "getting some good out of it." It is merely the translating into practice of the Latin phrase "*Do ut des*" (*I give in order that thou mayest give*). Sir James Frazer, thinking probably only of religion among very primitive people, does not take us much farther when he defines religion as "A propitiation or conciliation of powers superior to man." This merely amends the Latin phrase quoted above to make it read "*Do ut abeas*" (*I give in order that thou mayest go away*). Unfortunately this definition, too, corresponds with the religion of many modern people. Otherwise they would not speak so commonly of a calamity as a divine *visitation*. Another anthropologist, E. B. Tylor, speaks of religion as a "belief in spiritual beings" and leaves out at least two-thirds of the matter thereby. Matthew Arnold puts in the two-thirds, in his famous definition of religion as "morality touched with emotion," but he leaves out the element of belief. Pfleiderer leaves nothing but the emotion when he tells us that "the mark of real religion is sentiment." Herbert Spencer is characteristically abstract with his description of religion as "the idea of the absolute and unconditioned," while Edward Caird is scarcely less so when he says: "A man's religion is the expression of his summed-up meaning and the purport of his whole consciousness of things." Max Müller is trying to attain comprehensiveness when he declares that religion is "the mental faculty or disposition which, independent of, nay, in spite of, sense and reason, enables man to apprehend the Infinite under different names and under varying disguises." Réville is on the same lines with his definition of religion as "the determination of human life by the sentiment of a bond uniting the human mind to that mysterious mind whose domination of the world and of itself it recognizes and to whom it delights in feeling itself united."

All the above attempts at definition err by defect of statement. Not a few others err by over-precision. For example, we have Bishop Butler's well-known description: "Religion is the belief in one God or Creator and Moral Governor of the world and in a future state of retribution"—a definition which would exclude many more forms of religion than it would include. Nearer our own time is the not dissimilar definition by James Martineau: "Religion is a belief in an everlasting God, that is a Divine mind and will ruling the Universe and holding moral relations with mankind."

While on the subject two or three more definitions which will recur to the memory of some of my readers may be quoted. For instance, we have William James' statement that "Religion is the belief that there is an unseen order and that our supreme good lies in harmoniously adjusting ourselves thereto"—a better account than any we have hitherto used. Then there is Höffding's "Religion is faith in the conservation of values." More elaborate is Walter Gabriel's: "Religion ist das unverrückbare Etwas im Menschen, das keine Anstrengungen zu gross findet um zur vollen Entfaltung zu gelangen, und das die Seele nicht ruhen lasst, bis sie sich selbst gefunden, ihren Schöpfer und die wahre innere Beziehung zwischen ihm und sich selbst erkannt."[1] Much simpler are the hints in a number of other writers to the effect that, *e.g.* "religion is something vital to our pursuit of character, happiness and service of others"; that it is a "keeping open of the divine east window of surprise"; that it is "the anticipated attainment of God"; and the like.

What definition may we, at the outset of our survey, adopt, in order that we may include even the religion of the Russian Communist (who says he has none), and in order that we may find our proper material in all past time, as well as in all inhabited lands, above all in every aspect of man's complex personality—expressive, in fact, of his every need? So comprehensive an enquiry compels us to postpone yet a while the formulation of a definition which we could regard as satisfactory. Several pressing questions seem to invite our prior consideration.

The first is an enquiry as to the *geographical* scope of religion. Is religion of human interest universally? Or, is it something which has been intruded here and there by the perverse zeal of missionaries, bent upon "worrying savages" into the profession of faiths and the practising of cults which would never have occurred to them to adopt in the nature of things? Such a view has been many times set forth, sometimes as of authority. Travellers, at least in former days, were often wont to return from strange regions with the dogmatic announcement, "This tribe has no idea of religion." In reality, the traveller had probably no knowledge of the tribal language, and the tribe had little desire to break through its natural reticence for the benefit of an inquisitive stranger. To-day, of course, in the case of Russia, we have a whole country bent upon affording illustration of an entire nation educated out of the idea of religion. But what eventually will be the result of a campaign to make atheists of a hundred and fifty million people it would be premature to predict. Even here, in the process of eradicating Christianity, communists are

[1] See Walter Gabriel, *Gandhi, Christus, und wir Christen.*

giving proof of their need for religion. For Communism already possesses the emotion of a religion, the faith of a religion, the philosophy of a religion, and some of the institutions of a religion. The success of Communism would by no means prove the non-necessity of religion. Rather it would be the example of a new form of religion taking the place of an older.

The second of our questions concerns the scope of religion *historically* rather than geographically. If we admit, so far as the present is concerned, that religion pervades the whole field of human life, in some form or other, does it follow that this has always been the case? Moreover, will it remain so, rather than provide a stage in the process of human development, as Comte predicted? In other words, is there any period of human history in which religion is *added* to some previously existing state? Is it in the prehistoric, as well as in the primitive, or does it enter in some era of inherited culture? To put the matter in still another way, is religion a biological fact, or something superimposed? Is it coterminous with the age-long story of human evolution, from first to last? I have already expressed myself on this point in the *Introduction*, and the answer to the above queries is obviously, in any case, in the affirmative.

Such answer prepares us for the closely related query: Should a history of the kind we are attempting be a History of *Religions* or a History of *Religion*? I have, as already intimated, no hesitation in deciding for the latter. Those who write histories of *Religions* are describing a tree by its separate branches, but ignoring the trunk in which all the branches find their origin and their unity. To describe Religions by devoting a few pages to the lives of their several founders, followed by an account of their several tenets, and a sketch of their several careers in history, is to forget the larger fact. The larger part of a religion lies far back of the biography of any founder—other, of course, than of that Divine Spirit which is the source of creation itself. It is true that great religious geniuses mark the parting of many ways, stimulating the masses of men, and arousing them to adventures of faith of which they were incapable by themselves. But the essential hopes and fears and yearnings of mankind, such as make up the constant urge of religion, are present, however inarticulately, in the soul of man from the dawn of consciousness. Religion, then, is fundamentally one, the historically continuous expression of our common perplexities, our common problems, and our common hopes. It is also the common manifestation, in varied glints and glimpses of that eternal Light which "coming into the world, lighteth every man." We need this conviction as to religion as originally, and in all its present manifestations, a unitary thing, completely and universally human, if we are to sustain our faith that the ultimate goal of religion is to be universal too.

We have still to put our third question as to the scope of religion. This is: What is its range *psychologically*? Does religion concern merely one department of our personality, or must we regard it as applying to the whole? To answer this question we must be permitted to assume the common analysis of personality as including Feeling, Reason and Will, or (as they are sometimes described) the Emotive (or Æsthetic), the Intellectual (or Rational), and the Conative (or Moral) faculties. It is not necessary to insist upon these as representing three separate things. They are merely useful terms for the denoting of different aspects of our complex individuality. For, first of all, it is clear that religion does, and must, concern our *Feelings*. In any religion worthy of the name the emotions must necessarily be engaged. They serve to keep faith warm and to stimulate to action. Yet it is clear also that any exclusive preoccupation of religion with feeling is not a little dangerous. In such a case the result may easily be hysteria and even madness. From ancient times to the present the history of religion is prolific of instances in which men and women have been swept by waves of religious emotion from the mooring-posts of reason. In ancient times it is the story of the Bacchantes; in more modern times of the Holy Rollers. Nor is it merely the rational which, under such circumstances, is rejected; the moral, too, often goes overboard with the rest. In the second place, therefore, religion needs the cultivation of the *Reason*. To serve God with the *mind* is part of "the first and great commandment." Here, too, there must be balance. There have been rational interpretations of religion which have proved singularly barren in result, and leaders of highly intellectual cults have found themselves surprised and disappointed at the lack of appeal which their intelligence seemed to warrant, but did not secure. It is not that there is any excess of reason—there is seldom danger of this—but rather that reason is not carried beyond the limits of demonstration to the using of faith. For faith is not opposed to reason, but to sight, and faith no more destroys reason than a telescope destroys vision. It was in elevating reason to the position of a goddess, enthroned upon an altar dedicated to man's approach to God by faith, that the French revolutionists made their mistake. Reason, like knowledge, must "know her place"; "a higher hand must make her mild." So, in the third place, we must make room for *Will*. The conative, or ethical, element is as important as the others. No antinomian extravagance of emotion, no enlightened gnosticism, may dispense with morals, just as necessary under the Gospel as under the Law, though achieved through the working of grace rather than through the compulsions of legalism. And equally, of course, it must be remembered that mere moral philosophy is not religion and no system of ethics, even though it be pressed with the insistency of the Confucian, suffices to save or regenerate individual or nation. We must still insist that religion, if it is to be vital, cannot afford to ignore any one of the three elements we have mentioned. To quote St. Paul, in three separate passages of his *Epistles*: "Circumcision is nothing and uncircumcision is nothing, but the keeping of the commandments of God";[1] "Circumcision availeth nothing, nor uncircumcision, but faith working through love";[2] "Neither is circumcision anything, nor uncircumcision, but a new creature."[3] The supreme bliss of religion is not for the passionless, but for those who have reached the *apatheia* of which St. Clement wrote, the emotion of those whose passions are subdued to the dominion of a divine purpose—God's lovers, not

[1] I Cor. vii. 19. [2] Gal. v. 6. [3] Gal. vi. 15.

His slaves. The supreme bliss, again, is not for the irrational. Intelligence must be understood (as the Latin implies, and as we learn from Dante) as a higher form of love. And, once again, the supreme bliss is not for the weak of will, those who are, for their weakness, outside the possibilities of disciplinary pain and of ecstatic joy alike. To know at least this will save us from premature and inadequate definition.

If we are still looking for a definition, we know now for what to seek. For myself, I am prepared to accept that of Monsignor Le Roy, who describes religion as "the ensemble of beliefs, obligations and practices by which man recognizes the supernatural world, performs his duties towards it, and asks help from it."[1] Or we may take that of Dr. George Galloway, who tells us that religion is "Man's faith in a power beyond himself, whereby he seeks to satisfy emotional needs and gain stability of life, and which he expresses in acts of worship and service."[2] In order to adapt the formula to the use of religions which, like Buddhism and Communism, profess to be atheistic, we need, perhaps, merely to alter the words "Man's faith in a power beyond himself" to "Man's faith in an ideal beyond himself." Such a definition will in general suffice to cover the substance of the tremendous subject we have set ourselves to survey.

Just one further point before bringing this chapter to a close. As we shall find an evolution in the long story of religion as a whole, so we shall find one in the story of the three psychological aspects of individuality we have just considered. We may study the evolution of feeling, all the way from that vague sense of mystery which so commonly expresses itself as fear to the realization of a "love which casteth out fear." The passion which is base and dark has to be disciplined through many successive stages, providing room for emotions of the most varied sorts, until at length it becomes transfigured into that sublimated passion which makes the atmosphere of heaven:

[1] Monsignor A. Le Roy, *The Religion of the Primitives*, p. 33, New York, 1922.

[2] George Galloway, *The Philosophy of Religion*, p. 184, New York, 1914.

> So strong that love, could heaven bid love farewell,
> Would turn to fruitless and devouring hell ;
> So sweet that hell, to hell could love be given,
> Would turn to splendid and sonorous heaven.[1]

Yet the history of religion will have much to say as to the legitimate place for that kind of fear we call reverence, and for the kind of fear which shrinks from the *pœna damni*—the pain of loss. The query will present itself again and again as to how fast we dare go in ridding ourselves of fear, and at what point fear becomes needless and dangerous. At any rate, the purging of our emotions from their baser elements will constitute an important part of religious experience.

There must, again, be an evolution of reason, all the way from the making of myths (a faculty by no means to be despised) to the establishment of scientific generalizations, all the way from the ætiological guesses of primitive men with regard to things imperfectly observed, to that knowledge of Nature (still, of course, in the provisional stage) which, through observations by ourselves and others, we venture to formulate in so-called " laws." Every religion, apparently, has required a cosmogony and in the making of cosmogonies the mythopœic faculty has performed a religious function of value. Nevertheless, all along the road, reason has been constantly correcting her conclusions by enquiry, engaged in sloughing off exploded hypotheses and in making fresh hypotheses on which experience may continue to build. Moreover, always beyond the provable must be recognized the reasonableness of faith, which is the leap of the soul's surmise to heights whitherward knowledge only journeys ploddingly.

Then, thirdly, we have to take into consideration the evolution of the will. The ethical faculty has to be trained, all the way from the obedience of slaves to the obedience of sons, and thence to that connubial obedience which is the self-identification of the bride-soul with her bridegroom-lover. The question will often have to be asked, at various stages of religious history, as to how far the " being under law " must persist and just where " the freedom of sons "

[1] Algernon Swinburne, *Tristram and Iseult.*

commences. In the history of religion many types of *righteousness* will be discovered which have little to do with morality as we conceive it. But, all along, where religion is felt to be advancing, there will be perceived a development of the will towards freedom—in the sense of being free to fulfil the law of one's own being—and towards life in accord with that Supreme Will "which is our peace."

In conclusion, it is plain that such a subject as the history of religion brings us to the contemplation of things infinitely large. In all humility, we are attempting "from heights divine of the eternal purpose" a survey of that purpose, so far as finite minds are capable of grasping it, to the end that we may be intellectually enlightened and morally stimulated. For the most part, of course, our survey will keep its feet on the earth and deal with details we may reach by historical methods. Nevertheless, we must keep in mind throughout the plan—a plan which antedates time and stretches out to the full redemption of the Cosmos from its provisional Chaos, and to the perfecting of the individual organism we call the soul. And, though we say little about it, we shall have always in mind the operation of the primal Force which is nothing less than the Divine Love educating creation through the mysteries and tragedies of life for the final conclusive triumph. We shall also keep in mind the method of the education, a method which is revealed in the whole process of creation as well as in the sacrifice on Calvary. Behind all the story of development, in other words, is God, affirming in all the ages His purpose in man, first as the little child set in a new strange world to "embark on small adventures in the wild"; then the man confronting mysterious adventures of the spirit:

> And, when he is older, he shall be
> My friend, and walk here at my side;
> Or, when he wills, grow young with me,
> And to this happy world where once we died,
> Descending through the calm, blue weather,
> Buy life again with our immortal breath,
> And wander through the little fields together,
> And taste of love and death.[1]

[1] Alfred Noyes, *Creation.*

## CHAPTER II

### *What is Primitive Religion?*

WE will now, for the present, abjure metaphysics and confine ourselves, in the proper spirit of the historian, to the experience of man upon this planet. Yet, even on this planet, a large part of the history of mankind is outside the limits of history properly so-called. So far as time is concerned, the prehistoric period of humanity is almost infinitely longer than the historic. Man's life on earth probably goes back some 350,000 years B.C., to the Quaternary Period and the various sub-periods of the Glacial Age. Of all that lies between that remote date and the beginnings of recorded history, say, 5000 years B.C., we know nothing save what is gleaned from the scanty remains of burial mounds. This is enough to prove that even prehistoric man was religious in the sense of believing in a future life and in the worship of certain powers of Nature like the sun. But, while this agrees with our conviction that man has been incurably religious from the first, it affords us little in detail.

It will be seen, then, that the term *primitive* as applied to religion is only relative. We know only a little more of primitive religion than we know of primitive language. Even with the help of prehistoric archæology, with its megaliths and dolmens and long barrows, its ochre-graves and its assemblage of *life-givers*, we have little in the way of real criteria.

Nevertheless, what we do have suggests that man's general attitude towards the universe has not changed very radically. We may not accept the dictum of Tanquerey that " primitive religion does not substantially differ from the Christian religion "; we may feel it better to say with Otto, " What is potential in religion in general becomes in Christianity a pure actuality." But certainly we have cause to recognize the same kinds of reaction to the great encompassing mysteries of Nature. Thus, convinced that man in the Stone Age was striving to express the same kind of attitude to the universe, we are not so badly handicapped by our ignorance of the past as might be supposed. With some measure of imaginative insight, aided and corrected by the more or less laborious collecting of anthropological data, we find ourselves able to reconstruct, with some approximation to accuracy, the religion of the primitive, even though we only catch up with him when he is far advanced along the upward path. The two methods, used co-operatively, at least furnish us with valuable and suggestive material.

As an example of the former method, let us take that wonderful piece of imaginative reconstruction which Browning has given us in *Caliban upon Setebos*. Shakespeare had already given us one Caliban, a Caliban who is the primitive man presented for comparison with those vulgar products of civilization, Trinculo and Stephano. This Caliban shows us little or nothing of his religious side. But Browning offers us a Caliban who is not only potentially but actually religious, the man of the spirit. To begin with, however, it is not a promising picture, that of the savage

> Flat on his belly in the pit's much mire,
> With elbows wide, fists clenched to prop his chin.

Yet we are shown that Caliban, too, is among the prophets who prepare the way for fellowship with God. While, in the flesh, Caliban is kicking his heels in the cool slush, a spiritual sense is being awakened, and is becoming more and more responsive to the stimuli which prick him from without. His "dæmonic dread," in the presence of the unknown, contains the potentiality of a reverence which is "the raw material for the feeling of religious humility" and which will grow in time to love. Out of a respect evinced for tradition, as received from his mother Sycorax, awakens the capacity for a fellowship in faith such as shall create the Church. Out of the self-consciousness which postulates this or that hypothesis concerning God arises that sense of kinship so triumphantly vindicated at last in the doctrine of the Incarnation. Out of acts of propitiation, ritually organized, springs the entire system of sacrifice and prayer by which are fulfilled man's yearnings for communion with a living God. In the speculations of the man just emerging, as it were, from the slime, we discern anticipations and presentiments of the creeds and cults of advanced forms of religion, just as we might discern the limbs and viscera of the human being predictively present in the embryo.

Leaving a poetic reconstruction such as this of Browning's *Caliban*, and summarizing the data derivable from the widest possible survey of the anthropological field, we find in the comparison nothing essentially different. First, we find the emotion from which all religion may be said to have sprung. Petronius calls it fear, and asserts:

> Primus in orbe deos fecit timor, ardua coeli
> Fulmina dum caderent.[1]

Rudolph Otto describes it, in his *Das Heilige*, more accurately as " the sense of the numinous." He reminds us that emotion has two poles, the *mysterium tremendum* and the *mysterium fascinans*. One is the sense of horror in the presence of mystery, the horror which is more often illustrated in the religions of the Orient, as, for example, Indian Tantricism, than in those of the West.[2] The other is that sense of ecstasy, such as St. Catharine of Genoa expressed when she declared that but a drop of her emotion falling into Hell would turn Hell into Paradise. Certainly, though we cannot go astray in describing this " sense of the numinous " by the terser English word *awe*, we have to allow for the two aspects of the emotion. Undoubtedly, at first the element of fear may predominate, but it is a fear capable of ultimate transformation into the ecstasy of love. Fear of a sort will, of course, continue in religion as reverence and the sense of dread in the presence of the

[1] Petronius, borrowed by Statius, *Thebais*, III. 360. See also Lucretius, at length, *De Rerum Natura*.

[2] Yet appeals to the horrors of Hell have often enough been part of the revivalistic preaching of the West.

infinite mystery must be considered one of the permanent values of religion. As Goethe says:

> Das Schaudern ist der Menschheit bestes Teil.
> Wie auch die Welt ihm das Gefühl verteuere,
> Ergriffen fühlt er tief das Ungeheure.[1]

To supersede such an element too rudely is to rationalize religion mischievously and also to weaken its power over the consciences of men. Nevertheless, even from the first there is in awe the attractiveness of a great challenge, the incitement to a great adventure. Wonder is awakened by the sense of mystery as well as fear, and he who ceases to wonder soon ceases to be religious in the true sense of the word. The man who is forced to the confession, "I am so rapt in wonder I cannot speak," is not far from reverence for Him whose Name, according to the prophet, is *Wonderful*.[2]

Yet primitive man soon learned that his awe was the result not of a single mystery but of two mysteries equally awe inspiring. These are distinguishable from the first and have their separate developments, and each line of development has had an important part in moulding the creeds and institutions and practices of religion. The first of these (not necessarily in time sequence) is the mystery which man discovered outside himself in the phenomena and processes of Nature. Out of the awe thus inspired we get the idea of God as the Shining One, *Deus* (with its derivatives), the Divine Power in and beyond Nature, yet revealed especially in the heavens above. To the type of religion thus begotten we give the name of *Naturism*, and from it man gains his conception of both the transcendence and the immanence of God. The second mystery is that which man feels within himself, the mystery of his own being, of his life and his death. From man's sense of this we get the idea of God as the Spirit, *Theos* (with its derivatives), the Greek term ultimately derived from an old root signifying *to breathe*. We call this type of religion *Spiritism* and see in it the foreshadowing of what we shall later describe as the humanness of God. Both types of emotion

[1] Goethe, *Faust,* II. I. v. Cf. Job iii. 12–16.
[2] Isaiah ix. 6.

are in their essence anthropomorphic, but in the former case we have the material world conceived of as the visible vesture of a spirit like the wind (*anima*), vivifying the universe; in the latter case the human body is regarded as inhabited by a spiritual principle which is like the breath (*animus*) which inspires or, at death, forsakes, the body.

It is important to note that these two types of primitive religion are complementary rather than exclusive. They may both be present (and generally are) in one and the same religious system, though in varying proportion. It has been too commonly, and most unfortunately, assumed by some writers on religion that Naturism and Spiritism are to be reckoned antagonistic and mutually exclusive theories of religious origins. To some the awe produced by the sight of Nature's stupendous phenomena has sufficiently accounted for man's tendency to religion. The "spacious firmament on high," the glories of the rising sun, the moon swimming in a bank of clouds, the rolling storm-clouds—these are the things which first stirred man's soul to awe. To others religion sprang rather from the fear of ghosts troubling the visions of the night. It should be clear that either of these theories separately set forth is necessarily incomplete. To account for all the facts, both Naturism and Spiritism must be permitted their proper place, and to a large extent their separate developments. There must be room permanently for the awe which breeds its proud humility when we stand beneath the starry vault of heaven. There must be equal place for the awe we feel when we bend in the presence of the dead. The universal religion of which we are in quest must be a synthesis of both evolutions, not academically or artificially but naturally and vitally. We must find God manifested to us on the one hand through the mysterious operations of Nature, and on the other hand through the emotion engendered by the darker mystery of death.

Yet before we attempt to sketch the evolution of either Naturism or Spiritism something should be said with regard to the term *anthropomorphism* which was used a few paragraphs back and which requires explanation all the more because of the general tendency to undervalue the function it possesses in the evolution of religion. So far from being tempted to despise the use of anthropomorphic terminology in expressing our conceptions of God as the ultimate reality, or repeating the sneer that whereas God first made man in His own image men are now content to fashion God in their own, we should realize that the use of anthropomorphic terms is inevitable at certain stages of theological formulation and that its necessity by no means disappears when we advance to the highest conceivable apprehension of God. This is for two reasons : first, because in finding terms for expressing our theology we can only draw upon the knowledge we have of our own personality, the sole knowledge we have of personality at first hand. The word *Father*, permeated as it is with anthropomorphism, is still to-day more stimulating as a means of access to God than the most philosophic definition ever coined by man's intelligence. The terms we need to employ are, of course, not definitions but symbols, and they are, moreover, symbols which are effective only to the limit of their symbolism. For example, when I point my finger to the sun and say, "There is the sun!", my gesture is a symbol in that it suggests, not the end of my finger, as the position of the sun, but the line of direction which, followed up for millions of miles, will eventually reach the sun. Equally at fault is he who refuses to look beyond my finger and denies thereupon the existence of the sun, and he who, perceiving the inadequacy of the term *Father* as applied to God, rails at me for dealing in anthropomorphisms instead of definition. But, secondly, the use of the anthropomorphic has warrant since God does indeed touch man through Nature, just as man rises to communion with God through his immortal spirit. Where God and man are felt to be akin, the one to the other, why deny to man the assertion of the humanness of God or of the divinity of man ?

There is a further extension of this use of anthropomorphic symbolism which it is not out of place to mention at this point. With our modern enlargement of the idea of man's place in Nature, as having an inheritance from the world below us as well as a gift from above, even the use of *theriomorphic* (or *zoomorphic*) terminology is not without its justification in theology. With man's genetic relationship extended backward to the animal world, it follows inevitably that a completer Christology should take cognizance of the tremendous problems and perplexities which run down into subhuman regions in which life's earlier developments took place. The religion of primitive men, who felt themselves on intimate terms with the animal world, was bound, on the theological side, to employ the language of theriomorphism as well as that of anthropomorphism and, on the practical side, to use what we call *theriolatry*. On this subject, of course, much has been written from the anthropological standpoint. Theriolatry has been explained by all sorts of things, pastoral cults, hunting cults, the cult of dangerous animals, and the like. But the fact remains, which has been frequently overlooked, that for primitive man the transition from the theriomorphic to the anthropomorphic involved but the shortest of steps. To most primitives animals were not merely relatives but relatives to be respected and reverenced for many qualities. This will be more explicitly set forth when we come to the subject of *Totemism*: in the meantime it must not be forgotten that the language of theriomorphism, while it had great significance in the early stages of man's religious experience, has even to-day not entirely lost its validity. It ensures our recognition of the unity of all life, as derived from one source, as being subject to many of the same pains and problems, and expressing, as the Apostle implies, through the groaning of all creation, the same expectancy of an ultimate redemption. All Nature shares in the method by which life is exalted through sacrifice. In this method the brute creation, as we call it, has its very real, if unconscious, part. The swine that ran violently down a steep place to perish in the waters were nearer to the spirit of Calvary than the selfish drovers who complained of loss of wealth through the presence of Jesus. "The shabby old scape-goat" was nearer to the programme of Messiah inaugurated on Quarantania than were the priests and scribes at Jerusalem. The ass on which Christ rode into Jerusalem on Palm Sunday, though "the tattered outlaw of the earth," had a share alike in the Passion and its triumph. Christ

[1] Romans viii. 22.

accepted the title *Lamb of God* as well as that of *Son of Man*, and the completeness of redemption is illustrated by the association of Ox and Lion and Eagle with Man around the Great White Throne.[1] Such is the permanently valuable truth which we find in the theriomorphic stage of theology. The *forms* in which religion clothed itself in primitive times cease to be valuable, but the *truths* concealed behind the forms survive to find new vesture under new conditions. There is always predictively present that "fullness of time" in which truth shall appear no longer conditioned by temporal necessities.

When we understand this we shall exhibit a very generous tolerance for the symbolisms which other ages and other peoples find necessary for their expression of religious truths. It will be possible for us to pierce through the crudest of media and find thereby access to truths which words are inadequate to express. Even the satire of Rupert Brooke, in his description of the fishes' *Paradise*, will become for us significantly religious:

> Somewhere beyond Space and Time,
> Is wetter water, slimier slime!
> And there (they trust) there swimmeth One
> Who swam ere rivers were begun;
> Immense, of fishy form and mind,
> Squamous, omnipotent and kind;
> And under that Almighty Fin,
> The littlest fish may enter in.
> Oh, never fly conceals a hook,
> Fish say, in that Eternal Brook,
> But more than mundane weeds are there,
> And mud celestially fair;
> Fat caterpillars drift around,
> And Paradisal grubs are found;
> Unfading moths, immortal flies,
> And the worm that never dies,
> And in that Heaven of all they wish,
> There shall be no more land, say fish.[2]

*Satire*, we exclaim, upon our Christian ideas of heaven! Yet neither our crudest Christian symbolism nor the above quoted description of the fishes' elysium is ridiculous

[1] Revelation iv. 6 ff.

[2] Rupert Brooke, *Heaven*.

unless fish or men limit themselves to the letter of their symbolism. The old man's remark, "There's golding streets yonder, but I shan't think it natural unless there's chimbleys too," was only ridiculous in so far as the farther end of the man's symbolism was closed against the thing which "eye hath not seen nor ear heard." At the hither end every symbol must relate itself to the user's own experience. But, whether through the veil of Nature or through the mystery of his own being, man must continuously reach out towards touch with a Power beyond all Nature and towards a Spirit akin to his own. Moreover, in the quest and in the attainment alike, he must find the power which sets him on his feet and aids his advance "on to the bounds of the waste, on to the City of God."

## CHAPTER III

## *The Creed of Primitive Religion*

MANY will desire first to ask, What is a Creed? and further, Why a Creed? These are questions of permanent importance and deserve an answer. There are few errors in popular conceptions of religion more common or more serious than those prevailing on this particular subject. To some people a creed is something to be accepted solely on divine authority, as the result of revelation, a proclamation of ultimate truths which are altogether outside discussion or any appeal to reason. "Credo quia absurdum." To such the acceptance of a creed is simply an act of obedience to ecclesiastical authority, a test of orthodoxy rather than the use of a symbol. Where this idea prevails it is not strange that, while some yield to the proclaimed dogma an unquestioning faith, others are repelled by what appear to be gratuitous assumptions independent of or even contrary to reason and resting upon nothing more substantial than the decree of an ecclesiastical Council. It should therefore be understood from the start (as indeed has already been suggested) that a creed is properly (as the Greek synonym indicates) a *symbol*, that is, an attempt in the interest of practical religion to express our apprehension of truths which lie beyond our powers of definition. As we have already seen, the term *Father*, applied to God with the implication that it connotes all that is contained in our highest conception of human fatherhood, and then extends infinitely beyond into regions of thought where language fails, suggests belief of far nobler significance than the precisest definition we could frame. Words, even the most exact, are but counters, and when used of things which transcend experience can have no finality. They are true so far as they suggest the direction; they are false so far as they suggest the limitations of the original sense.

If creeds, then, are but symbols and in no wise definitions, why, it will be asked, use them? A little thought will convince us that a working hypothesis is always a stimulus to activity and a road towards completer intelligence. Experiments become experiences. Hence we might as well talk of a creedless business as a creedless religion. As the business man, trusting his acumen and the advice of his friends, essays an undertaking which he knows to be sound only after he has risked the experiment, or (to use an even simpler illustration) as a hungry person trusts those who have prepared a meal and only knows it to be wholesome after he has eaten it, so the man who craves a religious experience, and trusts a teacher who recommends himself as dependable, to the extent of making the venture, only verifies his faith when he has made trial of it. It is obvious, of course, that any theory of life on which a man is willing to stake something demands faith. In this respect the atheist, who rails at creeds, is quite as dogmatic *a priori* as the theist. In fact his inverted theology is a creed which is just as undemonstrable as that of any one else and is proclaimed with just as much confidence in its authority. Neither knows, to start with, of God as a matter of proof; each yields his life and its issues to the creed he esteems the best.

It should be added that when the reasonableness of faith has been conceded there will follow the fight to maintain faith. There is no more finality about faith than about physical life. As life is the moment by moment victory of the forces of growth over the forces of disintegration, so faith is the continuous victory of belief over the disposition to disbelieve. Those who plead for a "simple" creed, like that of the Fatherhood of God, forget that such an article of faith may under certain circumstances be the most difficult of all to maintain. None breaks down so often or so tragically in time of trouble. None needs a robuster confidence to sustain. Indeed, all formulation of truth works on the edge of mystery. Like Thor we essay a simple draught from the drinking-horn of the gods, only to find that we are in contact with the waters of the illimitable ocean.

Now when we ask ourselves concerning the creeds of primitive man we do not assume that doctrines were as clearly perceived and formulated as we shall here set them forth. Quite possibly, in the minds of most, there was nothing but what William James calls "big, buzzing, booming confusion." Probably most men, even as to-day, lived in one of the two twilights,

> The twilight of a seeking unto light,
> The twilight of a doubting unto night.

Not even Browning's *Caliban* could have held his views as "pat" as they are presented in the poem. Yet undoubtedly all the elements of a real creed were present, however vaguely, much as we shall here present them. If here they are given with some sort of logical sequence, it is, of course, merely for the sake of explicitness and for the convenience of the reader.

First of all a word is fitting in regard to that particular school of writers which rejects the evolutionary hypothesis and posits a primitive monotheism in the place of the series of developments presently to be described. Of this theory three things may here be said. First, that the evidence adduced for the theory is in a large number of cases exceedingly weak and even founded on misinterpretation of terms, such as *manitu*, and the like. Secondly, that much of the evidence is obviously the result of ideas imparted by missionaries themselves and mistaken by them for primitive tradition. Thirdly, that there is no reason to deny that a vague sense of unity did often lie behind the polydæmonism and polytheism of primitive man, even as the idea of *ṛita* lay behind the polytheism of Vedic India. We may well agree that the germ of a future monotheism (as well as the germs of other doctrines later to be manifested) is there, even though monotheism itself be absent.

Hence we begin, not with any tradition of a primitive monotheism, but with what Marett calls *Animatism*, or the belief in universal vitality. It is the conviction that the life of Nature corresponds with what man knows of himself. As it is natural for the child to attribute life to stick or stone, to chair or table, so it seemed natural to primitive man to assume that all Nature was instinct with life like his own. Thus in Chinese mythology we have the conception of the world as P'an Ku, the Chaos Man, whose head became the mountains, his breath the wind, his voice thunder, his limbs the four poles, his veins the rivers, his sinews the undulations of the earth's surface, his flesh the fields, his beard the stars, his hair the trees and his bones the rocks. Similarly primitive Teutonic cosmogony gives us the giant Ymir, product of the cold which came from Ginunggagap and the heat which came from Muspellsheim. Or, if another example be needed, we may find it in the Indian conception of Purusha.

Animatism, it is clear, soon developed into what we call *Animism*, a theory which not only recognized the presence of life but also that of a living spirit, independent of its material embodiment. The word *Animism* is first used by Stahl in the eighteenth century as the equivalent of a belief in the world-spirit, but since 1871, when E. B. Tylor employed it as "a minimum definition of religion," the word has been generally used in the sense mentioned above. It might, however, have been more accurate to describe it as "a minimum definition of theology" rather than of religion.

Just as the wind (*anima*) moving invisibly among the trees suggested the action of a pervading spiritual presence, so, by anthropomorphic analogy, is it with the primitive man's conception of everything in the material universe. By itself it is by no means an ignoble fancy. It postulates a sensitively organized universe in tune with our own emotions and not entirely separable from our own nature. It is a conception such as that which prompted the lines of a modern Japanese poet:

> So may I grow as pines upon her heights,
> And flow with all her rivers to the sea,
> And fall on her like dew on summer nights,
> And love and serve her through eternity.

From Animism it is but a short step and a natural development to what is known as *Dynamism*, that is, the belief that the spirit pervading material objects has a kind of mystic potency which may be exerted benevolently or malevolently upon those who come into contact with it.

For this power there are several terms employed. One of the commonest is *mana*, first used by Dr. Codrington of Melanesia and generally known throughout the islands of the Pacific. Codrington describes it as " a power or influence, not physical . . . which acts in all sorts of ways for good and evil, and which it is of the greatest advantage to possess or control."[1] Again: " If a man came upon a large stone with a number of small ones beneath it, lying like a sow among her litter, he was sure that to offer money upon it would bring pigs and such a stone would be thought to have *mana*."[2] *Mana* is thus ambivalent, bringing good or bad fortune to the man who possesses or touches the object in question. Of the effect of *mana* for ill we have an illustration in the Old Testament story[3] of the destruction of the men of Bethshemesh who looked into the Ark of God, whereas the house of Abinadab received it at the hands of the men of Kirjath-jearim without disaster. An Iroquoian word, meaning much the same thing, is *orenda*, literally *chant* or *song*, but actually denoting the supernatural power residing in trees, plants, stones, meteors, religious ceremonies and medicine men. Other Indian words of similar significance are the Siouan *wakan*, " the power that makes or brings to pass " and the Algonquin word *manitu*, which has sometimes been misinterpreted as referring to a personal deity.

Closely associated with the theory of dynamism is the system, with both theological and religious significance, generally known as *Fetishism*. The term is an ill-defined one and employed in too many diverse senses to be satisfactory, but is now commonly understood in the sense given to it by E. B. Tylor as denoting " the vessels or vehicles or instruments of spiritual beings." Goblet d'Alviella preserves the like sense in describing fetishism as " the belief that the appropriation of a thing may secure the services of a spirit lodged within it." For example, a man stubs his toe against a stone and, thinking of the stone as harbouring a grudge against him, possesses himself of it, henceforth

[1] R. H. Codrington, *The Melanesians*, p. 118, Oxford, 1891.
[2] R. H. Codrington, *op. cit.*, p. 183.
[3] 1 Samuel vi. 19.

controlling whatever properties there may be resident within. The word fetish, however, was originally used in an entirely different sense. It is derived from the Latin *factitius*, *i.e.* something made, and was applied by the Portuguese (in the form of *feitiço*) to relics, rosaries, images and the like, supposed to possess spiritual powers. The Portuguese term was brought into general use by de Brosses, in his *Du Culte des Dieux fétiches*, of 1760. For many years thereafter it was used in a very loose way of many different things. Comte even speaks of sun and moon and earth as being "grands fétiches," while Herbert Spencer thought of any "object with an indwelling ghost" as a fetish. If the word is to continue in use (which some would regret), it must be understood to imply a mascot or object carried to ensure luck, or, if too large for this, something of which the mere possession ensures control of its potency. Some fetishes will be used as *amulets* (from the Latin *amuletum*—root *amoliri*, to ward off),[1] that is, objects employed apotropaically, for the purpose of warding off evil. Others will be known as *talismans* (from the Arabic *telsam*, Gk. *telesma*, a magical figure), that is, objects used to secure good fortune. The African word *grigri* is applied to both the amulet and the talisman, an object which through a secret and mysterious power preserves the wearer from misfortune and disease or procures good luck in travel, war or fishing.

It should be remembered that, though the belief in mana and fetishes is associated with much superstition, it has yet a real survival value, since in the very nature of things the spiritual must use the material in a sacramental way. But, altogether apart from the appreciation of this, there is to-day a large use of fetishes of one sort or another, with varying degrees of belief in their efficacy. The negro carries his rabbit's foot, but many representatives of the "higher civilization" will be found more or less superstitiously attached to his lucky coin or the like.[2] Even our

[1] Some have derived the word from the Arabic *hamala*, to carry.

[2] In Paris a little statuette fetish, called *Argine*, is advertised at the price of $20—"to bring luck in bridge." It is also said to make "a charming seal that will bring happiness to a letter-writer and to the one who receives the letter."

respect for flags, ikons, crosses, photographs and pressed flowers is not unrelated to primitive beliefs of the sort we have been describing, though in most cases we transfer the idea of *mana* from the object itself to our subjective association with it.

The next step upwards from animism, in all its manifestations, was towards *Personalization*. Even Shakespeare's *Caliban* (not to speak of Browning's) was a poet, and the poet's faculty of personifying the phenomena of Nature was closely allied with the child's habit of dealing similarly with the objects he encounters. In either case it has a primitive character. The Psalmist who exclaims, "Why hop ye so, ye high hills?", Æschylus with his,

> O Sky divine, O Winds of pinions swift,
> O fountain-heads of Rivers, and O thou
> Illimitable laughter of the Sea,
> O Earth, the mighty Mother, and thou Sun,
> Whose orbéd light surveyeth all!

and Longfellow's "Nature, the old nurse," are all going back to the childhood of the race in adjurations of the sort. Such personalizations are often the achievement of men far advanced intellectually and spiritually, but they spring out of the same sense of admiration and wonder in the presence of natural phenomena.

There was further a very natural transition from personalization to *Personification*, or the imputing to separate phenomena of some specialized aspect of divinity. In certain cases and in certain stages there was some evident reluctance to go in this direction too far or too fast. It was a serious thing to give a *name* to any manifestation of divinity. Hence, as among the Keltic peoples, people often mentioned the godlings connected with Nature indirectly and by periphrasis. The *sidhe* of Ireland were, of course, probably spirits of the dead (cf. the Latin *sedes*) rather than spirits of Nature, but the reference to them as "the good people" and the avoidance of any definite nomenclature witness to this reluctance. The spirits of Nature are arranged in classes rather than referred to as individuals. To use the Greek terms, there were *oreads*, or spirits of the mountains, *naiads*, or spirits of the streams, *dryads*, or spirits of the trees. The Teutons, also, had their *trolls*, or giants of the obscure forest glades, *elves*, often lurking spirits of evil intent, and the like. Other peoples had their *fairies*, in all probability in origin the *fata*, or *norns*. All Nature was pervaded with spiritual presences, peeping between the leaves of the trees, dancing in the brooks, or slaving in the bowels of the earth. It was a striking testimony to the belief, primitive but essentially and religiously valid, that in the variety of Nature, as well in her unity, the presence of deity was to be discerned, bafflingly near to the life of man, both observant and observed.

Out of this stimulating imagination of primitive man, happily not yet lost to wonder, there developed at last a definite belief in many gods and the system we call *Polytheism*. The earlier stages of polytheism are frequently distinguished as *Polydæmonism*, a system which only differs from its successor in that the spirits worshipped are less objectively and personally conceived. In all polytheistic theologies we observe not only a sense of the variety which is so striking a characteristic of the phenomena of Nature, but also a sense of the many antinomies, or conflicts. It is plain that the storm-god, Indra, in Indian mythology, is often at issue with the sun-god, Surya, and that the temper of Rudra is of a more truculent sort than that of Varuna, the god of the cosmic ocean. So, again, in Greek polytheism, it is natural to set over against the deities favourable to Troy the gods who assisted the Greeks. There were supposedly divine elements on the side of some communities which to other communities were menacing or hostile. Later on, these antinomies would stiffen into this or that form of *dualism*, as in the Persian conception of the warfare between Ahura-mazda and Angra-mainyu, but in the more primitive communities the differences between divine forces seem more like the caprices of wilful children than the settled antagonism of mutually incompatible principles.

Several causes, in addition to the above, assisted the development of polytheism. One is the matter of *sex*.[1] Henry Adams, in his *Mont Saint Michel*, accounts for the

[1] On the large subject of sex worship see the Article, "Phallism" in *E.R.E.*, by E. S. Hartland, and the work of Clifford Howard, *Sex Worship*, Chicago, 1902.

passionate adoration of the Virgin Mary by speaking of it as the recovery of an element in deity which monkish generations (and, later on, a Puritan generation) had attempted to overlook. It was this same instinct for "the eternal feminine" which provided consorts for the gods of Egypt and Babylon and which mated the Baalim of Palestine with the Ashtaroth. It was, once again, the instinct which developed the *çakti* worship of India, with Sarasvati, Lakshmi and Kali the respective spouses of Brahma, Vishnu and Çiva. A second additional cause is to be found in the domestic character given to primitive polytheism. The idea of the *family* had much to do in determining the relation of the gods to one another and in explaining the supersession of one generation of deities by another. We may note this particularly in the polytheisms of Egypt and Greece. In the former the Divine Ennead is simply the genealogical tree of the gods traced from the ancestor Ra down to the two pairs of sister-brother spouses, Osiris and Isis, Set and Nephthys. In the other case, we see the generation of Kronos succumbing to that of Zeus and all the other deities finding their proper place in the domestic hierarchy. We have here a significant symbol of the social quality we are obliged to postulate of the Supreme Being, a quality ultimately to be expressed in the Christian doctrine of the Trinity.

Still a third cause is to be found in the realm of *political* ideas. It may not be exactly true to say, with Jevons, that "polytheism is the price which must be paid by political development." Nevertheless, we do find a parallel between political conditions and conceptions of the divine world, apart from the Chinese view of a terrestrial system of government reflected in the other world just as trees are reflected in a lake. While, as in the Euphrates Valley, there existed numerous city-states, it was easy to believe in a number of locally limited gods, with a city-god of the most immediate importance. But as federation of cities became common the gods of the various cities had also to be federated until, as in the case of Marduk of Babylon, the deity of the dominant city in a federation became the supreme god in a pantheon. Under this system there might be several nature gods all originally having the same function, but now subordinated to one or another through political conditions. There followed also from this circumstance that the discarding of certain gods and introduction of new ones was of frequent occurrence. In the former case, some gods would retire into what Caliban calls "The Quiet," through supposed change of celestial dynasty or the decline of popular support. Some, instead of disappearing, would sink into the position of a court of vassal godlings or angels, such as "the sons of Yahweh" who are introduced into the *Book of Job*. Some, again, would change their character, storm-gods becoming war-gods, and so on. In the latter case, foreign gods of special renown or potency would be adopted after conquest or borrowed in an emergency. Thus we shall see Rome borrowing gods from Egypt and Asia Minor and the nations of the Euphrates borrowing gods from the great Emperors of Egypt. Still another element in the development of polytheism may be usefully remembered, namely, that sometimes there was a reflex action on the theology from the ritual of worship. Much of the mythology of the Indian fire-god, Agni, for example, was created at the altar itself, and no small part of the mythology of the drink-god, Soma, is probably derived from the actual ritual of the brewing.

Primitive polytheisms, then, were anything but stable theological systems. They witnessed, not unhelpfully, to man's instinctive sense of the manifoldness and complexity of a world order which it was hard as yet to conceive of as a universe. But in the presence of a growing demand intellectually for such a conception of unity polytheism was bound at last to yield. As a matter of fact it yielded in several different directions—not, of course, in any strictly chronological sequence.

One of these directions is represented by what is called *Henotheism*, as a cult leading to a kind of monolatry. The word henotheism was coined by Max Müller in 1860, but was later confused by him with the new term *Kathenotheism*, a term which has quite lost favour at the present time, though it seems possible to make a valid distinction between the two terms. For there are two forms of henotheism, one which selects gods for worship in rotation, as in the idolatry of Mecca during the "days of ignorance"; the other implies the choice of one deity out of many to be a kind of tribal or national god, without any denial of the existence of other gods whom it is well for other tribes to recognize. A good illustration is furnished in the national period of Hebrew religion when Yahweh was the national god, a God of gods, though other nations were supposed to be content with their own particular deities. It may be observed that henotheism is the foundation of *nationalism* in religion, a theology which has had some good results in establishing among nations a sense of special mission, that is, in creating the belief that each nation is in a true sense "a chosen people" (chosen, that is, for service, not for exclusive privilege), but which at the same time has ministered much to race pride, to the belief that God is "unser Gott," and which in times of war has led men to attribute to God every imaginable atrocity and revengefulness. The survival value of henotheism needs very careful study and the whole subject of nationalism in religion may be profitably pondered.

Henotheism is called by Pfleiderer "the porch to pure monotheism," but there are yet two or three steps to be taken before that goal is reached. One is that obstinate and, to some, ineradicable conviction that natural facts compel belief in some form or other of *Dualism*. Living in a climate with conflicting seasons of summer and winter, or suffering in the body from attacks of disease intruding into periods of robust health, or experiencing reverses of fortune just when everything looked prosperous, men found it easy to imagine two antagonistic principles warring for the supremacy or disporting themselves benevolently or malignly, as the case might be, with human beings for their puppets. Sometimes the forces of evil were only half personalized, irresponsible malignities resistant to the divine control; sometimes the dualism was a more explicit one, almost a campaign between two powers on equal terms, as in Manichæanism; sometimes the struggle was less strongly dramatized or shot with gleams of hope, as in the later Zoroastrianism. Sometimes, again, as in the Chinese doctrine of the Yin and the Yang, there was a kind of

" bilateral symmetry " rather than war to the knife between hostile principles. Dualism dies out of a religion with great difficulty; even to many Christians the ultimate fate of the universe is determined by a kind of " tug God, tug Devil " competition, with some doubt as to the final issue.

Another step which has to be surmounted by religion on its way towards monotheism is over the tendency to merge all divine personalities and powers, complementary or antagonistic, into one impersonal solution, with the theological result to which we give the name of *Pantheism*. Practically this signifies the identification of Nature with God. The idea of the divine transcendency (stressed to the exclusion of all else in what is called Deism) is lost, and all manifestations of the divine in Nature are viewed as the self-revelation of the eternal World Soul. Philosophically we may distinguish between the pantheism in which God is the only reality and the universe is illusory, and that in which the conception of God is merged in that of the universe. The former is known as *acosmism* [1] and may be illustrated by the teachings of the Indian Vedanta; the latter is called *pancosmism*. In the one case the idea of the world is lost in that of God; in the other God is lost in His world. Of the popular form, closely associated with mysticism, which we call *panentheism*, that is, God in the All, we have an illustration in the familiar lines of Tennyson's *The Higher Pantheism*:

> Speak to Him, thou, for He hears, and Spirit with Spirit can meet;
> Closer is He than breathing, nearer than hands and feet.

In this last idea we have a much needed correction of the deistic idea prevalent in the eighteenth century, a correction which we owe largely to the nineteenth-century teaching as to evolution. Apart from the acceptance of a belief in the divine immanence, the Christian doctrine of the Incarnation lacked a vital element.

But the complementary truths of transcendence and immanence must be kept in their proper association with one another. Unless this is done we are apt to have a pantheism which blurs the distinction between the *I* of

[1] Or *Theopanism*.

Man and the *Thou* of God and (to quote Dr. A. E. Garvie) "robs human personality of its sense of freedom." The sense of sin," he adds, "the feeling of penitence, and the effort of amendment become, and must become, to the consistent pantheistic thinker, illusive."

It was by way of turning away from pantheism that theological thought was brought, in large part through henotheism, to *Monotheism*, that is, the belief in one only God. Many different circumstances aided this significant transition, one which was most momentous in the interest of science as well as for religion. In the case of certain peoples the advance from a somewhat narrow nationalism towards an Empire inclusive of many different nationalities made the need of a unifying principle obvious. So Amenhotep IV, in Egypt, tried, under the Empire, to unite his subjects in the worship of Atun. So the Roman Emperors found the need of going outside the pagan pantheon to find a universally accepted God in Mithra or Christ, or even in the *genius* of the Emperor. In the next place, we see the Jews, scattered through the lands after their loss of territorial nationality and compelled either to disown their national God, Yahweh, as a failure, or else to endow Him with larger and universal qualities. Thirdly, we must not forget to give credit to the Greek philosophers who sought to define God "as the source, or the explanation, or the correlate, or the order, or the reasonableness of the world." And, lastly, we must give weight to the witness of individual prophets who, sometimes with philosophic argument, as in Isaiah xl ff., lashed the folly of the polytheists with whips of satiric scorn.

With monotheism humanity reached two out of the three elements which make up the complete theology, namely, *transcendence* and *immanence*. There was needed further only something (as in the Christian doctrine of the Incarnation) to convince the world as to God's *humanness*.

Coincidently with the development of a complete idea as to the power, character and attributes of God, there had been growing up from primitive times the idea of a Sky-world, or *Heaven*, in which life would find its consummation in communion with God, in and yet above Nature. The religion of Naturism is uranic, or heavenly, rather than chthonic, or earthly. It gives God an abode in the heavens rather than upon earth. In the beginning, indeed, say many of the cosmogonists, heaven and earth were close together, as two deities lying prone one upon the other. The intervention of a third deity caused a "heaving" (whence the word *heaven*) of the sky, or, as in the Babylonian myth, Marduk, the sun-god, splits the chaos-monster in twain, one part forming the solid vault which Hebrew cosmogony calls the firmament. Here were set the sun, moon and stars, and, while the cosmic waters flowed round and below the enclosed space, above all, in the central height, dwelt God with his attendant deities. It was natural that primitive man, to whom the sky-god was long the first of the gods—in the case of China T'ien, or Heaven, is the one universal deity—should look to God in the skies and think of the stars as the "hosts" (*Tzebaoth*) who waited on the divine word. It was natural, too, that sun, moon and stars should become deities in their own right, especially in lands where they shone more brilliantly than in our cloudier West. Only the Japanese, for one reason or another, paid little attention to the stars.

In contact with the earth, through pillars at the cardinal points, or by means of mountain heights, the sky seemed immovable and it was natural that men would be led to "lift their eyes unto the hills" in order to commune with God. The sacredness of mountains everywhere is stressed in religion, from primitive times down to our own day. Sages sought access to God by pilgrimages to Meru, or Olympus, or T'ai Shan, or Sinai. Above these holy summits God dwelt in the thick darkness, or, as in Greek mythology, "lay beside their nectar." Hither in dreams, as in the story of Jacob, God was revealed at the crest of a mountain ladder. Hither men journeyed, as in the story of Yudhisthira pressing on to enter Elysium. Occasionally there were other routes open to the heroes of old; the Norse heroes passed to Valhalla by the path of the rainbow; the Chinese Emperors on the back of the Dragon; the Roman Emperors mounted *ad astra* without any special attention to the means. Where there were no mountains, as in the Euphrates Valley, there was erected the many-storeyed *zikkurat*, by which, as by the planetary spheres, man might ascend to fellowship with the Supreme. In other lands the pagoda served a like purpose. The Chinese poet, Yang I, exclaims:

> Upon the tall pagoda's peak
> My hand can nigh the stars enclose;
> I dare not raise my voice to speak,
> For fear of startling God's repose.

There is something of the same significance in the church spire of the Christian world and a familiar verse tells how "the parish priest of Austerity climbed up the high church steeple to be near God, that he might bring God down to the people." So through all the ages, from the days of Sumerian city-states to the days of the Persian *Book of Arda Viraf*, and on again to the time of Muhammad's *Night Ride to Heaven*, and thence again to the days of Dante, with his planetary spheres leading upwards to the Empyrean, we have preserved for us the primitive conception in all its essential features intact.

Nor is this without its survival value. If our use of the preposition *up* is a piece of mythology, and the article of the Christian creed, "He ascended into heaven" but a figure to express a fact, have we not hold all through upon a principle which Naturistic religion was indeed inspired to seize. Men may mock as they will about a "three-storeyed" conception of the universe, but, gazing upwards to the skies, we are assisted in the realization of the life of man as indeed linked with the order of the heavens, and that at any rate one law binds our hopes with the courses of the stars. If man physically seems but "a flea on the epidermis of the earth," yet the fact that the light of a guiding star shines "over the place where the young child lay" gives us not merely one law but points also to "one far-off divine event."[1]

[1] The Negrillos of Equatorial Africa bury their dead with face to the sky, "for it is to the sky that man must finally ascend."

So we take our leave, not unsympathetically, of the *Creed* of Naturism. If it be primitive to think of God as close at hand, if, again, it be primitive to place Him in a local heaven for His dwelling-place, we may yet remember that without these primitive conceptions we could not have our sense of God's abiding presence, nor could we look beyond the starved aspirations of earth to fullness of life in a heaven which, in the words of St. Bernard, is

Urbs Sion unica, mansio mystica, condita, coelo.

## CHAPTER IV

### *The Religion of Naturism*

If we cannot have a cult without a creed, it must be a foregone conclusion that we cannot have a creed without a cult. Out of beliefs which are quite ill-defined, even out of beliefs which are held quite conventionally, or even unconsciously, arises the main religious activity of mankind. People, so far as the ritual of their daily life is concerned, may be actually living on the capital of other men's faith, but they are, nevertheless, living on a working hypothesis of some sort. Among primitive men, however little they were disposed to reason on the matter, the practices of life were the direct outcome of the things they had learned to believe.

Much of this, of course, followed from the inevitable anthropomorphism of the popular theology to which we have referred. If, on the one hand, it was felt that every man " wears as his robe the garment of the sky, so close his union with the cosmic plan," on the other hand, Nature might well be represented under the figure of a cosmic man. It might therefore safely be postulated that the activities of Nature must betray the feelings and moods of a man. Nature, like man, was sometimes fickle and must be wooed; sometimes it was angry and must be placated; sometimes it was deliberately hostile and had better be evaded. Much of primitive religion, as distinguished from primitive theology, consisted of very human efforts to cajole or placate or outwit a Nature with which man, in his own interest, needed to be on good terms. On the whole, however, it was man's conviction that Nature was not unreasonable and might ordinarily be treated as one treated his fellow human beings. This sense of the general reliability of Nature, when its operations were not thwarted by failure of power, was from the first one of religion's great assets, and has been also the foundation of science. It corresponds with that primary postulate of our own philosophy that the operations of Nature are in the rational order and may be followed, at least up to a certain point, by our own rational faculty. Such a belief was bound to provide a tiny Ariadne thread which, held fast in human hands, would eventually bring men out of the dark cave of ignorance and set their faces towards the light. It is from this point that we start in order to follow aright the developments of practical religion from the days of primitive men to our own.

The first step, under the stimulus of naturistic awe, arises from the observation and interpretation of what we call Omens. The use of the term, which is derived from the Old Latin *Osmen*, but which is of doubtful meaning, should be carefully distinguished from that of Divination, which we shall discuss a little later. In the omen Nature is speaking of its own accord, making advances for the warning or guidance of mankind, the progeny of Nature. Where the information given implies ill-fortune, we often speak of omens as *portents* (Gk. *terata*), but in general the word signifies information conveyed without reference to its being good or bad. From certain indications, each of which might be regarded as a separate act of approach on the part of Nature, man in course of time learned either to anticipate success or to scurry away to shelter, as chickens learn to flee from the shadow of a hawk.

The subject is a big one and must of necessity be here treated with extreme brevity. It includes reference to the observation of all sorts of things, some of them "true" omens, others of the *post hoc ergo propter hoc* order. There were many bodily actions, of an involuntary sort, such as hiccoughing, sneezing, and the like, which needed interpretation. In this connection we shall recall the lines of *Macbeth*:

> By the twitching of my thumbs
> Something wicked this way comes

and many presentiments of the kind in Indian literature. There were also omens from the sight of birds, snakes and beasts of all kinds. Magpies suggested to the experienced:

> One for sorrow, two for mirth,
> Three for a wedding, four for a birth.

The Babylonian *Omen Tablets*[1] contain hundreds of examples of omens upon which men were wont regularly to rely. There are omens derived from symptoms exhibited by the sick, from the members of the body, from fire, flame, light and smoke, from the shape, colour and movements of clouds, from the appearance of scorpions, horses, asses, dogs, and, indeed, from almost every imaginable thing. The whole constitutes a huge generalization, of which some things are valid, others supported only by tradition or accepted through superstition. A description of Chinese omens, too, would fill a volume, embracing instances not unlike those common in the Euphrates Valley and many more besides. Japanese history, again, is full of reference to omens, from those referred to in the ancient story of the Empress Jingo and her invasion of Korea to those observed at the present day. In Roman history many an issue was determined by the appearance of some propitious or unpropitious omen. In the Bible, both in the *Old* and the *New Testament*, many an intimation was conveyed by dreams, altogether apart from the initiative of the dreamer. And, to show the extent to which omens have continued to win credence in comparatively modern times, we have only to turn over the pages of Shakespeare. Thus we have Hubert's warning to King John:

> My lord, they say five moons were seen to-night:
> Four fixed; and the fifth did whirl about
> The other four, in wondrous motion.[2]

In *Julius Cæsar* we have the omens predictive of the murder:

> A lioness hath whelped in the streets:
> And graves have yawn'd and yielded up their dead:
> Fierce, fiery warriors fought upon the clouds,
> In ranks, and squadrons, and right form of war,
> Which drizzled blood upon the Capitol.[3]

---

[1] See British Museum *Guide to Babylonian and Assyrian Collections.*
[2] *King John,* Act iv., Sc. 2.
[3] *Julius Cæsar,* Act ii., Sc. 2.

And in *Macbeth* we have the horses eating one another, against the use of nature, on the night of Duncan's "taking off."[1] Even the atmosphere of the plays of Shakespeare is charged with the ominous, as in *Lear*, where the storm on the heath corresponds with the inner aspect of the mad monarch's devastated life.

The belief in omens, moreover, still survives, not merely in generalizations which have a more or less tenuous thread of science for their support, but in fancies which are for the most part merely superstitious. In my own University, for example, the issue of a football game is quite frequently regarded as depending upon the flight of sea-gulls across the stadium.

A large department in the history of omens concerns the pseudo-science of *astrology*, that is, the belief that human destiny is controlled by the stars or by the conjunction of planets at the birth of an individual. It was at the core of much of the early religion of the Euphrates Valley and of Arabia and many men in modern times, in spite of the words of *Iago* and *Edmund*, have remained convinced that fate is "in our stars and not ourselves."[2] Napoleon III, for example, believed firmly in his star, and biographers of Robert Browning have connected the poet, both at birth and death, with stellar phenomena. Our dictionary, moreover, bears eloquent witness to man's erstwhile trust in the heavenly bodies in such words as *disaster*, *jovial*, *mercurial*, *martial*, and the like. The story of the birth of Jesus, too, would lack one of its most beautiful traditions if we discarded the incident of "the gray-haired wisdom of the East" led on to Bethlehem by the star.

Modern religion does not call upon us to discontinue our use of omens so much as to weed them out a little carefully and reject those only which show a misunderstanding of the wise words Nature intends for our attentive ear. So we pass to the consideration of a subject at least as vast in its range, namely, that of

DIVINATION.—The use of divination differs from the observation of omens in that in this case we voluntarily and

[1] *Macbeth,* Act ii., Sc. 4.
[2] *Othello,* Act i., Sc. 3; *King Lear,* Act i., Sc. 2.

of set purpose interrogate Nature as to what it has to say for our guidance or on our behalf. We are now no longer passive recipients of information, but earnest seekers, wooers of Nature's favours, suppliants at her tribunal.

The varieties of divination are practically endless and many of them are designated by the use of the suffix—*mancy*. This is derived ultimately from the Skt. root *man*, to think, but more immediately from the Greek *mantia*. The Greek *mantis*, or diviner, was regarded as not distantly related to the madman, and some *mancies* will appear to our modern science as mad as anything to which man has ever given his devotion. The instances here to be mentioned must be taken as merely windows opened upon a vast and bewildering landscape.

There is, for example, *oneiromancy*, or divination by dreams, that is, visions induced by the method known as incubation. The seeker, wrapping himself perhaps in the skin of a sacrificed animal, in order to ensure contact with his divinity, would resort to a particular temple, there to be visited by the god and oracularly inspired. Instances of such induced dreams will occur to the reader from almost any literature. For instance, the Keltic druid would glut himself with the flesh of a sacred white bull and sleep while four fellow priests chanted over him "the spell of truth," with the expectation of receiving nocturnal direction as to the choice of a king.

Then we have various forms of *augury*, in which the movements of living birds were deliberately studied by experts known as augurs. The bodies of the slain sacrifices were examined for marks of significance upon the viscera. This was the work of the haruspices and the examination was called *haruspicy*. In the temples of Babylon and elsewhere the study of the liver was almost a speciality, since the liver was regarded by many as a soul-seat. This form of divination is called *hepatoscopy*. Scores of species of divination are comprised under the general head of *sortilege*, or the casting of lots. This might take the form of tossing up a coin or stick, the drawing out of short or long pieces of paper or bamboo, the opening at random of a book in order to offer a significant passage to the eye—*sortes litur-*

*gicae*—or the placing of sticks in a vertical position in a bowl of water to watch the direction of their fall. Many choices, important and unimportant, were determined by such methods, from the finding of a lucky day for a funeral to the election of a Christian apostle.[1] It is worth noting in all this that men never supposed they were making an appeal to mere chance. It was rather the throwing of responsibility for a right choice on the unerring justice of Nature. Not luck but a divine providence ruled, and settled for man what he was unable to settle for himself. Under this same head would come *rhabdomancy*, or the divining with rods, as well as *belomancy*, the divining with arrows. This last-named method has many illustrations, including Nebuchadrezzar's use of arrows, as described in Ezekiel xxi. 31, that of the prophet Elisha's in 2 Kings xiii. 15, and perhaps that of David in 1 Sam. xx. 14. Then we have *hippomancy*, the divining by the neighing of horses, so picturesquely illustrated in the account by Herodotus of the choice of Darius Hystaspes to be King of Persia.[2] There are, again, *pyromancy*, divination by noting the flames rising from the sacrificial altar; *hydromancy*, divination by water, and *cylicomancy*, or divination by cups. This last is found in many forms, including examples as far apart as the divining cup of Joseph, mentioned in Gen. xliv. 5, the "seven-ringed cup" of Jamshid, mentioned by Umar Khayyam, and the divining cup of the Irish king Cormac, by means of which he discerned between truth and falsehood. A form of cup-divination is that of crystal-gazing, which also has illustrations in every part of the world.

Another wide-spread form of divination is that known as *scapulomancy*, or *omoplatoscopy*, in which the shoulder-blade of a sheep (in Scotland), or of a deer (in Japan), or a piece of tortoise-shell (in China) is scorched to provide the cracks which the diviner proceeds to interpret. We may also mention here the curious form of divination by the *last word*, of which we have illustrations in the Bible in such passages as Judges vii. 11, I Sam. xiv. 7–11, and in many places elsewhere.

One of the most important of all was the judicial test

[1] Acts i. 26.

[2] Herodotus, III. 85.

known as the *ordeal*, in which Nature was invoked to eke out the inadequate judgement of man. There were many varieties of ordeal, some of them simple, some of them quite impressive. In certain cases it consisted of nothing but the giving of a piece of bread to be swallowed, and, as to-day a self-conscious child finds it difficult to swallow a pill, so no doubt many a conscience-convicted criminal choked over the test. Sometimes the test was in drinking a medicated draught and of this we have illustration in the ordeal of bitter water prescribed in Jewish law for the woman suspected of adultery,[1] and in the many poison tests employed in Central Africa. Sometimes the accused person was thrown into the water to sink or swim. This is the test ordered in the Babylonian *Code of Hammurabi*, and this was the method used by the witch-hunters of Salem. In this case the *Code* was the more merciful, since in ancient Babylon the woman who floated was regarded as innocent, whereas in Massachusetts she was promptly put to death as guilty. The classical Indian ordeals were four in number, namely, by water, fire, poison or hanging. In Japan there was the walking across a hot bed of coals, a test still used, as described by Percival Lowell,[2] and one which in other lands provided us with the expression, "hauled over the coals." In Japan it appears to require chiefly a good nerve, as does also the test of the ladder of swords, which can be safely ascended unless the climber nervously slides his foot on the sword. A special form of ordeal, now happily discarded in most civilized lands, is that of the *duel*, or wager of battle, a contest which was not intended to favour the better shot or swordsman, but rather to throw the responsibility of revealing the juster cause upon God. A duel on the larger scale, but undertaken in the like faith, is *war*, but the ancient justification for the arbitrament of battle has been largely forgotten to-day and superseded by less defensible arguments.

In all the forms of divination there was a real reliance upon the essential justice and morality of Nature. A moral universe, it was felt, would not let her children down. Thus the survival value of all divination lies in the fact that natural law is indeed trusted to control the circumstances of man's

[1] Numbers v. 18. [2] See *Occult Japan* by Percival Lowell.

daily life. Our uprising and our down-sitting, our going out and our coming in, our eating and drinking, even our amusements, are all guided and assisted through the increasing articulateness of Nature. In this way we become more and more a part of the cosmic process, to co-operate with which is so important a part of our religion.

A step further takes us from the practices of divination to that of *Imitative*, or *Sympathetic*, or *Analogic Magic*. The question has been quite frequently raised as to whether Magic can in any respect be regarded as religion. Some writers have made religion begin only where magic ends. Jevons has described magic as a perversion of science as well as of religion. But this is hardly a fair statement. It ought to be clear that in what we call imitative magic, at any rate, there was no intention whatsoever of overriding natural law. It was rather the assumption that man was able, by imitating the natural process as far as he was able to understand it, to assist, or even speed up the operations of Nature. If he was able really to enter sympathetically into the methods of Nature's working, it appeared to him that he not only had the power to help, but that the obligation to help was his also. Indeed, he was but anticipating the conviction of Francis Thompson that man was "the great arm-fellow of God." Thanks to this primitive assurance, which some have desired to put outside the boundaries of religion altogether, man remains convinced that he has power to work together with God for the carrying out of the divine purpose.

With all primitive man's reliance upon Nature, he had behind him only a brief tradition of the regularity of natural processes, and therefore he could never be absolutely certain that the operations of Nature would continue unflaggingly without some aid from outside itself. If the Kelts of old were not without fear that the sky might at any time fall upon them, and if even John Ruskin could assert that he should never be surprised if the sun some morning declined to rise, it is not strange that early man had many a dread ere he could be entirely sure of the constancy of Nature in the matter of times and seasons. Yet he knew that upon this regularity depended not only the success of his quest for food but even life itself. What, then, was more natural than that he should bend himself to the task of co-operating with Nature in any way which seemed likely to be effective? It was not merely his responsibility; it was also his duty as a member of the group.

In the stage of nomadism it is probable that there was less need for imitative magic, since the nomad could always follow up the pasturage from one locality to another. Yet he felt it necessary to stand in some awe of the *moon* and from this developed in due time the institution of the Sabbath. The general belief that the moon was dangerous, which is reflected in such words as *moonstruck* and *lunatic*, made men unwilling to work till particular crises were reached or past. But, after the period of settled agricultural life was reached, there were several spheres in which the use of imitative magic was deemed a necessity.

There was, first of all, the need of bringing the *rain*. The rain-cloud was readily personified. Sometimes, as in China, it was thought of as the *Dragon*, who had to be encouraged to visit and fructify the earth. Sometimes, as in India, it was pictured as the divine *Cow*, whose milk was required for the refreshment of the thirsty soil. Elsewhere it was the *Thunder-bird*. In all cases something had to be done. There were many ways in which man might render assistance. In a great many cases all that was necessary was to imitate the thunder. For this purpose we have the use of the *Bull-roarer*, a piece of wood whirled in the air to give forth the requisite noise. This curious device is found in some form or another all the way from Australia to Ireland. In the latter country, in ancient times, it was known as the *voice of Fál*, or the *wheel of Fál*, or *Roth Ramach*. Another method, particularly in China, was the imitating of thunder by the smiting of gongs and the beating of drums. The imitation of lightning was thought equally effective. In many places, notably in Arizona and New Mexico, there were the *snake-dances*, in which the wriggling of the serpents upon the sand, or in the mouths of the performers, was supposed to simulate the lightnings which would presently rend the clouds and make the floods descend. In some other places it was thought sufficient to pour forth a little water on the ground as an imitative charm. It will be remembered that this was an important piece of ceremonial at the Jewish Feast of Tabernacles and had originally this significance. It was while this libation was being poured out on the Temple floor from a golden ewer that Christ made the great announcement of Himself as the Water of Life.[1]

Even more important for imitative magic than the rain was the *Sun*, in both its diurnal and its annual movements. One of the very earliest of charms, found in pre-historic graves, is the *sun-wheel*, which was supposed to have influence upon the solar chariot. Down to the present day the Swastika, arranged as a wheel moving from left to right, is for millions a sign of good fortune. Other solar symbols of a similar significance are to be recognized in the *Three-legged Crow*, or Yata-garasu, of Japanese myth, and the three-legged symbol which forms the arms of the Isle of Man, originally perhaps borrowed from the Hittites. But the round dance, prevalent everywhere, was the sun-wheel in practical use, in which men, keeping always to the right, maintained the sun on its course and brought good luck to the world. Thus was introduced into the marriage ceremony of ancient India the triple circling to the right, about the household fire, known as the *pradakshina*. This became the *dextratio* of the Roman ceremony and the *déisil* of the Kelts. The circuit of a kingdom, from the days of the old Indian *açvamedha* and the progresses of the High Chiefs of Ireland down to the going of modern judges "on circuit" was founded on this belief. To go in the opposite direction was to invite disaster. When King Loiguire set out to meet St. Patrick with hostile intent he drove his chariot "with a left-hand-wise turn." At Tara the term *déisil* was given to "a sward that brought luck before dying, where people used to make the right-hand-wise turn." "I know not where to turn" says a young man in Plautus, and his attendant replies, "Turn to the right, if you worship the gods." In India and elsewhere the "swinging ceremonies" were practised in aid of the sun; in Ireland and other

[1] John vii. 37.

places horse races became popular for the same reason. The result of many customs of this sort was to make, down to our own day, the right hand the place of honour for a guest, and the southern quarter, that is, to the right of the sun-rising, was the fortunate point of the compass.[1]

The seasonal positions of the sun were not less important than the diurnal. All the four quarterly positions, namely, the two *solstices* and the two *equinoxes*, were regarded as critical and calling for human assistance. At the midwinter and midsummer solstices, the one associated with the birth of Christ and the other with the birth of John the Baptist (illustrating the Baptist's declaration: "He must increase, but I must decrease"), the sun must needs be helped in his lengthening and his declining days alike with the gift of fire. The *Yule log* and the *Fires of St. John* have the same ultimate explanation and I have seen in the Yang-tze valley the lighting of the midsummer fires precisely at noon on the day of the summer solstice, though the Chinese seemed quite unaware of the significance of their act.

The observances at the time of the equinoxes are less stable, but in most religions one comes across the dramatic representation, in some form or another, at the spring season, of the annual passion and death of the earth (or fruit) god, and of his resurrection amid the rejoicing of all the faithful. In ancient Babylonia was enacted the myth of *Tammuz and Ishtar*, and as late as the sixth century B.C. Ezekiel reproves the women of Jerusalem for "weeping for Tammuz" within the Temple courts.[2] In Egypt *Osiris* took the place of Tammuz and *Isis* of Ishtar, while the women made little clay figures of Osiris and embedded therein seeds which the recovered vitality of the god would cause to sprout. Isis was the goddess of fecundity, through whose fidelity her brother-spouse was won back from the land of the dead. Similarly, in Syria, we have the myth of *Adonis and Venus*, in the old Irish sagas the legend of Tephi,

[1] Cf. the mistake of the Latin geographers in translating *Yemen* (the South) as Arabia Felix. Note also the giving by Jacob to his youngest son the fortunate name of *Ben-yamin* (right-hand son).

[2] Ezekiel viii. 14.

the Keltic Persephone, and Tea, the Keltic Demeter, and in the Teutonic lands it was the story of Balder the beautiful, slain untimely by his blind brother Hodir, and sent down to the dark halls of Hela until, amid the rejoicings of universal nature, life was restored. From the making of the old Adonis gardens to the sowing of sweet-peas on Good Friday in our own day, the same idea continued to find expression. In like manner, from the celebration of the death and resurrection of Bel-Marduk in Babylon[1] to the commemoration of the passion and resurrection of Christ, there has been the same continuity of thought. Not that the sanctions of the Christian Easter are invalidated when seen to rest upon a natural basis, but rather that Nature had from the beginning its "immanent *Telos*." The impressiveness of man's protest against death is thereby increased and man's contributory ministry to the victory of life over death enlarged. The Easter triumph is the more secure because human grief of old demanded the return of the earth-god. The observance of the autumnal equinox is concerned rather with the cult of the dead than with Naturism, so will not here be described.

Much importance is assigned in primitive religion to the assistance which man may give through imitative magic to the growth of the *crops*. Of course, we recognize this to-day in many practical ways, but early man had his own ways of rendering assistance. Frazer, in *The Golden Bough* gives us instances by the score. We have mention of the flax-sowers in Thüringen, walking with long strides through the fields, the seed-bag swaying from their shoulders, so that tall flax may sway in the wind. We are told of the women in Sumatra, letting their long hair hang loose, that the rice may grow luxuriantly. The peasants of the Franche-Comté are described as dancing and leaping at the Carnival that the hemp may grow tall. The peasants of Bavaria and Swabia and Baden leap over the midsummer bonfires, with the cry: "Flax, flax, grow seven ells high." Peasants in Norway and Sweden leap over the Balder's bale-fires, with the same intent. I myself have seen the girls in Korea, at the New Year Festival, leaping from a kind of spring-

[1] S. Langdon, *J.R.A.S.*, January 1931.

board or see-saw, in order that the crops may grow taller than the house. Customs of the sort abound the world over.

Space, indeed, would fail us were we to recall all the methods used in imitative magic. As one illustration out of many we may select the matter of *Knots*. From the Esquimaux woman, Oolahloo, who, as *angiakok*, takes her fur cord from a cariboo's neck out into the storm to tie knots in the wind to King Aeolus whom Jove empowers "foedere certo et premere, et laxas sciret dare jussus habenas," and so on to the commission given to St. Peter: "Whatsoever thou shalt bind on earth shall be bound in heaven; and whatsoever thou shalt loose on earth shall be loosed in heaven," we have real continuity of idea. Whether we think of the Norns spinning and crossing and cutting off the thread of life, or of Hardy's account of the "eternal artistries in circumstance" which the "Will has woven with an absent head," we find ourselves dealing with the same thought. Magicians in ancient Babylon tied man with the knots of disease; their fellows in Persia knotted up the limbs of King Gushtasp's charger—which Zoroaster healed with his counter-magic, as did Odin when he charmed away the lameness of "Balder's foal's foot." A wicked Jew bewitched Muhammad by tying nine knots in a string which he then threw into a well; witches in the Middle Ages prevented the consummation of marriage by fastening locks and knotting a charm, which the careful bridegroom sought to overcome by going to church with his shoe-laces untied; Queen Mab worked mischief by plaiting the "manes of the horses in the night;" the Quran invokes help from Allah against "the evil of the blowers upon knots;" the Shetland seaman buys winds from the wise women in the purchase of a knotted handkerchief. And so we might go on almost indefinitely, remembering all the while that these efforts of ignorant men to bind the Fenriswulf of evil were instinctive gropings towards the undeniable truth that we are indeed God's "arm-fellows," in union with Him who "ad liberandum hominem" became Incarnate.[1]

[1] H. H. Gowen, "Knots," *Anglican Theological Review*, July 1929.

It is tempting to refer to some other methods of assisting Nature, such as the making of clay or paper images of horses and other beasts of burden to serve either as *porte-bonheurs*, or, as is the more common, *porte-malheurs*. Steeds on which the plagues of cholera and small-pox might ride away are everywhere in evidence and touch upon the subject of the scape-goat. Miss Emerson found the peasants of Panchperwa, in India, using them with great conviction.[1]

It is not difficult to see the survival value of imitative magic. It is expressed in our own religious rites, as, for instance, in the celebration of the Christian Eucharist, where, in such words as, "Do this," there is of course far more intended than participation in a commemorative act. It is expressed, again, in all forms of social service, in which most people take part in the belief that they are co-operating with a divine providence for the amelioration of human ills. It is expressed in a larger way in the human instinct that the cause of cosmic evolution is itself served by our personal effort to achieve the highest. Our contribution as yet may be lamentably small, but "the intent's the thing."

Before passing from the subject something should be said as to the relation of imitative magic to the *Arts*. Other things have, of course, entered to determine the development of these, but certainly the utilitarian preceded the æsthetic. The "play"[2] element in the primitive world was small. Children played by imitating the acts of their elders, but the elders themselves "played" in grim earnest for the achievement of communal, or, more rarely, of individual ends. Thus, for example, in the *dance* and *drama*, the "acting" was not pretence but real "doing" (*dromenon*), not for the entertainment of an audience but for the service of a clan. Failure to participate was a public sin. "He does not dance," complained the Greek of the civic slacker. The round dance kept the sun in its orbit, the rain dance brought delectable showers, the enactment of heroic rôles made the heroism of the dead an asset for the living. So the dancing-ground, or *orchestrion*, became a social service centre for the antique world. To use another example,

[1] Miss Gertrude Emerson, *Voiceless India*, p. 90.
[2] Play is probably from *pflegen*, to do one's duty.

the art of *painting* was in like manner dependent on its utility as imitative magic. Men did not scratch the figures of bears or of foes transfixed with spears upon the dark walls of their caverns for the purpose of providing a picture-gallery: it was thus they captured the *mana* of the beast they hunted or the soul of the enemy they fought. Even the women assisted the magic, by dance or song or picture, while the men-folk were campaigning. *Music*, too, benefited by this practice. In general, perhaps, the intention was *apotropaic*, in assistance given to the sun to rid itself of the shadow of eclipse. But quite often the most unmusical din of primitive music was meant, as mentioned already, to imitate the thunder and so bring the needed rain to refresh the fields.

Probably one of the very earliest manifestations of primitive practice in religion is that intrusion of the negative in what we call

TABU.—This is a Tongan word which appears in its Hawaiian form as *Kapu*,[1] doubtfully derived from the primitive Polynesian words *ta*, a mark, and *pu*, exceedingly. It has the same general significance as the Greek *hagios* and the Latin *sacer* and represents the negative side of *mana*, the ambivalence of which makes the appropriation of certain things desirable and that of other things (or the same things under different circumstances) dangerous. It is to be illustrated all the way from the restrictions placed upon the kings of Tara, as to letting the sun rise on them in bed, as to crossing certain places after sunset, or dismounting at certain places on a Wednesday, and the like, or the ban placed upon the *Flamen Dialis* at Rome as to walking under a vine-trellis, eating beans, or naming a goat, down to the forbidding of the kings of Unyoro in Central Africa the use of beef or milk except from a special herd. Even Papal *Interdicts*, *Defence of the Realm Acts*, governmental regulations of many sorts, are forms of tabu. Voltaire says, satirically, of course, of the poems of Rousseau: "Sacrés ils sont, car personne n'y touche." But primitive man took the matter of tabus very seriously. We have already referred to man's primitive fear of the moon and to the

[1] In Samoan and Marquesan the word is *tapu*.

connection of the Sabbath with man's early refusal to work during the full of the moon. We have referred also to the incident in the story of the Ark, whose *mana* proved so destructive to the men of Beth-shemesh. Many tabus are recorded in the Old Testament, from the exclusion of the people from the shrine of the Tabernacle and from the neighbourhood of Mount Sinai during the giving of the Law to food restrictions and restraints placed upon labour. Indeed, the commandments of the *Decalogue*, with their reiterated "Thou shalt not," are largely of the character of tabus.

Tabus are either inherent or imposed, the former being the result of some age-long and general experience, the latter developing with the extension of kingcraft and the power of the priesthood. The many tabus of this latter sort which prevailed in Hawaii, until their abolition in 1819 by Kamehameha II, afford an interesting study. In the year just named, 1819, women were still being put to death in Hawaii for eating bananas, or other food prohibited for the female sex.[1] The protection of kings and priests by specially imposed tabus was due to the belief that these had more *mana* than ordinary folk. Some of the caste restrictions of India, such as the refusal of the Veda to the çudras, would probably come under this head.

As representing the earlier stages of law-making and law-enforcement, the tabu had its value. It was, in most respects, an evil day for Hawaii when the tabus were abolished without time being allowed for the growth of a higher law by way of substitute. We are still ourselves to a great extent under the dominion of tabus, personal, social and legal. It is, of course not intended that man should ever escape the incidence of law, or, like Ajax, defy the lightnings of a moral universe. But, if we are to become really moral, the day should dawn when respect for law should be without fear of the police and when the "Thou shalt not" should be imposed from within rather than from without. Eventually, no doubt, we shall find, with Dante, that "in His will is our peace." Meanwhile, we need to have the moral equivalent of the tabu in what is called

[1] There were very many tabus affecting the liberty of woman.

reverence. "Be ye holy, for I am holy, saith the Lord"; "serve Him with reverence and godly fear."

A step beyond the use of magic of the imitative sort—perhaps a little off the right line of development—is the use of another kind of magic to which we give the name of

MANTRAS.—The word is Sanskrit, from the root *man*, to think, but in the early Indian literature it is particularly applied to the Vedic hymns considered not so much as poems as spells. In the use of mantras generally we discern the attempt to go beyond the assisting of Nature towards the effort to force Nature's hand, to compel her, willy-nilly, to do anything we may require of her. Man asked, somewhat impatiently, whether there were not a secret key to the operations of Nature which, if known, would save him the trouble of ordinary co-operation. Might it not be possible to go beyond her somewhat pedestrian way of helping us if we could only get access to that secret? So Nature might be transformed into a "slave of the lamp," instead of an ally. This thought suggested all sorts of magical devices, among which the most highly valued was a species of asceticism, or *catharsis*, which would bestow upon men superhuman powers. In this there was no inevitable relation to morals, as we conceive them. A demon, such as Ravana, could, by standing on his head between five fires for so many thousands of years, achieve power over Brahma and all the gods. The proper charm, or mantra, would cause the sun to stand still in the heavens and death to stay its course. Mantras might enable men to storm the heavens and dethrone the gods.

There were all kinds of mantras, from simple and apparently meaningless words like *abracadabra* and *sesame* to the secret name of some mighty divinity. This last in itself touches a large subject, since the *Name* was regarded as part of the personality of a god or man. Isis, wringing from Ra his hidden name in order to dethrone him, Jacob exclaiming "Tell me thy name" to the mysterious stranger wrestling with him at the fords of Jabbok, and so on to children chanting their rhyme in the game:

What is your name?
Pudding and tame.

are all illustrations of this using of the name as a mantra. *Nomina sunt numina.* "We know thy name, O assembly!" says the author of the *Atharva Veda*, in a charm to get control of the town-meeting. So Alexander gained possession of the secret name of Tyre before he could subdue the fortress. To the Jew the name *Yahweh* was the secret title not to be used "for a vain end" (*Third Commandment*), and the *Toldoth Yeshu* tells the grotesque story of Jesus stealing the Divine Name from the Holy of Holies and hiding it in His thigh, in order to perform His miracles. "The Name" of God is always to be "Hallowed," and the Name of Jesus, in the New Testament, is "the Name above every other Name." But primitive men used the name, human or divine, as they might have used any other form of *mana*, to secure individual and sometimes quite selfish ends.[1]

The mantra idea has survived, unhappily, in certain un-Christian conceptions of *prayer*. Not a few pray to obtain what they think they want, even though the request may be in defiance of the divine will. Nor may we deny altogether the power of man to get, in a terribly literal fashion, the things he craves for. The *Psalms* describe the experience of Israel in the wilderness: "He gave them their desire and sent leanness withal into their souls." A picture by G. F. Watts represents a young man being dragged by a monster to the depths of the sea, and the motto runs: "Thou hast what thou hast desired with all thy heart."

Yet, after all, the mantra idea has its proper survival value. Man's control of Nature is in many respects real and often beneficial to the race. Man has harnessed the lightnings, bridled the cataracts, robbed many terrible dragons of their teeth, forced an apparently reluctant Nature to minister in the temple of his gods. In many rash attempts he has hitherto been frustrated and has failed; but man's Promethean rôle has not been wholly unworthy of the creature in whom is the divine spark, nor has it on the whole been played unsuccessfully.

There is only one more phase of the religion of Naturism which need be mentioned here and that is one which is

[1] H. H. Gowen, "The Name," *Anglican Theological Review*, April 1930.

rendered more than ordinarily complex through its involvement with things outside of Naturism. This is

SACRIFICE.—Sacrifice, as just suggested, has several diverse aspects, but from our present point of view it is man's effort to sustain the course of Nature by providing the requisite replenishment of power. It has therefore affinity with Imitative Magic. The powers of heaven may all too easily flag and fail:

> The sun himself grow dim with age,
> And Nature sink in years;

therefore it is necessary to furnish sustenance in the way of renewed force to Nature, just as we would give it to other things upon which we depend. We must do this even though we drain ourselves of our very life-blood in the endeavour. We do not need to say much on the subject now, as it will come up for discussion again under another head.

In conclusion, it will be seen that all the ritual of Naturistic religion bears witness to the homogeneity of life, the interdependence of all things cosmic. It was a truly great conception and one which necessarily entailed the ultimate doctrine of "all for each and each for all." As the clouds fed the sea and the sea again gave its waters to the clouds, so all men would feel bound to help the powers of heaven to fulfil their mighty task. This is the real significance of all uranic, as in some respects contrasted with chthonic, religion. The head of the victim which was offered to the skies was invariably lifted upwards, while the head of the victim offered to the powers below was bowed towards the earth. So sacrifice becomes our human way of eternalizing values. The thing offered is not, as some complain, "spilt like water on the ground:" it is life poured out for cosmic ends. Nurhachu did not lose his famous document of "the Seven Hates" when he burned it; he simply filed it in the eternal world. Man does not lose the thing he sacrifices; he simply lays it up "where neither moth nor rust can corrupt."

Our last thought, then, of Naturistic Religion is of something in the main cheerful and uplifting. It has inspired many to great hopes and to great deeds. It is the kind of influence (to which the prophet added the thought of One Who was Nature's Lord) to which Isaiah appealed when he bade the depressed Jews of the Exile period: "Lift up your eyes on high, and see who hath created these; that bringeth out their host by number; he calleth them all by name."[1] It is, again, the influence implicit in the appeal of George Herbert:

> Lift up thine eyes;
> Take stars for money, stars not to be bought
> By any art, yet to be purchased.

[1] Isaiah xl. 26.

# CHAPTER V

## *The Creed of Spiritism*

APART altogether from the controversy, waged with some heat in the nineteenth century, as to whether religion was the outcome of Nature worship or of Spirit worship, considerable discussion has been carried on over the question: Which was prior to the other? One might almost as well argue as to the priority of the chicken or the egg. Quite possibly primitive man did not think about the matter at all, but felt mystified in the presence of both mysteries impartially and as the mood took him. There is certainly no reason for denying that the " sense of the numinous " might easily be awakened in either direction more or less coincidently. The same mind which could respond to the sense of wonder with the words: " When I consider Thy heaven, the work of Thy hands," would also be able to express wonderment over the mystery within himself with the reflection: " What is man that Thou art mindful of him? " All the way from *Caliban* to the Psalmist and thence to *Hamlet* such questions would inevitably arise.

It will follow that in Spiritism, as in Naturism, there must be a creed before there could be a cult. Indeed the word creed is etymologically connected with the primary duty towards the dead which in India men called a *çraddha*. In the present chapter, therefore, we shall endeavour to state the several articles of this creed with as much explicitness as possible.

To begin with, it must have been exceedingly vague, an obstinate impression that man's nature was not wholly summed up in this body of flesh. It is not, of course, necessary to read back into the primitive past that complex psychology which induced the Egyptian to describe man's personality as consisting of nine different elements (*ba*, *khaibit*, *ka*, etc.), or which led the Chinese to distinguish between the varieties of *hun* and the varieties of *po*. It is not even necessary to assume as very primitive the idea of a tripartite personality such as we have in the Hebrew *basar*, *nephesh* and *ruaḥ*, or the Greek *sarx*, *psyché* and *pneuma*, an analysis made familiar to us by the translation of these terms respectively as *body*, *soul* and *spirit*. We have probably read into the ideas of primitive people a more formal analysis of personality than they actually possessed, though there is but little doubt that savage races were often perplexed as to the distinction between the " long " soul and the " short " soul, between the animal soul which was dissipated soon after death and the spirit which was believed to survive. As to this there was inevitably much vagueness and even the New Testament terms of *body*, *soul* and *spirit* are employed with some uncertainty. Yet apparent in all primitive psychology is at least the dichotomy which recognized the general distinction of soul (or spirit) from the body. If all outside things had a soul, it would be obvious that man was not less well endowed. Possibly the first idea of soul was no more than that of life, but the belief soon became prevalent that this life was in some way detachable from the body. There were times of unconsciousness when, as seemed certain in dreams, the soul appeared to wander. It was easy at such times to imagine that the soul had slipped away temporarily, perhaps in the form of a bird, or a mouse, or a serpent. It was therefore necessary to keep it, like the falcon, on a leash,[1] lest it escape permanently, or afford opportunity for some malign spirit or vampire to take possession of the body. Death was literally the departure of the soul. The words of the Emperor Hadrian will be recalled:

> Animula, vagula, blandula,
> Hospes, comesque corporis !
> Quae nunc abibis in loca,
> Pallidula, frigida, nudula,
> Nec, ut soles, dabis joca.

[1] Cf. the beautiful lines of Jalalu'din Rumi in Book I. of the *Mathnawi*, commencing :

> Nightly the souls of men thou lettest fly
> From out the trap wherein they captive lie.

So precautions against this departure must be taken, such as quenching the thirst ere going to sleep, or placing charms, in the way of ear-rings and nose-rings, upon the openings of the head. Especially must one use spells to prevent the violent expulsion of the soul in the acts of sneezing, hiccoughing or coughing.

Much thought was naturally given to the seat of the soul. Was it to be identified with the *breath*[1] (*animus*) as the soul of Nature was to be discovered in the wind (*anima*)? The possible connection of *soul* with *sea* and of *ghost* with *gust* would point in this direction. Was it, as some believed, in the *shadow*, which primitive man, not illogically, regarded as part of his own person? He resented the stepping on his shadow as an insult and even feared the taking of a photograph, lest thereby part of himself should pass under the power of another. Certain Negro tribes, we are told, fear the driving of a nail into the ground on which their shadow is cast, and Frazer mentions the terror of the Australian who "nearly died of fright because the shadow of his mother-in-law fell on his legs as he lay asleep under a tree." Others have supposed the seat of the soul to be in the *blood*. There was visible evidence of this when men saw life ebbing away with the streaming out of the blood. "The blood is the life," said the Hebrew, and the accusing voice said to Cain, "The voice of thy brother's blood crieth to me from the earth." It was a widespread belief down to quite modern times that a murderer might be convicted by the re-flowing of blood in his presence from the corpse. Empedocles affirmed: "The soul is the systasis of the blood." In the effort to restore life men used to put a daub of red paint on the forehead of the corpse or sprinkled it with red powder. There were in certain parts of Europe peoples whom we know to-day as the red-ochre folk because of the habit of packing the graves with that substance as a "life-giver." Other common life-givers were such things as gold, beads, cowry-shells, incense and jade. "He who swallows jade will exist as long as jade, and he who swallows gold as long as gold,"[2] it was said. But it was the actual

[1] Cf. Skt. *ātman*, the *breath*, that is, the *self*.
[2] Also: "Drink a pint of jade and you will live a thousand years."

gift of blood which men specially craved for the renewal of their life in the grave. So Odysseus fed the hungry ghosts of the under-world, as described in the 11th book of the *Odyssey*.

Many people were accustomed to seek the seat of the soul in the *hair*. This is one of the most widespread of primitive beliefs. Whether due to the knowledge that the hair often continued to grow after death or to the association, by imitative magic, of the hair with the rays of the sun, the idea prevailed that the hair (as in the case of Samson) was the seat of power and was also the residence of the vital principle. Witches were shaven to rob them of their unholy might, and Japanese wrestlers were accustomed, on retiring from the ring, to cut off their locks as an offering to the gods. "Hair! Hair! there is might in hair," says George Meredith in *The Shaving of Shagpat*, and a thousand illustrations conspire to confirm the assertion. Hair is even divine, said the Japanese, using the same word, *kami*, for hair as well as for the gods. Many a Japanese hero was buried or cremated with his body represented by but a single hair, even as a Chinese Emperor commuted his own death sentence by the sacrifice of his hair. The shaving of the head, whether through the vow of the Nazarite, the profession of the monk or the compulsion of a Manchu tyrant, was always regarded as the offering of life. For others to have possession of a man's hair was to gain control over his life; hence the protection of priest or king by the wearing of a fillet or a crown. Even prophets had their sacred commission associated with abundance of hair. Elijah was the more esteemed because he was "a lord of hair," while Elisha suffered by comparison even in the estimate of the children, who mocked his shorn locks with the cry: "Go up, thou bald head." [1]

By some, again, the *eye* was the soul seat and "the daughter of the eye," as the Hebrews called it, was the double of the person. In India, as E. V. Hopkins reminds us, the divine male was to be seen in the right eye and his *çakti*, or female principle, in the other. It was such a

[1] See E. V. Hopkins, *The Origin and Evolution of Religion*, 115 ff.; and H. H. Gowen, "The Hair Offering," *Anglican Theological Review*, January 1927.

belief as this which led to the fear of the evil eye and the dread of *invidia*, which we call *envy*, was something more than moral shrinking from one of the deadly sins. In Egypt we are able to follow the development from the idea of the Horus-eye, the symbol of life, to the eye of the goddess Hathor, the evil eye, the death-dealing avatar of the goddess of destruction.

Another commonly received soul seat was the *liver*, which was "the organ of divination" for many peoples, including Babylonians, Greeks and Etruscans. The Hebrews too, often identified the soul with the liver and we have passages in the *Psalms* which, if literally translated, would run, "Wake up, my liver!" rather than "Awake, my soul!" That the Hebrew word signifies alike *weight*, *liver* and *glory*, is in itself significant. In some passages of the *Psalms*, however, the *kidneys* (reins) are suggested as the soul seat and this may be the case in ancient India.

More common in India, as in many other places (including the lands of the West), is the thought of the *heart*, at least as the seat of feeling and affection. To some, according to Windisch (quoted by Hopkins), the soul might be supposed to have distributed its functions, using the liver for the passionate and sensual, the head for the mental and intellectual, and the heart for courage as well as for affection.

It has already been observed that the *name* was often regarded, at least in part, as a seat of the soul. This, however, was probably a somewhat late conception.[1]

An important consideration for primitive man was involved in the question, Was there not some secret place, external to the body, where the soul might be protected from the violence which was so common an incident in the life of mortal man? The doctrine of "the external soul" is one of unusual interest. The reader will recall Lafcadio Hearn's *Story of Aoyagi*, where the young wife suddenly cries: "I am dying. . . . Someone, at this cruel moment, is cutting down my tree—that is why I must die." As, in the Bible, there were "the witches who hunted souls," it was wise to have one's "bundle of life"

[1] H. H. Gowen, "The Name," *Anglican Theological Review*, April 1930.

laid up where no enemy could get at it. The safest place of all was, of course, with God; therefore the Psalmist exclaims, "Hide me in the secret place of Thy tabernacle."[1] In like manner St. Paul writes: "Your life is hid with Christ in God."[2] But many would fall short of security such as this and seek other hiding-places. The fine ladies of Jerusalem, according to Isaiah iii. 20, used, among other articles of jewellery, the amulets called "houses of the soul." For the souls of the dead little soul-houses were placed near the graves, a custom prevailing all the way from ancient Egypt to the Sea Dyaks of Borneo, and one which had not a little to do with the evolution of our own church building. We have in this an explanation of the use of "portrait-statues," also in use from Egypt of old to the megalithic tombs of ancient Britain and Brittany. The portrait statue was a "forma corporis," in which the spirit would naturally find a dwelling place. An old Egyptian scribe, one Qeni, once tied a papyrus to his wife's wooden statuette to serve notice of a law-suit in the underworld. But for the living as well as for the dead there were ingenious devices for providing a dwelling for the soul. Many of our fairy tales, such as the Indian tale of *Punchkin*, describe the soul of some giant, or ogre, hidden in a bird's nest at the top of a tree, in a coco-nut, or in some shell-fish at the bottom of the sea. The hero of the tale had first to learn the hiding-place of the ogre's soul before he could execute justice upon him.[3] Whether in the body or out of the body, it is plain that the soul needed careful watching over and guardianship.

The next article of belief in the creed of spiritism was that the soul *survived* the body when the separation took place at death. Death, for primitive man, was naturally a mysterious thing. It was, indeed, unnatural, and always considered as an act of violence, whether the instrument of violence were or were not capable of being detected. When by such violence the soul was expelled from the body it had occupied, the question was, Did it still exist? Primitive

[1] Cf. Psalms xxvii. 5.
[2] Col. iii. 3.
[3] See Frazer, *Folk-lore of the Old Testament*, Part III., ch. 7.

man said without hesitation, Yes, and supported his affirmation through the evidence of dreams, when dead relatives quite visibly appeared to the living, as in the case of Aeneas and Anchises and other heroes of classic literature. The soul disengaged by death became the *manes*, whence the belief in the disembodied soul is sometimes known as *manism*. With the advance towards deification of the dead the manes were frequently spoken of as *Dii manes*. But primitive man found evidence for the survival of the soul also in the spread of some contagious disease. Where some individual had died from such it was easy to explain the spread of the disease in the camp as due to the wrath of the deceased spending itself on the living. The soul expelled by violence, physical or occult, was presumably in an angry frame of mind and not to be lightly encountered. It is for this reason that in some countries, as in China, the ignorant are unwilling to relieve the dying or to interfere with the struggles of a drowning man. There was no telling what a disembodied spirit might not do to anybody near at hand. To meet a disembodied spirit was everywhere a sign of death or disaster; in some countries it brought lockjaw. Thus the dread of places thought to be haunted, even in civilized lands, has remained in the blood. In China, again, it was an excellent method of revenge for a man to commit suicide on his neighbour's doorstep or to wreck the fortunes of a railway by laying himself across the rails.

It is not, of course, necessary to believe that primitive man—still less primitive woman—felt no sense of bereavement. Such an idea would run counter to common animal instinct as well as to many facts of primitive life. Witness the efforts made to restore life by the pouring of water—or blood—upon the corpse, or the use of what the Chinese call the "calling back the dead." The shaking out of the little garments, hung on a broomstick, with the cry:

> Come back, little one, come back !
> Where are you hiding ? Where are you playing ?
> Come, come, we are anxiously waiting for you.

is as primitive as it is pathetically human. Yet, on the whole, there was a great fear of the dead, and a great desire that they should not return. Some of the signs of this fear we shall see a little later.

Where was the soul? we may now ask. The answer is variously given. For very many, possibly for most, there was the belief that the soul remained hovering above the grave for three days. Sometimes, as in the Avestan belief, it was supposed to hover in the form of a bird; others believed it was in the form of a butterfly, or perhaps that of some earth-dwelling animal, such as a serpent or a worm. Muhammadans believed that till the Day of Judgement the souls of men were in the crops of birds, green birds for the good, black birds for the bad, and owls for those who had committed murder. In China it was a common belief that one part of the soul—the more earthy part—was dissipated in the air, while a certain other part remained in the spirit tablet. There was yet another part in the grave; for most primitive peoples the grave was generally recognized as the abode of the soul. Ideas of the underworld, for the most part, developed from the conception of an enlarged grave, a vast subterranean vault. This is what we call *hell*, apart, of course, from all idea of a moralized after-life. Hell is literally the *hole*, the hollow, the Sheol of the Hebrews, the Hades of the Greeks. It is that chthonic realm of the dead so magnificently described in Ezekiel xxx. 17 ff.: "The mighty warriors in the underworld shall hail him and his allies: Down with you, down, to a shameful death, you, and all your host, amid victims of the sword. Assyria is down there, with all her folk, their graves round about their kings, buried in the abysses of the pit, all victims of the sword, who were a terror in the land of the living." There are also classic descriptions of this same realm in such passages as that of the 11th book of the *Odyssey*, where

> appear'd along the dusky coasts,
> Thin, airy shoals of visionary ghosts;
> Fair, pensive youths and soft, enamour'd maids;
> And wither'd elders, pale and wrinkled shades;
> Ghastly with wounds the forms of warriors slain
> Stalk'd with majestic port, a martial train.

A similar description appears in the 6th *Aeneid*, and Vergil shows some slight disposition to moralize the world of the dead in the words: " Quisque suos patimur manes " (We, each of us, suffer our own manes). It was not a cheerful outlook, by no means so cheerful as that of uranic religion, though a few of the dead were allowed the prospect of the skies, and some of the Polynesians believed in " leaping places " whence souls attained access to the stars or clouds. In some places, all the way from Egypt to Russia, soul ladders were provided from the graves, some of them with seven rungs suggestive of the ascent through the planetary spheres. Egyptian kings, in particular, were supplied with ladders that they might scale the skies. The four sons of Horus must bind a rope ladder, it was stated, " for this king, Pepi II; they join together a (wooden) ladder for King Pepi II." But most souls had to be thankful that they had " somewhere to go to," however gloomy. Gloomy it was assuredly, as the classic complaint of the great Achilles testifies. The Japanese creator-god, Izanagi, going down to hell to recover the soul of his dead wife, found it a place of such unspeakable corruption that he fled precipitately, pursued by the nine hags of hell. To the Greeks it was Aïdes, the land of the unseen. To the Hebrews the dead were the Rephaim, the *helpless ones*. To some the dead were pictured as half decomposed. From the *Epic of Gilgamesh* we learn that distinction was made between the dead who were fed by the oblations, and so were comparatively strong, and the dead who had been thrown out on the plain, and were unsustained, as also between these and the dead (such as the unmarried) who had died without the normal fulfilment of life. These became demons. At the best the world was " that low land where sun and moon are mute and all the stars keep silence."

The *accessories* of hell are quite clearly marked and for the most part recall old customs in connection with the disposal of the dead. To die was to go the way of the setting sun. Thus " going west " became (in Egypt) a synonym for dying, and men were laid to rest with their faces in that direction. The metaphor of the *river*, which we still employ in our popular hymns,[1] is one which is quite natural when we remember that a tribe, camped

[1] E.g. " *Shall we gather at the river?* "

along the shores of a stream, would prefer to dispose of their dead on the other side, to prevent return of the unwelcome ghost.

To transport the dead across the river there would be the *boat* or the *bridge*. The boat idea provided the funeral barge of ancient Egypt and the barque of Charon in Greek mythology. The bridge idea has a long history, from the use of a crazy log placed across a rushing stream to the impressive conception of the Chinvad Bridge of the Zoroastrian and the 'Al-Sirat of the Muhammadan, stretched across the Valley of Jehoshaphat, "sharper than a sword and finer than a hair." In between extremes such as these are the Snake Bridge of the Sioux Indians, the bridge in the Irish saga of Cuchulain, and that of the Yorkshire Lyke-wake Dirge:

> From Whinny-moore when thou may passe,
> Every night and alle ;
> To Brig-o-Dread thou comes at last,
> And Christe receive thy saule.

The Choctaw belief was that souls had to cross a dreadful deep and rapid stream over a long slippery pine-log, which had been stripped of its bark. People on the other side threw stones at those who crossed and it was in dodging these that the wicked fell thousands of feet into the gulf below. Allied with this is the belief of the Greenlanders that after death the soul has to slide for five or six days down a steep precipice, slippery with the blood of all who have gone before, a journey specially hard in the winter. It is not strange that *bridge sacrifices* came into vogue in order to expedite the soul's journey through these fearful ordeals, or that the word *Pontifex* (Bridge-builder) came to have a religious significance in pagan and even in Christian times. Children continued to play as games the dramas enacted by their terrified elders, as we may note in such a one as "London Bridge is falling down," with its forfeit of "a fair lady."

There was also the *dog*, or *jackal*, or (occasionally) the *pig*, as a kind of psychopomp, or soul-leader into the world of the dead. It is easy to see how the dog of the primitive man, which had shared his life above ground, might be

[1] See *Encyclopædia of Religion and Ethics*, art. "Bridge."

selected to become his inseparable companion in the grave. If the dog was the guardian of the home above-ground, might he not, as Cerberus, continue his functions in the grave? But, perhaps, the association of the dog, or jackal, with the underworld came about through the unpleasant interest which these beasts took in the shallow graves where the dead were laid. It is probable that Anubis, the jackal god, was a god of the dead before he was regarded as the psychopomp under the new deity Osiris. In any case, a family likeness exists between Anubis and Cerberus and between these and the Indian dogs of Yama and the Persian dogs of Yima. These last, mentioned in the *Veda* and *Avesta*, and which became still more important in the death rites of the Parsi, are "the four-eyed brindled" dogs who must be dragged into the presence of the dying in order that these might receive the *sagdid*, or "look of the dog." The *sagdid* served as a passport into the underworld and enabled the dead to rest in peace.

One other accessory must here be noted in connection with the underworld, namely, the *Hell-emperor*, who is generally identified with the first man, or the original head of a tribe, some early pioneer whose grave mound was in the centre of the family circle and whose early entrance to the world of the dead gave him place and power. Such is Yama in India, Yima in the Iran of the *Avesta* and Pluto (Hades) in the classic mythology of Greece.

It should not, at this point, be overlooked that many primitive peoples, and many, like the Hindus, quite advanced, believed in *transmigration* of souls. What could seem to these more natural than that the souls of men should pass into the beasts they resembled or admired? There was even some pride in the thought that a chief might return to earth as a lion, an elephant, a leopard or a buffalo. In such an idea there was no sense of humiliation, since, as Frazer observes, to primitive man "many of the other animals appear as his equals, or even his superiors, not merely in brute force, but in intelligence."

The final article of the spiritistic creed that calls for mention is the belief in the *deification* of the dead. If we ask whether this applied to all the dead or only to chiefs—

perhaps, in certain cases, only to males—the answer must be with hesitation. In most cases, probably, only the chiefs were supposed to survive as gods. Even in life certain men, chiefs and priests, were credited with certain powers (*orenda*) beyond those of others. Dynamistic as well as animistic views were widely current. Such powers were highly valued and regarded as contributing to the well-being of the tribe. In many cases, when these powers flagged, the former possessor was put to death, a subject treated with great particularity in *The Golden Bough*. But in other cases great men carried their *mana* with them to the grave. Hence ghosts easily passed to godhood. Euhemerus, a Greek mythographer who lived *c.* 300 B.C., interpreted the popular myths in his *Sacred History* as all based upon the traditions of heroes and rulers who lived and died and were thence raised *ad astra*. According to this system, known as *euhemerism*, Zeus was simply an old king of Crete who had forced the abdication of an earlier dynasty. Osiris, likewise, was an early king of Egypt who made wars and taught his people the arts of agriculture. *Euhemerism* is unsatisfactory as an explanation of all myths, but undoubtedly many of the gods are just deified human beings. The Roman emperors naturally became deities on their decease, just as the Egyptian Pharaohs had done before them. The Chinese emperors rode " the back of the dragon " to the heaven whence they had received their mandate. And the Japanese rulers—and many beside, both men and women—passed into the unknown as *kami* to be worshipped henceforth according to the rites of Shinto.

Such belief is by no means without its value to theology. If it was important to have the idea of a transcendent God and the idea of an immanent God, it was also important to hold the idea of a God who had projected Himself into humanity. The humanity of God, as already suggested earlier, gives us the third aspect of God which was needed to make theology complete. In this way the Christian doctrine of the Trinity, that is, belief in God as Father (God in His transcendence), Son (God in His humanness) and Spirit (God in His immanence) is found to have its ground in primitive religion.

## CHAPTER VI

## *The Religion of Spiritism*

ON the ground of the beliefs described in our last chapter a vast pre-occupation with death on the part of primitive man will appear to have been inevitable. We must not, however, jump to the conclusion that this preoccupation implies a surrender to the idea of mortality. Rather it serves to illustrate a profounder faith in life as the ultimate issue or, at the very least, an insistent protest against death as the ultimate issue. The thought of Sophocles, that

> Our last, our longest home is with the dead,
> Therefore let us praise the lifeless, not the living,
> For we shall rest forever there

is the outcome of a weary sophistication. Even more so is the pessimism of James Thomson in his *City of Dreadful Night*. To the natural man life was good and it was fitting that he should rebel against death as against something unnatural, an evil resulting from violence, whether the violence came from beast or man, or from the malignant powers which he called demons and we bacilli. As already noted, the attitude of man was towards death, and also towards the dead, an attitude of great fear. It was fear of the malevolent forces lurking invisibly near, perhaps in the form of some contagious disease; fear of the angry ghost torn untimely from all that he considered his; fear even of the place where death had taken place and where unknown dangers still remained in ambush. Even although occasionally we see fear and grief struggling together for expression, the fear had generally the upper hand and dictated most of the rites which gathered around the cult of the dead. The main elements of this cult we may now set forth in sequence. First there was—

THE DISPOSAL OF THE DEAD.—As might be expected in the case of people obsessed with fear, there seems to have been a very general desire to rid themselves as speedily as possible of "the body of this death." Sometimes this was effected simply by abandonment, even to the extent of leaving the locality where death had occurred. In the case of the early Japanese emperors, prior to the Nara period, A.D. 710–794, the capital was moved at every imperial demise. Sometimes the return of the dead was hindered by rites performed in connection with the funeral. These included the decapitation or dismemberment of the corpse, the fettering of the limbs by anklets or swathings, the placing of thorns beneath the feet, to make walking impossible, the closing of the eyes of the dead to render them blind, the effacing of the footprints of the men who bore the body to its last resting-place, or the placing of heavy stones on the grave. In the case of dangerous persons, suicides and murderers, or in the case of any suspected of vampirism, a stake might be driven through the corpse's breast. Even to recent times it was the custom in England to bury the body of one incurring the verdict of *felo de se* at the junction of four cross-roads with a stake through the breast, to make return impossible. In many cases, as among the Jews, criminals and lunatics might be cremated, with the original intention of destroying the soul altogether. In India efforts were made, in the *çraddha* ceremonies, to speed the *gati*, or going, of the spirit to the world of the ancestors. While many practices, some of which have been already mentioned, were adopted, as in the gift of hair, or blood, or other "life-givers" to furnish replenishment of vigour, it must always be remembered that this new life was in the other world, not in this. In this world no *revenant* was generally welcome, even by the relatives, but among the ancestors it was highly desirable to preserve identity by the making of masks, portrait-statues, and the like. Reference has already been made to these in Egypt and Britain, and Crete may be added to the localities where portrait-statues have been discovered. Even in East Africa, as Father Le Roy has recorded, "the natives make earthen statuettes" and put therein parts of the dead, their hair, skin, nails, or a small bone. While this desire for perpetuating the personality of the dead in the other world prevailed, there was also the ambition to obtain use of the *orenda* of notable persons by contact with the corpse which had been credited with unusual powers. The desire sometimes took strange forms, quite at variance with some of the fears which have been described above. On the death of a great chief or an enemy of unusual distinction, the living would rub themselves with the juices of the decomposing body, possess themselves of the head, scalp, ears or nose of the dead, or even engage in some sort of endocannibalism to transfer to themselves the qualities of the deceased. When Kamehameha I. died in 1819, the Hawaiian chiefs debated long what to do with the body and one exclaimed: "My thought is that we eat him."

The motives which have been described will account for most of the methods of disposing of the dead with which we are acquainted. First of all, there was simple abandonment or *exposure*, sometimes in the tree or cave which had been the primitive dwelling, sometimes in the jungle or on a mountain height. For a very large number it seemed fitting that the dead should rest, at least for a time, on the bare soil, as in the lap of the earth which had been their mother. It was in harmony with the custom of placing an infant on the ground for a while immediately after birth.[1] There are many survivals of this custom, from the Chinese practice of placing the body on the earth before it was coffined to the modern Parsi method of using the *dakhma*, or tower of silence, for exposure of the corpse to the vultures. Central Asia, too, furnishes many illustrations of the practice.

*Inhumation*, or earth burial, followed naturally where the hut was deserted and allowed to fall in upon the abandoned body. An old Chinese ideograph for burial seems to depict this falling down of the thatch upon the corpse in the hole which had served the living man for a home. Le Roy says: "Among several tribes of the Congo the chief on his death has his house for a tomb: his body is left there until the roof falls in; then the village is aban-

[1] See Albrecht Dietrich, *Mutter Erde*, Leipzig, 1925.

doned."[1] Burial was evidently the general practice as far back as Upper Palæolithic times, and we find graves of this period fenced round with the shoulder-blades of mammoths, while the body had been wrapped in a mat or skin and even placed in a coffin of wood or stone. The coffin was the natural development from tree-trunk burial. Some people, like the ancient Parthians, used slipper-shaped coffins of pottery. Others in Greece and pre-historic South India used large jars, or two jars set mouth to mouth. In certain cases burial became a rite to which men contributed their labour and wealth on the most stupendous scale. We have illustration of this not only in ancient Egypt, in the case of the Pyramid builders, but to almost the same extravagant extent among the makers of dolmens and long barrows and sepulchral mounds in general from Britain to China and Japan. To be "monumentally interred" was the general ambition of those who had been great in the land of the living.

*Cremation* came in with the Bronze Age and was doubtless employed in order to hasten the departure of the spirit or perhaps to destroy it altogether. In certain cases it was used particularly for criminals and other undesirables, but in some cases as a mark of honour to chiefs and men of high estate, to speed their souls upward to the stars. As a preventative of contagion it doubtless justified itself without primitive man being aware of the reasons for his success.

Whether the dead were deposited in a grave or upon the funeral pyre (but especially in the former case) care was generally taken to place them with the knees drawn up towards the chin. This is explained either through the desire to restore the dead man to the place he occupied as an embryo in his mother's womb, in view of an anticipated re-birth, or else by the desire to represent him as asleep. This last idea is confirmed by the apparent habit of Neanderthal man of placing a pillow of flint-chips beneath the head of the corpse. Other positions, however, are sometimes encountered, including the seated position, and even that of standing erect to which allusion was made in the last chapter.

[1] Monsignor Le Roy, *The Religion of Primitive Men*, New York, 1922.

Our next heading is that of

Gifts to the Dead.—The dead must not be left hungry or unattended, or otherwise unequipped for the ghostly life. If thus unprovided for, they might return. We have already noted the fact that the *house*, as in China and Japan, was frequently left for such occupation as the dead man might choose to claim. *Food* also was a necessity and must be placed where the soul might readily find it, before the spirit-tablet in the house, or periodically at the grave. Large legacies used to be left in ancient Egypt to provide the dead regularly with so many loaves of bread, so much meat, and so many jars of beer. Curses of the most horrifying nature were invoked on anybody who might attempt to steal the provender. Possibly some of the quaint bequests still honoured in English parishes for the provision weekly of so many loaves to be given out at the church originated in thought of the bequeathers rather than of the legatees. Certainly many early temples and churches were at first little more than altar shrines where food gifts were deposited for the dead, with an attendant priesthood to supervise the ritual. The taking of food to the graves in modern China at the Ching Ming festival is in line with the same idea, even as was the pouring of water upon the graves in ancient Babylon. *Clothing* also was supposedly needed for the dead. The origin of our modern funeral garb lies in the fact that originally the mourners went bare that the dead might take possession of the clothes in hand. Then came the use by the survivors of sackcloth and torn garments such as the dead would not be disposed to envy. Lastly came the making of special garments of funeral black. The funeral dress of the Chinese consists of garments which have not been dyed and are therefore unfinished. It is this which has given rise to the belief that white is the Chinese colour of mourning. Yet in some countries white is adopted for mourning for other reasons. For example, in certain parts of Africa the mourners paint themselves with paint made from white chalk or tapioca flour, mixed with the powdered bones of the dead. A traveller describes one such group of mourners: "covered with flour, as we prepare a cutlet for the frying-pan." In connection with the gift of clothing, it may be recalled that Herodotus tells the story of Periander, tyrant of Corinth, whose dead wife from the underworld reproached him for her lack of clothing. The king immediately commandeered the dresses of the Corinthian ladies and sent them to the shades below by means of a bonfire, thus silencing the complaints of his departed spouse.

*Implements*, again, of all sorts were despatched to the underworld for the use of the dead. Many vessels—broken in order to fit them for a realm where everything was dead—were buried in considerable numbers even in pre-historic times. "By a curious symbolism," says Le Roy, "the vases placed in the graves are always cracked or chipped, in a word, whatever is offered to the dead man must be 'dead.'" In the case of warriors and chiefs horses were slain and interred with the deceased. In the recent pictures of the funeral of Marshal Joffre the horse led behind the coffin is a reminiscence of this ancient custom. *Labourers*, too, to work in the fields of the dead, were slaughtered, or in later times (about the time of the twelfth dynasty in Egypt) replaced by the small clay figurines known in Egypt as *ushabti*, or *answerers*. The great stone avenues leading up to the Ming Tombs in China will remind us that ministers of state were not, in many cases, exempt from the duty of accompanying their dead lord to his last abode. The Japanese custom of *junshi*, or "following in death," will be recalled. It was supposedly abolished nearly two thousand years ago, by the substitution of clay figures (an arrangement suggested by the head of the clay-workers' guild), but it has sporadically persisted till the present day as may be illustrated by the suicide of General Nogi and his wife at the funeral of the Emperor Meiji. *Wives* were naturally not free from rendering such a service to the dead. The Indian practice of *sati* (lit. the *faithful woman*) was once (erroneously) supported by the authority of the *Veda* but was abolished by law in 1829. Yet Kipling's *Last Suttee* was by no means the last in India. Elsewhere the custom was common and often practised on the grand scale. The Chinese Emperor

Ch'in Shih Huang Ti included in the great holocaust which marked his funeral in 209 B.C. hundreds of women as well as thousands of workmen and slaves and immense treasure. At the funeral of Jenghiz Khan in A.D. 1227 the fairest women of Asia, as well as the finest stallions, were all slaughtered to provide the dead conqueror with an adequate entourage in the underworld. Gifts to the dead are still common in many countries, as, for example, in China where every city has its shops where nothing is sold except for the dead. Here you can buy even a papier-maché automobile with a papier-maché chauffeur. Indeed, our own use of flowers on the graves is not entirely the expression of our own affection. It should be added that ornaments as well as articles of utility were freely offered from the first and in Palæolithic graves we have anklets, necklaces, ivory figurines, bone amulets, etc., which had ornamental as well as magical reason for their use.

Commemoration of the Dead.—The commemoration of the dead is variously observed in different lands, but generally includes, first, a funeral service held shortly after death, as in the Indian *çraddha*, or the Christian *requiem*, and, secondly, an annual commemoration, commonly at the fall of the year, as in the Buddhist Bon and the Christian All Saints' Day. It is interesting to note as showing the perdurability of primitive ideas that to-day in America the Eve of All Saints', commonly known as All Hallow E'en, is much more generally observed after the old pagan fashion than in line with Christian ideas. In ancient Egypt, apart from the consecration of the tomb, which was generally prepared in the lifetime of its occupant, and the actual funeral ceremony, there seems to have been an annual commemoration service to secure the peace of the soul in Amenti. The Zoroastrians had their general feast for all the dead annually, as well as special services for the dead, not unlike those of the Indian *çraddha*, on the third, tenth, and thirtieth days after death, and also on the anniversary of death. The Romans, like the Greeks, had significant rites in memory of the dead, with speeches and games. The *exsequiæ*, or obsequies, included prayers and sacrifices in the house to the spirits of the dead and there was also a service on the anniversary. A general festival for the dead, known as the *Feralia*, or *Februalia*, was held on February 22 and was a service of purification. The *Lemuria*, held in May, were for the purpose of driving away the Lemures, or hostile spirits of the dead. Hebrew usage in ancient times is uncertain, but since the tenth century "there have been days prescribed for the commemoration of the dead." Islam has followed suit in pilgrimages and services at the graves of the saints. Christian usage has included many forms of commemoration, from the inscribing of an epitaph on the tombstone, or the writing of the deceased's name on the diptych on the altar, to the use of the anniversary, or *natalicia*, and the inclusion of the name in the martyrology, and ultimately in the calendar of the Church. Even outside of organized ecclesiastical life the instinct for the commemoration of the dead is shown in the observance of such days as *Memorial Day*, May 30, in the United States as a National Holiday, in the various services in widely separated countries at the grave of an "Unknown Warrior," and in the general disposition to observe anniversaries and centenaries.

The commemoration of the dead has often taken monumental form, from the time of the Pyramid Builders, as already noted, to our own day. The ancient Egyptians built their tombs, with a shaft for the victims sacrificed, and a chapel for the reception of the gifts. Absalom built his own tomb in the King's Dale, because he had no son to succeed and carry on the ancestral cult. To-day every city has its monuments to the dead and its cemeteries where men recall "the touch of a vanished hand, the sound of a voice that is still." It is an important part of life to link one's own generation with the past. Mrs. Browning asks: "Who dared build temples without tombs in sight?" and we have constantly occasion to recall the power of the dead to control the destinies of the living. The important thing is so to balance the rightful authority of the dead with the prerogatives of the living so as not to constrain the liberties of the present through the tyranny of "the dead hand." Past and Future struggle together for recognition in the ever-changing Present.

Communications with the Dead.—*Necromancy*, or divination by means of communication with the dead, is a primitive as well as a widely extended practice. It rests upon the belief that the dead are not wholly out of reach and may be conversed with under special conditions. There is generally a recrudescence of this belief in times of wide-spread mourning, as in the period of the Great War, when young life went untimely over the Great Divide in such abundance that there was a natural desire on the part of the bereaved to reach over to the farther shore. The methods of necromancy have not greatly varied from ancient times, though some religious systems have favoured some methods and discountenanced others. *Dreams*, induced in special ways, have been a common means of bridging the gulf. In China such various methods have been employed as *sacrifice*, to which the dead are supposed to come, the use of the *personator of the dead*, generally the grandson of the deceased, the use of the *spirit-tablet*, to which the ghost comes at the time of sacrifice, the use of the spirit-pencil, or *chi*, consisting of two long branches held by two people, with a short branch by which the writing is traced in the sand, the employment of the *wu*, or trance medium, and even by such methods as the calling back of the soul, referred to above, or the spreading of a table. The use of mechanical media, such as *planchette*, or *ouija*, is common the world over. Almost equally general is the use of personal media, in which the medium acts for the human enquirer, and a "control" acts for the spirit on the other side whom it is desired to consult. The case of the *Witch of Endor*, as described in 1 Sam. xxviii., is a classic instance, in which Saul calls up the spirit of Samuel through the wise woman of Endor to learn his fate in the morrow's battle. In still earlier times it seems probable from the mention of *teraphim*, as in Gen. xxxi. 34 and 1 Sam. xix. 13, that the dead were invoked by means of mummified infants used as media. In classical literature the dead are described as being consulted through special visits made to the borders of the underworld, as in the 11th book of the *Odyssey* and the 6th book of the *Aeneid*. In modern times communication with the dead has supposedly been attained, not only by methods mentioned above, but what is known as automatic writing or even by telaudition. The whole subject, so far as it is related to modern spiritism, must be regarded as highly debatable. Given the belief in the continued existence of the soul, there is nothing antecedently unnatural in attempts made from either side of the grave to establish communication. It is largely a question of evidence in support of the assertions made. Societies for Psychical Research on either side of the Atlantic have done much to clear away what was the result of mere credulity and superstition; they have done less to offer substantially constructive material on which to form a judgement.

To some minds the thought of being in possible contact with the dead has been undoubtedly of great solace. To others the dangers of necromancy are more obvious than its advantages. These dangers include loss of time spent in much vain effort; the possibilities of self-deception through the confusion of all sorts of psychological phenomena with genuinely spiritual manifestations; the possibility of deception through mediums financially interested in securing spectacular results; and even the possibility of being misled through the action of discarnate entities of a malevolent sort. Most serious, perhaps, of all is the danger of seeking to reverse the conditions of life by striving to know prematurely what we must die to experience. At least this was the thought of Dante when he put the soothsayers in the *Inferno* with their heads turned backwards. Some of these dangers are vividly depicted in Kipling's *Way to Endor* and, more dramatically, in Browning's *Mr. Sludge the Medium*.

The Christian position is adequately represented in the doctrine of the Communion of Saints, in which, without attempting to drag back the dead to the conditions of earth, we enter with them into spiritual communion with God. As for all that might minister to the gratification of curiosity, we may say, " the rest remaineth unrevealed." In any case, we have in the Christian teaching as to the possibilities of prayer and communion, enough to mark the survival value of one of man's oldest and most continuous instincts.

THE WORSHIP OF THE DEAD.—Ancestor worship was for primitive man quite natural. Ties which had been established on earth were not quickly loosed. There might be occasions when an old man, having lost his *mana*, was regarded as done with, and even buried alive, but the solidarity of the tribe nevertheless demanded that the father of the clan should be honoured in death as in life. Moreover, as to-day, a hero easily took on proportions after death which were greater than those attained in life. This is a feature of our own hero-worship, in which figures of men, like Washington and Lincoln, drop after death all human foibles and gain a certain fixity they never could have possessed while living. It is through such experience that they come to "belong to the ages." Indeed, by such steps we mount to the worship of Him who proclaims: "I am He that liveth and was dead, and, behold, I am alive for evermore." Naturally such a worship of the dead included *sacrifices* both for the dead and to the dead. Sacrifice, says Hopkins, is "the objective link between man and the spiritual world." From our present point of view it is primarily the feeding and sustaining of the dead, but it is also the common meal to which all are invited as well as the *manes*. That is, it is a communion feast as well as a sacrifice. By it the dead are enabled to "rest in peace" and by it the unity of the family is maintained.

But we cannot leave the subject of Spiritism without some reference to that very important extension of human relationship, backwards towards the animal, which we call

TOTEMISM.—The word *totem*, or *totam*, is an Ojibway word, first employed, that is, outside the tribe, by J. Long in 1791, in his *Travels and Voyages of an Indian Interpreter*. Since that time the word has been used in senses quite different from the original significance. Frazer says: "A totem is a class of material objects which a savage regards as with superstitious respect, believing that there exists between him and every member of the class an intimate and altogether special relation."[1] Reinach explains it as "the animal, vegetable and, more rarely, the mineral or heavenly body which the clan regards as an ancestor,

[1] Sir J. G. Frazer, *Totemism* (London, 1910), p. 1.

protector and a rallying sign. . . . The totem is not an individual, but an animal clan affiliated to the human clan." Le Roy says that "a pact by means of a visible creature is a pact with the invisible world" and explains totemism further as "an institution consisting essentially of a magical pact, representing and forming a relationship of a mystical and supernatural order, by which, under the visible form of an animal and, by exception, of a vegetable, mineral or astral body, an invisible spirit is associated with an individual, a family, a clan, a tribe, a secret society, in view of a reciprocity of services."[1]

It is clear that totemism, as now understood, refers not merely to religious beliefs as to ancestry traceable to the animal or vegetable world, but also that it implies a social system, with an often quite complicated arrangement for marriages, exogamic or endogamic, as the case may be. Or it may represent little more than the badge of a secret society, as in Africa, where we have "the society of the leopard" in Loango, and the "society of the hyena" among the Wanika. Here we shall use the term, doubtless to the dissatisfaction of the rigorists, simply of that form of ancestor-worship which carries the idea of ancestry back beyond the human to the animal or vegetable world.

There are, however, it must be conceded, many forms of totemism. Sometimes we have "split" totems, in which buffalo-tongues appear rather than buffaloes. Sometimes there are "linked" totems, as where snake, bird, fish, and plant are linked together. Sometimes there are "plant" totems, in which the ancestry is traced to a particular shrub or tree. And occasionally we have "abstract" totems, as in the adoption of the colour *red* for the totem of an Omaha clan.

The evidence probably is not quite sufficient for a confident generalization, but it seems likely that most clans had a totemistic stage. It is certainly the best explanation we possess for the animal-headed gods of Egypt to say that once upon a time the separate *nomes* had their separate totems, lion, baboon, ibis, etc., totems not so very unlike those which the African tribes to the south of Egypt still

[1] Le Roy, *op. cit.*, p. 87.

hold in reverence. The ancient Semites, as in the case of the Hebrews, had their tribal standards with totemistic names, the lion for Judah, the wolf for Benjamin, and so on. Many of the Old Testament names, such as Oreb, or *raven*, and Zeeb, or *wolf*, were derived from animals. Particularly was this the case with feminine names, as, for example, Zipporah, *sparrow*, Deborah, *bee*, Rachel, *ewe*, Huldah, *weasel*, Hoglah, Dorcas, etc. In Greece, again, many of the classical myths, such as those of Europa and Leda, may be best explained as of totemistic origin. Saxon England, too, had her Hengist, *stallion*, and Horsa, *mare*, while over Europe generally flourished such families as the Orsini, or *bears*, the Guelfs, or *wolves*, and the Colonna, or *doves*. The science of Heraldry is full of illustrations of the way in which men found their pleasure and their pride in tracing their ancestry to an animal origin.

Of the social implications of totemism, best studied in connection with the religion of the Australian aborigines, we need not now speak, but of its religious significance it should be said that this has been immensely heightened since the teaching of Darwin convinced man that his lineage is actually traceable backwards through the animal. As already pointed out, this doctrine carries with it religious consequences of the utmost importance. The new Christology must take cognizance of the animal world, with its own pains and problems, as well as of the world of humanity. It should now be easy to see why "the groans of all creation" await "the redemption of sons," and why it is that the earthly life of Christ is associated at His birth with "the beasts of the stall," His temptation with the "wild beasts," His working of miracles with the incident of the swine that "ran violently down a steep place into the sea," and His riding into Jerusalem for His Passion with the use of the ass borrowed specially for the occasion.[1]

* * * * *

From the many various beliefs and practices we have sketched in these last six chapters certain generalizations will be seen to emerge, such as not only contain indications

[1] See H. H. Gowen, "The Theriomorphic in Theology," *Anglican Theological Review*, April 1927.

of much that we still claim as the accumulated values of religion, but furnish even more broad hints as to what religion is to be when the primitive has completely yielded to the universal.

1. As to God.—God is revealed as transcendent, "the wholly Other," the Maker, anterior to and superior to His work. God is also revealed in the work itself, the visible, the idea fulfilled in creation, and most consummately in that supreme work of creation which the most perfectly reflects the Divine Idea, the human. God is, once again, the Immanent Spirit which abides in the work, the power by which creation is informed and inspired. Thus from the first we have in germ the Christian doctrine of the Trinity, no mere dogma of schoolmen and ecclesiastics, but a teaching necessary from the beginning in order to distinguish God from the "simple, impersonal force" to which some would reduce Him.

2. As to Man and his Destiny.—We find human destiny from the first prophetically described on the most generous and majestic scale. The material is at no point regarded as sufficiently explanatory of the mystery of manhood. There is a *mysterium tremendum* about Man as there is about God. Man's spirit rises above the limitations of time and matter. The future world as yet is but slightly moralized, but in death, as in life, to be a member of the family is to continue such; only the alien and the outcast have their portion "without the camp."

3. As to Society.—Here, too, there is the prophetic presentiment of something vast, catholic, undefined, mysterious. The very mystery of worship in the earliest times, like the mystery which still clings to the ritual and language of the Mass, or the mystery of the far distances in some great Gothic cathedral, suggests these large conceptions of what communion is in store for the souls of men. Primitive society might be bounded by the clan or the tribe, but, both here and hereafter, there was continuously hinted a solidarity which only sin—whatever the conception of sin might be—was able to break. To be a member of the human family necessitated the recognition of obligations which left no man free in the selfish sense. The higher the

position of leadership accorded to the individual, the more numerous and insistent became the ties. The rule was evermore, "He who did most shall bear most." And to be "gathered to the fathers"—even though within the narrow bounds of a desert grave—embodied something of the larger hope. The social morality which held within itself the power of inclusion or of exclusion possessed in a continuously increasing measure the promise of judgement to come, the promise of heaven and of hell.

4. Bloody, too, as were the rites which primitive man accepted as the condition of his security, the blood shed was, we doubt not, faintly envisaged as part of the sacrificial stream of life which flowed from beneath the altar of a living God with redemptive power. It was life poured out seemingly in vain, life as yet unvindicated, awaiting the revelation of a Divine Love as yet unknown. But, in the meantime, it was life crying, like the martyred saints of Judaism, for the answer which was by and by to speak from the Cross:

> How long, O Master, the holy, the true,
> Dost Thou not judge and avenge our blood,
> On them that dwell on the earth?

Out of the large amount of material available on the subject of these last six chapters, the following, for various reasons, may be consulted: Sir J. G. Frazer, *The Golden Bough* (second edition), London, 1900; (abridged edition) 1922; Ernst Grosse, *The Beginnings of Art*, New York, 1898; Gen. J. C. Smuts, *Holism and Evolution*, New York, 1926; L. B. Paton, *Spiritism and the Cult of the Dead*, New York, 1921; Shailer Mathews, *The Growth of the Idea of God*, New York, 1931; Albert Schweitzer, *Christianity and the Religions of the World*, New York, 1923; T. H. Robinson, *Introduction to the History of Religion*, London, 1926; A. S. Geden, *Comparative Religion*, London, 1922; E. V. Hopkins, *The Origin and Evolution of Religion*, New Haven, 1924; Edward Clodd, *Magic in Names*, New York, 1921; Carl Clemen, *Religions of the World*, New York, 1931; R. R. Marett, *Faith, Hope and Charity in Primitive Religion*, New York, 1932; W. Schmidt, *The Origin and Growth of Religion* (English trans.), New York, 1931; P. Saintyves, *Essais de Folklore Biblique*, Paris, 1922; Joseph Fort Newton (editor), *My Idea of God*, Boston, 1926; Eli E. Burriss, *Taboo, Magic, Spirits*, New York, 1931; G. W. Gilmore, *Animism*, Boston, 1919; Jane E. Harrison, *Ancient Art and Ritual*, London, 1913; W. O. E. Oesterley, *The Sacred Dance*, Cambridge, 1923.

# BOOK II

## THE PRIMITIVE RELIGIONS

### *Introduction*

WE have now discussed sufficiently the general principles of primitive religion. These principles will be found to be fairly constant in all the primitive religions which we are about to study separately. They seem to have applied likewise to all that we can discover of the religious beliefs and practices of pre-historic man and have certainly abundant illustration in such survivals of the primitive as we find in the advanced religions of the present day. This being the case, we might almost arrive at the conclusion that the elements of religion are universal from the start and that therefore separate treatment of the religions of different tribes and peoples is a work of supererogation.

But other considerations demand expression which at once reveal that our subject is one of much greater complexity than might appear from the preceding chapters. As in the history of art, and the history of human culture generally, we find ourselves compelled to allow for differences of climate, differences of occupation, differences of race and racial experience, differences of fortune in migrations hither and thither, differences such as show themselves in changed language and physical character, and a multitude of others. Quite important, too, is the fact that personalities arise (most of them, doubtless, quite unknown to history) whose thoughts, words, and deeds will stamp themselves ineffaceably upon the traditions and habits of certain tribes. Hence, men, whose general attitude towards the mysteries of Nature and the soul appears at first to be the same all the way from China to Peru, will be found gradually drawing apart from one another, exaggerating historic prejudices, elevating segmentary truths to the position of tribal and national slogans, till a multitude of conflicting religions usurp the place of a religion developing evenly along the line. It is to these separate experiences, with their many creeds and cults independently formed, and their many institutions independently developed, that we must now give our attention. This is the more necessary in that much less notice has been taken of the primitive religions than of those which we may call ethnic or historical.

Quite naturally the subject will divide itself into a survey under two main heads:

I. The religions which for the most part have remained primitive to the end of their course, or even to the present day.

II. The religions which, through certain historical circumstances, through political organizations of a certain sort, or through the rise of exceptionally gifted religious personalities, have become religions of a more highly specialized character and, in general, further advanced alike in faith and practice.

This second class we shall have to divide again under the two following heads:

1. The religions which have for the greater part run their course and are now dead. These will include the religions of Babylon, Egypt, Persia, Greece, Rome and the Amerindian empires. These are dead faiths, even though many elements of their belief and practice are found surviving or held in solution among the living religions.

2. The religions which, like Hinduism, Buddhism, Judaism, Muhammadanism and Christianity, are still active and maintain their hold upon many millions of people.

The following eight chapters are limited to the consideration of the religions of Class I, religions which have retained throughout their entire history a primitive character.

# CHAPTER VII

## *The Religions of Australasia and the Pacific*

STRESS has already been sufficiently laid upon the fact that even the most constant elements of primitive religion are found considerably modified by geographical, climatic, and other physical causes. Sir J. G. Frazer says: " Religion, like all other institutions, has been profoundly influenced by physical environment, and cannot be understood without some appreciation of those aspects of external nature which stamp themselves indelibly on the thoughts, the habits, the whole life of a people." Even where the same faith is carried from one continent to another there will necessarily develop, in connection with this faith, differences of detail and terminology of considerable moment. The Greek will find his abode of the gods on Olympus, the Hindu on Mt. Meru, the Hawaiian on Mauna Loa, and the Bornean on Kinabalu. The idea will be the same but the landscape will be vastly different.

Thus, in passing from the generalizations of the preceding chapters, it is necessary to survey, however briefly, the primitive religions of many peoples distributed geographically over the surface of our planet. And, first of all, we may study the beliefs and practices of the races occupying that enormous extent of land and water we call Oceanica, or Australasia, including the island peoples of the Pacific generally.

We may concede the original peopling of the Pacific as having resulted from the migrations of a limited number of stocks, all of them, to start with, emigrants from the continent of Asia. As to matters of detail there will, of course, be large variation of opinion, but it seems generally agreed that the first inhabitants of Oceanica were related to Pleistocene man, of whom we have the type in the Javanese *Pithecanthropos erectus*. This stock is now found surviving here and there over a wide area, as the negrito element, first of all, which still lingers in the Andamans, Philippines, Malay Peninsula, Java and elsewhere. Even the old *meles* of Hawaii seem to refer to some such stock as antedating the arrival of the Hawaiians. It is represented, in the second place, by the taller blacks inhabiting New Guinea and Melanesia, generally known as Papuasians. To these earliest elements were added two branches of the western Caucasian stock who, during the Stone Ages, passed from Europe to Eastern Asia. One branch, similar to the Ainus of Japan, passed by the northern route, through Japan, into the Pacific, and are conceivably the people who constructed the megalithic buildings of which remains exist on Easter Island and elsewhere. The other branch came by way of the south through Southern India and Indo-China. Yet later, in movements continuing into historic times, came the Mongoloid people whom we may call Malayan or proto-Malayan, who, though the latest comers, seem to have gone further afield than all the rest. By a series of movements, southward and eastward, with periods of conquest interrupting long periods of quiescence and isolation, it was possible for the ethnic and linguistic characteristics of the several groups to take form. Thus were gradually developed that extraordinary complex of peoples whom, for our special purpose, it is convenient to divide under the five following heads:

I. Australia and Tasmania.
II. Malaysia and the Philippines.
III. Melanesia.
IV. Micronesia.
V. Polynesia (in which, for racial and religious reasons, we shall include New Zealand).

I. Australia and Tasmania.—Since the Tasmanians have been practically extinct since 1876, and the last representative of the race died, we are told, in 1890, we may say what little needs to be said of these at once. They were a black or dark-brown people, with woolly hair, who never advanced to the agricultural stage, but remained to the end food gatherers, hunters and trackers. They used only wind-brakes for houses, clad themselves, when necessary, in skins, used stone implements, and obtained fire by the saw and grove method. They seem to have made rough drawings with charcoal, but betrayed no other signs of artistic development. Socially they were polygamous, but used no marriage ceremony. Their religion seems to have been well-nigh confined to a fear of spirits, whom they repelled in the dark with fire-sticks, but they also feared the dead, whose return they sought to prevent by piling stones upon the grave. Yet one story tells of a man leaving a spear by the corpse of another " to fight with when he sleep."

The Australian aborigines are chocolate-brown in colour and are apparently derived from two streams of Asiatic emigrants. Some describe the separate elements as three, represented by the three totems of crow, sparrow-hawk and emu. Others make Australian origins still more complex, due to " movements, combinations, dispersions, recombinations, variations, changes of interest and environment, changes of stress," as well as through the intrusion of foreign influences. All these considerations prevent us from seeing much likelihood of homogeneity in the culture of the Australian aborigines. For instance, there are said to be six methods of treating the dead, five or six different initiation ceremonies, three distinct methods of producing fire, and so on.[1] In general, however, the culture of the Australians is not unlike that of the Bushmen of Africa, or even the Patagonians and Fuegians of South America. They maintain a sort of gerontocracy, or government by the elders, who maintain their ascendency by an elaborate system of initiation ceremonies, including circumcision, the knocking out of teeth, combats, food restrictions, and the use of the bull-roarer. They have a very complicated system of social totemism, of which two exogamous groups form the chief feature. Each tribe is divided into two parts and each of the halves again into two or four. The marriage arrangements between these sections of society are of the

[1] See *Encyclopædia Britannica* (14th Ed.), II. 713.

most elaborate sort. The totem animal is sometimes eaten, in a quasi-sacramental way, by the headman of the tribe, but by no others, with the curious exception of outsiders. Yet restrictions as to the totem vary much in severity and are being gradually relaxed. As to religion some extreme statements have been made. Some have denied to the aborigines all religious belief, while others have ascribed to them a creed of such definiteness as must have been, at least in part, due to the Christian missionary. There seems to be at present a rather widespread belief in an All-Father, Baiame or Daramulun, but these two names are sometimes put in opposition to one another, and may only be deified tribal ancestors. There are also beings of malignant character who may be the souls of the dead. Certain magical power, or *mana*, is ascribed to certain men, also to things made by man, such as the bull-roarer. Objects possessing *mana* and capable of conveying that *mana* to men are called *churingas*. A person may acquire magical power by sleeping on the grave of a dead man. There is a belief in reincarnation, though rather vague. The soul is believed to be so small as to be able to pass through a chink. It is also believed to descend from the trees to feed on worms and grubs. Some believe that in a future state the black-fellow will be reborn as a white man. Others declare that at death the soul, which is generally associated with the shadow, goes west to an abyss or to a certain island of the dead. The dead are generally feared and are credited with the power of raising storms. Burial is either simple inhumation, or within a hut built upon the grave for a soul-house. Sometimes, however, the dead are exposed on a tree-platform, and sometimes a kind of cannibalism is practised in order to acquire the supposed powers of the deceased.

There are a few myths, though none exactly on the origin of the world. As to the origin of man, there are several types of myth, such as that which represents the two sky-beings fashioning men and women out of rudimentary beings with knives of stone. There are also myths accounting for the origin of fire and of the sun by the throwing of an egg against the sky where it broke upon a pile of firewood. A myth descriptive of the origin of death has a family likeness to myths which occur in Africa and elsewhere over a wide area. It describes the moon as offering immortality to men if they did what they were told. "See this piece of bark? I throw it into the water and it floats. So, if you obey me, when you die, you come up again." But they obeyed not, and the moon-god dropped a stone into the water which sank and came up no more. "Now you will be only a black-fellow while you live, and bones when you are dead."[1]

II. MALAYSIA AND THE PHILIPPINES.—1. *Malaysia.*[2] Under this head we shall include both the Malays, whom we take to be an Oceanic section of the Mongol family, and older elements represented by many of the pagan tribes. Geographically, we shall include most of the islands of the Malay Archipelago, with the exception of New Guinea, which, for our purpose, is best considered with Melanesia.

The primitive religion of Malaysia is a good deal intermingled with elements derived from Islam, Hinduism and even Buddhism. Most Malays to-day are Sunni Muhammadans, and were converted to that faith at intervals between the thirteenth and fifteenth centuries. Yet the primitive beliefs and practices still crop out everywhere and colour the later ideas. The general creed of the primitive Malay is a kind of animism, sometimes of a vague and general sort and sometimes developing into a belief in individual spirits. These may be present in man or they may occupy the bodies of animals. The elephant and the tiger and, in places, the mouse-deer are particularly open to possession. There is a general belief in wer-tigers, supernatural beasts endowed with weird and terrible powers. There is a general faith in the soul, which is known as a *sĕmangat*, a kind of homunculus, shaped like the individual who possesses it, but red in colour and the size of a grain

[1] Many similar legends are to be found in the folk-lore of the African races.

[2] For the religion of the Australian aborigines see the article by N. W. Thomas in *E.R.E.*, II. 244–48. Also such standard works as Spencer Gillen's *Native Tribes* (London, 1899), and *Northern Tribes of Central Australia* (London, 1904); A. W. Howitt, *Native Tribes of S.E. Australia*, London, 1904; and N. W. Thomas, *Natives of Australia*, London, 1906.

of maize. The soul of a man may be stolen by magic arts. For example, by taking soil from a man's footprints and treating it magically vengeance may be wreaked on the unlucky owner of the footprint. After death the soul is supposed to cross a bridge made of the trunk of a tree, from which, if he be bad, it may be shaken, or, if good, pass over to a Paradise in the west. Souls may also enter the bodies of animals and birds and it is often supposed that the soul of such and such a chief is in the body of an elephant. Even trees and other vegetable products have their *sémangats*. The cosmogony of the Malays, coloured as it is by elements from various sources, is rather mixed. It is believed by some that light came from the Supreme Being, was transformed into an ocean, from which the earth rose in seven stages (like a zikkurat), the sky above being a solid rock pierced with holes to permit the light to shine through as stars. A more primitive account of the origin of man includes a story of a woman carrying fire-logs under her arms to simulate children until she was instructed by a monkey. The worship of Malays, Muhammadan and pagan alike, is of the simplest sort, with prayers for material benefits and sacrifices offered as gifts to the spirits. Human sacrifices must once have been offered, and among some pagans there is still the sacrifice of a boy to obtain a soul for the war-idol. Omens are observed, sneezing being regarded as lucky in that demons are expelled, yawning as unlucky as giving opportunity for the soul to escape. Divination of many kinds is practised. Most religious observances are associated with magic and the magician, or *pawang*, has great influence. He is supposed to keep a familiar spirit and is consulted on every occasion for the discovery of the propitious moment. He also prescribes the tabus, or *pantang*. A special kind of magician is employed for the curing of diseases. Magic enters into most circumstances of life, even personal adornments having the character of charms and amulets. Magic is indeed necessary from birth to death. The ceremonies on the attainment of adolescence, such as tooth-filing, ear-boring, and the first head-shaving, are all of magical import. The burial customs are generally simple. Among the Malays proper there is little or no fear of the dead, but the pagan tribes are for the most part terrorized by death as much as any primitive people we know. The body is generally laid in a shallow hole, with three coco-nut shells of water at the foot and three of rice at the head. The grave is then roofed over with palm leaves and the structure deserted. By some of the pagan tribes tree burial is observed.[1]

2. *The Philippines.*—This archipelago, discovered by the Spaniards in 1513 and bought from Spain by the United States in 1898, after the Spanish-American War, consists of a large number of islands variously computed as from 1200 to over 7000, with a total area of 115,000 square miles. The largest island, Luzon, with 40,000 square miles, is the most northerly and the next largest, Mindanao, of 36,000 square miles, lies far to the south. The population, which has greatly increased since the American occupation, is now above 10,000,000, of whom 9,000,000 are Christian, about 500,000 pagan, and most of the rest Muhammadan. The population is divided among a large number of ethnic groups, 43 according to the *Encyclopædia Britannica*, 87 according to Beyer, and over 80 according to Worcester. These include, lowest in the scale, the Negritoes, or pygmies, in the mountain regions; the Indonesians, immigrants who have largely mingled with the Negritoes; the Moros, who, divided into seven groups, occupy the Sulu archipelago and are also found in North Borneo; the Pagan Malays, consisting of the tribes known as Tinggians, Bontoc, Igorot and Ifugao, in northern Luzon, all former head-hunters; and, above these in scale, the Filipinos proper of Malay extraction, though much intermarried with other elements, Chinese and Spanish. These Filipinos include eight principal tribes, as follows: Visayan, 4,000,000; Tagalog, 1,800,000; Ilocano, 1,000,000; Bikol, 700,000; Pangasinan, 400,000; Pampangan, 350,000; and Tarlac, 350,000; Ibanag, 156,000; and Lambal, 56,000.

[1] See W. W. Skeat, art. "Malay Peninsula," in *E.R.E.*, VIII. 345–72. Also Skeat, *Malay Magic*, London, 1900; and Skeat and Blagden, *Pagan Races of the Malay Peninsula*, London, 1906.

There is naturally great variation of culture and religious belief, due to the extraordinary amount of racial intermixture and also to the historical vicissitudes which the Philippines have experienced, including contacts with Japan and China as well as with Europe and America. The following notes, however, will apply generally to the pagan tribes and to such survivals of paganism as are elsewhere present.

Socially, the general type of organization is a division into small groups of from thirty to a hundred families. Each of these is called a *barangay*—now usually known as a *barrio*—and is under a kind of chief called a *dato*. Religious belief varies, but all the tribes believe in spirits called *anito*, who are appealed to for most material necessities. Some tribes acknowledge greater gods who are supposed to be beings of great stature living in the mountain cavities. A simple form of naturism accounts for most of the common phenomena. Thus the clouds are the breath of the wind, tides are caused by the movements of a great crab or a great fish, an eclipse is the result of the sun or moon being devoured by a crab, and monkeys are men who were once too idle to work, the sticks hurled at them having been transformed into tails. Disease is caused by evil spirits called *majalok*, who can fly through the air and devour the hearts and livers of the sick. When a man dies, his house is torn down and the body carried into the woods and buried, with broken pots and dishes strewn upon the grave. There is a kind of vampire known as a *balbal*, man-like in form, which sails through the air like a flying-squirrel and licks up the corpse. The Tagbanua believe that the souls of the dead go into a dark cave and there stand before a judge named Taliakood, who is informed of the good and bad deeds of the deceased by a louse from the corpse. The dead may die seven times, going deeper on each occasion into the earth. The mountain people of Panay believe that the dead need company, so they sally forth with lances and machetes to supply their lack by killing the first human being encountered. The Mangyans, on the authority of Dr. Worcester, have no belief in a future life, but declare "when a man's dead, he's dead." This tribe uses an ordeal consisting of a piece of red-hot iron to be grasped by the accused who wishes to protest his innocence.[1]

III. Melanesia and New Guinea.—Melanesia proper consists of five principal groups, namely, the Solomon Islands; the New Hebrides, with the Banks Islands; the Santa Cruz group; New Caledonia, together with the Loyalty Islands; and the Fiji Islands. To these I add, for our purpose, New Guinea, because of certain ethnic and religious resemblances. It should, however, be observed that, while the inhabitants of New Guinea are Papuans, the other island groups are occupied by an older Papuan element, upon which have been superimposed wave after wave of Indonesians from the mainland. Dr. W. H. R. Rivers has taken great pains to distinguish the different elements of Melanesian population, and endeavours to show that "all the chief social institutions of Melanesia, its dual organization, its secret societies, its totemism, its cult of the dead, and many of its less essential customs, such as its use of money, its decorative art, its practice of incision and its square houses, have been the direct outcome of the interaction between different and sometimes conflicting cultures."[2]

Thus the social system of Melanesia naturally presents different phenomena in the different groups. In the West Solomons there is a clan system of a rather definite kind. Descent is traced matrilineally in certain regions only, but there is general recognition of totemism, using the term as denoting a relation accepted between the community and certain animals, plants and objects, and the paying of honour to these by refraining from their use or using them sacramentally. The totems of the Melanesian groups are generally birds, aquatic animals, or shells. In some parts of the Solomons two of the six exogamic kindreds are named after the crab and the sea-eagle. In the New Hebrides one family is named after the octopus. In some groups the "guardian animal" (*tamanui*) is respected as specially concerned with a particular individual. Other individual

[1] See A. E. Jenks, *The Bontoc Igorot*, Manila, 1905; W. A. Reed, *Negritoes of Zimbales*, Manila, 1904; John Foreman, *The Philippine Islands*, New York, 1906.

[2] W. H. R. Rivers, *History of Melanesian Society*, II. 595, Cambridge, 1914.

totems are really fetishes, such as a stone kept for the purpose of preserving health.

Secret societies and the observance of mysteries are common throughout Melanesia. In Mota Dr. Rivers counted seventy-seven societies of this sort, organized, it has been supposed, to protect the secrets of the clan from the older stock on the islands. Quite a few of the groups possess the characteristic Melanesian institution of the *gamal*, or men's club-house, a long building divided into compartments to keep the initiations private and to separate the various grades of initiates. Some societies meet in the village and others, such as the tamate (or ghost-societies) in the bush. Initiation is rendered as mysterious as possible, with use of masks and weird sounds (*werewere*), produced by scraping a stick upon a stone. Kava-drinking is also a custom at these society meetings intimately associated with religion.

In general, Melanesian religion makes large use of magic, for increasing the supply of yams and fish, and of tabus, for the maintenance of law and order. Tabu marks are placed at the graves of the chiefs, at certain seasons near the coco-nut groves, to protect the places where food is stored, or to bar entrance to certain roads and houses. The cult of the skull is common in the West Solomons, but is absent from Southern Melanesia. Head-hunting in some districts once played an important part in the ceremonial dedication of a new canoe or house.

The quintessence of Melanesian religion is the belief in *mana*—a word already noted as of Melanesian origin, really a metathetic form of *nanama*, to be powerful—and in spirits. The latter are of two kinds, *tamate*, or ghosts, and *vui*, or spirits which have never been embodied. Both sorts are greatly feared, but especially the *vui*. In the South-Eastern Solomons the souls of the dead are fished for and placed in a relic-case, while in New Guinea images of the dead (*karwars*) are made and provided with food offerings. Of goblins, or ghouls, one of the most feared is the *atitigi*, a white monster with one eye in front and one behind, six fingers on each hand, and a sharp claw for tearing the bodies of the dead. Sacred images are believed to be possessed by spirits and there are certain trees, stones and streams in which spirits make their abode. Animals also may be possessed, as the frigate-bird and the shark in the Solomons and snakes in the New Hebrides. In some groups a "high" god seems to be reverenced, such as Qat in the Banks Islands and in the New Hebrides Tagaro, probably the same as the Polynesian Tangaroa (Hawaiian, *Kanaloa*). In the New Guinea archipelago there is much fear of "flying-witches." Certain women, known as *yoyova*, recognizable by their taste for raw flesh, are believed possessed by an immaterial spiritual principle called mulukwausi. These fly by night, feeding on corpses and destroying shipwrecked sailors.[1]

There is a general belief in the persistence of life after death, but with variant details. Sometimes the world of spirits is but an enlarged grave, beneath the earth; sometimes an island to which the soul goes in a "ship of the dead"; sometimes, as in the South-Eastern Solomons, merely "the land of no return." The New Guinea belief is that the dead go to the Isle of Watum, where their former life is continued. Dr. Rivers suggests that the disposal of the dead by inhumation was connected with the belief in an underworld; putting the dead out to sea in a canoe, or casting them into the water, with a conception of some island world of spirits; whilst cremation, which exists only on the extreme edge of the Melanesian area, was associated with the idea of an Elysium in the sky or in the air. Practically all the groups, nevertheless, believe in the possibility of the *tamate* haunting their former home. The world of the dead is but slightly moralized, though here and there we learn of a shark or a fierce pig which will bite the nose off the dead man guilty of some purely social offence.

There is naturally much resort to magic and sorcerers are believed capable of handing down their esoteric knowledge from generation to generation. Some of these sorcerers are adepts at making up parcels containing a hair from the person whom it is intended to destroy. In

[1] Bronislaw Malinowski, *Argonauts of the Western Pacific*, London, 1922.

Malinowski's elaborate description of the Kula[1] of the New Guinea archipelago we have given with much detail the spells (with or without rites) for the carrying out of canoe magic, love magic, garden magic, and the like.[2]

It may be added that ordeals of many kinds are employed, including the use of hot stones and the swallowing of magical objects. Divination is used to discover the causes of sickness, or to promote success in fishing. Omens, of course, both actual and imaginary, are as commonly observed here as elsewhere.[3]

In the *Fiji Islands*, which deserve a brief paragraph to themselves, we have illustrations of most of the usual beliefs and practices. The tribal system related everybody to an ancestral spirit and hence the term *matanitu*. Human sacrifices were offered on a large scale, especially at the founding of a temple, when men were interred beneath every post, or on the launching of a big canoe. There were square enclosures called Nang-a, in which altars were set up for sacrifice. Many totems were reverenced, including eels, lizards and snakes. There were superstitions connected with circumcision, tattooing, name-giving, and such like. Much *mana* was believed to pertain to the hair and accounts are given of the care taken to guard the locks of a chief. A kind of *puuhonua* (to use the Hawaiian term) was used as a Rock of Refuge for unintentional homicides. The souls of the dead were supposed to have "leaping places," precipitous cliffs from which the spirit went north-west to the far-off Isle of the Blest, known as Qaloqalo or Burotu.[4]

IV. THE MICRONESIANS.—The groups which fall under the head of Micronesia, or "the little islands," include the Ladrone, or Marianne Islands, now under Japanese mandate (with the exception of the United States island of Guam);

[1] The Kula is an elaborate system of exchange, in the borderland of the commercial and the religious, in which shell armlets and necklaces are employed. It is carried on throughout the New Guinea archipelago.

[2] See Malinowski, *op. cit.*, Chapter xvii., *Magic and the Kula*.

[3] See, in addition to the works above cited, R. H. Codrington, *The Melanesians*, Oxford, 1891; and W. G. Ivens, *The Melanesians of the S.E. Solomons*, London, 1927. Also the article by Dr. Codrington, "Melanesians," *E.R.E.*, VIII. 529–38.

[4] See A. B. Brewster, *The Hill Tribes of Fiji*, Philadelphia, 1922.

the Pellew (Palau) Islands; the Caroline Islands; the Marshall Islands; and the Gilbert Islands. The Carolines and Marshalls are now Japanese and the Gilberts British.

The inhabitants are of mixed race, with a foundation of Melanesian stock, to which has been added a strong Polynesian element in the east, and later, especially in the Carolines, an infusion of the Malay. The culture is in like manner mixed. In the Carolines, particularly at Ponape, there is a considerable area occupied by the ruins of old temples and palaces which seem to date from the time of the megalithic builders, who came from the north by way of Japan. The modern Micronesians, though lazy, make excellent navigators and possess charts enabling them to sail from island to island. The chiefs form a kind of caste by themselves and are honoured as semi-divine. The tabus imposed, such as "mourning tabus," on the death of a chief, are burdensome in the extreme. Tattooing on the body, for all but slaves, is in vogue and the Melanesian custom of using men's club-houses is also fairly common. As to religious beliefs, we have the account of the religion of Guam written by the Jesuit father Le Gobien as far back as 1700, but the so-called Chamorro religion is now extinct. There is, however, a very general faith in animism, with the usual dread of ghosts. Spirits, known as *anu*, are supposed to communicate with men through the medium of a *shaman*, whose office, however, is not hereditary. Ancestor worship is a cult maintained for the glorification of the chiefs, living or dead. The divinity of the chiefs, however, is not recognized until after death. Burial is in general under the dwelling-house, beneath which the body is allowed to shrivel. But warriors who fall in battle prefer to be buried in the sea in imitation of the hero Rassau, who has become the sea-god Arong, a deity worshipped in the form of a fish. It is probable that some of the myths prevailing in the Micronesian groups are of Indonesian rather than native origin.[1]

V. Polynesia and New Zealand.—Under the head of Polynesia, with which for racial reasons we associate New Zealand, is included a wide stretch of ocean territory

[1] See, for Micronesia, the article "Australasia" in *E.R.E.*, II. 236 ff.

and its island groups, extending to within two thousand miles of the American coast. The principal groups, apart from New Zealand, are the Samoan, Tongan, Cook, Society (Tahiti), Ellis and Hawaiian Islands. The population of all these groups is Indonesian, though including the remains of older populations. It seems derived ultimately through India, the Malay Peninsula and Java, and thence to have passed on across the Pacific at various times from the beginning of the Christian era to as late as the sixteenth century, for the last immigration movement of the Hawaiian islands. A very considerable part of the Hawaiian language, including many of its grammatical forms, may be traced back to Indian originals. A number of the Hawaiian myths, also, have Indian parallels.[1]

As there is a family likeness in all the religious beliefs and practices of the Polynesian groups, it will probably be sufficient to describe only the system which prevailed until the early years of the nineteenth century in the Hawaiian Islands, with a note or two as to variations in other groups and a more special reference to the religion of New Zealand. We are greatly assisted in our study of this system by the writings of the first Christian missionaries, by the considerable number of *meles* which were orally transmitted from older generations, and by lingering relics of ancient custom found here and there almost to the present day.

The social order of Hawaii (and of the Polynesian groups in general) included chiefs (*alii*), priests (*kahuna*), and the common people (*makaainana*). The chiefs were sacred (*kapu* or tabu) and alone had the right to wear the red feather cloak and helmet and the ivory clasp, or *palaoa*. The head chief of an island was called *moi*. It was not till the end of the eighteenth century that Kamehameha I. became king of the entire Hawaiian group. The kahunas, or priests, were also a class apart and were divided into many orders, *kilokilo*, or diviners, *kahuna anaana*, or sorcerers, *kahuna lapaau*, or physicians, and so on. Beside these general orders there were more specialized groups, such as necromancers, astrologers, prophets, and so forth.

[1] See A. Fornander, *An Account of the Polynesian Race*, 3 volumes, London, 1885.

The gods (*akua*) were of many classes, some of them nature-gods, deities of the volcano, thunder, meteors, and the like; others hero-gods, and seemingly spirits of the ancestors. There were also the great gods—apparently nature-gods—Kane, Kanaloa, Ku and Lono who, it was claimed, existed from the time of chaos (*mai ka po mai*). There were also local gods worshipped at various shrines to be found around the coasts; professional gods, such as Kaili, the famous war-god of Kamehameha; even animal gods, such as those supposed to inhabit the *moo*, or great lizard, or the shark. There were, again, family gods, *aumakua* (the *oromatua* of Tahiti). Some gods were in a class apart, such as Maui, the hero-god who fished up the eight islands from the bottom of the sea and lassoed the sun to prevent it from going too fast; Pele, who, with her numerous family, controlled the volcanoes and the lava-flows; and Kamapuaa, the demi-god who took the form of a gigantic hog.

The Polynesians, again as represented by the Hawaiians, had many temples, irregular parallelograms with thick walls and a high altar, like a scaffolding, on which the pig, or other sacrifice, was left to putrefy. In an inner court were the idols, some of them of ohia wood, others of wicker-work with eyes of mother-of-pearl and decoration of feathers. The common people had smaller idols, some of them merely pebbles supposed to contain *mana*. Human sacrifices were not uncommon and, as late as 1807, when Queen Keopuolani was ill, four men were sacrificed on her behalf. On great occasions a priest known as the "flesh-eating *mu*" would go round and select his victims. In certain parts of the islands were the cities of refuge, known as *Puuhonua*, enclosures of which the gates stood ever open, guarded with a white flag fluttering from a spear. Here the man guilty of unintentional (and even intentional) homicide might find a shelter under the protection of the priests. The *kapu* (tabu) was observed in the Hawaiian islands in many forms and with great rigour. There were food tabus, tabus on particular places, and tabus on particular times; a great variety of tabus applied specially to women. The abolition of the tabus by Kamehameha II., in 1819, was at once the breaking up of a terrible tyranny and also the demolition of a salutary system of restraint.

There were many beliefs and practices connected with the dead. On the death of a chief efforts were at once made by the kahunas to discover by magic the person guilty of the decease and a cruel revenge was taken on any suspected of responsibility. The mourning customs involved an almost complete moral anarchy, with many burdens and exactions placed upon the common people. The body of a chief was generally concealed in some cave, but in the case of a chief slain in war, the bones, made up into a bundle known as a *unihipili*, were carried about by the victor. It was believed that the souls of men went either to a place of happiness called Wakea, or else to an underground land known as Milu, where they lived on butterflies and other insects. For some, heaven was beyond the clouds, or beyond the western horizon. In some of the Polynesian groups the dead were buried in a canoe to suggest their long voyage beyond the sunset. In Hawaii there was a belief in a kind of psychopomp, Kaonohioka, "the eyeball of the sun," who led the soul to the underworld. Certain places, known as "leaping places," along the coast, expressed the general Polynesian belief in the soul taking its journey to the sea. Much more might be said of the Polynesian religion, but most of the notes given above will be found to have their parallels in other groups than the Hawaiian, while a few things, such as the use of bird omens in Samoa, may be regarded as distinctive of other parts of the Polynesian world.

New Zealand, a group of islands something over 100,000 square miles in extent, has a native population (excluding the 1,500,000 whites) of about 65,000. These are called Maoris, now somewhat increasing in number, and practically all Christianized. In the old religion most of the features resemble those of the Polynesian islands proper, with names somewhat changed through modification of language, as *rangi* (heaven) for the Hawaiian, *lani*; *ra* (sun) for Hawaiian, *la*; Tani for Kane, Tangaroa for Kanaloa, and the like. The Maori gods were sometimes great devils, working devastation through storm and lightning; sometimes they were small devils, like mosquitoes. Many were merely the ghosts of the dead. Souls were supposed to pass over the river Waioratane by means of a narrow bridge. Only the brave, however, could cross successfully and these passed upwards into the sky as clouds or stars.[1]

[1] On Polynesian Religion generally, in addition to Fornander, see Cook's *Voyages* ; W. Ellis, *A Tour through Owhyhee*, London, 1828 ; and H. Bingham, *Twenty-one Years in the Sandwich Islands*, New York, 1847. Also the article by Robert W. Williamson, in *E.R.E.*, X.

## CHAPTER VIII

# *The Primitive Religions of Africa*

IN no continent do we find such an enormous amount of material bearing upon the subject of primitive religion as in the continent which until recently has borne the name of the Dark Continent. Yet although "darkest Africa" is a territory where the early religion of the tribes has been less covered over, till recently, by missionary effort, than any other part of the world, it is by no means so virgin a field for the student as may at first sight appear. Apart from the early Semitic waves which so profoundly affected the religion of ancient Egypt, and apart from influences which may conceivably have crossed the Mediterranean from the north, the more modern introduction of Muhammadanism has done much to colour the ideas and practices of a large portion of the continent, north and east and central. Even the comparatively recent propagation of Christianity, so far as modern times are concerned, has introduced teachings which may very readily be so given back by the natives as to appear legends of their own. We have in this a warning much stressed by Bishop Callaway for the benefit of investigators, but which is still exceedingly important.

How much has been borrowed from one foreign source or another may never be known, but enough remains of the undoubtedly primitive to make the study of African religion a fascinating field.

In this chapter we shall find it convenient to consider our material under four chief heads, namely: (1) The *Bantus* of the south; (2) the *Berbers* of the north; (3) the *Hamites* of the east; and (4) the *Negroes* of the west.

But there are some generalizations of a preliminary kind which will assist us to cover a considerable portion of the field without the necessity of any such divisions, though we must make a few qualifications in respect to the Berber population in the north. These generalizations are:

1. That African religion is *bloody* beyond almost any primitive religion we know. Mr. Crawford says that we can add to the Bible statement, "without shedding of blood is no remission of sins" the corollary that, in Africa, "without shedding of blood is no—no anything." The horrible holocausts of human victims which have marked the "customs" in Ashanti and Dahomey have their counterpart in every part of Africa. Yet, Mr. Crawford reminds us, Do not *blood*, *bloom*, *blossom*, come from the same root?[1]

2. A second generalization will stress the fact that *witchcraft* also has in Africa a tremendously important place. "The witch-doctor," says Mr. Melland,[2] "is the curse of Africa," and the same writer has some lurid chapters on witches and witch-finding, though at the same time he is careful to recall that once in Geneva five hundred witches were burned in a single month.[3]

3. A third important element of all African primitive religion is the belief in *fetishes*. Fetishism, indeed, owes its first naming to an African traveller, Bosman, in 1705,[4] and also many of its most striking illustrations. Africa is full of *grigri*, *juju*, and the like, as examples of fetishism according to Mr. E. B. Tylor's definition of it as "the doctrine of spirits embodied in, or attached to, or conveying influence through, certain material objects." The fetish, explains Dr. E. V. Hopkins, differs from the idol in that "the idol works for the group, the fetish for the individual." African fetishism, says the same writer, is "rank with evil"; it is "the dominating religious factor." Nevertheless, it may be supposed to have a certain ethical value as guarding persons and places and things from unjust attack, as well as a certain religious value in its power to bring blessing. The fetish-log, smeared with oil or blood, is

[1] See D. Crawford, *Thinking Black*. Capt. Rattray, however, considers the "bloodiness" of African religion, at least in Ashanti, as overstressed.

[2] See F. H. Melland, *In Witch-bound Africa*, London, 1923.

[3] Cf. also the words of Martin Luther: "I would have no pity on these witches; I would burn them all."

[4] See Bosman, *Description of Guinea*, 1705.

sure to attract spirits who, in regaling themselves on the repast, take pleasure in the prosperity of their host.[1]

4. To the above may be added the general belief in the existence and survival of the *soul*. Major Leonard, in his account of the tribes of the Lower Niger,[2] writes (and his description applies generally to the African): "Among the Ibo and other Delta tribes the belief in the existence of the human soul is universal. To them it is an active principle that is awake and about when the body is asleep. Further, it appears as a something, indefinite and indefinable, an invisible and to some extent intangible essence apart from and of different texture to the material body, which leaves the latter during sleep, or for good at dissolution."

It is probable that as time goes on it will be possible to discern still more of unity in the entire scheme of African religion than we see to-day. Already it is being pointed out that the ancient religion of Egypt is in many particulars best explained by customs still persisting in Central Africa. For example, we have Monsignor Le Roy declaring: "We are struck by the curious analogy to be observed between the beliefs of the ancient Egyptians and those of the Bantus of to-day."[3] Something of this fundamental unity will, it is hoped, be discovered in much that is now to follow. This must be our excuse for what may appear to be a certain amount of repetition.

I. THE BERBERS.—Only brief mention needs here to be made of the Berbers, as the inhabitants of North Africa are called, for a double reason. First, these are distinctively a "white" race rather than African in the usual sense of the word. Secondly, their primitive religion has been so largely covered up with foreign elements, Phœnician, Greek, Roman, Christian and Muhammadan, that they are scarcely representative of primitive religion in Africa at the present day.

The name, which is possibly derived from the Greek

[1] Great care needs to be taken in noting the various implications of the term *fetish* in different parts of Africa. For this reason, as Mr. R. R. Marett reminds us, a committee of experts advised the discontinuance of the word "as a peculiarly dyslogistic and question-begging term."

[2] Major Leonard, *The Lower Niger and its Tribes*, p. 139.

[3] Le Roy, *Religion of the Primitives*, p. 94.

*barbaroi*, is applied to the different branches of the race known in classical times as Libyan. It stretches all the way from the Atlantic to Egypt and from the Mediterranean to the Sahara. It includes also the Guanches of the Canary Islands, from whom it is possible to derive interesting glimpses of early religious ideas. Dr. René Basset[1] says that, although the Berbers have a remarkable linguistic unity, the same is not to be said of their religion. Indeed, this seems largely influenced by the geographical location as well as by contact with the civilizations of antiquity. There was mountain worship with that special reverence for Mt. Atlas, "the pillar of heaven," to which the younger Pliny alludes. Maximus of Tyre, again, speaks of it as "both a temple and a god." There was also, it seems clear, rock worship, cave worship and the worship of streams. Sun worship was general, probably with the sun represented as a ram, whose horns also were regarded as themselves a solar emblem. Moon worship and star worship also were common, and there were myths about the stars, such as that of Orion, the hunter, dragging his foot out of the mire. Other natural myths include the story of the rainbow as the bride of the rain. There were also special gods to whom human sacrifices were offered and the native cruelty of the African was evident enough even before the primitive religion was superseded by the later cults. Some gods seem to have been deified kings and others were apparently mythical beings, ogres, and the like.

Among the religious practices which emerge from the somewhat sparse references in the works of ancient writers is the habit of induced dreaming on the tombstones of the dead, spoken of by Pomponius Mela, and sundry methods of divination and witch-finding which link us with the more purely African customs of the regions to the south. There was much sorcery performed by the use of plants for incantations; there was the use of a bag containing the heads of animals; and there was the uncovering of a thief by a secret writing passed round among the inquisitors. The agrarian rites performed at the periods of seasonal transition appear to have been much like those practised in

[1] *Encyclopædia of Religion and Ethics*, art. "Berbers."

other lands. An interesting rain charm involved the use of a wooden spoon which was dressed up in feminine garments and was supposed to invoke the coming of the showers. Another method was the tying up of animals away from their young, so that the cries of the separated beasts might appeal to the weather gods.

II. THE HAMITES.—The term Hamites is an unsatisfactory one at the best, and confusion has been made worse confounded by the diverse use to which the term has been put. Some writers have used the word of most of the inhabitants of Africa, including the Berbers of the north and east. Others have limited it to the Egyptian Bejas and the southern Ethiopian group which includes Agaos, Sidamas, Gallas and Somalis.

In this region, again, we encounter difficulty from the fact that the primitive religion has been greatly overlaid with Muhammadanism and with various forms of Christianity. But there are still a number of pagan tribes from whom we may gather the general character of earlier forms of religion. The Bejas are now entirely Muhammadan, the earlier Christianity having disappeared, so that we need not in this case say anything as to the character (purely hypothetical) of the earlier faith. As to the Agaos, Professor C. Conti-Rossini writes: "Little is known of the ancient Agao religion. Their chief god was the sky (Deban or Jar). Under him were many genii—some malignant, like the *zar*, and some beneficent. The latter dwelt in springs, trees and mountain tops, and were there venerated. A special worship was rendered to certain genii of the springs, as, for instance, to that of the source of the Blue Nile. Homage was paid to certain animals, especially the serpent, from which omens were sought. For defence against evil spirits, the intervention was permitted of special individuals, in whom exceptional faculties were recognized. The priesthood was hereditary from father to son. Life continued after death and food was offered to the dead."[1]

The religion of the Sidama was not greatly different. There was a supreme deity known as Hecco (or Deoc), supposed to be incarnate in the kings of the Kaffa. These

[1] *E.R.E.*, VI. 488.

had twelve high priests, among whom one was regarded as supreme. These healed the sick, prevented the effects of the evil eye and, by going into a trance, announced the will of the god. There were many food tabus, which prohibited the use of the flesh of horse, ass, mule, wild boar, hippopotamus and monkey. Men were not allowed to eat cabbages nor could women eat fowls, while priests were debarred from eating the flesh of the ox. Life beyond death was believed in, at least for the king, who was supplied with food every day for a year after his decease. One tribe, known as the Zinjero, worshipped the sun and regarded their king as a solar incarnation. They also worshipped a meteorite which had fallen from heaven. Human victims were offered on a mountain summit and one out of every ten strangers who entered the territory was sacrificed to the sun, a practice which, we are told, continued till the Abyssinians conquered the land in 1887.

The Somalis have been for the most part converted to Islam and the Gallas, less generally, to Christianity, but a number of tribes still remain pagan. By these, a supreme god, known as Waq, is worshipped, together with sundry *jinns*, a female deity of fecundity, and the spirits of trees and springs. There is also belief in a house-protecting genius known as a *qolo*. Serpents and birds are reverenced as assisting in divination, and for the same purpose the peritoneum of the victims offered in sacrifice is examined. There were also ordeals by means of boiling water and hot iron. No idols appear to have been used. Rossini says very much the same of the Kunama tribe and adds: "Their god is called Anna. Religious offices are handed down from father to son in certain families, as those of the Aula Manna . . . who have the duty of causing rain at suitable seasons; the Ula Manna, who keep the locusts at a distance from the Kunama country; and the Furda Manna, who indicate the time for beginning the ingathering of the grain, india-rubber and honey. The first two offices carry with them the pain of death if the charms turn out to be ineffective. But the religious practices of the Kunama consist in manifestations of a gross superstition rather than in the worship of Anna." [1]

[1] *E.R.E.*, VI. 492.

III. The Bantus.—The word Bantu, which is the plural of *Ntu*, or *Muntu*, merely a synonym for *man*, is a linguistic rather than a racial term, applied to a large number of tribes in South Africa which, from remote times, have been separated from the negroes of the Sudan and of the West. Their culture is generally tribal, each village having a chief of its own, but with groups of villages ruled by a high chief who is frequently a king and the founder of a dynasty. But these dynasties are very unstable and dependent almost wholly on the personality and vigour of the reigning monarch. In a great many of the tribes there is an exogamic system of some complexity. For instance, among the Hereros, of the former German S.W. African territory, there is an *eanda*, or system of mother-right, and at the same time a (more recent) system of *oruzo*, or father-right. Each has its own totem, as, for instance, the chameleon. Totemism is general and the totem may be an animal, a vegetable or even an agricultural implement, like the hoe. The Bechuanas, for example, have among their totems such animals as the monkey, the crocodile, the lion, and certain fish. In one tribe the mushroom is a totem. Among the Baganda and Banyoro, Sir Harry Johnston mentions twenty-nine different totems. Generally the totem is not eaten, or is eaten sacramentally. In most tribes circumcision, probably a relic of human sacrifice, is practised, while the girls are kept for a time in what is known as the " paint house " for instruction in the duties of married life. After the initiation rites, which are performed for both boys and girls, the newly initiated are supposed for a time to mark their " new birth " by pretended infancy, learning once again to feed, speak, and so on. For all people there are many tabus, called by the Bantus of the east coast *mwiko*, such as themselves point to a totemic origin. Many of these are food tabus and are frequently special for particular families. One family, for instance, is forbidden to eat the flesh of the buffalo; another similarly restrained from partaking of the antelope; still others denied the flesh of the pig. A royal family is debarred from eating the meat of the sheep or goat.

The Bantu conception of God is generally vague, but

it is stated by Mr. Milland that an habitual, all-pervading sense of dependence on a higher power "is a very fair summary of the religion of the Bantu peoples." Le Roy also finds "behind what is called their naturism, animism, or fetishism, everywhere there rises up, real and living, though often more or less veiled, the notion of a higher God, above men, manes, spirits, and all the forces of nature."[1] As a creator, however, God is but dimly apprehended, though the Yaos talk about Mulungu (or Mtanga), who pushed up the earth into mountains, dug channels for the rivers, and brought down the rain to fill the streams. Among other tribes the name (which seems to be applied to anything mysterious) appears as Milungu and Mulenga, a kind of rain-god. Mr. Milland speaks of the conception of Lesa and Nzambi as that of a creator god. Among the Zulus there is the belief in Unkulunkulu, "the great-great-grandfather," as the first man, originating the race from reeds, but this seems to point to ancestor worship rather than to the idea of a creator of heaven and earth. Myths of creation appear here and there, some of them no doubt a reflection of missionary teaching. Some of them, too, are mere poetic imagery, as, for instance, the explanation of the sun-spots and moon-spots as the result of a mutual mud-slinging in the course of a beer quarrel. The point may be sufficiently summed up by saying that in many places there is a belief in "a relatively Supreme Being," but that in general the tendency is towards a naturistic and spiritistic polytheism.

Certainly there are many nature deities. In fact, while the war-like tribes of the south and centre are nearly all pure ancestor worshippers, that is, worshippers of the spirits of the dead, the more settled agricultural peoples around the Great Lakes show considerable devotion to the divine powers of Nature. It has been suggested that this is perhaps due to the entrance of two different streams of population; it may equally well be the result of diverse habit of life. Among the Ekoi the two deities of earth and sky are reverenced and there are also acknowledged spirits of the streams and trees and mountains. The Zulus, and

[1] Le Roy, *op. cit.*, p. 114.

many of the other Bantu peoples, have a thunder-god. "We know him because he thunders" is no infrequent argument for the existence of the deity. Indeed, most of the tribes seem to have a sky-god who is at the same time a lightning- and thunder-god. In some places the spirit of a stream is appealed to by food placed between two small ant-hills made to lean against one another to form an arch.

More widely spread than the worship of nature-gods, however, is the belief in the spirits of the dead and in their reincarnation in the bodies of the living. To the chief while alive great powers are ascribed, as rain-maker, or as the performer of the rites by which war is to be won. This reverence is increased after death, with an added element of fear and dread of the released spirit. Souls were believed to have a perishable and an imperishable part. The imperishable part was fed with rice balls, as in the Indian *çraddha*, and in Mombasa was recognized in the first worm which came forth from the putrefying corpse. The funeral rites, which varied much in the several tribes, are described by Le Roy as a "mysterious bridge which leads the soul to its destination." In certain places the dead were buried in their own huts, or the house was duplicated in the grave, the village in the cemetery. In other places the bodies were abandoned to the hyenas, which might thus become, as in ancient Egypt, sacred animals. In still other places the dead were left on a river bank, or even eaten. In this latter case, the bodies were exchanged for those belonging to another clan. When buried, the body was placed in the position of the infant in the womb, to await a second birth. The chief was buried in a specially constructed barrow, with broken calabashes and other utensils, and such sacrifices as might seem meet. In some graves many valuables were sprinkled after having been ground to powder. Among the Hereros cattle were cut to pieces and their horns used to adorn the tree planted as a resting-place for the spirit. The Banyoro kings were placed in a pit, with nine living men all securely pegged down under a cowhide, and a temple was built upon the grave. In Uganda the king's underjaw was cut off prior to burial, ornamented, and kept in a special house, with a specially designated chief as guardian of the royal jaw—a pleasant custom only abolished as recently as the time of King Mtesa. In many parts of Africa still a peasant is slaughtered and buried immediately in front of the royal tomb. Among the Awemba the body was rolled in a mat and lowered into the grave. Then the nearest relation descended, cut a hole in the mat nearest the ear of the deceased, and whispered to him certain things expressive of hope that he would fare well in the land of spirits. Every man had his *chimvule*, or shadow-soul, which he could sometimes bottle up and carry with him in an antelope's horn. There was also the soul which could be placed in a *chipanda*, or stick planted outside the hut, to which prayers were addressed by the survivors. The underworld, according to some, consisted of villages like those on earth, where roamed many white cattle, or blue cattle spotted with red and white. Spirits could return in dreams or in the form of animals. Some chiefs were particularly anxious to return in the shape of lions, and took medicine to secure that desirable result. Others were believed to come back in the form of snakes. Belief in transmigration was general. But there were also evil spirits which might enter into corpses where these were left unprotected. The act of sneezing was regarded by many as a sign that the spirit of the dead was present; some declared that the spirit voices twittered like birds.

Practices of a more or less religious character included the use of divination, the observation of omens, the offering of sacrifices, and, of course, all the functions of the priests and witch-doctors. Witches were sometimes believed to be the unconscious carriers of evil influences, "plucking out the soul of someone asleep," or, without intent, being the cause of some similar calamity. Poison ordeals were common, especially the use of the *mvavi*, given a man to drink in order to prove him guilty or innocent of the charge of witchcraft. Sacrifices in some tribes are performed by the head of the family, but in general form but one of the many functions of the priests, who may be witch-doctors, witch-finders ("smellers out of witches"), rain-makers, healers, fortune-tellers, mad doctors, consecrators of weapons, family priests, prophets and prophetesses, or necromancers. Divination is performed in many ways, such as the use of "the first word," water-gazing, placing of a basket over the head, using the divining-rod, and so on. Names were chosen for children by divination and the practice of *teknonymy*, or the parent taking a name from the child, was common. Powerful charms were made from the hair, nail parings and teeth of persons against whom harm was designed. Spittle was regarded as a "soul holder" and might be given as an honour to convey *mana*. It should be added that among the tribes of the south-west, south-east and centre idols are practically unknown, unless we include the little dolls carried about as amulets.

IV. THE NEGROES.—Under this head we include generally the black races of equatorial and Western Africa, as distinguished from the Berbers of the north, the Hamites of the east, and the Bantu-speaking peoples of the south. Of course, there is much intermingling with all three of these groups. Although much has been contributed on the subject of West African religion by such competent writers as Miss Mary Kingsley, Mr. R. E. Dennett, Captain R. S. Rattray,[1] and Mr. Mockler-Ferryman, it cannot be said as yet that any very systematic treatment of the whole field has been produced. This is partly due to the comparative paucity of the investigators and to the natural reticence of the negroes themselves, who dislike to be interrogated on matters which seem to them to be subjects of mere curiosity or even amusement to foreigners.

The general culture of the negro peoples of Africa is agricultural, but they are expert in iron-smelting where such is possible, and show considerable skill in the arts of weaving and carving. In West Africa the Yorubas are the most advanced, the Dahomians coming next, with the Ashantis a rather bad third. Totemism is generally prevalent and polygamy is common, with many food tabus applying to different families and tribes. Cannibalism is

[1] See R. E. Dennett, *At the Back of the Black Man's Mind*, London, 1906; M. H. Kingsley, *Travels in W. Africa* (1897), and *West African Studies* (1899); R. S. Rattray, *Religion and Art in Ashanti*, Oxford, 1927; and A. F. Mockler-Ferryman, *Up the Niger*, London, 1892.

rife, more in some parts than others, and in some places from natural taste, in others as a method for disposing of and assimilating the *mana* of their dead relatives.

In religion, according to Miss Kingsley, there are four main schools, namely: (1) from Sierra Leone to the Niger mouth; (2) thence eastward to the Cameroons; (3) the Mpongwe country; and (4) the Loango country north of the Congo. The distinctions of religion, however, in these regions do not seem to be very clearly drawn. Many gods are acknowledged, national gods like the Bobowissi of the Gold Coast, or Mawu, the sky-god of the Ewe-speaking peoples; local deities, such as the long-haired, malignant Sasabonsum and the female monster Srahmantin; local spirits connected with trees, rocks, rivers, springs and hills, such as the friendly goddess Fohsu, who assists her devotees in the gathering of salt; family gods, such as the *bohsum* (or *obosom*), who are supposed to protect the family line; and individual gods, which are really but slightly different from charms and fetishes. Fetish worship is universal and the West African *grigri* and *juju* have wide repute. It is interesting to note that most of the gods worshipped are malignant beings, since the benignant ones are not supposed to require any attention. Among different peoples, in addition to the above, there are special cults, as that of the moon in Guinea and that of the thunder bird in Dahomey. Nature myths of all sorts abound, though they concern rather the origin of man and questions of human destiny than the creation of heaven and earth.

There is a very general belief in the soul, though great variation as to the whereabouts of the soul-seat and the number of souls a man possesses. The equatorial negroes believed the soul to be resident in the liver and hence sealed blood-brotherhood by eating a piece of goat's liver. The Yorubas acknowledge three souls and locate them respectively in the hand, the stomach and the big toe—that they may have strength, wisdom and the power to move. Some believe in four souls, the immortal soul, the bush soul, the shadow soul and the dream soul. The last named may easily escape and will then have to be brought back by the witch-doctor. On the Gold Coast it is believed that a man has a *kra* (or *okra*), or wandering soul, which goes forth to seek another body when the other soul goes to ghost-land, though Rattray uses the word *okra* as merely a synonym for soul in general. Ghost-land is apparently as little to the taste of the negro as it was to Achilles, for a saying is quoted: "One day on earth is better than a year in *saman-dazi*." In Ashanti the *saman*, or ghost, is guided to the spirit world by the sacrifice of a fowl. The sacrifice of human beings at the funeral of the great was common, as a kind of "following the dead," and sometimes the sacrifice was repeated at an annual commemoration, perhaps for the purpose of ensuring the fertility of the land. The bones of the dead were generally collected, preserved and marked, but in some places the dead were merely floated down a stream. Most, however, were buried, among the Bongos the men facing the east and the women to the west. In Ashanti the dead were commonly buried with their feet away from the village, but, since the dead were believed sometimes to turn around in the grave, sometimes the other position was adopted to deceive the spirit. Among the Fans the dead were eaten. The ceremony of "making a father" equivalent to the making of a *pitri* in India, involved certain complicated rites. The skeletons of chiefs were preserved and food offerings continued to be placed before them. The skulls of ancestors were frequently kept by families on a shelf in small earthen pots.

In addition to the ceremonies at burial there were many associated with birth. The new-born child was regarded at first as a ghost-child, that is, the result of a death in the spirit world. "When a child is born in this world, a ghost-mother mourns her child in the spirit world." For this reason it was very guardedly received and a name given known as the "god's name." Later, on the fortieth day, another name was given and there was a kind of baptism. Later still the earlier name was dropped and "a strong name" bestowed. Other "rites de passage" (as certain ceremonial customs are called by Arnold van Gennep) were performed in connection with arrival at puberty and marriage, though the former was regarded as naturally connected with the latter. Sacrifices were offered on most occasions, the scale of sacrificial values being in the following order: man, bullock, sheep, fowl.

Religion in West Africa had little to do with morality as we conceive it, but many offences were restrained by the various oaths and tabus, and by the influence of powerful secret societies, as to the organization of which there is still much mystery. The members of these societies were at once police, judges and executioners. Some crimes, such as adultery, were restrained by very severe punishments, as, for example, the terrible "dance of death" made the penalty for an offence against the royal harem.

The religion of Ashanti has been so carefully observed and described by Captain Rattray that a paragraph may be permitted to summarize some of his observations. He gives the supreme god of Ashanti as Nyame, a sky-god, who is associated with an earth-goddess, Asase-ya. The *obosom*, or "high gods," are probably the ancestral deities. These may have their shrines in trees and other natural objects. The *suman*, or fetishes, are objects, containing *mana*, often used as a kind of scapegoat to take away the evils endangering their possessors. The spirits of the dead are the *saman-fo*, worshipped to secure the fertility of nature and man. A native is quoted as saying: "The *obosom* and *suman* are like the white man's cannon and lesser guns." The main power of an *obosom* comes from Nyame; the power of a *suman* from plants and trees. An *obosom* is the god of the many; the *suman* is the god of an individual. In addition to the above, there are fairies (*mmoatia*), whose feet point backward, and whose speech is a kind of whistling, and monsters such as the Sasabonsam (mentioned above), with long hair, bloodshot eyes, long legs, and feet pointing both ways (possibly a reminiscence of the gorilla).

Captain Rattray gives an elaborate account of his observations on the various *Rites de Passage*, but for these the reader must be referred to his *Religion and Art in Ashanti*.

A very gruesome form of the primitive religion of West Africa passed from the Gold Coast to Jamaica, Haiti and certain parts of the United States. This form of devil-worship, as it really is, is known as *Obeah*, or *Voodoo*. What is termed "Red" Voodoo involves the sacrifice of a girl-child, euphemistically described as "a goat without horns." Where circumstances make this sacrifice impossible a white kid is accepted as a substitute. "White" Voodoo limits its sacrifices to black dogs, or black cocks and hens, cruelly slashed and slain. A fire-dance, often termed the Dance of the Old Master (that is, the Devil), is performed at the summer and winter solstices. There is often maintained a secret and powerful priesthood, male and female, known as *papaloi* and *mamaloi*, and these witch-doctors specialize in charms, herb-remedies, luck-balls, fingers of death, hands of love, and such like. In certain black communities of the Western Hemisphere Voodoo undoubtedly exercises a terrorizing influence upon the ignorant and is a menace to many others.[1]

[1] See *E.R.E.*, XII. 640–41.

# CHAPTER IX

## *The Primitive Religion of Asia*

### I

ALL the great historical religions of the world—Brahmanism, Confucianism, Taoism, Buddhism, Zoroastrianism, Hinduism, Judaism, Islam and Christianity—are of Asiatic origin. Therefore, to write the story of the religions of Asia would almost be to write the entire history of religion. Yet I may once again remind the reader that behind all the above-mentioned movements, considered historically, there lies an infinitely larger mass of belief and practice pertaining to the field of primitive religion. Of the countless clashes and interminglings which have been going on in Asia for thousands of years, of the countless migrations, along the lines of least resistance, or enforced by climatic changes, or by pressure of armed attack, we shall probably have to be content with ignorance. Thousands of important but unknown personalities may have contributed to the expression of this or that belief, the formation of this or that habit, or the creation of this or that institution. These must remain in enforced oblivion. What we see in the remote abysm of time, or in those jungles of to-day where the shadows have been only partially lifted, is a widely extended religious system which forms a dense tropical mat out of which the tall trunks and spreading branches of the historical faiths stand out as things apart. Yet the undergrowth out of which these faiths have sprung contains values which no subsequent developments altogether superseded. The historical faiths themselves depend for their elucidation on a knowledge of the soil, climate and vegetation of which they are the outstanding expression.

In different parts of Asia and under different conditions this oldest of all religions will present very different features and will bear many different names. Some of these separate features we shall reserve for description when we come to the conditions under which religions like Confucianism in China, or Islam in Arabia, arose. For this reason the present chapter and the next will make no attempt to examine in detail the primitive religion of every portion of the vast Asiatic continent. It will suffice if, without confining ourselves to the specific thing which goes under the name, we here consider that important type of primitive religion, extending from the Ainus in the east to Asia Minor in the west, and from Siberia in the north to Arabia and Malaysia in the south, which goes under the convenient name of *Shamanism*. To this we shall add such notes on the early religions of certain peoples such as are more conveniently treated here than under the head of the historical religions.

The word *shaman* has had many suggested derivations, including the very dubious one of the Persian *shemen*, an idol. The most likely etymology connects it with the Sanskrit *çramana*, an ascetic, from the root *çram*, *to be weary* (that is, of this illusory world). In its Chinese form the term becomes *sha-mên*, and so we get to the immediate derivative, the Tungus *saman*. In a highly specialized sense the word is now used of one who, through the possession of particular endowments, is able to control a familiar spirit or spirits, and so becomes the intermediary between the spiritual world and a needy humanity.

Though Shamanism is a religion of the widest possible extent, ranging, as we have suggested, throughout the entire continent of Asia, and beyond that, extending into America, its most specialized form is found in northern and eastern Asia, where in fact it is the real religion of the Ural-Altaic peoples, and accords nicely with the polydæmonistic beliefs of that region. The shaman is sometimes born into his office, much of Asiatic shamanism being hereditary. Among the Buriats it is believed that the first shamans, ninety-nine males and seventy-seven females, were chosen and consecrated by a deity named Mindiu. But some shamans are such by predisposition, particularly if they possess the highly neurotic temperament which makes it easy to manifest, in reality, or by simulation, the frenzies and epileptic fits which mark the successful practitioner. To this end they practise diligently until it is clear that they have vocation and can undergo initiation and consecration. The initiation consists in bestowing upon the candidate a drum and drum-stick, decorating him with a varied collection of rattles, rings, rags, and other charms, and performing a sacrifice which includes the sprinkling of the novice with blood. Then the full-fledged shaman is ready to become a public servant in a large variety of ways. As a diviner he will use the shoulder-blades of sheep or deer, after the manner known as scapulomancy; he will also divine by the casting forth of arrows; and in the hundred or more ways which might be illustrated from the story of primitive religion anywhere. As a healer he will use his own soul, or a familiar spirit, to go in search of the departing soul of the sick man, pursuing the ghost even down to the realm of Erlik, the prince of evil. Or he will suck out the evil spirit by his incantations, or bribe the evil one with sacrifice, or scare the demons with mad efforts on his drum. An important preliminary to the cure is the diagnosis, so, in serious cases, a white ram may have to be offered to the good spirits and a black ram to the evil spirits.[1] In still more severe cases the offering has to be a horse.

The *horse sacrifice* is the highest function in which the shaman is likely to be called upon to take part. The horse is chosen and brought to a certain hill, on which is a grove of birch-trees. After birch branches have been waved over the animal, the shaman uses his drum to collect the spirits. Sitting on the figure of a goose, on which he intends to ride to heaven with the spirit of the sacrifice, he then superintends the slaying of the horse. Dr. Radlof[2] says that the horse was strangled, and this may have been the case where strangling was the Mongol method of execution, as among the Gilaks. But Jeremiah Curtin describes the horse sacrifice among the Buriats, in which the horse was first fettered and thrown, then slain by an incision which

[1] Cf. Eusebius, *Præp. Evang.*, IV. 9: "Dark victims to the powers of darkness, light to the powers of light."

[2] W. Radlof, *Ency. Rel. and Eth.*, III. 17, IV. 177.

enabled the shaman to extricate the heart of the beast. Two fires had meanwhile been lighted near the sacred grove, known as the "senior" and "junior" fires. Over the senior fire are boiled the fore-quarters of the animal and the hind-quarters over the other. Then each head of the family—women were not allowed to be present—ties a long thread of flax, to which feathers are attached, to a birch-tree, in order that by this "ladder" the incantations may rise to the sky. The boiled flesh from the senior fire is then carried round the circle in the sunward direction, and afterwards consumed in the fire. The flesh from the junior fire, on the other hand, is distributed and ceremonially eaten. All remains, as in the Passover of the Jews, were carefully committed to the fires. If the smoke of these went up straight to the sky, it was a good omen for the year. It is plain that the horse sacrifice was here, as in other parts of the world, from Scandinavia to India, a solar rite, for the winning of the year's prosperity. Curtin tells us that, among the Buriats, the prayer at the sacrifice was addressed to such deities as the "Pure Heaven," the "Creator of Cattle," and the "Golden Sorrel," that is, the light of the sun. He describes the fires as not two but fifteen, all roaring beneath the iron kettles in which the flesh was stewing. He adds that the gods were supposed to participate in the pleasure and sociability of the feast.[1]

The gods of shamanistic Asia are of many sorts and many names, according to locality. Some of them are good, like Ulgen, and some of them malevolent, like Erlik. Possibly the cosmogony of the shamans was coloured by views derived from Buddhism, or even from Nestorian Christianity. In any case, there was belief in a kind of three-storeyed universe, with seventeen realms of light above, seven or nine hells below and between the earth. The evil being Erlik, a kind of fallen angel, lived in one of the hells; the supreme god, Kaira, lived in the topmost heaven; and the nine great ancestors lived in one or another of the lower heavens. In the fifth was a kind of demiurgus; in the third lived Ulgen and his two sons. It was the function of the shaman to have control over the nine ancestors or,

[1] Jeremiah Curtin, *A Journey in Southern Siberia*, chap. iv.

on the other hand, to be able to placate Erlik. It was the specialty of the "white" shaman to do the former, while the "black" shaman was supposed competent for the latter task. While sacrifices might be offered to Erlik anywhere, the sacrifices to Ulgen had to be in secret. It will be seen that most of these sacrifices were of the nature of ancestor worship, though many of the good spirits, known as Tengri, would come into the category of naturism. Beneath the outward forms of shamanistic religion, moreover, may be found a great deal of totemism, often suggested by the *tamgas*, or clan crests. The horse, for instance, may well be a *tamga*, or totem sign. Erlik, again, is sometimes represented as a bear, while other animals venerated include the wolf and (among birds) eagle, hawk and goose. Mr. Curtin describes the use, among the Buriats, of fetishes he calls *ongons*, little bags sometimes made of the skin of an ermine and containing small images, to which people pray for rain and crops. These are fixed to a post, but after the death of the owner are carried to the forest and allowed to rot.

Most of the events in a man's life, from birth to death, are controlled by shamanism. There is a special goddess, Umai, who is supposed to preside over birth. When a child is born, a cow or sheep is killed, partly for sacrifice and partly for a feast. If it be a boy, another boy or if a girl, another girl stands by the cradle to answer questions and in this way it is decided whether to rock up or down and what name is to be given. The placenta is then buried and libations made to it as to a recognized ancestor. The dead are sometimes burned, but more often buried. In the case of the Buriats there are elaborate ceremonies for nine days after death, and those gifted with second sight are able to see the spirits of the dead clad in the "ghosts" of their old clothes. By the Karzuk the dead are buried in solid structures of wood, clay and brick. Burial mounds, known as *kurgans*, are to be found in thousands from the Irtish to the Orkhon, some of which go back to the Bronze and Iron Ages. In many cases burial masks were used to preserve the lineaments of the dead, or even rude stone figures buried with the corpse. The absence of the skull from the skeleton—which in many cases was buried in an erect position—has been frequently observed. In some instances there seems to have been a grouping of the graves, with one mound a little apart from all the rest. There was a general belief in the survival of the soul. It was supposed that at birth a good spirit was sent to guard the new-born individual and an evil spirit to mislead him, but that at death both spirits accompanied the soul to judgement. It is difficult, however, to say how much of this may be due to the Buddhism, or Muhammadanism, or the Nestorian Christianity, with which the original shamanism has been overlaid.

If we travel from Northern Asia to the islands of the extreme east, now composing the Japanese archipelago, we come upon that curious survival of an ancient race known as

THE AINUS.—These are the aboriginal people of the Japanese islands, numbering now but 20,000 souls, and confined to the coast of the northern islands. Some ethnologists have convinced themselves of the existence of a still earlier stock, now extinct, known as the *Koropok-guro* (earth-hiders), but these were probably Ainus of an earlier and still more rudimentary culture. Dr. A. C. Haddon describes the Ainus as " the relics of an eastward movement of an ancient mesocephalic group of white cymotrichi who have not left any other representatives in Asia, though travellers often refer to the resemblance of the Ainu to the Russian mujik."[1] They were originally white people who migrated across the entire Euro-Asiatic continent and are probably related to the aborigines of Australia. They are very hairy people, with beards falling to the waist, a circumstance accounting for the name Yemishi, or prawn-people. The word *Ainu* means *man*, though, by folk etymology, it has been associated with the Japanese *inu*, a dog. Their culture was neolithic and is illustrated by the contents of some thousands of kitchen-middens (some of which may go back six thousand years) around the coast of Japan.[2] It seems probable that their early organization was totemistic, though this has been denied. Even Archdeacon Batchelor,

[1] A. C. Haddon, *Races of Man*, p. 89.
[2] N. Gordon Munro, *Primitive Art of Japan*, Trans. As. Soc. Japan, 1906.

a defender of the general theory, acknowledges that the people seldom talk of themselves as being connected with bear, wolf, turtle, snipe, hawk and eagle, and never of any vegetable. The best evidence for totemism is found in the interesting bear-cult, but Dr. E. V. Hopkins believes the bear sacrifice rather a " sending " of the bear to its ancestors to secure more bears for the next season's hunting than an actual indication of Ainu descent from the bear. The bear sacrifice is, in any case, exceedingly striking and reminds us forcibly of the similar sacrifice described in the Finnish *Kalevala*[1] and also said to exist among the Lilloet Indians in British Columbia. The bear-cub is suckled by the women, treated with every care as " the dear little divine thing," and then sent, by strangling, to join the great bear ancestor to influence the powers above in favour of the sacrificers.

As to the religion of the Ainus, there are very diverse opinions. Mrs. Isabella Bird Bishop who, however, was only among the Ainus a few weeks and only communicated with the people through an interpreter, believed that they had little or no religion. On the other hand, Archdeacon Batchelor, who has known the Ainus and their language for many years, has too high an estimate of their beliefs, even crediting them with a primitive monotheism. Dr. Hopkins, who seems a little prejudiced against Batchelor, declares, much too sweepingly, of the Ainus: " They have neither gods, temples, nor priests." It seems probable that Batchelor's Supreme God, *kamui*, means much the same as the Japanese *kami* (the one above), and implies belief in a large variety of spirits, the spirits of the dead, and spirits which are merely " potencies " in nature. The bear, as we have seen, is worshipped, possibly as an ancestor. Much the same is true of the cereal, or millet worship. Fire is also worshipped and the word *Fuji* (applied to the mountain) is probably an Ainu word for *fire*. Fire would naturally be worshipped also as a culture deity. Indeed, all nature was full of " potencies "—earth, air, rivers and seas. The sun and moon also were worshipped, the sun being regarded as masculine and the moon as feminine—

[1] The *Kalevala,* Runo xlvi., Wainamoinen and the Bear.

contrary to the Japanese reckoning. There were, again, many demons, of whom the swamp demon (*aunt of the marshes*) was particularly malevolent.

Various myths have been transmitted to us, but it is impossible to say what influence may have coloured them. One represents the sun and moon as husband and wife and explains the invisibility of the moon at certain times by saying: "she has gone to visit her husband." Another describes the wagtail as having been sent down from heaven to create the earth out of the waters and as accomplishing this by trampling the mud from the sea-bottom into a solid mass.

Only vague ideas seem to have prevailed with regard to the state of the dead and the future life. The dead were much feared and it is said that only the women were permitted to speak to them. When burial had taken place the bows and arrows and other implements of the deceased were broken over the grave and sometimes the hut in which the dead had lived was burned over the corpse. Some believed that the dead went into the bodies of animals, while others, possibly as the result of foreign contacts, held that there were six heavens and six hells to which people went, according to their conduct here upon earth.

One of the most interesting features of Ainu religion was its concern with fetishes. The fetish, or god-stick, known as an *inao*, was quite elaborately fashioned of a piece of willow or lilac wood, fantastically dressed up with shavings, provided with a slit for a mouth, and a warm, black cinder for a heart. It may have corresponded with the backbone, which was regarded as a soul-seat, and so suggests the Lares and Penates of ancient Rome. But there were distinctions among the *inao*. There might be a private *inao*, fixed in the hearth on the birth of an individual and holding his fate. Or there might be a household, or even tribal, *inao*, guarding the fortunes of the entire family. There might, again, be an evil fetish, to which a noisome mess was offered known as the evil-stew. This probably represents an attempt to placate the evil spirits. There is a rather close connection of Ainu fetish worship with ancestor worship and this constant concern of men with the "potencies" of nature and the spirit world, in spite of the absence of professional shamans, links Ainu religion very definitely with shamanism. The shaman, however, is not unknown and may be called in for a variety of purposes. Indeed, the frenzy of the Ainu shaman, in which all sorts of prophecies are uttered, seems to prelude the appearance of the Shinto priest and the phenomena of "possession."

Magic was, naturally, in general use and some use of fox-skulls was made for the purpose of giving oracles. Closely associated with magic were the various forms of ordeal and tabu which were from time to time enforced. The ordeals included the use of fire, hot water, hot stones and medicated water. A common form was the throwing of a cup over the shoulder, the guilt of the thrower being determined by the position of the cup when it reached the earth. The tabus involved the practice of *couvade*, by the father on the birth of a child betaking himself to bed. A ban was placed upon a woman uttering the name of her husband and there was also a ban placed upon the shedding of blood in the bear sacrifice. The strangling of the bear seems to suggest that the same rule may have applied to the horse and other sacrificial animals.[1]

Let us now pass westward, through the great territories of China, whose early form of religion we will leave untouched for the present, to the passes of the Hindukush. Traversing these we enter the Indian peninsula and give our attention briefly to the religion of

PRE-ARYAN INDIA.—Under this head we include those primitive elements of Indian religion which are characteristic of the aboriginal Negrito population and of the prehistoric waves of immigration known generally as Kolarian and Dravidian, which entered the land respectively from the north-east and the north-west. The terms Kolarian and Dravidian are linguistic rather than ethnological, but they designate for our purpose the tribes, on the one hand, Bhils, Kols, and so forth, and, on the other, Tamils, Telugus, Malayalim, Kanarese, and the rest, spread over

[1] The religion of the Ainu is exhaustively described by Archdeacon John Batchelor in his *The Ainus in Japan*, and in *Ency. Rel. and Eth.*, Vol. I., art. "Ainu." See also Isabella Bird Bishop, *Unbeaten Tracks in Japan*, 1885.

the peninsula from the Ganges southward to Ceylon and occupying the territories of Madras, Hyderabad, Chota Nagpore and the Central Provinces.

The present-day religion of all these peoples is Hinduism, as that religion is generally understood, but it must be realized that the basis of all popular Hinduism is something vastly older than the faith imported by the Aryans and that the average Indian peasant to-day is anything but an orthodox Hindu except in the sense that he feeds the Brahmans and in general accepts the restrictions of caste. The general culture of the representatives of this older population is totemistic, though it may be hard to distinguish between totemism as a social institution and mere animal worship. Risley tells that among the Oraons the tribal names are those of animals and plants, and where this is the case the animal or plant (or some part of either) becomes tabu. In Central India, at any rate, the totem tree is never cut. Animism was the prevailing belief and the control of particular spirits was often rigidly localized. Boundaries between the realm of spirit and spirit were defined, and boundary ceremonies included the use of a goat, which was led around until certain symptoms of shivering revealed that it was trespassing upon the domain of another spirit. Many of the old Dravidian gods were subsequently adopted into popular Hinduism as avatars of Vishnu and Çiva. Çiva himself was regarded as a survival of the older gods, and identified with the Vedic Rudra. In general the coarser and more tantric elements of popular Hinduism are derived from this older worship. The worship of earth (Pritthivi), as the Great Mother, is due specially to the old matrilinear agriculture rather than to the Aryan immigrants. The fertility cults, with their obscene orgies, in connection with the marriage of the earth-deities, are also Dravidian rather than Aryan. Mother Earth had her benevolent as well as her malignant aspect, and might be invoked as "the hope-fulfiller." But in general the Earth was a goddess to be propitiated by dread rites, and the cruelties and sexual excesses connected with the cult of Kali, the spouse of Çiva, may be traced to these primitive ideas.

The Dravidian peoples distinguished many kinds of spirits, friendly and hostile. There were tree spirits, which were often regarded as village gods, and great care was taken to preserve such and such a tree or grove for the reverence of the indwelling spirits. These had no special names, but they were often believed to be potent to heal. Rags were frequently hung on the trees to obtain something of the *mana* of the resident deities. Water spirits were specially respected and thought able to ward off the menace of a flood. The coco-nuts offered to these, as in the Punjab, have been suspected of being a modern commutation of the old sacrifice of human heads. Wind spirits and hail spirits were likewise recognized, naturally so, because of the power of the elements to destroy a growing crop. To the mountain spirits sacrifices were offered, to placate them before an attempted ascent. Sun worship was another feature of Dravidian religion, with the use of sympathetic magic to sustain the solar power at the critical seasons. Some of the fire ceremonies, such as those connected with leaping through the flames, were for aspurgation. In any case, much that survives in the Hindu *Holi* festival is vastly older than Hinduism itself. Moon worship and star worship were doubtless in vogue at a still earlier date, but they are not important in Dravidian religion to-day. There were certain fixed sanctuaries for the local and village gods, as among the primitive Semitic tribes. Some of these were little but a heap of stones under a tree, or a hut for the spirit to dwell in. This was only repaired when the occurrence of an epidemic suggested the anger of the godling. An interesting feature of this oldest of Indian cults is the implement worship, such as we see in ancient Rome and elsewhere.[1] Ploughs, corn-sieves, baskets and brooms were all objects of worship; the palm-tappers in certain districts present offerings to their sickles; the potters decorate their trade tools; and many similar customs might be adduced.

Not only are nature-spirits recognized and worshipped, but also the spirits of the dead, as might be expected. Though ghosts were sometimes looked on as benignant, as in the case of a woman who had performed *sati*, most of

[1] Cf. in the Old Testament, Habakkuk i. 16.

them were thought of as angry and had to be propitiated. There were large numbers of *bhuts*, or *bhutas*, roaming round ruthlessly because of lack of proper funeral rites. Animals were naturally worshipped in the totemistic communities, though not always as totems. The horse was thought of as a steed for the dead, or for the carrying away of disease, and pottery figures of horses, with holes for the entrance of the spirit, were placed here and there to rid the locality of an unwelcome presence.[1] The tiger, known often as "Lord Tiger," was worshipped, mainly out of fear, and a "man-eater" was specially dreaded as adept in "shape-shifting." Among the Marathas the dog was worshipped and at the Malhari shrine in Dharwar the priests were wont to assume the dress of dogs and meet the arriving pilgrims with barking. The monkey-god, Hanuman (long-jaw), was worshipped as a hero of the epic Ramayana, but the cult evidently goes back to an older theriolatry and was later adopted by Hinduism. In connection with animal worship it should be noted that the shrinking from an animal as unfit for food was not always due to the beast being thought unclean. Sometimes, on the contrary, it was because of special sanctity as a totem. This may explain even the rejection of the pig as food by the Semites.

The Dravidian peoples were not without a mythology, which included a myth as to the way the sky escaped its first contiguity with earth. This reminds us strongly of similar myths, all the way from Egypt to New Zealand. In the present case an old woman, annoyed through knocking her head against the too lowly firmament, took her broom and pushed the sky upwards out of reach.

The working religion of pre-Aryan India was, as in other parts of Asia, shamanism. The shaman constituted no regular priesthood, but was sometimes hereditary. The essence of the cult was the worship of powers, benevolent and malignant, through a contact established by frenzy attained in the usual ways—very often by the use of a whip, or even a chain, for purposes of self-flagellation. The shaman, if not a regular priest, was at least exorcist, sorcerer

[1] Gertrude Emerson, *Voiceless India*.

and medicine-man. He was surrounded by many tabus, and in many cases the *mana* was supposed to be resident in his carefully protected hair. As a disease-curer, for example, in dealing with a case of snakebite, the shaman would consult a vessel full of water, waiting for the troubling of the water (as did the sufferers at the Pool of Bethesda)[1] to betoken the arrival of the spirit. He would also use a goat or buffalo as a scape-animal, drawing a little blood from the ear of the beast and then sending it forth from the village to bear away the disease. Religious festivals were observed at the chief agricultural seasons, particularly in connection with ploughing, sowing and harvesting. Sometimes the rites were for purgation, and sometimes for the promotion of fertility. Obscenities were common, as in similar agricultural rites all the world over. Omens were carefully observed and, among many common to all lands, we may note those revealed in the eggs and entrails of fowls and in the appearance of grains of rice. Sacrifices were offered on the *do ut des* principle, and also as a feast in which friendships were ratified with the placated gods. The victim offered had always to be considered willing, and the better to ensure this the animal was garlanded and fed before being slain. Human sacrifices apparently had once been common, but had been commuted by the substitution of a buffalo or a goat. Magic had a large part in early Dravidian religion, as may be inferred from what has already been stated. For the carrying away of diseases there were many devices, in addition to those already mentioned. Toy carts were employed to remove the spirits of cholera and small-pox. Scape-animals, marked with vermilion and driven away with violence, were frequently used for the same purpose. And in the Dekkan the custom is recorded of sending forth a woman, who was, however, permitted to return next day, to render like service to the community. Much else of the popular Hinduism of to-day will be found to belong to the underlying shamanism of the earlier period, but the above sketch will suffice to describe its general character.

[1] See St. John v. 7.

We may conveniently include one other region in this present chapter, namely:

TIBET.—As might be expected, from the fact that Buddhism only entered Tibet as late as the seventh century, and that the land is so walled about with mountains, as well as by a climate so terrifically severe as to be very uninviting to strangers, the religion of Tibet retains many features such as without doubt go back to the first arrival of immigrants in the post-glacial period.

The culture of these first inhabitants was simple even to barbarism, a barbarism which continues to crop up through the veneer of Buddhism with which manners have in general been covered. Polyandry was prevalent, for economic reasons, though monogamy is the more general rule. As far as occupation is concerned, the people were divided into traders, peasants and herdmen, but a large number—from one-eighth to one-fifth—are monks and nuns, thus earning for Tibet the reputation of being the most "religious" country on earth.

The old pre-Buddhistic religion is termed *Bon* (*Pön*)—a word of unknown meaning, but signifying the same kind of shamanism that we have encountered elsewhere in Asia. The shamans had many functions, as explainers of omens, namers of lucky days, arrangers of marriages and burials, exponents of planetary influences, and casters of horoscopes. In brief, the shaman played very much the rôle which in China is assumed by the Taoist priest. In addition to reverence for the shaman or medicine-man, the follower of Bon (the *Bonpa*) was given to the use of prayer-flags—often seen fluttering from the house or bridge—and to the making of pilgrimages. As might be predicted from the severity of the weather, and the frequency with which the flocks and herds and crops of the Tibetan were destroyed by snowstorms and avalanches, most of the spirits to whom prayers were addressed were devils. Devils, too, took up their dwelling in human bodies as diseases and had to be expelled by means which must have been as unpleasant to the patient as to the demon. Sometimes, indeed, the demon was treated quite considerately, being provided with clothes, hat, boots and steed, so long as he would go. The Abbé

Huc has described some of the exorcisms of which he was himself the witness. Although Buddhism, in the form of Lamaism, has been in control of Tibet since the ninth century of our era, the Bon is still probably more extensively accepted than Lamaism. Mr. W. W. Rockhill estimated that two-thirds of the people were still Bon-pa. Of the Bon priests there are now few in western and central Tibet, but in eastern Tibet they are quite numerous and have monasteries of their own. Here they display much evidence of actual antagonism to the Lamas, using the Buddhist formula (*Om-mani-pad-me-hum*) backwards as *Muh-em-pad-ni-mo*, and turning the swastika into a left-hand symbol. Mr. Waddell supposes this to indicate an earlier lunar cult. In early times there appear to have been many bloody sacrifices, including the offering of man, horses, oxen and asses, but at present these are generally represented as images of dough. Lamaism itself is not free from rites which were originally Bon. The unreformed Red Hats show most evidence of these survivals, but they are not absent from the practices of the reformed Yellow Hats. The devil-dances which are exhibited at the Lama Temple in Peking are, of course, shamanistic in origin, though as now performed only " stunts " for the edification of tourists.

The remaining regions of primitive Asia we must reserve for another chapter.

# CHAPTER X

## *The Primitive Religion of Asia*

### II

IN the present chapter we shall consider the primitive religion of certain other parts of Asia and, first of all, must devote several pages to that of

THE ABORIGINES OF CHINA.—Of some primitive elements in the religion of the Chinese themselves we shall have something to say later. Here we confine ourselves to the beliefs and practices of the tribes whom the Chinese dispossessed or pushed aside and who are now found in the south-west provinces of the Middle Kingdom. When the Chinese first entered the country they are described as subduing the Man in the south, the Yi in the east, the Tih in the north, and the Jung in the west. Whatever the distinctions between these tribes once were, they have now disappeared. Consequently, in describing the present aboriginal population, we can only refer to them as a Mongoloid race, now occupying the provinces of Yunnan, Szechuan and Kweichau, and from whom have been derived the main elements in the population of Annam, Siam, and other parts of the Indo-Chinese peninsula. In Yunnan about two-thirds of the people are aborigines and as many as 141 tribes have been listed, distinguished as Lolos, Miao-tzu, and Shans (or Tai). The term Lolo is considered objectionable, a word of contempt used by the Chinese. It is better to speak of them as Nosu. A term of a general nature, often employed, is that of Man-tzu, or " wild men." The Nosu, to use that convenient term, are found principally in Yunnan, the Miao in Kweichau, to a less extent in Yunnan, with only a few in Szechuan. The Shan, or Tai, are principally in Yunnan and on the Burmese frontier. So far as language is concerned, the Nosu and Miao may be classed together, while the Shans must be kept apart.

It will be noted that, with 53 separate tribes in Kweichau and as many as 180 in the whole region, the ethnological field is a paradise of vast scope.

The religious ideas and practices of the population of these provinces closely resemble those we have already described as Asiatic. That totemism was general is plain from the names of some of the tribes: Miao-tzu, sons of the cat; Ma-tzu, sons of the horse; Kwei-tzu, sons of the tortoise. Many practices reveal the separateness long maintained from the Chinese population all around them. No Buddhist temples are to be seen on the hills, nor are there any of the horrible Temples of Hell in the cities. Chinese customs, such as the binding of the girls' feet, are rejected and Nosu have been heard to say: "We would sooner marry a daughter to a dog than to a Chinese." The white towers which are frequently seen crowning the hills have been built to strike terror into the hearts of the Chinese and keep them at a distance. Even the custom of cremation is followed, not merely through long habit, but because it contrasts with the "cold burial" of a Chinese. It is difficult to say whether any high gods are recognized; the evidence is rather that only the spirits of the dead and spirits of natural phenomena are known. Most of these are malevolent, and the worship offered is generally of the apotropaic kind. A future world is accepted and sacrifices are sent into this other world to secure certain results. In one case a murderer is described as being sent to make his peace with the dead, after he has been bound, gashed with wounds into which candles were burned down, and the tortured body divided and thrown to the dogs and wolves. Malevolent spirits are greatly feared, and believed capable of pursuing their victims as beasts of prey. By the Miao the underworld is supposed to be a sort of barnyard, in which people are turned into fowls and slaughtered by the Hell-emperor for the entertainment of his guests.

For all the aboriginal peoples of south-west China religion lays stress on omens, such, for instance, as may be deduced from the observation of magpies, and on the use of ordeals, of which those by boiling water and oil are common. In the former the slaves representing two opposing families seek to snatch an egg from a cauldron of boiling water without ill result. A few myths have passed from generation to generation on such matters as the origin of rain, snow, sun and moon, though some have doubtless been influenced by the teaching of missionaries. One curious myth describes the snow as having produced twelve men, of whom three were the first to introduce the art of ploughing.

Most religion, however, was mere shamanism and witchcraft. The wizards, who are called *Pee-mo*, have an elaborate technique for the sending off of their mana, to achieve its good or evil purpose. Mr. Pollard[1] describes the shaman as despatching a curse through the smoke of a fire kindled for the purpose, with the killing of a chicken as a sacrifice to the spirit. Elsewhere he describes the slaying of a dog in order that the spirit of the animal might go hunting in the other world to secure justice. When called in to see a sick man, the wizard will make the patient breathe on an egg, which the demon is then supposed to enter. Then the malignant power is conjured into a small straw doll, which is carried out to the high road and lost. Mr. Pollard tells us that he could never give his Nosu children a doll because of this fear of witchcraft and because it had been the practice of the wizards to use dolls as *porte malheurs*. The circumvention of demons was an important part of life, and in some places the hair was plucked out in early manhood to prevent some demon from getting control. Happily, as in China, the demons were often as stupid as they were malevolent, and could be generally disposed of in some simple fashion.

From aboriginal China it is but a short step to

INDO-CHINA.—The peninsula of Further India includes French Indo-China, Cambodia, Siam and Burma. All of these are Buddhist countries, but from beneath the surface layer of Buddhism, and from beneath the still earlier stratum of Brahmanism (where such exists), come seeping up the elements of a far older faith. This is quite irrespective of race, though, of course, the older the race the more archaic is the religion represented. In Indo-China there are many

[1] S. Pollard, *In Unknown China*, p. 250.

of these very primitive tribes, Muongs, Mois, Penongs and Khas, all words synonymous with *savages*. Generally speaking, the culture of these tribes is matrilinear and in their marriage customs endogamous, though some go outside the tribe for their wives or husbands.

In general religion is animistic, with a strong leaven of fetishism and polytheistic naturism. The spirits are good or bad, and are believed to live in large rocks or trees. Care is taken, before cutting down a tree, to kill a dog, dip an arrow in the blood, and draw it across the tree to be felled. Villages are supposed to be protected by a special spirit or genius, who is represented by a roughly carved figure, decorated with a plume of grass, armed with bow and arrow, and sprinkled with the blood of a chicken. This guardian of the village is replaced annually. Many sacrifices are offered, graded downwards from the buffalo to the pig, and thence to the goat and the chicken. Some tribes, however, still remember when human sacrifices were offered at the funeral of a great chief.

While naturally there were feasts held at the time of the fructification of the rice, the great feasts were in honour of the dead, who were buried and not cremated. The corpse was invariably bound around the jaw and then with bands around the hands and feet. The coffin was filled with the deceased's choicest possessions and communication was established between the dead man and the upper air by the insertion of a bamboo tube, down which gifts of rice, alcohol and soup, or even tobacco-smoke, might be sent and up which it was believed the soul escaped in due time. After a year it was believed the soul was ready to depart far from the grave, so a final great feast was held, with offerings of many sorts, the setting up of a kind of portrait statue, and with games. After this there was no further observance. The world to which the spirits passed was but dimly envisaged. Some tribes believed it was necessary for the dead to pass between two huge stones in continual motion, and thence between two gigantic moving scissor-blades, and then over a precarious bridge of tree trunks spanning an awful precipice, with a gap which had to be overleaped. Beyond all this was a life not unlike that on earth, with slaves to do the work of the great ones—slaves represented by little wooden figures placed upon the grave.

There was universal belief in sorcery. The sorcerers were believed to have awful powers, particularly over fire and water, and were accordingly dreaded. Ordeals were commonly practised, most of them of the kinds generally in vogue, but including an egg test in which the accused had to break an egg between his thumb and forefinger. There were many fetishes, especially pebbles of a peculiar shape, or prehistoric flints and axe-heads. These were sprinkled with blood and highly reverenced. Tabus were naturally numerous, including a particular tabu placed upon the road by which a village had been evacuated. Totemism is not clearly defined, but it is natural to suppose it must have existed, since certain tribes refuse to eat the flesh of the domestic elephant and others decline the flesh of the tiger, except by way of showing a spirit of revenge. Quite a few of the tribes have a vague kind of cosmogony, but it is difficult to separate imported ideas from those which may have been primitive.

Over the whole of the Indo-Chinese peninsula Mongol tribes have descended in successive waves of invasion and, though the culture of these tribes is not in the strictest sense of the word primitive, yet we may regard their religion as coming under that head, in order to distinguish it from the Brahmanism and Buddhism beneath which it was later submerged. We shall find it convenient to make a brief survey of the religion of these invading Mongol peoples under the separate heads of Cambodia, Siam and Burma.

Cambodia.—Three-quarters of the population of Cambodia is of the Mon-Khmer stock and represents the race which once founded a state whose former power is attested by the stupendous ruins of Angkor. The country has had long periods during which Singhalese Buddhism was dominant and earlier in which the main religious influence was that of Brahmanism. But the first animism was never uprooted and is still widely prevalent. All kinds of supernatural beings are believed in, ghosts, ogres, and spirits masquerading as lions, serpents (*nagas*) and birds. Some spirits, called *nak-ta*, are thought to be good, the local guardians of trees, rocks and streams. Oblations and sacrifices are offered to these, some of the latter being of a cruel character. It is believed that the prosperity of the offerer, or the success of his intention, is greatly enhanced by the prolonged groaning of the victim. There are also individual tutelary spirits, such as the *arak*, which are probably the spirits of ancestors. Many of the worst spirits are those of the wicked dead, or of women who died in child-birth. Some spirits take the form of wer-wolves or wer-tigers, both male and female. Happily these fearsome monsters may be reduced to powerlessness by striking them on the shoulder with a hook, though the operation may be something like that of putting salt on a bird's tail.

Wizards, sorcerers, and diviners are legion. The *kru* (*guru?*) exorcises in many quaint ways, such as by sending a charm into the body of the afflicted one by means of a worm or a black beetle. Others confine themselves to astrology, the finding of lucky days, or the averting of the evil effects of an eclipse. Of the festivals observed some are undoubtedly Buddhist, but others, such as the cutting of the top-knot, the new-year festival, the water festival, and festivities in honour of the dead, must go back to much earlier times.

Siam.—The Siamese are in the main a branch of the Tai, Mongol immigrants who came originally from the high plateaux of Tibet and Yunnan, driving the earlier Khmers, Mons and Burmese towards the coast. Buddhism was introduced about A.D. 442, but there was an older reign of Brahmanism and beyond that a general animism of much the same character as that already described. Spirits known as *phi* were reverenced. They were both benevolent and malevolent, but the malevolent were much more numerous and powerful. The *phi-nang-mai*, or female tree-spirits, were regarded as good and were supposed to replenish the bowls of wearied pilgrims. Of evil spirits there were three kinds, the spirits of the dead, spirits of nature, and spirits belonging to another world than our own. Most dangerous of all were the *phi-lok*, or spirits of the dead, giants in stature, with a tiny mouth, from whence came only a whistling kind of speech, and who were wont to pull people from their beds at night. The worst of all were the spirits of the still-born or of people who had died through cholera. To escape the malignancy of the dead it was the custom to bury the corpse in a large pot, folded up and bound to prevent return. A special kind of spirit was the guardian of the house, frequently heard whispering in the dark, and sometimes accommodated with a small house of its own. Sorcerers (*modu*), sorceresses (*thao*) and diviners (*mothai*) had an important place in society. Many of them were supposed to use, for the bewitching of men, a familiar who could be reduced to the size of a pea. Clay figurines were also employed in order that the insertion of a pin or a nail might ensure the torture of the intended victim. Love philtres, as well as potions of more certain (and more fatal) efficacy, were often mixed with the food of anyone whom it was desirable to attract or to destroy. Many Siamese superstitions go back to primitive types of religion, such as the use of charms to secure invulnerability, the use of rice as a symbol of fecundity, the general fear of having a picture taken, the use of foundation sacrifices, with the victim (obtained by lot) buried alive beneath the building, and a number of ceremonies connected with birth and marriage, some of them possibly Buddhist.

Burma.—Burma is usually regarded as the Buddhist country *par excellence*. But Dr. Hackmann[1] says of Burma: "The real acting religious force is not Buddhist at all." He adds that it is "a factor dating from pre-Buddhist times, and which Buddhism, notwithstanding the powerful hold which it has obtained over this people, has been entirely unable to supersede." Bishop Bigandet writes to similar effect: "The Buddhism of the people has but little or no part in their daily life. In common life, from the day of birth to that of wedding, or even of death, all the customs or formulæ made use of by the Burmese originate with demon worship and not with Buddhism."

The Burmese are of mixed race. The oldest element is that known as Mon, or Mon-Khmer (also spoken of as Peguan) in Talaing. Next to this comes the Shan or Tai

[1] H. Hackmann, *Buddhism as a Religion*, p. 147.

element, from south-west China, and last of all the Burmese. No one of these elements presents what might technically be called a primary culture, but their religion is sufficiently near the primitive for our purpose. Buddhism was introduced in the fifth century and with it a little Brahmanism, and to-day all profess Buddhism except the (approximately) 340,000 Muhammadans, the 300,000 Hindus, and the 150,000 Christians.

Nevertheless, as already pointed out, the census figures are misleading, and nat-worship is the true religion of Burma. The *nats* (from a word derived possibly from *natha*, *a lord*) represent something like the old Indian *devas*, but are of all sorts. Every house has its *nat*, with an established place at the hearth, as in the homes of the early Slavs. The *nat* is also provided with a vessel of holy water, and offerings of rags and coco-nuts. Villages also have their *nats*, spirits for whose benefit festivals and dramatic representations are staged. The women who perform in the nat-dances are believed to have powers of exorcism, divination and necromancy. The nats themselves are classified in thirty-seven divisions. The idea of a universal creator god is certainly foreign to the Burmese and in its stead is this all-pervading faith in nats as tutelary spirits, ghosts, and supernatural beings from other worlds. A number of other spirits find credence, however, such as do not come under the category of *nats*. There are the ordinary spirits of the dead, independent, immaterial entities which are supposed to hover for a time over the corpse, or which may, during the life of their owner, be kept within a charm. People with the evil eye have two souls. The spirits of the dead are feared and ceremonies are performed for the purpose of keeping them at a distance. The other world is conceived of rather vaguely, but a man who has been slain on earth is supposed to remain a slave in Hades until his murder has been avenged. Some ghosts, known as *tase*, are particularly malignant, especially those of suicides or women dying in child-birth. Evil spirits may take possession of a house and bring about fevers and agues.

There are, however, nature spirits, representing sky, sun, moon, rain, wind and trees. Many festivals celebrate the processes of nature, such as the seed-time, with its maypole, or the harvest, with the sending forth of the scape-animals and the driving forth of the straw-woman round the fields, or the New Year, characterized by dowsings of water, for a rain-charm.

Ancestor worship is not strongly stressed, except along the Chinese frontier. Totemism is indicated in numerous ancient customs. Some tribes, like the Kachins, decline to eat snakes, wild cats, dogs or monkeys, except those of the white-eyelid variety. Some tribes, again, describe themselves as descended from the tiger, the wild goat, the monkey, or the bear. The Kachins think themselves derived from a kind of gourd which fell from heaven and split open on reaching the earth.

Sacrifices of propitiation are offered to the *nats*, and the buffalo, pig, dog, cow, goat, chicken, are the animals most favoured, as well as fish and eggs. Human sacrifices were employed till recent times, and both foundation and boundary sacrifices were offered to protect buildings and frontiers. The posting up of heads had much the same object. There were many methods of divination, mostly along lines already described, unless it be in the special use of chicken-bones and the entrails of cattle and pigs. Wizards were necromancers, exorcists, magicians and averters of the evil eye, as well as diviners. There was no particular ceremony at marriage, but many rites had place in death, mainly to prevent return of the dead for the injury of the living. The ghost was driven into the jungle and the temporary shrine which had been erected destroyed, to deprive the spirit of a home. All methods of disposing of the dead were used, from simple neglect of the corpse to crematory rites and the building of elaborate tombs.

Much else might be written with regard to the beliefs and practices of the varied racial elements making up the population of the Indo-Chinese peninsula, but the general character of the religion will be sufficiently evident.

It is now necessary to take a long journey across the continent westward, to consider briefly the primitive religion of a region even more a museum of racial interminglings than the Asia of the south-east.

Western Asia.—By Western Asia I have in mind three extensive pockets of land in which certain peoples of Asia found their home, bringing thither in all probability a culture elsewhere developed. These are, respectively, the peninsula of *Asia Minor*, the most westerly of all, the regions at the head of the Persian Gulf, mainly in the *Euphrates Valley*, and the vast peninsula of *Arabia*. With these we must associate the narrow strip of land along the eastern shore of the Mediterranean we call *Palestine*, which was the corridor linking together the three territories mentioned.

The student of ethnology will recognize in these regions a veritable jungle of races, an area within which races of the most various kind, Aryan, Turanian and Semitic, have jostled one another through countless centuries, until the component elements have become wellnigh indistinguishable the one from the other. The historian, too, will find these ancient clashings and interminglings continued through the historical period with complications which defy a conscientious analysis. It is not therefore surprising that the student of religion should find the same difficulty in the many elements which form the dense undergrowth out of which the later religions of South-west Asia arose.

It was in this region that at least four great historical faiths first appeared, namely, Zoroastrianism, Judaism, Christianity and Muhammadanism. It might therefore appear that to deal with these, with some attention to the several cultures from which they sprang, would be sufficient, and that no need existed to call further attention to what someone has called "the miry clay" in the feet of religion. But it would be fairer to use another metaphor and to speak of primitive religious elements as the living protoplasm out of which future religion was to grow. Or, to use a still different figure, it is well to remember that primitive religion constitutes "the tap-root which sinks deepest in racial human experience and continues its cellular and fibrous structure in the tree-trunk of modern conviction."

Nevertheless, subsequent references which will be inevitable in descriptions of the historical religions, make it unnecessary to be otherwise than brief, especially in regard to those primitive religions which antedate the Semitic movements over the larger part of Western Asia. In respect to the earliest religions of Asia Minor, we find ourselves in very close contact with the beliefs and practices belonging to the old Ægean culture, on which, in part, was founded the civilization of ancient Greece. This religion has left no literary history and we must be content to rely on archæological evidence of the Bronze Age or earlier. Certain salient features, however, emerge as to which there can be little doubt. The idea of God seems to have been connected for the most part with its expression in female divinities, of whom we have representations with the characteristic Minoan flounce, and guarded by lions. We have here probably a picture of the Great Mother, who in Cappadocia bore the name of Ma, and with whom is generally associated a younger male divinity who is to the Great Mother what Attis is to Cybele, or Tammuz to Ishtar. There seem to have been no proper temples, but stones, baetyls, and triliths represented the abode of divinity, or the sacred mountain, while trees also served in some degree as shrines. Rivers and springs were also sacred, especially such fountains as the famous one of Aflatun Bunar, near Iconium, and that on Mt. Argaeus. There were, again, a number of sacred animals, especially the bull, lion, goat, serpent and dove. The bull's skull, or *bucranium*, often pictured as "the horns of consecration," was one of the commonest of symbols, and the *bipennis*, or double axe, known as the *labrys* (whence the word *labyrinth*), had also special significance. Another symbol in general use was that of the knotted tie.

Had we more knowledge of the Hittites and their language we should doubtless find much in common between these and the Minoans. As it is we get glimpses of a powerful Earth-mother cult, together with the associated reverence for a son or a younger deity. We do not know much about the Hittite gods, but of male deities there were Teshub, a storm-god, and Tark, who may have supplied us with such words as *Teucrian*, *Tarquin* and *Etruscan*. Animism was as general here as elsewhere in the region; divination by the liver reminds us of the Babylonian practice;

burial customs show interment in large jars after partial cremation. It is regarded as some indication of Aryan affinities (or contacts) that there are Hittite references to several Aryan gods, such as Varuna, Indra, Mithra and (probably) the Açvins.

Apart altogether from archæological evidence we have strong reason for believing that the primitive religions of Asia Minor had much of what Hinduism calls *çakti*, or worship of the female principle. The mænads, or "raving" women, were as much a feature of ancient Phrygian religion as were the frenzied devotees of Dionysos characteristic of the Thracian cult. Indeed, the two movements may well have been closely connected. Certainly Asia Minor was many times in history the scene of impassioned outbreaks of emotional excess of this sort.

The religion of the Euphrates Valley in Sumero-Akkadian times will be dealt with in a later chapter. It remains for us here to acquaint ourselves somewhat with the general principles of religion as they are reflected in the primitive history of the Semitic peoples, particularly as they show themselves in the probable cradle of the race, Arabia. It is, of course, not certain that Arabia was the original home of the Semites. Other theories of origin have been maintained, including those which derive the stock from Africa, or even from Armenia. But it is clear that, since the fourth millennium B.C., Arabia has been the prolific mother of peoples who at intervals, approximately, of a thousand years overflowed the limits of a land which produced more than it could support. These periodic migrations continued till all Western Asia was coloured in its culture and religion by the Semite, even though he was obliged to borrow many of the higher elements of this culture from the peoples he dispossessed. In all this territory the Semite, nevertheless, remained as a conqueror till the arrival of the Turk and the Mongol.

It is a fairly accurate generalization when we say, as we have said the same of so many other regions, that the primitive religion of the Semite was animistic. We may add that it is this religion which has in large part survived to the present day, cropping up through the superimposed

Muhammadanism as a similar faith has cropped up through the Buddhism of Eastern and Southern Asia. "The Moslem," says Gottfried Simon, "is naturally inclined to animism; his animism does not run counter to the ideal of his religion." Later on we shall find illustrations of this saying.

Arabia is the best locality for the study of primitive Semitic religion since its isolation gave particular strength to its conservatism in creed and cult. Here the old matriarchal tribalism lingered long and the tribal gods long maintained their authority against occasional attempts at innovation or reform. The fact that each tribe worshipped one deity in the main as a kind of tribal god had frequently led to the supposition that we are here face to face with a primitive monotheism. In reality the tribal god was but one deity in a primitive polytheism, a god deemed to be akin to his worshippers and the owner of the springs and pasturage which were the source of their livelihood. This sense of kinship was frequently stressed by the use of theophorous names asserting the fatherhood or the brotherhood of the god. While the tribal god was known as the Baal (*master*), or Melek (*king*), or Adon (*lord*), or 'El (*mighty one*) of the tribe, it must be remembered that the tribe did not grudge service to many other divine beings. There were, for instance, feminine deities not a few. There was a sun-goddess named Allat, accommodated with a male consort, Allah, afterwards taken up by Muhammad, a planetary goddess, Al Uzzat (the Mighty), who corresponds with Venus, a god of storms, Qozah, and many stellar deities, such as the Pleiades, the constellation worshipped as a rain-bringer. Hubal, the god of Mecca, was another rain-bringer, and has been identified with Allah. Another well-known god was Wadd, the divinity of the firmament. In the form of animals, too, were many deities, the lion-formed Yaghuth, Ya'uk, in the shape of a horse, and Nasr, the vulture god. Some gods appear to have been deified heroes and others are evidently the personification of abstract qualities, such as Friendship, Goodwill, Time and Fortune (Al Jadd).

Beside deities proper there were large numbers of

spirits good and bad, such as *jinns*, *afrits* and the *lilith*. The jinns were made of fire prior to the creation of man, and lilith was the nocturnal monster who infested the waste with the jackals and ostriches.[1] There were also fearful hairy monsters known as the *shĕ'erim* (satyrs) who were greatly dreaded. The many forms of reverence given to animals suggest the prevalence of totemism, and this suggestion is confirmed by the number of tabus in the matter of food. The old Semitic word for *holy* (*qadesh*) itself implies a cutting off from prohibited things. It is not known whether the pig was rejected because it was originally holy or because it was merely unclean. But many instances may be cited of animals which became an "abomination"—that is, something *ab-ominous*—because originally sacred to a deity. Thus the fish was sacred to Atargatis and the dove to Astarte—later, of course, to Venus. The mouse (and rat) may have been first of all sacred to a plague demon and the horse was practically everywhere sacred to the sun. It will be recalled that at the annual solar feast at Rhodes (largely Semitic) four horses were thrown into the sea. In South Arabia the camel was particularly sacred, possibly in connection with a pastoral cult, and this sacrifice still retains a special significance in Arabia.

Sacrifice was regarded as at once the food of the gods and as a means of sustaining sacramental fellowship with them on the part of man. It constituted further a blood-bond between the several members of the tribe and their gods. Many things connected with the sacrifices were highly regarded, and the wearing of the skin of the victim as a garment enabled the offerer to enter into a very special relationship with his totem. To use the sacrificial fat for the anointing of the members of the tribe, or of the chiefs, constituted a rite for the imparting to them of the vigour of the sacrifice. Foundation sacrifices, with children as the usual victims, were thought necessary to give strength to the different stages of a wall or building, from the laying of the first stone to the setting up of the gates. The case of Hiel, the Bethelite, as described in the *Books of Kings*, will recur to the reader.[2] It is the Semitic rite corresponding

[1] Cf. Isaiah xxxiv. 14.

[2] 1 Kings xvi. 34.

to our own custom of placing valuables in the foundation-stone of a new building. But we should remember that in Arabia the slaughter of infants had an economic aspect, since families were generally larger than their means of support. Human sacrifices seem once upon a time to have been numerous, but the victim was generally redeemed at the cost of so many camels or sheep. It will be remembered that Muhammad regarded himself as one who had been twice redeemed. The slaughter of an animal, even when required for food was always regarded as a sacrifice and the cutting of the victim's throat was accompanied by a kind of praise-shout, or *tahlil*, a cry to the spirit of the place: "Permission, O possessor of the ground!" In some parts of the Semitic world human sacrifices lingered to a late period, as is suggested by the Bible story of Jephthah's daughter. In all probability, the rite of circumcision is a relic of this ancient mode of sacrifice.

Other religious rites included the circling of sacred spots, keeping sunward, much after the fashion of the *tawaf*, or visiting of the holy places, later authorized by the Prophet as the Haj. Such a circuit, often accompanied by whistling and clapping of hands, was (as the word *haj* suggests) a synonym for a festival.[1] There were many festivals, both pastoral and agricultural, and these exhibit many of the features common at the equinoxes and solstices all the world over. The shaman, or holy man (Ar. *kahin*), in early Semitic religion showed little promise of developing into the ethical prophet of later Judaism. There was indeed little that was ethical in their profession and the close relation of the prophet to the madman was attested by the use of the word *majnun*, or one inspired with a *jinn*. It was theirs to advise as to the use of charms, mainly directed to the harming of an enemy, such as the burying of an image with a date-palm thorn thrust into its body, or the sewing up of a charm into the mouth of a toad, which, in its own wasting and eventual death, brought about a like calamity for the person against whom the charm was devised.

The extent to which all this was deeply implanted in

[1] Cf. I Samuel xxx. 16.

the manners and customs of the ancient Semites is plain from the persistence with which the same practices and beliefs maintain to the present day. "Islam," says Dr. Zwemer, "at its very centre has remained pagan,"[1] and this estimate will be confirmed by any survey of the tree worship, well worship, rock worship, serpent worship, and even worship of the dead, now prevailing in Moslem lands. Many of the concessions made by Muhammad to the stubborn paganism of his time witness to the fundamental character of Semitic animism. We have, for instance, not only the practices condemned, such as the "blowing upon knots," the use of rain-making charms like "giving the cat a bath," divination with arrows, the use of hair offerings, the binding of the dead by tying thumbs and toes together to prevent return, or the placing (for the like purpose) of ashes on the eyes, eggs under the armpits, and thorns beneath the feet, or the use of familiar demons, invisible to all but idiots and prophets. These things, though condemned, are still popular. But we have other things such as are condoned if not actually recommended—the worship of the Black Stone fetish at the Ka'aba, the use of Quranic texts as charms and amulets, the divining by the beads of the rosary, and the use of water in which a rosary has been washed for healing. Many practices in modern Islam have come about quite naturally through the infiltration of superstitions from other countries such as India, or even China, but it must be confessed that most of them are vigorous survivals from that dark background of religion which hangs like a heavy curtain between us and the unknown beginnings of Semitic history.

[1] S. M. Zwemer, *The Influence of Animism on Islam.*

## CHAPTER XI

## *Primitive Religion in the Americas*

THERE is almost universal agreement that the population of both North and South America entered the western continent by way of Behring Straits, and that the nearest relatives of the Amerindians—as it is convenient to call them—are the Mongoloid peoples of North-eastern Asia.[1] Dr. A. H. Keane, however, believes that somewhat earlier than this immigration came certain long-headed European people by way of the Faroe Islands, Iceland and Greenland. Others suppose there was a westward movement across the Atlantic by a more southern route; and others, again, that, by way of Oceanica, some hardy voyagers crossed the Pacific and reached the western coast. In regard to this last theory, however, it must be observed that the Polynesian migrations are of too recent a date to have affected Amerindian culture to any extent. It seems fairly certain that, in historical times, and until the discovery of America in modern times, there has been no cultural contact between the Amerindians and the peoples of the Old World. The first immigrants brought only the first elements of culture such as the use of the fire-drill, the art of stone-chipping, the bow, throwing-stick, harpoon, nets, the arts of basketry, and the domestication of the dog. They developed independently pottery-making, agriculture (with the digging-stick), weaving, the working of the softer metals and the domestication of the llama and alpaca.

The arrival of these proto-Mongoloid tribes probably took place more than ten thousand years ago and proceeded so slowly, with small bodies of people crossing the straits at considerable intervals, that an unusually large number of linguistic stocks had time to develop, as many as a hundred

[1] See Clark Wissler, *The American Indian*, New York, 1917, 355 ff.

and fifty altogether, and a disproportionately large number on the Pacific coast. All show the same general features and their holophrastic character contrasts them markedly with the languages of the Old World. No Amerindian peoples created a true script, though pictograms were employed among many tribes, wampum records among the Algonquins, quipus among the Peruvians, and calendric and astrological codices among Mayas and Aztecs. On the continent itself the pathway of migration was generally southward, following three main lines, along the coast, across the inner plateaux, and by the main channels provided in the east. That many bloody encounters took place between the different waves of migration is shown by such defence works as were erected by the mound-builders of Ohio and by the constructions of the Pueblo-builders of the south.

A first survey of the primitive religions of North America—and indeed of America as a whole—incline one to regard them as presenting a quite uniform character, that of a shamanistic system of faith and conduct closely resembling that of North-east Asia. But closer acquaintance with the field reveals distinctions and shows that, while the religions of certain peoples of the extreme north and the extreme south have remained crudely primitive, midway between these extremes has been developed a considerable amount of reflective philosophy. There are also, naturally, differences due to the climatic and economic variations between the several areas. The plains tribes are warlike, hunters by occupation and dwellers in *tipis*. The tribes of the plateaux are agriculturists, living in stone houses and peacefully inclined. The North-west Indians, again, are fishermen, living in wooden huts and making some ostentation of their wealth in the potlatch.

For such reasons we shall find useful Dr. Kroeber's division of the field of North America into ten culture areas, as follows: (1) Arctic, or Eskimo; (2) North-west Pacific coast; (3) California; (4) Inter-mountain plateau; (5) the Mackenzie-Yukon region; (6) Prairie region, or Central plains; (7) North-east forest region; (8) South-east woodland region; (9) South-west plateau; (10) Mexico.[1]

[1] See A. L. Kroeber, *Anthropology*, New York, 1923.

We might profitably discuss each of these areas separately, but, for the sake of brevity, it will be better to take a general view of Amerindian religion, so far as the areas present features in common, and then proceed to note features here and there which may seem to call for separate notice.

It will at once appear that totemism has played an important part in the history of Amerindian religion, though whether the totem was first respected because of its relation to the food supply and then reverenced as ancestor, or the stages were the other way about, may remain uncertain. At any rate, the word *totem* is an Amerindian word and denotes an Amerindian characteristic. Sometimes a tribe treated its totem as an ancestor and sometimes as a badge. Sometimes the totem was eaten and sometimes it was not. In many cases there seemed more disposition to trace descent from animal than from human ancestors. The Delawares derived themselves from "the great Hare"; the Mohegans from the bear, wolf and deer. On the other hand, the Algonquin "Foxes" are said to have had seven totems, without tracing descent from any.[1] Totems naturally had close relationship with the fauna of particular districts. In Alaska the totems were bear, wolf, whale and frog, while in California the raven (master of life), crane, owl, wolf, hare and snake were favoured. In the middle east and west there were some vegetable totems.[2]

The conception of God is naturally vague all over the continent and a number of statements—most of which emanate from the early missionaries—as to the worship of a Supreme Being must remain suspected of foreign influence. Where a "high god" is reported it will often be found that we are dealing rather with the personification of some natural phenomenon or with some deified ancestor. The word *manitu*, moreover, which has often been described as a synonym for God, means no more than a spirit, which may be either good or bad. Similarly, the supposed "high

[1] See E. V. Hopkins, *History of Religions*, New York, 1918, chap. VI.

[2] It must be remembered that the totemic complex is intimately bound up (as in some parts of Oceanica) with the belief in a certain animal as an individual guardian. The youth who went out to fast and pray and so put himself into relation with the spirit world expected to be visited by the spirit in the form of an animal, which from that time became his guardian. See Wissler, *The American Indian*.

god" of the Dakotans, called *Wakanda*, is not a god at all but rather a force like that which we call *mana*. As for the *Michabo* of the Algonquins and the *Ioskeha* of the Iroquois, these were deified heroes rather than gods in our sense of the word. Nature-gods, of course, there were in plenty—sky-gods, earth-gods, gods of the four cardinal points, gods of the four winds, corn-spirits, spirits of animals and spirits of trees, springs and rocks. But the almost universal theology, if we may use the term, of the Amerindian tribes was essentially animistic and their worship was that of animal and human ancestors, with a somewhat higher kind of polytheism prevailing in Mexico and Central America.

As in primitive religion elsewhere, there was much concern over the dead and their state in the other world, though according to E. V. Hopkins, the Pend d'Oreille Indians have no word for soul and know nothing of a future life. Such assertions, however, are frequently based on imperfect information. In general the soul is taken for granted. Some tribes, such as the Algonquins and Iroquois, believe in two souls, while the Siouans have a "third soul," which goes either to the sky-heaven or to the ice-bound hell. Evidently many views might be collected from different parts of the continent, varying all the way from sheer agnosticism to a joyous certainty. The dead were exposed on trees or stagings, buried or burned.[1] Sometimes both burial and cremation were used by the same tribe, according to the rank of the deceased. The souls of the dead were supposed to start out from the grave for a goal which took four days to reach. There was a "snake-bridge" to be crossed, corresponding to the Chinvad Bridge of ancient Persia, and this bridge was by some, like the Hurons, supposed to be guarded by a dog. But some coast-dwelling tribes preferred to think of souls as going to their final abode by boat.[2] For most tribes there was a sky world, where life went on much as on earth, the

[1] Cremation was, however, rare and in some places inhumation was feared as hindering the passage of the dead to the world of spirits.

[2] In some parts of the west the "western trail" was mapped out very definitely, with a long log to be crossed immediately before arriving at the world of the dead.

Eskimo busy with his kayak and harpoon, the hunter busy with bow and arrow in pursuit of ghostly bisons, and so on. At a period which perhaps can hardly be considered primitive, the other world became moralized, and the sky world was reserved for the good, while the bad found their "own place" in a world of storm and snow. A lightning flash was supposed to separate good from bad on the way towards their proper abodes. Some tribes held a belief that there might be vouchsafed a return of the dead to earth for a second chance. Mourning rites included the usual self-mortifications, mutilations, dishevelling or cutting of the hair, stripping off of garments, and the offering of blood and property at the grave. By such rites the mourners were supposed to light torches, corresponding to the corpse-candles of the West, for the guidance of souls along the pathway of spirits.

The shamans naturally differed in function and authority from tribe to tribe. It is hard indeed to say where the shaman ended and the priest began, unless we decide that the shamans were an unorganized priesthood, each man in direct touch with the power of the spirit world. In some tribes the shamans were merely irresponsible medicine-men; in others they had a certain amount of official standing. Among the Algonquins they formed an hereditary order, confined to a single family. In general the description holds good that the shaman possessed a sevenfold function, curative, preventive, inquisitive, malefic, operative, prestidigative and prophetic. In any case his talents ran the complete gamut, from the lowest kind of trickery, including the use of hypnotic power, to a genuine healing skill, often through the employment of vegetable remedies. Great importance was attached to dreams, induced visions, and the interpretation of the same. Some shamans, particularly the women of the profession, worked mainly through trances and waking visions; some by the use of a familiar spirit; still others by taking the form of some animal, often a bear.

The mythology of the Amerindians, in part due to the working of a poetical imagination, in part to indulgence in a species of ætiological guesswork, in its interpretation of cosmic phenomena shows certain general features. The deluge myth is found almost everywhere, and usually the world is recovered from the waste of waters by the mission of some animal, such as a crayfish or a musk-rat. The universe was sometimes conceived of as a many-storeyed structure and sometimes as modelled after the *tipi*, with a flat earth, a tent-like heaven, and a door towards the east. The relations of sun and moon and stars were patterned on those of the family, and it was common to talk of Father Sun and Mother Moon, with the Morning Star as the child, though sometimes Sun and Moon are thought of as brother and sister.[1] Sometimes, too, the sun was depicted as "the old man of the dawn," almost a personal deity. The idea of the Thunder-bird is also a common element of Amerindian mythology, with the Plumed Serpent in the south along the Mexican border. Almost everywhere we have the conception of the Trickster Helper, who may be the demiurgic Raven of the western coast, the Coyote of the western plains, the Great Hare of the Algonquins, or the Rabbit (cf. the *Brer Rabbit* stories) of the Cherokees and others. Many myths treat of the origin of death, some of them with a pathetically beautiful spirit of acquiescence. Thus in the far north two old women are represented as debating whether they should choose both light and death rather than neither light nor death, and they accept the former alternative. Among the Blackfeet an old man and an old woman argue the same high theme, with the result that the old man refers the decision to the throwing of a buffalo chip into the water to sink or swim. But the old woman turns the chip into a stone, remarking, "Unless we die we shall not pity one another." So, once again, on the Pacific coast, Coyote persuades men to accept death rather than access to the fount of eternal youth, declaring, "Joy at birth and grief at death is better."

Religious practices are naturally varied, but embrace certain typical rites or usages such as the following: the *Dance*, *Prayer*, *Fasting*, the *Sweat-bath*, the *Smoke*, and *Sacrifice*.

[1] Sometimes we find the relation expressed as Father Sun, Mother Earth and Daughter Corn.

*Dancing*, which is universal, has in all probability several objects. It is a means of auto-intoxication such as induces religious ecstasy or arouses physical courage before battle. Occasionally, perhaps, it is a mere effort at "showing off." It is often, however, a species of imitative magic, used, together with self-torture, for the purpose of keeping the sun in its course or stimulating the growth of the crops. Sometimes, with the actors masked, and accompanied with song, the dance imitated the actions of animals and brightened the prospects of a projected hunt. The Algonquins had their tribal dances for planting and harvesting, for the declaration of war, the making of peace, for the restoration of health and for honouring the dead. In California there were victory dances over a fallen foe, and adolescence dances for girls and boys. In Arizona and New Mexico the Snake and Antelope fraternities have their remarkable rites for the bringing of rain. And among the Zuni the impressive Hako or Holy Rites of the Corn-maiden have been found worthy of imitation by Dr. William Norman Guthrie in the Church of St. Mark's in the Bowerie, New York.[1]

*Prayer*, too, is wellnigh universally used, including the silent meditation of some of the tribes in certain moods, the crude petitions for material favours from the gods, such as the Huron prayer: "Spirit of this place, we give thee tobacco; so help us, save us from the enemy, bring us wealth, bring us back safely," and the more spiritual supplications of Navajos and Pawnees.

*Fasting* also has a great variety of aims. Sometimes it is a simple purgation, the result of taking an emetic (the "black drink"), for the cure of physical ills. Sometimes it is a discipline to make possible the dreaming of vivid and inspired dreams. "To be able to fast long," said the Algonquins, "is an enviable distinction." This is an idea confirmed (to take an illustration from another continent) by the Zulu proverb: "The continually stuffed body cannot see secret things." It is possible also that fasting was believed to assist the attainment of ecstasy, and even

[1] William Norman Guthrie, *Offices of Mystical Religion*, 1927.

that it was apotropaic in preventing evil spirits from entering the body.

The *Sweat-bath* was closely associated with fasting as a means of warding off evil influences. It cured sickness, assisted ecstasy, and expelled demons. It is remarkable that the use of the sweat-house extends all the way from Canada, except among the Eskimo, southward. The Mexicans, like the Mayas and Incas, resorted to bleeding instead.

*Smoking* is a characteristically Amerindian rite. The pipe was regarded as a kind of portable altar and smoking a kind of sacrifice, offered to heaven and earth, and to the gods of the four quarters, with the four ceremonial puffs to the north, south, east and west. It was also a rain charm, an inducer of trance, an invitation (as among the Blackfeet) to spirits, a means of establishing friendship with spirits (as with men), and also a method of propitiating the ghosts of animals slain in the chase. For this last reason the hunter filled the mouth of the slain bear with smoke and begged the beast to harbour no grudge against the slayer.

*Sacrifice* proper had a wide range both of purpose and also in the material offered. It was the offering of food to the spirits, the presentation of a friendly gift, an act of propitiation, or an act of imitative magic to stimulate the food supply. All sorts of things were offered, from vegetables to dogs and other animals, and from these to human beings, though human sacrifices were more in vogue in the highly developed systems of Mexico than in the religions we more properly entitle primitive.

But before speaking of the special form taken by religion in Mexico under the Aztecs, it is well to mention a few stray facts as to the characteristics of more northerly cultural areas to which so far we have had no occasion to allude. Most northerly of all we have the Eskimos, or (to use the term preferred by themselves) the *Innuits*, that is, *men*. Though divided into several ethnical groups, religiously they are much on the same level. Bancroft speaks of the Eskimo religion as "vague fear, finding its expression in witchcraft." Spirits inhabit all things, inanimate as well as animate. Some acknowledge a kind of deity called

*Tornassuk*, who rules over the *tornat*, or helping spirits, but it is hard to think of Tornassuk as a " high god." The spirit of the food supply is the goddess *Sedna* (at least among the central Eskimo). She causes storms and controls the supply of seals, which are considered as her " fingers," amputated by the act of her father. There are also rock spirits and hill spirits and, of course, the spirits of the dead, who are apt to be exceedingly wrathful when offended. Death itself is a bad spirit who robs men of their souls. Men are believed to have several souls, but after the dead are buried not much attention is devoted to them by way of mourning rites. The medium between man and the spirits is the witch-doctor, or *angiakok*, generally a man, but sometimes of the other sex. Women are sometimes employed to go from house to house stabbing the demons who may be in possession, after the manner of the Taoist priests in China. The angakok is used to discover any who have broken tabus and so provoked the wrath of the spirits. The discovery is often made by induced visions. Along the Pacific coast and southward to the four sub-culture areas of California, religion, while the same in its main features as that already described, tends to become more communal, with more numerous and more elaborate ceremonies. Its shamanism centres, as usual, in the phenomena of disease and death, but its festivities include not only the post-victory tribal dances and initiation rites, but also such specialized rites as those of the first salmon and the jimson-weed. The dead are either buried or cremated and the mourning rites are restricted to one day until the annual tribal commemoration comes round. The mourners cut off their hair, burn the hut of the deceased, together with such valuables as he may have left behind, including his shell-money and his baskets. The name of the deceased is henceforth avoided and drops out of the language, a significant fact in trying to understand the differentiation of tribal dialects. Some of the dead are supposed to go above and some below, while some are believed to cross the ocean to the west. Occasionally, however, they return in the form of animals.

One of the highest developments of primitive religion in

North America is to be found among the Algonquins, who include the Blackfeet of the west, the Cree-Ojibways of the middle west, and the so-called Wabanaki or "easterners." They are now mostly Christianized, but the early shamanism shows plainly through the adopted faith. Many spirits were recognized, both benevolent and malignant. One of them was the rather clownish *Kuloskap* (Glooscap), who has been sometimes described as a Supreme Being. Together with Kuloskap is that spirit's evil genius Malsum, the wolf. As the mythology is generally given, a certain missionary colouring is more or less obvious. Kuloskap is really (as Dr. J. D. Prince describes him) "a supernatural Indian and the father of all the conjurors." To the old Algonquin the other world was either above the firmament or in the bowels of the earth where a company of gigantic, immortal animals—their own totem animals—lived in beatitude.

South of the Algonquins and north of Mexico lived the important group of tribes known as the Denés, a group of very varied culture, embracing the fierce Apaches of the south, the timid Hares of the north, the industrious Navahos and the lazy Dog-ribs and Slaves. These tribes are all primitively shamanistic and zootheistic. The powers of Nature all originally spoke and fought amongst one another, and kindly spirits still communicate with men in dreams as animals, becoming from that moment personal totems. The thunder-bird idea is strongly held, the idea of a spirit who causes lightning by the winking of his eyes and thunder with the flapping of his wings. The tricky creator-hero appears in some myths, and there is also a flood story (possibly derived from the missionaries [1]), in which the earth is ultimately reconstructed by the efforts of a musk-rat and a beaver. The dead are never buried but exposed on a platform or hidden in hollow trees. The other world is underground and is watered by a river in which the shades catch fish for their subsistence. If any do not receive the proper funeral rites, they are compelled to feed on mice

[1] Dr. Boas thinks that some Old World themes got into Amerindian mythology through the early Spanish missionaries. But the deluge story is rather too general to be accounted for in this way.

and vermin, while the more fortunate dance away their days upon the grass.

In all that has been said so far there will be observed a certain resemblance, not only of the religion of one American tribe as compared with any other, but also with the primitive religions of the continent of Asia. That evidence exists of development towards the higher types of religion I should be the last to deny, and, indeed, it is plain that an immense distance separates the shamanism of the Eskimos from that of the Iroquois and the Algonquins. There is also the fact that out of the religion of the peoples we have described developed the organized faiths of the highly sophisticated civilizations of pre-Spanish America, that of Aztecs and Mayas and Incas. Of this, however, we shall treat in a later chapter, in dealing with the religious systems of the dead empires.

To complete the present chapter it remains only to sketch briefly the primitive religion of South America. Dr. Kroeber divides this continental area into four cultural fields, namely, Columbia, or Chibcha; Andean, or Peruvian; the tropical forest land of the Orinoco, Amazon and La Plata drainages; and Patagonia. It is somewhat difficult, of course, to get back with any certainty to primitive conditions in these regions, since some districts made great cultural advances beyond their neighbours, and since the original Indian population has been in many places largely intermingled with the Spanish and other European invaders and, later, as in Brazil, with imported negroes. In some parts, as in Uruguay, the Indians have practically disappeared; in Bolivia they form from 60 to 70 per cent. of the population; Ecuador is 50 per cent. Indian; and the population of Paraguay is mainly Indian. Comparing one part with another, and reserving reference to those organized religions which accompanied the advance of the Incas to empire in the centuries preceding the Spanish conquest, it is possible to make a general conspectus. By way of summary it may be said that the furthest advance was made by tribes in the north and centre, while least progress was made by the Patagonians in the south. The general average of culture among the savage peoples was in early times not greatly superior to that of the Australians and Papuans, with almost entire absence of the forms of worship or with the worship of beings who can hardly be considered as having the nature of gods. A rather low form of animism was the general rule, with stress on the worship of ghosts, who were usually considered hostile. The dead were believed to reincarnate themselves as animals, jaguars, snakes, hawks, and so on. Or they went to the land of the " fathers " in the sky, where warriors were supposed to give evidence of their continued existence in the fall of shooting-stars or in fighting within the thunder-clouds. There was also a naturistic worship showing itself in reverence paid to the moon and stellar bodies. *Tupan*, " the god of the eastern Tupi," was really a thunder-god, whose voice was simulated in the magic rattle. Dances, some of them masked, were performed in the case of initiation ceremonies, at funeral rites, or in the establishment of a new settlement.

In Guiana, and other parts of the north and north-west, the dead were buried in the house, which was then deserted, while the possessions of the deceased, his hammock and other necessities, were interred with him. Sometimes a slave was strangled and buried at the same time with his master. In the Andean region, in the Tiahuanaco period, prior to the rise of the Incas, there does not seem to have been any sun-worship, but there was a rain- and thunder-god (that is, a fertility god), called *Viracocha*, to whom great honour was paid. There were also moon- and sea-gods, and clan gods generally in animal form. The dead were frequently mummified and made into tightly corded packs, with the needed utensils and adornments included in the bundle.

The Araucanians, who held up the advance of the terrible Incas and also, for a couple of centuries, resisted the conquering Spaniards, illustrate much the same kind of culture. Here we find tribes with a social organization based on totemism, without temples, but with a ritual which laid great stress on clan totems and the ancestors. There were also puberty rites, the latter being accompanied with human sacrifice and ritual cannibalism.

The Patagonians, who called themselves *Aoniken*, or *Patak-aoniken* (corrupted by Magellan into *Patagonian*), consist of some much diminished tribes who have in part become intermingled with the Araucanians and Puelches. Information as to their religion is neither extensive nor exact, but they recognized a number of family tutelary spirits, with whom communication was established through the shaman, and, according to some, two or three powers of a higher sort of whom one was a good spirit, *El-lal*, a kind of creator-god, but in all probability a culture-hero, who taught the use of fire and the bow. There was also an evil wind-demon, Maipe, and another, the dreaded Keron-kenken, who was wont to devour new-born children, drinking the tears of the disconsolate mothers. The tribal groups identify themselves with the ostrich, puma, guanaco, and so on, and old tales tell of wars of totem against totem, possibly only an echo of intrusions upon tribal hunting-grounds. The shamans were (and are) much sought after for healing disease and extracting evil spirits. As sorcerers they seek to expel the malefic spirit with loud din and shouting and ferocious pursuit. There seems to be a belief in transmigration, but while one spirit of the dead is thought to traverse a mysterious ocean, a secondary spirit is believed to prowl around the former habitation. The dead are buried in a squatting position, with food and utensils. After a year the bones are exhumed and painted red, before being restored to the grave. Persons who die away from home are generally cremated.

It is hard to say how much or how little all these beliefs affected the religion of the Incas, or how much of the religion of the Incas really developed earlier ideas. But we can at least discern in the later beliefs a number of things which belong to primitive religion the world over. These include the annual ritual renewing of the fire, the seasonal dances, communion with the dead and the gods in the sacred drink, the idea of the dead being led across a hair-fine bridge by a black dog, the carrying of mummies into battle as fetishes, the setting up of temple posts on the bodies of men sacrificially slain, and the use of many forms of divination, such as haruspicy, augury, games of odd and even, little heaps of maize, and many others which will be recognized as common in widely separated lands.

Our conclusion is that, whether or not the original settlers from North-eastern Asia were subsequently reinforced or not from across the Atlantic or the Pacific, the religion they all alike professed and practised was that we have already described as prevailing in the settlements of the older world.[1]

[1] On the general subject of this chapter see the *Encyclopædia of Religion and Ethics, passim* ; Hartley Burr Alexander, *The Mythology of North America*, Boston, 1916 ; the same author's *The Mythology of Latin America*, Boston, 1920 ; Clark Wissler, *North American Indians of the Plains*, New York, 1912 ; and the same author's *The American Indian*, New York, 1917.

## CHAPTER XII

### *The Primitive Religion of the Kelts*

A SURVEY of the primitive religion of the Kelts, however brief, should afford a good introduction to the study of the religions of Europe prior to the rise of Christianity. The Keltic waves passed over territories which had been occupied by still earlier populations and probably absorbed from these a considerable amount. Yet the indigenous elements of pre-Keltic religion probably made no essential difference to later beliefs and practices, and we may confidently see among the Kelts the religion of the older branches of the Indo-European family, little changed by the influx of a new religion. This is particularly true of Ireland, where no Roman conquest occurred to overlay or destroy the earlier culture. Thanks to this fact, Ireland has, even through her superstitions, rendered service to those who desire to get back to a near view of her most ancient faith.

As to the earliest populations of the west of Europe we are almost entirely in the dark and at any rate have no recorded history. Irish legend speaks of several pre-Keltic invasions following the Flood, of which the third was that of the *Fir-bolg*, possibly a Mediterranean people similar to the Basques of Spain. These were conquered in due course by a race known as the *Tuatha Dé Danann*, or People of the Goddess Danu, generally supposed to be the legendary deities of the Kelts themselves. Following on these came the *Children of Míl*, or Milesians, who are to be identified with the first Irish Kelts.

The main Keltic wave seems to have begun its westward march about 2000 B.C. On the way certain branches turned aside from the main body and formed pockets in southern lands. One such entered Asia Minor where, some centuries B.C., it formed the people known as Galatians, to whom St. Paul wrote an *Epistle*. Other branches affected the history of Greece and Italy. Gaul was probably reached about 800 B.C., Spain three centuries later, and Britain and Ireland a century or so still later. The final result was a group of Keltic tribes in the west of Europe, distinguished in the matter of language as Erse (in Ireland), Gaelic (in North Britain), Cymric (in South Britain), and Brezonec (in Brittany).

A good deal of the religion brought to these lands by the Kelts probably differed but slightly from that which they found on their arrival. That is, it was animistic, involving the worship of many powers which were but vaguely personalized, recognized both in the world of nature and in the world of the dead. It is likely that many of the spirits worshipped and feared were the ghosts of the dead, who were supposed to haunt the mounds and barrows made by the former population of the land. These barrows, known as *síd* (cf. Latin, *sedes*, seats) were supposedly inhabited by *aés sidhe*, who were to the Irish Kelts what the "Rephaim" were to the Hebrew invaders of Palestine. It was quite natural that in course of time these should, by a use of hypochoristic language, diminish to the fairies, brownies, and "good people," whose presence had become familiar, though it was not wise to name them rashly.

Many of the "high" gods of Ireland (to confine ourselves for the most part to the mythology of the western island) were the result of euhemerization, though it is scarcely possible now to separate with any certainty the divinities due to the personification of natural phenomena from those due to the blurred memory of ancient kings and heroes. Probably not a few of the gods were the result of a merging process in which both spirit worship and nature worship played an equal part. Such, no doubt, were the Tuatha Dé Danann of whom we have spoken, "tribes of the goddess Danu," who herself may have been a sky divinity. In any case, even at a late date, there was close association between gods and kings, since the kings preserved in themselves a certain divine power which had to be protected by all kinds of tabus, called *geasa*, and which had to be transmitted safely from one generation to another. Indeed, it was sometimes difficult to distinguish between the *mana* of a king and the " soul " which had to be hidden for security in some sacred tree. The slaying of a king and the cutting down of a tree might have the same magical end in passing on the sacred vigour to a successor or to the solar orb.

All this makes it exceedingly difficult to say where euhemerism ends or where naturism begins. Was Dagda just a thunder-god, or was he, as the " clever " god, the reminiscence of some long-dead chief? How far, again, was Manannan, the three-legged god, lord of the Isle of Man, a mere legendary hero, or a solar myth, reminding us of the three-legged crow of old Japan? We know not, again, how far Ler (the Llyr of the Welsh and the origin of the place-name *Leicester*) was a god of the sea, or how far he was some really human Lear. Nor do we know, once again, whether Lug, from whom is derived the name of some sixteen places called *Lugdunum* (cf. *Lyons* and *Leyden*), was a sun-god, or whether in Lug, of the Long Arm, son of Cían, lord of many arts, sleep-strain, wail-strain, and laughter-strain, we are to recognize the hero of some ancient saga.

While we are mentioning these " high " gods, we must not omit some others of importance. For instance, there was the Cumhal of the Irish, who is to be identified with the Camulos of the British, evidently a sky-god (cf. *Himmel*). Another is the Brigantia of the British, who is identical with the Brigindu Danu, mother of the gods, lady of fertility, goddess of poetry, and who survives under the Christianized name of St. Brigit. Then we have the Nuada of the Irish, who is the Lud of the British, from whom we derive such place-names as *London* and *Ludgate*. There are, again, Bran the Blessed, whom we shall mention again later in connection with the Isles of the Blessed; Taranis, the Keltic thunder-god, who gave his name to Tara; and so on, right into the circle of heroes who gathered around the Table of Arthur. In addition to these are any number of nature divinities, from those of sun and moon (in early days more important than the sun) to those of mountains, rivers, springs and wells. Some things later on gained a Christian significance, as, for instance, the *Holy Grail*, originally that "divine cauldron from which none goes unsatisfied and which restores the dead, the enchanted cup in tales of Fionn which heals or gives whatever taste is desired to him who drinks from it, and which is sometimes the object of a quest."[1]

Fertility goddesses were common throughout the Keltic field and especially "the mothers," worshipped by the women, and represented with fruit in their laps or with cornucopias. The "matres" were usually three in number and in certain parts of Europe were subsequently confused with "the three Marys." As a counterpoise, the men worshipped war-deities like Camulos, Teutates, Albiorix and Caturix.

Animal gods, too, were strongly in evidence, including Epona, the horse-goddess, a fertility god, the swine-god, Moccus, the bull-god, Torvus, the stag-god, the bear-god, the horned-serpent god, and others. Bird divinities were common, generally associated with the spirits of the dead. But some were thunder-birds and fire-birds. Even the robin and the wren fall into this category, and the doggerel rhyme of the Wren-boys, with its "Though he's so little, his family's great," is connected with old superstitions of this sort. Many trees, also, were reverenced, the ash and the yew especially in Ireland, and the oak in Britain. The cutting down of a tree for the purpose of burning was a piece of imitative magic, to stimulate magically the heat of the sun. The cutting of the mistletoe (a parasite still regarded as bringing good fortune) from the oak with a golden sickle, as described (somewhat vaguely) by Pliny, was for the purpose of taking "the soul of the tree," before felling its protective host. In addition, there was a cult of weapons, such as the sword and the hammer. Indeed, Keltic countries were territories where almost anything might be a god or the habitation of a god.

Whether the worship of animal deities indicates totemism, or merely the propitiatory reverence of animals hunted or reared, we do not know for certain, but some tribes took their name from the red deer, the beaver and

[1] John A. MacCulloch, *Celtic Mythology*, p. 203.

other animals. Such names, moreover, as *Brannogenos* (son of the raven), and *Artigenos* (son of the bear), suggest at least a totemistic tendency. The great name of Arthur itself has been derived from the word for bear (cf. Gk., *artos*), though some etymologists have ventured the opinion that it is rather from the early Aryan root *ar*, *to plough*. In favour of the totemic theory we may mention that exogamy and the tracing of descent matrilineally were common in Ireland and that certain totemic animals were forbidden as food, or only eaten sacramentally. We may also note the use of animal figures as military badges and the British custom of tattooing animal figures on the body.

The Keltic priesthood had great importance and prestige, whether considered as sacrificial priests, as bards, or as diviners. Of the so-called Druids various opinions have been entertained. There is not even certainty as to the meaning of the term, since, while some derive the word from the Greek *drus*, an oak, and adduce the Welsh *derw* (cf. *Derry*) as confirmation, others explain it as *dru-vid*, the very wise. Undoubtedly much of the lore once ascribed to the Druid, partly on the authority of Cæsar, is now generally discredited. The theory that the Druids built the megalithic monuments, of which Stonehenge is the best surviving example, is likewise recognized as an invention of the seventeenth century. In extant literature they appear only sporadically from 52 B.C. to A.D. 385, and this literature includes Cæsar's *De Bello Gallico*, where we have the references to human sacrifices and the doctrine of transmigration; Cicero's *De Divinatione*, as to certain Druidical forms surviving in Gaul; Diodorus Siculus, again on the subject of transmigration; Pliny's *Natural History*, on the cutting of the mistletoe and the sacrifice of white bulls; Tacitus, on the destruction of the Druids; and scattered references in Strabo, Ammianus Marcellinus, Suetonius, and Pomponius Mela. As to whether Druidism was an essential feature of Keltic religion opinion varies. Many believe the Druids to have been an earlier priesthood absorbed by the Keltic conquerors, while Mr. Kendrick holds that they originated with the Keltic priests in Gaul about the fourth century B.C., and that in Britain they represented the grafting on of a Kelticized institution upon an autochthonous element.[1]

Keltic worship was carried on in sacred groves rather than in temples, but temples were not unknown and often in their architecture simulated the grove. Idols were not common and were often nothing but roughly carved tree trunks. The festivals were in the main those of a pastoral rather than of an agricultural people, though marking the four quarters of the year but not the solstices and the equinoxes. The year began, in Ireland, with the great feast of *Samhain* on November 1 (our All Saints' Day). This was the day of beginnings, the day for moving the flocks to winter quarters, and also the times for the "assemblies." These assemblies were marked by the ritual drinkings, which correspond to the soma-drinking in India and the "mead-circling" in Teutonic countries. Triennially they were the occasions for equalizing the solar and the lunar year, since in the course of three years eleven extra days would be accumulated for the assembly. There are still conventions held triennially out of obedience to this ancient habit. The next great feast was *St. Brigit's Day*, February 1, but of this we have but the slightest knowledge. The greatest of all was *Beltane*, on May 1, when the flocks returned to pasture. Dr. Macalister says that the morning of May-day was "one of those critical moments of the year when supernatural events might be expected to happen." Then on August 1, came *Lugnasad*, the solar festival, sacred to Lug, when magical rites were used to supply vigour to the orb of day, when the harvest was begun and when horse-racing (dear ever since to the Irish heart), lustration, and the performance of the *deasil*, were the vogue.[2]

The practical religion of the Kelts included most of the observances already noted as common everywhere in primitive life. There was divination of many sorts, including the interpretation of cloud movements, the behaviour of flame and smoke in the sacrifices, the cry and flight of birds, signs noted in the entrails of sacrificial victims, and

[1] See T. D. Kendrick, *The Druids, passim.*
[2] See R. A. S. Macalister, *Tara, passim.*

the manner in which the victims, animal or human, fell and died. The chewing of acorns by the diviners was a favourite method of obtaining the gift of prophecy, and oracles of various sorts were given through the leaves and other parts of the oak. The mystic ceremony of "saving the soul" of the oak by removing the mistletoe has already been noted. The gift of prophecy was a special prerogative of the priestesses, who seem to have been highly reverenced as seers. Sacrifices of all sorts were offered to the gods, including the heads of foes slain in battle. Some human sacrifices were offered to the *manes* of the dead; others seem to have been fertility rites designed to ensure an abundant harvest. Among the latter was the burning of human beings (as well as animals) in a great hollow effigy made of branches and reeds. This horrid sacrifice was to utilize and preserve the powers liberated by death for service in the spiritual world. Much the same idea was involved in the sacrifice of an ox or goat, whose skin was immediately worn by the sacrificer to obtain the *mana* of the victim. Tabus, known in Ireland as *geasa*, were common, and generally imposed for the protection of the king's life. Many *geasa* were restrictions voluntarily accepted to tide over a dangerous moment. There was a characteristically Keltic use of fasting as a tabu directed against an enemy. "If B," says Dr. Macalister, "allows A to starve to death, the ghost of A will haunt B continually." Illustrations of this belief will be recalled in the hunger-strikes employed as a weapon in Ireland in quite recent years.

A very important part of Keltic religion concerned itself with the world of the dead, that *orbis alius* of which such frequent mention is made in the sagas. This other world was situated in different places according to the geographical and intellectual standpoint of the various branches of the Keltic family. For some it was simply an underground abode where the dead enjoyed a bodily immortality resembling in most respects their terrestrial estate. Hence the burial mounds were not only places where the dead were interred, together with the necessities of life, even to wives, slaves, horses and implements, but were also spots haunted by the disembodied spirits. So a mystic atmosphere prevailed productive of all kinds of superstition. For it was well understood that the dead could and did return, sometimes in wraith-like simulacra of the former body and sometimes in the shape of an animal or bird. The doctrine of transmigration was deeply rooted, as Julius Cæsar himself reported. An interesting illustration is afforded by the tale of Tuan MacCarell, who was in one life a deer, in another a wild boar, then a sea-eagle, after this a salmon, which being eaten by the wife of Carell, was reincarnated in her son. Even within the bounds of a single life transmigration could be effected, hence the singular transmigration combats which form so characteristic an element in Keltic literature.

Others believed the abode of the dead to be beneath the waves, possibly an echo of some great catastrophe in the sinking of a coastline or the engulfing of a group of villages. A very general belief was that in the *Isles of the Blest* beyond the western seas.[1] It was that *Paradise* of which Claudian wrote:

> There soft movements are heard of shades that uncertainly hover,
> Moaning and sighing in sadness ; there too the peasant sees ever
> Beings with faces so pale, figures of those who have gone hence,

or like that Isle of Avallion, tempest-free, to which Arthur was borne to be healed of his grievous wound. The Bretons spoke of the Isle of Tevennic and the Bay of Souls, to which the dead pass from Cape Race. The settlers at the mouth of the Rhine, says Procopius, saw the dead depart from the Isle of Brittia. And very numerous are the Irish references to that Isle of Bresail (whence comes the name of *Brazil*), of which we read in the half-Christianized sagas of the *Voyage of Bran the Blest*, or in the *Adventures of Cormac MacAirt*. It is one of the great Irish tales which tells how Bran heard from a woman of wondrous beauty the story of the Blessed Isles, fifty in number, beyond the western horizon, and how he sailed on till he was met by the sea-king, Manannan MacLer, who guided the weary mariners unto the desired haven. When Bran at length

[1] See S. A. Coblentz, *The Answer of the Ages*, chap. xiv.

returned to Ireland, generations had been born which remembered him not.

In all these legends of an Elysium beyond the waves there is naturally a family likeness. It is a land of unfading beauty, with nothing rough or harsh, where the flowers bloom perennially and birds sing celestial melodies, where divine women minister to the newly immortal the food and drink of gods, and where the dead may be visible or not at will. To the Irish especially this Tir nan Og is a living reality, as real as the brownies and other fairy-folk who linger around the mounds and forts of their beloved land.

The end of Keltic paganism is supposed to have come with the preaching of St. Patrick, but it is by no means certain that some features of that paganism have not survived in the story of the saint himself. As for St. Brigit, she is but the old Brigindu, the British Brigantia, rebaptized, as already noted. One need not go far to find other survivals just as significant. Even the influence of the priesthood in the Ireland of to-day reflects the authority of the Druids who in ancient times had so much to do with the election of chiefs and kings. In other parts of the Keltic world Druidism was harshly treated by the Romans and died before the advance of Christianity. Yet even in these regions much of the old religion surrendered outwardly to the new only to survive in thin disguise.[1]

[1] See Douglas Hyde, *A Literary History of Ireland*, chap. xiii.

## CHAPTER XIII

## *The Primitive Religion of the Teutons*

AS we might expect, the border line between the religion of the Kelts and that of the Teutons is difficult sometimes to see and always easy to pass without suspecting it. We have to keep in mind throughout the common descent of these two branches of the Indo-European family. Even the name Teuton has been derived from that of a Keltic war-god, *Teutates*. In the second place, we have to remember the extent to which both religions, and not least that of the Teutons, have been coloured by the Christianity which superseded them. It is for this reason that such myths as that of Odin's hanging for nine days over Niflheim and that of "the Twilight of the Gods" must remain suspect as to their purely pagan origin. A third consideration enters into the discussion when we reflect upon the fact that, just as Greek mythology modified almost to transformation that of the Romans, so the Roman mythology did much to transform the religious ideas of the countries subjugated by the Empire. The result is that we cannot wholly trust the equation of Teutonic with Roman divinities which was made by the conquerors, or even the equation of the terms used in designating the days of the week.

Once again, we have to give weight to the very considerable variation in mythology and religious practice which existed in different parts of the Teutonic world, even though all the regions may present a generally well-defined and similar type. In the early history of Europe the Teutons are represented by such well-marked movements of men as are suggested by the terms Visigoth, Ostrogoth, Vandal, Burgundian, Alaman, Bavarian, Frank, Longbeard, and English. Eventually these settled down in the territories now known as Germany, Scandinavia, Iceland, and

England. From these territories smaller groups went forth as Angles and Saxons from the shores of the Baltic, to take possession of South Britain, and others in like manner to found new states or empires. But for the purpose of this chapter we shall limit our analysis of the Teutonic stock by thinking of it only under the three heads of Scandinavian (inclusive of Norse, Swedish and Danish), Germanic and English Teutons. Up to the time of the seventh century most of the tribes forming these divisions were barbarous and savage, and many centuries had to elapse before it could be said that their conversion (even nominally) had been actually achieved. For though the evangelization of the Teutons began as early as the fourth century with the preaching of Ulfilas to the Goths, paganism was not yet overthrown among some tribes of the stock until after the eleventh.

For our knowledge of the primitive Teutonic religion the sources are rather scanty. In the first place we have some outside information, as it might be considered, such as the *Germania* of Tacitus, written about A.D. 98, the *Lives of the Saints*, like the story of St. Boniface, and a few hints in the *Baptismal Formularies*. In the second place, we have information from the more truly native literature, such as the sagas, and particularly the poetical and prose *Eddas*, though these latter, in their present form, come to us from a time well into the Christian period.

From all sources, taken together, we get the impression of a "crude cult with a crude belief," and yet one which is not without gleams of poetic fancy and philosophic discernment. The Teutonic gods form a fairly complete pantheon, though it is by no means easy to assign to each its proper importance in different parts of the Teutonic world. Most of the deities are nature gods, but here and there distinct hints of euhemeristic influence may be detected. Cæsar has described the Germanic tribes as worshipping the three great divinities of Sun, Moon and Fire, but it is hard to equate these with the chief gods of the Teutonic pantheon. The moon, of course, was widely reverenced, on account of its supposed influence on the vegetation. The sun, also, "moon's bright sister" (for the sun was regarded as feminine), was worshipped because of its importance in connection with agriculture. In the native literature, however, many divinities are more strongly personalized than the sun and moon.

In general, we may divide the spiritual beings reverenced into several classes. There were, first of all, the Aesir, with which we may probably compare the Indian "strong ones," the Asuras. These included Odin, his son Thor, Balder, Vali, Vithair, Vili and Vi. Then, in the second class, there were the Vanir, who included Njörthr (the Gothic Nerthus), here regarded as masculine, and his children, Freyr and Frejya. These were under the overlordship of Odin. The third class was that of the Jötuns, a monstrous brood of giants—frost giants and cliff giants—who, as in the case of Freyr and Gerd, are supposed to have intermarried with the gods. One of these giants was Thrymr, the adventurer who stole the hammer of Thor. Some of these divinities are represented as theriomorphic, such as the Midgardsworm and the Fenriswolf, or even the Grendel who figures in the great poem of Beowulf. The dragon, too, or serpent, appears now and then, as in the story of Fafnir, guardian of treasure, and in the myth of the two serpents, Ofnir and Svafnir, into whose form Odin was sometimes changed. Many animals, too, are associated with the gods, without being regarded as divine. Such are the raven and wolf associated with Odin, the boar and cat with Freyja, the horse and boar with Freyr, and the goat with Thor. Then, again, there were dwarfs, as, for example, the Miming who becomes the famous *Wayland, the Smith*, in Anglo-Saxon mythology. To these must be added the Alfar, or Elves (A.-S., *Ylfe*), who dwelt in Alfheim, the realm of Freyr. Volund, or Wayland, was the prince of Alfar, though whether we are to regard the elves as the souls of the dead, as dream people, as a reminiscence of extinct races, or as nature gods of lesser dignity, we cannot tell. Of a more abstract character are the Norns, or Fates (the *Weird Sisters* of *Macbeth*), and the Valkyries, "choosers of the slain," who rode forth to the battlefields to seize the dead. One strange figure, a little apart from the rest, is Loki, a son of the giants, the evil one, the foe of the gods, "the ender."

He is represented also as the blood-brother of Odin and may have been originally a fire-god, possibly a deity of the subterranean fires. After the death of Balder Loki was bound in Hell and the poison of serpents made to drip over his face. But Sigyn, his wife, held a shell to receive the venom so that only when she turned aside to empty the vessel did the poison reach him. The story of Loki's breaking loose before "the Twilight of the Gods" possibly owes something to Christian influence.

Of the great gods, Odin (Wuotan, Woden), seems to have been originally the chief, at least in Scandinavia. In Germany he was known as Woden, from *wode*, the wind, and was pictured as the frenzied rider on the grey eight-legged steed, Sleipnir, the very spirit of the storm. Later, as in the parallel case of the Vedic Indra, he passed from the rôle of a storm-god to that of a war-god, and as such became Val-fadir, the god of the slain. As the god of the dead Odin was the psychopomp, or leader of the spirits to the underworld, Valhalla, "the hall of the slain." He was reputed to be well versed in runes, a skill gathered from his nine days' hanging over Niflheim on "the wind-stirred tree," and he was also reverenced as the divine physician. As the husband of Freyja (Frigg) Odin had added prestige in the north and received in sacrificial tribute offerings of horses and men. In the south his cult was not so prominent, as may be gathered from the use of the term *Mittwoch* for the fourth day of the week instead of *Wodens-tag*. It will be remembered that the worship of Odin was suppressed among the Saxons by Charlemagne with particular severity.

The influence lost to Odin became the heritage of Thor, who in course of time became the national god of the north and was highly reverenced elsewhere, in Germany under the name of *Donar*, and in Saxon England as *Thunor*. It seems probable that the supremacy of Thor came about as the result of a rebellion against the more aristocratic followers of Odin. In consequence the Thing met on *Thors-day* instead of *Odins-day*. In all cases the name, with which we may compare the Keltic Taranis, denotes the thunder-god, to whom the oak was especially sacred. We have in this the explanation of the fact that the Romans identified Thor with Jupiter and that the famous oak of Geismar (cut down by St. Boniface) was called "*robur Jovis*." Thor was visualized as a huge, red-haired, red-bearded giant, drawn in a car by the two he-goats, Tooth-gnasher and Tooth-gritter, and bearing with him his terrible hammer. This latter suggests his connection with a fertility cult, especially as we find that Thor was the "king" of the May-pole festival. Yet this need not prevent us from thinking of the hammer as having originally been the thunder-bolt. Thor was the last of the old Scandinavian deities to acknowledge the victory of the "White Christ."

Tiu, whose name (otherwise written as Tyr, Ziu, or Tyu) suggests the Indian *Dyaus* and the Greek *Zeus*, was evidently an old sky-god, whose power waned before the vigour of a younger generation. Yet it is Tyu who lost his right hand in the great contest with the Fenriswolf and succeeded in binding the monster with the fetter Gleipnir, made out of six non-existent things. Possibly he is to be identified with Nuada, the sky-god of the Keltic peoples. At "the Twilight of the Gods" Tiu fought the Hel-dog Gar and each slew the other.

Of Freyr (or Frey) and Freyja, respectively the son and daughter of Njörd, there are many interesting myths. Freyr was a fertility-god, to whom the wild boar was sacred and the ceremonial bringing in of the boar's head at Christmas in England and the making of Yule-cakes in the shape of a boar in Sweden are to be regarded as reminiscences of the old boar sacrifice. Frey was also the possessor of the famous magic barque, Skidbladnir, "swiftest and best of ships." The sister of Freyr was Freyja, the "lady" (cf. *frau*) queen of the fertility rites, the Norse Venus, whose necklace is the dawn, the rainbow, and the sunset in the sea. Freyja,

> thin-robed, about her ankles slim
> The grey cats playing,

is a symbol of the fecundity of nature and her day (*Friday*) was a favourite day for marriages till the custom was repressed out of Christian reverence for the death-day of

Jesus. The cat, with its "nine lives," still recalls the gift of the nine worlds to Freyja by Odin.[1]

Other divinities include Njörd, whose sister-wife was probably the Nerthus of Tacitus, "the mother of the gods," whose image was carried for a bathing ceremony by slaves who were subsequently drowned; Balder, "the beautiful, the fairest of the gods," a solar or year god, whose death through the treason of his half-brother, Hodr, caused all Nature to mourn till he was recovered from the abode of Hela—a deity referred to but seldom, yet familiar to all through Matthew Arnold's beautiful poem, *The Death of Balder*; and Heimdall, the foe of Loki, the Teutonic Izrafil, announcer of the judgement, guardian of the bridge of the dead, deity of light and of the beginnings.

It should be added that, in addition to the above-mentioned, many things were worshipped as supposedly the residence of divinity. Thus there was Ran, the sea, Mimir, the spring where Odin pledged his eye, and other springs, trees and even weapons of war, so dear to the heart of the viking. Some hills were sacred to Odin, as to the lord of the dead, and some to Thor. Some were regarded as personifications of the giants who were believed to inhabit their hollows. Not only groves but single trees were held to be sacred and in springs near by human sacrifices were sometimes offered by drowning the victims. Sometimes a sapling was split to allow a sickly child to be passed through it, in the belief that healing would ensue.

Wood-spirits of wild and shaggy mien, with meeting eyebrows, were known as Schrat (whence our *Old Scratch*). So sacred were trees that the man who wished to fell one must first do obeisance, with bended knees and folded hands, just as the Japanese artists pay reverence to the cherry-trees they use for their wood-blocks. Water-spirits were as numerous as wood-spirits, and these, too, as at Upsala, were honoured with human sacrifices. One of them was the German Nix, the Old Norse Nykr (whence our *Old Nick*), dangerous to children. It is when we realize the thoroughness with which Norse paganism peopled the world of Nature that we can understand the query of

[1] See M. Oldfield Howey, *The Cat in the Mysteries of Religion and Magic.*

the old tenth century *Penitential*: "Hast thou gone to any place other than the church to pray—to fountains, stones, trees, or cross-roads . . . or sought there the welfare of body or soul?" In this connection we must not omit mention of the Landsväetter, or tutelary spirits, related to the land as the Fylgja to the people, and against which the figure-heads on the ships were designed to be protective.

The cosmogony of Teutonic religion is shown in its most highly systematized form in the *Eddas*, though our hint as to the possibility of Christian influence must not be overlooked. First, we have the impressive conception of Ginnunga-gap, "the yawning chasm," north of which was Niflheim, the land of snow and ice, and to the south Muspellheim, the land of warmth and light. Here life was quickened and took form as the giant Ymir, who may be regarded as the equivalent of the Indian Purusha and the Chinese P'an-ku. From the melting frost came the world-cow, whose licking of the ice produced Buri and Borr and Borr's three sons, Odin, Vili and Vi. Then came the slaying of Ymir and the creation of the visible world from his blood and bones, and teeth and hair and flesh. Henceforth we have the triple world, consisting of Midgard, the earth, a vast disc on the ocean, around which lay coiled, like a gleaming girdle, the Midgardsworm; secondly, Utgard, or Jötunheim, the world of the giants, beyond the ocean; and thirdly, at the summit of a mountain, Asgard, the abode of the Aesir. Resting on this, and overarching all, was Heaven, and between Heaven and Earth the rainbow bridge, Bifröst, over which the gods ride to keep tryst at Urda's well. In Asgard is Valhalla, the palace of Odin, where the high gods feast with the victorious dead. In the *Voluspa*, and elsewhere, we have reference to "the nine worlds," as follows: Asgard, Vanaheim, Alfheim, Midgard, Jötunheim, Muspellheim, Svartalfheim, Niflheim, and another of uncertain name and significance. Through all these nine worlds grows the great ash-tree, Yggdrasil, over Urda's or Mimir's well, the well of fate, with its three roots fixed in earth and hell and the world of the frost-giants. In the branches of Yggdrasil dwell the eagle, hawk and squirrel, while four harts feed on the topmost twigs and the Nidhog gnaws at it from below. It is possible that in these various mythological features we may catch gleams of ancient rites performed in the forest sanctuaries of which the very memory has otherwise passed away. Myths of a world-tree, of course, are common everywhere, reflected in nursery tales like Jack and the Beanstalk as well as in the sublimest of apocalyptic visions. In the case of Yggdrasil, however, Christian writers discovered a too tempting opportunity to find the shadow of the Cross. One other piece of Teutonic mythology already mentioned has, at least in equal degree, been affected by later Christian ideas. This is the story of Ragnorok, "the Doom of the Gods." The *Eddas* describe this terrible catastrophe as the breaking-up of laws, the universal wreck of the world involving the revolt of Loki, the death of Balder, and the ending of life through the advent of an awful winter, like that described in the *Avesta* as coming upon mankind in the days of Yima. Not only the death of mankind but also the death of the gods was the fruit of the disaster; yet out of the ruin emerges a new world and the final stanzas of the *Voluspa* depict the return of Balder at peace with his blind brother, and

> A hill I see brighter than the sun,
> O'erlaid with gold, on Gimle stands;
> There dwell for ever the righteous hosts,
> Enjoying delights eternally.

The world of the dead is less consistently envisaged, though some of the confusion may be due to the contacts with other systems of belief, both earlier and later. There was a general faith in the survival of the soul, which was conceived of as a Fylgja, or "follower," or "co-walker," that is, a kind of *döppelganger* of the body. Souls could apparently return in the form of animals and could also pass into the bodies of animals as wer-wolves, that is, man-wolves, and the like. The world of the dead was known as Hel (with many variants), conveying the general idea of a "hollow" world. The queen of the dead, the Teutonic Persephone, was known by the same name, or as Hela. It is often quite difficult to tell whether the goddess or the place is intended. Hel is deep in the earth and enclosed on every side, guarded also by the dog Garm, "best of hounds," and the rust-red cock who gives warning of the approach of souls by crowing. The approach is by the Helveg, or Hell-way, and a bridge which must be identified with the *brig-o-dread* of the Yorkshire ballad. Men were buried with shoes known as hel-shoes, so that—to quote the *Lyke Wake* ballad—when they came to Whinnymuir, they might not arrive "wi' shoonless feet."

Apparently Hel was the abode intended mainly for the common folk who died what was called "a straw death." The souls of the warriors went to Valhalla, where they fought all day and were renewed at night, feasting after the fray on boar's flesh which replenished itself miraculously, and quaffing huge quantities of intoxicating mead.

Nevertheless, in spite of Hel and Valhalla, the dead were also believed to reside in the barrow-mounds where their bodies were laid to rest. Here they might be approached for necromantic purposes in order to furnish information such as only the dead could give. Here, too, spells might be woven for the laying of an unquiet ghost, since "a barrow wight" could be dangerously troublesome to the living. It was in any case dangerous to have too much to do with the dead and their dwellings; therefore great care had to be exercised to avoid the lure of female spirits and to observe the proper *tabus* in case of the offer of food or drink.

The rites of Teutonic worship were not in essentials different from those of the Keltic communities. In the Norse lands especially there was general belief in magic and particularly in the spells or runes which, coloured with blood, were carried on all kinds of objects from swordhilts and drinking horns to mythological ideas such as the teeth of Odin's horse, Sleipnir. Magic songs and cursing-spells were also known and used with entire conviction. Witches and wizards were supposed to be able to go forth from the body and as night riders speed forth on staff or broomstick to their nocturnal assemblies. Divination was extensively used and in Germany took form in the casting of lots and deductions from combats, dreams, smoke, the flow of blood, the flight of birds, and the neighing of white horses. There was also abundant use of imitative magic, much of which was for the purpose of obtaining fire or increasing the power of the sun and moon. In the case of the latter we have the witness of the old Saxon prayer,[1] *Vince*, *luna*, uttered at the time of eclipse. To assist the sun fire-wheels were rolled down the hills and bonfires lighted. A fire ritual was also performed to establish a claim to land, in carrying the fire around the plot or shooting fire over it. Need-fires, kindled by friction, were also lighted to drive the cattle through them as a rite of purgation and other consecrated fires were used to heal diseases.

The temples, as with the Kelts, were generally groves, but there are also instances of temples constructed of wood or stone and of these as containing idols. So far as Saxon England is concerned, we may recall the letter of Gregory the Great to St. Augustine requesting him to destroy the idols but to leave the temples standing, and also the story of the conversion of Coifi after the preaching of Paulinus in Northumbria. As to the use of groves, reference has already been made to the cutting down by Boniface of the oak of Geismar. Confusion is sometimes caused by the carrying over of the term grove to a constructed temple built upon a site once occupied by a sacred tree. Grove or temple, the Teutonic sanctuary was esteemed so sacred that, among the Semnones, no one was allowed to enter except in chains to mark his humility in the presence of divinity.

The priests were originally guardians of the groves, but had many functions. While not generally so powerful as their Keltic co-professionals, the Teutonic priests had considerable authority in politics, especially in connection with the choice of the chiefs. There were priestesses, too, and a high priestess was often very influential, as in the case of Velleda ("the prophetess"). Tacitus speaks in his *Germania* of the large number of women with prophetic power. Priests were also sacrificers and the importance of the horse-sacrifice gave point to their influence, as we may gather from the story of St. Boniface and again from that

[1] See the "Indiculus Superstitionum," *Ency. Rel. and Eth.*, I. 466.

of the conversion of the Norsemen. In Anglo-Saxon England the influence of the priests was only indirect and moderate. They were not allowed ordinarily to bear arms and were forbidden to ride except on mares.

The chief festivals of Teutonic religion were the Midsummer feast on June 24, the Autumn feast on November 10 (afterwards Martinmas), the Winter Solstice, December 25 (and on till *Twelfth Night*), and May-day, or *Walpurgis*, on May 1. Most of these had close connection with imitative magic, and were solar in character. The festival at the Winter Solstice (our Christmas Day) had to do both with the revival of the sun, as may be inferred from the use of the Yule log, and also with the dead. During the twelve days after Christmas the dead were supposed to ride forth with Odin. In this connection the eve of the feast was sometimes known as Mothers' Night and involved a kind of ghost ceremony—a circumstance which perhaps accounts for the fact that ghost-tales are still popular in the Christmas stories.

Taking it all in all, as we have seen, there was in Teutonic religion plenty of cruelty and superstition, to show the need of a milder and more merciful as well as of a purer and juster creed. But there were also elements of nobility, of virility and honesty, of chivalry towards womanhood and of honour among men, which promised well for the race when more adequate ideas of God should dawn upon the Teutonic world and blossom in more spiritual realization of the significance of life.[1]

[1] On the general subject of this chapter see the following: *E.R.E.*, XII. 246–58; J. Grimm, *Teutonic Mythology* (Eng. trans.), London, 1880–88; P. D. Chantepie de la Saussaye, *Religion of the Teutons* (Eng. trans.), Boston, 1902; E. E. Kellett, *The Religion of our Northern Ancestors*, London, 1914; P. B. du Chaillu, *The Viking Age*, 2 vols., London, 1889; J. A. MacCulloch, *Eddic Mythology*, Boston, 1930.

## CHAPTER XIV

## *The Religion of the Primitive Slavs*

THE present chapter must be a short one, not because of any lack of literature on the subject, but because when the material of this literature has been conscientiously sifted it is found that we really know much less about ancient Slavic religion than men imagined they knew in the seventeenth, eighteenth, and even the greater part of the nineteenth centuries.

The peoples commonly designated as Slavic occupy almost the entire region of Eastern Europe, from the Baltic and the Elbe in the west and north to the Adriatic and the Black Sea in the south and eastward to Kiev and Novgorod. They may conveniently be divided into the Baltic, or West, Slavs, who include the Letts, Lithuanians and Prussians, and the True Slavs, who include the Russians, Czechs, Poles, Wends, Slovaks and Serbians. Both of these divisions belong to the one linguistic family and have a very close affinity with the earliest of the Aryan-speaking stock. Yet with all that they have in common there are many differences observable and special care is necessary to distinguish between Baltic Slavs and South Slavs.

Given the comparatively recent date at which all the Slavic tribes separated from the parent stem and the comparatively limited range of their migrations since, it would appear on the surface that the task of ascertaining and describing their primitive religion should be an easy one, especially since these tribes were the longest to remain pagan of all European peoples. In the south it is true that the conversion of the Slavs commenced as early as the sixth century, but the South Slavs generally were not evangelized till the end of the ninth century, the Russians not till the end of the tenth, and some of the tribes along the Baltic not till a still later date. Unfortunately, however, we have little in the way of available tradition and although Christian writers were not always averse to giving us certain information of an historical character they seem to have been deliberately unenlightening with respect to the paganism they sought to eradicate. A considerable body of information has, of course, survived through the medium of folk-lore and language, and archæological research has revealed something more. Yet in general we must with some humility admit that our success in unveiling the past of Slavonic religion has not been conspicuous.

The main difficulties in the way are, naturally, precisely those we encountered in dealing with the religion of the Kelts and the Teutons. On the one hand it is exceedingly difficult to separate what is natively Slavic from what has entered into Slavic beliefs and customs from contact with the Teutons, contact which was at once intimate and long continued. And, on the other hand, it is particularly hard to penetrate beneath the veneering of Christian tradition to the genuinely old conceptions which Christianity was supposed to displace. It is plain that in a considerable number of instances old Slavic divinities have been transformed into Christian saints or the histories of Christian saints have been read back into the legends of pagan deities. As an illustration, we have the popular confusion of the thunder-god, Perun, with Elijah (St. Ilya) who called down fire from heaven upon his foes. A still more complete confusion has been made between the god Svantovit, a deity of the Elbe Slavs, and St. Vitus. There was also the general disposition to identify the god Volos with St. Blasius. Even the keeping of the midsummer festival of Ivan Kupalo, among the Letts, shows an inextricable jumble of ideas about St. John the Baptist and pagan fertility gods. The Virgin Mary herself is in many places confused with the pagan figure of "the Mother of Cattle."

Probably we get nearest to the primitive Slavic religion when we go back beyond the names of the greater gods to the recognition of nature spirits and the spirits of the dead, as in the other systems we have considered. Among all the Slavic tribes the most generally accepted belief is that in the tutelary spirit known as *dedŭ*, or grandfather, *deduĭka domovoy*, " grandfather house-lord," and other names of like import. He is conceived of as an old man with bushy hair and body covered with fur, a mere thumbkin in size, whose proper place was behind the oven or under it. When the family moves its members are supposed to take the *domovoy* with them. In certain districts the *dedŭ* is a hobgoblin much like the Teutonic *schrat*, and by the Slovaks and others called by that name. Elsewhere he is a kind of house serpent or *genius loci*, a kind of luck-guarder. But almost everywhere the *dedŭ* has a malicious and demoniac side and may be exceedingly troublesome or even dangerous to unwary sleepers.

There were hosts of other spirits. Some were known as Vili, or Wili (cf. *peri*, *fairy*), spirits of the dead and yet doomed themselves to death should they lose a single hair. The Rusalken also were spirits of the dead and potentially hostile. Souls of unbaptized infants were called Navky, Navy, Mavky, Navji, etc. They were liable to entice the wanderers on moonlight nights and bring about their death by drowning, leading them astray into deep waters. If anyone heard them singing it was the part of wisdom to exclaim: " I baptize thee in the name of the Father and of the Son and of the Holy Ghost," in which case the spirits would turn into the Rusalky, or water-nymphs. It might seem that this baptizing for the dead was scarcely worth the trouble, since the water-nymphs played upon travellers much the same tricks themselves. Besides these, the Russians had sylvan spirits called Lešiy, whom one encountering could only escape by turning his clothes inside out and putting the left-hand shoe on the right-hand foot. There were also wild women and (more rarely) wild men, field-spirits, and a special kind of water-spirit known as Vodyanik, to whom a horse smeared with honey was sacrificed. There were, once again, gnomes known as Barz-dukai, or bearded men, living under the earth and generally benevolent. The Fates were much worshipped under such various names as Rožanice, in Russia, Narŭčnici (destinies) in Bulgaria, and in the north Udělnicy, or " dispensers " (of fate). They were supposed, like the Norns, to spin, measure out, and cut off the thread of life.

Beyond these very vaguely personalized beings, the ancient Slavs worshipped the Sun, reverenced by the use of the endearing diminutive *sulniče*, the Moon, believed to be the residence of the spirits of the dead, and likewise worshipped with a term of endearment, " dear moon," and the stars, which were closely linked with the destinies of individual men. Fire was also held in great reverence and was deified as Ugnis, or Ogni. The gods, properly so called, are not very well defined, and even of those we know most about the functions are by no means clear. The word for the gods is *bogŭ*, from the Iranian *baga*, and the Sanskrit *bhaga* (from the root *bhaj*, to shine). The discarding of the old pagan deities has given us our word *bogy*, with such derivatives as *bug* and *humbug*.

The best known of the gods to us is Perun, or Perkunas, though the latest authorities do not regard him as so important as did earlier writers. He does not seem to have been worshipped by Baltic and Southern Slavs alike, though it is reported that the ancient Prussians prayed during a thunderstorm, O Perkunas, pass us by. The name Perun, doubtfully equated with the Vedic Parjanya, the rain-cloud, signifies "the beater," or " the striker." He was evidently a thunder-god or a lightning-god, worshipped especially in ancient times in the neighbourhood of Kiev and Novgorod. Some recent authorities regard him as having been borrowed from the conception of the Teutonic Thor. It will be remembered that Vladimir celebrated his baptism into the Christian faith by having the image of Perun dragged ignominiously, attached to a horse's tail, to the river. Yet in certain districts sacrifices were offered to Perun as late as the seventeenth century.

Other gods mentioned here and there include Veyopatis (cf. the Vedic Vayu-pati), lord of the wind, turned into a " mother-god " by the Letts, who entitle her Veya-mate; Svarog (cf. the Skt., *svarga*, heaven), probably a sky-god or a fire-god (Hephaistos), and Svarožič (son of Svarog), one of the common terms of endearment; Svantovit, identified with St. Vitus, a chief god of the Elbe Slavs who sacrificed to him a white horse and derived omens from the sacrifice; Veles, or Volos, a god of flocks, identified with

St. Blasius, who was a shepherd and a martyr of Cæsarea in Cappadocia; the Lithuanian Sauli-le, or *Little Sun*, probably the Vedic Surya, to whom the peasants at the solstice cried, *Ligo, ligo, O sun!* (Swing, swing, O sun), with waving torches—a piece of imitative magic similar to the swing-ceremonies of other lands; another solar god, worshipped by the pagan Russians, Dažbog, "the giving god"; Stribog, a god of another sort, lord of frost and cold; the three-headed god, Triglav, perhaps only a local form, in Stettin, of Svantovit, worshipped with the dedication of a black horse and used for divination; and Černobog, the Black God, personification of the forces of evil and perhaps influenced by Christian ideas. A more obviously imported divinity is the Trojan, who is really a reminiscence of the Emperor Trajan, conqueror of the Dacians in A.D. 101–2, and to whom divine honours were paid.

Temples for worship were not common and the idols in most places, as in Russia, were placed in the open air, preferably on the slope of hills. The sacrifices, which were of animals, grains and food, were generally offered by the princes and householders. Only among the Elbe Slavs was there a highly developed priesthood. Divination was in common use, by all the usual methods, including a special kind of fortune-telling by means of cakes.

The chief feasts were the quarterly *dziadys*, which corresponded approximately with the equinoxes and the solstices. These festivals were both a commemoration of the ancestors and connected, through imitative magic, with the agricultural processes of the year. The Whitsuntide festivities, known as Rusalye (cf. the Greek *rousalia*), are probably of foreign origin. At this feast a doll, called the Rusalka, is thrown into the water and ceremonially drowned, as an offering to the spirits of the dead. In some particulars the ceremony reminds us of the familiar pre-Paschal rite of "driving out the death."

Everywhere among the Slavs the belief existed in the soul, its power and its survival after death. In leaving the body it might take form as a bird, bat, or butterfly. The desertion of the body might take place at any time, as, for instance, through thirst. At death its escape was aided by the opening of a door or window, for the soul that was thwarted in its desires might prove troublesome to the survivors. The souls of sorcerers could not leave in the ordinary way, so that a board in the roof was generally loosened for their accommodation. Most souls hovered around the familiar neighbourhood for forty days and then departed for the woods, or waters, or clouds. The common desire was to get rid of them as speedily as possible, or at any rate to restrain them from haunting the old home. For this reason the souls of suicides were supposed to be hindered from return by a stake driven through the breast of the deserted body. There was a widespread belief in metempsychosis, and even in the ability of souls to take animal form as wer-wolves, though horses, cows and other animals might be similarly possessed. Some people were specially predisposed to this habit of shape-shifting, and in Lithuania the child born with teeth was regarded as almost a predestined wer-wolf. It was also believed that a person over whom fell an unclean shadow, or one upon whom a cat or dog jumped, was a potential vampire, whose body would not corrupt in the grave, because sustained by the power of the spirit to suck the life from other beings.

Burial and cremation were both used for the disposal of the dead and sacrifices of slaves and women were often made at the funeral ceremony. The world of the dead was not clearly envisaged, but by many Veles or Volos (cf. O.N., *valr*), whose image, like that of Perun, the converted Vladimir ordered to be thrown into the river, was regarded as an actual god of the dead. Some customs concerning the dead remind us of Persian usage, such as the use of a dog to catch the expiring breath of the dying, and the provision of a ladder to enable the spirit to climb up from the confining grave. Other things, such as the ship-like form of the coffin, seem to suggest the influence of Scandinavia. Of the Slavic mythology, properly so called, it is difficult to write clearly. What Dr. Louis H. Gray writes of "the pitifully scant remnants of what must once have been a great mythology," in the case of the Baltic Slavs, applies very generally to the whole family. "Yet fragmentary as they are, they possess a distinctive value. They help to explain the migrations of important divisions of our own Indo-European race . . .; they cast light upon and are themselves illuminated by, the mythologies of far-off India and Iran; they reveal the wealth of poetic imagery and fantasy inherent in the more primitive strata of our race. . . . We may lament the paucity of the extant Baltic myths; yet let us not forget to be grateful and thankful that even a few have survived."[1]

[1] See the chapter on Baltic Mythology by Louis H. Gray in Jan Machal's *Slavic Mythology*, p. 330. The "Bibliography" at the end of Dr. Gray's volume is the best guide possible to the literature of the subject. See also the "Index" (*sub voce* Slavs) to the *Encyclopædia of Religion and Ethics*. Other useful references will be *The Slavs*, by G. F. Maclear in the series, *The Conversion of the West*; "Slavic Religion" by Karl H. Meyer, in Carl Clemen's *Religions of the World*; and chapter ix. in E. V. Hopkins' *History of Religions*.

# BOOK III

## THE STATE RELIGIONS OF ANTIQUITY

### *Introduction*

IN the following chapters we pass from the religion of the primitive peoples to the more highly organized faiths of the world's first great Empires, excepting only the religions of the Orient, which we shall have occasion to deal with in a separate section.

Religion and government were always closely associated, even in the tribal stage. It was inevitable that the authority of rulership should find its sanctions in the will of the gods and in their power to enforce that will in the obligations of society. As, moreover, society advanced from the tribal towards the national and thence towards the imperial, it was certain that these sanctions would be pressed more and more insistently and that the form of government itself would be reflected in new conceptions of the divine order and of the character of the gods themselves. The closer a secular government approximated to the idea of a true empire, the nearer men must come to the conception of God as one and supreme. The very conception of a universe, as distinguished from a multiverse, or from the thought of the world as chaos, must arise from experience of a rule in which all differences of race and language and nationality were obliterated under the comprehensive and unchallenged authority of a single ruler. And, as a natural consequence of this expanded conception of God, must arise new ideas as to the largeness of human society, as something inclusive and catholic, and new ideas as to the range and significance of human life.

In this section we shall treat of six of these more or less systematized forms of state religion, as follows:

1. The religion of the *Euphrates Valley*, from the days

of the Sumerian city states, on through the period of Babylonian, Kassite, and Assyrian dominion, and down to the fall of the neo-Babylonian dynasty in 539 B.C.

2. The religion of *Egypt*, from the beginning of the dynastic history down to the time when the Nile Valley came completely under the rule of the foreigner.

3. The religion of the *Persians*, from the founding of the Achæmenian Empire by Cyrus down to the fall of the Sasanids about A.D. 641.

4. The religion of the *Greek* communities, from the first establishment of the Greek states till their absorption into the Roman Empire.

5. The religion of *Rome*, from the beginning of the Roman kingdom down to the conversion of the Empire under Constantine.

To the above, for the sake of completeness, we shall add:

6. The state religions of the *Amerindian* empires, namely, those of the Aztecs in Mexico, the Mayas in Guatemala, and the Incas in Peru.

# CHAPTER XV

## *The Religion of the Euphrates Valley*

WE need not be greatly concerned as to the relative priority of the civilizations of the Euphrates Valley and Egypt. So rapidly is the scroll of history being unrolled backwards both in Mesopotamia and in the Nile Valley that any decision we might make on the question would be premature and open to speedy unsettlement. If Egypt to date seems to have yielded the more impressive evidence of the antiquity of civilization, it is only fair to remember that climatic conditions in the Nile Valley have been much more favourable for the preservation of this material than those of the Euphrates, and that the very materials on which the Sumerians inscribed their records were, under ordinary conditions, uncertain and perishable.

In any case, it is hardly likely that the civilization of these two districts was, in either instance, developed *in loco*, unless it be that the hottest climates in the world were in some past age within what we call "the zone of initiative." The whole history of the Euphrates Valley, at least, has shown a constant tendency to decline apart from continual infiltrations of a more vigorous stock from the colder north. These always found the more civilized people to the south an easy prey and their culture a desirable form of loot. Hence, apart altogether from archæological evidence, it is probable that a considerable part of the Sumerian civilization was developed somewhere in Central Asia, before the increasing aridity of that territory forced its occupants, to the loss of their "fighting edge," to find a line of least resistance in the direction of the tropical "pocket" to the south.

The matter is not irrelevant to our discussion of Euphrates Valley religion, since it is evident that long before the establishment of the Sumerian city states, the inhabitants of the valley enjoyed a considerable culture, including the art of writing in the cuneiform character and the religious ideas intermediate between those of a primitive religion and those of an organized state cult.

It may be well first of all to refer to some of these early beliefs and practices, especially as they seem to have remained more or less stable, however overlaid, in subsequent periods, and may be observed still cropping up through all the more advanced conceptions of religion which have been superimposed.

The general type was that of polydæmonism, with spirits, good and bad, but mostly bad, on every hand, to assist or thwart the desires of men. The evil spirits, who were often invoked by use of the symbolic number *seven*, were responsible for all sorts of disease and for death. To gain relief from them, either by the use of spells or by appeal to some power more divinely potent, it was necessary first to know the name of the assailant. The idea of the future life was not highly developed, but, as early as 3000 B.C., vases, arms and ornaments were laid with the corpse in the narrow trench which served as a grave. The funeral cist, which at first was of brick, was superseded later by the use of two large earthenware jars and the funeral furniture amplified to include knives, weights, beads and arrows. Food sacrifices were offered once a month. The underworld was envisaged as a vast, dark grave, " the house of darkness," where the profoundest gloom reigned and the dead, " clad like birds in a garment of feathers, had dust for food and mud for drink."

The worship of the earliest times consisted largely in the use of sorcery and apotropaic magic. The exorcism texts which have come down to us from the earliest times afford an interesting study. An example is the Sumerian " locust charm " (one of the oldest pieces of writing in the world) which records the expulsion of locusts and caterpillars from a certain piece of land by the breaking of a jar, the muttering of a curse, and the cutting open of a sacrifice. The fee for this particular operation was " one tall palm-tree." Of omens we have copious examples in the tablets preserved in the British Museum.[1] In the matter of divination there is ancient evidence of the use of hepatoscopy, or divination by means of the liver of a sheep —the liver being (as earlier noted) a seat of the soul and revealing clearly the attitude of the god towards the proffered sacrifice; of lecanomancy, or the telling of fortunes by the dropping of oil into a vessel of water; and of oneiromancy, the ascertaining of the will of the gods by dreams. Astrology, also, was in common use and star-gods must have been recognized from very early times, as is clear from the use of the star as an ideogram. Imitative magic was general and there can be little doubt that the observance of the seasonal feasts, for the purpose of promoting the processes of nature, goes back to the remotest periods. Sacrifices, both bloody and unbloody, were general, the former using as victims bullocks, sheep, goats, fish and several kinds of birds, and the latter using bread, fruit, wine and milk. We see also the beginning of such institutions as that of the sabbath, the earliest *shabitum* being a tabu day, at the full of the moon, when men ceased work for superstitious reasons. There can be but small doubt that religion of the usual sort was never displaced by subsequent developments, and that, moreover, it produced a number of pseudo-sciences which long dominated the Mesopotamian civilization.

To approach nearer to the religion of the region which we may properly designate as a state cult it is necessary to remind ourselves that from very early times people of different racial origin occupied the lower part of the valley of the Euphrates and Tigris, which were at this time streams pursuing their separate ways to the Persian Gulf. In the most southerly part were the Sumerians, a people of Turanian stock, occupying such cities as Ur, Eridu, Uruk, Nippur and Lagash, while further to the north were the Semites, the so-called Akkadians, whose chief cities were Babel, Sippar, Kish, Kutha and Akkad (or Agade). The government was that of independent city-states—independent, but frequently at war with one another, though

[1] See the British Museum *Guide to the Babylonian and Assyrian Antiquities*, 77 ff.

enjoying a common culture. This generalization will hold, even though as early as 2700 B.C. Lugalzaggisi of Uruk did succeed in uniting under one sway some of the smaller city states. The government was so closely connected with religion that each city had a territorial god who was the invisible ruler and a visible priest-king, or *patesi*, who was believed to be the son of the invisible god and of the priestess who occupied the upper storey of the temple tower, or zikkurat. The city-god was known to the Sumerians as En, and in the Semitic tongue as Bel (*lord*) or Melek (*king*) of the city-state, though he had different names in the different cities, as En-lil in Nippur, Marduk at Babylon, Shamash at Larsa, and so on. The god had his female consort, so that for every En there was a Nin and for every Bel a Belit. The goddess was sometimes personified by the high priestess who was regarded as "the Bride of God," symbol of a humanity in fellowship with the invisible.

The city-god—or earth-god—is generally found associated with two other high gods to form a divine triad. The most ancient triad seems to have been that of Anu, Enlil (the city-god of Nippur), and Ea. Anu was the supreme sky-god, worshipped especially at Uruk, and associated with a female counterpart, Antu. He reigned at the pole-star where the universe was at eternal equipoise and around him circled the stars, the homes of the lesser gods. Ea was the god of the watery waste, revered particularly at Eridu, which long maintained its reputation for magic, since Ea was the lord of wisdom, the knower of all the spells.

As time went on, this triad, formed doubtless by the association of father, mother and child in the human family, was supplemented by others. One important triad was that of Sin, Shamash and Ishtar. Sin was the moon-god, who with his wife Ningal represents one of the oldest of the Mesopotamian cults. Shamash, the sun-god, is represented as the son of Sin, and was regarded as the god of justice, the supreme judge of heaven. Ishtar, in her earliest form, was probably a fertility goddess, through whom the earth renewed itself periodically, but later became identified with the planet Venus. Sometimes, in this triad, Ishtar is replaced by Ramman (or Adad), the Babylonian thunder-god, the Rimmon of 2 Kings 5. 18.

Other deities of the Sumero-Semitic mythology which may here be mentioned include Marduk, the city-god of Babylon, who, on that city becoming the capital of an empire, displaced his father Ea as a supreme divinity, becoming conqueror of chaos and creator of heaven and earth; Nabu, the city-god of Borsippa, who became the god of oracles, patron of writing and science; Ninib (as to the pronunciation of whose name we are uncertain), a war-god, who—as well as his wife Gula—is accepted also as a divinity of healing, a kind of Babylonian Æsculapius; and Nergal, the old Sumerian god of the underworld, appealed to by the necromancers. We may mention also Tammuz, or Damuzi, the Sumero-Babylonian vegetation god (corresponding with Osiris, Adonis, Balder, etc.), who died annually to be lamented by the women (cf. Ez. viii. 14) and was resuscitated by the power of Ishtar. It should also be mentioned that many divinities are associated together under the name of Igigi and Annunaki, the former name referring to the star-gods above the horizon and the latter to those below. It must, of course, be remembered that many of the old Sumerian gods, even such as Tammuz, may have been euhemerized human beings as well as personifications of the powers of Nature.

The temples of the region and time with which we are dealing were many and some of them were magnificent. We are fortunate in being able to supplement the extensive information derived from archæological exploration with such accounts as are given in the famous *Cylinders of Gudea*, the priest-king of Lagash about 2500 B.C. The description of the dream through which Gudea was led to build the great temple to Ningirsu, with the details respecting the construction and the dedication remind us of many subsequent instances of temple-building, from the building of Solomon's temple at Jerusalem to that of Westminster Abbey by Edward the Confessor.[1]

The temple area consisted of a large rectangle, in which

[1] See L. W. King, *A History of Sumer and Akkad*, London, 1910.

at a point opposite to the entrance, was a curiously small sanctuary, before which was probably placed the altar for the sacrifices. Closely associated with the sanctuary was reared the characteristic feature of the Sumerian temple, the artificial mountain, or zikkurat, a towering structure of brick, generally of seven storeys, to represent the planetary spheres, and coloured variously with glazes of blue, red and black. We are reminded of "the City of God" in the New Testament Apocalypse (xxi. 14) and its twelve "foundations" or courses of different colours and all manner of precious stones. Like "the Bride City" the zikkurat was designed to be the meeting-place of the divinity with the priestess, his spouse. No other was privileged to pass the night in the sacred abode.

The priesthoods in ancient Babylonia must have been exceedingly powerful. At the head of them was the king himself (like Melchizedek, the king-priest of Gen. xiv. 18), proclaiming in his own person the divine right to rule. Like Solomon at Jerusalem, we find Gudea officiating at the dedication ceremonies of his temple to Ningirsu. Below the king were the three large classes of priests, magicians, soothsayers (an hereditary class) and musicians, or singers. Priestesses also were endowed with much influence, from the high-priestess who was the consort of the god down to the three classes of *hierodouloi*, or temple prostitutes. These were chosen by means of special omens. It will be remembered that the arts of reading and writing and the keeping up of the sciences (or pseudo-sciences) were almost entirely in the hands of the priesthoods.

Great developments in the religion of the Euphrates Valley came with the transformation of the Sumerian city-states into an empire. One of the many ways in which Mesopotamia contrasts with Egypt is in the comparative immunity enjoyed by the latter country from invasion by a foreign foe. In the Euphrates Valley invasions were of regular occurrence. One of the earliest of these was that of Sargon of Agade, who about 2800 B.C., or according to Nabonidus a thousand years earlier, attempted to make a Semitic state in which the Sumerian cities should be parts of a federated system. His efforts, however, and those of his successor Naramsin, seem to have had but a brief success, and it was not till the time of the great Hammurabi, about 2100 B.C., that the Semite attained the consummation of his plan to consolidate the various elements of the Empire, with Babylon as the capital.

The result of Hammurabi's victory over his neighbours was of extraordinary significance from several points of view. The world's first real imperialism had been created, something different in kind as well as in degree from anything hitherto attained in Egypt or in China. It was something more than the achievement of a political confederation, for the federation now had a capital, and a real master at its head. The consequences were politically, culturally, commercially and religiously of vast and enduring importance.

To confine ourselves to the religious aspects of the transition from the Sumerian to the Babylonian system, we may note first the theological developments. As there was a head to the Empire so that must now be a head to the pantheon. It was no longer satisfactory for each city to have its own gods, even though these could be readily equated with those of other cities. The god of the capital must be supreme, even as Babylon had become supreme over her former rivals. Thus Marduk entered upon his reign as victor over the ancient chaos and the creator of heaven and earth, with his father Ea, of Eridu, and his son Nabu, of Borsippa, placed in their proper relation to one another. All the gods, moreover, who had lost prestige with the declining power of their old shrines, might now be admitted as members of an organized hierarchy of gods. The systematization of the divine hierarchy is manifested in all sorts of ways, including the ticketing of the several deities with numbers, so that the designation of the moon-god, Sin, became 30, and that of Shamash, the sun-god, 20.

Coincidently with the reorganization of the gods arose the reorganization of the traditional mythology, in order to ensure the awarding of the proper dignity of Marduk. It is probably from this time that we get some degree of cohesion in the stories which make up the substance of the *Gilgamesh Epic* and other like sagas. At any rate it is in the atmosphere of Babylonia that we contemplate them more intelligently than of yore.

There is, first of all, the Creation story, which begins with telling of the primeval father, Apsu and Tiamât, the personification of the watery chaos, which dwellers at the head of the Persian Gulf saw as the primal source of the land's life and of the civilization which had arisen upon it. Together with their son, Mummu, these deities reigned alone, and then sprang from them the gods. When Apsu died Tiamât was remarried to Kingu, who receives from his wife the tablets of destiny. So arose the war of the gods, with uncertain result, till Marduk proclaimed to the assembled deities his willingness to fight Tiamât. The story goes on to describe the arming of the divine hero and his eventual combat and the victory over Kingu and his evil allies. Splitting open the body of the monster Tiamât (cf. the *t'hom*, or *abyss*, of Gen. i. 2), Marduk fashions from one part the heavens and from the other the earth, following up the first creative act with the creation of the various forms of life, with man as the crowning result. It is interesting to compare the old Babylonian myth with the spiritualized Hebrew version of Gen. i. 1–2, 4, in which the fight between Marduk and Tiamât is softened to "moving," that is, "stirring" (not without struggle) of the Divine Spirit over *T'hom*.

One of the greatest pieces of Babylonian literature, the *Gilgamesh Epic*, has more than one aspect of religious interest. We may pass over the story of the friendship of Gilgamesh, a hero two-thirds divine and one-third human, and Engidu, the story of the war with Khumbaba, and other exploits. More interesting to us is the story of the fashioning of Engidu by Aruru and of the passion of the goddess Ishtar for Gilgamesh. We get interesting flashes of older story in the description of the death of Tammuz and of the descent of Ishtar herself into the underworld. There is poetic beauty in the goddess' demand for admission by the doorkeeper and of her stripping herself garment by garment at the seven gates of hell. We are reminded of the story of Balder when we hear of the cessation of love on earth till the deity is restored to the upper air. Then we have the strange story of Engidu's sickness and death, and the passing of our hero through the portals of the western mountains that he may himself recover the means of revival for his friend. The passing across the western sea is graphically and grimly told, as is the meeting with the immortalized ancestor, Ut-napishtim, the hero of the Babylonian Flood story. There is much pathos in the account given of the discovery of the plant of life, by which old men become young, and of the snatching from him of the plant by a serpent just when he is about to return. Gilgamesh came back after a futile pilgrimage to the world below and the poem ends, unsatisfactorily enough, with the hero's resort to Nergal, the god of the dead, for the purpose of gaining at least one glimpse of the dead Engidu. It is a sad picture we get at the last of the condition of the dead, with the one moral drawn as to the importance of attending to the burial rites of those who pass hence from our sight. Yet beyond the sadness we have, for the first time in literature, the revelation of that Promethean spirit which persists in demanding the fulfilment of a spiritual vision.

As for the *Flood* story, it is natural to make a comparison between it and the Hebrew accounts in the two separate documents of Genesis. We note such likenesses as the building of the ark, the gathering together of the seeds of life, the landing upon the mountain, and the sacrifice. We note such differences as the briefer time assigned to the flood in the Babylonian story and the addition of the swallow to the raven and the dove sent out from the ship. But beyond this, we note the distinctly purposeless nature of the catastrophe in the older narrative as against the moral atmosphere prominent in *Genesis*, as well as the polytheism which gives us a picture of distracted deities howling like dogs to their kennel or crying aloud like a woman in travail. The spirituality of the Genesis account, while not complete, shows great advance on the attitude of the old Babylonian poet.[1]

Some other pieces of Babylonian literature should be mentioned for their religious significance. For example, the fragment of Adapa myth (by some supposed to show

[1] See Sir J. G. Frazer, *Folk-lore in the O.T.*, London, 1901, I. 104 ff.

affinity with the Genesis story of Adam[1]) seems intended to explain why man did not become immortal like the gods. Called upon to explain damage inflicted upon the west wind, Adapa, warned by his father Ea, mistakenly declined the food and drink of life offered by Anu. In the story of Etana, again, we find the hero mounting to heaven on the eagle to obtain the plant of life, and when almost on the verge of success, falling back, out of misgiving and fear, earthwards. In all these myths we have flashes of insight which betray the germs of a higher religion awaiting the proper season to exhibit their maturity.

The creation of the Babylonian empire gave not merely a systematized theology and a systematized mythology but also a systematized ethics. It is probable, of course, that the famous *Code of Hammurabi*, set up in the market-place of Babylon, reflects in many respects the custom laws of earlier times, and even the existence of older Codes, such as that of Urkagina. But, in formulating, promulgating and enforcing uniform regulations which operated even in the case of agents travelling in distant lands, a notable service was rendered by Hammurabi to the cause of world ethics.

There is no need to claim for the Code virtues which were beyond the possibilities of the place and period. There were many inequalities due to the division of men into the three classes of nobles, freemen and serfs. There were many barbarities tolerated due to inadequate conception of the aim of punishment and to rigid application of the *lex talionis*. Death was inflicted for many offences, including the casting of spells upon others, the sheltering of runaway slaves, the pursuit of brigandage, defaulting from military service, selling drink at a tavern for too high a price, and so on. Slavery had its own inevitable injustices, including the ear-marking of a slave who accepted a lifelong servitude. There was no such thing as international morality, but, on the other hand, there was a place for woman in the business world and proper protection for her

[1] The *m* of Adam is, as a labial, etymologically equivalent to the *p* of Adapa. For the story see A. T. Clay, *A Hebrew Deluge Story in Cuneiform* New Haven, 1922, 39 ff.

rights. There were many laws—some of them excellent—dealing with property and the cultivation of land, inheritance, divorce, wages, the carrying on of agencies, and the like. While there was little of the transcendental about these laws, and little even of the specifically religious, it was clearly indicated that all law was divinely derived, transmitted by Shamash, the god of justice, to the king.[1]

We may infer even more than what is suggested above from literature outside the *Code*. We have, for instance, proverbs which reflect ethical ideals, as follows:

> Upon a glad heart oil is poured out of which no one knows.
> When thou seest the gains of the fear of God, exalt God and bless the king.

Or such a passage as this from *A Moralist's Counsel:*

> Thou shalt not slander—speak what is pure?
> Thou shalt not speak evil—speak kindly!
>
> . . . . .
>
> Daily approach thy God,
> With offering and prayer as an excellent incense![2]
> Before thy God come with a pure heart,
> For that is proper toward the deity!

Or, yet once again, the following *Interrogative Code*, from an old ritual:

> Has he estranged father from son?
> Has he estranged son from father?
>
> . . . . .
>
> Has he not released a prisoner, has he not loosened the bound one?
> Has he not permitted the prisoner to see the light?
>
> . . . . .
>
> Has he for "No" said "Yes," for "Yes" said "No"?
> Has he used false weights?
>
> . . . . .
>
> Was his mouth frank, but his heart false?
> Was it "Yes" with his mouth, but "No" with his heart?

This, together with the testimony of the Babylonian *Psalms of Penitence*, affords evidence that Babylonian ethics were by no means low. The sense of sin was definitely present and prayers for forgiveness often reached a high standard of spirituality.

[1] See R. F. Harper, *The Code of Hammurabi*, Chicago, 1904.
[2] Cf. Ps. cxli. 2.

Meanwhile the Babylonians were losing vigour, as the Sumerians had done before them, and new peoples were triumphantly moving to the south. These invaders had no native culture of any importance, but they had ability to appreciate and absorb that of the peoples they conquered. Hence, while the population of the Euphrates Valley suffered change, there was no interference with the prevalent civilization or religion. The conquerors represented three stocks, Kassite, Hittite and Assyrian, but although Kassite influence lasted five centuries and the Hittite intermingled with the Assyrian, it was through the last-named empire that the downfall of the Babylonian state came about. The Assyrian, of mixed Semitic and Hittite origin, appears on the horizon of history as early as 2400 B.C., entrenched in the mountain region to the north-east of the Tigris, and occupying cities among which Ashur, Nineveh and Calah are the best-known capitals. It was not till about eleven centuries B.C. that, under Tiglath-Pileser I., the conquest of the territory to the south was achieved, and not till 689 that Babylon was destroyed—though presently to be rebuilt. Nevertheless, for five hundred years "the throned tigers" of Assyria occupied a position which made them the terror of the contiguous states, so that no event in ancient history was hailed with such pæans of exultation[1] as the end of "the bloody city," when Nineveh at last fell beneath the combined attack of the Medes and the rebel governor of Babylonia, Nabopolasar, in 606 B.C.

Religiously, Assyria introduced a few new gods, especially Ashur, originally the city-god of the Assyrian capital, but now elevated to the place occupied by Marduk in the Babylonian sagas. Adad, the storm-god, the equivalent of Ramman, also comes to the front, and the war-god whom we know as Ninib won likewise a prominent place in the pantheon. Special honour, again, was given to Anu, Sin, Shamash and Ishtar, the latter in her character as a war-goddess. Gods were freely equated with one another, as, for example: "Sin is Marduk as giver of light in the night"; "Shamash is Marduk in the sphere of the law";

[1] Cf. the "taunt-songs" of the prophet Nahum.

"Adad is Marduk with reference to rain"; etc. Under the Assyrian, too, the gods were depicted in colossal animal forms, hewn out of the rock which now took the place of the clay employed by the earlier civilization. The main differences between the expression of Assyrian religion and that of Babylonian was the fiercer and more ruthless spirit of the northerners, their preoccupation with war, and the horrible nature of the punishments they inflicted upon their foes. Yet towards the end the spirit of the southern culture seemed to be winning its way, and in the work of Ashur-bani-pal there is evidence of a milder attitude as well as of greater appreciation of the religious literature of the past. But to the end Assyrian religion was strongly nationalistic and the gods of Assyria were foes to the divinities of other lands. We have only to recall, by way of illustration, the taunt of Rabshakeh before Jerusalem: "Where are the gods of Hena, of Ivah, and of Sepharvaim?"[1]

The recovery of the south, under what is called the neo-Babylonian empire, 606–539, was a revival of the old Babylonian temple worship as well as a revival of the older nationalism. That it was a time of great splendour we may learn even from the literature which mocked it, as in Isaiah xl.–lxvi. The very names of the kings, moreover, Nabopolasar, Nebuchadrezzar, Nabonidus, reveal a return to influence of the old god of prophecy, of the stylus, of scholarship. Nebuchadrezzar was the builder of splendid palaces and of splendid temples, and that he followed the old religious customs is shown from many references in the Old Testament.[2] As to Nabonidus, the last of the line, his zeal for religious organization and for recovery of the monuments of the past made him an antiquary as well as a restorer of the older cult. He tried to restore the supremacy of Marduk, but the lesser shrines resented the endeavour, and the royal zeal produced discord rather than unity. It was at this time too late to achieve a renaissance of permanent value, but it may at least be said that the last

[1] 2 Kings xviii. 34.
[2] Cf. Ezekiel xxi. 21; see also the novel by G. R. Tabouis, *Nebuchadnezzar*, English edition, New York, 1931.

rulers of Babylonia did their best for Marduk's honour and for the ancient order generally.

In a general survey of the beliefs and practices of the Euphrates Valley religion we come across many things which belong to "the beggarly elements" of religion. "The crude procedures of savage sorceries" were indeed so deeply rooted that many of them still persist, in the form of a kind of black magic, to the present day. We find also expressions of pessimism cropping up from time to time, as in the complaint of the so-called "Babylonian Job," with its hopeless outlook upon life during his period of trouble.[1]

Yet, on the other hand, there were, from the earliest Sumerian ages, germs of vital religious truth which it became the special mission of Judaism in later days to accept, preserve and develop, in order that they might be part of man's ultimate faith. Some of these elements we may here present:

1. The idea of creation as a struggle between the forces of light and darkness, with the victory resting ultimately on the side of the light. However physical may be the materials of this tremendous duel, dramatized from the observed conflict between sea and land at the head of the Persian Gulf, it is plain that the contest between Marduk and Tiamât furnished the Bible writers with the conception of the apocalyptic warfare between good and evil which had in the future such significant spiritual result.

2. In the Babylonian *zikkurat* worship, with its effort to reach the abode of the gods, by means of temple towers suggestive of the planetary spheres, there was symbolized, first, the possibility of God's descent to communion with mortal men, and, secondly, the possibility of man's ascent to fellowship with God. Crude as was the imagining which placed the dwelling-place of deity on a mountain height, or, in default of the mountain, at the top of a man-erected tower, it had in it the germ of all subsequent conceptions of the City of God, with its courses of vari-coloured gems, and its open gates, within which God might dwell and man live in God's presence. Whatever half-way errors the idea

[1] The "Babylonian Job" was the governor Tabi-utul-Enlil. The poem is given by Professor M. Jastrow, in his *Civilization of Babylonia and Assyria*.

contained such as we associate with the Gnostic theory of emanations, æons, and the like, it was an idea most precious and suggestive for the future of religion.

3. In that topmost chamber where the high-priestess resided, regarded by all as the spouse of God, we find the first intuition of man as to the relation between the divine and the human, described in the New Testament as the marriage of the Lamb. It is a picture of redeemed society, in which "the King woos His glorious Queen." It is, moreover, a picture of the human heart prepared to be the dwelling-place of "the high and lofty One that inhabiteth eternity," the Bridechamber of the soul:

> The hold that falls not when the town is got,
> The heart's heart, whose immured plot
> Hath keys yourself keep not. . . .
> Its keys are at the cincture hung of God;
> Its gates are trepidant to His nod;
> By Him its floors are trod. [1]

4. In the divine rulership through the *patesi*, or priest-king, represented as the Divine Son, we have the earliest germ of the Messianic doctrine. Without human father or mother, "a priest for ever," the patesi is the Shepherd. He is, almost in the language of Isaiah (ix. 6), "exalted king, chief counsellor, the subduer, princely leader, great lord."

5. In the quest, already commenced, for immortality we have an element of religion which leads straight on to the ultimate satisfaction of that quest in the Christian religion. The words of Sabitu to Gilgamesh:

> When the gods created mankind
> They fixed death for mankind.
> Life they retained in their own hands.
> O Gilgamesh, let thy belly be filled,
> Day and night be merry, daily arrange a merry-making;
> Day and night be joyous and contented;
> Let thy garments be pure, thy head be washed;
> Wash thyself with water;
> Regard the little one who takes hold of thy hand;
> Enjoy the wife lying in thy bosom.

[1] Francis Thompson, *The Fallen Yew.*

are as little final to the hero of the Babylonian epic as are the similar words of the Hebrew sage to the Jew (cf. Eccles. ix. 7–9). The mention of the water of life, whereby Ishtar is restored by Namtu, the very failure of Gilgamesh to retain the plant of immortality, or to raise up more than the ghost of Engidu, represent the seriousness of this age-long quest. Moreover, the seasonal myth, in the story of Tammuz and Ishtar, made nature a partner with man in the demand for faith in the more abundant life beyond the changes and chances of mortality. And the bitter regrets of Adapa at his failure to receive the proffered "bread of life" and "drink of life" at the hand of the gods serves to emphasize still further this mighty truth.

6. The laws of Hammurabi, resting as they do on codes and customs long anterior even to the first Babylonian dynasty, must be regarded as part of that revelation of law which we rightly call divine, a revelation given from Shamash as well as from Yahweh, and in both cases preparatory to a higher law written not on "tables of stone" but on "the fleshy tables of the heart."

7. Lastly, the moral and spiritual aspiration, expressing itself in prayer and in hymns of penitence, or in such phrases as the already quoted:

> Daily approach thy God,
> With offering and prayer as an excellent incense;
> Before thy God come with a pure heart,

show men as already on the rungs of that ladder of sunbeams which "slopes through darkness up to God."

Babylon and all its secular splendours passed away, or remain humbled in the dust, but the "word" which belongs to the religion of the future was destined to survive, never to pass "till all be fulfilled."[1]

[1] For the subject of this chapter the reader may consult, in addition to the books referred to above, the following: *The Cambridge Ancient History*, Vols. I., II. and III.; R. Campbell Thompson, *The Epic of Gilgamesh*, London, 1928; M. Jastrow, *Hebrew and Babylonian Traditions*, New York, 1914; L. Delaporte, *Mesopotamia*, New York, 1925; R. W. Rogers, *History of Babylonia and Assyria*, sixth edition, London, 1915.

## CHAPTER XVI

# *The Religion of Egypt*

TO have a fair idea of Egypt geographically it is only necessary to think of a rope some six or seven hundred miles long, tied into a knot here and there to represent the cataracts, and with the northern end frayed out to show the Delta. This rope will suggest both the river Nile and the country which is little more than the strip of mud formed by the sediment of the river gradually spreading out fanwise towards the Mediterranean.[1] Herodotus was correct in describing Egypt as " the gift of the Nile." In Homer the word *Aiguptos* (Egypt) is actually used of the river, but the true derivation of the word is from *Het-ka-Ptah*, " the temple of the *ka* of Ptah," a term originally applicable to the city of Memphis. In the Old Testament Egypt is generally spoken of as *Mizraim*, " the two Musri," a reminiscence of the period of the Double Kingdom. In the poetical books the phrase " *Land of Ham* " is frequently employed. Ham (derived from *Qem* or *Qemt*, *black*) is an old name for the land in allusion to the black soil of the river valley in contradistinction to the red sand of the desert. The word *Nile* is actually a Semitic word for river, or rather gully (*nahal*).

The Nile is one of the great rivers of the world in physical proportions, but it is still more important as the channel of Egyptian culture and religion. Laid down at the rate of about four inches a century, the sedimentary deposit brought down from Central Africa has made the present area of cultivable land and has indeed carried this area out into the Mediterranean far beyond the ancient limits. Three great branches, the White Nile, the Blue Nile and the Atbara, swell the main stream, and the only drawbacks to its importance are the six cataracts which obstruct navigation here and there. The real Egypt is

[1] But see Sanford and Arkell, *First Report of the Prehistoric Survey Expedition*, University of Chicago, 1928.

below the first cataract, a limit marked by the trading station of Assouan, the ancient Syene (*market*), which the Greeks called Elephantine, from the ivory offered here for sale. The Delta of the Nile, marking the opposite limit, has an area of no less than 14,500 square miles.

As intimated in an earlier chapter, the Egyptian people are the result of much miscegenation. The general opinion is that the oldest stock is the Hamitic, or Punt, as represented by the modern Somalis. To this, in prehistoric times, came migrations of Semites from Arabia and Syria, and also a more or less constant infiltration of Berber (or Libyan) people, of Mediterranean origin, from the west. Allowance must be made also for the inevitable pressure from the south of the blacks of Nubia and Central Africa. Pictures on the old monuments show the ancient inhabitants of Egypt with their pointed beards, loin-cloths, and belts of skin, often with an animal's tail hanging down behind, a somewhat close resemblance to certain present-day inhabitants of Africa to the south.[1]

The Egyptian *language* belongs to the class known to philologists as proto-Semitic, that is, a tongue from which both the Egyptian and the Semitic languages have sprung, the various branches having separated before either the grammar or the vocabulary became established.[2] Later on, in the days of the Empire, many new Semitic words were introduced. In a written form the language crystallized very early, perhaps by 4000 B.C. The hieroglyphic script was at first purely pictorial, but later on was reduced to a kind of alphabet. It was lavishly used for inscriptions on tombs and temples, and so became standardized. A more cursive form of writing, comparable to our writing hand as distinguished from print, is known as hieratic and was used by the priests from the fourth and fifth Dynasties downward for the copying of literary compositions on papyrus. After the Ethiopian period a still more cursive form appeared to suit the needs of business, known to the Greeks as demotic. Still later the Greek script became

[1] For fuller accounts see Moret, *The Nile and Egyptian Civilization*, London, 1927; and S. A. B. Mercer, *Études sur les Origines de la Religion de l'Egypte*, London, 1929.

[2] See Édouard Naville, *L'Évolution de la Langue égyptienne*, Paris, 1920. But the classification is doubtful.

common, and the most modern of all, known (in the Church books) as Coptic, was one using the Greek letters eked out with seven characters from the demotic.[1]

To confine ourselves to the history of Egyptian *religion* (though the above-mentioned details are not impertinent in the case of a faith making such large use of written forms) we have first to ask as to the character of this religion in prehistoric times. As the first date in Egyptian history —that for the establishment of the calendar by the heliacal ascension of Sirius (Sothis)—is given as July 19, 4241 B.C.,[2] it will be seen that we have to go back some seven thousand years for such a period. Even then we do not find ourselves in an age of absolute barbarism. The dead were buried in the sand with a certain amount of funerary ritual, in a contracted position, with hips and knees bent, hands before the face, and face turned westward. Sometimes they were dismembered or decapitated, and the women seem to have had (either before or after death) the left arm broken.[3] A dab of red was frequently put on the forehead, apparently as a life-giver. With the dead were buried amulets of many sorts, slate palettes and paint for toilet purposes, ointments and jars containing the ashes of offerings made at the grave. We are evidently in the neolithic age and face to face with burial customs such as we find common with many other primitive peoples.

The earliest stage of Egyptian history, politically, is that of a small community state, known to the Greeks as a *nome*, a stage corresponding very well to the Euphrates Valley city-state. There were about forty of these nomes, strung out north and south along the Nile valley. The religion was of the same general character in all, except that local circumstances involved the use of different names for the divinity and divinity itself was identified with some different object, generally an animal. The animal worship of ancient Egypt, whether rising from fear, or affection, or belief in relationship with some particular animal as a totem, was practically universal. It is tempting to describe

[1] See *Guide to the Egyptian Collections* in the British Museum, London, 1909.

[2] The date is disputed by some, as by Arthur Weigall, *History of the Pharaohs*, I. 26 ff.

[3] This has been explained by some as the result of the wife's defence of her head from the blows of her husband's club. But burials were not always as described. See V. Gordon Childe, *The Most Ancient East*, London, 1928.

this as totemism, but at present it is wise to accept the statement of Dr. W. Max Müller to the effect that "the Egyptians in historic times were not conscious of a totemistic explanation" of their animal symbols.[1] On the other hand it may be said that the older view that the animal gods of Egypt were adopted as symbols of divine attributes in a system of much profundity is now generally discarded. Manetho (third century B.C.) says that animal worship was introduced by the second king of the second Dynasty, but it is evident that the practice goes back much beyond any date we may assign to the beginning of dynastic history. It is, indeed, quite possible that the animals were originally personal totems which in course of time were promoted to the rôle of community gods. The districts in which particular animals were reverenced will often furnish a clue to the reason for the reverence. The bull Apis, of Memphis, was worshipped as "the second life of Ptah" the creator, but other similar communities had their bull-gods, such as the Mnevis of Heliopolis and the Bekh of Hermonthis. At Dendereh was the cow-goddess, Hathor, equated with the sky. At Mendes, in the Delta, was Ba, the ram-god, later a deity of reproduction. At Bubastis the favourite divinity was the cat-god, Bast, or Pasht,[2] earlier, perhaps, that much more formidable feline, the lion. At Abydos, ages before the development of Osiris worship, the jackal, Anubis, was worshipped as a god of the dead, possibly from its habit of prowling around the graves. In the south were animal gods such as Sebek, or Sobk, the crocodile, at Crocodilopolis, killed at Elephantine but worshipped at Thebes, and (according to Strabo) actually bred in the temple tanks; the baboon, later identified with the moon-god, Thoth, and esteemed as a god of wisdom; and the hippopotamus, Taurt, with the hippopotamus goddesses, Rert, Apit, and Shepuit. Then again there was the mongoose, or ichneumon, Khatru, or Shedeti ("the one from the city of Shedit"), worshipped especially at Heracleoppolis. Among birds were worshipped the phoenix,

[1] See W. Max Müller, *Egyptian Mythology*, Boston, 1918.

[2] See M. Oldfield Howey, *The Cat in the Mysteries of Religion and Magic*, p. 66.

or bennu bird; the vulture, Nerau; the hawk, Horus, later identified as the sun; the ibis, also worshipped as Thoth, the scribe of the gods; the goose; and the swallow. The cobra was reverenced among reptiles; and among insects the scorpion, the scarab beetle, the grasshopper and the praying-mantis. Even fish were included among the deities, especially those which were supposed to predict the rising of the Nile. Nor among the animal gods must we omit the name of Set, later identified with the principle of evil. With what particular animal he was originally associated is doubtful, as it was to the Egyptians themselves. Okapi, jerboa, greyhound, oryx, giraffe and ant-eater have all been suggested, and it is not impossible that he was identified with the pig, the totem of some primitive tribe which warred against the Horus or hawk people.

It may be assumed that even in the time of the monarchy there was coincidently with the worship of animal gods the worship of the powers of nature, and that these forms of worship were readily equated, even if as yet there were no systematized theology. No doubt, with the moon serving as chronometer, as among primitive people everywhere, that luminary had a very early place in the respect of the race, even before the identification of the moon, as measurer, with Thoth, the scribe of the gods. But in a land like Egypt sun worship was inevitable from the first. Many local names were employed for the sun, and there were many things with which the orb of day might be equated. In the eastern Delta the oldest sun-god was probably Atum, of Heliopolis; in Memphis appears Ra, who, after the fifth dynasty, became supreme and superseded Atum. Nevertheless, Ra, who had risen so triumphantly over the dark ocean of Nu, in time grew old and feeble, with his bones turned to silver and his flesh to gold. He spent half his days in the world of the dead and was presently forced by magic to yield up his secret name to his daughter Isis. In the twelfth dynasty Ra is displaced by Amen, a local sun-god of Karnak, who becomes the supreme god with the ascendancy of Thebes. Other solar gods were popular in particular communities or in a diffused way for certain periods. Horus, the hawk, was a sun-god in the early dynasties; less popular but still widely recognized, was the scarab-god, Khepra; both the lion-headed goddess Tefnet and the cat-headed deity of Bubastis were regarded as daughters of the sun; and even Hathor, the celestial cow depicted with the sun between her horns, and the goddess Isis had their solar aspects. About 2000 B.C. almost every deity was in some way identified with the sun and it was usual to speak of Ra as having his fourteen "doubles." With the great religious revolution of Ikhnatun towards the close of the eighteenth Dynasty Atun, the god of the solar disc (or rather ray), was proclaimed as the one god, the source of all life. In addition to the identification of the sun with some humanized deity or an animal, there were, again, frequent representations of the sun in the form of an eye or a boat.

Other early nature-gods include Nu, the god of the primeval, watery waste; Shu, the air-god, with Tefnet, the rain-goddess, as his wife; Qeb, the earth-god, with Nut, the sky-goddess, represented both as woman and cow; Min, a kind of primitive father-god, and Hathor, the primitive mother; and the Nile god, Hapi, represented in various guises. Among nature-gods are also to be reckoned the creator-gods such as Ptah, the fashioner, and Khnum, the first creator's assistant. Thoth, who produced the world by the word of his mouth, is also, from one point of view, a nature-god, as are the stellar-gods and the gods of the wind. Outside of both these and the animal-gods are certain deities of an abstract character, such as the gods and goddesses of birth, fertility, harvest and justice. Possibly, too, in this last category we may include the name of Menthu, an ancient and celebrated god of war.

Foreign gods begin to appear about the time of the Hyksos invasion, and particularly after 1600 B.C. From Africa to the south came such deities as the grotesque Bes, Dedur, Anqet, and Sati; and from Asia (especially by way of the Hittites and peoples of the Euphrates Valley) the Baals and Ashtaroth, Reshpu, the lightning god, and Sutekh. It is even possible that Ikhnatun's Atun himself was an importation from Syria (cf. the Hebrew *Adon*).

Fabulous beings of various sorts, typhons, chimæras,

sphinxes, may for the present conclude our list of Egyptian deities. The systematization of these various elements of religion, distributed among the nomes, begins with the formation of the Double Kingdom, before the thirty-seventh century B.C. This consisted of Upper Egypt, represented by its symbol of papyrus, and with white as its distinctive colour, and Lower Egypt, with its symbol of the lotus and its colour red. No doubt the war between the Set worshippers of the south and the Horus worshippers of the north, ending in the victory of Horus and the branding of Set as the principle of evil, has some relation to this period. The first two dynasties of Egyptian history ruled from Abydos, but in 3407 B.C. Menes united the kingdoms, accepted the double crown, and made Memphis the capital. The inevitable result was a development of religion corresponding to the transformation of the land from a duarchy to a monarchy.

Now for the first time we have a more or less consistent cosmogony. We have, for instance, the fashioning of the earth by Ptah out of clay, with the assistance of Khnum, after the word of creation has been uttered by Thoth. Also we have the conception of the sky (Nut) as being originally associated closely with the earth (Qeb), but raised to the form of a vault—represented both as cow and woman—by the air-god Shu. The mythology includes also the attempt of Ra to destroy mankind, through the agency of the goddess Sekhmet, and, on the repentance of the sun-god, the brewing of beer from the dada fruit to make a sleeping-draught for the irate goddess. The aging of Ra and the plot of Isis to rob him of his secret name have already been mentioned. The cosmogony of Egypt of this time also includes that weird conception of the underworld, the Duat, a region haunted by unimaginable terrors, guarded by bars and doors, defended also by demons such as *Flame-hugger*, *Shadow-eater*, *Bone-breaker* and *Eyes of flame*, a region where souls were tormented by fire-spouting dragons, demons with sharp knives and claws, and monstrous monkeys catching souls in phantom nets. Yet through this world passed the sun, even Ra himself, during the hours of night.

The theology of Egypt now began to systematize itself

in a series of triads and enneads. The complete ennead (or *Great Ennead*) was as follows, starting with Atum or Ra, the sole self-originated god, and giving us, first, Shu, the air-god, and Tefnet, the rain-goddess, from whom were born Qeb, the earth, and Nut, the sky. From these again were born the two pairs of brother-husbands and wife-sisters, Osiris and Isis, Set and Nephthys. The ennead may be diagrammatically set forth as follows:

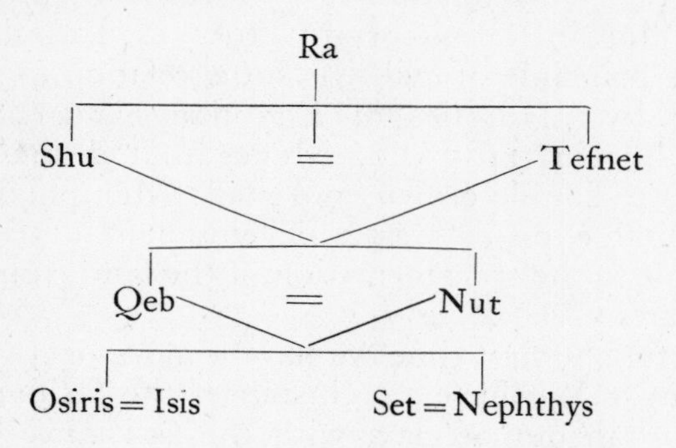


The Osiris cycle was possibly at first the local cult of Abydos, where Osiris, Isis and Horus, father, mother and child, formed a triad of their own. Later a special myth arose connecting the births of Osiris, Isis, Horus, Set and Nephthys with the five epagomenal days at the end of the year, since Ra had sworn a mighty oath to Nut that none of her children should be born on any day of the true year. It is evident from this myth (as from others) that there were two deities of the name of Horus, one the brother and the other the son of Osiris.

The Osiris cycle is also responsible for the story which is one of the most striking of all the seasonal myths and may at the same time have some historical nucleus back in the days when the Set tribes and the Horus tribes contended for supremacy. Osiris was the victim of a plot concocted by his brother Set and untimely slain. But Isis, sister wife of the dead king, discovered the coffin at Byblos and hid it. Not long after came Set and by the light of the moon perceived the painted chest. He tore it in pieces and scattered the members of the embalmed body over the land of Egypt. Great was the grief of Isis when she learned of the outrage, but she searched patiently from place to place till the dismembered body was recovered and the funeral rites were duly performed. From this time Osiris, displacing the older god Anubis, reigned as king of the dead, " first of the westerners." The story of the death of Osiris and the tears of Isis is annually dramatized to symbolize the restoration of the earth's fruition through the divine power of the spring. The whole tale is beautifully told in Plutarch's *De Iside et Osiride*, but we must remember that by the time of the Greek writer the story had lost much of its first simplicity. The myth itself, however, had very practical consequences, for, as Frazer reminds us, the Egyptians believed " that every man would live eternally in the other world if only his surviving friends did for his body what the gods had done for the body of Osiris. Hence the ceremonies observed by the Egyptians over the human dead were an exact copy of those performed over the dead god."

The mention of Osiris brings us at once to the fascinating subject of Egyptian views as to the world of the dead, and to that of Egyptian eschatology generally. But first a few words should be said as to Egyptian theories of psychology. According to some these were simply " savage" in no respect more advanced than those of some Central African tribes; according to others they were elaborate and complex beyond those of any other people. Certainly the terms used for various aspects of personality are unusually numerous, but our difficulty in defining these clearly and unmistakably may just as well be the result of confusion in the mind of the early Egyptian as of our own ignorance. In the beginning it is probable there was nothing more complicated than the ordinary primitive distinction between body and spirit. In the fifth dynasty we find the statement: " The soul belongeth to heaven and the body to earth." A dynasty later it is said to King Pepi: " Thy essence belongeth to heaven and thy body belongeth to earth." Later still we find as many as nine different terms employed to distinguish the elements of human personality, as follows: *Khat*, the body, which by mummification must be made to retain its form and identity; *Sahu*, the glorified body; *Ka*, the genius, or double, the actual individuality, which must be sustained after death by offerings of meat and drink, and which, if deprived of these, is apt to become malicious and dangerous, "like a wild fowl";[1] *Ab*, the heart, or seat of life, comprising also, apparently, the will and intent—it was very necessary to preserve the heart (possessed of both a material and a spiritual character), lest it be stolen through the use of magical arts; *Sekhem*, or vital power, something closely associated with the ka; *Ba*, the soul, an element also associated (in a manner difficult to understand) with the *ka*; *Khu*, best translated as spirit, but hard to define; *Khaibit*, the shadow, regarded (as also in the case of the Greek *skia* and the Latin *umbra*) as possessing independent existence; Ran, the name, always supposed to carry with it some connotation of personality. The preservation of personality was of the greatest concern to the Egyptians; hence their constant preoccupation with death. But though they unceasingly echoed the thought of Sophocles that "our last, our longest home is with the dead," yet they were thinking less of death than of continued life. The Egyptian would have agreed:

> 'Tis life of which our nerves are scant;
> 'Tis life, not death, for which we pant,
> More life, and fuller, that we want.

Kings, at any rate, could not endure the thought of mortality. Hence the pathetic (if amusing) bluff of King Unis, of the fifth dynasty, when (in the *Pyramid Texts*) he tries to persuade the gods that he is a terrible fellow who eats big gods for his morning meal, middle-sized gods for his dinner, and little ones every night, while the older (and presumably tougher) divinities serve as fuel to keep his kettles boiling—all this to compel the yielding of entrance to that sky-world on which his heart is set. In the time of King Unis it is asserted again and again: "The King has not died the death; he has become one who rises from the horizon."

But if kings and the great ones of earth were bent on reaching the stars, commoner folk had to be content with

[1] In view of the various views advanced on the subject, this description of the *Ka* may be received with caution.

the belief that their souls, or some part of them, hovered about the tomb and the cemetery. Here provision was made to feed the hungry ghost, and vast legacies of bread and beer were left, with dire threats against marauders who might misappropriate the offering. Some had the idea of an underworld more spacious than the grave, and allusion has been made to the fields of the dead where the *ushabti*, or "answerers," toiled for their masters. Some again thought of the underworld as a pleasant land where milk was given from the breasts of goddesses, where grapes and figs abounded, "bread from the divine granaries and fruit from the tree of life," amid cool breezes and rippling streams. The usual life above-ground was also reproduced, and groups of bakers, butchers and brewers deposited in the tombs were thought to work magically for the comfort of their dead lords. Meanwhile, if the proper charms were forthcoming, the soul might take shape as a bird or butterfly to revisit occasionally "the glimpses of the moon."

Some enlargement of the idea of the underworld as the grave is to be seen, again, in the conception of "going west." For many this was nothing but the last grim voyage across the Nile, in charge of the ferryman, Mr. Facing-backwards, to find rest in the sands of the western desert. For others it became the highly mythologized conception of joining the boat of the sun in its westward journey, and so on to the mysterious land of the caverns of the night. Here was the residence of Sokar, the abode of the serpent Apop, the burial mounds of Atum, Ra and Tefnet, and the realm of Osiris.

The world of Osiris furnishes us with the first moralization of the underworld in religious history. The dead have their hearts weighed against an image of truth; they run the gauntlet of the forty-two assessors; they make what is called "the negative confession"; they have their deeds transcribed by Thoth, the scribe of the gods; they stand before the judge, Osiris, who is clad in mummy clothes to show that he had died and was alive; they receive at last the verdict of justification, taking henceforth the name *Osiris N. or M. Justified*. The life of bliss envisaged beyond the judgement, however, seems to have been little more than the renewal of the normal activity of the agriculturist, with the element of sordid toil eliminated.

For this post-mortem experience great preparation was needful. First there was the preparation of the body, so that recognition was possible in the other world. In prehistoric times nothing more was deemed necessary but to lay the corpse in the sand to become desiccated by natural means. Later, various systems of mummification, differing in different localities, were devised, some of them of a very elaborate kind. The word *mummy* (Arabic, *mummia*, bitumen) merely implies the keeping of the body from decay by the use of spices, gums, natron or bitumen. But, according to Herodotus, three methods were employed. The most expensive involved the removal of the viscera through an incision in the abdomen and of the brain by means of a hook inserted through the nose, after which the cavities were filled with powdered cassia and myrrh, the openings sewed up and the body steeped for seventy days in a tank filled with a solution of salt or soda. Then the body was taken out, dried, anointed, and (with the application at each stage of the proper formulæ) swathed with layers of linen. Beyond this it was only necessary to paint the outer casing and inscribe on the covering the name of the deceased. A less expensive method removed the viscera by the use of oil of cedar, and the flesh was thereupon dissolved from the bones with a preparation of soda, leaving the body merely skin and bone. For the poor the body was merely steeped for seventy days in a preparation of soda and then handed over to the relatives for burial. The common people did not obtain the privilege of mummification proper till Saite times. In the case of the wealthy the viscera were embalmed separately and placed in what are known as Canopic jars, each jar dedicated to one of the four gods of the cardinal points. Many kinds of professionals were employed in the embalming process, including those known as the *paraschists*, or cutters, who were supposed to flee away after making the incision, ceremonially pursued, and the *taricheutes*, or swathers. In comparatively late times brightly painted cartonnage cases were used and in Greek times it was usual to paint the portrait of the deceased on the coffin. Embalming did not completely cease till several centuries after the beginning of the Christian era.[1]

Coincidently with the development of the process of embalming we note the evolution of the tomb, all the way from sand-burial to the building of the Great Pyramids. In all cases the idea was to protect the body from prowling jackals and marauding men as well as from loss of identity. To begin with, the body laid in the sand—the fertile land was too valuable for such a purpose—was covered with a simple slab and a hut erected close by to receive the offerings. Soon the slab became more massive, till we get the mastaba, or bench, type, concealing a chamber for the ka, a chamber for the mummy and the offerings, and a shaft or pit for the victims selected to accompany the deceased. In course of time we arrive at the "stepped pyramid" type, of which the best example is the tomb erected by King Zoser, of the third dynasty, a structure not unlike a six-staged zikkurat. After this it was but a matter of time to reach the true pyramid, of which we have the world-famous examples at Gizeh. These are the Pyramid of Khufu, of the fourth dynasty, a vast pile 451 feet high, containing 65,000,000 cubic feet of masonry; the Pyramid of Khufu's son, Khefre, only slightly less in height than the former; and that of Menkaure, only 210 feet high. It is a pathetic fact that in spite of all the efforts of the Pharaohs to make their last home inviolable, by the use of false doors and misleading passages, the ingenuity of the thieves, not to mention the archæological zeal of modern times, has in every case succeeded in breaking in on the diuternity of their mortal slumbers.[2]

It should be added that, beyond the provision made to satisfy the elemental necessities of food and drink, by the compilation of magical formulæ, there was also furnished a *Book of the Dead*, a *vade mecum* to meet every emergency, such as opening the mouth, breathing the air, remembering the name, keeping the heart, with spells for the overcoming

[1] See G. Elliot Smith and Warren R. Warner, *Egyptian Mummies*, New York, 1924.

[2] See G. Maspero, *Manual of Egyptian Archæology* (Revised Edition), New York, 1926.

of the ghostly crocodiles and snakes which might be lurking in unexpected places.[1]

In the observances of Egyptian religion the priesthoods naturally played an important part.[2] First, no doubt, they were but the humble guardians of the food offerings at the tombs, but in course of time they developed into imposing hierarchies which, as in the case of the priests of Ra at Memphis and those of Amen at Thebes, became extremely wealthy and powerful. They were divided into many classes, bore different names, and were obliged to observe special rules for ritual purity, being clean shaven, clad in white, or wearing ritual robes, as of leopard skin. The feeding, washing and dressing of the gods was their particular concern, as well as the pouring of libations and the reciting of the magic spells.

Side by side with the evolution of the priesthoods was that of the temples, from the crude huts of primitive times to the magnificent structures of the Empire period, with their splendid pylons, their avenues of sphinxes, their paved courts, and their *adyta*, or shrines, for the performance of the secret mysteries.

The festivals, too, were splendid and numerous, including the observance of the great calendric days, the feast of the New Year, and the observance of the five epagomenal days. The seasonal festivals laid special stress on the story of Osiris and the recovery of the earth's fertility through the divine agency of Isis.

While the priestly religion consisted largely in the performance of rites in the temples, from the breaking of the seals at dawn till the evening fell, the religion of the people generally was largely based on the use of magic. Magic indeed attracted the attention of all, high and low, from early times to the latest. From the *Tales of the Magicians*, as told by the sons of King Khufu, to the story of the *Magic Book of Thoth*, in the nineteenth dynasty, we find much preoccupation with magic, as we might gather from the references to Egyptian magic in the Bible.[3] Magic was worked in many ways, through the knowledge of

[1] See E. A. W. Budge, *The Book of the Dead,* London, 1910.
[2] This includes the part played by the Pharaoh as priest.
[3] See Exodus vii. 11 ; 2 Timothy iii. 8.

secret names, through the use of wands, or through the use of spells for the curing of disease. Spells, sometimes oral and sometimes accompanied by manual acts, or by the application of amulets, recited over herbs and mixtures, became the means by which the Egyptians groped their way towards the knowledge of drugs and medicine such as was later to benefit mankind. There were also what were called "magic shoutings" and one Hemi describes himself as "high-voiced in shouting the name of the king in the Day of Warding-off."

As to Egyptian ethics, though we know but little of the standards actually observed, we conclude that on the whole there was a clear insight into what was wrong and what was right. The old "ethical wills," such as the *Instructions of Ptah-hotep*, and *Kegemne*, and *Intef*, naturally bear on the surface indications of a prudential philosophy reminding us of Lord Chesterfield's *Letters* and the advice of *Polonius* to *Laertes*. But, though such maxims as: "Render homage to the great man"; "Fill not thy mouth at the house of thy neighbour"; "She (thy wife) will be attached to thee if her chain is pleasant"; trend in this direction, there is much of another sort. Counsels such as: "Make a lasting monument for thyself in the love of thee" touch a higher note. Moreover, while the items of the *Negative Confession* are negative, such an admission as: "I have not destroyed the joy of others" is more than conventional morality. The unit of society is plainly the family and the family finds its sanction in the relation of Osiris, Isis and Horus. The king is divine and despotic, and a large part of the population is in slavery, yet there is much sense of charity and justice and even Khufu is defended from the charge of harshness to his subjects in the building of the Great Pyramid.[1]

Speaking of the kings, it is interesting to watch the development of Pharaoh worship. Kings were also from the first priests, but in course of time they became more and more sacrosanct, and their holiness had to be guarded by the brother-sister marriages which are so curious a feature of ancient history. The idea that the Pharaohs

[1] See S. A. B. Mercer, *Journal of Oriental Research*, January 1926.

were children of the sun may have prevailed as early as the fifth dynasty, 2750 B.C., at Heliopolis, while the first use of the term "Son of Ra" occurs in connection with Isesi, 2645 B.C. Later it became a fixed dogma of Egyptian state religion.

In what has been said above we have in many particulars outrun the age of the Old Kingdom, but historical developments from that time on are easily summarized. A great shifting of Egypt's centre of gravity came at the end of the eleventh dynasty, about 2111 B.C., at which time it may be assumed that Abraham was deported, with other Semites, as described in the Book of Genesis.[1] The twelfth dynasty inaugurated a period of political change, in which negroes were confined to Nubia and the capital removed from Memphis to Thebes. The literature, however, shows at first a considerable atmosphere of pessimism, and poems like the *Song of the Harper* and the *Misanthropist* contrast strangely with earlier writing. Death is now, at least to some, not so much a step on to communion with the gods as a release from the wretchedness of living.

Then, about 1680 B.C., came the invasion of the Hyksos, with Egyptian ideals for a while submerged beneath those of the Semite. It was natural now that new gods should enter from Syria and elsewhere. But a century later the victory of Ahmes ended the eclipse of the Egyptian and launched the new dynasty on adventures in foreign lands which would have been incredible at an earlier period. The next centuries are the great days of the Empire, the days of the Amenhoteps and the Thothmes, of Queen Hatshepsut, and especially of Thothmes III., greatest of all the Pharaohs. During this period Palestine came under Egyptian sovereignty and Semitic influence once again flowed in apace.[2] Out of the spoils of war the priesthoods of Amen at Thebes accumulated untold wealth and possession of a large part of the lands of Egypt. Possibly it was this which led towards the religious revolution inaugurated by "the world's first idealist," Amenhotep IV., who called himself Ikhnatun, a movement, however, which lasted

[1] Genesis xiii. 1.
[2] See George Cormack, *Egypt in Asia*, London, 1908.

beyond the seventeen years of his reign, from 1375 B.C. to 1358 B.C. Young as he was, Ikhnatun, aided by his mother and his wife, who have been suspected of some foreign strain, made heroic efforts to supersede the religion of Ra and Amen with the worship of Atun, the god of the solar ray. It is disputed whether Atun worship was, strictly speaking, a monotheism or merely a form of henotheism, but as to the stupendous nature of Ikhnatun's effort there can be no question. Almost alone, he braved the arrogance and prestige of the official priesthoods, built his new city of Akhetatun, away from the influence of Thebes, moved thither the machinery of government, and endeavoured to turn the stream of Egyptian religion into new channels. The fact that Atun worship eventually failed and that the new capital was deserted less than sixty years after Ikhnatun's demise must not blind us to the significance of what was actually accomplished. The glorious hymn of Atun as the giver and sustainer of life, often compared with the Hebrew 104th Psalm, is enough in itself to show the height attained by the religious idealism of Ikhnatun. Take, for example, the paragraph:

> Creator of the germ and maker of the seed,
> Thou givest life to the son in the body of the mother,
> Soothing him that he may not weep,
> Nursing him in the womb,
> Giving breath to animate all.
> When in the shell the fledgling chirps in the egg,
> Thou givest him breath to preserve him alive,
> And when thou hast brought him to burst the shell,
> Then cometh he forth from the shell to chirp with all his might.
> Manifold are thy works, thou sole God, whose power none other possesseth.[1]

One may gather the nature of the change effected not only from the literature but also from the art of the period, since there is needed but a comparison with the art of pre-Ikhnatun times to show the sincerity and realism with which Nature is now portrayed as contrasted with the stiffness and conventionalism of earlier periods. One almost forgives Ikhnatun the fatuity of his foreign policy for the sake of those gleams of idealism which, amid the arid patches

[1] See J. H. Breasted, *History of Egypt*, pp. 371–75, New York, 1905. For later translations see Erman's *Egyptian Religion* (translated by Blackman), and Scharff, *Aegyptische Sonnenlieder*, Berlin, 1928.

of dynastic history, lighten the story of the Pharaohs at this point.

Alas, when Ikhnatun died, his reforms withered and perished. His sons-in-law, Senenkhere and Tutenkhamen, who succeeded him, were but poor creatures, and the superseded name of Amen returns to the annals of Egypt. The discovery of Tutenkhamen's tomb, on November 22, 1922, in the Valley of the Tombs of the Kings, serves mainly to reveal the extraordinary lavishness with which the royal sepulchres were furnished, with couches, portrait statues, crowns, maces, garlands, jewellery, ornaments, canes, bows and arrows, undergarments, and even the mummified game, meat and fowl, the hungry soul was supposed to crave.[1]

Under the New Empire of the nineteenth dynasty, in which Rameses II. is the most conspicuous figure, great wealth once again accrued to the official cult and the priesthood of Amen. We learn from the Harris Papyrus that 750,000 acres, or one-seventh of the area of Egypt, together with the service of 100,000 slaves, were the property of the Church. Rameses II. attributed his much-vaunted victory over the Hittites to the help of the gods and acknowledged especially his indebtedness to Menthu, the war-god. Egyptian gods even obtained reputation in lands beyond the border, as we learn from the curious story of the "possessed" princess who obtained from Rameses a loan of the Egyptian god Khonsu for the healing of her malady.[2]

But the days of decline were approaching. We need only read the adventures of Unamen to perceive that the old prestige of Egyptian religion, at any rate in Syria, is on the wane. The priest of Amen, seeking for timber for the repair of his shrine, is but shabbily treated at ports where once all would have bowed humbly as before their suzerain. Moreover, the taint of decay shows itself even in the domestic field. Animal worship is revived with more and more grossness and the discovery of the sacred Apis is surrounded with manifold superstitions. The more

[1] See S. A. B. Mercer, *Tutenkhamen and Egyptology*, London, 1923.

[2] The story is a pious forgery, but is paralleled by the actual borrowing of the Ishtar of Nineveh to cure the sickness of Amenhotep III.

barbarous elements of the old religion gain renewed popularity and the *Coffin Texts* become more and more a collection of meaningless *abracadabra*. Perhaps a notable exception may be made for certain remains which reveal the religion of the poor, in a spirit of self-abasing and sorrowful appeal reminiscent of some of the Hebrew *Psalms*. On the whole, however, the period of foreign conquest and political decadence is at the same time a period of religious decline. The feeble line of the twentieth dynasty Ramessids gave way to the twenty-first dynasty when a union of the priesthood of Amen with the Pharaonic line expressed some concern over the royal mummies. Then came the twenty-second dynasty, whose most notable monarch, Sheshonk (Shishak) married his daughter to King Solomon. The twenty-third dynasty is Ethiopian and reveals one interesting individual, Piankhi, whose concern over the horses is picturesquely expressed.[1] So we move on to the time of the Assyrian invasion, and thence to the Pharaoh Necho of the twenty-sixth dynasty, against whom Josiah made his fatal stand and fell at Megiddo.[2] After this the history of Egypt becomes a more or less continuous record of foreign invasion and conquest. Some of the invaders, like Cambyses, despised the Egyptian gods, and some, like Alexander, honoured them for political effect. But it is plain that many of the gods are being superseded by, or identified with, the deities of Greece, though at the very last Egypt had the ironic satisfaction of seeing some of her ancient divinities transplanted to Rome to allay the restless syncretism of the Imperial city.

In conclusion, we may ask what Egyptian religion contributed to the future, even if, as a national cult, its end was determined. First of all, there was a renewed expression of the quest for life. The Babylonian myth of Tammuz and Ishtar finds its parallel in the Egyptian story of Osiris and Isis. There is infinite pathos in the cry which forms the Easter anthem of the Nile Valley: "He wakes, Osiris wakes, the weary god awakes and stands; he controls his body again. Stand up, thou shalt not end, thou shalt not

[1] See E. A. W. Budge, *Annals of the Nubian Kings*, p. lxx., London, 1912.
[2] 2 Kings xxiii. 29.

perish." There was, again, that moralizing of the after life such as for the first time offers a vision of the final judgement. However much of magic might be associated, too, with the progress of the soul, the ethical values were by no means altogether obscured. And, once again, there is that new conception of God of which one catches glimpses in the religious revolution of Ikhnatun. It even seemed for a time as if the theology which had commenced with something closely resembling a primitive totemism was passing through the polytheistic stage towards a pure monotheism, such as the world had not hitherto seen. Lastly, it is not without significance that in the *Hymn to Atun* and the *Instructions of Amenemope* we find passages which are reflected in our own sacred literature, in the 104th Psalm and the *Book of Proverbs.*[1] It may even be true, as some have suggested, that old pictures of Isis and Horus afforded to Christian artists their conception of the Madonna and Child, that the doctrine of Thoth's creation of the world by his word had something to do with the development of the *Logos* idea, and that the asceticism of certain stages of Egyptian religion was in part responsible for the appearance of the eremites of the Thebaid.[2]

[1] The section of the Proverbs apparently borrowed from the *Instructions of Amenemope* is from xxii. 17 to xxiii. 11.

[2] In addition to books referred to above the reader is advised to consult the article in *E.R.E.*, Volume V., on "Egyptian Religion," by W. Flinders Petrie; A. H. Gardiner's article, "Egypt, Religion," in the 11th edition of the *Enc. Brit.*; A. Erman and Rabke, *Aegypten und aegyptische Leben*, 1923; and J. H. Breasted's *Religion and Thought in Ancient Egypt*, 1912.

## CHAPTER XVII

## *The Religion of Ancient Persia*

THE story of the religion variously described as Magianism or, more correctly, Zoroastrianism begins with the separation of the eastward moving Aryans into the two branches distinguished as Indian and Iranian. That these two streams were originally one in their main religious characteristics is clear from the number of terms which are their common property and the number of beliefs and practices which were identical or similar. But that the separation which is an important incident in the Aryan story carried with it religious as well as economic disagreement is apparent from the diverse way in which the religious terms common to the undivided stock are later employed. On the economic side differences arose manifestly because the Iranians wanted to settle down to the cultivation of the soil, whereas those who had hitherto been their comrades on the march desired to drive their cattle yet further to the east. On the religious side the differences are still more significant. Two terms for the divine powers of Nature had hitherto been in general use, the one "*devas*," or "shining ones," the other "*asuras*" or "mighty ones." Whether some antagonism had developed between the *asura* worshippers and the *deva* worshippers prior to the separation of the Indo-Aryans and the Iranians we do not know, but with the separation it would appear that the *deva* worshippers became abhorrent to the ancestors of the Persians and the "*daevas*" (to use the Iranian form) synonymous with devils. Moreover, while the term *asura* (Iranian *ahura*) was preferred to the term *deva*, a reaction against polytheism led to the singling out of one *asura* for special worship. Henceforth Ahura-mazda, the Lord of Wisdom, became the God of Iran. This deity is probably to be identified with the ethical god of the Veda, Varuna, whose prestige declined in India to the same extent that it advanced in Persia. The other Vedic gods, for the most part, became demons, and Indra, Rudra, and the Açvins were numbered among the arch-demons. Some escaped this fate and became spiritual beings subordinate to Ahura-mazda. One of them, Mitra (Mithra), the sun in his friendly aspect, survived to play an important part in the last stages of the Zoroastrian religion.

Thus arose in Western Asia, at some period later than that of the Vedic penetration of India, the closest approximation to monotheism the world had hitherto seen, if we except Ikhnatun's brief experiment at the close of the Egyptian eighteenth dynasty. Herodotus, writing, of course, after the time of Zoroaster, describes the religion of the Persians as follows:

"It is not their custom to make and set up statues and temples and altars, but those who make such they deem foolish, as I suppose, because they never believed the gods, as do the Greeks, to be in the likeness of men; but they call the whole circle of heaven Zeus, and to him they offer sacrifice on the highest peaks of the mountains; they sacrifice also to the sun and moon and earth and fire and water and winds. These are the only gods to whom they have ever sacrificed from the beginning; they have learnt later to sacrifice to the 'heavenly' Aphrodite, from the Assyrians and Arabians. She is called by the Assyrians Mylitta, by the Arabians Ahlat, by the Persians Mithra." [1]

With the exception of the confusion in this last sentence of the old solar deity Mithra with the female deity of the waters, Anahita, there is nothing in the above account which forbids us to believe that the pre-Zoroastrian religion had already taken the step of isolating Ahura-mazda from the ruck of Aryan deities and had come fairly close to the conception of ethical monotheism.

The theology which eventually prevailed was no doubt gradually evolved. Behind all the divine beings there was conceived to exist that eternal order of things which the Persians called *arta*, as the Vedic Aryans called it *rita*.

[1] Herodotus, Book I. 131.

Then came the great figure of Ahura-mazda, the Greek Ormuzd, a personal god of the moral order, and a remarkable advance on Vedic theology. He is the god of light, wisdom, righteousness, the creator of heaven and earth. With him are associated the spiritual beings which were in part the survival of the gods of earlier days and in part the personifications of the divine attributes. As the Amesha-spentas, or Amshaspands, "the holy immortals," they are sometimes six and sometimes seven, thus corresponding with the seven Igigi of Babylonian mythology and the "seven spirits of God" in the Bible.[1] Three of these are represented as masculine and as standing at the right of the eternal throne, Vohumano, or Good-will, Asha-vahishta, or Best Truth, and Kshathra-vairya, or Desired Power. Three of them are feminine and are stationed at God's left, Spenta-armaiti, or Holy Piety, Haurvatat, or Holiness (Wholeness), and Ameritat, or Immortality. Between these two groups and opposite to the throne stands Sraosha, the angel of Faith, or Obedience. And beside these great archangels of the presence are other holy ones, the Yazatas, of whom the greatest were the divinities borrowed from the other Aryans, Mithra and Anahita.

But the monotheism of Zoroastrianism was not so absolute as to exclude expression of that cosmogonic struggle which was recognized as part of the moral and physical worlds alike. People living in a region which included such extremes as the winter of the Caucasus and the summer of the Persian Gulf were not likely to ignore the apparent dualism which Nature herself seemed to illustrate. So in the world of spirit, even though Ahura-mazda were deemed omnipotent, there was present everywhere the work and influence of a Counter-worker, a Lie-demon, whose effort was ever to frustrate the will of the God of truth. Of course, the term *dualism* may be very loosely applied, and it is fairly certain that in early times the Iranian used it of a moral struggle apparent in the individual life, as well as in the universe at large, rather than in the assertion of a philosophical antinomy. Moreover, where good was regarded as "the final goal of ill," it is hard to see that

[1] Cf. Tobit xii. 15; Rev. v. 6.

rigid division of the universe into two eternally warring spheres such as marked the later teaching of the Manichæan. But in many respects the language of the early Iranian scriptures is unguarded enough to excuse our use of the term as applied to Persian religion. God was matched all too evenly with Angra-mainyu (whom the Greeks called Ahriman), and his work parodied all too successfully the work of Ahura-mazda.[1] Angra-mainyu also had his angels, archangels of evil, multitudes of *druj* awaiting a chance to harm mankind, from "the dasyu-slaying Indra," thus transformed into a demon, to the 99,999 diseases which were all attributable to evil spirits. And besides the evil spirits who were definitely such there were mythical beings such as the Pairikas, or fairies, and the great serpent Azhi Dahaka, not to speak of the three-legged ass, Khara, or the demons of a later age like Aeshma-deva, the Asmodeus of the *Book of Tobit*.

As to religious practice, we may suppose that many things were carried over from the common usage of the undivided Aryan family. Certainly the fire-cult had a special place in the thoughts of man, and the brewing of the *Haoma*, corresponding to the Soma, or sacred drink, of the Vedic Aryans, preceded and outlasted the reforms of Zoroaster, who abhorred the practice.

Many elements may have been taken into the system of Iranian religion from that of the Euphrates Valley, as it existed prior to the Achaemenian conquest, but these may be the result of accommodations made after the time of Zoroaster, and will be mentioned later. It is sufficient at present to assume that the disposal of the body by exposure, the use of consanguineous marriages, and the larger place given to magic, may be due to Median influence rather than to anything present in the undivided stock. It is the predominance of this later element which is more properly described as Magianism.

At some period to which it is difficult to assign a date there entered on the scene one who, with all allowance made for the legendary, must be regarded as an heroic figure, a reformer of the first importance, a prophet and an

[1] Cf. Kipling's fragment, *The Seven Nights of Creation*.

organizer in one. This is Zarathushtra, whom the Greeks called Zoroaster, and the modern Persians Zardusht.[1]

Though some have thought Zoroaster an entirely legendary figure, and some have even thought the name a term signifying an hereditary priesthood, there can be little doubt as to his historicity. But it is another question when we try to fix a date or even a definite region for his birth. Xanthus, the Lydian, who wrote about 450 B.C., describes him as having lived six thousand years before the time of Xerxes and others have put the same gulf between the prophet and Plato, or even made his date six millennia prior to the Trojan war. Masudi, however, places Zoroaster 280 years before the time of Alexander, and the *Bundahish* diminishes this date only about twenty years, so that we may with some confidence, with the majority of modern scholars, put the birth of the great Iranian about 660 B.C. Yet, for linguistic reasons, there are not a few who would prefer an earlier date, say, about 1000 B.C. As for the place, some, with Jackson, hold that he was born in the district of Azerbaijan, between L. Urumiah and the Caspian; others see his birthplace further to the east, in Bactria. It may very well be that Zoroaster was a native of Media who migrated to Bactria and there won his first successes as a religious teacher. Some information we gather from the *Gathas* and from early tradition, as, for example that his father was Purushaspa (*Purusha*, a man, and *aspa*, a horse), of the Spitama, or "Whiting," family, and that his mother was Dughdhova. The name Zarathushtra is of uncertain meaning, but *ushtra*, a camel, like the name Purushaspa, betrays agricultural associations. Legend adds nothing as to the name, but surrounds the story of the birth with much miraculous detail. We are told of the bringing of the *fravashi*, or *genius*, of the future prophet, at his conception, by two angels who conveyed it in a stem of *haoma* plant and deposited it in a bird's nest, while his material part, also brought by angels, was placed in milk drunk by his parents. Pliny repeats the familiar story that the child laughed on

[1] See A. V. W. Jackson, *The Life of Zoroaster*, New York, 1899; also J. H. Moulton, *Early Zoroastrianism*, chap. iii., London, 1913.

being born, a legend supposedly alluded to by Vergil in the line: "Incipe, parve puer, risu cognoscere matrem."[1]

Very early in his career the predestined prophet was assailed by demons, particularly by Buiti (cf. the Skt., *bhūta*, a ghost). There were attempts to burn him, to strangle him, to have him trampled underfoot of oxen, to deliver him to the wolves. But from all perils he was providentially protected, became notable for his love of animals, passed through a five-year period of tutelage under a famous sage, and at twenty left his father's house, like Gautama, to deliver his soul. Other accounts speak of his marriage and the birth of three sons, who in time became heads respectively of the three Iranian orders of priests, warriors and herdsmen. He remained in the desert seven, or, according to Pliny, twenty years, having communings at intervals with Ahura-mazda. The supreme revelation came at the age of thirty—"the year of the revelation"—and in the next ten years he was vouchsafed seven other visions and underwent his "temptation," during which the demon Buiti, sent by Angra-mainyu, tested him to the uttermost. Connected with this time of preparation is the story referred to by Shelley, as the utterance of Earth in *Prometheus Unbound*:

> Ere Babylon was dust,
> The Magian Zoroaster, my dead child,
> Met his own image walking in the garden.
> That apparition, sole of men, he saw.

When Zoroaster commenced his preaching, he had at first as small success as, long centuries after, fell to the lot of Muhammad. His cousin, Metyomah, was his sole convert and the legendary visits to India and China were as scantily productive. The turning point came with the visit to Balkh in the twelfth year of the ministry, when the prophet came to the court of King Gushtasp, or Vishtasp (Hystaspes), whom some have tried to identify with the father of Darius I. Here his preaching was at first in vain and the plots of the Magian priests caused him to be cast into prison. But the miraculous cure of the famous Black Charger, whose legs by witchcraft had been drawn up into its belly, brought

[1] Vergil, *Eclogue*, III. 60.

about the conversion of the court and the slaying of the prophet's foes. The story is told, with much curious circumstantiality, in the *Dabistan*.[1]

With the patronage of Gushtasp, and the support of the brothers Jamasp and Frashaoshtra, whose daughter Hvovi Zoroaster married, the prophet's cause now flourished apace from Iran to Turan, and a Holy War was inaugurated in which the king's son, Isfendiyar, bore an heroic part. Missionaries, moreover, were despatched far and wide, and fire temples founded throughout Iran, some of which probably owed their fame to the naphtha wells which were here and there discoverable. The last twenty years, which correspond with the last decade of the life of Muhammad, were years of great success, politically and militarily as well as religiously. Then the prophet paid the penalty for his fame by a violent death at Balkh at the age of seventy-seven. Though the Greek accounts speak of Zoroaster as having been slain by lightning, the more normal story is that he was attacked and killed by a Turanian who forced his way into the fire temple, where the aged prophet was at the time officiating.[2]

By the Zoroastrians of later times Zarathushtra was regarded as the inaugurator of a new era in the history of mankind. According to this belief, world chronology was divided into four periods of three thousand years each. In the first period Ahura-mazda's word prevailed over the power of Angra-mainyu, and Yima (the Indian Yama), known also as Jamshid, ruled in the name of the Highest. Then came the age in which the Evil Will, represented in Azhi-Dahaka, the great serpent, the Zohak of the *Shah Nama*, appeared to triumph. The third period was one of struggle between the two powers of Light and Darkness, culminating in the appearance of Zarathushtra. Thus the Zoroastrian age inaugurates a struggle which must continue till the appearance of Saoshyant, the Messiah, when God becomes "all in all."

Towards the consummation of this desired ideal Zara-

[1] Shea and Troyer, *The Dabistan*, 116 ff., London, 1901.

[2] A good (imaginary) description of the prophet's death is given in F. Marion Crawford's novel, *Zoroaster*.

thushtra contributes in various ways. He is a practical monotheist, one of the earliest of apocalyptists, a great moral teacher, a fighter not beyond the use of magic and the arm of the flesh, strongly interested in the cultivation of the earth, a friend of the animals which are serviceable to man, particularly of the ox, the dog and the domestic fowl. He is also revealed as a great organizer and establisher of fire-temples, not quite strong enough to resist certain reversions to old practices, as in the case of the *haoma* drink, but nevertheless keeping the face of mankind towards the coming of the expected Messiah.

The teachings of Zoroaster are to be found in the *Avesta*, the discovery of which in modern times we owe to the zeal of the Frenchman, Anquetil Duperron, who, after seeing a fragment of Avestan writing in the Bodleian Library, went out to India in the latter part of the eighteenth century and brought back a translation which he deposited in the National Library at Paris. The story is familiar of the ridicule thrown upon the discovery by Sir William Jones and it was indeed a long time before scholarship condescended to become interested. Since the nineteenth century, however, great progress has been made in Avestan scholarship.[1]

The *Avesta*,[2] sometimes erroneously named the *Zend-Avesta* (a term really denoting the *Avesta* with its Pahlawi commentary), is now known only through the portions which survived Alexander's sack of Persepolis and were subsequently restored through the zeal of the Sasanid king, Shahpur I., in the first half of the third century A.D. Alexander is supposed to have destroyed the famous copy of the whole, written on prepared cow-skins, in letters of gold, and the part saved is regarded as but one-twentieth or less of the entire work. What we have is arranged under four heads: The *Yasna*, including the *Gâthas*, or songs, generally conceded to be contemporary with Zarathushtra himself, and full of signs of the conflict of the time; the *Yashts*, containing twenty-one hymns used on sacrificial occasions; the *Vendidad* ("anti-demonic"), consisting of

[1] See article "Avesta" in *E.R.E.*, II. 266 ff.
[2] Probably from the same root (*vid*, to know) as the word *Veda*.

twenty-two sections known as *fargards*; and certain fragments known as the *Khorda* (or Little) *Avesta*.

The *Gâthas*, as mentioned above, are full of evidences of an early date. They contain an account of Zarathushtra's marriage to the daughter of Frashaoshtra and of the marriage of the prophet's daughter, Puruçishta, to Jamasp. They describe also very vividly the appeal of the Ox-soul to Ahura-mazda, which is answered by the appointment of Zarathushtra as protector, though the Ox-soul at first demurs to having "the ineffectual word of an impotent man for my protector."

All the rest of the *Avesta* belongs to the period from about the fifth to the third century B.C. The most interesting portions are in the *Vendidad*, where, for example, we have, in *Fargard I.*, the creation of the sixteen good lands by Ahura-mazda, with an account of the marring of that work by Angra-mainyu, "who is all evil." In *Fargard II.* we have an account of the increase of the population of the world under Yima and its subsequent limitation by the coming of the great winter—a catastrophe corresponding with the Flood of the Euphrates Valley legend. *Fargard III.* contains the eulogy of the earth and of the work of the agriculturist. *Fargards IV.* to *XII.* deal with various forms of uncleanness and their purification, with advice as to the avoidance of the Druj Nasu, or corpse-demon. *XIII.* is the *Fargard* of the dog, the quaint survival of a much larger literature dealing with the sacredness of the dog. In *Fargard XVIII.* we have the praise of the cock, the bird of the angel Sraosha, "the drum of the world," and the special enemy of the sloth demon, whose significant name is "Going-to-be." And *Fargard XIX.* describes Zarathushtra's victory over the tempter by the recitation of the sacred formula, the *Ahunaver*—"the will of Ahura-mazda is the law of righteousness." We have also more than one reference to the famous Bridge of Decision, the Chinvad-bridge, across which the souls of men must pass to the final judgement.

How far the Achæmenians were in the strict sense of the word Zoroastrians is a matter of doubt. They do not seem to have known of Zarathushtra himself and there is ample testimony to the effect that Cyrus worshipped, or claimed to worship, the various deities of his subjects in the Euphrates Valley. But Darius Hystaspes mentions Ahura-mazda and seems to have been more nearly a Zoroastrian than his predecessors. Meanwhile, there had been interminglings with and accommodations to the older religions of the region. Artaxerxes Mnemon names both Mithra and Anahita, the goddess of the fructifying waters, side by side with Ahura-mazda. The practice of exposing the dead, moreover, does not seem to have become general, since the Achæmenian kings were buried, their bodies encased in wax.

From the time of the destruction of the "golden book" by "Iskander Rumi" to the time of the Sasanids Zoroastrianism was only followed in secret, as under both the Seleucids and the Arsacids (Parthians) the culture of Persia and much of its religion were Greek. Nevertheless, there must have been much latent devotion to the older cults, since it was precisely at this time, in the first century of Sasanid rule, that Mithra-worship became popular in the Roman Empire and attracted the attention of Emperors like Diocletian and Julian. By the Roman soldiers it was borne westward and Kipling has interpreted the devotion of the legionaries in the "*Song of Mithra*":

> Mithra, God of the midnight, here where the great bull dies,
> Look on thy children in darkness, oh, take our sacrifice!
> Many roads thou hast fashioned : all of them lead to the Light.
> Mithra, also a soldier, teach us to die aright ! [1]

From Shahpur I., A.D. 240, and on through the reign of Shahpur II., 310–380, there was great zeal for Zoroastrianism, and Khosru I. was called Nushirwan, the Just, because of his severity towards other religions. Much neo-Zoroastrian literature was produced, such as ultimately formed the *Bundahish*, or Book of Beginnings, and the *Book of Arda Viraf*. The former is a vast, rambling work descriptive of the creation of the world, and running on to its final destruction by fire, which to the good will appear to be only like warm milk. In this general conflagration

[1] In *Puck of Pook's Hill*.

"the stench and pollution which were in hell are burned, and hell becomes quite pure." The *Book of Arda Viraf* is important for its views on eschatology and its influence on Muhammad's Night Ride to Heaven, and (ultimately) on the *Divina Commedia* of Dante. To allay the doubts of a sceptical age, it is decided by the *dasturs* (an order of priests) to send one of their number, through the use of hashish, to the other world, that he may report on his return as to the realities of future reward and retribution. Arda Viraf, chosen by lot, makes the journey and awakes to tell of his journey across the Chinvad-bridge, guided by the angel Sraosha, and meeting at the bridge the personification of good thoughts, good words, good deeds. He followed the souls of the pious through the realms of bliss and describes the happiness of those in the star-track, the moon-track, the sun-track, and so on, the bliss of the liberal, of those who contracted next-of-kin marriages, of the warriors, the agriculturists, the shepherds, and all the rest. Then Arda Viraf had his experience of the Hell world and saw the dread river which, like Dante's Styx, was made of the tears of men, was met by the personification of ill thoughts, ill words, ill deeds, and witnessed the punishments of the damned. What the effect of Arda Viraf's revelation was upon his time we know not, but the stimulus was evidently needed to revive the faith of men.

Then, in the middle of the seventh century, came the overwhelming flood of Islam and from thenceforth Zoroastrianism was virtually extinguished on its native hearth. Many died as martyrs, a larger number conformed, a few succeeded in maintaining the faith under Muhammadan rule. Dr. A. V. W. Jackson, in *Persia, Past and Present*,[1] gives an interesting account of his visit to Yezd and his entertainment there by the Zoroastrian colony. He found in that city over 8000 of the faithful, heard the *Ahunaver* recited and the sacred texts read, witnessed the celebration of the fire-sacrifice, by priests who still wore the ancient veil, or *paitidana*, and used the *barsom*, and was presented with a branch of the sacred *haoma* plant, that earthly representative of the heavenly tree of immortality.

[1] Chapter XXIII.

Many Zoroastrians, naturally, fled from Persia before the invading Arab horde, and some reached China quite early in the seventh century, where they established the first fire-temple of the Middle Kingdom. Others fled to India, where, under the name of Parsis (Persians) they form, in the city of Bombay, a flourishing, wealthy, and enlightened community. As we learn from the *Kissah-i-Sanjan*, a Persian work of about A.D. 1600, the first colonies landed on the coast of Gujerat in the eighth century, subsequently settled in the city of Surat, where Duperron found them in the eighteenth century, and then, at the beginning of the nineteenth century, removed to Bombay, where to the number of over 80,000 they live at the present day. They are divided into the two classes of Athorvans, or fire-priests, and Behdins, or laymen, all alike known for their wealth, benevolence and interest in education. They still preserve most of the old Zoroastrian customs, especially those connected with birth, marriage, death and the disposal of the dead. The fire-temples, known as *dar-mihr*, or palaces of Mithra, are still kept open, and the *dakhma*, or tower of silence, is a grim reminder of the custom of exposing the dead. Parsis still observe the New Year festival, stress the virtues of good thoughts, good words, and good deeds, profess the old beliefs as to the resurrection and final retribution, though in truth many are agnostic or inclined to various forms of theosophy.

But it is now time to give a clearer, though condensed, account of the Zoroastrian religion, without overmuch reference to the various modifications and accommodations made from age to age. We have already noted the Iranian belief in the world as a battlefield between the forces of good and evil, set in array one against the other. Originally there was much to suggest a true dualism, and occasionally Ahura-mazda and Angra-mainyu are spoken of as brothers from one womb. But as time went on what at first was a kind of "bilateral symmetry" was envisaged as an ethical monotheism, in which the power of Ahura-mazda was expected to triumph through the appearance of Saoshyant, the Saviour. Meanwhile, it is every man's duty, to the full extent of his power, to help the good and hurt the evil.

Hence its frequent intolerance, as in the reign of Khosru Nushirwan.

Two expressions of faith may be quoted, one of them quite old, and one comparatively modern, to bring out the creed of the Zoroastrian as clearly as possible. The first is from the *Twelfth Yasna*:

"I repudiate the Daevas. I confess myself a worshipper of Mazda, a Zarathushtrian, as an enemy of the Daevas, a prophet of the Lord, praising and worshipping the Immortal Holy Ones (Amesha-spentas). To the Wise Lord I promise all good; to him, the good, the beneficent, righteous, glorious, venerable, I vow all the best; to him from whom is the cow, the law, the (celestial) luminaries, with whose (heavenly) luminaries blessedness is conjoined. I choose the holy, good Armaiti (Humble Devotion), she shall be mine. I abjure theft and cattle-stealing, plundering and devastating the villages of Mazda worshippers."

The second is the confession known as the *Patet Erani*, as follows:

"I believe in the good faith. I believe in the coming resurrection, in the later body, in the passage of the bridge of judgement, in a future recompense of good deeds, and in the punishment hereafter of evil deeds; in the perpetual state of Paradise for the good, and in the annihilation of hell, of the Evil One, and of all the evil demons. I believe that Ormuzd will at last be victorious and that Ahriman will perish, together with all the offshoots of darkness. All that I ought to have thought and have not thought, all that I ought to have said and have not said, all that I ought to have done and have not done, all that I ought to have commanded others to do and have not commanded, and all that I ought not to have thought and yet have thought, and all that I ought not to have said and yet have said, all that I ought not to have done and yet have done, all that I ought not to have commanded and yet have commanded,—for every thought, word and deed, whether of the body or of the spirit, whether of earth or of heaven, I pray for forgiveness and repent of every sin with this Patet."

The Zoroastrian conception of personality is scarcely

less complex than that of the Egyptian. A man consisted of his perishable body, his *ahu*, or vitality, his *daena*, or *ego* (thinking conscience), his *baoda*, or intelligence, his *urvan*, or soul, and his *fravashi*. This last term, of uncertain derivation, appears at first to have been applied to the ancestral spirit, or *manes*, and corresponds somewhat to the Indian idea of the *pitri*. But, later on, the word is used as more closely correspondent with the Egyptian *ka*, or the Roman *genius*, a kind of double, sometimes not unlike the Hebrew conception of the guardian angel.[1]

The public rites of the Zoroastrian religion preserve in some respects a continuity from the time of the undivided Indo-Iranian period, especially in such matters as the fire-cult and the use of the *haoma*, which latter Zoroaster was apparently, as we have seen, unable to suppress. The fire was always kept alive in the urn within the temple and five times a day the *mobed* entered, wearing on his face the *paitidana*, or sacred veil, to prevent the sacred element from being contaminated by his breath. He wore at his girdle the bunch of twigs, now represented by a bunch of wire, known as the *barsom*, or *baresma*, which is supposedly referred to in Ezekiel's charge against the Jews: "They put the branch to their nose."[2] Probably, however, the *barsom* was originally the litter on which the fire was laid, as in the case of the kusa-grass used in the Vedic sacrifices. On each visit to the shrine the priest laid a log of sandal-wood upon the fire, with the threefold formula: "Good thought, good word, good deed." He had also among his duties the daily recitation of the Avestan texts. The priest-hood was hereditary in certain families and the High Priest was known as the Magupat, or Head Magian. The *haoma*, like the Indian *soma*, was the sublimation of some early intoxicating drink, now conceived of as the sacramental expression of the drink of immortality, brewed from the "Tree of All Seeds," the Gaokerena, or Ox-horn, which as the "White haoma" was the heavenly counterpart of the "Yellow (or Green) haoma," obtainable on earth. In one of the *Hymns* the *haoma* is thus invoked: "I call down upon me thy intoxicating inspiration, O Golden One;

[1] Cf. Matthew xviii. 10; Acts xii. 15. [2] Ezekiel viii. 17.

send down power, victory, health, well-being, prosperity, increase, strength to fill my whole frame, knowledge of all things." Nowadays, the *haoma* is, in general, drunk only by the priest, who pours a portion into an adjacent well in order to assist the fruitfulness of nature. Beside the rites performed at the fire-temples, there are many of a domestic or personal character, such as the touching of a child's lips at birth with *haoma*, the awarding of the *kushti*, or girdle, to the boy of twelve, the celebration of marriage, the use of the *sagdid*, or " look of the dog " at the moment of death, and the performance of the funeral rites at the *dakhma*. There are also festivals to be observed, particularly that of the New Year (Nau-roz) and those of the equinoxes.

The eschatology of Zoroastrianism has already been alluded to in connection with the *Book of Arda Viraf*. It was the general belief that the soul survived and in a disembodied state, on the third day after death, met its good or bad thoughts, words and deeds, personified as beautiful maidens or horrible hags, at the head of the Chinvad Bridge, or Bridge of Decision. The bridge was supposed to be stretched from Mt. Daitya to Mt. Elburz, and is mentioned several times in the *Gâthas* and frequently in the later literature. It had a certain moral significance, since it was nine fathoms wide for the good and as fine as a hair for the ungodly. The Yazata, or Holy One, charged with the meting out of justice was Rashnu, associated with Mithra and Sraosha, but Zarathushtra himself also was held to be the guide of the faithful to the realm of bliss. The Paradise of Zarathushtra had its various felicities, starting with the limbo where dwelt those whose virtues exactly balanced their vices and going on thence to the heaven of the supremely obedient. Hell, the abode of the demons, was in the north, and here too there were different compartments for the avenging of different offences. The damned were crowded together in one indistinguishable mass, and yet each one wailed in the darkness, " I am alone." The rich who refused charity to the needy here suffered from hunger and thirst and the untruthful hung suspended, head downward, with twisted tongues. At the very vortex of hell, as with Dante, was the prince of evil,

Angra-mainyu, who continually mocked the damned by asking, "Why did you eat the bread of Ahura-mazda and yet do my work?" But apparently the punishments of hell were not everlasting, since hell itself, with all its pollutions, was destined for destruction by devouring fire, after which the world, purified and renovated, would become an immortal home for mankind.

As we have already seen, the ethics of Zoroastrianism had, to use the phrase of Dr. G. F. Moore, "a strenuous and militant quality." The Mazdean lived to help the good and hurt the evil to the full extent of his power. The greatest virtue of all was to tell the truth, as we see illustrated by the remark of Herodotus, the inscription of Darius at Behistun, and even in the well-known story of 1 Esdras, where the people affirmed the verdict of the young Jew Zerubbabel with the cry: "Great is the truth and it shall prevail!"[1] Next came the insistence on physical purity. "Next to life," ran the saying, "purity is man's greatest need." Hence we have laid down the multitudinous and meticulous rules as to avoiding impurity and as to purifications. The corpse-druj, or Druj-nasu, was particularly feared, visible often in the form of a carrion-fly, as might well be the case, and to be driven away by the glance of the demon-averting dog. Other demonifuges were the placing of a drop of *haoma* on the lips and the burning of fragrant woods. Constant emphasis was put on the threefold duty of *humata*, *hukhtva*, and *hvarshta* (good thoughts, good words, good deeds), and the avoiding of their opposites. Only a little behind the moral virtues were placed what we may call the economical virtues. Of these the care of the land was the chief. "Who makes glad the earth?" it is asked in the *Vendidad* (III., 23 ff.). "He who plants the most grain, grass, and fruit-trees, who brings water to a field where there is none, and draws it off where there is too much. . . . He who sows grain sows good; he makes the religion of Mazda progress." After this comes care of the useful animals, such as the cow and the dog, and correspondingly the destruction of pests and the reclamation of the waste. Some practices regarded as ethical are less

[1] 1 Esdras iv. 41.

in accord with western ideas, such as the permissible polygamy and concubinage and the custom of consanguineous marriages which was highly praised, and rewarded with celestial bliss.

In conclusion, something must be said as to the contributions made by Zoroastrianism to some of its rival religions and to world religion in general. That the religion of Persia influenced Buddhism in a certain degree has been generally believed. Mr. D. B. Spooner, in his papers on *The Zoroastrian Period in Indian History*,[1] doubtless went beyond the evidence furnished by his excavation of the old palace of Açoka at Patna. But the impression still remains that a good deal in the Buddhism of the Mauryan dynasty is best explained by the theory of Achæmenian contact. Of course, there may have been currents in the reverse direction, and the reference to "the heretic Gaotema" in the *Yashts* may imply that the Buddha's teaching was as obnoxious to the Persian monotheists as to the polytheists of India.

As to Judaism, the relation of that faith to Zoroastrianism has been alternately exaggerated and minimized. The fact that for two hundred years Judah and Jerusalem were under the Achæmenian Empire make the influence historically more than probable. It was an influence which was likely to work both ways. But in the development of Judaism it would certainly appear that the angelology and eschatology of post-captivity times were very essentially affected by Iranian ideas.[2] And these ideas passed on into the Christian era, influencing both Christians and pagans. On the one hand, we find the Roman soldiers, as already observed, extending the glory of the bull-slaying Mithra, and, on the other hand, we find Zoroastrian ideas expressing themselves in the heresies of Christendom, some of which we shall have later to discuss. Here we may just refer to Manichæanism as a particular example. Though embodying a starker form of dualism, such as goes back to an earlier period of Euphrates Valley religion, Manichæanism affords a striking illustration of the Persian habit of expressing

[1] See Journal of Royal Asiatic Society, 1915, 63–89, 405–445.
[2] Cf. Isaiah xliv. 28 ff.; see also Menzies, *History of Religion*, 406.

itself eclectically by combining genuine Persian ideas with the tenets of other creeds. In this way Mani (A.D. 215–273) was in the right line of succession from some of the earlier prophets of Iran.[1]

To world-religion Zoroastrianism contributed the following elements of permanent value:

1. The idea of a God no longer a mere Nature God, but One who is Spirit, Light, Wisdom and Righteousness.

2. Religion as moral choice, the assertion of the great principle: "The Will of the Lord is the Law of Righteousness."

3. The doctrine of a future life, even more consistently moralized than in the religion of Egypt.

4. The confession of a faith which made man a co-operating partner with God in the establishment of His Kingdom and a hastener of "the time of freshening," when the Saviour, Saoshyant, should appear for the redemption of man.

Surely those who supposed that of the Wise Men who came to the cradle of Bethlehem one, at least, was a disciple of Zoroaster did not greatly err.[2]

[1] See F. C. Burkitt, *The Religion of the Manichees*, Cambridge, 1925; A. V. W. Jackson, *Researches in Manichæanism*, New York, 1932.

[2] In addition to the works referred to above, the general reader will find useful the following: Martin Haug, *Essays on the Religion of the Parsis*, London, 1884; E. G. Browne, *Literary History of Persia*, Vol. I., London, 1902; D. J. Irani, *The Divine Songs of Zarathushtra*, New York, 1924; G. F. Moore, *History of Religions*, Vol. I., chapters xv. and xvi.

## CHAPTER XVIII

### *The Religion of Ancient Greece*

UNTIL recently most educated men would have declared with little hesitation that of all ancient religions we knew best that of the Greeks. The intensive study of the Greek classics, from the time of the Renaissance to the present, seemed to have so familiarized the mind of man with every detail as to the beliefs and practices of this gifted race as to make dogmatism quite excusable. To-day we are more hesitant or more modest. We are even uncertain with regard to etymologies which were once regarded by philologists as completely established.

The present uncertainty arises because of the new knowledge acquired during the past generation as to the comparative modernness of what was once regarded as ancient and as to the great complexity of what was once regarded as simple. In two particular ways we have had to correct our view of Greek religion. First, we have found ourselves obliged to trace it back to several intermingled strains of different racial provenance. Secondly, we are now compelled to recognize in the grossness and savagery of many early aspects of this religion elements which are more in harmony with the primitive religions we have been discussing than accordant with that exalted conception of Greek culture derived from the sculptors and dramatists of the fifth century B.C.

To begin with, we find ourselves in the presence of racial elements which are both Indo-European and non-Indo-European. We may indeed distinguish three separate strata of population. First of all we have the final stage of that remarkable civilization, with Crete and Cyprus as special centres, which we call Minoan or Ægean. This civilization seems to have spread from Crete to the Cyclades and thence to the mainland of Greece. Next we have that ancient native population to which we give the name of Mycenean or Pelasgic, the evidence of whose high culture and skilled artistry is open to inspection in the Museum at Athens. Then, lastly, we have the successive waves of Aryan invaders, Achæans, Dorians, and Ionians, breaking from their home beyond the Balkans, and finding their way gradually to all parts of the Greek peninsula and to the adjacent shores of Asia Minor.

Each of these important ethnic elements had a primitive religion which made contributions to the pan-Hellenic religion of later times, and much of which remained almost unmodified through subsequent periods of history. Some features readily lent themselves to the shaping of the religion which was later so conspicuous a characteristic of the Hellenic state, and many others helped to swell the current of popular religion, with its magic, mysticism, and worship of the dead. As to the last, the famous domed sepulchres of the Mycenæans, with their furniture provided for the spirits, are sufficient witness. As for the deities which formed later so highly systematized a pantheon, it is easy to see that some of these derive from the goddess cults of the Cretan world, or from Semitic cults which had found lodgment in Cyprus, while others were the product of the same poetic fancy which had given the personified forces of nature to the Vedic pantheon.

Thus the first period of Greek religion, lying wholly within the field of the primitive, may be said to extend all the way from the Stone Age, at the close of the third millennium B.C., through the Bronze Age, which may be put roughly as extending from 2500 to 1200 B.C., and on through the period of the Indo-European invasion which introduced the ancestors of the Achæans, Dorians, Ionians, and Æolians.

In earlier chapters we have already sufficiently described the religion of this first period. It is enough to say here that it contains all the usual features. There was a kind of fetish worship, in which springs, and trees, and stones, and shapeless pieces of wood, called *xoana*, were reverenced for their supposed possession of spiritual power. What we call *orendism* was a very general belief. Primitive animism, too, peopled the mountains, rivers and air with beings scarcely personified, but thought in their totality to present some evidence of the divine. If there was no totemism in the technical sense, there was abundant evidence of animal worship, and later representations and legends of the gods bear constant witness to the fact. So we have the cow-eyed Hera, the association of Athene with the owl, of Apollo with the wolf, of Zeus with the eagle, and of Artemis with the bear, not to speak of the shape-shiftings of Zeus as ox or swan. Human sacrifices were offered at the tombs of heroes, and at stated times in the calendar the dead were fed. Of the gods some were survivals from the goddess cult of Minoan times, such as Hera, Aphrodite, Athene, and Artemis; others were the strongly anthropomorphized personifications of the Aryan mythology. Until recently it was taken for granted that most of the Greek gods belonged to the latter category, and nature myths were held to account for the entire theogony. But a more cautious philology prevails to-day and now the Indo-Hellenic equations are reduced to a few, such as Dyaus-Zeus, Ushas-Eos, the Açvins-Dioscuroi, and possibly Varuna-Ouranos. But, of course, up to the time of the systematization, every locality had its own gods, who might quite easily be identified with any other deities resembling them in function, as political or religious unification developed. Perhaps, to start with, many of the gods were just as departmental as the Roman *indigitamenta*, but, as time went on, there would be a Zeus on every hill, distinguished only by adjectives of local significance. Such was the case when Homer and Hesiod carried out the great work of systematization which made their writings almost a Bible for the theologians of ancient Greece. This systematization, of course, was not accomplished at a stroke; separate *orenda* had gradually been acquiring the character of special gods; but Homer did humanize and stabilize the conception of the gods, and, moreover, made them members of a family which had much to do with shaping a religion which was pan-Hellenic rather than local. He also gave a setting to the Olympians which made for them a place distinct from that of the older and displaced dynasty of Kronos, and at the same time left the impression of certain forces behind and beyond all the gods, such as Moira, or Fate, and Themis, the principle of law and social order.

Greatest of all the Olympians was Zeus, the syncretism of an old Cretan god, the native sky-god of the undivided Aryan peoples and the local sky-gods worshipped on every high hill throughout the land. Though Zeus had, as under the circumstances was natural, many fabled birth-places, he came nearest to providing the Greek with the conception of monotheism and also nearest to providing the basis for an ethical conception of religion.

Of the other Olympians, since their names are not self-interpreting, it is impossible to say which were foreign and which were native. Hera, the wife of Zeus, came originally (superseding the older Dione) from Argos where, from the epithet cow-eyed, she may originally have been connected with a pastoral cult. But, in the Homeric system, she becomes the goddess charged with the government of the household, for which she does not seem in Homer too well qualified, on account of her nagging and interfering ways.

Athene, the greatest of the Olympians next to Zeus, is one of the old gods. Homer does not describe her, as does Hesiod, as born from the head of Zeus, but makes her the goddess of civilization and the useful arts, wise not in a speculative way, but in the arts of spinning and weaving, the giver of the olive-tree to Athens after a contest with Poseidon. Apollo, generally regarded as the sun-god, did not attain that character till comparatively late, though from the beginning the brightest of the Olympians. He had, indeed, very varied characteristics, as the giver of oracles, the slayer of the Python (in commemoration of which originated the Pythian games), the patron of music, friend of shepherds and their herds, and healer of the diseases of men. His chief shrine at Delphi was one of the unitive forces in Greek religion, though Apollo never threatened the supremacy of Zeus. In comparatively late times Artemis, the virgin huntress, goddess of wild nature both animal and vegetable, was made the sister of Apollo. She was probably a goddess of the older world, one of the mother-goddesses of Mycenæan times, and connected with some form of totemism which revered the bear. Another foreign god adopted by the Homeric system is Ares, the Thracian war-god, who was made the son of Zeus and Hera and the lover of Aphrodite. Hermes, again, was not originally an Hellenic god, but the humanization of the old fetish stone-heap, known as a herm. In the Homeric theology he becomes the son of Zeus and Maia, famous from his cradle for his cunning and thievery, perhaps for that reason becoming the god of markets, and for some other reason the herald of the gods, and eventually the psychopomp, or leader of souls into the nether world. Aphrodite, the foam-born, was doubtless, to start with, a Cyprian, or Semitic, fertility-goddess, like the Ishtar of the Euphrates Valley. In Homer she becomes the wife of Hephaistos, and in other literature (not Homeric) the mother of Eros. Hephaistos himself was an old fire-god, especially of the fire in the forge, the lame artificer of the gods. When the hearth-fire crackled it was as natural for the Greek to say, "Hephaistos laughs," as, during a shower, to say, "Zeus rains." Hestia, the hearth-goddess, ruled over the relations of the human family as Hera ruled over those of the Olympians. Poseidon, the son of Kronos and Rhea, and brother of Zeus, was at first the god of sweet waters, then of inland lakes and brackish springs, and ultimately the ruler of the sea. He was also the god of horses, and in his original character may have had something to do with the horse-sacrifice. Another brother of Zeus was Hades, god of the underworld, but he may have been added as a chthonic deity to produce a measure of symmetry in the Olympian family. Other Homeric gods of minor importance, such as Dionysos, "the frenzied" Thracian divinity associated with the invention and use of wine, and Demeter (Ge-meter), a goddess of fertility and tillage, are of distinctly foreign origin. The last named is referred to in Homer rather as a symbol than as a personality. In addition we have a whole multitude of lesser divinities, attendants on the gods, like Hebe and Ganymedes, Graces, Muses, Hours, and spirits of ocean, air, winds, springs and rocks. Olympus where the gods "lie beside their nectar" is for Homer the centre of the universe, from which all things human and divine are surveyed.

Hesiod, writing possibly several centuries later than Homer,[1] is still more bent than the older poet upon playing the part of the theologian and of affording men a consistent answer to the question, Whence came the world, the gods and men? Though following the authority of Homer, he is more resolutely set on consolidating the rule of Zeus over the pan-Hellenic world. The *Theogony* has probably been altered since it left the poet's hand, but its main features are clear. First, we have Chaos, and then out of the abyss "the broad-bosomed earth," Tartaros and Eros. From Chaos, again, spring Erebus and Night. Night bears to Erebus the Ether and the Day. Earth, of her own power, produces the starry Sky. This last pair, Heaven and Earth, as in other mythologies, become the parents of all that follows. The story of three generations is given, namely, those of Ouranos, Kronos and Zeus. From the blood of the mutilated Ouranos are born the giants, the Titans, who wage war against the progeny of Kronos and Rhea, Hestia, Demeter, Hera, Hades, Poseidon and the last-born, Zeus, who is saved by a ruse from being devoured by his cannibalistically disposed sire. Then follows the story of the battle of the Titans with Zeus, which possibly conceals under a veil of mythology some struggle between earthly dynasties ending with the triumph of the sky-god and his worshippers.

The religion of the Heroic Period may be briefly summarized as follows: Many of the old practices still persisted, including theriolatries in which the bull of Zeus, the owl of Athene, the bear of Artemis, the dove of Aphrodite and such like, were much in evidence; human sacrifices, of which the echo still remains in the literature;[2] magical rites, such as the beating of the human scapegoats (*pharmakoi*) at the Thargelia through the streets of Athens. But some of the darker features of the older cults were disappearing,

[1] Modern opinion tends to regard Hesiod and Homer as being nearly contemporaneous.

[2] As, for example, the actual sacrifice of twelve Trojan youths at the funeral of Patroclos.

though in a religion so local and disintegrated any generalization is unsafe. Yet the Greek had an inborn sense of the reasonable, he was less than most under the sway of religious authority, whether exercised by an official priestly caste or by a sacred literature. There was an almost complete absence of dogma (in the usual sense) and there were no religious "founders" to overawe by the prestige of their personality. Every city had its temple, or *temenos*, and here with simplicity, and for the most part with joyousness, the rites of religion were carried out. The gods were not abstractions but highly humanized and, with the growth of artistic experience, we see the divinities transformed from rude *herms* and *agalmata* to statues of the finest physical perfection. The festivals were numerous and followed the changes of the calendar. Many of them were at great shrines, such as those of Delos and Delphi, and helped the cause of pan-Hellenic unity. Here also were performed rites of a more personal character, such as the interpretation of omens through the entrails or thighs of the sacrificial victims, or the enquiry from famous oracles, an enquiry sometimes stimulated by "induced" dreams at the shrine. There were also many placation rites to be performed, involving often the casting of beans, or eggs, or even pigs to the avenging ghosts, or to turn aside the wrath of the Erinyes and the Keres. The sacrifices were both uranian, when the throat of the victim was pressed upwards, and chthonian, when the victim's throat was pressed towards the earth. The animals offered were sheep, goats, swine or cattle, and there were also offered dough, honey, poppy-seeds and grain. The victims were led forward adorned with garlands, sometimes with their horns gilded, and the sacrifice was always regarded as the occasion for a common meal. The plunging of an altar-brand into a bowl of water and the sprinkling therewith of the worshippers were regarded as a kind of baptismal ceremony uniting them in the joy of a family celebration.

As to the ethics of Greek religion at this time there is much that might be said to its disadvantage, but on the other hand, in addition to the reasonableness and the joyousness to which allusion has already been made, there was a sense of public obligation which had, as we shall see, important consequences in the next period. In the way of sin the vice most disliked was the *hybris*, or overweening pride, which men felt was bound to bring down upon them the wrath of the jealous gods.

The second period of Greek religion, which we may call the Middle Ages of Greece, extends from about 900 to 500 B.C. It shows the work of the Homeric and Hesiodic systematizations now complete, with all the old functional gods identified with members of the Olympian pantheon and these highly anthropomorphized. As particular cities, such as Athens, increase in importance, particular deities also grow in public favour, and civic duty becomes nearly identical with religious obligation. Zeus, Athene and Apollo become especially important, and the temples and shrines of these deities become civic centres. The family cults are now largely taken over by the *polis* and festivals organized on the civic scale. The worship of heroes has assumed almost the proportions of an American Memorial Day, while reminiscences of the older practices remain, as in the Feast of Pots on the last day of the Anthesteria, when the spirits of the dead are placated with pots of porridge and dismissed again to their dwelling in the nether world. Even the market-place has now become sacred ground, the duties of citizens have become religious obligations and the priests and diviners have become public officials, on whose ministrations the welfare and even the safety of the state may depend. At the same time games and festivals held at various important centres have taken on a kind of national or pan-Hellenic character.

There now enter into Greek religion two elements of the greatest possible significance, corresponding in a certain broad way with parallel developments we find in the religious life of the Middle Ages of Europe. The first is the appearance of the so-called redemptive religions in the form of the *Mysteries* of Demeter and Dionysos, and in the movement known as Orphism. The other is the appearance of a kind of scholasticism by which the philosophers attempted to construct a reasoned view of the universe and of the place of religion therein. Both of these movements spring out of that spirit of enquiry which reflection upon the Homeric theology was bound to engender. But whereas the philosophic movement was an effort to rationalize life and in general an appeal to the mind, the *Mysteries* made their appeal to the conscience and to feeling. Religion to the followers of the *Mysteries* was no longer civic but personal. There arose a sense of sin and of need for expiation in ways which these strange sacramental dramas seemed to make possible. Thus, while the old altars were growing cold, a new religion was being born of immense consequence to the future.

One of the striking features about the history of the Mystery religions is the lowliness of their origin and the apparent ease with which they made headway against the strongly entrenched cults of Zeus, Athene and Apollo. Originally the Mysteries were nothing but tribal manifestations of imitative magic, rustic festivals at the turn of the seasons designed to carry the failing forces of nature over the critical periods and recover the vigour of the year for the uses of men. Thus they are in line with the similar Mysteries associated with the stories of Tammuz and Ishtar, of Osiris and Isis.

In the case of Demeter, the earth mother, we have the beautiful myth, as reflected in the Homeric Hymn to Demeter, of the goddess forcing from the cold embrace of Hades, god of the nether world, her daughter, Persephone, that she may gladden again for a season the hearts of men. The maiden, gathering flowers with her companions, has been seized by the grim god of the underworld and carried off. But the bereaved mother held back the fertility of all the earth till the will of the gods sent Hermes down to Hades as a messenger. Thus Persephone was released, but as she had partaken of the food of Hades, she must spend below one-third of her time, returning again with the annual miracle of the spring. The solemn drama, representing the maid's abduction, the sorrow and search of the mourning mother, and the joyous thrill of the resurrection, must have been deeply impressive, even when performed by peasant tribesmen as a piece of imitative magic.

It must have been vastly more impressive and a performance of national significance when carried out at Eleusis, with all the accessories that the best of Hellenic art could afford. Eleusis had originally been an independent community, but about the seventh century B.C. it came under the dominion of Athens and from that time on till several centuries after the beginning of the Christian era was a place of pilgrimage to which even princes and emperors travelled with expectation. Even the Christian Emperor Valentinian I. found himself unable to forbid his subjects to set forth upon a pilgrimage hallowed by long tradition and by associations of the most solemn sort. So far as we know the Eleusinian rites occupied several days during which time the initiates who had previously obtained permission to participate from the noble families in charge went through the various stages of the drama. One day—the rites took place in the middle of September—known as "To the sea, O mystics!" (ἅλαδε μύσται), they purified themselves by a sea-bath; the two following days they spent in Athens, whence they came in procession along the sacred way, calling on the name of the god Iakchos. At Eleusis itself the rites were concealed from the gaze of the profane. That it was possible to ridicule them is plain from the way in which Demosthenes taunts Æschines for having once acted as an acolyte in the Mysteries: "In the night time wearing a fawn-skin and mixing the bowl; purifying the candidates, and swabbing them off with mud and bran; then making the man arise from his purification, and bidding him say, 'I have escaped evil, I have found a better thing'—priding yourself that no one ever shouted so loud. . . . By day leading the five companies marching through the streets, wearing the chaplets of fennel and poplar-leaves, hugging their brown snakes and raising them above their heads, bawling *Euoi saboi!* and dancing to the tune of *Hues attes! attes hues!* while old women salute you by the titles of Leader, Guide, Ark-bearer, Sieve-bearer, and the like. For such services you were paid with sops and twisted rolls and fresh-baked cakes—who would not count himself a lucky dog to fare so well?"

Nevertheless, a Pindar could sing: "Blessed he, who having seen (the Mysteries) passes beneath the hollow earth; he knows the end of life, and knows its god-given origin." And a Sophocles: "O thrice-blessed those mortals, who having beheld these mysteries descend to Hades; to them alone it is given there to live; for the rest all evils are there."

Dionysos also was a foreign deity, a wild, Thracian vegetation-god who, entering Attica from Bœotia, prior to the Ionian invasion of Asia Minor, gave renewed opportunity to the sober-minded Athenians to let themselves go emotionally at certain seasonal crises, namely, at the winter solstice, and on towards the spring equinox. Dionysos was originally a vegetation-god of the usual kind, but was later identified with the spirit of the vine and was even represented, euhemeristically, as the discoverer of the vine and the introducer of its culture into lands as remote as India. In the tribal rites out of which the Dionysiac revels developed the god was torn to pieces by wild women known as Mœnads in order that, by imitative magic, the earth, fertilized by the dismembered body, might recover from the winter's sleep. In the earliest times it was a mad orgy in which clashing music, ecstatic dances, savage ululations, with the eating of raw flesh, were the distinctive features. But in course of time the rites became softened, disciplined, and to a certain extent spiritualized through the influence of the normal reasonableness of the Hellenic mind. Some indication of the part played by Dionysos and his cult in Greek life may be perceived in the *Bacchae* of Euripides. It is interesting, moreover, to note that out of savage and barbarous practices belonging to the sphere of primitive religion emerged at last the stateliness of the Attic drama, the spirituality of the Orphic brotherhoods, and eventually the lofty moral teachings of philosophers like Plato.

Orphism may, indeed, be regarded as a special form of the cult of Dionysos, though it may have sprung from the sympathetic magic of a tribe in which the death of Orpheus at the hands of the Mœnads, because he had despised Dionysos and held Helios the greatest of the gods, had the place usually occupied by the story of Dionysos. In connection with the latter it was believed that Zagreus, son of Zeus and Persephone, had been killed by the Titans, who devoured him. His heart, however, rescued by Athene, was swallowed by Zeus, and Zagreus was reborn as Dionysos, son of Zeus and Semele. Out of the ashes of the Titans consumed by the lightnings of Zeus sprang mankind, who henceforth celebrated the death of the god as a means of entering through death and burial upon a life of resurrection bliss. It is clear that Orphism, propagated by the *thiasoi*, or Orphic brotherhoods, with a missionary zeal hitherto unknown among the Greeks, was something new in Hellenic religion. The old physical ecstasy was superseded by an emotion of the spirit, something esoteric was introduced into the old tribal and communal rites, a certain democracy entered the hitherto restricted circles, and, though much charlatanry prevailed here and there, there was evidently something very genuine at the core. As Dr. Macchioro puts it: "Orphism . . . became a primary element in Greek culture, and constituted one of the most important spiritual upheavals which history has ever witnessed." [1] To quote Dr. L. R. Farnell: "It proclaimed a theory, unfamiliar to native Greek mythology and religion, that the soul of man is divine and of divine origin; that the body is its impure prison-house, where it is in danger of contracting stain; that by elaborate purifications and abstinences the soul might retain its purity, and by sacramental and magic methods the pure soul might enjoy in this life and in the next full communion with God. Preoccupied with the problem of life after death, the Orphic mysteries evolved the concept of purgatory, a mode of posthumous punishment temporary and purificatory; also, if we can trust certain indications in Pindar and Plato, the dogma of reincarnation or more specially of a triple cycle of lives both in this world and in the next." [2]

As to the cathartic side of Orphism probably nothing more needs to be said, but a few further words may be useful as to modifications entailed in the Greek eschatology. Primitive Greek religion differed little in this respect from other early systems that we have considered. Mycenæan graves of the tenth century B.C. depict the spirits of the dead, and an early Spartan relief "shows a dead man seated

[1] V. D. Macchioro, *From Orpheus to Paul*, p. 165, New York.
[2] *E.R.E.*, Vol. VI, *sub voce* "Greek Religion."

with his wife, holding out a cup for libations, and accepting offerings from the living." But the later Greeks, unlike the Egyptians, avoided the thought of death as much as possible. To them, for the most part, "the cup of death was empty." Though not absolutely immaterial the soul was thought of as an attenuated and devitalized thing which could only be kept in being by periodical draughts of blood supplied by the sacrifices. As to the dwelling-place of the ghosts, while primitive opinion took it to be the grave and its neighbourhood, there was gradually elaborated the doctrine of an unseen world, Hades, a dismal land, like some Thracian morass, in which miserable souls wallowed unceasingly. For most this infernal region was definitely localized as a great subterranean vault, inhabited by a monstrous brood of serpents and dire terrors of the darkness. Some placed the entrance at Cape Taenaros, in Laconia, others at Troizen in Argolis, others again, at Heracleia, in Pontos. Occasional visits were paid by mortals, for special reasons, as in the case of Odysseus and Orpheus. Their experiences are told in many famous passages. Achilles, for instance, tried to clasp the shade of Patroclos:

> Away like smoke it went with gibbering cry ;
> Down to the earth Achilles sprang upright,
> Astonished, clasped his hands, and sadly said,
> " Surely there dwell within the realm below
> Both soul and form, though bodiless."

At the spring festival, known as the Anthesteria, the world of ghosts as well as the world of vegetation was believed to be quick with desire for the upper air, but when the festival was past the cry: "Out, ye ghosts, the Anthesteria is over!" was sufficient to banish them to their dark abode. Moreover, the doors were smeared with pitch to prevent return.

Some exceptions were made in the case of the very bad and the very good. Hopeless sinners, and in particular perjurers, were from the first consigned to Tartaros, where was carried out the punishment of "many and terrible deeds of murders foul and violent." Here Ixion laboured eternally with his wheel, and Sisyphus groaned beneath his stone. But there was also Elysium, with its boundless plains, and its endless banquets for those enjoying the favour of the gods, though one seeks for something other than moral reasons for the inclusion of Helen, Menelaos and Achilles. The character of Elysium may be judged from the famous speech (in Homer) of Proteus to Menelaos: "But thou, Menelaos, son of Zeus, art not ordained to die and meet thy fate in Argos, the pasture-land of horses, but the deathless gods will convey thee to the Elysian plain and the world's end, where is Rhadamanthys of the fair hair, where life is easiest for men. No snow is there, nor yet great storm, nor any rain; but always Ocean sendeth forth the breeze of the shrill west to blow cool on men."

The growth of interest in philosophy and in the Mysteries brought about considerable change in the way of regarding the dead. There was, in the first place, a disposition to consider the soul as divine, but as temporarily imprisoned, as in a tomb, within the mortal body. The Orphic rituals expressed dramatically the eagerness of the soul to escape from bondage back to its pristine freedom and purity. So Empedocles described the soul as a fugitive from God and a "wanderer," and proceeded to suggest those successive embodiments in human, animal, or even vegetable form, which at this point link Greek philosophy with the Indian doctrine of metempsychosis. This idea was, as we know, largely accepted by Plato.

In the second place, the conception of judgement, which had appeared earlier in Pindar, is more definitely stressed. Plato gives us the names of the three infernal judges, Minos, who reminds us of the Indian Manu, Aiakos and Rhadamanthys, to whom later was added the name of Triptolemos. The judgement scene is enlarged also by the introduction of new divinities as participators. Hermes is, of course, the psychopomp, as Anubis was in Egypt. Charon, the grim ferryman, is provided to ferry souls across the Styx at an obol per head, while to the Styx and Acheron are added the names of other infernal streams, such as Kokytos, Phthlegthon and Lethe. Kerberos, the three-headed hound of hell, guards the infernal portals, and within reigns Hades, now a god, "the discipliner of mortals." Later Pluto appears as the occupant of the infernal throne. Nothing is said as to any limitation of the sufferings of the dead; to all appearance they are doomed to an eternity of misery.

All this while the old polytheism was probably as strong as ever and no attack on traditional institutions or ritual was permitted. Even in the fourth century Lysias declared: "It is prudent to maintain the same sacrifices as had been ordained by our ancestors who made our city great, if for no other reason than for the sake of the city's luck." But among an increasingly large number of the thoughtful the spirit of enquiry was abroad and, with no obstacle in the nature of sacred books or organized priesthood, even began to flourish. The course of national history itself strengthened the consciousness of moral agencies at work to fulfil the destinies of Greece. The influence of the victories over the huge armaments of Persia was particularly unifying and stimulating. A new patriotic religion appeared in which Zeus was now Zeus Hellenios and Zeus Eleutherios. Even the winds and the sea-nymphs were praised as divine instrumentalities, employed to increase the glory of Hellas. Further stimulus came through the resplendent art of Pheidias, by whose genius the Athene of the Acropolis and the Zeus Olympios gave even to strangers like Emilius Paulus "the thrill of a real presence."

The philosophers were indeed no rebels against the established order, but sincere prophets of "Zeus however called," and enlightened interpreters of the world in which gods and men alike found themselves resident. In the main they were both reverent and constructive and it was not without reason that Clement of Alexandria placed them with the Hebrew prophets as heralds of the Christ. Even the least conservative were at least religiously bent on purging mythology of absurdity and obscenity.

We have no space to discuss the teachings of the philosophers in detail; it will suffice to refer to some outstanding features and personalities. Pythagoras (sixth century B.C.), head of a school at Colophon in South Italy, taught that the universe was permeated "by a prodigious intelligence, of which the intelligence of individuals is but a reflection or a part." He presents us with "a genuine theory of evolution, even though its foundations were psychic rather than physical." Xenophanes of Colophon, also of the sixth century, resident for many years in Sicily and Italy, founded the Eleatic school of philosophy. He denounces the inadequacy of former religious ideas in the words: "Homer and Hesiod ascribe to the gods everything that among men is a shame and disgrace—theft, adultery and deceit," and, on the other hand, he affirms: "There is one God, greatest among gods and men, neither in shape nor in thought like unto mortals." There is again Herakleitos (540–475), of Ephesus, "the dark philosopher," who asserts the supremacy of intelligence, of which he declares: "One, the only wise, is unwilling and yet willing to be called by the name of Zeus," and relates religion to life in the saying: "The law of things is a law of universal reason, but most men live as though they had a wisdom of their own." Then comes Parmenides (born about 539 B.C.) of Elea, with his doctrine of reality founded on the teachings of Xenophanes—a teaching which through him passed into the writings of Plato and Aristotle and the Christian schoolmen. Empedocles (490–430) expounded his doctrine of metempsychosis and his conception of the soul as a divine element working its way back to unfettered fellowship with God. About the same time Anaxagoras, at Athens, taught his doctrine of the *Nous* (mind) and insisted on the presence of mind in the universe, even though, as Socrates complained, he gave it but little to do. Then came Democritus (born about 470), greatest of the physical philosophers, with his atomic theory—atoms moving ceaselessly in the void and by their collisions and combinations integrating the sun in heaven and all the stars. Protagoras (481–411), first of the sophists, introduced his theory of knowledge and his denial of the possibility of valid truth, asserting that "man is the measure of all things." Socrates (470–399) was the younger contemporary of Protagoras and also a sophist, suspected by the orthodox, but really no radical. He revered the Delphic oracle, and his prayer (in the *Phædrus*): "Beloved Pan, and all ye other gods, who haunt this place, give me beauty of the inward soul, and may the outward and the inward man be at one" goes to the heart of religion. Moreover, as a martyr to the truth, "Socrates drinking the hemlock" is no unfitting herald of "Jesus on the rood." The importance of Plato (428–348) in the religious history, not of Greece only but of the world, has been generally recognized. As Dr. G. F. Moore puts it: "In making goodness the dominant element in the conception of the godhead, Plato goes a long step beyond those who tried to explain the dealings of God with men from the point of view of justice."[1] It was the reliance upon God's goodness which led him to confident assertion of the immortality of the soul—the soul which brings from afar a memory of the ideal world of which it is a part. Plato held with Wordsworth that "our birth is but a sleep and a forgetting," that we come "not in entire forgetfulness" and "not in utter nakedness" from the heaven which is our home. This is the constructive side of a teaching which did more to purify the traditional mythology than anything that had hitherto appeared in Greece. The consequences for the future, under Christianity, are obvious. Scarcely less important for that future is Aristotle (born about 384), "the master of those who know," one whom later on we shall see coming into a position of authority among the mediæval schoolmen. With little or nothing to say on many questions either of theology or of popular religion, he stands for ever in the front rank of the sages of ancient Greece.

We cannot pass from this period without reference to the poets and dramatists whose influence, if not so far reaching as that of the philosophers, was at the time wider and more popular. Though they preached no new religion, they yet tended in theology towards monotheism, proclaiming the justice and majesty of Zeus, and they were all moralists, affirming the surefootedness of an avenging fate following hard on the steps of the sinner. This influence goes back beyond the Attic poets to Pindar, "an original thinker who spoke words of power," and emphasized the wisdom and justice of the gods. The three great tragedians, Æschylus, Sophocles and Euripides, were all alive at the time of the battle of Salamis, and contributed to the emotions

[1] G. F. Moore, *History of Religions*, Vol. II., 499, New York, 1913.

of that wonderful era. Æschylus, who, like his successors, shows no interest in Orphism, taught clearly the sovereignty and justice of God. "Zeus," he said, "is the ether, Zeus is the earth, Zeus is the heaven, and what is beyond the universe," a striking declaration of both the immanence and the transcendence of deity. Sophocles is more concerned with the retribution which follows sin. Euripides raises other problems and has been accused of being agnostic. But it is clear he is just scornfully sceptical as to the truth of the old myths and bent on the excoriation of sin, even though gods themselves are the offenders. It is plain that he has thrown over the traditional polytheism and is desirous of warning men against a debasing anthropomorphism. On the positive side, moreover, he betrays a real human sympathy, declaring that "the whole earth is the good man's fatherland."

A few words must suffice for the period of Greek history which commences with the amazing adventures of Alexander the Great, through whom the dominion of Greek culture, and in large measure Greek religion, extended to regions of which the older Greek states never dreamed. There were, in truth, many developments on which it would be possible to dwell. With the familiarizing of men as to the names and nature of a multitude of foreign gods, there grew up not only the possibility of syncretism in religion, but the more wholesome possibility of a catholicity both in theology and practical religion of which the rule of dynasties like the Seleucids was the earthly shadow. It was now possible for a poet like Aratus (third century B.C.) to write the famous lines used on Mars' Hill by St. Paul: "All the ways are full of God, and all the gathering places of men, the sea and the harbours, and at every turn we are all in need of God, for we are akin to Him." There entered also into the hearts of the religious that longing for salvation which was in part the sequel to the grant of Greek rule to some of the downtrodden peoples of the East, a salvation which was freedom and healing from the ills of life. The idea of a ruler as *Soter*, or Saviour, was a

[1] See Acts xvii. 28.

real pointing towards the fact of the Incarnate Son of God, the Saviour of the world.

Other movements, of course, such as Epicureanism and Stoicism, are characteristic of the age, but these may be conveniently referred to under the head of Roman religion. It is time to conclude the chapter with some summary of Greek contributions to the religion of the future.

Among these we have, first and foremost, the gift by Greece of her superb language, which was to become the language of the Bible carried by evangelists and apostles to the world, that the thoughts of the Hebrew poets and prophets might become intelligible to the Gentiles.

There was, secondly, the ideal of beauty, the conception of the *kalos*, which, blended with the Hebrew idea of the good and the Roman idea of the true, was to suggest the full morality of the Christian. In the words of Plato: " It is the clear view of truth, the possession of eternal beauty, the contemplation of absolute good, which makes up the life of the just and happy."

There was, thirdly, the gradually evolved conception of God which led men's thoughts away from the gross, the savage and the crude to the idea of a God

> who leadeth men in wisdom's way,
> And fixeth fast the law,
> Wisdom by pain to gain.

To use again the words of Plato: " What a pilot is to a ship, a driver in a chariot, a leader in a chorus, law in a state, a commander in a camp, this is God in the universe, except that to those ruling is wearisome and full of effort and full of care, but to Him it is without worry, without toil, and free from all bodily weakness."

Once again, in many a myth as well as in the *Mysteries*, there is more than suggestion of the victory over death, a hopeful creed sometimes dramatized and sometimes expressed confidently in song. Still again, in the story of Socrates, we have a moral teaching which was a genuine gift of religion to the world. It has been well said that " not only in the Man of Sorrows, as depicted by the Evangelical Prophet, but in the anticipations of the

Socratic dialogues, there was the vision, even to the very letter, of the Just Man, scorned, despised, condemned, tortured, slain, by an ungrateful and stupid world, yet still triumphant."[1]

And, lastly, there is a touch of the inevitable Cross upon the very religion which, among all ancient religions, was thought to have turned its back upon that Cross most definitely. Hear the last words of Socrates before his judges: "You, too, O judges, it behooves to be of good hope about death, and to believe that this, at least, is true—that there can no evil befall a good man, whether he be alive or dead, nor are his affairs uncared for by the gods."

Is it not plain that the Jew Philo was not false to the mission of his race in receiving from the religion of the Greek ideas which it was possible for him to blend with the revelation vouchsafed to his fathers to form the doctrine of the Logos, through which the world of the divine and that of the human are set at one?[2]

[1] Dean Stanley, *Lectures on the Jewish Church,* III. 200, London, 1883.

[2] On the whole subject covered by this chapter it will be useful to read Angus, *The Mystery Religions and Christianity,* New York, 1925; the same author's *Religious Quests of the Græco-Roman World,* New York, 1919; Chapter VI. of Carl Clemen's *Religions of the World,* New York, 1931; L. Campbell, *Religion in Greek Literature,* London, 1898; E. Caird, *Evolution of Theology in the Greek Philosophers,* Glasgow, 1904; J. Adam, *The Religious Teachers of Greece,* Edinburgh, 1908; and the article on "Greek Religion" by L. R. Farnell in *E.R.E.,* Vol. VI.

## CHAPTER XIX

### *The Religion of Ancient Rome*

THE difficulties we found in discussing the religion of ancient Greece are present in even larger measure in any survey of the religion of Rome, partly because of the greater area covered by the Roman state in its palmier days, and partly because of the more extensive intermingling of peoples which has to be kept in mind. Indeed, at the very start, the blending of Etruscan, Italic and Greek elements out of which Roman religion arose appears so complex as to be beyond the possibility of any satisfactory disentanglement. Yet a careful study of the entire period enables us to discern certain elementary facts and a certain nice adaptation of these to the successive political " patterns " evolved from the days of the early Italic communities to the period of Imperial decadence.

There emerges, moreover, the impression—largely justified—of a religion specially suited for a hard-headed, practical, unimaginative people, little given to fancy, creative of little or no mythology, and inclined to make small distinction between the *jus sacrum* and the *jus civile*.

The main elements which go to make up the Roman religion are the Etruscan, the Italic and the Greek, but it is not ordinarily recognized that Greek influence is early as well as late. Greek colonies appeared in Italy as early as the eighth century B.C. to such an extent that the southern portion of the peninsula was commonly known as Magna Græcia. Greek influences also affected the Etruscans with whom the history of the Romans commences.

The origin of the Etruscans is still very obscure, though it is generally conceded that they were non-Indo-European, and probably came (as Herodotus suggests) from some part of Asia Minor. Many have supposed them intimately connected with the Hittites, as such similarities as those between *Tarq* (the Hittite war-god), *Teucer* and *Tarquin* might seem to imply. The Etruscans had gods like Tinia and Turan, who were later identified with Jupiter and Venus. They had also a demon of the underworld in Tulchulcha, and it has been surmised that Saturnus had an Etruscan forerunner in Satre. The Etruscan mythology, of unknown antiquity, expressed creation as a process involving the passage of twelve millennia, of which six are already over and six still to come. The first man, created at the beginning of the sixth millennium, was a clod turned up by the plough and thereupon transformed into a child named Tages. The Etruscan religion made large use of different forms of divination, stressing the value of odd numbers; it employed human sacrifice on a somewhat large scale; and emphasized the worship of the "twelve gods." It is not clear how much of the old Etruscan religion entered into the ultimate religion of Rome, but it is possible that the name *Rome* is itself Etruscan and therefore that the community was strongly affected by this influence.[1]

It is clear that much more was supplied from the Indo-European communities we call Italic, of which Rome was at first by no means the most considerable. In these communities there were many deities who were taken over subsequently into the Roman pantheon, but it is not clear to what extent these were anything more than local variations of a very few and it seems probable that many of the names used were mere adjectives descriptive of different aspects of one and the same divinity.

Without being precise as to the historical order of these Italic deities, it may be convenient to group them somewhat as follows. Of the nature-gods the most prominent is Jupiter (or Juppiter), the Latin equivalent of Zeus, a deity of the open sky, and the chief god of most of the Italic states. His might is shown in the thunderbolt, which was exhibited by the Fetiales and used for the administration of oaths, much as the Bible is used in our own law courts. In this connection Jupiter was moralized as Deus Fidius. But he bore a large number of names indicative of his main characteristic, such as Fulgur, Fulmen, Feretrius, while as

[1] Some of the kings of Rome were probably Etruscan.

the light-bringer he was known as Lucetius, Elicius, and so on. Another nature-deity was Mater matuta, the goddess of the dawn, also worshipped as a sea-god and a divinity of birth. The many seasonal divinities—some of them of later birth—are also to be noted under this head, such as Vertumnus and Pomona. There may also be mentioned, of the same order, the Earth-mother, Tellus mater; the fertility-god, Liber, afterwards identified with the Greek Dionysos, the god of sowing; Saturnus—from whom Italy was named by the poets, Saturnia; Consus and Ops, deities of the harvest and the granary; Faunus, the kindly spirit of the out-of-doors (cf. *favere*, to favour); Silvanus, the god of the woodland; Diana, an original tree-spirit, one of the first of Italic gods to be adopted by the Romans; Venus, originally a goddess of productivity, specifically of market-gardens, eventually identified with the Greek Aphrodite and the Semitic Ishtar, and raised to highest honours as the reputed mother of Æneas and ancestress of the Julian family; and Flora, the goddess of the springtime flowers. Even Mars (Mavors), afterwards the most famous of war-gods, was originally a vegetation-god, who was looked to for stimulating the growth of the grain. Of water-gods there were deities like Neptunus, the divinity of moisture, belonging to the oldest cycle of the Italic gods, and such lesser deities as Lympha, the goddess of the stream. Fire-gods also appear, such as Volcanus or Vulcan, gods of the underworld like Vediovis (commonly invoked in oaths), and disease-gods, like Febris appealed to for the avoidance or cure of malaria.

Gods of human life and gods of society, again, were common, often described as in pairs, male and female. Every individual had his *genius*—the power of reproductivity—or the corresponding feminine, *Juno*, not originally associated with Jupiter. In the order of the household the deities particularly invoked were Janus, the god of the entrance gate, and Vesta, the goddess of the hearth. Janus was reputed to have had an affair with a nymph, Carna, who was rewarded by being made the goddess of hinges and renamed Cardo, with the gift of whitethorn that she might banish mischief from the threshold. Besides these, the Dii Penates were worshipped as the family gods, guardians of the things kept in the alcove, while the Lares were reverenced as the gods of the ground, later more specially as the deities of street-corners. There was also Minerva, the goddess of the household arts, later to be identified with the Greek Athene.

The abstractions which are frequently mentioned as among the earliest of Roman divinities are probably the invention of later and more reflective times, but it is not beyond the bounds of possibility that gods such as Pavor (fear), Pax (peace), Concordia (concord), and Spes (hope) had objects of reverence corresponding to them in the early days. The same thing is true of the functional or departmental gods, described by the Germans as *Sondergötter*. Of these there is a vast array, of which a considerable number were thought to preside over specific agricultural operations. Thus we have Subruncinator, the weeding; Vervector, the ploughing of the fallow; Occator, the harrowing; Reparator, the preparing of the soil; Imporcitor, the drawing of the furrow; Messor, the mowing; Convector, the gathering; Segesta, the sowing; Matura, the ripening; Tutilina, the storing of the grain; and Terminus, the preserving of the boundaries. Many of these were inscribed in lists known as the *Indigitamenta* (from *indigito*, to point with the finger), and were called *Dii indigetes*, or native gods, by way of contrast with the imported foreign gods, *Dii novensides*. Childhood alone had its forty-three guardian deities, such as Cunina, the cradle god, Statura, the god of standing up; Edula, the god of eating; Locutius, the god of speaking; Adeona, the god of coming to one; and Abeona, the god of going away. Of course some of these titles may easily have been mere adjectives applied to more important deities, but by the common folk they were distinguished, even as by the ignorant Our Lady of Lourdes is distinguished from Our Lady of Loretto.

There were no temples, in the sense of buildings (*ædes*), much before the end of the monarchy, but sacred places became known as *templa*, or spaces marked off, and images were in course of time erected with their faces set towards the west, by way of contrast with the eastward facing images of the Greeks.

The father of the family was the first priest and then the king of the community. After a while, to relieve himself of responsibility, the king appointed a *rex sacrorum* and gradually there was developed the whole hierarchy of *collegia* and guilds, augurs, flamens, fratres arvales, luperci, or wolfmen, salii, or leapers, vestals, to watch over the sacred hearth flame, pontifices, and the rest.

Though not entirely independent of the state religion, there were *sacra privata* as well as *sacra publica*. The central point of family religion was the *atrium*, or hall, and of this again the *focus*, or hearth. Behind this was the *penus*, or store-closet, which was the seat of the Penates, or family divinities. The Lar familiaris was not, as sometimes represented, an ancestral spirit, but the spirit of the holding, a hallowing of the place rather than of the person. In all probability the *lares* were first worshipped at the *compita*, or street corner. On the other hand, as already pointed out, the *genius* was the generative force of the paterfamilias, the numen residing in a person—not his soul—upon which depended the continuance of the line.

Family religious rites took place on many occasions, as, for example, at a marriage or on the birth of a child. The child had to be guarded against the wild, untamed powers of nature by the wearing of an amulet, or *bulla*. So far as the death-bed was concerned, the offices of religion were not much invoked, but the piety of the living was relied upon to protect the dead and to keep them supplied with food. There were annual rites at the grave, on as many as nine different occasions, corresponding to the Christian use of All Saints' Day. Much of the family religion, apart from this, consisted of rites designed to increase the productivity of the fields and to ensure the security of the beasts employed in agriculture.

Something should here be said as to the authorities from which we derive knowledge of the early Italic religion. These consist, first, of the *Fasti*, or Kalendars, which, though mainly dated between 31 B.C. and A.D. 51, take us back in substance to several centuries beyond the Christian era. We have fragments of some thirty of these *Fasti* and are thereby enabled to reconstruct the old Italic year, with its *Dies fasti* (lucky) and *nefasti* (unlucky). Apparently the Kalendars were drawn up almost purely for agricultural purposes and confirm our estimate of the early Roman religion as one of fields and woods, with a multitude of functional deities. The primitive Kalendar shows a year of ten months, but with the Numanic, following the reign of Numa Pompilius, came in the year of twelve months and no further reform was introduced till the time of Julius Cæsar, to whom we owe the Julian Kalendar. Secondly, we learn much as to the early religion from men like Varro (116–27 B.C.) and Verrius Flaccus (*c.* 10 B.C.), later, of course, from such writers as Ovid and Pliny, and something from references in the Christian Fathers.

Roman religion, as distinguished from its more primitive components, may be conveniently divided into four main periods, as follows:

1. From the earliest time of which we have knowledge to the end of the regal period, about 500 B.C.
2. From the time of Tarquinius Superbus to the wars with Hannibal, 200 B.C.
3. From the age of Hannibal to the reign of Augustus, shortly before the Christian era.
4. From the establishment of the Empire under Augustus to the conversion of Constantine, A.D. 323.

In the first period the general "pattern" is that of a religion adapted to a race of agriculturists and stock-raisers. All the festivals seem to imply the importance of this aspect. We have, for example, the *Cerealia*, in honour of Ceres, on April 19; the *Robigalia*, on April 25, when a red dog was sacrificed to avert the danger of rust in the crops; the *Ides* at certain times of the year sacred to Jupiter, and the *Kalends* similarly sacred to Juno. In March the Salii leaped to assist the growth of the crops; in October (on the 15th) there were rites in honour of Mars, to protect the community from the menace of war and disease, with a horse offered in sacrifice on the Campus Martius.

The gods worshipped at this period were *numina* of a

very undefined personality and it was advisable to keep on good terms with them nevertheless. Jupiter was, as pointed out above, the numen of the sky and the bearer of the thunderbolt. Mars and Quirinus were probably but different names for the same god, worshipped by Romans and Sabines alike. Janus and Vesta were the house-gods, deities of the gate and hearth, protectors of the sacred entrance and the sacred recess. At the same time there was a widespread cult of the dead, as represented by the *Dii parentes* and the *Dii manes*. This cult had ample expression at the various calendric festivities. The *Parentalia* were observed from February 13 to 22 as a kind of ghostly home-coming, when, with temples closed, business suspended, and even marriages uncelebrated, people went forth with roses and violets, or with offerings of oil, milk and honey to the tombs. The celebration culminated on February 22 in a "feast of love" when place was made for the effigies of the dead in seats of honour. Three months later, on May 9, 11 and 13, the *Lemuria* were held, when the head of the house rose at midnight to cast black beans over his shoulder and repeat nine times the words: "With these beans I redeem myself and mine." At the stroke of a gong the spirits were then bidden to depart. Again, at the *Compitalia*, there was the hanging outside the doors of the woollen effigies of the inmates, which it was believed the prowling ghosts would bear away instead of their living originals.

The temples, as already noted, show a gradual development from the use of sacred groves to the erection of special buildings, or *ædes*. In these was enacted a primitive ritual, with its sacrifices, both bloody and unbloody, all designed for the purpose of making over a value to the deity there adored. One of the most significant of these sacrifices was the *suovetaurilia*, or the sacrifice of sheep, swine and bulls in one oblation. With these were offered the salted meal, or *mola salsa*, from whence we derive our word *immolate*. The officiating priest acted with his eyes covered, with music sounding in his ears (to prevent distraction), and amid the silence of the multitude. Ill effects would follow to the land and the community were the perfection of any rite marred, deliberately or inadvertently, and a *piaculum*, or "apologetic sacrifice" was necessary to atone for errors of this sort. One of the most remarkable of all rites was the *lustratio*, when prayer and sacrifice were combined with processions, to cut off the intrusion of evil from the land. The rite arose doubtless from a very primitive fencing off of the farm by the use of magic, but the typical illustration of the *lustratio* is that which took place at the *Ambarvalia* of May, when the threefold sacrifice was three times driven around the given territory before being offered to the gods by the Fratres arvales. There is naturally much in the religion of this period which is barbarous and superstitious, and much that was founded on fear, but it had, nevertheless, its good side in that duty to the community was strongly stressed.

The second period, from about 500 to 200 B.C., saw many changes. The last of the Etruscan kings had already given certain religious privileges to the plebeians which had hitherto been restricted to the patricians, so it is not surprising to see certain steps towards democracy. But a much greater change came about through Rome's absorption of the surrounding communities and the desire shown to systematize religion in a large way as compared with what had been hitherto deemed possible. Thus, while the list of *Dii indigetes* was now closed, the process of Hellenization commenced with a view to the creation of an inclusive and homogeneous pantheon. First of all, we find the goddess Diana brought from her famous shrine at Aricia by Lake Nemi to occupy her new home on the Aventine Hill, while the grove itself remained a sanctuary for the whole Latin federation for many generations yet to come. Then followed the introduction of the Greek divinities. The Dioscuroi, under the name of Castor and Pollux, came by way of Tusculum, and Heracles was introduced to become the Latin Hercules, a deity of trade profits and of booty taken in war. Then the original Etruscan triad of Tinia, Thalna and Minerva, which had later become Jupiter, Mars and Quirinus, was superseded by the new triad of Jupiter Optimus Maximus, Juno and Minerva, and the new temple raised upon the Capitoline

Hill became common ground for the worship of plebeians and patricians alike. In 493 B.C. the Greek triad of Demeter, Dionysos and Persephone was introduced and identified with the Latin divinities Ceres, Liber and Libera. Meanwhile, the Sibylline Oracles had been imported from their ancient home of Cumæ and, closely associated with these, in 431, came the Greek Apollo, as a god of healing in time of plague, but destined to find no Latin equivalent. The Greek Aphrodite, brought from Mt. Eryx in Sicily, was now identified with Venus and Artemis with Diana, while in the third century B.C., on the advice of the Sibylline Oracles, an entirely new foreign god was introduced in Æsculapius, the sacred serpent being brought with honourable escort from Epidaurus to its new habitation on an island in the Tiber, where it swam ashore. It remained only to identify the Latin Neptunus with the Greek Poseidon, to equate Orcus with Pluto, and to introduce Hermes under the name of Mercury to make the pantheon complete. Mercury was regarded as the protector of the routes by which the grain was imported and so naturally a god appealed to against the failure of the crops.

Certain changes in ritual inevitably accompanied the expansion of the Roman theology. The *ritus Græcus*, in which the priests officiated with uncovered heads, took the place of the Latin rite, in which they remained covered. An important innovation was the use of the *lectisternium*, or couch for the banquet of the gods, with the richly attired puppets reclining to partake of the provided feast. The first use of *lectisternia* appears to have been in 399 B.C. and was ordered by the Sibylline Oracles to rid the land of pestilence. Of a more native sort was the development of the two great *collegia* of Pontifices and Augures. The pontifices were now increased from three to nine and thence to fifteen, and found new occupation in drawing up the lists we have mentioned as *Indigitamenta*, in which all kinds of new gods (of a rather academic sort) are mentioned. These include such divinities as Salus, Spes, Fides, Pudicitia, Victoria, Fortuna, and the like. They were never personalized in any proper sense of the word, but it is important to remember that though many of the so-called *Sondergötter* are primitive in character many of those here indicated are of priestly rather than of popular provenance. The Augurs were frequently magistrates, who had always the right of *spectio* in the performance of their official duties, and had much occasion, in their own uncertainty, to depend upon indications furnished them by the flight of birds or the feeding of chickens.

The third period of Roman religion extends from the end of the second Punic war, about 204 B.C., to the time of Augustus. The Punic wars proved a turning point in the history of religion since, under stress of the conflict (to use a phrase of Sir Gilbert Murray, applied to Greece), Rome "lost nerve." Either the gods were impotent or angry and there was every justification for the people to seek relief in any direction charlatanry or superstition might suggest. So there were endless supplications and paradings of *lectisternia* for three entire days in honour of the twelve Greek gods. There was even resort to human sacrifice in the case of certain Gaulish and Greek prisoners. In 206 B.C. an event took place which marks the beginning of an Orientalizing process in the Roman religion. On the recommendation of the decemviri, aghast at the progress made by Hannibal, there was imported from Pessinus in Asia Minor an image of the goddess Cybele, Mater Deum Magna Idæa, the Attis of Asiatic religion. The festival held in Rome on April 4 proved the prelude to Scipio's great victory over the Carthaginians and the timely triumph had the effect of popularizing the foreign superstitions. Mathematici, soothsayers and Chaldæans began to flourish on Roman credulity and other foreign deities were immediately sought. Ma, or Bellona, was welcomed from Cappadocia, Isis and Sarapis (*Osar-hapi*) from Egypt, Adonis and Atargatis from Syria, and Mithra from Persia, though the oldest Mithræa in Rome are not earlier than the time of Trajan. Many of these cults, however, including the dangerously emotional worship of Bacchus imported from Thrace, were regarded with considerable misgiving, and here and there prodigies seemed to show the wrath of the Roman gods. In B.C. 58 the Senate gave orders for the destruction of the altars of Isis, though the consul, L.

Emilius Paulus, in the following year, found no workmen willing to carry out the order. Augustus gave command in the case of the Egyptian gods that they should only be worshipped outside the Pomerium. It was not till the third century A.D. that this restriction was removed. Together with the worship of the Oriental gods there was displayed an increased tendency to consult the stars and astrologers multiplied to meet the demand.

Meanwhile, many of the intelligent classes, repelled by popular superstition, took refuge in one or another type of philosophy. The two favourite schools were those of the Epicureans and the Stoics. The best Roman example of Epicureanism is Lucretius, who confounded all religions with superstition and put aside alike the native and the foreign gods. Stoicism was much better calculated to bring out the nobler side of Roman character and from this time on to the conversion of the Empire many of the finest Romans were Stoics, holding fast to the ideal of duty, however much the sea of faith had ebbed.

But the prevailing attitude of men was sceptical, even in regard to virtue. Cicero, though proud to be an augur, was a thorough-paced sceptic, till he lost his daughter Tullia, when natural affection restored his belief in immortality. So was Varro, in spite of his academic interest in the religious tradition. The festivals, such as the *Lupercalia*, were now kept without real understanding of their origin or significance. Temples went to pieces till Augustus undertook their restoration. The priesthoods fell into contempt. Mucius Scaevola, though holding the office of Pontifex Maximus, declared that there were three kinds of religion, the poetic, the philosophic and the political. Of these only the last, he said, was of consequence, and this was not true. Religion was plainly at a low ebb, with immorality rampant and all classes selfish and callous to the corruptions of the time.

Just prior to the opening of the Christian era it may well have seemed that Roman religion had lost whatever savour it had anciently possessed. But, while we may think of that " hard pagan world " as spiritually dead, we shall have to award Augustus the credit for a *tour de force* in the way of religious revival which is almost unique in history. It is true that this revival was part of a political scheme. The Emperor rightly discerned that the prosperity of the State was inseparable from the attention to be bestowed upon religion. A reflection of this is to be seen in Horace's famous *Carmen Seculare*, written for the great Secular Games of 17 B.C. The occasion was meant to be the beginning of a new *seculum*, the turning over of a new leaf. Not only in the mind of the Emperor, but also in the consciousness of the people, there was a feeling of weariness and disappointment which almost amounted to a sense of sin. Yet out of the darkness a new era might be born and the wellnigh Messianic expectation of Vergil's *Fourth Eclogue* reflects the felt possibility of the situation. At the same time the extension of the Empire gave a new sense of destiny, and it was considered worth while to make an epic of the story of Æneas in order to trace the generation of Rome to the gods and to exult in the glory still to be revealed. Together with this was the stress on the *pietas* of Æneas which was to reproduce itself in the character of her citizens if Rome was to fulfil her mission.

It was on this wave of hope that the Emperor rode to carry out his wonderful series of reforms. Waiting patiently till the death of Lepidus, Augustus became Pontifex Maximus in 12 B.C., having long been a member of the colleges of augurs and pontifices. He immediately proceeded to revive other ancient *collegia* such as those of the Luperci, Salii, and Fratres arvales. Eighty-two temples were restored through the imperial bounty, including that of Apollo Palatinus, the Temple of Mars, and the Temple of Vesta on the Palatine Hill. Later the Emperor made still further approach to the religious unification of his realm by associating the *Genius Augusti* with the two *Lares compitales*, with the symbol of this new trinity placed at the intersection of all the streets. What paganism could do for the creation of a catholic religion, such as called for the loyalty of all to one idea, and co-operation in a common service, was done by Augustus. It is well to note that, while the effort failed, some ideas were so strongly entrenched in the popular mind as to make the transference of certain celebrations easy from the pagan to the Christian calendars and the transition possible from a catholic paganism to the beginnings of a catholic Christianity.

It is not here necessary to describe the various stages by which the Roman ideal passed on towards a tragical *debâcle*. The fall came in spite of many an attempt to stem it, both from the political and the religious side. If there were Emperors who strove loyally to weld together this great organization of diverse peoples into a unity by pressing on their subjects the importance of worshipping the Imperial *Genius*, there were others who, seeing in this direction failure, were already casting about for some other faith, whether it came from Persia or from Egypt, which by its adoption might save the State from disintegration. And if there were philosophers like Seneca and Epictetus and Marcus Aurelius striving to steady themselves amid the general drift by adherence to the Stoic ideal, there were also many others genuinely seeking illumination and strength through attendance at the grottoes of the Mithraists, or feeling after a Saviour God and regeneration through the Mysteries or purification through such rites as the *Taurobolium* and *Criobolium*, or endeavouring to purge out the grosser part of nature by fasting and enforced chastity, or to strengthen the spiritual element by participation in a sacramental meal.

The religious system had already been revealed which was to offer fully what was thus being ignorantly sought, though the majority knew it not or sought the way to salvation amiss. Hence it was that the Roman religion which tried to retain its authority by archaic revivals or by despotic use of the imperial power became the blasphemous parody of what might have been its proper line of development. It was terribly easy for Rome, in failing to become the Bride-city of the New Dispensation, to become the Harlot-city, the doomed Babylon instead of the New Jerusalem. Setting herself to secure her strength through material force, she set in array against her those spiritual forces which the apocalyptists of the time saw coming down out of the heaven of the absolute world. Setting herself to secure unity by forcing all men to offer incense to the *Genius* of the Emperor, she left men to worship the shadow of a

Beast which had already been slain and whose body had already been given to the devouring fire. Setting herself to secure peace by crushing out the free life of the peoples she had subdued, she roused against her that spirit of freedom through whose breath she was destined to perish.

Yet, though we are accustomed thus to see Rome as the antithesis to that city of redeemed humanity which had been revealed from heaven, we must not forget that her religion, like that of Greece, had its contributions for the future, and that the language of Rome, like the tongues of the Greek and the Hebrew, witnessed to Christ's Kingdom on the Cross. We need not stress overmuch the witness of the Stoics. Whether Seneca, Epictetus and Marcus Aurelius are, as thinkers, in the right line of descent from Cleanthes, or whether they were themselves touched with the golden ray of the newly arisen Sun, in either case we cannot put them outside the category of the minds "naturally Christian," such as illustrate the continuity of the divine leading. If even "the fierce Tertullian" could speak of "Seneca, saepe noster," it does not become us to be catholic in a lesser degree.[1]

But, outside the witness of the Stoics, we have contribution to the religion of the future from the Roman in the following particulars:

1. Rome gave to the first Christian apostles that vision of *catholicity* which is so powerfully reflected in the missionary strategy of St. Paul. With her divine representative Augustus, Divus, ruler over what appeared to be the World, Rome was at once the symbol, as she, alas, became the parody, of the œcumenical dominion of the Christ. That "the kingdoms of the world" were to become "the Kingdom of our God and of His Christ," that "all peoples, nations, kindreds, tongues" were to accept His authority, was a vision which was not a little assisted by the spectacle of political achievement which had welded nations, east and west, into one great imperial entity, all elements of which paid tribute to the Lord who reigned from the Seven Hills of Rome. Presently, of course, the symbolism

[1] See F. W. Farrar, *Seekers after God*, London, 1868.

would bring into strong relief the contrasts between the brutishness of the material Rome and the vision of the City of God. But, in the years preceding the Neronian persecution, it is not to be overlooked that it was Rome which gave St. Paul the sense of the scope of his evangel; it was Rome which offered to his eager feet the roads which linked city to city within the Empire; it was Rome, again, whose even-handed justice ensured his protection time and time again against the violence of the mob.

2. In the second place, it was from Rome that, with the vision of catholicity came also the expectation of universal *law*, an order like that of Camelot,

> Where all about a healthful people moved,
> As in the presence of a gracious king.

The sense of law which pervaded the Roman system, when divorced from other things, had its mischievous influence, in later days making too rigid and precise both the thinking and the conduct of Christian men. But, in these early days, in its influence on the organization and the administration of the Christian communities, we cannot fail to recognize it as a providential gift for the extension of that spiritual kingdom which, first inspired by the conception of so vast an Empire, was destined in time to proclaim its message to "regions Cæsar never knew."

3. To the expectation of universal empire under the reign of universal law was added the hope of universal *peace*, the beginning of that new age which, after all the troubles of the Republic, seemed predicted by the auspicious accession of Octavius Cæsar. It makes little difference what the immediate occasion may have been for the writing of Vergil's *Fourth Eclogue*. The poet prophesied better than he knew:

> A mighty line of ages springs anew;
> The Maid returns and Saturn's golden prime;
> From heaven on high a new-born race descends.

In course of time, as has been said, Rome became the parody rather than the type. Nevertheless, through all the smoke of apocalypse, she still emerges as a wonderful and inspiring idea. We can well understand how the

Abbé Pierre Froment, in Zola's *Rome*, could take his stand upon the hills outside the Sacred City, and "in the soft and veiled light of the lovely morning" dream of "the Rome of that first meeting, the Rome of early morning," suggested to his sanguine soul. "What a shout of coming redemption seemed to arise from her house-roofs, what a promise of universal peace seemed to issue from that sacred soil, twice already Queen of the World."

Perhaps, having in mind the impressive story of her religious development, we, too, with the Abbé, may dream of what that "third Rome" might be, if we could see all that its history suggests placed at the feet of the Christ who became heir of all that it achieved. Then, indeed, while we should still continue to sing our "Jerusalem, the Golden," we should also hold in our hearts and upon our lips the greeting: "Ave, Roma Immortalis!"[1]

[1] On the general subject of Roman religion the reader is referred to W. Warde Fowler, *The Roman Festivals of the Period of the Republic*, London, 1899; the same author's *Religious Experience of the Roman People*, London, 1911; Carl Clemen, *Religions of the World*; G. F. Moore, *History of Religions*, Vol. I., chap. xxi.; E. V. Hopkins, *History of Religions*, chap. xxiii.; W. S. Fox, *Greek and Roman Mythology*, Part III., Boston, 1916; and the article "Roman Religion" in *E.R.E.*, Vol. X., by W. Warde Fowler.

# CHAPTER XX

## *Religion of the Amerindian Empires*

THE more settled civilizations of the American continent, prior to the Spanish Conquest, had four centres, namely, Mexico, Guatemala, Yucatan and Peru, but we may describe their civilization, and the religion which, at least in part, expressed that civilization, under the three heads of Aztec, Mayan and Inca.

Whether any part of this culture was the result of overseas contact in historical times has been a moot question. Some have maintained the theory of communication with Europe by way of Greenland; others have been zealous to prove the establishment of communication with Oceanica by means of canoes. For either of these hypotheses there seems but slight evidence. Mr. Stuart Chase [1] expresses himself as follows: "I am inclined to cast my vote . . . with those who, like Dr. Franz Blom, hold that American culture in its more advanced phases was a purely American phenomenon. It took nothing from Egypt, nothing from China, nothing from Angkor. Granting the invasions, they came before old-world civilizations had developed, or from races out of contact with them. Peru, Mexico, and the rest hammered out their own destiny from their environment. Diffusion took place within the Americas, but hardly from the old world, unless we go back to stone hatchets and wooden dugouts. Any bright morning, however, this patriotic theory may be overturned. A stone Asiatic elephant that is obviously not a macaw or tapir may be found on a newly excavated temple, thus proving beyond peradventure cultural diffusion from Asia. Until that definitive discovery is made, I shall continue to ascribe Mexico to Mexicans and not to Egyptians, Chinamen or Polynesians."

[1] Stuart Chase, *Mexico, a Study of Two Americas*, p. 3.

In any case, whether the civilizations we have in mind are independent creations, due to the emergence of important personalities, or whether they are the natural development, in communities of exceptional intellectual and physical vigour, of primitive ideas, the primitive ideas, such as we have discussed in earlier chapters, were never completely overlaid by the subsequent religious experience of Aztecs, Mayans or the Incaic Peruvians.

Dealing first with what may be called the " higher " religion of *Mexico*, it is easy to see that the Aztec civilization is something which has been superimposed on that of the earlier Toltecs, many of whom seem to have been driven south into Central America when the Aztecs established their empire somewhere about A.D. 1000. The old Toltec gods were, as was usual after the conquest of one people by another, imprisoned, but even as " prisoned gods " they retained much of their old authority. The general character of the superseded religion may very well have been as bloody and filthy as that of the conquerors which Bernal Diaz found, so far as its temples bore witness, a good imitation of hell.

Yet it cannot be denied that there must have been a certain intellectual quality about the cult which produced a calendric system of fifty-two years and which embodied a certain amount of astronomical lore in the worship of the gods of the Four Quarters. It may be noted that some tribes preferred to speak of the five points of the compass, recognizing (as did the Chinese) the place where you stand as well as the direction to which you look. Others, again, raised the number to seven, the perfect figure, by including the zenith and the nadir.

The " high gods " embraced many of the deified powers of nature. There was, for example, Huitzipochtli, originally the morning star, " lord of the south," the war-god, often represented by his symbol, the humming-bird. Then came Tezcatlipoca, the sun-god, or fire-god, represented by a smoking mirror. Best known of all (to the Spanish) was the famous Quetzalcoatl, " the bright-feathered snake," god of the eastern quarter, a culture-god, and probably, to begin with, a deified ancestor. Equally important to the

Aztec was Tlaloc, the thunder- or rain-god, to whom babes were sacrificed (afterwards devoured in cannibalistic feasts), that the tears of the little ones and their mothers might act as a rain charm. Mictlantecutli, represented as a fearful skeleton, was the god of death and guardian of the north. To him the dead were commended with passports such as remind us of Egyptian charms in the *Book of the Dead*. Tlauizcalpantecutli was guardian of the west and Venus as the evening star. In addition to these we have an important deity in Xipe-Totec, "the flayed one," represented as clad in a skin stripped from a human sacrifice. At his festival, which was in the spring and meant, by imitative magic, to assist nature to acquire her new vesture of green, many human beings were sacrificed and youths appeared in the skins of the victims.

In addition to the high gods, there was an almost infinite number of lesser divinities, including (in very early times) moon-goddesses, gods of merchants, weavers, potters, fishermen and metal-workers, water-gods, fire-gods, mountain-gods, and volcano-gods, gods of medicine, and gods of disease, animal-gods, and even flower-gods.

The worship of the Aztecs was elaborately ceremonial. The huge pyramids, or *teocalli*, with their many storeys and varied colours, reminding us of the old Babylonian zikkurats, must have been strangely imposing. Even with their horrible sacrifices and cannibal feasts, they could hardly have suggested to the people what they did to Bernal Diaz, when he described an Aztec temple "such as one pictures at the mouth of Inferno, showing great teeth for the devouring of poor souls." The terraced pyramids were often of enormous size, rivalling even the Pyramids of Gizeh in bulk. As parts of a sacred city, with their towers and perennial fires, they must have been exceedingly impressive, especially at Tenochitlan, the capital (now Mexico City), which was founded in 1325. Altars smoked by their hundreds through the land and priests by thousands busied themselves with the offices of their profession, as diviners, guardians of the idols, thurifers, musicians, and singers, as well as sacrificers. In Mexico City were two chief priests, and special priesthoods were attached to the service of various gods, such as Huitzilopochtli and Tlaloc. Some of the priests were esteemed as so charged with dangerous *mana* that they had to be kept secluded for the sake of others. Of the prayers used some have been preserved and are striking enough to invite comparison with the liturgies of other faiths, but Dr. Hartley B. Alexander speaks of "a kind of world-weary melancholy" as being generally typical of Aztec supplication. Enough has already been said of the sacrifices to show the place occupied by the offering of men and women—sacrifices as horrible as any recorded in the history of religion. Some victims were prisoners of war, but many were selected from the youth of the land. Specially in vogue was the offering of human hearts, torn from the bosoms of their still-quivering victims, in order to supply vigour to the sun and other powers of nature. Many sacrifices were followed by cannibal feasts, though "eating the god" was often a sacramental rite in which the god was represented in paste, divided and distributed to the worshippers.

There were naturally many seasonal festivities, of which the Great Spring Feast was one of the most important. It was in connection with this that an unblemished youth was chosen, provided with four selected maidens as wives, feasted and reverenced till the day when, after the new fire had been kindled on his breast, his heart was torn from his body and presented to the sun-god, Tezcatlipoca. Then swift runners carried brands lighted from the new fire to rekindle all the hearth-fires of the land.

The Aztecs had a rather detailed cosmogony, such as included the idea of four ages preceding the creation of man. First there was the jaguar age; this was followed by the ape age, the bird age, and the fish age. After this fourth epoch the fallen sky was raised and the earth revived; then came in succession the kindling of the fire and the creation of man. After men began to multiply wars arose, for the purpose of supplying the human hearts necessary for the sun's support. Only when this support had been assured was the sun itself created.[1]

[1] See Hartley B. Alexander, *Latin-American Mythology,* chapters ii. and iii.

There were supposed to be thirteen regions of heaven above the earth and nine regions of hell below. In these regions the souls of men were distributed after death. Warriors went eastward and mounted to the zenith; women went westward, but climbed in the morning towards the zenith to receive the sun from the hands of the warriors. On the death of a king the corpse was provided with a jug of water for the journey, a bunch of cut papers to pass him through the dangers of the road, garments to protect him from the wind, and a little dog to guide him across the nine rivers. The souls of men are often represented as passing between clashing mountains and knives of obsidian, to stand before the skeleton god, Mictlantecutli, for judgement. Thence they fare over "the ninefold stream" to their final abode. On this fearsome journey the dead man is guided by the red dog which was sacrificed at the grave, and this becomes his psychopomp, corresponding to the Anubis of ancient Egypt. It may be added that the bodies of the dead were wrapped like mummies and sprinkled with water from the vessel placed beside the grave.

In conclusion, we may say that, in spite of the awful cruelty which characterized the religious ritual of Mexico, the morals of the people, so far as observed, show a rather high ethical standard, and a conception of life by no means so debased as we might have expected.

THE MAYAN RELIGION.—For our present purpose we may consider the ancient civilization of Yucatan and the (Quiché) civilization of Guatemala and parts of Honduras as one. With some tribal interminglings, the peoples of these regions represent one linguistic family and one religious type conveniently described as Mayan. The Mayan Empire seems to have been founded in Guatemala about the beginning of the Christian era and reached its high point between 450 and 600 A.D. It was early in the seventh century when the Mayans migrated into Yucatan and built cities like Chichen Itza. Whether, as some suppose, these people are to be identified with the Toltecs driven south by the Aztecs, or not, it is clear that they developed an impressive knowledge of astronomy—one to which modern mathematicians "take off their hats."

Though the time record of the Mayans begins on August 6, 513 B.C., astronomical studies extending back for centuries before this were necessary to secure the data requisite for this calculation. The Mayan calendric system is, moreover, singularly complete. Each year was divided into eighteen periods of twenty days, with five nameless days at the year's end when sacrifices were offered to the Gods of the Four Quarters. Fifty-two of these years formed a cycle, or "bundle." In several other ways beside astronomy the Mayans seem to have been far in advance of other Amerindian peoples. In architecture and sculpture certainly, though they never knew the principle of the keystone to the arch, they show extraordinary ability. It is from these architectural survivals, as at Chichen Itza, we obtain a fairly clear idea of the Mayan religion, though we should know much more had not the Spanish Bishop, Diego de Landa, in the middle of the sixteenth century, destroyed the Mayan records. A recent traveller, Mr. Phillips Russell, writes of the Chichen site: "Here we found everything which could provide (the Mayan) with a complete emotional *katharsis*—bloody human sacrifices to arouse his terror, processions to gratify his love of spectacle, cavernous temples to provoke his awe, naturalistic representations of gods to create his submission, and ball games to divert and excite him." [1]

On the whole, however, the Mayan religion was not nearly so bloody as that of the Aztecs. Dogs, rather than human beings, were customarily offered in sacrifice, though the ceremonial tearing out of the heart of a human being, after smearing the body with stripes of blue, was still performed on special occasions. For example, in time of drought, a virgin was chosen to hurl herself into the Sacred Well at Chichen, to propitiate the rain-god, while the devout followed up the sacrifice by throwing in their jewels. Imitative magic was much in vogue, as is clear from the feasts which were kept at the seasonal crises. The year began about July, when the "new fire" was obtained by friction, all the implements of labour consecrated by anointing or colouring with blue, and other rites used to

[1] Phillips Russell, *Red Tiger*, p. 33.

promote the year's prosperity. In October there was a feast to "the feathered snake," which among the Mayans was named Kukulcan (identifiable with the Aztec Quetzalcoatl). To quote Alexander:[1] "They say and hold for certain that Kukulcan descended from the sky the last day of the feast and personally received the sacrifices, the penitences, and the offerings made in his honour." About December came a festival for the initiation and strengthening of the youth (a kind of Confirmation service), and a month later all the ceremonial utensils were renewed. March was the month for the feast of extinguishing the fire, when fires were first of all lighted into which all manner of animals (and especially their hearts) were thrown. When the victims were consumed water was poured over the holocaust till all was thoroughly extinguished. This, of course, was a rite for bringing rain. April contained the feast in honour of the god of caravans and merchant adventurers, and May witnessed another rain festival, when a dog was slain and its heart placed in a bowl over which another bowl was put as a cover. Then jars full of water were dashed over the spot and the rain was invoked.

Many Mayan myths have been preserved for us in the *Popul Vuh*, an heroic saga written down in the Quiché language in the seventeenth century by a Christianized native of Guatemala. Though the narrative is suspected of Christian colouring, we learn much from its four books as to the Quiché theology, as well as Mayan ideas as to creation. The Quiché equivalent for the Quetzalcoatl of the Aztecs (the Kukulcan of Yucatan) is Gucumatz. Here also we learn of Huragan, the one-legged[2] god of wind and storm, and of Camazotz, the bat-god, ruler of subterranean caves and the underworld.

THE INCAS.—The period of the Incas, conquerors of Peru and the neighbouring territories of an empire attaining, prior to the coming of the Spaniards, an area of 300,000 square miles, and culminating in the reign of Huayna Capac (1482–1529) is, of course, but the last of a whole series of Peruvian culture periods, and cannot be considered as

[1] Hartley B. Alexander, *Latin-American Mythology*, p. 136.
[2] Whence our word *hurricane*.

independent of the Chinin and Tiahuanaco periods which preceded it. The country from the mountains to the sea was favourable enough to agriculture to make possible the cultivation on a large scale of the potato, maize and cotton, and the energy (or the necessities) of the people had succeeded in taming and adapting to their needs such animals as the llama and the guanaco.

The religion of these earlier peoples was mainly one of intermingled fear and gratitude, fear in the presence of mysteries which were probably hostile, and gratitude in the presence of powers from which they derived their sustenance. All things, animate and inanimate, were supposed to have resident in them some spiritual power, capable of doing harm or good to mankind. Such objects were known as *huaca*, a Quechua word for "holy thing." They included springs, rivers, mountains, cliffs, rocks of curious formation, gnarled trees, fierce or uncommon animals, and the like. The "irreflective wonderment" of men before these objects made of them gods. At special times particular reverence was given to one *huaca* or another. For example, when the planting time came round the women spoke pleadingly with Mother Earth, and when a voyage had to be made similar supplications were addressed to the sea. *Huacas* were the objects reverenced by the tribe, but there were also household or personal fetishes (Lares and Penates), known as *conopas*, worshipped by families and individuals as house-guardians.

Religion as thus described naturally persisted into the Incaic period—and beyond it—as a kind of "undying, archaic culture," but there were gods which played a larger rôle than the *huacas* and the *conopas*. One of these was the deity known as Viracocha in the mountain regions and Pachacamac on the coast. He was possibly a deified ancestor, a circumstance suggested by Don Felipé Huaman's remark that "the first race of men in Peru bore the name of Viracocha." But Viracocha was also (if not originally) a kind of sky-god or rain-god, identifiable with the so-called "weeping god" of Peru, whose tears provide the rain. The Viracocha (Pachacamac) worship of the coast was low and fetid, but in the highlands it presented a more philosophic aspect and it was this last which was adopted as a kind of superior religion by the Inca Pachacutec. The Inca religion officially was, however, sun-worship, superimposed on the older cults of Peru. Temples of the sun rose in many places, notably at Cuzco, and here the sanctuary was so holy that anyone who had recently visited the temple took precedence of the man who was journeying towards it. At the Inca Passover all evils were ceremonially expelled from the land, including strangers, deformed persons, those " whose ears were broken," and all dogs. The solemn festival was at the June solstice, to which the tribes came up in picturesque array, some in puma skins, some in feather plumage, and some dressed as condors with outspread wings. A black llama from the herds of the sun was sacrificed, with its head turned towards the east, and its heart torn out while still alive. Many other animals were at the same time offered to the sun and omens drawn from the hearts and other viscera. A little cotton wool was then lighted by means of a metallic mirror and the anger or pleasure of the deity deduced from the time taken to kindle the flame. From the " new fire " the households of all the land were supplied.

Naturally there were other festivals, such as the sowing festival in September, when brown llamas were sacrificed at various shrines, the farms of the sun ploughed by priests and priestesses, and maize beer sprinkled over the fields. There was also a moon festival in October, to ward off sicknesses and other evils. At this time all dogs, and people suffering from infirmities (as noted above), were driven forth and the prayer: " O sicknesses . . . go forth from the land " repeated again and again. Coincidently thirty white llamas were sacrificed, and with the blood and maize little loaves were made which were distributed to the worshippers to form a kind of sacramental meal. By this fellowship was supposed to be established both with the gods and among themselves. In November the brewing of the maize beer took place, as a rain charm, and a black llama was tied out in the fields of the sun to remain unfed till the gods relented and sent rain on the land. In January was celebrated the feast of " breeching " or knighting the youths, who were subjected to severe ordeals and fasts, followed by races and sham battles to teach the enduring of hardness. Other festivals, manifesting the characteristic Amerindian knowledge of astronomy were held at intervals in the year, and the local shrines held their own observances in honour of the moon, Venus and the thunder-god.

Among the priests there were quite a number of orders. Some priests were appointed by the Inca and some were hereditary. The high priest was called Villac-umu, "the soothsayer who speaks." An important place in Inca religion must be assigned to the consecrated virgins, or "chosen women" who, like the Vestal Virgins of Rome, suffered burial alive if guilty of any neglect of their sacred duties.

In the reign of the Inca Pachacutec (1400–1448) a royal effort was made, reminding us of the efforts of the Egyptian idealist Ikhnatun, to secure a higher religion than sun-worship, by the making of Viracocha into a supreme deity. The sun, he declared, was not illimitable in power and not always able to penetrate the clouds. Why not worship a god more adapted to the respect of reflective minds? The effort came too late to save the Inca Empire from decline and ultimate conquest by the Spaniards, but it must be recorded to the credit of one of the best of the Peruvian rulers. It is quite possible to see in Viracocha the making of an *Ens Supremum*. One of the prayers addressed to him begins as follows:

> Viracocha, lord of the universe,
> Whether male or female,
> At any rate commander of heat and reproduction . . .
> Where art Thou?

And it ends:

> O hearken to me,
> Listen to me,
> Let it not befall
> That I grow weary and die.

And another hymn ends:

> Give us life everlasting,
> Preserve us and accept this our sacrifice.

The Andean religion, such as it was, was quenched in blood by the Spanish conquistadores, but not a little of what it believed and practised still survives and maintains itself as intermingled with the religion of its conquerors.[1]

[1] For the history of the Inca dynasties see especially Philip Ainsworth Means, *Ancient Civilization of the Andes*, Chapters VI. and VII.

The general works to be consulted on the subject of this chapter should include: H. H. Bancroft, *History of Mexico*, San Francisco, 1883–88; H. I. Priestley, *The Mexican Nation, A History*, New York, 1923; Eduard Seley, article, "Mayans," in *E.R.E.*, VIII. 505 f.; C. R. Markham, *History of Peru*, Chicago, 1892; W. H. Prescott, *History of the Conquest of Peru*, New York, 1847.

## BOOK IV

## THE RELIGIONS OF THE ORIENT

# CHAPTER XXI

## *The Religions of India—I.*

GROUND has already been prepared for some description of the great historical religions of India. In Chapter IX. a sketch was given of the religion of the pre-Aryan peoples, particularly that of the Dravidians, who, as Tamils, Telugus, and the rest, still hold an important place in Indian ethnology. It was noted that many features of the old shamanistic cults of the Kolarian and Dravidian races remain as elements in present-day Hinduism.

Somewhere about 1500 B.C. the most significant event in the whole history of India took place in the invasion of the peninsula by the people generally described as Aryans. Little enough is known of the origin and course of this migratory movement, but we have already, in Chapter XVII., said something of its relation to the beginnings of Iranian as well as of Indian history. We have seen what the relations were between the people we call Indo-Aryan and Iranian; we have seen the probable circumstances under which the two parts of the great stream separated; and we have seen something (from the Iranian point of view) of the religious consequences of that separation, through which the gods of one section became the devils of the other.

It is now our task to describe as briefly and simply as may be the religious developments which followed the Aryan invasion of India, starting with the revelation of Aryan theology and religion afforded by means of its earliest literature, the *Veda*, and proceeding thence to the remaining stages. The subject will thus arrange itself under four heads, in their historical sequence as follows:

I. The Vedic Age.
II. The Age of the *Brahmanas*.
III. The Age of the *Upanishads* and of the Philosophies generally.
IV. The Age of the great Heresies, particularly those of Jainism and Buddhism.
V. The Age of Hinduism.

Of Indian Muhammadanism and other religious developments we shall speak in later chapters.

I. VEDIC RELIGION.—"In India," says Dr. L. D. Barnett, "there is no twilight before the dawn. In the darkness the eastern sky suddenly flushes and the ruddy edge of the morning sun swiftly leaps upon the horizon." This break in the darkness comes with the emergence of the Vedic Aryans through the passes of the Hindukush in the north-west of India. We know not whether they came in small detachments or in large but, by the light of the *Rig-veda*, we see them gradually advancing from the Indus valley to the valley of the Ganges, crossing river after river, fighting with the "noseless," non-sacrificing aborigines, and more than occasionally with one another, even as English, French and Spanish fought one another in the intervals of subduing Indians on the North American continent.

Though a fighting and aggressive people, these Vedic Aryans were by no means barbarous or primitive. They had domesticated the cow, bull, sheep, goat, swine, dogs and horses. They loved pastoral work among the flocks as well as to follow the plough. Among the arts of life they used spinning, weaving, plaiting and dyeing, and wore woollen clothing as well as skins and furs. They had blacksmiths and goldsmiths, and their weapons of war were of metal as well as of bone and wood. They employed no coined money, but used ornaments as a sort of currency. They did not practise child-marriage, nor as yet the horrible rite of *sati*, but they had, nevertheless, many of the vices of a considerable civilization as well as its virtues, drinking and gambling recklessly. Altogether the Vedic Indians were a virile, flesh-eating, hard-drinking, hard-fighting stock, who found little difficulty in extending their sway beyond the region of the Sapta-sindhavas into the Duab, and further to the south.

Their literature, the *Veda* (*knowledge*), is the oldest Aryan literature we possess, and is the source of almost all we know about the people socially and religiously. When the first assemblage of the hymns was made and the whole collection (*samhita*) first regarded as of religious authority we do not know. The careful preservation of the text, and the counting of lines, words and syllables, resulted, however, from the use of the hymns as spells, or *mantras*, rather than from any purely literary valuation. As the *Veda* stands, we speak of the *Four Vedas*, or sometimes (omitting the *Atharva*) as Three. These are the *Rig-veda*, the *Yajur-veda*, a collection of sacrificial hymns, divided into the *Black and White Yajur*, the *Sama-veda*, or book of songs, and the *Atharva-veda*, a later collection which, however, contains much ancient material of a magical character. The most important, of course, is the *Rig*, a collection of 1017 hymns, or *suktas* (plus eleven supplementary hymns known as *Valakhilyas*), divided into ten books, or *Mandalas*, and assigned to a number of mythical seers known as *rishis*. As poetry, there is already great attention paid to form, and various metres are employed, while the substance of the hymns is a sincere and devout nature worship, the result evidently of genuine emotion produced by the experience of the march.

The religious attitude of the poets—with which we are chiefly concerned—is that of men still obsessed with many of the superstitions of primitive people, yet in the main with hearts uplifted to the beneficent powers of nature in the common human prayer, "Give us this day our daily bread." Thus, while there are spells for the curing of a cough, or for the prolongation of life, most of the *suktas* are in praise of kindly powers in and beyond the sky, from whom the gifts of rain and sunshine and fruitful seasons might be hopefully requested.

The theology of the *Veda* is a well-defined polytheism, though with the clear-cut divine personalities of the Homeric pantheon lacking. Back behind all the gods appears the conception of *Rita* (the Iranian *Arta*), a kind of moral law to which the gods themselves were subject. Then we have the familiar dualism of Heaven and Earth, Dyaus-pitar, the Sky-father, and (much less prominent in Vedic times) Pritthivi-matar, the Earth-mother. Next we have the sublime conception of Varuna, who might so easily have become the god of an Indian monotheism had the trend been that way. Varuna probably represents the old idea of a cosmic ocean above and below the earth—the "sea" of the Babylonian mythology. But to-day he has degenerated into a mere godling concerned with pools and puddles. In the *Veda*, however, Varuna is the ethical god, to whom the worshipper addressed himself in penitence:

> What gift of mine will he enjoy unangered ?
> When shall I, happy-hearted, see his mercy?

Varuna is often invoked together with Mitra (the friend), an old, displaced solar deity, who later came again into his own as the Mithra of Persia and the Roman soldiers.

Most powerful of all the Vedic gods was Indra, to whom are addressed 250 hymns in the *Rig-veda*. He is, first of all, the storm-god of the pantheon, but later was India's war-god, the slayer of the monster who dried up the rivers and pastures, and the leader of the mighty host of conquering Aryans against the Dasyus. With Indra are associated other storm-gods. There was Rudra (*the ruddy*), the wild boar of the sky, the lightning flash, whose distinctiveness made it natural that he should later be transformed into Çiva. There were also the Maruts, or *Crushers*, the storm-angels who, with golden helmets, and wielding lightnings, drove their swift, tawny horses across the wind-blown heavens. There was, again, Parjanya, the rain-cloud, invoked in but three hymns, which, nevertheless, are notable for their beauty. Once again, we have Vayu, or Vata, the wind-god, the breath of the gods, which "comes rending the air, with noise of thunder."

Next in importance to Indra is Agni, the fire-god, whose praises are chanted in 200 hymns. We see here the importance of the fire cult, upon which, indeed, civilization itself was in large part founded. Agni has many forms; he is the god of the hearth-fire, the god of the funeral pyre, the god of the fire in the air and in the sky. But he is especially the god of the sacrifice, the priestly god, now appearing in his avatar as a dwarf to win back the universe from the demons, now making his circuit through the heavens as the sun. So associated with Agni we have the sun-god Surya (known also as Savitar), to whom many beautiful hymns are addressed; Ushas, the rosy-fingered goddess of the dawn, the Eos of the Greeks and Aurora of the Latins; also the divine Twins, the Açvins, or Horsemen (the Dioscuroi of the Greeks), who probably represent the two twilights, or the morning and evening star.

A god of a quite special character is the drink-god, Soma, to whom all the hymns of the ninth book of the *Rig-veda* are addressed. Soma was probably the deified juice of the moon-plant, *Sarcostema viminale*, or *Asclepias acida*, a milkweed out of which an intoxicating liquor was brewed to take the place of the barley beer brewed by the Aryans in their earlier habitat. It is easy to realize that the use of such a drink would in time take on a sort of sacramental significance, as in the corresponding use of *haoma* with the Iranians. In course of time Soma came to represent the invigorating sap of life with which the moon was supposed to charge herself gradually during the month. Hence the custom of planting seeds at the full moon, when nature reached her climax of vigour. Gods such as Indra were described as quaffing huge quantities of soma, and many wonderful properties were ascribed to the beverage by its participants, mortal and immortal alike.

There still remain a number of lesser gods belonging to the Vedic system. There is Pushan, originally perhaps a solar god, but here approached by the devout as a pathfinder, to whom shepherds and wanderers looked for guidance in the night. There is, again, Brihaspati, lord of prayer, naturally associated with Agni, the god of sacrifice. We have also Yama, god of death, originally a king, with his wife Yamī, and his spotted, broad-snouted, four-eyed dogs, the children of Sarama. It was his work to lead the dead along the road, a psychopomp, like Anubis. Once again, there are the Pitris, or ancestors, and many divinities of yet lower degree, including the horses of Indra, the cows, the waters, even the dice-gods, and the gods of medicinal herbs.

Towards the end of the tenth book of the *Rig-veda* it is obvious that we are already beginning the passage from polytheism towards pantheism. Dr. Macdonell considers the famous hymn, X. 90, as "the starting-point of the pantheistic philosophy." It commences:

> A thousand hands has Purusha,
> A thousand eyes, a thousand feet;
> He holding earth enclosed about,
> Extends beyond, ten fingers' length.

Even more striking is the magnificent cosmic hymn: *To the Unknown God:*

> The Golden Germ arose in the beginning,
> Born the sole lord of everything existing;
> He fixed and holdeth up the earth and heaven;—
> Who is the god to worship with oblation?

But there is not much in the *Veda* like this. On the whole, the deities are more or less highly anthropomorphized physical forces, endowed with the virtues and the vices of their worshippers, and appealed to for things which belong mostly to the material world.[1]

Let us now see what type of cult found its sanctions in such a theology. It is plain from what has been said that the attitude of men in Vedic India was profoundly religious. Everything done in the home was a religious act. The lighting of the household fire, indeed, was the laying of the foundation of the home, and the leading of the bride around the fire, in the ceremony known as the *pradakshina*, was an important part of the marriage rite. The god of marriage, Viçvavasu, was appealed to for his presence on such an occasion. Similarly, the funeral rites, or *çraddhas*, were of religious importance, both for the sake of the dead (to hasten their *gati* towards the world of the pitris), and for the sake of the survivors. Both burial and cremation were at first used, as may be seen from such hymns as R.V.X. 18. Satī, as already remarked, is not supported by the correct

[1] On the theology of the "Veda" see H. D. Griswold, *The Religion of the Rigveda*, Oxford, 1923; also A. A. Macdonell, *Vedic Mythology*, London, 1897.

reading of R.V.X. 18, 7, but was nevertheless of ancient authority. The Vedic hymns, however, declare: "Rise, woman, and go to the world of living beings: come, this man near whom thou sleepest is lifeless; thou hast enjoyed this state of being the wife of thy husband, the suitor who took thee by the hand."

Primitive and popular religion soon came under the direction of an organized ecclesiasticism and the Brahman, who had at first been inferior to the warrior, gained an ascendancy he has succeeded in retaining to the present day. There were four orders of priests (all, of course, Brahmans), namely, the Hotar, or *Caller*, whose business it was to recite the verses in praise of the gods; the Udgatri, or *Singer*, who accompanied the offering of the sacrifice with song; the Adhvarya, who was expert in the muttered formulæ suitable for each particular sacrifice; and the Brahman proper, who was the overseer of the entire ritual. Of the ritual itself we shall speak presently.

The institution of Caste, which plays so important a part in the subsequent history, does not seem to have been originally Vedic. As its Sanskrit equivalent, *varna* (*colour*) denotes, the observance of caste was originally the precaution taken by the white-skinned Aryans to prevent assimilation with the darker-skinned aborigines. As time went on, however, the caste divisions became four, and in the last book of the *Rig-veda* (X. 90) we have the suggestion that the four castes of Brahmans, or priests, Kshatriyas, or warriors, Vaiçyas, or people generally, and Çudras, or non-Aryans, were derived respectively from the head, arms, thighs and feet of the immolated divine being, Purusha. It is perhaps needless to say that in later times these four castes multiplied themselves indefinitely and now constitute India's major social problem.[1]

II. THE BRAHMANIC PERIOD.—With the achievement of the ascendancy of the Brahman we reach a stage of Indian religion which we may call Brahmanic, commencing at some rather uncertain epoch following the Aryan conquest and attaining its height about the seventh century B.C. It

[1] On the civilization of Vedic times see Zenaide Ragozin, *Vedic India*, New York, 1895.

should be explained that while the word Brahm denotes the impersonal element out of which the world periodically evolved, and while the word Brahma signifies that manifestation of Brahm which is concerned with creation, the Brahman is the "prayer-man," or representative of the divine among men. As the technique of his priestly office became too elaborate to be easily retained by the unaided memory, it came in time to be embodied in ritual commentaries on the *Veda* known as Brahmanas, and it is from these that most of our knowledge of Brahmanic religion is derived. Each of the Vedas has its Brahmanas, the *Rig-veda* the *Aitreya* and the *Kaushitaki*, the *Yajur-veda* the *Taittiriya* and the *Çatapatha*, the *Sama-veda* eight, of which the best known is the *Chhandogya*, and the *Atharva-veda* the *Gopatha*. They represent, says Eggeling, "the intellectual activity of a sacerdotal caste which by turning to account the instincts of a gifted and naturally devout race, had succeeded in transforming a primitive worship of the powers of nature into a highly artificial system of sacrificial ceremonies." [1]

Naturally much of the concern of the *Brahmanas* is with sacrifice and the linking up of the Vedic songs with the ritual. Sacrifice was regarded not so much as an expiation for sin as a means of strengthening the exhausted gods. It was also a means for gaining power—entirely apart from moral considerations. Some were thereby enabled, by sacrifices on the grand scale, for example, the hundred-horse sacrifice, to obtain power over the gods. In this way the demon Ravana made himself invulnerable, except through the agency of men or monkeys. Three great groups of sacrificial rites are described, each group with seven separate sacrifices. There was the Great Sacrifice, with its three fires, its games, chariot-races and drinking bouts. There was the Havir Sacrifice, with its oblations of butter, milk, rice and meat, at which all four orders of priests had to be present. There was also the seven-fold Pāka Sacrifice, performed at the domestic hearth at certain seasons of the year. In early times there had undoubtedly

[1] Julius Eggeling, Introduction to the *Çatapatha Brahmana,* Vol. IX., Sacred Books of the East.

been the use of human sacrifices, as is plain from the story of Çunaçepa and from the order [1] to make the altar in the shape of a human being. But for man had been substituted the horse, in the greatest of Vedic sacrifices, known as the *açvamedha*—where the horse was a symbol of the sun. Later still the goat was substituted for the horse. The place of sacrifice was normally a room in a Brahman's house, or in a large shed. The floor was first covered with the sacred *kusa* grass, the couch of the gods. Much attention had to be paid to all the implements used, such as the sacrificial pillar, which must be hewn with an axe, while the axe itself was entreated: "O axe, hurt it not." The earthly sacrifice was supposed to have its counterpart in the heavenly sacrifices of Prajapati, lord of creatures, whose strength, exhausted by the act of creation, had to be recuperated by the Brahmanic ritual. At the same time the worshipper had to do his best to identify himself with the animal offered to the gods, and this he achieved by wearing the skin of the victim and by a sacramental feast, so as to feel himself reborn to a more highly vitalized relation with his god and his community.

The *Brahmanas* have much of interest apart from their character as textbooks for the priestly order. They give us old myths and legends, such as that of the Flood from which Manu was saved through the intervention of Vishnu, and that of Indra's defeat of the demons' attempt to raise a fire-tower to the heavens. They explain curious questions of ritual by such apologues as that of *Mind and Speech*, and in other ways they throw light on the systematization of religion in the priestly stage. They reveal religion as what is termed *Karma-kanda*, the religion of doing things, a type in which all depended on the meticulous exactness with which every detail of a ceremony was performed.

It is obvious that such a conception of religion threw enormous power into the hands of the priestly caste and many, some of them grotesque, are the illustrations given of enormous fees earned by the Brahmans in the performance of their responsible office. For example, one worshipper is said to have given 85,000 white horses, 10,000 elephants,

[1] *Çatapatha Brahmana*, I. 2, 5, 16.

and 80,000 slave girls to a Brahman as a fee. When King Janaka offered to Yajnavalkya 1000 cows, each with ten pieces of gold fastened to its horns, the Brahman's only notice of the generosity was an order to his pupil to drive home the cows.

That the power of the Brahmans has never since that time—except during the supremacy of Buddhism—been broken is one of the salient facts of Indian history, but even the seventh century B.C. was not without its revolts.

III. The Upanishadic Period.—A very broad distinction has been commonly made between the *Brahmanas* and *Upanishads*, or philosophic commentaries on the *Veda*, as though these represented completely opposite poles of thought. It is true that the *Brahmanas* give us the religion of works, the *Karma-kanda*, while the *Upanishads* are concerned with *Jnana-kanda*, or the religion of knowing. But the transition is not so abrupt as has sometimes been described. As Dr. Edgerton has shown, even the intellectual quests of India have always been associated with practical ends—" If one could only know everything, he could thereby get everything."

Thus the *Upanishads* are not so much experiments in a direction opposite to that of the *Brahmanas*; they rather continue the Indian effort to achieve release, or *moksha*, by the way of knowledge instead of by way of works.

From this point of view an interesting and significant transition is marked by the books known as *Aranyakas*, or " forest *Brahmanas*." As men decided to abandon the preoccupations of domestic life, and to settle down to the ascetic career, it became necessary to provide these with textbooks in the art of meditation rather than manuals of ritual. And these forest *Brahmanas*, in turn, formed a bridge by which men might pass to meditate on the one reality in the true Upanishadic sense.

The word *Upanishad* probably signifies " a sitting down under " (*upa-ni-shad*) a teacher, and it may be remembered that the teacher need not be a Brahman. The books probably belong to a period about 600 B.C., and must have been very numerous. The number has been reckoned from 150 to nearly 250, some so late that there is even a Muhammadan *Upanishad*, the *Alla Upanishad*. They are not always easy to analyse, since they show abrupt change of manner and subject, and (as Professor Geden says) "the entire treatment is suggestive rather of intimate oral instruction than of methodical exposition."

They stress the use of the syllable *Om* (really *Aum*) as the symbol of the highest self. They suggest the spiritualization of much of the old ritual, as, for instance, when the *Chhandogya Upanishad* declares: "Man is sacrifice. His first twenty-four years are the morning oblation. The next forty-four years are the midday libation. The next forty-eight years are the third libation." They speak much of the hidden self, which is contiguous to the absolute self, and show that here dwell all our true desires and our power to attain them. They reveal the steps which have been taken from the old polytheism towards the pantheism of the future. When Yajnavalkya is asked, How many gods are there? he replies at first, Three and three hundred, three and three thousand, but when the question is repeated he declares ultimately there is but one. The general attitude of all the Upanishadic writers is the idealistic monism which we shall presently note as *Vedanta*. The beautiful prayer of the *Brihad-aranyaka* is:

> From the unreal lead me to the real:
> From darkness lead me to light:
> From death lead me to immortality.

It is unnecessary here to describe the influence which the *Upanishads*—among the first Indian writings translated into a western tongue—have had on the philosophy of the West, through Schopenhauer and his successors. It is as important to know the influence they still possess in Indian religion, as witness the words of Rabindranath Tagore (in *Sadhana*): "The writer has been brought up in a family where the texts of the *Upanishads* are used in daily worship. . . . To me the verses of the *Upanishads* have ever been things of the spirit, and therefore endowed with boundless vital growth."

In the *Upanishads* the general drift of Indian philosophy is sufficiently apparent. But there are important variations of interpretation such as lead eventually to the creation of differing and even antagonistic schools. But before giving a necessarily brief account of the *Six Orthodox Schools* it will be useful to mention certain principles common to all the schools.

Foremost among these is the practically unanimous belief in *samsara*, or metempsychosis, a doctrine probably not originally Aryan, but borrowed from the aboriginal population. It took such complete possession of the Indian mind as to become everywhere an accepted postulate. On the theory of *samsara* no unmerited punishment could befall a man. "As among a thousand cows a calf follows its mother, so the previously done deed follows the doer." Closely connected with this was the belief in a cyclical creation and dissolution of the material world, the process requiring a kalpa, or period amounting to 4,320,000,000 years. Other ideas were the eternity of the soul, though distinction has to be made between the *paramatman*, or supreme, universal soul, and the *jivatman*, or individual soul. Some schools believed in the existence of an uncountable (though not infinite) number of individual souls, eternal retrospectively as well as prospectively, while others held that the Universal soul alone existed, and that individual souls only existed through *avidya*, or ignorance. Another general belief was that in the eternity of matter, though here again a distinction must be made between the belief in gross matter, as maintained by the materialist, and belief in matter as an illusion of the soul overspread by *maya*. It was accepted by all that consciousness could only arise when the soul was invested with bodily form, through association with a physical particle known as the *manas*—translated as *mind*. This union of body and soul was, however, uniformly productive of misery and while, in view of preceding beliefs, heavens and hells were necessary for working out the consequences of acts, known as *karma*, beyond all heavens and hells lay the only desirable bourn, *Nirvana*, which was release (*moksha*) from bondage to matter. This hoped-for consummation is not to be interpreted as extinction, but rather the surrender of all supposed separateness—the sliding of the dewdrop into the ocean.

It is easy to see that, even with certain ideas held in common, there was much room in the above-mentioned beliefs for diversity. A Buddhist writer speaks of as many as sixty-two varieties of Upanishadic thought. But very early a distinction was made between philosophies which were orthodox and those which were heterodox. Strangely enough, the distinction was not based on theologic belief, since even among the orthodox schools some were atheistic, some pantheistic, and some dualistic. Orthodoxy was rather a matter of compliance with custom as to the acceptance of the Veda and of the authority of the Brahmans.

As to the six orthodox schools, known as the *Shad Darçanas* (*Six Views*), it is perhaps unfortunate that we cannot treat them in their historic sequence. This is due not merely to the fact that we know so little of the authors, but also to the fact that early and late elements appear in every system. Here it will be sufficient to name them and indicate briefly the characteristic feature of each. They may be remembered best by thinking of them as three pairs, namely, the Nyaya and Vaiçeshika, the Samkhya and Yoga, and the Purva-mimamsa (Mimamsa) and Uttara-mimamsa (Vedanta).

1. The *Nyaya* (*analysis*) is really a system of logic rather than philosophy, and is based on a textbook by one Gautama (not the Buddha) called the *Nyaya-sutra*. It furnishes a "correct method of philosophical enquiry into all the objects and subjects of human knowledge, including, amongst others, the process of reasoning and the laws of thought." It may be noted in passing that Indian logic differs from the Greek in using a syllogism of five members rather than one of three. For example (to use a common illustration), it states a proposition as follows: "The hill is fiery; For it smokes; Whatever smokes is fiery; This hill smokes; Therefore this hill is fiery." Nyaya is to Indian thought what Aristotelianism is to the thought of the West. It provides the tools for the thinker, so that the latter may do his work understandingly. From false notions, it was believed, spring false activities of the soul, and thence *samsara*. So salvation, after all, was held to depend upon a correct logic. For the rest the philosophy accepted an

ultimate reality of " things," of souls, and of God as distinct from His creation.

2. *Vaiçeshika* was so named from the particularity (*viçesha*) which is emphasized in a theory of atoms ascribed to one named (or nicknamed) Kanada (*the atom-eater*). The system extends the logical method of Nyaya to physical investigations, maintaining the reality, not only of souls, but also of such things as space, time and atoms. The world is supposedly formed by the aggregation of atoms, which, although eternal and innumerable, are not infinite in number. Their constant combination, disintegration and recombination are due to the activity of a hypothetical force called *adrishta* (*the unseen*), which is in turn the result of the accumulated *karma* of all sentient beings. Though impersonal, this adrishta became for many of the followers of Kanada a kind of blind deity. It will be observed that in the atomic theory of this philosophy there is something not wholly unlike Nietzsche's doctrine of " the eternal return."

3. *Samkhya*, which signifies *synthesis*, and is probably the oldest of the philosophical schools, is ascribed to Kapila, a semi-mythical sage, whose historical reality is now being generally abandoned. He was supposed to have made the first protest against monism and to have taught that primordial matter was the basis of the universe. The school is frankly dualistic. On the one hand, there is postulated an innumerable number of uncreated souls, eternally separate one from the other, and yet (since what is eternal is incapable of disintegration) omnipresent. On the other hand, there is the ever-active potentiality of nature, Prakriti (the producer), the eternal, rootless evolver, a subtle essence made up of three constituent qualities, or *gunas*, namely, *sattva* (goodness), *rajas* (passion), and *tamas* (darkness, or stolidity). When Prakriti is in union with the soul (Purusha) then everything is produced, as milk is secreted by the cow. To use the illustration of Monier-Williams, " the soul is a looker-on, uniting itself with unintelligent Prakriti, as a lame man mounted on a blind man's shoulders, for the sake of observing the phenomena of creation, which Prakriti himself is unable to observe."

Samkhya, in its classical form, is thoroughly atheistic, but some later thinkers, dissatisfied with the apparently accidental harmony between the interacting souls and natural possibility, assume a kind of god in an omniscient spirit. The system was, of course, held within the poles of orthodoxy by its profession of belief in the *Veda*.

4. Intimately related to the Samkhya philosophically is *Yoga*, or "yoking," *i.e.* with the divine, a practical concession to those unable to endure the stark pessimism of the older system. A proverb says: "No knowledge like the Samkhya, no power like the Yoga." It is a concession, first, in its acceptance of a Supreme Being and, secondly, in providing a practical discipline whereby the soul may find union with this Being. In brief, Yoga is an art for the securing of larger vision and the powers—latent in all men—through which the lower self is conquered and the higher self set free for fellowship with God. Some of these methods, though unduly subjected to the Indian obsession for classification, are suggested by common sense rather than by any particular system of philosophy. Some of them have been over-enthusiastically hailed in the West for the benefit of the esoterically minded. Others consist of practices which have made the Yogi in India an object of pity if not of contempt. Yet these eccentricities of self-mortification have for others represented the summit level of spirituality. The *Bhagavad-gita* declares:

> That holy man who stands immovable,
> As if erect upon a pinnacle,
> His appetites and organs all subdued,
> Sated with knowledge secular and sacred,
> To whom a lump of earth, a stone, or gold,
> To whom friends, relatives, or acquaintances,
> Neutrals and enemies, the good and bad,
> Are all alike, is called "one yoked with God."[1]

The Swami Vivekananda describes the Yogi as revealing to the world the living power which lies coiled up in every being, the Giver of eternal happiness. On the other hand, Sir M. Monier-Williams declares that the system is "a mere contrivance for getting rid of all thought, or rather

[1] Translation by Sir M. Monier-Williams, *Hinduism*, London, 1885.

for concentrating the mind with the utmost intensity upon nothing in particular." The sober truth probably lies somewhere midway between these extremes. The textbook of Yoga, the *Yoga Sutra*, is ascribed to Patānjali, though the practices associated with the system undoubtedly go much further back than the second century B.C.

5. The *Mimamsa*, or *Purva-Mimamsa*, *i.e.* "the earlier investigation," is ascribed to Jaimini, and, like the Yoga, is a practical system, teaching the ceremonial duty of man in reference to the sacrifices, while in its theological attitude it is either agnostic or polytheistic. "The Supreme Being might exist, but was not necessary to the system." On the other hand, the *Veda* was eternal, as are all articulate sounds. "The echoes of a word once uttered vibrate in space to all eternity."

6. Connected philosophically with the above is the *Uttara-Mimamsa*, or "later investigation," generally known as the *Vedanta*, or "end of the Veda." It represents a definite gathering up of the doctrine of the *Upanishads* and in its various formulations extends over a long period of history, down to the time of the great Çamkarachārya, in the eighth century, and even to the time of men like Ramkrishna Parahamsa and the Swami Vivekananda in modern times. Vedantism is really a kind of pantheistic monism, expressing its main tenets in such terms as *advaita*, or *non-dualism*, and in such phrases as "Brahma exists truly, the world falsely; the soul is only Brahma and no other." All else but Brahma is *maya*, or illusion, but by reason of ignorance (*avidya*) the living soul mistakes the world and his own body and mind for realities, just as a man walking along the road may mistake a piece of rope for a serpent. To remind man of his constant need for a right comprehension of his relation to the universe, the Vedantist employs the catchword, *Tat tvam asi* (*Thou art that*). When man has ceased to distinguish between the soul and God, he attains *moksha*, or release.[1]

It must be observed, however, that some teachers, such

[1] On the "Vedanta" see especially Paul Deussen, *The Philosophy of the Upanishads*, Edinburgh, 1906; also Rudolf Otto, *Mysticism, East and West*, New York, 1932. In the latter book is an elaborate comparison of Çamkara and Eckhart.

as Çamkara, taught an unqualified monism, others, like Ramanuja and Ramananda, a monism which was qualified by many concessions to the less advanced. It was natural that, in addition to the orthodox schools to which allusion has been made there should be shadings off here and there in the direction of eclecticism.

One of these eclectic systems must here be mentioned since it produced one of the best-known religious poems of India, the *Bhagavad-gita*. This is a long philosophic poem set in the midst of the great epic, the *Mahabharata*, as the discourse of the god Krishna, acting as the charioteer of Arjuna, in answer to his master's question as to the moral right of kinsmen to engage in mortal combat with one another. The battle is set in array, the Pandavas and the Kauravas are about to fight, when Arjuna puts the query. Then the god, who is attached to the side of the Pandavas, launches into a disquisition in which he declares that every caste, including that of the warriors, was bound to fulfil its obligations and that, moreover, there was no serious harm done by slaughter, since both "the red slayer" and the man who thinks he is slain are merely the victims of *maya*.

The poem, eighteen cantos in length, is probably the work of a pious Brahman, writing subsequently to the opening of the Christian era, who endeavours to reconcile the contradictory principles of Samkhya, Yoga and Vedanta, and who has probably included also some sentiments originally Christian. In large stretches of the poem the philosophy is pure Vedanta in which the god reveals himself as the manifestation of all in heaven and earth:

> The life in all, the father, mother, husband,
> Forefather and sustainer of the world,
> Its friend and lord.

It should be added that, in addition to the philosophy, the poem reflects that new type of religion we call *bhakti*, in which the devotion of the soul to God, through one of the avatars of Vishnu, notably that of Krishna, has become a prominent feature of religion. It was a daring thing to take the legendary, human Krishna, with all his faults thick upon him, and transform him into a revelation of the

Supreme God. Yet who will deny the grandeur of the conception? It is with good reason that Dr. Kenneth Saunders writes:[1]

"Here indeed Upanishadic thought comes very near to that of the *Prologue* of the Fourth Gospel; the Logos doctrine finding its fulfilment in the Incarnate Christ is a doctrine of divine immanence, of the creative power of God which is in all things, and which is the light that lights all men."

Here we must pause in the long story of the development of Indian religion to take note of the rise of movements which the Indian called heresies, notably the two great heresies of Jainism and Buddhism.[2]

[1] Kenneth Saunders, *The Gospel for Asia*, pp. 90–91.

[2] For a fuller treatment of the *literature* embraced in this chapter see H. H. Gowen, *History of Indian Literature*, New York, 1931. The chapters covered are from iv. to ix. inclusive. For further material on the "religion" of the period consult: Sir Ananda Acharya, *Brahmadarsanam*, New York, 1917; Auguste Barth, *The Religions of India*, London, 1882; S. Dasgupta, *Yoga*, London, 1924; John N. Farquhar, *A Primer of Hinduism*, Oxford, 1912; Richard Garbe, *The Philosophy of Ancient India*, Chicago, 1899; E. W. Hopkins, *The Religions of India*, Boston, 1895; A. A. Macdonell, *Vedic Mythology*, London, 1897; Nicol MacNicol, *Indian Theism*, London, 1915.

## CHAPTER XXII

# *The Religions of India—II.*

### THE GREAT HERESIES

IT has been already pointed out that not all Indian schools of philosophy were orthodox, in the sense of accepting the authority of the Brahmans. In certain cases, as in that of the Nastikas (from *na-asti*, *it is not*), negation was carried to an extreme point and the *Veda* was denounced as foolish and untrue. The legendary founder of this school is one Charvaka, whence the school was known as that of the Charvakas. It was also called Lokayata, that is, directed toward " the world of sense." The theory was an entirely naturalistic one and may be gathered from the following quotation from the *Sarva-darçana-samgraha*:

> There is no heaven, no final liberation, nor any soul in another world.
> Nor do the actions of the four castes, or orders, produce any effect . . .
> While life remains let man live happily, let him feed on ghee, even though he runs in debt.
> When once the body becomes ashes, how can it ever return again? . . .
> All these ceremonies for the dead—there is no other fruit anywhere.
> The three authors from the Vedas were buffoons, knaves and demons.

As a sect the Charvakas are now extinct, but there are other heterodox schools which have shown great vitality. Two of these we must consider somewhat at length, Jainism and Buddhism.

JAINISM.—The religious movements of the sixth century B.C. are not to be taken as a mere perverse revolt against the power of the Brahmans. They may quite well have had some relation to that mighty current of religious awakening which passed across the entire continent of Asia, giving Lao Tzu and Confucius to the East even as it gave Zoroaster and the Hebrew prophets to the West. In India itself we have exuberant illustration of unwonted interest at this time in the things of the spirit. Seventy or more movements have been referred to, most of which have perished unsung and unwept. But two were destined to survive, in a strikingly diverse way. Jainism was fated to find no home outside of India but, nevertheless, in its native land to attain permanent status. Buddhism was destined to become a world religion, though practically banished from the country of its origin.

It is not possible here to present a complete account of the Jain philosophy and religion, but a few things must not be overlooked. The word *Jain* is derived from the root *ji*, *to conquer*, and signifies the religion of those who have overcome the lust of living. Dr. Farquhar says: "Jainism was originally merely a specialization and intensification of the old ascetic discipline under the influence of an extreme reverence for life and of a dogmatic belief that not only men, animals and plants, but even the smallest particles of earth, fire, water and wind are endowed with living souls. Consequently, a very large part of the Jain monk's attention was directed towards using the extremest care not to injure any living thing. So eager were the Jains to part with the world to the uttermost that many of their monks wore not a scrap of clothing. Twelve years of most severe asceticism were necessary for salvation. After that, if a monk did not wish to live, he was recommended to starve himself to death." [1]

Jainism seems to represent a teaching long antecedent to the career of its most distinguished teacher, Mahavira. Indeed the Jains always speak of their faith as eternal. Nevertheless, it is convenient to start consideration of the system with some account of this Vardhamana Mahavira, whose life seems to have extended from 599 to 527 B.C., dates which make him an older contemporary of the Buddha. Like Gautama he was a *kshatriya* and hailed from the region of Magadha. He is said to have been the son of a nobleman of Vaiçali and related to the royal family of his native state. Many legends are told of his mother Triçala and of her dreams concerning her progeny, but we pass these over to mention the bare facts of his vocation to the ascetic life, his marriage to the Lady Yaçoda, the birth of his daughter,

[1] J. N. Farquhar, *Primer of Hinduism*, p. 50.

who eventually married Jamali (the first schismatic), his initiation as a monk in the thirtieth year of his age, his fasting under the Açoka tree, and other episodes closely paralleling the career of his younger contemporary. Born with three degrees of knowledge, Mahavira attained the remaining fourth at his *kevala*, or enlightenment, and then for forty-two years of monkhood preached the message of deliverance to his generation, till "the two terrible ones" who dog the soul, birth and death, ceased to have power over him and he passed away quietly and alone.

Mahavira is regarded by Jains as the latest born of twenty-four historical "conquerors" known as the Tirthankaras (or Tirthakaras), or "ford-makers." Of the early Tirthakaras there are endless, and frequently grotesque, legends. The nineteenth is said to have been born as a woman owing to deceitfulness in a previous life. This one "little rift within the lute" marred the perfection of the ascetic life in its twenty particulars, and Mallinatha became, in spite of all else, a woman. The immediate predecessor of Mahavira was Parçvanatha, said to have been born at Benares about 817 B.C. It is possible that, like his successor, he was an historical personage.

In addition to the twenty-four Tirthakaras, Jain mythology speaks of twelve Chakravartins, or world-monarchs, of nine Vasudevas, nine Baladevas, and nine Prativasudevas, making altogether the sixty-three great personages, as celebrated in more than one piece of Jain literature.

Mahavira gathered around him in his lifetime 14,000 disciples, divided into four orders, or *tirthas*, of monks, nuns, lay-men and lay-women. But difference of opinion appeared early and eight great schisms are recorded, beginning with that of Mahavira's son-in-law, Jamali, and ending with the permanent split of A.D. 83, which produced the Digambaras. The schism of Jamali was over the question as to whether a thing was perfected when it was begun, but the real discussion concerned the more practical matter of the right way to make beds. The eighth schism came about through the influence of Vajrasena, and henceforth the Digambaras, or "sky-clothed," held to the principle of nakedness, and such other matters as the impossibility of women achieving deliverance, and the need of food after a saint has obtained "complete knowledge." The older body of Jains were known as the Çvetambaras, or "white-clothed."

The Jains built many shrines, some of which are *stupas*, or towers, and some cave-temples, hewn out of the solid rock. The best known are those of Mt. Abu in the Aravalli range. Sir Richard Temple writes of this famous place: "The numerous cupolas, obelisks and spires, often bright with the whitest marble, seem to pierce the sky. The shrines are laden with the weight of gorgeous offerings, sent by wealthy members of the sect from almost every populous city of the empire."

Jain literature is quite extensive and includes, beside the *Canon* and its commentaries, much in the way of poetry and moral tales, as also a number of works on lexicography and grammar. The Digambara *Canon* differs from that of the Çvetambara, the latter having been fixed in A.D. 454. The Jain books were written in both prose and verse and originally in a vernacular known as Ardha-Magadhi, but for the last thousand years it has been customary to use the Sanskrit. It is difficult to convey in a few words the teachings of the Jain *Canon*. The leading ideas approximate to the Samkhya philosophy, but much emphasis is laid on the "indefiniteness of being" thus explained by Dr. Jacobi:

"Existing things are permanent only as regards their substance, but their accidents, or qualities, originate and perish. To explain: any material thing continues to exist for ever as matter; this matter, however, may assume any shape and quality. Thus clay, for example, may be regarded as permanent, but the form of a jar of clay, or its colour, may come into existence and perish."

Souls also are eternal and are infinite in number, good Jains being ever engaged in freeing these from their association with matter along the threefold way of right faith, right knowledge, and right conduct. The monk takes five vows: not to kill, not to lie, not to steal, to abstain from sexual intercourse, and to renounce all earthly possessions. When these vows are completely fulfilled, the Jain, as already noted, may commit suicide by self-starvation.

In general, it may be said that the rules laid down for the Jain do not greatly differ from those laid down for the Brahmanic ascetic, but whether one copied from the other, and which one, are matters of uncertainty.

The Jains to-day number but 1,178,596, according to the latest figures, but they have exercised an influence out of all proportion to their numbers. In the south a good deal of Tamil literature has been much coloured by the faith of Mahavira, some of the finest of Tamil poems being distinctively Jain. And they form still quite an important religious community, found in all parts of northern Hindustan, but especially in the West, in Mewar and Gujerat. Unfortunately, however, their literary activity is to-day wellnigh confined to journalism and pamphleteering.[1]

BUDDHISM.—Historically the story of Buddhism in India is little more than an interlude, and even religiously the faith seems from the first to have revealed currents at variance with the general trend. Some years ago the exploration of Açoka's old capital of Pataliputra (Patna) by Mr. D. B. Spooner suggested that the palace of the first Buddhist Emperor of India was "a Mauryan copy of the entire Persepolitan design" of the palace of Darius Hystaspes. On this archæological foundation Mr. Spooner built the theory that Buddhism stood for the spiritual acclimatization of Iranians domiciled in India after the invasion of Alexander the Great, and that even before this Gautama represented the beginnings of "a Zoroastrian period" in Indian religion. Of this interesting hypothesis not much has survived, and we can offer other reasons for the success of Buddhism than the supposition of its foreign origin.[2]

First and foremost, is the undoubted appeal made by the personality of the founder. This appeal not only made Gautama the centre of a considerable circle of devoted disciples, but it later compelled the Hindus to include him as one of the ten avatars of Vishnu, and it had the even

[1] On Jainism see Hermann Jacobi, *Gaina Sûtras*, Vol. X., S.B.E.; Mrs. Sinclair Stevenson, *The Heart of Jainism*, Oxford, 1915. Also *Encyclopædia of Religion and Ethics*, art. "Jainism."

[2] See D. B. Spooner, "The Zoroastrian Period in Indian History," *Journal Royal Asiatic Society*, 1915, pp. 63–89, 405–445.

more remarkable result of securing the canonization of the Buddha, under the name of St. Josaphat, in the Christian Church, in the Calendar of the Eastern Church on August 26 and in that of the Western Church on November 27. This came about through the popularity of the romance, *Barlaam and Josaphat*, written by St. John of Damascus, on the basis of materials borrowed from the *Lalitavistara*.

We may be doubtful as to the precise date of Gautama's birth and death; yet we feel that the India of the sixth century B.C. was a soil well prepared for such a life and such a teaching. It was in this significant time, within what is known as the Nepalese Terai, in the raj of one Çuddhodhana, whose capital was Kapilavastu, that the child was born, whose personal name was Siddhartha, his family name Gautama, and the name of his clan that of the Çakyas. The actual birthplace is marked by a pillar erected by King Açoka, in the third century B.C., which is first referred to by the Chinese pilgrim Fa-hien 1500 years ago, and was rediscovered in December 1896.

We need not pursue the fantastic sequence of legendary lore with which a pious fancy has embroidered the story of Prince Siddhartha. It will be found in all its exuberance of detail in Sir Edwin Arnold's *Light of Asia*, which is itself based on a Sanskrit work:

> The Scripture of the Saviour of the World,
> Lord Buddha, Prince Siddhartha styled on earth—
> In Earth and Heavens and Hells incomparable,
> All-honoured, Wisest, Best, most Pitiful;
> The Teacher of Nirvana and the Law.

We may just recall the legends making known to Mayadevi the miraculous birth to be; the story of wonders attending that birth; the shout of victory and the seven steps; the story of the mother's death seven days after; the coming of the grey-haired sage, Asita. Then, with epic wealth of detail, follows the account of the young kshatriya's education, his supernatural athletic skill, the tossing of the elephant over the wall, the creation of a spring where the miraculous arrow fell, the discovery on his body of the thirty-two marks which betokened the arrival of a world-ruler or a Buddha, the making of the "five great observations" which designated him as born of the right family, in the right continent, the right district, at the right time, and of the right mother.

Now appears the father's anxiety lest Siddhartha's choice should lead him into the path of the ascetic rather than into that of the warrior. To influence the youth's destiny he is married to his cousin, Yasodhara, and of the union a son, Rahula, is born. Further to fence the prince from brooding over " the weary weight of this unintelligible world," all things suggestive of misery were carefully concealed by the king's command. But destiny proved too strong. So we come to the familiar story of the " Four Seeings," *i.e.* the four expeditions with his charioteer in the course of which, by the intervention of divine providence, Siddhartha beheld in sequence the spectacles of age, sickness, death, and the ascetic. With full force the Hindu conviction of the essential sorrow of existence smote on the hitherto untroubled calm of a sheltered manhood. So came about the " Great Renunciation." Siddhartha was twenty-nine years old when he carried out his far-reaching resolution, rose in the night, stepped lightly over the sleeping forms of wife and child, and attended by his charioteer alone, mounted the horse Kantaka to forsake for ever the white domes of Kapilavastu. When he reached the edge of the jungle the future Buddha took off his royal robes, cut the long locks which were the symbol of his freedom, and sent back chariot, horse and servant to the deserted palace. Then, facing with unaverted eyes the mystery of sorrow, with all the trappings of life surrendered, Siddhartha attached himself to five ascetics from Benares, to find perchance in the accepted way release and peace.

Alas, six years of struggle passed without spiritual result; it was " like time spent in tying the air into knots." So Gautama left the anchorites as he had left the palace, and went forth alone to take his place beneath the Bo-tree at Buddhagaya, there to wrestle with the principalities and powers of evil till peace should crown his conflict. The temptation of Gautama has been many times described, and in fullest detail; suffice it here to say that the triumphant result was the " illumination " which made the Çakya prince henceforth the "enlightened," the Buddha. The enlightenment is embodied in what are called the *Four Noble Truths*, which may be succinctly stated as follows:

1. The truth that life is sorrow, that all happiness is illusory and vain.

2. That the cause of sorrow is desire, *trishna*, as to which the philosophers had already had much to say.

3. That the way out of sorrow is *Nirvana*, that sliding of the dewdrop into the ocean which ends at once the illusion of personality and the pain of consciousness—the glad city of peace, the final rest.

4. The "Eightfold Way" to Nirvana consists of right belief, right resolve, right speech, right behaviour, right occupation, right effort, right contemplation and right concentration:

> So is the Eightfold Path which leads to peace ;
> By lower or by upper heights it goes.

The Buddha did not believe in a soul; man was but a concatenation of physical and mental experiences. There could be no permanent "I" even as there was no Oversoul. It is difficult to see in Gautama's conclusions aught but the starkest pessimism. Even so sympathetic an interpreter as Rhys Davids writes: "Thus is the soul tossed about from life to life, from billow to billow, in the great ocean of transmigration. And there is no escape save for the very few who during their birth as men obtain a right knowledge of the Great Spirit and then enter into immortality, or, as the later philosophies taught, are absorbed into the Divine essence." Yet Buddhism was not particularly indebted to its philosophy. Much more attractive was the social gospel, which came to India like an outburst of spring, that religious privileges which had hitherto been monopolized by the Brahman might now be the portion of all, without distinction of caste, or race, or sex. It was like the voice of a great bell suspended from the heavens, proclaiming a common consolation to be won, if men willed it, even in this life, through the gaining of Nirvana.

That the ministry of the Buddha for the next forty and more years was fruitful is clear, even if we do not admit its spread beyond the borders of Magadha. After seven days of delirious bliss, following upon his victory, the Buddha started his "turning of the Wheel of the Law." He delivered his first sermon to the ascetics of Benares, gathered into a *Samgha*, or community, his first converts, sent them out to beg and preach during the fine season of the year, and during the rains kept them around him in retreat. So the Buddhist trinity of *Buddha*, the Teacher, *Samgha*, the Society, and *Dharma*, the Law, appears early in the movement. Outstanding men, like Kaçyapa, Ananda and Upali, joined the ranks. Women also flocked to listen and were eventually permitted to join the order as nuns. The preaching even gained the honour of opposition, especially from a cousin of the Buddha, Devadatta, who, moved by jealousy, repeatedly endeavoured to bring about the teacher's death.

So passed years of devoted and unremitting labour till, now an old man, Gautama arrived at the city of Vaiçali and was overtaken by his last sickness. The traditional story is that a blacksmith named Chunda, out of hospitality, offered the sage some dried boar's flesh, of which the Buddha partook and presently died. Buddhists have argued sometimes that the "boar's flesh" was really a kind of mushroom, or that perhaps Gautama did not wish to repel the man's hospitality. But it must be remembered that at this period India had not completely turned its back on flesh food.

The death of the Buddha took place about 487 B.C.—some say 477—at Kuçinagara. Here between two sala trees Gautama lay down "after the manner of a lion" for his last sleep. And "the trees bloomed out of season and scattered their flowers on him as he lay." Even the hour of dying was not without its act of ministry, for it was at this time that Gautama solved the doubts of some of his disciples. The body was cremated and an eightfold division made of the ashes, with two extra portions from the embers after the fire had been extinguished. We are once again indebted to a reference by Fa-hien, the Chinese pilgrim, for the discovery, in 1907, amid the ruins of the old stupa at Purushapura, of the little box of silver filagree work, containing a golden casket, within which one of these portions of the Buddha's dust has survived.

Immediately after the Buddha's death the first General Council of the order was held at Rajagriha, at which, according to tradition, 500 monks were present. The whole *Canon* was recited, Ananda rendering the *Sutras*, Upali the *Vinaya*, and Kaçyapa the *Abhidharma*. It must be remembered that the organization was from the first primarily monastic. The regîme of the monk included the five ordinary commandments, obligatory also to laymen, namely, not to steal, not to take life, to refrain from unlawful sexual intercourse, not to lie and not to drink intoxicants. But it had three supplementary obligations: only to take food at certain specified times, not to take part in music, dancing or theatrical performances, and not to use perfumes or unguents. Lastly, completing the rules, it was forbidden to sleep on a high or wide bed, or to possess gold or silver. Women had been admitted to the order only after much debate, and on the intercession of Buddha's aunt, Mahaprajapati, who cut off her hair, put on yellow garb, and used the sympathetic aid of Ananda to secure her end. For laymen the rule was made easy to prepare for the higher path in some succeeding incarnation. "The quintessence," says Hackmann, "of this moral code for laymen is that their conduct should be governed by a careful observance of the moral norm prevailing in their days."

A second General Council was held about 377 B.C., at Vaiçali, seventy miles north of Rajagriha, and here the first sign of a line of cleavage made itself apparent, such as later led to the development of the two schools of *Hinayana* (Little Vessel), sometimes called Southern Buddhism, and *Mahayana* (Great Vessel), known also (not quite accurately) as Northern Buddhism. But at this time the dispute was on small points, for example, as to whether the *bhikshus*, or monks, could drink unfermented liquors. A committee of four on each side tried to arrange a compromise, but in general the southern school retained the orthodox position, while the northern favoured modification of the conservative view.

Soon after this came the great event which transformed

the entire history of India and made possible the entrance of other religious ideas beside those connected with the teaching of the Buddha. This was the invasion by Alexander the Great in 330 B.C., in the endeavour to complete the conquest of the Achæmenian Empire by the subjugation of the two north-west provinces of India. The incident only concerns us in that shortly after the return of Alexander to Babylon an insurrection took place against Seleucus Nicator, his general, headed by an Indian who had been a camp-follower in the Macedonian army. This was Chandragupta, founder of the Mauryan dynasty, which lasted from the time of the revolt till 184 B.C. Chandragupta has been claimed by the Jains, but our present interest is in his grandson, the great Açoka, one of the most notable rulers in the whole history of the peninsula. Açoka (274–236 B.C.) started out with conquests which carried his domain southward to Madras. Legends of his ruthless cruelty, including a probably fictitious story of the massacre of his brothers and sisters, are of later invention, but it seems true that, some eleven years after his accession, Açoka came under the influence of Buddhism and from thence was enthusiastically active in the support and extension of the faith. He had inscriptions made on pillars and rocks all over the land, in order that he might announce the principles of religion he desired to recommend to monks and laity. He also dug wells for the benefit of travellers and provided hospitals and medicines for animals and men. He made quinquennial circuits of his dominion for the purpose of stimulating the administration of justice, and sent missionary envoys as far as the Seleucid realm of Antiochus. One famous piece of missionary work was the sending of his son (or younger brother) Mahendra to Ceylon, following it up with the despatch shortly after of his daughter, Sanghamitra. Of this mission I shall have somewhat to say in a later chapter.

Açoka reigned thirty-six or thirty-seven years, founded the city of Çrinagar in Kashmir, beautified his capital of Pataliputra, and died about 236 B.C. in the fulness of his powers and in the odour of sanctity. That he was subsequently ignored must be set down to the revival of

Brahmanism, to which religion the name of Açoka was naturally *anathema*. Fortunately, however, his fame has been saved by the rediscovery of the *Rock and Pillar Edicts* and by the sympathetic references to the great Buddhist emperor in the writings of Fa-hien. It is probable that in this reign, about 250 B.C., the Third General Council was held at Pataliputra. The historicity of this assembly is not beyond doubt, but there is support for the tradition in the Singhalese *Chronicles* and in the writings of Buddhaghosha.

The end of the Mauryan dynasty, as stated above, came in 184 B.C., and from this time we have scanty knowledge of the fortunes of Buddhism in India. Gradually in the south, and in the Pali language, was accumulating that vast mass of material which in course of time was fashioned into the *Canon*, known as the *Tripitaka*, or, in the Pali, *Ti-pitaka*, that is, "*the Three Baskets.*" This name is given to the whole collection of speeches, stories, rules and reflections which were, according to tradition, put into form as early as the reign of Açoka. The *Three Baskets* are respectively the *Vinaya*, or Basket of Discipline, the *Suttas* (*Sutras*), or Basket of Teaching, and the *Abhidhamma* (*Abhidharma*), or Basket of Metaphysics. A brief word will suffice for the *Vinaya*, since this was kept secret by the monks, concealed even from the knowledge of the Buddhist laity. It comprised rules for the reception of members into the Samgha, for the periodical confession of sin, for the retreat during the rainy season, for simple medicinal treatment, and rules of a legal sort for the settlement of controversies and discords.

The *Suttas* form the "Sermon Basket" and are divided into five smaller collections known as *Nikayas*, or "lectures." In *Nikaya I.* we have the famous *Mahaparinibbana Sutta*, generally known as the *Book of the Great Decease*. Many of the *Suttas* are series of verses, with repetitions and refrains, designed for recitation by the whole monkish community. Such are the *Snake Sutta*, where every verse ends with the refrain, "as a snake casts off its decayed, old skin," and the *Rhinoceros Sutta*, of which the refrain is, "Let one walk alone like a rhinoceros." The *Suttas* known as *Thera-gatha* (*Songs of the Monks*) and *Theri-Gatha* (*Songs of the Nuns*), are well known to us through Mrs. Rhys Davids' *Psalms of the Brethren* and *Psalms of the Sisters*, and show much more of spiritual joy than most pieces of Buddhist literature. One of the best-known pieces of Buddhist literature of this class is the *Dhammapada*, or *Path of the Law*, a work written about 70 B.C. It is an anthology of maxims, arranged in over four hundred stanzas, with the maxims frequently illustrated by stories of the Buddha and his disciples. Under the twenty-six headings of the Pali version we have treated such objects as Twin Verses, Reflection, Thought, Flowers, the Fool, the Wise Man, and so on. Ere leaving the *Suttas* we must not forget the *jatakas*, or " birth stories," which are tales of the previous lives of the Buddha as a Bodhisattva, or one on the way to Buddhahood. Many of them are beast-stories and show how Gautama, as a tortoise, or a hare, or in some other form, outwitted Mara, the prince of evil, or performed praiseworthy acts of compassion and self-sacrifice.

The *Abhidhamma*, or *Third Basket*, contains the Buddhist scholastic, a better term on the whole than metaphysics. Mrs. Rhys Davids declares that our knowledge of Buddhist philosophy would not greatly suffer were the whole of the *Abhidhamma* to be lost. " The burden of the *Abhidhamma* is not any positive contribution to the philosophy of early Buddhism, but analytical and logical and methodological elaboration of what is already given."

While in the south Buddhism gradually passed out of India by way of Ceylon, in the north it gravitated towards the north-west and became distinctly of the Mahayana type. Following upon the collapse of the Mauryan dynasty we have several rather short-lived semi-foreign dynasties, all of which were favourable to Buddhism. First came the Indo-Bactrians about 147 B.C., in which line appears Menander (known to Indian literature as Milinda), famous for a Buddhist book in Pali, *The Questions of Milinda* (*Milinda-panha*), a series of seven dialogues between the king and the sage Nagasena. At the close of the third dialogue Menander is converted, but he continues to ask questions and to receive instruction till the end of the book. After the Indo-Bactrians came the Andhras, or Indo-Parthians, whose king Gondopharnes (or Gondophorus) is said to have received both the Christian apostle St. Thomas and the emissaries of the Chinese emperor Ming-ti, who carried back with them to the Middle Kingdom the first Buddhist books and images. It is quite possible that at this point there was some intermingling of the two streams of religion. The Parthian power gave way before the end of the first century to the Kushans, or Indo-Scythians, of whom Kanishka, famous alike in international trade and in the history of Buddhism, is said to have called together, at his capital, Purushapura, the Fourth General Council. Mahayana Buddhism was now in full control in the north, and Kanishka was probably much influenced in his views by the great Mahayana teacher, Açvaghosha, famous also as dramatist and as the biographer of Gautama.

It may be convenient here to point out that Mahayana Buddhism differs from the original teaching in four special particulars. First, in its theology, as making out of the original Buddha-essence, the Adi-buddha, a kind of god, whereas the original doctrine was atheistic. Secondly, in its soteriology, as offering to men salvation through the help of beings known as Bodhisattvas, that is, beings on their way to Buddhahood, whereas, according to Gautama, every man was his own saviour. Thirdly, in its eschatology, as offering to men, through its doctrine of the Western Paradise, a future less blank than had been suggested by Nirvana. And, fourthly, in its practical ethics, as stressing the advantage of becoming a Buddha, or teacher, in some future life, rather than an *arhat*, whose whole interest was in securing release from the wheel of existence.

In spite of all changes, Indian Buddhism was now in a state of decline, through the reasserted dominance of the Brahman caste. With the rise of the Gupta dynasty, about A.D. 360, there are many signs—as in the revival of the *açvamedha*, or horse-sacrifice—that the days of Buddhism in India were numbered. It is true that the Chinese pilgrims, from Fa-hien to Hiuen-tsang, found in India much of interest to them as Buddhists, but to the latter the apostasy from the faith was plain, while even to the former the heresies (as he considered them) were numerous. Yet Harsha, "the last native lord-paramount of India" (A.D. 607–

647), was more than fair to the Buddhist cause, whatever were his own personal convictions. Some say that he was converted by Hiuen-tsang from the Hinayana to the Mahayana school. At any rate, he was the pilgrim's patron and protector and saw to it that in the debates staged between the Chinese visitor and the Brahmans the Buddhist should have fair play. Harsha, who was dramatist as well as king, has left us the one Buddhist play, the *Nagananda*, which has survived in Indian literature.

But no favour shown by Harsha, or others, could avert the end. The Gupta rulers were worshippers of Vishnu, the Gupta dramatists invoked the benediction of Çiva, and the Brahman ascendancy was ere long completely re-established. The large amount of Buddhist literature written in Sanskrit was gradually carried across the frontier to be translated into Chinese and the languages of Central Asia, and the one poor consolation left to the Indian Buddhist was the acceptance by the Hindu of Gautama as the ninth *avatar* of Vishnu.

To-day the total number of Buddhists in India (including Burma and Nepal) is about 11,000,000, and most of these are outside of India proper. The last stronghold of Buddhism in India, Magadha, fell before the sword of Islam rather than before the power of the Brahman. But by this time the missionaries of Gautama had carried (if not the exact teachings) at any rate something of the spirit of the Blessed One over all central, eastern and southern Asia. In later chapters we shall give some account of developments in these regions. Meanwhile, we must finish the story of Indian religion (except for the part concerned with Islam) with some description of the revival of Brahmanism, under the name of Hinduism.[1]

[1] On Indian Buddhism generally see T. W. Rhys Davids, *Buddhist India*, London, 1880; J. H. Kern, *A Manual of Indian Buddhism*, London, 1896; J. B. Pratt, *The Pilgrimage of Buddhism*, New York, 1928; Moritz Winternitz, *Geshichte der indischen Litteratur*, Vol. II., Leipzig, 1909–1920; Samuel Beal, *Buddhist Records of the Western World*, 2 Vols., London, 1884; J. M. McPhail, *Asoka*, Oxford, 1918; R. Mookerji, *Harsha*, Oxford, 1926; H. H. Gowen, *History of Indian Literature*, chaps. xix.–xxiv., New York, 1931.

## CHAPTER XXIII

# *The Religions of India—III.*

### Hinduism and its Developments

THE decline of Buddhism in the sixth and following centuries A.D. was followed by a revival of Brahmanism for which, doubtless among many others, the great Vedantist Çamkaracharya has been by many held responsible. Çamkara lived and taught between A.D. 788 and 850, and wrote commentaries on the principal *Upanishads* and the *Bhagavad-gita*. But he is best known as the teacher of the unqualified monism, or non-dualism (*advaita*), referred to in Chapter XXI. He taught that " beyond Brahman nothing exists save an illusive principle called *maya*," by means of which the supposedly individual soul is kept back from union with the Oversoul. At the end of each *kalpa* Brahman rests, free from the power of *maya*. Then all individual souls are merged in the Eternal. " This Eternal," says Dr. Rudolf Otto, " is wholly and purely *Atman*, or spirit (*chit* and *chaitanyam*), pure consciousness (*jnana*), pure knowledge. Similarly, because it is without division, this spirit, or consciousness, or knowledge is beyond the three antitheses of Knower, Known, and the act of Knowing. Thus it is at once ' anantam,' without end, and beyond space and time." [1]

But although Vedantism, either in its unqualified or in its qualified form, remained the generally accepted philosophy of thoughtful Indians, and much else that belonged to pre-Buddhistic habits of thought—notably in the matter of caste—again raised its head, in strict truth Brahmanism never did return, nor did the philosophic schools regain the sincerity and simplicity of the Upanishadic period. Instead of the *karma-marga*, or way of works, and the *jnana-marga*, or way of knowledge, we find now the religion of

[1] Rudolf Otto, *Mysticism, East and West*, New York, 1932. See p. 3.

*bhakti*, that is, of devotion to a multitude of gods and goddesses.

For the origins of *bhakti* men have looked in many directions. Some have suspected indebtedness to Christianity, while recent Muhammadan writers believe that, at least in the second period of its development, much is owing to the Sufistic philosophy of Islam.[1] Others are satisfied to regard it as the natural reaction of the Indian mind from the Brahmanic ritual and from the speculations of the *Upanishads*. At any rate *bhakti* found much to feed upon in the local village cults, where some particular deity attracted to itself the homage and affection of its votaries, unwilling to go further back for their theology. So we arrive at that mixture of elements we call Hinduism, a huge syncretistic system in which complicated polytheisms are united with an involved series of caste usages, and something borrowed from almost everything, even down to the superstitious beliefs and practices of the Negrito fetish-worshippers. From Buddhism itself everything was accepted except its atheism, its denial of the eternity of the soul, and its opposition to caste.

Although it is a difficult thing to systematize so particoloured a religion, yet the systematization is found as nearly as possible in the scriptures known as *Puranas*, which have the same kind of authority for Hinduism that the *Veda* has for the earlier religion.

The *Puranas* signify literally "old things," or *archæologica*, but though the contents of the books may go back to quite early times, the books themselves belie their name. Probably none of them is older than the sixth century A.D., and so, of course, could have had nothing to do with their traditional author, Vyasa, also regarded as the traditional author of the *Mahabharata*.

The *Puranas*, however, are almost entirely concerned with things fabulous and mythical. According to the *Canon of Amara Sinha*, each had to deal with five subjects. These are: (1) The *Sarga*, or creation of the universe; (2) the *Prati-Sarga*, the destruction and recreation of the universe; (3) the *Vanica*, the genealogy of the gods and patriarchs;

[1] See Yusuf Husain, *L'Inde Mystique au Moyen Age*, Paris, 1929.

(4) the *Manvantara*, or reigns of the various Manus; and (5) the *Vamçyanucharita*, or history of the solar and lunar kings.

A few words on these several topics will serve to present the distinctive features of Hinduism. Creation was the outbreathing of worlds from the mouth of Brahma—to return to their original nothingness at the expiration of a *kalpa* of 4,320,000,000 mortal years. The *kalpa* was divisible into fourteen periods, each governed by one of the many successive Manus. Indians believe they are now living in the Kali-yuga, or evil age—an age of degeneracy described in the *Vishnu Purana* as one in which

> the rights of men
> Will be confused, no property be safe,
> No joy and no prosperity be lasting.

All the successive *kalpas* are governed by Manus, the first of whom was Manu Swayambhuva, whose seven sons ruled over the seven continents, of which the central one was Jambudwipa (India). These seven continents were separated one from the other by six oceans, respectively of salt water, sugar-cane juice, wine, melted butter, curdled milk and milk.

The eighteen *Puranas* are divided into three series, each of six. The last six serve to honour Brahma, the creator, and are intended to express the quality of *ragas*, or passion; the next six are in honour of Çiva, the destroyer, and represent the quality of *tamas*, or gloom; and the first six exalt Vishnu, the redeemer, and express the quality of *sattva*, or reality.

All these deities are manifestations of the impersonal Brahm, and form together what is known as the Trimurti, or "threefoldness." In theory Brahma, Vishnu and Çiva are equal, as is expressed in the lines:

> In those three persons the one God was shown—
> Each first in place, each last—not one alone ;
> Of Çiva, Vishnu, Brahma, each may be
> First, second, third among the Blessed Three.

But in practice, so far as the teaching of the *Puranas* goes, the chief honours are with Vishnu. Brahma, as the god of creation, which is past and done with, has small recognition in India at the present day, and but one or two temples in the whole land. Çiva has a very much larger share of India's allegiance, as the Hindu continuation of the Vedic god Rudra, the god of nature's destructive forces. By some he is regarded as the primal creator, who by his austerities has won the right to be the lord of life. As the typical Yogi, Çiva embodies for many all that is austere. He is the ideal of the naked ascetic. He satisfies, moreover, the religious ideas of the wild aboriginal tribes, and has become the substitute for their primitive deities. As "the lord of spirits and demons," with his string of skulls for a necklace, and serpents for a garland, he is the delight of the more uncouth element of the populace. And, again, as the representative free-liver of the Tantric rites, he is the wild, jovial god, given to drink and dancing, surrounded by troops of buffoons and dwarfs. The Çaivite temple is everywhere to be seen, even though the Çaivites themselves are not so commonly beheld outside the ranks of *yogis* and *sunnyasis*. Their sect-mark consists of the three horizontal strokes of white or grey ashes on the forehead.

But Vishnu was the god who satisfied most the longings of the Indian heart and the religion of *bhakti* was predominantly Vaishnavite. Everywhere might be seen the worshipper of Vishnu with his sect-mark of two perpendicular strokes, ending below in a curve, which was supposed to represent the footprint of the god. The preference given to Vishnu is somewhat grotesquely set forth in the *Bhagavata-purana*, where the sage Bhrigu is described as going forth to test the temper of the three deities of the Trimurti. When Bhrigu omitted the customary obeisance to Brahma, the god's anger blazed forth terribly and it was with difficulty restrained. Then the sage passed on to Çiva and deliberately failed to return the god's salute. Çiva's eyes flashed fire and he raised his trident to destroy the impertinent visitor, but Parvati, the divine spouse, interceded and won forgiveness for the sage. Then Bhrigu went on to Vishnu, whom he found asleep, and awakened the god with a kick in the breast. Immediately Vishnu arose, asked the sage's pardon for not having greeted him on his arrival, and expressed the honour he felt at having received the imprint of Bhrigu's foot upon his breast. Thus it was revealed that Vishnu was the greatest of the gods.

Vishnu, whose name is derived from the root *viç*, *to pervade*, was originally a god of the solar ray, but came later to be regarded as a form of the Supreme Spirit, under the name of Narayana, or he that moves upon the waters. As the divine pervader, he infused his presence into all created things and these self-projections came to be known as *avatars*, or descents, undertaken to preserve the world of gods and men in certain dangerous crises. The story of these *avatars* is a considerable part of the substance of the *Puranas*. They are arranged under the five following heads:

1. Full *avatars*, in human form, as, for example, when Vishnu was born as Krishna.
2. Half-human *avatars*, as when Vishnu imparted 50 per cent of his essence to Rama, the son of Daçaratha.
3. Quarter *avatars*, as in the case of Rama's brother, Bharata.
4. Eighth-part *avatars*, as in the case of Rama's other brothers, Lakshmana and Çatrughna.
5. The diffusion of the divine essence into ordinary men, animals, and other sentient beings.

According to the general Puranic conception, the *avatars* of Vishnu are ten in number—the ten being, as elsewhere, the symbol of development, that is, $1+2+3+4=10$. The upward trend in the sequence will be obvious. The ten are:

1. The *Matsya*, or *Fish avatar*, when, as related in the *Mahabharata*, the *Çatapatha Brahmana*, and the *Vishnu Purana*, Vishnu saved Manu by appearing in the form of a fish and ordered the building of the ship wherein Manu was saved.
2. The *Kurma*, or *Tortoise avatar*, which took place when Vishnu descended to the bottom of the sea to recover the things lost in the deluge and made himself a pivot for Mt. Mandara, with Vasuki, the serpent, as a rope, for the churning of the *amrita* from the sea of milk.
3. The *Varaha*, or *Wild-boar avatar*, in which form Vishnu descended into the abyss to fight the demon Hiranyaksha, who had seized the world and borne it away.

4. The *Nara-sinha*, or *Man-lion avatar*, when Vishnu delivered the world from the demon Hiranyaçipu, who was invulnerable to gods, men and animals, but not to a composite of all three. Vishnu entered a stone pillar in the demon's hall and came forth, half-man and half-lion, to tear his antagonist asunder.

5. The *Vamana*, or *Dwarf avatar*—the familiar story of Vishnu's three strides when the god, appearing with the other gods before Bali as a dwarf to claim as much territory as he could step over in three paces, overpassed heaven and earth, but left the infernal regions to the Daitya king.

6. The *Paraçu-Rama avatar*, when Vishnu as Rama-with-the-axe slew the Kshatriyas and established the supremacy of the Brahmans.

7. The *Rama*, or *Rama-chandra avatar*, when Vishnu became Rama, son of Daçaratha, and slew Ravana, the demon king of Lanka.

8. The *Krishna avatar*, probably the most popular of all, when Vishnu became Krishna, the dark god, one of the heroes of the *Mahabharata*, and the subject of innumerable legends.

9. The *Buddha avatar*, arranged as a concession to the Buddhists, and to counteract their influence as a religion separate from Hinduism.

10. The *Kalki*, or *White-horse avatar*, of the future, when, at the end of the Kali-yuga, Vishnu shall appear, riding a white horse and wielding a sword blazing like a comet, to create, renew and establish purity on the earth. Some have advocated the recognition of this *avatar* as fulfilled in Christ.

It should be added that the *Bhagavata-purana* speaks of twelve other *avatars* of Vishnu and indeed declares that his *avatars* are innumerable " like the rivulets flowing from an inexhaustible lake."

Another side of Hinduism than that presented in the *Puranas* is that which concerns the worship of the gods in their *çakti*, or female essence. This is given especially in the works called *Tantras*, a word which may be explained as, first, *web* or *woof*, next, an uninterrupted *series*, and lastly, as *rule* or *ritual*. The *Tantras* are esteemed by

Hindus next after the *Puranas* and date in general from the sixth or seventh century. Though some thus place the authority of these books very high, they are in general devoted to low and magical conceptions of religion. Each of the gods of the Trimurti has his *çakti*. That of Brahma is Sarasvati (the watery), the old lost river of India, deified as Vach, the goddess of eloquence. Vishnu's çakti is Lakshmi, or Çri, the goddess of good fortune, and mother of Kama, the Indian Cupid. She is sometimes identified with Sita, sometimes with Radha, and as Mombadevi she has given her name to Bombay, of which city she is especially "Our Lady." Çiva's *çakti* is the dread goddess Kali, known also as Durga, the inaccessible, Parvati, the mountain goddess, Bhairavi, the terrible, and as Devi, the goddess *par excellence*. As Kali she is depicted with a black skin, a hideous and terrible countenance, dripping with blood, encircled with snakes, hung round with skulls, and in all respects a fury rather than a goddess. She has given her name to Calcutta, *Kalighat*, the temple steps of Kali, and as Kumari, the maiden, to Cape Comorin, the southernmost point of India. She is the mother of the elephant-headed god Ganesha and of Karttikeya, the god of war.

Tantric worship is frequently of the grossest description, particularly that which is known as left-handed *tantra*, in which the five requisites are the five M's, *Madya*, wine; *Mamsa*, flesh; *Matsya*, fish; *Mudra*, parched grain, or mystical gesticulation; and *Maithuna*, sexual intercourse. In left-handed Tantric worship we reach the lowest depths of religious degradation. Tantric worship generally is most commonly encountered in Bengal and in the Eastern Provinces. From this last-named region a native writer declares: "Two-thirds of our religious rites are Tantric and almost half our medicine."

The doctrine of *bhakti*, developed in the cult of both Vishnu and Çiva, has had enormous consequences in the history of Hinduism during the past thousand years and has done much to give to Hinduism its distinctive character. It has broken the force of the old pantheistic philosophy for many millions and has made these millions worshippers of a countless number of deities with a devotion rising in many cases to an emotional mysticism of the first order. Much of the worship of India is, it is true, exceedingly superstitious and in many cases gross. In every city the temples are filled with the images of the gods, many-headed and many-handed, and often represented with a symbolism which, to westerners at least, is distasteful. Not only are the chief gods of the pantheon represented, but such deities as Hanuman, the monkey general of Rama, and Ganesha, the elephant-headed son of Çiva. The villages teem with shrines to gods still lowlier in the mythological hierarchy, and many animals share in the reverence awarded to the human and superhuman deities. The cow is naturally a sacred animal, while monkeys and serpents also have their numerous votaries. Even trees and stones, the fetishes of primitive folk, are adored by many in the hill districts. Pilgrimages are acts of worship which are exceedingly popular and rivers are especially sought as goals in these religious adventures. Supreme in the heart of all Hindus is the river Ganges, on which the maidens float their love-lamps and the bereaved their dead. But the confluences of rivers, such as the seven *sangamas* (*confluences*) are the favourite resorts. India is full of holy places, like the four residences of the gods, of which that of Jagar-nath in Puri is one of the best known, or like the twelve places marked by the phallic symbol of Çiva. Hinduism permeates the life of its professors in every act all the year long, but there are many festivals of peculiar sanctity, most of them regulated by the moon, such as the great Indian *Saturnalia*, known as *Holi*, which takes place on the ten days before the full moon of February-March.

Hinduism, like other religions, has a multitude of sects, apart from the broad distinction made between Vaishnavite and Çaivite. Many of these sects originate with the great religious revivals of the twelfth and subsequent centuries and were certainly influenced by the more spiritual aspect of Islam which we call Sufism. There is little doubt that many Hindus were unconsciously affected by the monotheism of Islam and it is possible also that the situation was influenced by Christian teaching.

Some of these movements are deserving of careful

attention, but we must be content to mention but a few. Earliest are the Nimbarkas, founded by Nimbarka, an enthusiastic votary of Vishnu and Radha in the eleventh century. Their sect-mark consists of two yellowish perpendicular lines joined below in a curve. In this sect we may probably reckon the great lyric poet Jayadeva, writer of the *Gita-govinda*. In the middle of the eleventh century comes Ramanuja who, in opposition to Çamkara, espoused the doctrine of modified monism. He wrote numerous commentaries on the *Brahma-sutras* and the *Bhagavad-gita* but gained the popular ear most by the hymns in which he sang of the Supreme Soul manifested in Vishnu. The two perpendicular marks which form the sect-mark of the Ramanujas is white. Not long after Ramanuja came Madhava, born possibly in 1197, founder of the Madhavas. Madhava was originally a Çaivite, but was converted to Vaishnavism and held that the Supreme Soul was manifested in Vishnu. He lived in the Kanarese country and by some has been regarded as the last of the great southern teachers. But he travelled extensively in the north and left behind him numerous disciples distinguished by the red perpendicular sect-mark. The Madhavas by some have been supposed to have received influence from the Nestorian Christians. In 1299, probably at Allahabad, was born Ramananda, whom two million Ramanandis to-day accept as their master. Ramananda is regarded as the fifth guru in descent from Ramanuja. A child prodigy and a pundit at twelve, he made pilgrimages over the greater part of India, gathered together his twelve apostles, of whom one was a weaver, and preached everywhere the pure doctrine of Rama as distinguished from the more erotic teachings connected with reverence for Krishna. Many held that Ramananda was himself an incarnation of Rama. Another great teacher and the founder of a sect bearing his name was Vallabhacharya, born about 1479, and looked upon by his followers as an incarnation of Krishna. He was Vedantist in his general outlook, but preached a doctrine called *Pushti-marga*, the *way of enjoyment*, as contrasted with the usual recommendation of asceticism. Vallabhacharya gained a large number of adherents, not merely at Benares, where he lived, but also in Bombay and Gujerat. One other great Vaishnavite sectary was Chaitanya, who was born in 1485 and was likewise regarded as an incarnation of Krishna. He was a revivalist preacher of great power and influence and a thorough-going ecstatic who often became self-entranced. Some accounts describe him as translated to the heaven of Vishnu without dying.

In the life and teaching of men such as these we get sight of a quality in religion which transcends Hinduism and links its representatives with the mystics of all times and climates. The same thing is true of some of the poets who belong to the period we call mediæval in India. The religious poetry of some of these possesses a sincerity which atones for the defects of their theology. There is for, instance, Namdev, who worshipped the village god of Pandharpur, Vithoba, and yet found a revelation of the Supreme which he had failed to discover in *Vedas* or *Puranas*.[1] There was the çudra woman Jamabai, the voluntary drudge of Namdev, who found poetry as well as piety in her drudgery. There was again the Maratha poet Ekaṇath, who learned that:

> God dwells in all and yet we find
> To Him the faithless man is blind.
> Water or stones or what you will—
> What is it that He does not fill?

There was Tulsi Das, who wrote a great poem on Rama—the popular *Ramayana* of Bengal—and thought of the hero as a great father in heaven through whom all men on earth were brothers. There was, to mention but one more, Tukaram, the çudra grain-dealer, who wrote hundreds of hymns in praise of his god which have become as familiar on the lips of the Marathas as the *Psalms of David* to us.

In all these many converging influences have produced their proper result in making Hinduism at once more popular and more spiritual than the older religion. But in certain cases there was a more or less deliberate effort made to synthesize the religious elements which, through the Muhammadan conquest, had found place in Indian life

[1] See C. A. Kincaid, *Tales of the Saints of Pandharpur*, Oxford, 1919.

side by side with old customs and old beliefs. Two of these instances require our attention, first, that of Kabir and his following, the Kabirpanthis, and, secondly, that of Nanak and the religion which came to be known as Sikhism.

Kabir (1440–1518) was born in or near Benares, probably of Muslim parentage, and in his early life was cared for by a weaver and his wife. He became a disciple of Ramananda and was by him, through the success of a simple stratagem, initiated into the cult of Rama. From that time on Kabir was the enthusiastic preacher of a theism to which there was neither temple, church nor kaaba. The child alike of Allah and Rama, he maintained: "There is nothing but water in the sacred bathing-places; and I know that they are useless, for I have bathed in them. Lifeless are all the images of the gods; they cannot speak; I know it, for I have called aloud to them." He was naturally much opposed by the Brahmans, and on one occasion they sent a woman of ill-fame to tempt him. But, instead of yielding, Kabir converted the courtesan. Though a genuine mystic, teaching that God had spread his form of love throughout the world, "he earned his living as a weaver, finding industry in no way incompatible with vision." Kabir's poetry on the subject of *bhakti* introduces an element of passion into Indian literature which is Semitic rather than Aryan, as will be felt by those who have read the *Songs of Kabir*, translated by Rabindranath Tagore.[1] When Kabir died, so runs a beautiful legend, both Muslim and Hindu desired his body, the Muslim to bury it, the Hindu to consume it on the pyre. Long they wrangled over the matter, until the shroud was lifted and found to cover nothing but a mass of flowers. These were then reverently divided and the share of each disposed of in the accustomed way. The Kabirpanthis number less than a million in all India, but their influence is out of all proportion to their numerical strength. Some other sects, such as the Dadupanthis, followers of Dadu, the cotton-cleaner of Ahmadabad, derive their theology from Kabir.

It was the influence of Kabir to which, at least in part, is due the religious movement of Nanak Shah, the founder

[1] *The Songs of Kabir,* translated by Rabindranath Tagore, New York, 1919.

of Sikhism. Nanak was born in 1469, in the Punjab. He became early acquainted with both *Quran* and *Sutras*, but only gradually formed the resolution to purify religion by the elimination of formalism and corruption. In his pilgrimage to Mecca he was rebuked for sleeping with his head to the house of God and replied: " Tell me, pray, in which direction the house of God is not." Soon he became convinced that Hinduism had to be emancipated from the fetters of mythology and that neither sacrifice nor pilgrimage was so meritorious as the search for truth. Salvation must be won by devotion to God, together with good conduct towards men. Nanak died, at the age of seventy, in 1538, and the leadership of the reforming sect fell to a series of Gurus, of whom the fourth built the famous lake temple at Amritsar, henceforth the centre of Sikhism. The fifth Guru, in 1601, compiled the sacred book known as the *Adi Granth*[1] which is now reverenced almost as a god. Arjun also organized the faith on such a scale that later on it attracted the bigoted Aurungzīb, who imprisoned the ninth Guru and waged a war of suppression against the faith. The tenth Guru answered the challenge of persecution by creating the Khalsa, or inner circle, the nucleus of a militant nation, with each individual under a vow to wear steel, slay the Muslim on sight, and use the common name Singh (lion), as an indication of resolve to fight and die. When the tenth Guru died the succession was regarded as closed and the *Adi Granth* remained the sole authority. To-day the Sikhs number about 3,250,000, but they have lost much of their importance since the annexation of the Punjab and show themselves much more complacent towards the customs of Hinduism.

An influence of an entirely different sort and one which is due to Christianity and the West, is that which produced the *Samaj* movements of the nineteenth century. The real founder of this movement was the famous Ram Mohun Roy (1772–1833), who co-operated with Lord William Bentinck in the suppression of *sati*. Becoming convinced of the many corruptions in Hinduism, Ram Mohun Roy formed the *Brahma Samaj*, evolved a kind of Protestant service com-

[1] Translated by Ernest Trumpp, London, 1877.

posed mainly out of the *Upanishads* and the Gospels. After the premature death of the founder, the movement, with less leaning towards Christianity, was taken up, first by Dvarkanath Tagore (grandfather of the poet) and later by Debendranath Tagore, the poet's father, who continued as its *Maharshi* (*great rishi*) until his death. In 1857 the movement was joined by the brilliant Keshub Chunder Sen who, however, disagreed with the Tagores on the question of caste and formed in 1866 a new *Samaj*, leaving the older society to function as the *Adi* (original) *Brahma Samaj*. Then Keshub for a time fell under the influence of Ram Krishna and showed a trend towards Hinduism which, together with certain inconsistencies of conduct, cost him his influence in the movement. Yet he made one last effort to contribute to the cause of Indian theism by founding in 1881 the *Naba Badhan* (*New Rule*), a peculiar mixture of Christian and Hindu ideas which has not outlived the death of its founder in 1884.

By this time many Hindus had become genuinely alarmed over the interpretation of their religion given to and by foreigners. So we have the rise of certain movements designed to save Hinduism from disintegration through attack direct or indirect. The first of these was the *Arya Samaj*, founded by Dayananda Sarasvati (1824–83), with his slogan of *Back to the Vedas*. Here we have asserted the absolute adequacy of Hinduism to the needs of modern life and the absolute infallibility of the *Veda*. Other Hindu teachers who have rallied to the defence of the Indian religion include Ram Krishna, mentioned above, who, though trying to absorb the ideals of Christianity and Islam, was really a devotee of the goddess Kali and a professor of Yoga. Among the followers of Ram Krishna was the Swami Vivekananda who attracted much attention in America at the time of the Chicago *World Fair* of 1893, and laboured till his death in the cause of religious nationalism. Since Vivekananda's time other teachers have arisen such as Bal Gangadhai Tilak, who died in 1920, and Mohandas Karamchand Gandhi, whose religious nationalism has played a startling rôle in recent history.

It is easy to take a one-sided view of Hinduism. To

many it will recall nothing but superstition, cruelty and grossness, social backwardness and political ineptness. To others it will be the one thing needful to rescue the West from the grip of materialism, the fragrance of a sacrifice that rises for the benefit of all humanity. To most thoughtful people it will be apparent that Hinduism cannot fulfil itself until it has been Christianized. Only a "genuine" God such as St. John presents as the antithesis to the "shadow gods" of the heathen (1 John v. 21) can satisfy the yearning of Indian *bhakti*. Many indeed are the saints of India who by true faith have risen to the seeing and doing of noble and inspiring things. But for the salvation of India (to quote Dr. J. N. Farquhar): "A new religion must be found, a religion which will provide a religious foundation for the wider and truer ideas which now dominate the Hindu mind; satisfy the religious instincts of the people, and stimulate them to purity, progress and strength. Christianity is unquestionably the source of the new explosive thought which is recreating the Indian character and intelligence to-day. There is no other religion which contains these master ideas. Only in the realm of Christianity, Christ and His Cross, the Fatherhood of God, the Brotherhood of Man, and the Kingdom of God, can Hindus find the universal principles needed for a new intellectual, moral and social life."[1] [2]

[1] J. N. Farquhar, *A Primer of Hinduism*, Oxford, 1912, p. 202.

[2] Other books on this subject which it will be useful to consult are as follows: Sophia D. Collett, *Life and Letters of Ram Mohun Roy*, London, 1900; W. Crooke, *Popular Religion and Folk-lore of Northern India*, 2 Vols., London, 1896; John Dowson, *A Classical Dictionary of Hindu Mythology*, London, 1879; Francis Kingsbury and G. E. Philips, *Hymns of the Tamil Saivite Saints*, Oxford, 1921; Margaret MacNicol, *Poems by Indian Women*, London, 1923; H. Mitra, *Hinduism, The World Ideal*, London, 1916; Sir M. Monier-Williams, *Hinduism*, London, 1885.

# CHAPTER XXIV

## *The Religions of China—I.*

### To the Advent of Buddhism

A FAMOUS living Chinese philosopher expresses the opinion that the Chinese are not naturally a religious people. The basis of his idea (which is rather widely held) is that, first, the Chinese are not emotional in their expression of religion and, secondly, that religion is so tied up for them with their entire philosophy of life that it seems to occupy no special place. Yet there is little doubt, on reflection, that the Chinese attitude towards life, as having cosmic significance and as involving definite relations with the family and the state, is essentially religious.

It is a common error, in treating of the history of Chinese religion, to commence with the teaching and career of the great sages Confucius and Lao Tzu, in forgetfulness of the fact that these simply represent different strata of a system which was many centuries old when they appeared, and that neither of them claimed to be the originator of the philosophy he expounded. Indeed, Confucius and Lao Tzu, and others after them, only gave system and stability to beliefs and practices which they desired to transmit to their posterity.

No doubt many personalities unknown to us did contribute to the earlier religion. The names of culture-heroes like Fu-hsi, of " model Emperors " like Yao and Shun, and of philosophers like Chou Kung, do not appear in the early annals without justification. But, in the main, Chinese religion developed all along from popular appreciation of those two aspects of the numinous sense which we have labelled respectively Naturism and Spiritism. It may be that in describing these developments we shall introduce unconsciously ideas which belong, in their formulated stage, to later times, but it would not be difficult to show that even these are probably discoverable in germ at the earliest period to which we can penetrate.

Let us treat first, as briefly as may be, of the naturistic side of Chinese popular religion. Viewed as " a *collectanea* of all the powers of Nature " was the sky, or *T'ien*. To many T'ien was a real god, while to the Taoist T'ien was but the equivalent of Tao. But in popular religion T'ien was never personalized and stood rather for the law behind all the gods than for a deity such as shared with earth the honours of a primitive dualism. A much more personal view of God as lord of nature is suggested by the term *Shang-ti*, or *Supreme Being*, though the actual worship of Shang-ti was restricted to the Emperors. There is, however, a popular conception of Nature as a kind of god in itself presented in the myth of P'an-ku, which Dr. Carus declares is " a Chinese version not only of the Norse myth of the giant Ymir, but also of the Babylonian story of Tiamât." P'an-ku is represented as dying for his handiwork, so that his head became mountains, his breath wind and clouds, his voice thunder, his limbs the four poles, his veins the rivers, his sinews the undulations of the earth's surface, his skin the herbs and trees, his bones the rocks and metals, his sweat the rain, and the insects which infested his body men and women.

It was generally recognized—though not systematically expressed till much later—that the Universe was the result of the interplay of the two eternal principles of *Chi* (gaseous matter) and *Li* (form). These combined in varying proportions of finer and grosser matter, so that the world, and all things in it, presented the opposite but complementary aspects of the *Yin* and the *Yang*. The former was feminine and negative, specially represented by the earth; the latter was masculine and positive, and identifiable with the heavens. In the monad, or world-egg, the Yin is the dark part of the circle, represented in divination by the broken line and the even number; the Yang is the light segment of the circle, and is represented by the unbroken line and the odd number. From this symbolism originated, first the use in divining of the four bigrams, as follows: ⚌, ⚏, ⚎, ⚍; and later the use of the eight trigrams, as follows: ☰ (heaven), ☷ (earth), ☳ (thunder), ☶ (mountains), ☲ (fire), ☵ (water),

☱ (steam), and ☴ (wind). The invention of these is ascribed to Fu-hsi about 2852 B.C. Later still, about 1122 B.C., the system was further extended by the use of the sixty-four hexagrams, upon which is built up the volume of the Classics known as the *Yi-ching*, or *Book of Changes*.

The general belief in the harmonious adjustment of form and matter finds multifarious expression. It explains, for instance, the Chinese resort to the five sacred mountains, by which approach is possible to the world of heaven. These are T'ai-shan in Shantung, Hua-shan in Shensi, Hêng-shan in Shansi, Nanyü-shan in Hunan, and Sung-shan in Honan. It explains also the place given to the pseudo-science of *Fêng-shui*, literally, *wind and water*, a kind of geomancy, based on the belief that the harmony of wind and water currents makes fortunate the building of a house or the digging of a grave in one spot rather than in another. Much trouble for foreigners has arisen from ignorance or disregard of this strongly entrenched superstition. In the third place, out of the Chinese reverence for the supposed dependence of man upon harmonious co-operation with the powers of nature has arisen a vast complex of methods in the way of divination. Only a few of these may be mentioned, in addition to those already referred to, such as the use of the whole and broken line in the bigrams and trigrams. Variations of this are to be noted in the bringing out of lines upon a piece of scorched bone or tortoise-shell, and in the use of the stalks of the *Achillea millefolium*—grown especially on the grave of Confucius. Other forms of divination include a kind of juggling with the names of the twelve animal "branches" and the ten elemental "stems," used in the construction of the calendar; indications from human physiognomy, or from the shape of the ears, and the length of the arms; the tossing of coins and the throwing of oyster-shells; the use of lucky ideographs; the placing of sticks in a bowl of water; and the use of omens derivable from the song of birds, the cawing of crows, the burning of a lamp-flame, the twitching of the fingers, the casting of horoscopes, and the like.[1] One of

[1] See Henri Doré, *Recherches sur les Superstitions en Chine*, Shanghai, 1911–19.

the commonest of present-day methods is the use of a piece of bamboo-root, split in the middle so as to be flat on one side and curved on the other. Favourable omens are indicated by the falling of one half stick with the flat surface uppermost and the other reversed.

Naturism involves also the belief in many protective agencies such as are now commonly associated with Taoism. Such are the various talismans against fire, sometimes consisting of the mere ideograph for *water* painted on the wall and sometimes of more elaborate formulæ in blue, green, red, yellow and violet posters placed north, east, south and west of the house, and in the centre. Healing talismans often consist of simple spells to be burned and mixed with a soup or drink; others belong to the scape-goat order and are representations of man, horse, pig or ox, to receive the disease and bear it away. These are just illustrations taken from a vast body of popular practices, all bearing witness to man's sense of dependence on, and trust in, Nature, as also to the necessity for creating and maintaining harmony between her multitudinous manifestations. [1]

No less important than the Chinese attitude towards Nature is the attitude towards the world of spirits. In China, as elsewhere, there was a general belief in the continuity of existence after death and a cult based on the belief. Chinese views as to personality were quite complicated. According to some, man had just two souls, the lower (corresponding to the *psyche*), in which there was a predominance of *Yin*, and the higher (*pneuma*), in which the *Yang* was in control. Others maintained that man possessed seven animal souls (*po*), which gradually evaporated and ceased to be, and three spirits (*hun*), one of which stayed with the body in the grave, while a second remained in the spirit-tablet, and the third departed to Hades. Those who held the simpler theory believed that at death the lower soul was reabsorbed in matter while the higher ascended to the celestial regions. Popularly the spirits of the dead were considered as " rough " or " mild," good or bad, *shên* or *kwei*, according to the manner in which

[1] See J. J. M. de Groot, *The Religion of the Chinese*, New York, 1910.

they were treated by the survivors.[1] Mourning customs were all the development of concern on the part of the living lest the dead should return to plague them. Hence the care taken to provide the dead with what was supposed to be necessary for their repose. Many of the graves were constructed in imitation of the hut and images of the things needed by the dead were therein deposited. It will be remembered that when the great Ch'in Shih Huang-ti, 210 B.C., was interred, a tumulus 500 feet long and nearly two miles around was built to contain the utensils, slaves, women and workmen who were buried with him. To most Chinese the other world was a vast grave in which the departed constituted a kind of hierarchy, reflecting the conditions prevailing above-ground much as a mountain is mirrored in the clear waters of a lake. There are not a few to-day who believe that the underworld changed its form of government with the setting up of a Republic and that Lao Tzŭ is at present the Hell President.

A large part of Chinese life in early times was lived as it were in the presence of the dead. Ancestor worship held together both the family and the State. In the family a living descendant, generally the grandson,[2] was chosen to be "the personator of the dead." The spirits of the departed were then believed to enter through the open door. To quote the *Shih-ching*:

> The spirits come, but when and where
> No one beforehand can declare.
> Therefore we should not spirits slight,
> But ever live as in their sight.

Large collations were prepared of which the spirits were supposed to partake. At the close the "prayer officer" announced the satisfaction of the dead. Sometimes pantomimic dances were performed "to give pleasure to the august personators of the dead." The annual festival of *Ching-ming*, in the spring of the year, when men and women resort to the graves of the ancestors, after a visit to the

[1] See W. E. Soothill, *The Three Religions of China*, Oxford University Press, 1924.

[2] On this see especially Book II. of Marcel Granet's *Chinese Civilization*, New York, 1930.

temples, is still impressive testimony as to the solidarity of Chinese life, in which death is felt to make no real break. Communication with the dead, moreover, was maintained in other ways than by offerings at the ancestral tablets and at the grave. Some employed the *wu*, or wizard, to bring men into contact with the dead; others used the *chi*, or spirit-pencil, to obtain written communications inscribed upon the sand.[1]

Beyond the spirits of the ancestors was a multitude of other spirits, for the most part non-human and discarnate, though it is sometimes hard to be precise as to their nature. The work of driving away the malevolent spirits, or *kwei*, was a serious business and produced a busy and lucrative profession. Methods employed varied from crude forms of disinfection, such as the vapourizing of red vinegar, to the burying of figurines (supposedly representing the cause of the evil), sword strokes in the air with a magic sword made out of cash, the careful construction of houses with a spirit-screen, or without opposite doors and windows—this because spirits (unlike humans) could only move in a straight line—or even by the use of the seal of a mandarin, who in ancient times was credited with authority in both worlds.

There were also spirit animals of significance in mythology and practical religion alike. These included the tortoise (*kwei*), the phœnix (*fêng-huang*), the unicorn (*chi-lin*), and the dragon (*lung*). Other animals were also feared as easily possessed by the spirits; one had specially to be on guard against fox-devils and devils occupying the bodies of apes and tigers.

At some unknown period in Chinese history a special form of religion became the *State cult*. This deserves careful consideration, all the more because, since the time of Yuan Shih-k'ai, the Temples of Heaven and Earth have remained deserted shrines and to-day no national rite exists to exercise a unifying influence, unless we so regard the worship at the tomb of Sun Yat-sen at Nanking.[2] The Emperor as the Son of Heaven—in his representative rather than in his personal character—had special relations

[1] See J. J. M. de Groot, *The Religion of the Chinese*, New York, 1910.
[2] Since Sun's death in 1925 there has been much falling off in the acceptance of his ideology.

with T'ien and with Shang-ti. Indeed, he was "the representative man" in a kind of Chinese Trinity of Heaven, Earth and Man. He officiated as the High Priest of the nation in the three grades of sacrifices, Great, Medium and Inferior. The four Great Sacrifices were those of Heaven and Earth, the Great Temple of the Ancestors, and to the gods of the land and grain. The Medium Sacrifices were nine in number, offered to Sun, Moon, the Imperial Manes, Confucius, the patron deities of Agriculture and Silk, and the gods of Heaven, Earth and the Cyclic Year. The third grade included a crowd of sacrifices offered to the Clouds, Rain, Wind, Thunder, the Sacred Mountains, and so on, down to the gods of gates and flags. In the performance of the sacred rites the Emperor was assisted by a Board of Rites, but he himself was the *Pontifex Maximus*, wearing for the worship of Heaven a blue robe, yellow for the worship of Earth, red for the Sun, and pale white for the Moon.

One of the most impressive of all State rites was the worship at the Temple of Heaven at the time of the winter solstice. At the dead of night the Emperor and his attendants went out through the deserted streets to the beautiful park in which stands the Altar of Heaven, "a beautiful pearl set in an emerald ocean." The son of Heaven prepared himself for his solemn duties in the Hall of Fasting, which still—though rebuilt in modern times—rears its roof of blue a hundred feet into the sky. Everything in the ceremony of the day was marked by impressive symbolism, the form of the buildings being circular, and the steps arranged in series of threes and nines. The Emperor knelt on a single round stone at the top of the altar and there made his supplications for the prosperity of the nation. The rites performed at the Temple of Earth at the summer solstice were similarly striking, with their own appropriate symbolism, the square buildings, the yellow colouring, and the use of the even numbers instead of the odd. In fact all the details of State worship are deserving of the serious study of those interested in the history of religion. Few are alive to-day who ever witnessed them, and the fact that ceremonies so free from idolatrous implication and so fitted to remind the nation of its essential unity have now passed away for ever add an interest which is almost unique.[1]

In the provinces there was some attempt made to give official recognition to religion by special observances, and during periods of drought and famine resort was had to extraordinary rites to secure the intervention of the gods, but these too are going the way of the worship of Shang-ti under the Empire.

It is as an ardent supporter of the official religion and all that it connoted that K'ung-fu Tzŭ, that is, Master K'ung, the Philosopher, whose name was Latinized by the Jesuits as Confucius, appears upon the scene. Attention has already been drawn to the fact that Confucius made little or no constructive contribution to Chinese religion. We may, indeed, say that he contributed less to religion than any religious founder whom we can call to mind. But he is, nevertheless, a very great force in the history of his people, though at the present time his system is exposed to a double attack, on the part of the less intelligent type of missionary, and on the part of the more hysterical type of modern student.

K'ung was born in the state of Lu, in the present province of Shantung, in 551 B.C. The K'ungs of Shantung are probably members of the oldest nobility on earth, the present holder of the family name having passed the seventieth generation. The sage's father was already the father of nine daughters and one crippled son when he married the woman who became the mother of China's most illustrious son. The birth took place in a cave on Mt. Ni, whither the mother had gone on a pilgrimage. His father having died, Confucius was brought up from his first to his seventh year by his mother. Early in life he became distinguished for the gravity and formality of his deportment, and a familiar story tells of his playing at "rules of propriety" with his child companions. At school he soon became a monitor and so remained till the age of seventeen, when he accepted an under mandarinate,

[1] See chapter xiii. of E. T. Williams' *China Yesterday and To-day*, New York, 1927.

the inspectorship of the sale of grains. This office he filled with such success that a regular agricultural school was the result. At the age of nineteen he married, but the match turned out unfortunately, and a divorce took place after the birth of a son. The child was named Li (*Carp*) in allusion to the present—a good augury for the future of a boy—received that day from the Duke of Lu. Probably Confucius was but a cold father, as he had been a cold husband. A story tells of the question addressed to Li by a disciple of the sage: "Have you learned any lessons from your father different from those received by us?" The youth replied that he only remembered two questions addressed to him by his father, namely, Have you read the *Odes*? and Have you studied the rules of propriety? From which answer the questioner deduced that "the superior man" always shows reserve towards his children. For a time Confucius acted as inspector of fields and herds, but his mother's death necessitated three years of retirement which the sage devoted to study, music and archery. He then became a teacher and in course of time rallied to him three thousand disciples, by whom he was deeply and sincerely reverenced. According to his own account, he was not patient with stupid scholars; he expected a pupil, when he himself had lifted one corner of a subject, to lift the other three himself. Raised to the position of a minister of crime in his native duchy, he brought about notable reforms. Those who gave the sheep much water to drink before taking them to sell, those who decorated the cattle to get better prices, and those who lived extravagantly, were brought to justice. As in the days of King Alfred, people became so honest that jewels dropped on the highway were untouched; all men were faithful and all women chaste. The Duke and his people, however, became tired of this moral severity, and when the Duke of a neighbouring State, jealous of the sage's influence, sent to Lu some female musicians and thirty teams of fine horses, the era of reform came to a sudden end. Confucius, who had himself been wearied by the Duke's inconsistencies, and who felt as much a stray dog as did Dante at Verona, retired in despair. It had been, as he put it, a case of

"Virtue in the rear and Vice in front," so he was not unwilling to seek a new sphere for his politico-moral experiments, or else to confine himself to the instruction of his disciples. His own life he summed up as follows: "At fifteen I was bent on learning; at thirty I stood fast; at fifty I knew the will of God; at sixty my ear was open to the truth; at seventy I could follow my desires without transgressing the 'square.'" Nevertheless, the last years of Confucius were saddened by a sense of failure and he died in 479 B.C., at the age of seventy-two, with the discouraging confession: "The great mountain must crumble, the strong beam must break, the wise man wither away like a plant." He was buried at Ch'u-fu, where his grave is still visited by a multitude of pilgrims. Dead, Confucius was mourned even by those who in his life-time had despised him. His work was carried on by others and the sage's fame owes much to the loyalty of disciples who, like Mencius, upheld the principles he had taught. After a brief period of persecution during the Ch'in dynasty, 249–210 B.C., the influence of Confucius experienced a great revival. He was made Duke and Earl under the Han dynasty; Perfect Sage in the fifth century A.D.; King (*Wang*) under the T'ang dynasty; Emperor (*Huang-ti*) under the Sungs; while Mings and Manchus paid him reverence under the title *Perfect Sage, Ancient Teacher*. As late as 1907 the great Empress Dowager—in reply to the Christian doctrine of the deity of Christ—raised Confucius to a position of equality with Shang-ti. The sage's own grandson wrote the impassioned eulogy which represents not unfairly the deliberate opinion of most Chinese, at least till recent years: "His fame overflows the Middle Kingdom and reaches the barbarians of north and south. Wherever ships and wagons can go, or the strength of man penetrate; wherever there is heaven above and earth below; wherever the sun and moon shed their light, or frosts and dews fall, all who have blood and breath honour and love him. Wherefore it may be said that he is the peer of God."

Probably the greatest service Confucius rendered his countrymen was in the part he took in collecting the books which have come to be known as the Confucian *Classics*, in which the general principles of Confucianism are embodied and expounded. These are generally reckoned as nine in number and though some have supposed the bulk of them to be forgeries of the Han period the general consensus of scholarly opinion has favoured their genuineness. The nine consist of two groups, the *Five Ching*, sometimes described as the Old Testament of Confucianism, and the *Four Shu*, which may be called the New Testament of the system. The *Five Ching* are: (1) *The Shu Ching*, or *Book of History*, a compilation of fragmentary annals extending from the days of Yao and Shun, about 2400 to 619 B.C.—all put together to show that the maintenance of Confucian principles brought prosperity while their neglect always entailed disaster. (2) The *Shih Ching*, or *Book of Odes*, a collection of 305 poems, historical, lyrical, religious, and miscellaneous, brought together by the zeal of the sage. (3) The *Yi Ching*, or *Book of Changes*, already alluded to as an elaboration of the system of the Hexagrams ascribed to Wên Wang and the Duke of Chou, with certain appendices contributed by Confucius himself. (4) The *Li Chi*, or *Book of Rites*, the *vade mecum* of the "superior man" and the textbook of the Board of Ceremonies. (5) The *Ch'un Ch'iu*, or *Spring and Autumn*, a rather dull chronicle (expanded by a more readable commentary) of the State of Lu for a period of 250 years prior to the time of Confucius. The *Four Shu* are: (1) The *Lun Yu*, or *Analects*, an entertaining compendium of the table talk of Confucius, containing dialogues between the sage and his disciples and a variety of remarks on government and human affairs in general. (2) The *Ta Hsueh*, or *Great Learning*, an interesting little outline of Confucian ethics, with an analysis of the process whereby man becomes, first, the sage and, secondly, the ruler. (3) The *Chung Yung*, or *Doctrine of the Mean*, compiled by K'ung Chi, the sage's grandson, an enthusiastic exponent of his ancestor's teaching. (4) The four books of *Mencius*, a treatise of political science such as the student of to-day can hardly afford to neglect.[1]

As Mencius contributed so much to the subsequent fame

[1] See F. Max Müller (Editor), *Sacred Books of the East*—Volumes on China.—Oxford, 1899.

of Confucius, a word or two ought in fairness to be devoted to this illustrious philosopher. Mêng K'o, as he is called in China, was born in the province of Shantung about 372 B.C. and was brought up by a mother who is generally regarded as one of the model women of Chinese history. She moved her dwelling-place successively from the neighbourhood of a cemetery, a slaughter-house and a market because her boy seemed overmuch affected by an unfavourable environment. In the neighbourhood of a school she finally found satisfaction and there devoted herself to the upbringing of the future philosopher. Mencius was both philosopher and political economist, a thoroughgoing democrat and a pacifist. He insisted that if taxes were light and the people were well governed a nation ought to be able to repel an invader with sticks and stones. Mencius died, after twenty years of retirement, about 289 B.C.

It will be obvious that, while Confucianism could be by no means the last word in Chinese religion, it made certain contributions of considerable significance, such as "the Master of all good workmen" will surely acknowledge. First, there is the emphasis on individual virtue. The "superior man" must constantly cultivate the moral sense. In this way he gains "a nature constantly right." That a man should daily judge himself in the forum of his own conscience is a fine conception, however infrequently the idea may have been realized in practice. The story of the *Four Knowings* tells how an official replied to one who had tempted him to accept a bribe with the plea, "No one will know it"; "No one know? Why, I know; you know; Heaven knows; Earth knows. How can you say that no one will know it?" Secondly, there is the emphasis on those social obligations which are comprised in the doctrine of the *Five Relations*, namely, the relation of the subject to the ruler, that of the son to the father, of wife to husband, of younger brother to older brother, and of friend to friend. All this has had its effect not only on the Chinese character but also on Chinese culture, which, largely through Confucianism, became a venerable tradition staying the disintegrating tendencies of political tyranny and anarchy, binding together family with family and village with village, even moulding the incoming hordes of barbarians into conformity with Confucian ideals.

Nevertheless, something different and something better was needed to complete what had been begun and to save China for her mission to civilization. Confucius, though esteemed by his disciples, was in general cold and unsympathetic, even (as we have seen) to wife and son. "Knowing God only as majesty and never as Father, the spring of his affections could not bubble joyously forth."[1] The love which Christ offered to the world of men would have seemed to Confucius unworthy of a philosopher. Moreover, he could put in no valid claim to know the Way, the Truth, or the Life. He "did not know the ford," for knowing less than perfectly the meaning of life, he was unable to expound the mystery of death. And, once again, Confucius was by no means satisfied with the travail of his own soul, or able to glimpse the victory ahead. We have already quoted the last despairing utterance, the cry of the disappointed:

> The great mountain must crumble,
> The strong beam break,
> And the sage wither like grass.

But we must now pass from the man and the system which have had most influence on the ethical ideals of China to the man and the system which might very easily, in combination with the other, have made possible for China a more vitalizing experience in religion than it has hitherto been her lot to know.

Little is known of Lao Tzŭ, to whom is ascribed the origin of the religion known as *Taoism*. His personal name was Li Erh, and his posthumous name Li Tan, but some have regarded him as a purely legendary character. Most scholars, however, accept him as historical and give his birth as about 604 B.C., thus making him a somewhat younger contemporary of Confucius. A picturesque story tells of an interview between the two sages in which Lao Tzŭ was curt and enigmatical, and Confucius so perplexed that he could only compare the older philosopher to the dragon,

[1] W. E. Soothill, *The Three Religions of China,* Oxford University Press, 1924.

whose mounting of the winds and clouds was beyond the understanding of men. Lao Tzŭ was for a time Keeper of the Archives in the old capital of China, but official life was distasteful and he withdrew eventually towards the west. Here he was besought, according to tradition, by the warden of the passes to put his precious teachings into writing before retirement from the world. Thus was written the *Tao Tê Ching*, or *Classic of the Way of Virtue*, the Bible of Taoism. It is not certainly the work of the sage, but is in any case an exposition of early Taoism which, as Dr. E. T. Williams remarks, is as different from the teachings of Taoism to-day as the teaching of Spinoza is from that of Madame Blavatsky.

The word *Tao* has been translated in a variety of ways, as *Way*, *Nature*, *Logos*, even *God*. Perhaps the word *Way* is as satisfactory as any, since Lao Tzŭ had in view a certain principle—a kind of *Ewigzeitgeist*—or *élan vital* coincident with the universe, with which man only needed to harness himself in order to find happiness and success. Thus, instead of learning by heart the multifarious legalism of the Confucian system the Taoist was urged to get at once into harmonious relations with Nature and then "by doing nothing all would be done." Lao Tzŭ himself, if he were the author of the *Tao Tê Ching*, did not say expressly what the Tao was. "The Tao," he said, "which can be defined is not the eternal Tao; the name by which it can be named is not its eternal name. When nameless, it is the origin of the universe; when it has a name it is the mother of all things. Therefore only he who is ever passionless may behold its mystery." Practically, Lao Tzŭ taught a doctrine of grace as opposed to a doctrine of law. He said: "The crow does not become black through being painted, nor the pigeon white through bathing." The general attitude of the Taoist was that of the mystic and the quietist, as is plain from such sayings as the following:

> Keep behind and you shall be put in front. Keep out and you shall be put in.
> Mighty is he who conquers himself.
> He who is conscious of being strong is content to be weak.
> He who is content has enough.

To the good I would be good. To the not good also I would be good in order to make them good.
Recompense injury with kindness.
The weak overcometh the strong ; the soft overcometh the hard.

What Mencius was to the system of Confucius Chuang Tzŭ, one of the most delightful characters among the Chinese sages, was to Taoism. He belongs to a time two centuries later than that of his master, but still reflects the spirit of "the old philosopher." So entirely did he identify himself with Nature that having on one occasion dreamed that he was a butterfly he declared that he was thenceforth uncertain whether he were a man who had dreamed he was a butterfly or a butterfly which had dreamed it was a man. All official life was distasteful to him, so much so that when approached with the request that he should become the Prime Minister of Ch'u he reminded the envoys of the stuffed tortoise in their master's hall while he pointed to the little live tortoises waggling their tails in the mud and asked which they would prefer to be. When Chuang Tzŭ was dying he forbade his disciples to bury him, saying: "I will have Heaven and Earth for my sarcophagus; the sun and moon shall be the insignia where I lie in state; and all creation shall be my mourners." Chuang Tzŭ left voluminous writings behind him from which a single quotation will suffice to illustrate his point of view: "The command of armies is the lowest form of virtue. Rewards and punishments are the lowest form of education. Ceremonies and laws are the lowest form of government. Music and fine clothes are the lowest form of happiness. Wailing and mourning are the lowest form of grief. These five should follow the movements of the mind." [1]

It is convenient here to give a brief summary of the history of Taoism on to the days of its present decline. Some have felt disposed to restrict the term *Taoism* to the subsequent developments, using for the early system the name of *Laoism*. But it is better to use a single term and to divide the history of the religion into three periods or stages. The first is that of philosophic sincerity and covers the age of Lao Tzŭ and his better-known disciples. The

[1] Lionel Giles, *Musings of a Chinese Mystic*, London, 1911.

second is that of imperial patronage, at its height in the time of the great Ch'in emperor 249–210 B.C. The third is the modern period of superstition and charlatanry. During the Ch'in period the Emperor himself expounded Taoism to his courtiers and those who yawned were turned over to the executioner. The first of the Han emperors also was devoted to the cult which by this time had become largely a quest for the two secrets of the *Elixir Vitae* and the *Philosopher's Stone*. The hierarchy of Taoist Popes dates from this era and the first Pope was Chang Tao-ling, who ascended to heaven at the age of 123 from the Dragon-Tiger Mountain in Kiangsi, where his descendants have resided ever since. "He had acquired power to walk among the stars, to divide mountains, and seas, to command the wind and the thunder, and to quell demons." Later Taoism received the worst of Buddhism from that system and perhaps imparted to Buddhism the best that had once been its own. Taoism is now little better than a system of magic, though much resorted to by the superstitious of all ranks. The present Pope or "Great Wizard," is employed to expel evil spirits from the dwellings of the wealthy. "All new gods are declared by the Emperor" so it was said prior to the Revolution of 1911, "through him, and on the first day of every month he gives audience to an invisible host of gods and demi-gods who come to present their compliments."

It has thus come about that the system which promised so well for China is now but another illustration of the proverb: "Corruptio optimi pessima est." The *Way* of Taoism was, after all, not a Living Way. Taoism, instead of promoting spirituality, sold itself to man's craving for magic. What might have been at least the complement and corrective of a mere moral philosophy degenerated into a mass of stupid futilities. No more than its rival system has the religion of Lao Tzŭ been able to supply the full answer to its questionings for which the soul of China has so long been waiting.

The same thing is true of the several philosophies which arose in China independently of both Confucianism and Taoism and which have left but a small impression on the

China of to-day. They deserve mention, however, if only to show that the Chou period did not follow the ways of K'ung and Lao exclusively. Yang Tzŭ, or Yang Chu, for instance, of the fourth century B.C. is mentioned by Mencius and Chuang Tzŭ as having founded a school of extreme ethical egoism. He has sometimes been compared with Epicurus, who was his contemporary, and apparently shared some of his opinions. Again, Mo Ti, or Mo Tzŭ, Latinized as Micius, preached the opposite doctrine of communism and mutual love. Mencius declared that, while Yang Tzŭ would not have parted with a single hair of his head to save the world, Mo Tzŭ would willingly have sacrificed all. "He was vigorously opposed," says Giles, "by Mencius, who exhibited the unpractical side of an otherwise fascinating doctrine." Another contemporary philosopher mentioned by Chuang Tzŭ is Lieh Tzŭ, or Licius, but it is now supposed that he is merely a man of straw used in a kind of allegory by Chuang Tzŭ for the purposes of argument. Later historians were misled into taking him for an historical personage.

Certainly China was not without her many doctors and doctrines offering spiritual solace to the heart of men in the centuries prior to the appearance of Christianity. All alike, however, were impotent in the effort to stay the plague of misery and corruption which during these ages swept over the body politic. In our next chapter we shall consider the new competitor which arose to challenge the attention of the Middle Kingdom. While Buddhism by no means supplied what Confucianism and Taoism so obviously lacked we shall see that it recommended itself so far as to be in time included in the San Chiao, the Three Religions, of China.[1]

[1] Other useful books to which the reader of this chapter may be referred will include the following: Abel Bonnard, *In China*, London, 1926; Richard Wilhelm, *A Short History of Chinese Civilization*, New York, 1929; H. G. Creel, *Sinism*, Chicago, 1929; S. Wells Williams, *The Middle Kingdom*, 2 Vols. (Revised Edition), New York, 1907; R. K. Douglas, *Confucianism and Taoism*, London; Edwin D. Harvey, *The Mind of China*, Yale University Press, 1933.

## CHAPTER XXV

# *The Religions of China—II.*

### BUDDHISM

SOME time after the first half of the first century of our era, in the reign of Ming Ti, A.D. 58–76, an important incident, according to the common tradition, brought about a great religious change in the Middle Kingdom. The Emperor dreamed that a great golden image, its head surrounded with a halo of light came flying from heaven and hovered over the imperial palace. Summoning his soothsayers, Ming Ti learned from them that a great teacher had been born in the west, and he was advised by his brother to send envoys immediately who might bring back a true report of the great event. Eighteen men were sent who visited the court of the Indo-Parthian ruler of North-west India, Gondophorus, or Gondopharnes. From this ruler they received a sandal-wood image and the *sutra* supposed to be Açvaghosha's life of the Buddha. It has been surmised that, since the Christian apostle St. Thomas was at this time, according to tradition, present at the same court, the Chinese emissaries may very conceivably have borne back with them Christian as well as Buddhistic ideas. In any case, they returned to the Imperial capital, Loyang, about A.D. 68, accompanied by two Indian teachers, Kaçyapa Matanga and Gobharana. This, says the generally accepted story, was the beginning of Buddhism in China. The White Horse Temple was erected in Loyang as a reminder of the white horse on which the precious images and books were transported.

Naturally we ask whether the Emperor had anything to go by beyond supernatural guidance or intuition. Some believe that Buddhism was probably not unknown in China two centuries earlier. A record in fact exists which describes missionaries of the Indian faith as coming to China about

217 B.C. and of their imprisonment by the reigning monarch. It is readily seen that from the beginning of the Han period, about 200 B.C., Chinese contact with Buddhism was more than possible, not only in North-west India, Kashmir and Nepal but also in Central Asia. During the reign of Han Wu Ti, 140–87 B.C., Chinese generals had extended the imperial domain westward almost as far as the Caspian, and it is certain that soldiers of this "far-flung" empire must have brought back reports of the rapidly expanding faith, even though the account which describes the bringing back of a golden image be not literally true.

Once introduced, Buddhism did not at first spread widely or rapidly. There were certain obvious drawbacks in the eyes of the Chinese, such as the emphasis placed on the monastic life, an emphasis which did not well accord with ancestor worship or the doctrine of filial piety. There was also the revolt from that official preoccupation which to the majority of Chinese was as the breath of life. And there was again the worship of relics which was distasteful to the mind of the Chinese, not to speak of the general anti-foreignism of a conservative people to whom it was a sufficient condemnation of Buddhism to assert that Gautama was one who buttoned his coat on the wrong side.

Nevertheless, there were features of Buddhism which gradually gained Chinese approval. The new religion was a literary system and brought a new type of culture to a people already strongly obsessed with reverence for the written word. There was also inherent in Buddhism a transcendental value entirely lacking in Confucianism and at least in the later stages of Taoism. It was shown, moreover, by experience that Mahayana Buddhism was exceedingly tolerant of the older beliefs and that the deities of Chinese polytheism could be without difficulty retained as Bodhisattvas, or future incarnations of the Buddha. It is not to be forgotten, too, that early Chinese Buddhism produced not a few saintly lives such as went far towards thawing the cold hearts of stolid Mongolians and inclining them to the Gospel of Gautama.

Nevertheless, for three hundred years the faith spread but slowly and it was not till A.D. 333 that some of the

States gave permission for the taking of the vows. The edict of tolerance seems to have been followed by a period of rapid growth, since we are told that in 381 nine-tenths of the people in North-west China were Buddhists. Even an emperor, of the short-lived Ts'in dynasty, took the vows, and alarm was presently excited by the stream of people deserting official life for the monasteries. Then followed a period of persecution, due partly to the discovery of a conspiracy in which monks were involved, as a result of which many monasteries were destroyed and nuns forbidden to enter the palace. After a few years, however, about A.D. 451, the edict was revoked and a more friendly feeling for the foreign faith prevailed for several centuries. One emperor, Liang Wu Ti, 502–550, took so much interest in the propagation of Buddhism that he is sometimes called the Chinese Açoka.

It was in this reign that Buddhism, which in India had now entered upon the period of decline, transferred its headquarters to China. In 526 came the twenty-eighth patriarch in succession to Gautama, Bodhidharma, known to the Chinese as Tamo (whence the confusion with St. Thomas) and to the Japanese as Daruma. Bodhidharma arrived at Nanking, where he much displeased the Emperor by the brusque announcement: "I am heaven and you are hell." Then he crossed the river to visit the capital Loyang, where he made himself famous as "the wall-gazing saint," from the meditation protracted through nine years, during which time his feet were worn away and the rats gnawed off his ears. A popular legend makes him the discoverer of tea, since, having cut off his eyelashes to keep himself awake, the tea-plant immediately sprang up and afforded the beverage which dispelled his somnolence at less personal inconvenience. Notwithstanding the story about his feet being worn off, Bodhidharma is said to have left one shoe in his coffin, from which his body disappeared—transferred supposedly to celestial regions. The saint was the founder of the sect of meditation, known as Dhyana in India, as Ch'an Tsung in China (where it remains one of the most influential schools) and later introduced into Japan as Zen.

During these centuries, from the fourth to the seventh,

we must not overlook the important contributions made to literature and religion by the Chinese pilgrims who left their monasteries, sometimes for many years at a time, to add to the treasures of their temple libraries by visits to the Holy Places of Buddhism in India. The most famous of these pilgrims are Fa-hien, a simple and sincere man who travelled, mostly on foot, for fifteen years and brought back the books of the *Vinaya* for his temple library at Ch'ang-an; [1] I Tsing; and, perhaps the most important of all, Hiuen Tsang, who became a favourite of the Indian king Harsha, in the middle of the seventh century, and staged debates against the heretics with great credit to Buddhism.[2] It is along the track of Hiuen Tsang's journeys through Central Asia that Sir Marc Aurel Stein has laboured for so many years. The discovery by Stein in 1907 of the famous "polyglot library" at the Tun-huang oasis is a good illustration of the work of these Chinese pilgrims down to the end of the ninth century.[3]

All through this period Buddhism had been spreading in Central and Southern China and a very large mass of literature had been translated from the Sanskrit into Chinese. It was in connection with this work of translation that a method was devised by the Hindu missionaries for grouping the Chinese ideographs under the radical forms; also, to assist knowledge of the Chinese pronunciation, each monosyllable was given with an initial and a final sound. These features have been ever since retained in the standard Chinese dictionaries.

Buddhism, as already suggested, found favour with the early T'ang rulers, in the seventh century—as did also the other foreign faiths, Magianism, Islam, Manichæanism, and Nestorian Christianity. But from time to time there were anti-foreign reactions. Kao Tsung, for example, was influenced by his minister, Fu Yi, to oppose Buddhism. A little later, in the eighth century, the emperor sent 12,000 monks home from their monasteries, though the same monarch subsequently relented and issued an edition of the

[1] See James Legge, *Record of Buddhist Kingdoms*, Oxford, 1886; Samuel Beal, *Buddhist Records of the Western World*, London, 1884.

[2] See S. Beal, *Life of Hiuen Tsang*, London, 1911.

[3] See Sir Marc Aurel Stein, *Ruins of Desert Cathay*, London, 1912.

*Tripitaka*. The worst of all the persecutions came about 819, when a double attack was made on Buddhism, by the Taoists, jealous of the increasing prestige of the faith, and the Confucianists who were moved to protest by the worship of relics. It was on this occasion that the philosopher Han Yü presented his "Memorial on a Bone of Buddha," and was in consequence exiled to the South.

After this Buddhism remained a tolerated religion, gradually achieving a position as one of the *San Chiao*, or "Three Teachings." Under the Mongols, in the time of Kublai Khan, the form of Buddhism known as Lamaism was introduced and flourished. (Of this type we shall speak later.) Under the Mings (1368–1644) Buddhism was favoured, though at the same time the growing wealth of the monastic establishments was looked at somewhat askance. The Manchus, who followed the Mings in 1644, were not quite consistent in their attitude, favouring Lamaism in Mongolia and Tibet, while in China proper dislike was expressed for all religions but the Confucian. For some years before the Revolution of 1911 a very vigorous propaganda was directed from Japan, but in recent years this has lost some of its force and much of modern China professes itself hostile to Buddhism as to other religions. Of the present condition of Buddhism in China something will be said presently.

It has been pointed out that Mahayana Buddhism showed considerable willingness to accommodate its beliefs and practices to those of the peoples among whom its lot was cast. This is particularly true of Buddhism in China, and in order to understand the religion as compared with the faith taught by Gautama some account of the various theological and sectarian developments is necessary. Already, ere leaving North-west India, the reverence manifested to Gautama as the Buddha was largely superseded by worship rendered to various Bodhisattvas, or future Buddhas, whose characteristics in certain cases may owe something to the religions of the West. Then in China itself it became natural to identify some of these Bodhisattvas with gods already in the pantheon, or to increase the number of worshipful beings by deifications and canonizations of various grades. Ultimately we get a hierarchy of gods and near-gods in Chinese Buddhism which may be thus systematized:

1. The *Heavenly Buddhas*, which include Gautama (*Shih-chia-mo-ni*, that is, Çakyamuni), who is represented as the glorified Buddha, sometimes standing in an attitude of teaching, and sometimes seated in the act of meditation; Amitabha (*O-mi-to-fo*), the Buddha who leads souls into the Western Paradise; and Yao-Shih Fo, who is probably the same as the Sanskrit Bhaisajyaguru, and is connected with medicine. He lives in endless light and draws all creation out of the darkness of error into the light of peace. (In parenthesis it should be said that the various triads of Chinese religion may easily be the source of confusion. Sometimes we have represented the Three Founders, Confucius, Lao Tzŭ and Gautama; sometimes the old Buddhist triad of the Buddha, the Law and the Society; sometimes the Taoist triad of the Three Agents, Heaven, Earth and Water; and sometimes even the Three Model Emperors, Yao, Shun and Yü. It is by no means easy to separate in these triads what is Buddhist from what originally had a place in other systems.)

2. The *Bodhisattvas* (*P'u-sa*), generally given as Kuan-yin, the goddess of mercy, who corresponds with the Indian Avalokiteçvara (probably "the down-looking god"); Ta-shih-chih (Mahasthana), a deity of power, sometimes represented as Amitabha's second son; Maitreya (*Milo-fo*), the Buddha expected at the close of the present era, represented as a jolly, *bon-vivant* kind of a god, with round and protuberant stomach and smiling face; Wên-shu (the Sanskrit *Manjusri*), the god of learning, represented as seated on a lion; and P'u-hsien (*Samantabhadra*), a god of mercy, seated on an elephant. Of these Kuan-yin, though identified with Avalokiteçvara, has a purely Chinese tradition. Her real name was Miao-shan and she had two sisters, Miao-chin and Miao-yin. The two latter married, but Miao-shan from the first, braving her father's anger, felt a vocation for the religious life and fled to a convent. The father sent soldiers to burn the convent and for this outrage was stricken with blindness. For this there was no cure

except that a near relative should tear out her own eyes. This heroic act Miao-shan performed for her sire and it was for this that she became a Bodhisattva in a subsequent birth. Kuan-yin's special shrine is on the island of P'ut'o, in the Ningpo Archipelago, a great resort for pilgrims from all over China.

3. The *Arhats* (in Chinese *Lohans*), or saints of Buddhism, including sometimes only the closest of Gautama's friends, Ananda and Kaçyapa, sometimes the ten, sometimes the twelve, sometimes the eighteen, and in some cases the five hundred disciples. At the famous temple of the five hundred *lohans* at Canton the figure of Marco Polo seems to have been included. The image at any rate has a very un-Chinese appearance. In some classifications the *Patriarchs* of Buddhism, such as Bodhidharma, are comprised under this head.

4. The *Tutelary Deities*, a very motley collection of worshipful beings, including the Four Heaven Kings (*Lokapalas*), that is, the old Indian gods, Indra, Agni, Varuna, and Yama, placed as guardians at the entrance of Buddhist shrines; the Twenty-four Devas; the two Door-gods, who were originally two famous soldiers of the T'ang period; and other deified individuals, such as the popular Kwan-ti (the God of War), originally a general of the period of anarchy which followed the Han dynasty in the third century A.D.[1]

The sects, or schools, of Chinese Buddhism present a rather complicated problem, since many of them represent the teachings of individual monks whose following rapidly disintegrated. Even as to the variations of teaching represented in these schools there is often an inextricable confusion. Ten schools are generally recognized, but for practical purposes half of them may be disregarded. The three most important are the *Ch'an* Tsung, the *T'ient'ai* Tsung, and the *Ching-t'u* Tsung. The Ch'an is the sect of meditation known in India as Dhyana and in Japan as Zen. It was founded (in China) by the first Buddhist patriarch, Bodhidharma, who aimed at the "emptying of consciousness" to the exclusion of other religious activities. As "the wall-gazer" Bodhidharma is the subject of many

[1] Made a god in 1594, when the Ming dynasty was declining.

popular legends. The sect itself is now broken up into five subdivisions, though each section claims the title of *tsung*. The T'ien t'ai, known later in Japan as Tendai, was founded by the monk Chih-k'ai, who died in A.D. 597, in the T'ien-t'ai Mountains. He tried to create a system which harmonized the various traditions—an "all-ways" school. So, in addition to the practice of meditation, he advocated the study of the scriptures. In their zeal for copying the sutras it is said that some monks opened their veins and wrote the sacred books in their own blood. The favourite sutra of the sect was the *Lotus Scripture*, the *Saddharma-pundarika* (in Chinese, *Miao-fa-lien-hua ching*). The Ch'ing-t'u, or Pure Land Sect, known later in Japan as Jodo, is by some reckoned the oldest of all, tracing its teachings back to Vasabandhu, the pupil of Nagarjuna. It was established in China in the fourth century by Hui-yuan, who had been converted from Taoism to a belief in Amitabha (O-mi-to-fo) and the Western Paradise to which Amitabha was supposed to lead the soul. With Amitabha reign the Bodhisattvas Kuan-yin and Ta-shih-chih, the "three holy ones of the western land." Beside these principal schools may be mentioned the Lu-tsung, or school of discipline, occupied with the *Vinaya*; and the Hien-shou-tsung, founded by Tu-fa-shun, who died in 640 and followed the text-book prepared by Nagarjuna, the great Indian exponent of *Mahayana*.[1]

Buddhism in China is properly a monastic religion, though there are, of course, many millions of Chinese who follow Buddhist teachings and practices without taking the vows. The monks and nuns probably number considerably over a million, but it is hard to obtain accurate figures. The monasteries are for the most part outside the cities, on mountain tops, and surrounded by trees. They follow in their structure a general plan, which often includes several great halls around a central court, beside smaller buildings for guest rooms, store rooms, kitchen and dining hall. The

[1] For the general subject of Chinese Buddhism see R. F. Johnston, *Buddhist China*, London, 1913; K. L. Reichelt, *Truth and Tradition in Chinese Buddhism*, Shanghai, 1918; H. Hackmann, *Buddhism as a Religion*, London, 1910; W. E. Soothill, *The Three Religions of China*, Oxford, 1924; Joseph Edkins, *Chinese Buddhism*, London.

temple bell is a characteristic feature, as is also the fish-pond, often beautiful with lotus blossoms. The images are arranged in the order already described, Buddhas, Bodhisattvas, Saints and Patriarchs, and Tutelary Gods. Many of the images have a small hole at the back, through which a living animal has been inserted to give life to the statue. The monks are mainly recruited from the ranks of children vowed to religion by their parents, not infrequently at a time of illness. They are not, however, formally admitted to the monastic order till after their twentieth year, when they pass successively through the three stages of initiation, in certain cases undergoing very severe and painful tests. In addition to the regular monks there are Buddhist hermits, who live in mat sheds in close connection with a monastery. Some monasteries have great fame, as, for instance, those of the T'ien-t'ai Mountains, and those connected with places of pilgrimage like Pu-to-shan, Chiu-hua-shan, Wu-t'ai-shan and O-mi-shan.

On the surface at least, Chinese Buddhism seems to have lost much of its former vigour. Few of the monks seem to have much acquaintance with the *Canon*, or even with the names of the images under their care in the temples. Their morality, again, is said to be of a low order. The present-day practice of Buddhism includes much that is grossly superstitious. The cult of the "dried priest" who, under a special regime, starves himself to death and is henceforth carried around the village or placed in the temple as a holy relic, is much in vogue in the Yang-tze valley. Not infrequently one comes across the fanatic who immures himself for a term of years, bricked up in a narrow place, within which he will neither change his clothes, or wash, or cut his hair. The keeping of the birthday of the Buddha in one of the large cities of China seemed to have as its principal feature the purchase of live eels in the market that, as an act of mercy, these might be set free in the river. The temples generally are loathsome with the presence of lepers and other diseased persons, while the common adornments concern the torments of the ten hells, realistically portrayed in stucco groups around the court. It is, indeed, in preoccupation with the future life that the Chinese Buddhist is to be distinguished from his Confucian or Taoist brother. Everywhere in the temples one finds the figure of the Hell Emperor, T'i-tsang-wang, who was once a saint of the T'ang period, zealous for the welfare of souls in the other world. Compassion is not exactly the feature of the Hell Emperor which manifests itself in the temples of China to-day. The various punishments meted out in the ten departments of Hades exhaust in imagination the possibilities of human cruelty. Yet it is to be remembered that the punishments of the Buddhist hells are not eternal, but rather the fulfilment of a man's *karma*, and preparation for a new incarnation to which he goes forth presently through the gates of oblivion.

Though the above picture of Chinese Buddhism is that which will recur to the memories of most people acquainted with conditions in the Middle Kingdom, it is only fair to say that some have discerned recent signs of revival. Where these exist they are due in part to the impact of Christian teaching and Christian institutions, in part to the influence of Japanese Buddhism, which has lent its help for the increase of knowledge and improvement of morals, and in part to the new movement towards the defence of religion, forced by recent events on the professors of all the faiths.

As to one section of Chinese Buddhism, however, little can be said that is good. This is *Lamaism*, to which we must devote a few words before concluding the chapter.

Lamaism is so called from the title given to the monks of Tibetan Buddhism. It is a Tibetan word (*blama*) meaning "superior" and was applied originally to the head of a monastery. Tibetan religion, as stated earlier, was in the earliest period what is called *Bon*, a form of nature worship, with reverence paid to the dead, carried on by shamans who were experts in magic. But in the seventh century A.D. a change occurred which marks not only the introduction of a new religion but also the beginnings of authenticated Tibetan history. A certain prince named Srong Tsan Gampo had succeeded in subjugating the neighbouring tribes and, to mark his newly acquired prestige, married two wives, one from China and one from Nepal. Both of these ladies were Buddhist and, once again in the history of religion, we are called upon to mark the influence of woman in the propagation of a faith. The devotion of the Nepalese princess, however, seems to have been the dominant one and in consequence, when help was asked in the extension of Buddhism, India was the direction to which the Tibetans turned. But at this time Buddhism in India was decadent almost to the point of extinction, so that the doctrines introduced were rather reminiscent of Tantric Yoga than of the teachings of Gautama. One has only to look at the picture of the Tibetan Judgement, with Yama-raja, the king of the dead, adorned with human skulls, a serpent necklace, for a cape a human hide from which protrude the head, a hand and a foot (and other grim accessories), to mark the difference between this and the genuine Buddhist art. The missionary who came at this time was one Padma Sambhava, known to the Tibetans as Guru Rimpo Che, and under his leadership monasteries were founded, books translated, and, in course of time, new sects created. In the eleventh century a new doctrine was propagated by an Indian teacher named Atiça, and at the height of the Mongol supremacy, in the thirteenth and fourteenth centuries, Lamaism was carried from Tibet into Mongolia and even found favour with the Great Khan, Kublai, who saw in it a useful tool for the political unification of his vast realm. By this time the organization of Lamaism had attained much of its later character as a politico-religious system governed by a " living Buddha." With the fifteenth century, however, came a more far-reaching movement in the reformation under Tsong Kapa, whose new sect, the Gelugpa, may conceivably be indebted to Christian missionaries. This sect is known as that of the *Yellow Caps*, in distinction from the earlier Lamaists, the Ningmapa, or *Red Caps*. The fifth of Tsong Kapa's successors became so powerful that he was able to obtain from China the acknowledgement of his sovereignty over Tibet, with the title of *Dalai* ("*ocean*") Lama. The Dalai Lama was supposed to be a reincarnation of the Bodhisattva Avalokiteçvara, and was chosen by an elaborate piece of divination in which the fresh incarnation was indicated. Other sects followed the example of the monks resident at Lhasa and found in the heads of their respective monasteries incarnations of other Bodhisattvas. The Grand Lama at Tashi Lhumpo at Shigatze even obtained a position scarcely inferior to that of the Dalai Lama. And as Lamaism spread through Mongolia, the head lamas of different districts, about a hundred and sixty (it is said) in number, were recognized as Living Buddhas under the general title of Hutukhtu. It will be remembered that, at the Revolution of 1911, the Hutukhtu of Outer Mongolia, at Urga, became the ruler of the territory which is now a part of the Soviet system. As the persecution of the Red Caps by the Yellow Caps increased during the seventeenth century, the Manchu sovereigns were led to intervene and both K'ang Hsi and Ch'ien Lung assumed the overlordship of Tibet together with the patronage of the Lamaist Church. The Tibetan War during the reign of Ch'ien Lung was in consequence of this intervention. A further result was the erection of the Lama Temple at Peking (Peiping), where the so-called "Devils' Dance" takes place at the New Year. But the temple and its occupants have now fallen on evil days; the hangers-on have much diminished in number, and most of the "dancing" consists of rather vulgar "stunts" put on for the edification (?) of foreign tourists. Not much needs to be said of Lamaism as a religion except that, with some few exceptions, the monks are ignorant and superstitious beyond most other Buddhists. Most of the men of Tibet are monks of one sort or another, sometimes "home" monks, who live on farms with their families, with little to mark them as "religious"; sometimes "vagabond" monks wandering from lamasery to lamasery and supporting themselves by begging; and sometimes genuine monks living in vast establishments such as are found throughout Tibet but especially at Lhasa. In these there is much use of charms and *mantras*, much dependence on prayer-flags and prayer-wheels, much use of sacred symbols such as the *swastika*, much use of finger-twistings (like those employed in the Shingon sect of Japan), use of religious dances, and other observances in general due to the ever-present fear of devils and the desire to escape the terrors of the Buddhist hells.[1]

It is perhaps an unduly pessimistic vision of Buddhism with which we finish our sketch of Chinese religion, but it will be allowed that the facts as given above are not distorted. We shall do well to keep in mind the distance between Buddhism at its best and degradations of the best such as we see, for example, in Lamaism. But even Buddhism at its best was proved to be a very undependable Way. Sir Edwin Arnold was not exaggerating when he placed on the lips of his Buddhist visitor to Galilee the words:

> I do discern that, forth from this fair life
> And this meek death and thine arisen Christ,
> Measureless things are wrought ; a thought-dawn born
> Which shall not cease to broaden, till its beam
> Makes noon of knowledge for a gathered world,
> Completing what our Buddha left unsaid ;
> Carpeting bright his noble Eight-fold Way
> With fragrant blooms of all-renouncing love,
> And bringing high Nirvana nearer hope,
> Easier and plainer.[2]

There was, after all, more about pity, human and divine, than it was possible for Gautama to discover for the remedying of the ills of men. In the eternal issue, moreover, there was fuller content than what the negations of Nirvana suggested. Buddhism, considered as a finality, was an utter failure. It was quite powerless to lift the individual above the insurgent ills of life; it was powerless to deliver the Orient from its many social and political miseries. Only too obviously, in the grossness and superstition of modern China, one realizes how Buddhism has sunk into ready connivance with the charlatanry of a debased Taoism. Nor is it difficult to assign reasons for such a failure. God, under whatever name, even in polytheistic or apparently monolatrous forms of Buddhism, is Himself but part of the great illusion. Amida, Maitreya, this one or that, all sink back ultimately into Maya; they fade away just when

[1] For Tibetan Buddhism see H. Hackmann, *Buddhism as a Religion*, London, 1910 ; W. Y. Evans-Wentz, *The Tibetan Book of the Dead*, Oxford, 1927 ; *Ency. Rel. and Ethics, sub voce* "Lamaism."
[2] Sir Edwin Arnold, *The Light of Asia*.

human hands most yearn to touch them. "Amida's Paradise is indeed a very concrete heaven to the average believer. But as the believer grows in intelligence and begins to delve in the deeper teachings of his sect, his vision of Paradise begins to fade. He learns that for practical purposes he should act and live as if the achievement of an enriched personality were the goal of all our strivings and the one value which abides the wreck of time, but in reality personality and all individuality cannot be a permanent state."[1]

Hence the cure of sorrow, except to those who have taken despair to themselves as a bride, must be illusory too. As in the familiar story of the woman and the millet seed, Buddhism has no comfort to give save that "loss is common to the race," and that misery is inseparable from life. No wonder we find that, at its very best, Buddhism is tinged with ineffaceable sadness, the sadness of those who panted for life, yet were offered consolation only in the abnegation of life; of those who craved for peace, but were offered peace only in the dreamless sleep of Nirvana. As it has been put by a non-Christian Chinese writer, quoted by Dr. Soothill: "Buddhism abandons the world, Christianity would redeem it."[2]

Surely Prince Siddhartha, had he lived in Galilee instead of India, and had he been able to share the lot of Jesus of Nazareth, rather than that of the ascetics of Benares, would not have fled to bleak negations as a refuge from the world's sorrow. Rather, hearing the invitation: "Come unto Me, all ye that are weary and heavy-laden, and I will give you rest," we may reasonably suppose he would have been among the first to follow in the Way. And thus following he would have learned how to exhaust pessimism at its very source.

[1] W. E. Soothill, *The Three Religions of China*, Oxford, 19 4.
[2] W. E. Soothill, *op. cit.*, p. 111.

## CHAPTER XXVI

### *The Religions of Japan*

THE population of the Japanese Archipelago, in addition to the Ainus, whose religion we have discussed in Chapter X, was in early times made up out of ethnic contributions from three different directions. First, there was an inconsiderable migration by way of Kamchatka and the north of people known as Sushen, or Siberic, a stock with some affinity to the race we know later under the name of Manchu. Next, we have a much more important movement, probably in three or more separate migrations, known as the Yamato, which came from the Continent by way of Korea and settled first of all in the region bearing that name on the western shores of the main island. Lastly, from the south, possibly from South China, possibly from the Malay Peninsula or Borneo, possibly even from as far afield as the Polynesian Islands, came the virile and warlike stock known as the Kumaso. These settled first in the southern island of Kyushu. It was from these last two elements—the Anglo-Saxons and Normans respectively of the Japanese population—that the ultimate race descended. The Empire was actually founded by the incursion of the Kumaso, some centuries before Christ, into the main island and by their subjugation of the older population. Culturally, too, though many elements were transmitted from the Continent, it was the Kumaso stock which became dominant, as one may see by a study of the food and the houses which became habitual.

The traditional date of the accession of Jimmu Tenno, the first emperor, is February 11, 660 B.C., but this precision is uncritical and due to later arrangement of the chronicle. During this period of legend it is probable that Japanese religion was a simple form of nature worship, in which appreciation was more conspicuous than fear, and in which the worship of ancestors had as yet found little or no place. This religion we call *Shinto*, from the Chinese *Shên-tao*, the *Way of the Gods*, though the proper Japanese term (meaning the same thing) is *Kami-no-Michi*.

Who are the gods, known to the Chinese as Shên and to the Japanese as Kami? The word itself, which is similar to the Ainu word for God, *kamui*, means literally "that which is above" and is applied to many different things, including the chiefs of clans (believed to be divinely descended) and even the hair of the head (a recognized soul-seat). As applied to the gods it may be translated as "heaven-dwellers." The *kami* may be grouped under three heads, though the first must be regarded as in all probability the original. This first group includes the large class of deities who are the personifications of natural forces. Among these are the creator pair, Izanagi (the male-who-invites) and Izanami (the female-who-invites), who produced the islands when Izanagi, from "the floating bridge of heaven," dipped his spear into the Pacific and turned the congealed drops into islands as they fell. One myth, however, declares that, even before the time of Izanagi and Izanami, a reed sprouted from the ocean of chaos from which deities, personifying the germinating powers of Nature, were produced in pairs. Izanagi and Izanami also produced new gods and it was at the birth of the Fire-god that Izanami died and descended to the Japanese Hades, "the land of gloom." In an effort to rescue his spouse Izanagi himself went down to Yomotsu-kuni, but was so horrified at the corruption of the place that he fled incontinently, pursued by the nine hags of hell. While purifying himself after his escape Izanagi produced still more gods, including the Sun-goddess, Amaterasu, from the washing of his left eye, the Moon-god, Tsuki-yomi, from the washing of the right eye, and the Storm-god, Susa-no-wo, from the washing of his nose. The Moon-god ceased to have a place in Japanese mythology, and there were never any star-gods—there is no mention of the stars in Japanese poetry. The Sun-goddess soon acquired the supremacy she afterwards maintained as the Divine Ancestress, and all princes and princesses were known as *hiko* and *hime*, that is "sun-child."

The mythology goes on to tell of the pranks played by Susa-no-wo upon his sister, the Sun-goddess, of his tearing off the roof of the house where she sat weaving with her maidens, of her flight to the cave where she sulked till by various dances and charms the myriad gods lured her forth and decreed the exile of the Storm-god to Idzumo. It becomes clear as the mythology proceeds that Izanagi and Izanami represent the old dualism of heaven and earth, that the two eyes of the sky are the Sun and the Moon and that the nostrils of the sky is nothing but the typhoon, dreaded in ancient times even more than to-day. Subordinate nature deities are described as sea-gods, wind-gods, mountain-gods, and such poetic creations of the imagination as Konohanasakuya-hime, the Lady who makes the trees to bloom, and Tatsuta-hime, the Lady who weaves the brocade (of autumn leaves), but these last belong more to the realm of poetry than to that of mythology. The second class of gods are really personified abstractions, such as the god of growth, and the food-god, though this last, Ukemochi-no-kami, is by some thought to be one of the most ancient of all. The third class is that of the deified men and women who represent the ancestor-worship introduced from the Continent. It is, however, a very large class, and includes gods figuring in Japanese history all the way from the Empress Jingo, in the third century A.D., down to General Nogi and others in our own time. It should be added that besides these three classes there is a countless host of other divine beings such as fairies, vampires, fox-spirits, and dragon-spirits, but in the larger number of cases it is impossible to determine how far these were originally Japanese or merely importations (in Buddhist times) from India and China.

For the worship of the gods, or the spirits of the dead, there were built the severely simple shrines known as *miya*, or "august houses." As the word denotes, the Shinto shrine was first of all nothing but the dwelling-place of the reigning sovereign (the high-priest of the nation), and the depository of the sacred insignia of Shinto, the mirror, the sword and the jewel (*magatama*). After a while, with the delegation by the emperor of his religious duties to special clans such as the Nakatomi and the Mononobe, the *miya* multiplied, till now, scattered over the Empire there may be as many as 200,000, great and small. The approach to the shrine was a gateway known as *torii*, which has sometimes (by folk-etymology) been explained as "fowl-perch," but is more probably derived from the Indian *turan*, or gate, and may correspond thus with the Chinese *pao-lao*. The temple is plain and unpainted and generally fenced about with paper fringes, known as *gohei*, hung upon a hempen rope. There are no idols, but the *shin-tai*, or god-body, is an object which is supposed to enshrine the invisible god-presence, or *mitama*. In addition to the *shintai* the temple may contain some of the insignia referred to above as the Three Treasures. Of these the *magatama*, or jewel, is thought by some to represent an old bear's-claw fetish.

The ministers of the temples, and of the Shinto religion generally speaking, are represented by numerous orders. There are *kataribe*, or reciters, *urabe*, or diviners, and *kangahari*, the god-possessed ones, while the priests of the local shrines are known as *kannushi*. The powers of some of these in the region of the occult are described by some as very remarkable.[1]

In Shinto worship there is considerable variety. Much of it is extremely archaic and shows the survival of pantomimic dances described in the mythology. These were originally, no doubt, rites connected with imitative magic. There is the use of prayers, called *norito*, but these seem to have little relation to supplication properly so-called. *Imi*, or abstentions (*tabus*), *misogi*, or cleansings, and *harai*, or exorcisms, are common. The crowning rite of the year is the *O-harai*, or Great Purification, a kind of scapegoat ceremony, by which, at the beginning of the year, the sins and pollutions of the year are transferred to paper patterns of the body which are then taken out to be sunk in deep water. The idea of sin (*tsumi*) seems to have relation to ritual offences rather than to moral delinquencies. Pilgrimages have great importance and are health-giving excursions to the mountain shrines, especially to Fuji-san, Ise and Idzumo, in special garb and supported by the

[1] See Percival Lowell, *Occult Japan*, Boston, 1894.

pilgrim staff, which bears the name of the Buddhist saint, Kobo Daishi. Naturally to-day the pilgrimages are quite as much a vogue with Buddhists as with Shintoists.

Beliefs in the future, too, are highly coloured from Buddhist contact, but it seems clear that the early Japanese believed in a soul, which they called *tama-shii* (*ball-wind*). This soul was divided into two parts, one mild and gentle, such as stayed with the body and ministered to its happiness, the other rough and inclined to go away on adventures of its own. After death one of these souls remained in the neighbourhood of the body for a while, and the other, as a shade, journeyed towards its abode in the Land of Gloom, or, as a *kami*, to the Plain of High Heaven. The idea of coming to the River of the Three Routes, where the soul had to make its choice between hell, the world of beasts, or the world of hungry ghosts, is obviously Buddhistic.

The history of Shinto may be summarized as passing through three stages. First, we have the period of Primitive Shinto, prior to the introduction of Buddhism, when it was merely a rather bizarre kind of nature worship, which inculcated personal cleanliness and loyalty to the Emperor. It is to be noted that the word *matsurigoto* has the double sense of government and of religious observances. After the coming of Buddhism in A.D. 552 we have what is known as *Ryobu*, or the "twofold doctrine," a mixture of the two faiths by the identification of the old gods with the Bodhisattvas. It originated with the visit of Gyogi, a priest of the Hosso sect, to the shrine of the Sun-goddess at Ise, and his return with the announcement from the goddess: "I am Vairochana (Dainichi)." Though the fusion of the two religions was never complete, Ryobu remained generally acceptable till the eighteenth century, when there came a revulsion against things Chinese, including Buddhism, and the attempt of scholars like Motoori, Mabuchi and Hirata to bring about a revival of Pure Shinto. Lastly, since the beginning of Meiji, in 1868, has come the official effort to present Shinto as a political philosophy and to evacuate it as far as possible of its religious content. Many Japanese, including a number of the most distinguished Christians, have accepted this view and use the elaborately beautiful rites of Shinto to rally the people to imperial unity and loyalty to the emperors. Thus the ceremonies connected with the enthronement, marriage and burial of the emperors are Shinto. In spite of their archaic character many of these rites are profoundly impressive and well worthy of study on account of their symbolism. As a religion, however, Shinto will probably have little place in the future of the Japanese people.[1]

Ere outlining the story of Buddhism in Japan, from the time of its arrival in the sixth century to the present day, it is necessary to say something about Buddhism in Korea, or Chosen, from whence it passed to the archipelago. The peninsula was first reached by the religion of Gautama in A.D. 372, when a monk called by the Koreans Sundo arrived from the present province of Shensi with sutras and images. Contact with the Continent was at this time much more constant than has been generally supposed. Korea was at this time split up into three kingdoms, a northern one called Kokurye, one in the south-west, Pakché, and one in the south-east, Silla. Sundo came to the northern kingdom and had such success that two monasteries were erected as a cradle for the new faith. The kingdom of Pakché, anxious not to be behind its northern neighbour, then sent to the Chinese Emperor, and presently, in 385, came a missionary, Marananda, with ten monks, to undertake the conversion of the kingdom. Then last of all, Silla, yielded to the new propaganda and by the beginning of the sixth century the whole peninsula was religiously Buddhistic and culturally, of course, Chinese. The golden age of Korean Buddhism, however, came with the tenth century and with the unification of the country as Korye, an accomplishment due largely to the efforts of a Buddhist monk who was, however, murdered and left the fruit of his labours to a successful rival. From 912 to 1392, with Song-do as the capital, Korea was zealously Buddhist, claiming one out of every three sons for the monastic life. Just before and after this period the two Korean alphabetic systems were invented, the *Nido* system

[1] See W. G. Aston, *Shinto, the Way of the Gods*, London, 1905; D. C. Holtom, *The Political Philosophy of Modern Shinto*. Transactions of the Asiatic Society of Japan, Vol. xix., Part II., 1922.

as early as the ninth century, and the present *Un-men* script (" the most simple and perfect alphabet in the world ") about the middle of the fifteenth. By this time, however, Buddhism was on the decline. It lost State support and suffered from the attempt to replace it with Confucianism. So it lost its initiative and presently sank to its present condition of ineptitude. Nevertheless, some large monasteries still retain importance, especially those in the Diamond Mountains, and around Keijo, the capital. In the Korean Buddhism of the present day much of the older cults of sun, moon, stars, mountains, rivers and caves crops up and the witch, or *mudang* is so frequently employed for exorcism as practically to have driven the monk out of the field. It is possible that the Japanese regime in Chosen may do something to revive Buddhism and return to it some of its former authority.[1]

It was in A.D. 552, in the reign of the Emperor Kimmei, that envoys came from the kingdom of Pakché (or Kudara) with presents of books and a letter stating: " This doctrine is hard to understand, but marvellously excellent. It furnishes men with treasure to their heart's content. Every prayer may be fulfilled and every wish granted." King Seimei was not entirely disinterested in his missionary work since he asked for a *quid pro quo* in the shape of military assistance against his enemies, a singular request in the passing on and recommendation of a pacifist religion. Whether this were so or not, the Emperor, after his first enthusiasm, was as suspicious of the new cult as was Ethelbert of the missionary, St. Augustine, when, for fear of magic, he insisted on hearing the monk in the open air. To test the faith Soga-no-Iname, head of the clan specially charged with the care of foreigners, was ordered to afford hospitality to the Korean visitors. It was a foregone conclusion that the Nakatomi clan, who (with the Mononobe) formed the high priesthood of Shinto, would be ranged in opposition to the new cult. So we have a struggle inaugurated between the conservatives (*o-muraji*) and the innovators (*o-omi*), with the Emperor endeavouring to be

[1] See H. Hackmann, *Buddhism as a Religion*, pp. 85 ff., 257 ff., London 1910.

neutral. At first fortune favoured the Nakatomi since the envoys had brought with them small-pox as well as *sutras* and the plague caused a summary dumping of the images into the Naniwa Canal. But, the plague continuing, the fearful were inclined to think their judgement premature, so the images were dredged up and the experiment continued. The rumour that a wonderful log of camphor wood had floated in from the sea, to strains of heavenly music, gave fresh prestige to the faith. Then, in 577 and 584, came more missionaries and, after a brief civil war in 587, a test on the anvil triumphantly vindicated the indestructibility of a Buddhist relic—said to have been the pupil of one of the eyes of Shaka—and patronage of the foreign faith soon became open and unashamed.

One more struggle, however, was necessary, involving the determination of the succession as well as the respective claims of the Soga and Nakatomi clans. In this struggle the remarkable man came to the front who was destined to be the Constantine of Japanese Buddhism. This was Prince Umayado, regent under the Empress Suiko, and known generally as Shotoku Taishi, that is Crown Prince Shotoku. This illustrious individual, the thirteenth centenary of whose death was observed throughout Japan in 1921, was from the beginning inclined toward the Sogas, but his activity was the result of a vow that, if victorious over the rebel Moriya, he would further the faith of Shaka.[1] Placing the images of the *Four Heaven Kings* in his helmet, Prince Umayado went valiantly into the fight and emerged as conqueror. One may still see the Temple of the Four Heaven Kings, the *Shi-tenno-ji*, at Osaka on the site where Shotoku raised his memorial of the victory, and in the Temple of the Guiding Bell it is still believed that the souls of children are guided by the compassionate prince into the presence of their playmates, who invoke the aid of the saint by pulling a bell-rope made of the bibs of dead children. Here too is the conduit of running water which is supposed to bear letters and prayers for the dead into Shotoku's presence. One story reminds us of the legend of St. Martin of Tours. It tells how Prince Umayado covered

[1] Dr. Anesaki says Shotoku was possibly a Buddhist of the third generation, certainly of Buddhist parentage.

a dying beggar with his cloak and how subsequently when the beggar's tomb was opened no body was found therein but only a cloak neatly folded. It was thus revealed that the saint's charity had been bestowed upon a divine being. Another story speaks of Shotoku as an incarnation of the Goddess of Mercy, Kwannon, who had proclaimed: "Wherever a gnat cries, there am I," a tribute probably to the fame of the prince's generosity rather than the affirmation of a dogma. When Shotoku died it was said: "All the princes and *omi*, as well as the people of the Empire —the old, as if they had lost a dear child, had no taste for vinegar, the young, as if they had lost a beloved parent, filled the ways with the sound of their lamenting." The tribute was neither insincere nor undeserved.

Though in A.D. 645 the Soga family was overthrown and wellnigh exterminated, the future of Buddhism in Japan had now become secure and, as in other lands, the religion of Shaka brought with success important consequences for the art, literature and government of the land as well as for religion. The introduction of Chinese writing and Chinese books had enormous effect in stimulating the intellectual life of Japan, even though it was several centuries before the development of native scripts, the *kata-kana* and the *hira-gana*, to add to the Chinese ideographs. As for art, to quote Professor Asakawa, "Almost every branch of industrial and artistic development owes something to the influence of the (Buddhist) creed." And Mr. Saito declares that in the Horiuji, built by Shotoku, one may study the influence of Chinese, Indian, and even Greek ideas upon the art of Japan, all alike transmitted by Buddhism. The bare simplicity of the Shinto temples was now superseded by the warmth of colour and the splendour of gold and lacquer which we associate with the Buddhist *tera*. There was a sort of common impulse towards the making of beautiful things, as when the Empress Suiko, in 592, founded the majestic shrine of Miyajima, or as Emperors and Empresses vied with one another in the casting of great images of Buddhas and Bodhisattvas.

Much of this advance we see in the eighth century, when for the first time the Empire created a fixed capital.

This was Nara, where some seven sovereigns ruled from 710 to 794. It was a great time for Japan, "the few bright decades of political ardour, æsthetic awakening and religious exaltation."[1] There was an enthusiasm for temple building and image making for which it is difficult to find a parallel, save in the cathedral building of thirteenth-century Europe. It was now that the *Daibutsu* of Nara, still standing, though after many restorations (in the course of which everything of the original except a part of the trunk and legs, with a few petals of the lotus on which the Buddha sits has been lost) was cast under the orders of the Emperor Shomu. Certain Empresses carried enthusiasm for Buddhism so far as to forbid the taking of any form of life, even of fish, and the poor fishermen, all but reduced to starvation by the edict, had to be relieved by imperial subsidies of rice. The Empress Komyo vowed to wash the feet of a thousand beggars, and finding among these a beggar hideous with leprosy discovered later that she had ministered to a god in disguise. It was about this time that the priest Gyogi, famous otherwise as the inventor of the potter's wheel, and himself the builder of forty-nine temples, invented also a way of reconciling the old religion with the new by proclaiming, as the result of a vision, that the Sun-goddess and Vairochana were one.

Nevertheless, Buddhism had its own sectarian developments, more or less independent of the Shinto. In Nara times there arose six denominations of Buddhists, as follows: 1. *Sanron*, the school of the *Three Treatises*, brought over by Ekwan from China in 625; 2. *Jojitsu*, a Hinayana sect, brought over from the Korean kingdom of Pakché; 3. *Hosso*, brought over from China by Dosho; 4. *Kusha*, established by two Japanese priests who had studied in China; 5. *Kegon*, which held that the original Buddha, from whom arose all the Buddhas of history, sat on a lotus of a thousand petals, each petal a universe and each universe consisting of a myriad worlds. This sect was introduced in 736; 6. *Ritsu*, a Hinayana sect brought over in 754, and particularly strict in the matter of discipline and regularity of ordination. Of the six Nara sects only Hosso and Kegon survive, but

[1] G. B. Sansom, *Japan, A Cultural History*, New York, 1931.

it should be remembered that sectarian differences did not involve rancour and that varying doctrines were frequently taught in the same monasteries. As it was said:

> From various sides the paths ascend,
> Many and far abreast,
> But when we gaze on the calm, full moon,
> Single's the mountain's crest.

Generally speaking, the influence of Buddhism on Japan was good. Manners were much ameliorated and, as Dr. Harada puts it, Buddhism "optimized Japan." But there is another side, bearing on the subject of political development. As the Emperors became more and more interested in the practice and propagation of religion they became less concerned with the conduct of State affairs and the management of a military campaign was generally relegated to the clan leaders. So we have presently a number of Emperors known as "learned emperors," because of their almost exclusive preoccupation with the sutras rather than with affairs of State. A little later the "learned emperors" pushed their devotion to religion further and became "cloistered emperors." At times there were three or four of these abdicated sovereigns living at the same time and it became a temptation to some of the more aggressive daimyos to "save face" in an otherwise seditious movement by putting a "cloistered emperor" at the head of his faction. Naturally, when adult emperors, almost as a matter of course, took the vows soon after their accession, it became difficult to find heirs except minors. So "child emperors" became common and proved a source of serious weakness by playing into the hands of ambitious daimyos. It was out of such conditions that the Shogunate, or military government, arose—an institution which, with brief intervals, held sway from 1186 to 1867.

From 804 to 1186 we find ourselves in that period of Japanese history known as the Heian, or Kyoto, era. The new capital was very likely chosen that the emperors might get away from the overshadowing influence of the Buddhist priesthood. Priests, like Dokyo, had interfered seriously in politics and had acquired a large amount of property in the name of their temples. But the move, if it had this reason, proved in vain, for Buddhism continued to flourish and new contacts were established with the faith in China. Some notable Japanese scholars visited the T'ang capital in the early ninth century and brought back new ideas, some of which were possibly coloured by Manichæan and Christian influences prevalent in China at this time.[1] Two scholars merit special mention since they became the founders of two new sects and were greatly influential in other ways. Saicho, afterwards known as Dengyo Daishi—the first to receive the title of "Great Saint" (*Daishi*)—went to China in 802 in the train of an ambassador of the Sugawara family. He returned in 805 to introduce to his native land T'ien-tai Buddhism, under the name of *Tendai*, and established on Hiyeizan, a mountain north-east of Kyoto, the famous monastery which in course of time became a nursery for hosts of swaggering bonzes who occasionally terrorized emperors into compliance with their demands. Tendai, indeed, became worldly and corrupt, though Saicho's identification of the Shinto divinities with the *avatars* of the Buddha popularized the work commenced by Gyogi, and completed the triumph of Ryobu. Kukai, later known as Kobo Daishi, painter, poet, sculptor and traveller, is one of the great figures of Japanese Buddhism. He went to China in 804, with one of the Fujiwara princes. When he returned, about 807, he brought with him a syncretism, in which Manichæan influences probably find place, known as *Shingon*, the True Word sect. It belongs to the *mantra* school, is related to the Indian system of Yoga, and but faintly reflects the teachings of Gautama. It was supposed by talismanic devices to assist enlightenment and used particularly the five-syllabled charm, *a-bi-ra-un-ken*. Kobo became in 816 the abbot of Koyosan, a famous monastery in the mountains between Kishu and Yamato. Thousands of pilgrims visit the monastery annually, along the "Road of Many Turnings," chanting as they go the hymn: "May our six senses grow pure as we climb the heights!" In the "Hall of Ten-thousand Lamps" is shown the "Poor Woman's Single Lamp," the gift of one who sold her hair to buy the precious offering. Though all the rest are the gifts of the rich, it is said that

[1] So it is contended by Arthur Lloyd in his *Creed of Half Japan* Dr. Anesaki doubts it.

in a high wind all blow out except the woman's lamp, which burns steadily through the gale. Kobo Daishi is honoured by all pilgrims, who call their pilgrim staff by his name. To be buried in the same ground as Kobo is to obtain rebirth in Paradise. Thus, after cremation, the "Adam's apple" of a dead man is often sent to be cast into the hall of bones at Koyosan. Many legends persist in the neighbourhood, of which a specimen is the story that soil from India has been dropped at each of the eighty-seven stations, or that which declares that the fire at Koyosan has burned unquenched for a thousand years. Kobo Daishi's fame extends to the realms of art and literature as well as to that of religion. But that is another story.[1]

In the periods we have so far discussed most Buddhist teaching came by way of China. But in the thirteenth century religious movements were initiated of great significance but of genuinely native origin. It is interesting to notice, however, that these are contemporaneous with religious movements which swept over the entire Euro-Asiatic Continent, affecting alike Western Europe, India and China as well as Japan. At this epoch, though the emperors resided at Kyoto, the administrative capital was Kamakura, three hundred miles away, and here the Hojo Shikken, or Regents, ruled in the name of Shadow Shoguns and they at least as shadowy emperors. The period, extending from 1199 to 1333, is known therefore as the Hojo period. The Buddhistic movements of the time began with the rise and teaching of certain distinguished reformers who were reacting strongly from the "prosperous and degenerate" Buddhism of the Kyoto court and also from the prevalent pessimism of the time. Most of the new teachers came from the Tendai school. Such was Genshin who, though he never left the Tendai, must be considered a forerunner of the Amida sects. Of him, says Dr. Reischauer, "His three small volumes on Paradise, the Intermediate State, and Hell have exerted a great influence and should be of special interest to Western readers,

[1] For Japanese Buddhism see especially A. K. Reischauer, *Studies in Japanese Buddhism*, New York, 1917; Arthur Lloyd, *The Creed of Half Japan*, London, 1912; Kishio Satomi, *The Discovery of Japanese Idealism*, London, 1924; J. B. Pratt, *The Pilgrimage of Buddhism*, New York, 1928.

especially to students of Dante."[1] Then came Ryonin, 1072–1132, with his clear-cut teaching as to Amida Buddha and the reiterated formula, *Namu Amida Butsu*, which gained the name of *Nembutsu* for the sect. Both of these teachers are outside the Kamakura period, but may be regarded as heralds of the dawn.

First among the real founders of the epoch is Genku, commonly known as Honen Shonin. He was born about 1130 and as a child was about to slay the assassin of his father when the dying parent besought him rather to seek enlightenment. So Genku entered Hiyeizan and studied Tendai, only somewhat later to turn away from what seemed a religion of despair to a religion which offered hope and salvation through the merits of Amida. So Honen, in 1175, became the founder (in Japan) of the *Jodo*, or "*Pure Land*" sect, with its doctrine of future blessedness in the Paradise of Amida. Japanese Buddhism makes a clear distinction between *ji-riki*, or salvation by one's own merits (as taught by Gautama), and *ta-riki*, or salvation by the merits of another. Jodo was not entirely one or the other, since the use of the *Nembutsu* was necessary. Nevertheless, it marked a clear advance towards Amidaism and was so welcomed by multitudes, including some of the emperors. To-day Jodo is the second largest Buddhistic sect in Japan.

A certain disciple of Genku, Shinran, soon passed beyond his master's position by rejecting the *ji-riki* doctrine altogether and proclaiming salvation through faith in Amida alone. "We have nothing to do," he said, "with salvation; we have but to believe." Shinran Shonin, 1173–1262, is one of the most interesting of the Buddhist fathers. Visitors to the great Western Hongwanji at Kyoto may still see the image of Shinran, carved with his own hand as a gift to his daughter—for the *Shin-shu* priests need not be celibate. After the saint's death the ashes remaining from the cremation were mixed with lacquer and used to varnish the effigy. Shinran entered one of the Hiyeizan monasteries at an early age, but was converted to Amidaism by the preaching of Honen and two years later founded the *Jodo Shinshu*, or True Pure Land sect, now the largest of the

[1] A. K. Reischauer, *Studies in Japanese Buddhism*, p. 103.

Japanese Buddhistic schools. A story tells that while Shinran was still at Hiyeizan he met a charming princess who showed him that the scattered rays of the sun could be gathered together at a focus by means of a burning-glass, and asked him if he could not do the same for the teachings of Shaka. Shinran, who has been termed the " Luther of Buddhism," did his best to achieve this unification. He died at the age of eighty-nine, " true to the end to his determination not to know anything but Amida and salvation in his Western Paradise." He wrote a famous book, the *Kyogo-sho-monrui*, or the Analects of Doctrine, Practice and Attainment, as an exposition of his teaching. Justification by faith in Amida is still the central truth of Shin-shu and dying men still lay hold upon a coloured cord connected with the image of Amida to be drawn in death towards the refuge of his compassion.

Just prior to the establishment of Shin-shu another sect arose destined to have great influence upon Japanese religion. In this case the provenance was foreign, for the new sect was no other than the *Zen* Buddhism associated with the name of the patriarch Bodhidharma, which in India had been known as *Dhyana* and in China as *Ch'an*. Bodhidharma, of whom many wonderful tales are told, is the original of the toy known as Daruma, so weighted that nothing can destroy its poise. It was to afford spiritual poise that meditation was recommended, and the tea-ceremony (*cha-no-yu*) was developed to illustrate as well as to assist the winning of this steadiness of mind and heart. Zen became for this reason the special cult of soldiers, who became also the most famous connoisseurs of the tea-cult. In Japan Zen was first preached by Eisai, about 1191. This sage, like the others mentioned, had resided at Hiyeisan, but remained unsatisfied till he revisited China and became converted to the doctrine of Bodhidharma.

In some respects the founder of the fourth Kamakura sect is the most interesting of all. Professor Lloyd calls *Nichiren* " the greatest and most striking personality in the whole of Japanese Buddhist literature." Dr. Anesaki opens his biography thus: " If Japan ever produced a prophet or a religious man of prophetic zeal, Nichiren was the man.

He stands almost a unique figure in the history of Buddhism, not only because of his persistence through hardship and persecution, but for his unshaken conviction that he himself was the messenger of Buddha, and his confidence in the future of his religion and country." Born in 1222, the son of a fisherman, Nichiren early passed from under the influence of Shingon to that of Tendai and thence to the denunciation of all the current schools. In striking contrast to the tolerant attitude of other sects, this "strong man of combative temperament" denounced the other sects as treasonable inventions of the devil. He called Kobo "the greatest liar in Japan" and described the Zen as teaching a "doctrine of fiends and devils." Yet it is not easy to find anything precisely new in Nichiren's teaching. He advocated a return to the "pristine purity" of the Buddhism of Gautama, but betrayed ignorance of what this was by pinning his faith to the *Hokkekyo*, a scripture of later time and of a very different doctrinal trend. Nichiren's significance is not, however, that he taught new truths so much as that his belligerent attitude brought him into stormy relation to the political events of the time. More than once his uncompromising preaching brought him within the shadow of death. In 1271 he was arrested and tried for high treason. "Behold, the pillar of Japan is falling!" he cried as the soldiers closed around the giant monk and bore him to the execution ground near Kamakura. But as he passed the temple of Hachiman, Nichiren addressed the war-god in a famous prayer, in which the monk threatened to denounce the god's ingratitude in the presence of the Buddha, on the Vulture Peak, immediately after his death. "And what will you do then?" he added. Legend goes on to describe the coming of a lightning flash which paralysed the executioner and secured his victim's reprieve. Nichiren's great opportunity came with the menace of the Mongol invasion. His predictions gave him a tremendous popular vogue and in course of time the "Ishmael of Buddhism" became the "Lotus of the Law" and the founder of the sect called after his name. Famous as "an eloquent preacher, a powerful writer, and a man of tender heart," he died on November 14, 1282, surrounded by his disciples and reciting with them the "stanzas of eternity." Where he died is now the Hommonji, and the saint's bones, enclosed in a reliquary of rock crystal, repose on a jewelled table supported by eight green tortoises, before which burns a perpetual lamp. Under the influence of Nichiren Buddhism in Japan became truly national.[1]

The four Kamakura sects mentioned remain to-day the strongest of the fifty recognized by the Government and occupy 53,000 out of the 72,000 existing temples. Buddhism had now a clear field in the Empire until the end of the Ashikaga Shogunate in 1573, when Oda Nobunaga was given a commission to rescue the Empire from the chaos into which it had fallen. Nobunaga found his chief opponents in the "turbulent shavelings" of Hiyeizan, with their centuries of immunity from control. He therefore put the whole community to the sword and burned the great temple, Yenryakuji, with historical materials of irreplaceable worth. The burning of Hiyeizan, on St. Michael's Day 1571, was an event giving satisfaction to the Jesuits, who were favoured by Nobunaga out of his desire to encourage a religious influence in the land such as might act as a check upon the power of the Buddhists.

Hideyoshi, Nobunaga's successor, cared nothing for Buddhism, though he occasionally wrote letters to the gods for the sake of their effect on the public mind. As a boy he had been turned out of a Buddhist shrine for smashing the idols which did not consume the offerings he placed before them. On the accession of Iyeyasu, however, in 1600, Buddhism came again into its own, though the seventeenth century is also marked by the rise of a Chinese school of learning which was devoted to the neo-Confucianism of the Sung philosophers. The Tokugawa Shoguns were earnest Buddhists, who in their efforts to eradicate Christianity compelled all Japanese to enroll themselves in their respective Buddhist parishes. The founder of the line was reverenced after death as a god, and lies in his sumptuous shrine at Nikko—"Noble of the First Degree of the First Rank, Great Light of the East, Great Incarnation of Buddha."

[1] Masaharu Anesaki, *Nichiren, the Buddhist Prophet*, Harvard, 1916.

Space forbids our pursuing further the story of Buddhism in Japan, except to say that at the Restoration in 1867, when Shinto became a political philosophy, Buddhism was disestablished. The result has not been as harmful to religion as was at the time anticipated. Thrown upon their own resources the priests and congregations have made notable steps towards a great revival. This revival has manifested itself in a variety of ways. Many old and dilapidated temples have been restored and many new ones built. The building of the great Hongwanji at Kyoto is said to have cost several million dollars, not to speak of the ropes of hair contributed by thousands of Japanese women that the great beams might be hoisted into place by the strongest of cables. Buddhist universities have also been established and the present writer can vouch for the comprehensive character of the literature used in their libraries. Young Men's Buddhist Associations have been founded in obvious imitation of the Western Y.M.C.A. The methods of Western religion have been in many cases adopted, even to what seems almost the parodying of familiar Christian hymns. Much has been done in the way of Social Reform and almost every agency known in the West has been reproduced in Tokyo and other cities by Japanese Buddhists. Even missionary work to foreign lands has been attempted. As early as 1876 Japanese missionaries were sent to China and in more recent years to Honolulu and to the Pacific coast, mainly, of course, to their own fellow-countrymen.

The situation, naturally, is not without its anxieties. Okuma said in 1909: "Japan at present may be likened to a sea into which a hundred currents of Oriental and Occidental thought have poured, and, not having yet effected fusion, are raging wildly, tossing, warring and roaring. . . . A portion of our people go neither by the old code of ethics and etiquette nor by those of modern days, while they are also disinclined to conform to those of foreign countries, and such persons convey the impression of neither possessing nor being governed by any ideas about morality, public or private." That anxiety exists is proved, again, by the calling of the Tri-Religion Conference (with

Shinto, Buddhist and Christian representatives) in March 1912 to discuss how they might best meet the spiritual needs of the nation.

So far as Buddhism is concerned, Professor Inouye, of the Imperial University, Tokyo (quoted by Dr. Reischauer) suggests the following five reforms:

1. The raising of the standard among the priests, "though Christian rivalry has stirred some of them to emulation in educational and charitable enterprises of recent years."

2. The abolition of idols and the substitution of the Japanese language for the unintelligible Sanskrit and Chinese in the ritual and scriptures.

3. The shedding of the pessimism which is characteristic of the Indian faith, since "pessimism is the creed of a decaying nationality, in the hour of adversity when the world looks dark and life has no hope to offer us."

4. The reform of ethics, so as to "bring the ethical system into harmony with present-day needs."

5. The abandonment of the many superstitions which "the ignorant accept blindly and the educated laugh at."

Perhaps I may add to this Dr. Reischauer's comment that "if Japanese Buddhism cannot lay hold on the Living God without undergoing a radical change in its fundamentals, it does not follow that Japanese Buddhists cannot fling away their pessimism and lay hold on Him and so find satisfaction for their hopes and aspirations."[1, 2]

[1] A. K. Reischauer, *Studies in Japanese Buddhism*, p. 327.

[2] Other books recommended are: M. Anesaki, *Japanese Mythology*, Boston, 1928; B. H. Chamberlain, *Things Japanese*, London, 1905; H. H. Gowen, *An Outline History of Japan*, New York, 1927; W. E. Griffis, *The Religions of Japan*, New York, 1907; G. W. Knox, *The Development of Religion in Japan*, New York, 1907; J. A. B. Scherer, *The Romance of Japan*, New York, 1926. The most authoritative work on Japanese Religion is Dr. M. Anesaki's *History of Japanese Religion*, London, 1930. We have here not only an adequate account of Shinto and Buddhism, but also a description of Confucian influence, an account of the popular religious movements at the end of the eighteenth century under two women, Kino (1756–1826) and Miki (1798–1887), an account of the modern religions known as *Tenri-Kyo* and *Konkokyo*, and sympathetic reference to such Japanese Christian leaders as Joseph Neesima, Paul Sawayama, and the still living Toyohiko Kagawa.

## CHAPTER XXVII

## *Buddhism in Southern Asia*

SO far our account of Buddhism has concerned itself mainly with the extension of the faith in its Mahayana form, and in the countries of Central and Eastern Asia. But it must be remembered that what is generally, and perhaps inaccurately, termed Southern Buddhism has even more claim to be regarded as a genuine outgrowth from the teaching of Gautama and that it passed beyond the borders of India proper at an even earlier date than did the Buddhism of the North. There is a hint of allegory in the fact that the Bo-tree under which Gautama sat has perished and yet, nevertheless, lives and flourishes in the shoot transplanted into Ceylon. For the religion which, after a thousand years of life in India, has there died, probably beyond hope of revival, is still, through the zeal of the great Buddhist Emperor, Açoka, a powerful influence in the lives of millions and millions of people in the countries of Southern Asia. It is now our task, therefore, to describe, with necessary brevity, the fortunes of the faith in these interesting lands.

The first result of Açoka's missionary work is to be seen in Ceylon, the Lanka of the epics, supposedly inhabited by demons of whom Ravana is a specimen. These "demons" probably are the original inhabitants of the island, people such as the Veddas of to-day, or Dravidians who had invaded Ceylon at various epochs.

It is quite possible that rumours of the preaching of Buddhism had reached Ceylon even prior to the mission of Açoka in 250 B.C., and that the envoys sent by King Tissa to the court of the Mauryan really went to obtain definite instruction in the faith. In any case, Açoka immediately despatched a mission under his son (or younger brother) Mahendra (Mahinda), who, accompanied by a number of monks, flew through the air (according to the legend) and alighted on Mt. Mahintale, just when Tissa was drawn forth from his capital at Anuradhapura by divine providence to meet the emissaries. The preaching of the young prince was so effective that the ladies of the court at once demanded a provision for nunneries as well as monasteries. Their petition was granted by the sending of the princess Sanghamitra (Sanghamitta), who brought with her a shoot of the Bo-tree (already referred to). This was planted and still lives among the ruins of Anadhurapura, the oldest historical tree in the world.

Buddhism flourished in Ceylon from the first. Many availed themselves of the land grants of King Tissa to build monasteries and dagobas. Images were made, gardens were laid out and relics imported. In the fourth century was brought the famous relic purporting to be the left canine tooth of the Buddha, saved from the ashes after his cremation. A special shrine was erected for it, but in the eighth century it was removed to the new capital, Pollanaruva, and later still transferred to the Temple of the Holy Tooth at Candy. Fa-hien, at the end of the fourth century, speaks of it as having been carried about in procession. In 1560 it was burned by order of the Portuguese Archbishop of Goa, but a new tooth (miraculously, say the Singhalese) was immediately forthcoming. Those who have seen it report that it resembles the tooth of a crocodile rather than that of a human being.

For some centuries the fortunes of Singhalese Buddhism remained set fair, but a period of stagnation supervened, from which the religion was only rescued by a great revival which took place in the twelfth century, under King Parakrama Bahu II. Several centuries later came the Portuguese, after them the Dutch, and later still the British, who have been in possession of the island since 1796. During this period of foreign control Buddhism has sometimes fallen on evil days and at one time was so near extinction as only to be saved by the arrival of ten Siamese monks, who re-established the succession of the order. Naturally, under foreign rule, Buddhists could no longer bask in the favour and under the patronage of kings. On the other hand, however, many were driven by disaster to a deeper loyalty, and the faith of Gautama is still the chief religion of Ceylon. Yet the number of monks, which Fa-hien reported to be 20,000, was at the census of 1901 only 7331 and it is probable that this number is diminishing.

The monkhood is largely recruited from children given into the hands of the priests from an early year. Their education may begin as early as the eighth year and the novitiate is undertaken at the age of eleven, when the novice's hair is cut and his robes assumed. The novitiate is spent in the service of the priests and in the study of the sutras. Then, in the twentieth year, there is admission to full monkhood, though, it must be remembered, the vows are not lifelong and at any time may be cancelled. The monks live in monasteries which contain, first of all, the *pansalas*, or huts, for the dwelling-place of the monks; secondly, the *vihara*, or temple, with its statues of the Buddha, standing, sitting, or lying, its images of the disciples and even of some of the Brahmanic gods; lastly, the preaching-hall, an adjunct to all the larger establishments. In the court are the usual Buddhist features—lotus-pond, bell, and generally a Bo-tree. Ceylon contains a number of important and historically interesting sanctuaries. The year of the monks is generally divided into a period of nine months of preaching and three months of retreat and study, the latter period corresponding with the rainy season. Lay adhesion to Buddhism is usual, but the layman is only Buddhist to the extent of accepting the tenets of the faith and taking upon himself periodical vows of a temporary character.

Though Singhalese Buddhism follows in the main the teachings inculcated in the Pali literature of India, it is much intermingled with dark and sinister forms of demonolatry. The general verdict as to the effect of Buddhism on the Singhalese is not favourable. Dr. T. W. Rhys Davids sums up the matter as follows: "There is no independence of thought in Ceylon Buddhism; and, as in most cases where a pagan country has adopted a higher faith from without, the latter has not had sufficient power to eradicate the previous animism. But Buddhism has had a great attraction for the better educated, and has led to remarkable literary results. The nation as a whole has undoubtedly suffered from the celibacy of many of the most able and earnest; but, on the other hand, there is very little crime, and, in certain important particulars, such as caste and the position of woman, Ceylon is in advance of other parts of our Indian Empire, with the single exception of Burma, where the same causes have been at work and the same disadvantages felt." [1]

BURMESE BUDDHISM.—The introduction of Buddhism into Burma took place under very uncertain circumstances. The Singhalese chronicle, the *Mahavamça*, is authority for the statement that the first missionary was Buddhaghosha, about A.D. 450. This saint came from Magadha, where he had been converted from Brahmanism to Buddhism, to Ceylon, where he engaged with zeal in the translation of the Singhalese commentaries into Pali. Thence he is supposed to have gone to Burma for the propagation of his beliefs, but the tradition of this visit is generally discredited by scholars. It is far more probable that Buddhism filtered into Burma from Northern India, together with other elements of Indian culture, and that the first Burmese Buddhism was of the Mahayana school. One tradition is explicit enough to declare that, following upon the Council of Pataliputra, 250 B.C., two missionaries went from India to the country of Suvarnabhumi (the Gold-country), supposedly to be identified with Burma. Açoka's missionaries are said to have found an uncultured people, who were only too glad to receive ideas from so civilized a land as India, though they blended these ideas naturally enough with the *naga*-worship, *nat*-worship, and magical practices of which their religion had heretofore consisted. The result was a syncretism of which we see more than occasional traces to the present day.

At this early time the population of Burma consisted of four main elements, the Shans in the north, Telaings (or Mons) in the south, Arakanese in the west, and Burmese in the centre. War between these elements was of frequent occurrence and in these wars Buddhism often fared badly. It was not till the reign of the great king Anawrahta, 1044–

[1] *Encyclopædia of Religion and Ethics*, III., p. 334.

1077, that the conflict between Burmese and Telaings was terminated, at least temporarily, by the establishment of Pagan as the capital. The king also ensured the ascendancy of the Hinayana and the use of the Pali scriptures. From this time on to the destruction of Pagan, with its 9999 dagobas, several centuries later, Hinayana continued to triumph and the devotion of the people knew no bounds. "For two centuries," says Mr. G. E. Harvey, "Pagan had witnessed the spectacle of a whole population filled with a passion for covering the earth's surface with pagodas, and now she was perishing to the drone of prayer." [1]

Several circumstances contributed to the decline of the enthusiasm which had been awakened by Anawrahta's "rape of the king and of the religious books" and his victory over the earlier *ariya* (Aryan) priests. One was the invasion of Kublai Khan in the thirteenth century, and another was the constant warfare between Burma and other parts of further India till the unification of the country under the strong Toungoo dynasty in the sixteenth century, and then on to the rise of the Alaungpaya dynasty from 1752 to the period of British annexation. During much of this time the land was in a state of practical anarchy, with periods of tyranny and cruelty wellnigh beyond belief interposed. If one laments the fact that Buddhism was unable to avert the cruelty, it may at least be said that the religion of Gautama did something to ameliorate it. To quote Mr. Harvey again: "The harshness of the rulers was mitigated by the humanity of the monks: if the distressed mariner wandered into a monastery, he was safe, for the monks would bind up his wounds, feed him, clothe him, and send him as if in sanctuary with letters of commendation from monastery to monastery till he reached Syriam, there to await the chance of some passing ship." [2]

Since Burma became part of the British Empire Buddhism has naturally lost some of its former prestige, especially as there is no longer a king to appoint the chief abbot, known as the Thatanabaing, but in other respects Buddhism has gained, and has even to many become a

[1] G. E. Harvey, *History of Burma*, p. 63.
[2] G. E. Harvey, *op. cit.*, p. 205–6.

symbol of the lost nationality they regret. In general it has entered deeply into the life of the people and has, with this cheerful and contented folk, cast off much of the pessimism so characteristic of the faith in India.

There are said to be as many as 75,000 monks in Burma, but, as a matter of fact, every man in Burma is admitted at least for a short time into the order, as a kind of initiation into manhood. Since the monasteries are schools, the boys will begin attendance at the age of eight or nine and will continue to study the Burmese and Pali languages, the *jatakas*, and, in general, to get as adequate a knowledge of the *Tripitaka* as possible till they have decided on a career. If the vocation is to be permanent, the novice will take special vows at the age of twenty, otherwise he returns to the world. The professed monk puts on the yellow robe, has his head shaved, receives his new name, and is given the utensils which are the monk's sole possessions. The ceremony of ordination takes place at a great festival held about the month of July. After ordination the occupation of the monk consists of begging, copying the sutras, teaching, and also (it must be said) spending a considerable time in more or less edifying gossip. The monk who has gone through ten *Was*, or July festivals, is known as a *hpongyi* (man of great renown); the abbot of a monastery is a *sayadaw*; the head of a number of monasteries in a district is a *gaung-douk*, a kind of bishop; and the chief abbot of the whole country is the *thathanabaung*, who is elected by the monks, but must have his appointment confirmed by the British Government.

Burmese monasteries and temples are very numerous, so much so that it has been estimated there are two temples for every village. The principal building, generally built of teak, is called the *kyoung*, and is divided into two parts, one serving as a dwelling-place for the monks and the other as the image hall, containing images of the Buddha in the three conventional attitudes of standing, sitting and lying down for the entrance into *Nibbana* (Nirvana). Beside the *kyoung* there is the *thein*, or storied pagoda, used for various purposes. Many of the shrines are reliquaries rather than temples and correspond to the Indian *chaitya*. They were built to secure merit for the builder and to afford shelter for some supposed relic of the Buddha or his disciples. The typical dagoba is a kind of four-sided pyramid, culminating in a lotus-bud, of which the finial is a kind of umbrella known as the *hti*. Burma possesses many celebrated dagobas, of which the most famous are the Shwe Dagon at Rangoon, the Shwe Maw Daw at Pegu, and the Shwe San Daw at Prome. The old capital at Pagan is said to have contained 9999 of these sacred buildings and the ruins of many of these still remain.

The question is often raised as to how far the religion of Burma may still be called Buddhism, seeing that obviously the worship of *nats* is much more deeply entrenched in the habits of the people than the following of the precepts of Gautama. The *nats* are variously explained, as the spirits of the dead, or as Indian *devas*, whose worship antedates the introduction of Buddhism. Some of them are regarded as protecting the *dagobas*, much as the four heaven kings of Indian origin protect the temples of China or Japan. Most people show a disposition to propitiate the *nats*, even where there is no actual belief in their existence, following the principle of the legendary Englishwoman who bowed to Satan because "civility costs nothing and you never know what may happen." On this point Bishop Bigandet (quoted by Hackmann) declares: "The Buddhism of the people has but little or no part in their daily life. In common life, from the day of birth to that of wedding, or even of death, all the customs and formulæ made use of by the Burmese originate with demon-worship, and not with Buddhism. If a misfortune befalls him, he attributes it to the *nat*; if he wishes to undertake an important matter, he tries to enlist the favour of the *nat*. Even the monks frequently give in to the influence of this strong undercurrent of animistic religion which underlies their Buddhist faith." [1]

In the Shan states the evidence for the persistence of the primitive religion is still stronger than in Burma proper. But Buddhism in Burma has not only retained elements from the far-distant past, but has also assimilated a considerable amount through contact with the West. Some

[1] H. Hackmann, *Buddhism as a Religion*, p. 148.

of this assimilation comes from the adhesion of Europeans and other foreigners, who, in exchange for the retreat from the challenge of life afforded by the shelter of a monastery, have, unconsciously, contributed ideas from their own cultural past. There has been also no small influence as a result of the more conscious imitation of Western ways for which Burmese trained abroad must be held responsible. Dr. Saunders illustrates this by quoting such parodies of Christian poetry as:

Glory, laud and honour
To our Lord and King,
This through endless ages
Men and devas sing.

or

Buddha loves me, this I know,
For the Scriptures tell me so.[1]

Various estimates have been made of the effect of Buddhism on the life and character of the Burmese. In general it has left them cheerful and contented, has given a much higher place to women than in most Oriental countries, and in the judgement of one competent to judge, is "harmless and antique, kindly and considerate." It has quite obviously not stuck too closely to the principles of the founder, for, though Burmese Buddhism is of the Hinayana type, there is much looking for the next Buddha, Mettaya (Maitreya), "The Loving One."

There has also been observable considerable laxity in the matter of begging, while the desire for money (a not exclusively Oriental failing) seems on the increase. A Government *Report* for 1912 reads: "The moral sense of the people is diminishing with a slackening of religious observances. With the decay of ancient beliefs the Buddhist religion is losing its moral sanction as an inspiring force in the lives of its adherents. Drunkenness, gambling, drug-taking and vicious habits, increasing as they all are, tend to produce a weakening of self-control and a loss of self-respect which in favouring circumstances easily create the criminal."

Some reform movements have been initiated, one of

[1] K. J. Saunders, *Buddhism in the Modern World.*

them by a Scotsman, Mr. Allan B. MacGregor, who was converted to Buddhism from Roman Catholicism nearly thirty years ago. Another movement of the sort is the Chulla-gandi, which has endeavoured to bring about greater severity of discipline in the monasteries, but has not succeeded in disarming the hostility of the Maha-gandi. As to the part taken by European and American converts in the promotion of Burmese Buddhism, Dr. K. J. Saunders has something interesting and suggestive to say in an *Appendix* to his *Buddhism in the Modern World*.[1]

Siamese Buddhism.—Siam is the "one officially Buddhist state" of Asia, but we know very little of the circumstances under which Buddhism was introduced. As the Siamese are a Mongol people, and closely related both geographically and ethnically to the Chinese, it may well be suspected that Buddhist missionaries from China entered Siam at an early date. One tradition has it that the faith came by way of Cambodia about A.D. 422. On the other hand, the contacts with India were early and constant, and the oldest ruins in the land show plenty of signs of Brahmanism, signs which diminish in number as we approach modern times. The first Buddhism was of the Mahayana type, but when the Siamese people pushed their way, in the thirteenth and fourteenth centuries, into Burmah, they very soon, from contact with the Telaing folk of the south, accepted the teachings of the Hinayana. In 1260 the king was so anxious to validate the succession of the order that he sent to Ceylon for assistance and an abbot was sent back who was able to link up the line of the order in Siam with that descended from the illustrious Mahendra. At the same time relics were imported and a branch of the Bo-tree. After this Siamese Buddhism so flourished that in 1750 the Singhalese monks returned the compliment which had been paid them by sending to Siam for clergy to strengthen their own organization. The new dynasty which was inaugurated in 1782 showed great enthusiasm for the cause of religion—an enthusiasm which has been fully maintained to the present day.

Since Siam has been, until recently, an absolute monarchy

[1] K. J. Saunders, *Buddhism in the Modern World*, Appendix I.

it may well be understood that the support of religion by the king gives Buddhism great prestige. The king is not the high priest, or chief abbot, but by his nomination of the chief abbot, called *sangkharat* (Skt., *sangharaja*), he wields great influence. One of the king's chief duties is to attend the feast held between the eleventh and twelfth months, for the purpose of bestowing upon the monks the gift of "holy clothes." On this occasion all the people are supposed to make patched garments—monks are not supposed to wear any other—but the king's gift naturally throws all the rest into the shade. The monarch comes in his royal barge with great bales of cloth which he presents, after he has made his threefold obeisance to the image of the Buddha, the sacred books, and the monkish assembly, and after he has taken the five vows of the Buddhist layman, together with the three vows special for the day. This homage rendered by the king to the representatives of religion gives the monks power as well as prestige, and it cannot be complained that the power conferred has been to any extent abused.

The monks, who are known as *talapoins*, numbered in 1924 114,349, of whom only 110 came from other countries. In spite of their numbers they are held generally in high regard. Dr. Pratt tells us that their ten vows include the wearing of the yellow robe, the begging day by day of food just sufficient for the day's needs, charity towards the poor, refraining from scolding, the paying of courteous attention to those who address them, constant self-reminders as to the impermancy of living things, recollectedness as to the states of future retribution, earnest effort for self-improvement in virtue, frequent meditation in some lonely place, and the pursuit of learning.[1]

The temples in Siam are known as *wats* and are numerous and splendid, especially in the capital, Bangkok. The largest of these houses as many as 250 monks. Four kinds of *wats* are recognized, built respectively through the generosity of kings, princes, nobles and the common people. Within the *wats* are images of the Buddha, almost exclusively in the familiar seated or standing attitude. One reclining

[1] J. B. Pratt, *The Pilgrimage of Buddhism*, p. 163.

figure, however, about 160 feet in length, is to be found in one of the Bangkok temples.

From early times Siamese Buddhism has been devoted to literature. In the eighteenth century, under King Phaya Tak, 1767–80, there was compiled in Siamese a commentary on the Pali Canon, known as *Trai Phum*, the *Three Places*, dealing first of all with the universe in general, then of the heavens and their inhabitants, and lastly of the hells. A good deal was accomplished in the way of printing the Buddhist classics in the nineteenth century by the king Chulalongkorn and his father, and sumptuous copies of the Pali *Tipitaka* were made, some of which were presented to Western universities and libraries. Under Prince Damrong the Vajiranana National Library has continued this good work and carried out research of considerable extent and value.

The influence of Buddhism on Siam generally has been good, though much superstition and ignorance naturally underlie the tolerant and undogmatic faith of this singularly attractive people. The prevalent Hinayana is much intermingled with belief in Maitreya as the coming Buddha, there is little stress placed on the *Four Noble Truths*, Heavens and Hells are more in the minds of men than the longing for Nibban (Nirvana). Yet more than one scholar has approved Dr. Pratt's respect for " the religion of that sunny land." " Its marble wats, its golden shrines, and much more of the simple steady faith of the laity, the training given them by the monks in the fundamentals of morality, the impress, still so deep, of the Founder's limitless devotion—these rather than the undoubted defects of his teaching, fill one's thoughts as one embarks once more upon the tawny Menam and sails slowly downstream, past the jungle vistas, past the native huts, past the last little wat on the banks of the widening river, out into the gulf, until Siam has become again merely a thin green line between sky and sea, and the ship turns with its steady course towards Cambodia." [1]

BUDDHISM IN CAMBODIA.—Cambodia is a remnant of the most extensive Khmer Empire, to which we owe the dead splendours of the Angkor *wats*. Situated as it is

[1] J. B. Pratt, *The Pilgrimage of Buddhism*, p. 187.

geographically we naturally find, together with the remains of the ancient Brahmanism, much that shows the slight distance which separates us from China. Indian influence entered very early and has remained to the present day as a kind of Çaivistic colouring observable in the architecture and decorative art as well as in the religion. Also, naturally, there are remains of the primitive worship of the *neaca-ta*, or spirits of the land, such as correspond with the *nats* of Burmah.

Buddhism, in the Mahayanist form, was introduced to Cambodia somewhere between the fifth and seventh centuries, but had a long struggle with the Çaivism which represented the official cult of the Khmers, before its triumph in the thirteenth and following centuries. The Chinese traveller Chon To-kuan witnesses to the fact that in 1296 the Hinayana had completely superseded the teachings of the other school. From that time Cambodia has remained enthusiastically Buddhist, devoted to the Pali *Canon* and the Singhalese type of Hinayana. When Cambodia became French in 1862 the conquerors allowed the king to remain as the temporal head of the Church and by him the two "archbishops" of the "right" and the "left" are nominated who divide the oversight of religious matters in the kingdom between them.

The monks are a highly privileged class, on the whole less learned and intelligent than their fellow-clergy in Siam, but rendering service in the education of the young, in performance of the services at the *wats*, and in expounding the Law several times in the month. Boys begin their education at the temples at a very early age, becoming "disciples" by a kind of confirmation rite at the age of twelve, and (if they choose) full-fledged monks at the age of twenty-one. The monks are exempt from military duty, taxes and public works, and subsist on the alms of the faithful. There is also an order of female devotees, or nuns, drawn partly from the ranks of widows and partly from those who have been vowed to religion from childhood.

The *wats*, usually erected in the middle of a wooded park, are familiar objects throughout the land, though not on so magnificent a scale as in Burmah or Siam. The kings have vied with one another and with Siam in the building of these, but have not greatly succeeded. The images in the *wats* are generally of the seated or standing Buddha, but occasionally an image of the Chinese Mi-lei-fo (Maitreya) obtrudes itself and reminds one of the nearness of the Middle Kingdom.

The Cambodians are practically all Buddhists, but know little of Buddhist doctrine. As in Siam, the Heavens and Hells are much more strongly stressed than Nirvana. In concluding this chapter I cannot do better than give a summary of Southern Buddhism as a whole by Dr. K. J. Saunders: " Such, in bare outline, is Southern Buddhism—in its origin a stoical agnosticism which ignored the gods and bade men rely upon themselves in following the paths of goodness that lead to happiness. Because it thus ignored the deepest instincts of humanity, first by turning the thoughts of men away from God, and again by glorifying celibacy, these instincts, refusing to be snubbed, have taken a revenge, so that to-day Buddhism survives, largely because of the teachings it has been compelled to adopt in the process of moulding itself ' nearer to the heart's desire.' This may be illustrated in two ways. Nibbana at best, originally an ideal of negative, solitary bliss, has been replaced by an ideal of social life hereafter. Moreover, faith in self-mastery has given place to prayers for help, or, among the most conservative, to the belief that there is a store of merit gained by the sacrificial lives of the Buddhas throughout the ages, which may be tapped by the faithful. Buddhism has thus passed through an interesting history of adjustment. It is important for the student of religion to give close attention to this history, one of the most amazing and fascinating chapters in human thought." [1]

[1] K. J. Saunders, *Buddhism in the Modern World*, pp. 41 ff.

# BOOK V

## THROUGH JUDAISM TO THE CHRIST

### *Introduction*

IN this last and—I fear—lengthy portion of the volume it is my purpose to show how all the different elements of a potentially universal religion are gathered together into one somewhat narrow stream, thence to broaden out for the uses of all the world, or (to change the metaphor) brought to a single focal point of revelation, in order that from this point the gains of all prior history, as exemplified in one Divine-Human figure, accepted as the heir of the ages, are made available for all mankind.

The four sections of this concluding book may be described as follows:

I. The story of the evolution of Judaism—the middle term in the history of religion.
II. The rise and extension of Christianity up to the preaching of Islam.
III. The story of Islam as a Judæo-Christian development.
IV. The history of Christianity from the rise of Islam to the present day.

Several points may be preliminarily noted to make clear my general attitude. First, though I believe that the witness of Judaism was practically complete with the opening of the Christian era, I hold it important to follow the continued bearing of that witness—not without the Cross—through the troubled centuries which have passed since the Fall of Jerusalem.

Secondly, I conceive of Islam not so much as a separate religious system as a reform movement in Arabia strongly influenced by Jewish and Christian ideas and maintaining the character of its origins down to the present day.

Thirdly, since man is a " billion-year plant " rather than

a "century plant," I do not conceive of the Christian story as much more than begun. Two thousand years, I judge, make but a brief period in which to realize ideals which have been slowly dawning for the spirit of man through the countless ages of the past. When as much time has elapsed for the reproduction of the Christ as was deemed necessary for the production of the Christ, then we may find excuse for impatience with the slow grinding of the mills of God. But—not till then.

SECTION I

JUDAISM, THE MIDDLE TERM

# CHAPTER XXVIII

## *The Evolution of Hebrew Religion*

RENAN once declared that only three ancient histories were really deserving of the study of intelligent men, namely, those of Greece, Rome, and the people of Israel. The statement to-day hardly carries conviction, for several reasons. The peoples referred to might even find themselves excluded from the field of ancient history altogether, when their story is put alongside that of nations now known to be immensely more venerable. But from the point of view of religious history the story of the Jew cannot be dismissed so cavalierly, even though we may not attach the importance to the subject assigned it by the Great Frederick's chaplain who, asked by his master in a hurry for a proof of Christianity, responded, equally in a hurry, "The Jews, Your Majesty, the Jews!"

We have assumed throughout the preceding pages that the record of revelation given to the Jew in the Old Testament is but one Old Testament among many designed to prepare men's minds for the dawning of the new spiritual day. This is a point of view essential to the modern exposition of Christianity as the universal religion. Nevertheless, the assertion needs qualification. Even if the Hebrew Scriptures did not exist to be their own witness, it would be difficult to overlook the special rôle the Jew has played in establishing a *liaison* between the old and the new.

The reasons for ascribing such a distinction to Judaism —using the term for the present of the religion of Israel in all its stages—may be assembled as follows:

1. Because the human lineage of Christ is traced for us, in the main, from the seed of Abraham. I say "In the

main," since St. Matthew, most Jewish of the evangelists, takes pains to reveal to us the intrusion of the foreign element in the case of the three named ancestresses of Christ, Rahab, the Canaanitess; Ruth, the Moabitess; and Bathsheba, the wife of Uriah the Hittite. This strong statement is made for the definite purpose of proclaiming Christ as the heir of all humanity, with its sins and frailties as well as its racial differences. It is of no small significance that of the four women mentioned in the legal genealogy of Jesus three were alien in blood and three bore a blot on their character. Nevertheless, the genealogy is a Jewish one, intended to mark Christ as the Son of David. Not all the Nordic zeal of a Houston Chamberlain is ingenious enough to prove the contrary.

2. The geographical and historical contacts of the people of Israel made them the inevitable recipients, carriers and distributors of ideas from, and between, the great world-powers of the pre-Christian epoch. Like a full stream fed by many tributaries, Judaism bore the waters collected from these many sources towards the ocean of their goal. "The giant forms of empire," with which Israel was brought into contact, were indeed "on their way to ruin." Yet, ere they fell, they yielded up gifts of the spirit which had been their dower, such as we have referred to in earlier chapters, to the Jews whom they despised and on whom they had trampled. All these manifold contributions, which some have even feared to acknowledge, lest they should seem thereby to be doing violence to the unique claims of Christianity, from the creation myths of Babylon to the angelology of Persia, or to the philosophies of Greece, must, on the contrary, be regarded as essential to the completeness of the Hebrew witness. The Jew was a guest, or a captive, in every land, in order that he might become the link between what had already been revealed and the new things yet to appear.

3. What Israel was able to receive from the Gentile world—what by reason of her geographical position in that corridor between the continents along which ran the chariot-ruts of history, she was able to gather—she was able, by reason of the same conditions, to distribute. As we shall

see later, she possessed a centripetal force which compelled her to concentrate and retain; she possessed also a centrifugal force which compelled her to distribute. In her little hill-fort of a capital, Jerusalem, or " Security-burg," loyalty to the talent which had been committed to her became a passion—wellnigh a fanaticism. In her other capital, Alexandria, she developed a sense of responsibility for diffusion and became, almost in spite of herself, the great apostle to the Gentiles.

While stressing this important point as to the uniqueness of Judaism, in preparation for the propagation of a universal faith, we must, nevertheless, be careful to remember in the history of religion Israel was a kind of *liaison*-officer with a responsibility at either end of the story. At the point where the developed product of the faith of Abraham, as an accumulated fund of trust and experience, is poured into the life of the New Dispensation, there are links which have not failed to obtain more or less general recognition. The nationality of the first apostles, the use of the Hebrew Scriptures, the emphasis put on the fulfilment of the Jewish sacrificial system, the dramatic passing of the priesthood and the Temple order—all this has made the fact inescapable. " In Novo Testamento patet quod in Veteri Testamento latet."

But the *liaison* is equally significant at the other end, where the religion of Israel is first beginning to differentiate itself from the religion of the contiguous Semitic tribes. At this point, too, we have a contact, less recognized, but providentially ordered and equally suggestive.

Let us try, at the outset of this brief sketch of the development of Hebrew religion, to link the story with that of the primitive religions we discussed earlier in this volume. Noting the salient points of this relation we shall see how the truths glimpsed in primitive religion were changed, as by a subtle alchemy, in the laboratory of Jewish experience, to become serviceable at last for the religion of all mankind.

It is a very distinct gain to religion that the supposed separateness of early Israel in race, language, and religion, can no longer be defended. The older (and now discarded) idea was in part due to the chauvinistic pride of the Jew, in part to our own traditional misconception of what was to be understood by the term "chosen people." Now that archæology, philology and comparative religion have all alike thrown light upon the subject, we see how little in the Hebrew Scriptures themselves the traditional view had in its favour. It is much more significant to recognize with Isaiah [1] that the Hebrew language was "a tongue of Canaan," an ordinary Semitic dialect, than to think of it as the primal, sacred language spoken by our first parents in Eden. It is much more significant, again, to appreciate the brutal force of the prophet Ezekiel [2] when he reminded the Jew: "Thy birth and thy nativity is of the land of the Canaanite; the Amorite was thy father and thy mother was an Hittite," than to think of the Jew as unrelated to the ethnic world in which he moved. So in religion we must bear in mind that the quality of Hebrew faith and its value for the purposes of the divine plan are in no wise conditioned by the advanced character of its theology and the supposed superiority of its morals.

If we enquire as to the true reasons for the special place Judaism was destined to occupy in the field of religious history, even as Greece was assigned her special place in the field of art, and Rome in the field of law, we find the answer in two main facts. The first is that a consistently spiritual outlook, in spite of the defection of the many, kept the essential soul of the nation watching for God "more than they that watch for the morning." The story of Jacob is the historical illustration of how the Jew, carnal and material as he might be in appetite, trickster and mean as he might be by inclination, nevertheless, struggles on, until by wrestling, as it were with God Himself, he wins his new nature and the new name which is its sign and reward. The second is in that intensity of moral earnestness, amounting sometimes to a fanaticism, such as insisted on the turning of vision into conduct.

Of course, it is obvious that not all Israel was "of Israel." To quote Samuel Taylor Coleridge, there was an Israel which produced the "old clo' man" and there was

[1] Isaiah xix. 18. [2] Ezekiel xvi. 3.

an Israel which produced the Evangelical Prophet. Zangwill says:

> Hear, O Israel, Jehovah, the Lord, our God, is One,
> But we, Jehovah, His people, are dual and so undone.

Yet, after all, it was the soul of the nation which determined its religious experience, and though "the remnant" dwindled and dwindled till "the Servant of Yahweh" became an ideal Person rather than the nation as a whole, yet of that ideal it was still true:

> Wheresoe'er a Jew dwelt there dwelt Truth,
> And wheresoe'er a Jew was there was Light,
> And wheresoe'er a Jew went there went Love.

Having recalled to ourselves, then, the fact that the Jew was called upon to be an apostle, exactly as the first Christian apostles were called by the Lake of Galilee, not for what they knew, or were, or could do, but because of what they were capable of becoming, and knowing, and achieving, let us see what that same Jew did with the primitive conceptions of religion he received as the inheritance of his race and through the circumstances of his environment.

The primitive, or patriarchal, stage of Hebrew religion extends from the time that Abraham and his descendants first appear on the field of history to the religious revolution under Moses. Though the patriarchal narratives are, in their present form, the product of a later age, and have read into them the ideas and manners of that later age, they yet reflect more or less accurately the beliefs and practices of the primitive stage. So we gather thence a conception of God not far removed from the animistic. The plural name *Elohim* suggests a vaguely personalized aggregation of "powers," which must be recognized and propitiated at all likely places, such as springs, rocks and trees. We gather also at this time a primitive morality such as makes it credible that God may on occasion demand the actual slaying of a son in sacrifice; lying is not highly reprehensible when a foreigner is the victim; and there is little in the way of injury which it is unlawful to inflict upon the alien. There is also revealed a primitive conception of society as tribal. For all the purposes of social morality society is confined to the clan or family. Intertribal morality is unknown and even "the stranger within thy gates" is accepted only when, separated from his own kin, he comes to throw himself upon the hospitality of the camp. There is, once again, a primitive conception of human destiny, the idea of a future life which is simply the passing of the disembodied ghost into the underworld of the grave. As in the case of the pagan Semites, the life beyond the present was but the reunion of the spirit with the spirits of ancestors in some dim, shadowy simulacrum of life beneath the soil. It was from such beliefs and such attitudes of mind that the moral earnestness and spiritual vision of the potential "Servant"—illustrated so wonderfully in the faith of Abraham and his seed—broke the way towards the great revolutionary step which marks the transition from the first to the second stage of Hebrew religion.

The national period begins with the appearance and leadership (under God) of the great law-giver, Moses. Here, as so often in the history of religion, personality plays its significant part. In its every incident, while the subordination of Moses to the great "head of the army" is clearly acknowledged, we get the sense of a great personality assisting a laggard people through the wilderness, a true shepherd who feels himself charged with leading a foolish and reluctant flock to their proper goal.

Nevertheless, there were other elements in the situation which were to produce their fruit in due season. Just as Abraham's experience in the city-states of the Euphrates Valley, though it provoked revulsion against the materialism of the Babylonian, transmitted seeds of finer things which were presently to germinate and flourish, so the experience of Israel in Egypt, though its bitterness of bondage brought revolt against the tyranny of the Pharaohs, absorbed ideas which later contacts were to make abundantly fruitful. Furthermore, the henotheism of Midian, with its more personally conceived deity of storm and war, Yahweh, introduced a new element into the religion of Israel, or at least re-emphasized one which had hitherto been vague and local.

The recognition by the people, through the teaching of

Moses, that they had been adopted by a god to whom they were not akin, defective as the conception will appear to modern theology, marked an immense advance beyond the worship of the Elohim. There was about Yahweh, enthroned murkily on Sinai, something more personal, more anthropomorphic, at once more passionate and more tenderly concerned, than anything they had hitherto conceived in deity. To be taken up by Yahweh, led and sustained, championed and fought for, even punished and afflicted, brought about an entirely new sense of the relation between God and mankind. To return to Canaan behind the standard of such a one was the very stimulus to heroic endeavour they needed to lift them to a sterner conception of moral values. For this God was not merely a mighty God; he was also a " holy " God. And just because he was so holy, they too must be dedicated to Him and wage a holy war against the idolatrous naturalism of the agricultural tribes, whose fertility cults they now perceived to be, in the light of their desert experience, filthy and abominable. In brief, the word " holiness " was in process of taking on a new and more transcendent meaning. Can we wonder that this great adventure, in which Yahweh left the clouds and darkness of His dwelling-place on Sinai to march before the people till they were able to give Him a new abiding place on Zion, assumes an aspect of enormous importance for the future of religion?

The national period was not destined to be of long duration. It was only in the lull that followed the decline of the Babylonian Empire, the withdrawal of Egypt and the Hittites alike, after the dubious victory of Rameses II. at Kadesh, and which preceded the rise of the Assyrians, that the territorial nationality of Israel was politically possible. Nevertheless, the period lasted long enough to accomplish what it was providentially prepared to achieve. For a while, under the conditions of the new life, it seemed a struggle to the death, a struggle between the nomad and the settled folk, between Yahweh and the male and female fertility gods, the Baalim and Ashtaroth, between moral ideals and the licentious rites which, along the lines of imitative magic, were supposed to stimulate the reproductive powers of the soil. In this struggle the general tendency of the masses and their rulers was to assimilate themselves in belief and practice to the older habits of the land. But the vital force of religion, what one may call "the law of vital procedure," that "tendency towards perfection" by which life seems to direct itself towards better things, shows itself in the rise of the prophetic order. Few more striking illustrations of evolution in a religious organism are to be found than the way in which the *shaman*, or medicine man, is enabled to lend himself to divine uses, until he becomes the spokesman for God of the highest religious truths. Beginning as the mere clairvoyant minister to the secular necessities of a village community, uncouthly clad, eccentric in conduct, emotionally controlled and affected by music, used as a finder of lost cattle and the like,[1] we see the prophet in Israel gradually transformed, through right spiritual attitude and intensity of moral earnestness, into the prophet as we see him in the pages of *Isaiah*. Thenceforth there is no great crisis in Hebrew history, to the beginning of the Christian era, which is without its prophetic interpretation, an interpretation, moreover, which has significance for all ages and for all mankind.

From the struggle between the entrenched forces of the older naturalism and the new Yahwism we come to the interpretation of the Assyrian menace of the eighth century B.C., which the prophets were the first to perceive and the first to understand. *Amos*, the wool-grower of Tekoa, brought into contact with world politics in the cities to which he took his wool, and brooding over those politics in his pastures and among his fig-trees, becomes convinced of an overruling Power, to whom all the nations were subject, about to break in upon the fancied security of Israel in a storm of judgement. *Hosea*, the poet-prophet of Galilee, out of his experience of love and grief, adds to the announcement of judgement the proclamation of divine love which uses judgement as an educative discipline to purify and redeem. *Isaiah* and *Micah* bear their witness in the southern kingdom, shaken as that kingdom is by the

[1] See 1 Samuel ix. 6 ff.; x. 5 ff.

downfall of the northern capital. Isaiah stresses the assurance of that divine presence which makes Jerusalem safe, even amid the confident truculence of the hitherto victorious foe. Micah, in the light of that same passage of the Assyrian through the land, is concerned with the need of social penitence and the revival of faith. Then appears *Zephaniah*, scenting from afar the terror of the Scythian and proclaiming the near advent of Yahweh's "Day," a proclamation which coloured the visions of apocalypse for ages to come. *Nahum* raises his voice in taunt-songs, at once hailing and anticipating the downfall of the "bloody city," Nineveh, which had so long tyrannized over the surrounding States. Then—a new step for prophecy—*Habakkuk*, "the first sceptic in Israel," ascends his lonely watch-tower to fight out the battle of faith, even when truth seemed slain in the streets. Suppose, he asks, Isaiah's optimism to be ill-founded, and the assault of the Chaldean to succeed where the Assyrian had failed, what then must be the relation of the soul to God? And the prophet wrings out of hostile circumstance the sublime affirmation—such as strengthened religion for all time to come—that the life of the just man was still bound up with fidelity to Yahweh.[1]

By this time the period of territorial nationality, with its national religion—now beginning to be discredited as a religious "pattern"—is drawing to a close. Much has been accomplished since Moses accepted his mission. A more personal and a more ethical conception of God has been proclaimed; a higher morality, and one more consonant with the character of "a holy God," has been preached and practised; there has been a deliberate renunciation of the primitive traffic in necromancy and a refusal to look beyond the grave, for the time being, for signs of the divine government and the divine favour; and there has been a strengthened sense of the nation's *raison d'être* as an instrument in God's hands for the working of His will.

But these truths had now served their purpose and were begging to be regarded as outworn. Already Amos had

[1] Habakkuk ii. 4.

heralded a larger conception of God and a larger conception of human society than Yahwism made possible. For a time we watch the breaking down of the old philosophy. Two great prophets found themselves doomed to look upon and explain to a depressed age the calamity which was all too obviously imminent. *Jeremiah*, in the unpopular *rôle* of one who knew the captivity to be inevitable, had to vindicate faith in God in a time of ruinous catastrophe, and to be himself an illustration of that faith. *Ezekiel*, among the first band of captives by the canal Chebar, far off from the scene of the fatal *dénouement*, had to endure, for himself and others, the shock and the reverberation of Jerusalem's fall, and thenceforward to brace himself to the vision and task of reconstruction.

It is in this time of reconstruction that we find the religion of Israel passing from nationalism to internationalism, from henotheism to monotheism. Following upon the capture of Babylon by Cyrus, who seemed to the Jew a true "Messiah," the "Evangelical Prophet" appears, singing the return of the "remnant" in immortal poetry, making monotheism secure for all the ages to come, and proclaiming, as no other human voice has done, the heartening mission to which the Servant People had been called in the providence of God. It is true that after the Return sordid years elapsed, years of disillusion and disappointment. But, while some, with eyes upon the past, asked whether any revival of nationalism, with the restoration of David's line, were possible, others were straining their eyes to behold in Israel's mission some grander end than had yet been dreamed of. So the old man *Haggai* appears, to proclaim the future glories of Judaism in her ministry to the world, and the young man *Zechariah*, in a series of striking visions, to reassure his people as to the validity of the worship and witness of Hebrew religion.

In truth, the double mission of Judaism was beginning to be made clear: first, the mission to condense, concentrate, hold and defend to the very death what was essential; secondly, the mission to distribute and transmit, even to the dissolution of what had been provisional, the message which summed up the religious experience of the race.

The centripetal aspect of this mission has given us the Law, the Temple, the Priesthood, the Sacrificial system. It provided that wonderful pentagonal idea of Holiness, as represented in the ceremonies of the *Day of Atonement*, in which the holiness of all Mankind was represented by the High Priest, the holiness of all Time by the symbolism of the Day itself, the holiness of all Space by the symbolism of the Holy of Holies, the holiness of all Matter by the symbolism of the sacrificial Blood, and the holiness of all Acts by the sprinkling of the blood upon the Mercy-seat. It was as though the entire religious system of the Jew was an intensification by specialized emphasis in the five regions of Person, Time, Space, Matter and Act, such as might enable the conception to flow back upon the world with redemptive power. Thus all men might become High Priests, all days time in which God and Man might meet, all space filled with the glory of God, even the bells upon the horses become consecrate to God, and every act reckoned as sacrificial service at the altar of God. The centrifugal aspect of the mission of Judaism is thus seen to spring out of the significance of the centripetal. As there was a mission to conserve and defend, so there was a mission to disperse and evangelize. The nationality which is so passionately defended in the book of *Esther* the Jew must be prepared to cast into the crucible in order that books like *Ruth* and *Jonah* may become possible—books in which place is found for the Gentile in the manifest purpose of God.

Hence there opens for Judaism a new era in which the chosen people is no longer the little, pent-up, struggling nation, striving to maintain precarious foothold on its narrow isthmus between Asia and Africa, but rather an influence of world-wide significance, spreading out from Alexandria as well as from Jerusalem, at once receiving and distributing the treasures she had accumulated in the days of her obscurity. Of what she had received we have already spoken in the chapters on the religion of peoples in historical contact with the Jew. What she was inspired to contribute must be summed up in a few paragraphs. As the prophet had been moved to touch the moral conscience of mankind, and as the priest had been led to organize ritually the symbolism of religion, so now the sage was employed to be the instrument for establishing and maintaining touch with the wisdom of the nations and to address these nations in a tongue easy for them to understand. So, too, came the new language of Israel to the world in the Greek (*koiné*) into which the sacred Scriptures were translated. It is, of course, merely one among the many evidences of the appearance of that "fulness of time" when it was the part of the Jew, by the sacrifice of himself, to dim the torch of his own national life, in order to pass on a brighter light to the Gentile world.

Ere, however, we reach this point, it is needful to note that the two more or less contemporary aspects of Jewish religion, the one with its centre at Jerusalem, the other at Alexandria, contradictory as they sometimes seem in their literature and their attitude to life, were yet working together towards giving to the world another gift of transcendent import for the cause of the world's religion. This is the new sense of the largeness of life. Both the sage at Alexandria and the martyr at Jerusalem, under stress of the persecution of Antiochus, had come to recognize the falsity of the old philosophy which made all divine favour, to nation or individual, measurable by the degree of material prosperity enjoyed. It was now necessary to transcend this philosophy of the Deuteronomic Code, as it applied to the nation, and the doctrine of Ezekiel, as it applied to the individual, that justice was meted out by the divine Judge invariably within the limits of three score mortal years. The problem was faced by some of the Psalmists (cf. 73) and in the book of *Job*, and, while no certain conclusion was possible for the Old Testament mind, light appeared from two directions. On the one hand, Job's demand for a God akin to himself in sympathy and in a common sense of right and wrong became the link which made all earlier anthropomorphic elements of religion predictive of the Incarnation. And, on the other hand, the sense of the divine kinship made credible the sharing of the divine life beyond the grave, and gathered up all the intuitions of primitive men, as preserved in various forms of spiritism and necromancy—intuitions which, as we have seen, were suppressed by Yahwism as, by themselves, morally fruitless—into one great conviction as to a quality of life which it would be good to enjoy for evermore.

Under the stimulus of hopes such as these it was possible for the Jew, out of the very furnace of his affliction, to see, through the fervid eyes of the apocalyptist, the triumph of that kingdom which was at once Theophany and Theodicy, the world-wide rule of righteousness and of a righteous God, in partnership and kinship with humanity.

In such a development as we have thus briefly sketched, what are the special elements of religious truth which Judaism has gathered out of the chaotic beliefs and practices of primitive men to lay at the feet of a world awaiting the fuller revelation of God?

1. There is clear advance made towards an adequate conception of God. We see the tribal idea of God, not far removed from animism, displaced by the more anthropomorphically conceived Yahweh, war-god and champion of tribes now welded into nationality. Satisfaction with a national divinity eventually gives way before the larger vision of a God who has been concerned with the exodus of the Philistines from Caphtor as well as with that of Israel from Egypt.[1] From Amos onward this feeling grows, until the henotheism of the national stage is superseded by the genuine monotheism of the "Second Isaiah," the proclamation of a God whose dominion is universal and absolute, and beside whom is no other.

2. There is a corresponding development of the conception of the Church or Society. In the beginning the elect element was the tribe alone, and outside was a humanity always alien and generally hostile. The necessities of defence against the tribes of Canaan, and of loyalty to Yahweh who had adopted them as His people, enabled the people of Israel to create the monarchy, centralized at Jerusalem, and to maintain its integrity until its peculiar task had been accomplished. The patriotism thus engendered furnished the world with a still living symbolism and "Jerusalem" remains still to the spirit something beyond the power of speech or imagination to express.

[1] Amos ix. 7.

But, even before the tragedy came which dissolved the nation as a territorial unit, the Jew learned that there was something greater than patriotism. When the triple bond of God, Land and People was so rudely severed—just as the idea of God rose to nobler proportions instead of perishing—the ideas of Land and People, by the aid of an inspired symbolism, became vaster and more wonderful. What a communion became possible for those who had eyes to behold the nations of the earth bowed before a common God and engaged in a common service! What a Zion rose before the vision of men as they thought of the Gentile taking hold of the skirts of the Jew and demanding participation in the privileges of a common faith! Gradually all those elements of humanity which had been, as it were, eliminated while the specialization of Israel's function was in process, are seen to be coming back in order that they may enjoy the fruits of that specialization. The "chosen" people is indeed chosen, not for the enjoyment of a splendid isolation, but in order that it may become "a light to lighten the Gentiles."

3. In the third place, continuously with the expansion of the idea of the national into the human, we see the development of the sense of the individual. The failure of the old philosophy of material reward for religious fidelity, to which allusion was made above, led necessarily to discrimination within the nation between those who kept and those who violated the law of God. Surely justice must dictate the recognition of some other principle beside that of the solidarity of the family or tribe. It could not be fair that for ever the fathers would eat sour grapes and that the children's teeth must thereby be set on edge. Solemn as was the certainty that evil consequences followed the evil doer to the third and fourth generation, there must be another side. This other side, first announced by Jeremiah, is formulated by Ezekiel in the famous words: "The soul that sinneth it shall die."[1] With the enunciation of this great truth, there opened on the world possibilities of personal religion and personal freedom of which earlier generations had not dreamed. As there was a world outside

[1] Ezekiel xviii. 20.

the nation which was under the direction of the Spirit of God, so also within the nation was, as it were, a microcosm, in which, equally as in Jerusalem, God could set up His throne. By and by it would come to pass that a truer nationalism would find place for a truer individualism, even as nationalism would have found for itself an abiding place in the true internationalism of the Kingdom, when "the glory of the nations" should enter within the open gates of the City of God.

4. Fourthly, Judaism brought to birth, in the train of the prophetic teaching as to the significance of individualism, a larger conception of life itself. As we have seen, Ezekiel's teaching that God rewarded or punished the actions of individual men here and now for a while sufficed. In many of the circumstances of the normal life it did actually appear that it paid to be pious. "I have been young and now am old, yet never saw I the righteous forsaken or his seed begging their bread," said the Psalmist. But circumstances soon revealed contradictions to so optimistic a creed. Another Psalmist, perplexed by the prosperity of the wicked, exclaims: "They are not in trouble like other men; neither are they plagued like other men." The book of *Job*, as already pointed out, took up the subject with great boldness, even with an audacity which to some seemed blasphemy, carrying opposition to the traditional orthodoxy up to argument with God Himself. The solution, only faintly glimpsed in the poem, in course of time began to grow clearer. If life is to be judged justly, the judgement must take cognizance of a larger conception of life than one confined to thought of the mortal body. So the old view as to survival of the soul, which had been suppressed in the interest of practical morality, now returns charged with new significance. "The glory of going on and still to be" becomes credible if men have some share in the life of the Eternal. In such a case, a theodicy may be hoped for such as shall not outrage the sense of justice in the martyr who lays down his life for the sake of truth.

5. Fifthly, all these enlarged conceptions of God, of Society, of the worth of the Individual, and of the largeness

of Life, meet in the comprehensive doctrine of the later Judaism as to the Coming of God in the Person of His Anointed to judge the world, for the avenging of wrongdoing and for the establishment of the divine Kingdom. The apocalyptic dreams nourished in the Essene communities and elsewhere during the last two centuries of the Old Testament dispensation, bring to a focal point not merely the hope of Israel but also "the desirable things of the nations" which it was the mission of Judaism to clarify and interpret. There were, of course, pagan throwbacks not a few, revivals of old dreams of a restored nation with its secular monarchy. There were manifold differences and inconsistencies in the visions received and proclaimed. Some looked for a kingdom both of and in the world; others had their eyes lifted beyond the grave and the resurrection of the dead. But the essence of the hope was in all the same, however crude the terms in which that hope was clothed. Men knew that God was drawing near to give answer to the universal yearning. They knew that out of that shaking of heaven and earth which His appearing must bring about there would dawn the beginning of a new and better day. As in their own experience the veil had been taken away from many of the things in which the heathen believed concerning God and human life, so a new rending of the veil was about to happen, and beyond it a new revelation of God. The primitive world together with the Jewish world—*David cum Sibylla*—are ready to unite in one sublime acclamation:

> Say among the nations, The Lord reigneth :
> The world also is stablished that it cannot be moved :
> He shall judge the people with equity.
> Let the heavens be glad and let the earth rejoice ;
> Let the sea roar and the fulness thereof ;
> Let the field exult and all that is therein ;
> Then shall all the trees of the wood sing for joy
> Before the Lord, for He cometh ;
> For He cometh to judge the earth.[1]

[1] Psalm xcvi. 10 ff.

From the Christian point of view, Judaism as a whole turned its back upon the great commission—the privilege of being the missionary, trained from the beginning, to be the apostle to the Gentiles. Thus she did not enter the Promised Land prepared for her dwelling. As, after the forty years' trial in the wilderness, only a scanty remnant entered into Canaan, so, after the forty years of opportunity between the Crucifixion and the Fall of Jerusalem. The result was that her "house was left unto her desolate"—the Temple destroyed and the Priesthood and sacrificial system rendered for ever obsolete.

Yet the work of Israel in the world was not brought altogether to an end. The fate of Israel was to be something more than that of "the Wandering Jew" of the legend. Judaism rejected the Cross, but she could not remove its weight from her own shoulders. She bore about with her throughout the world the witness of a people who had won power by martyrdom. In a sense never intended by the utterers, the words, "His Blood be on us and on our children," have proved true. But for healing rather than for hurt. In a very real sense the best power of the Jew has come from his sharing the Cross with Him whom the rulers rejected. The victims of "the Ghetto's plague" and the Inquisition might well plead:

> Thou! if Thou wast He, who at midnight came,
> By the starlight, naming a dubious name!
> And if, too heavy with sleep—too rash
> With fear—O Thou, if that martyr gash
> Fell on Thee coming to take Thy own,
> And we gave the Cross, when we owed the Throne—
> Thou art the Judge. We are bruised thus.
> But the Judgement over, join sides with us!
> Thine too is the cause.[1]

The Christian will, I believe, gladly acknowledge that in that tragic but heroic history of Judaism, from the beginning of the Christian era to the present day, the method and the secret of Jesus have not altogether been obscured. Many a time in that long story the Jew may be regarded as

[1] R. Browning, *Holy Cross Day*.

appealing confidently to the Christ of Calvary in the words: "Thine too is the cause." [1]

[1] It has not been thought necessary in the above sketch to give more than a few references or to quote authorities. But for the sake of those desiring more detailed treatment of the subject of Hebrew religion the following books are recommended: George Adam Smith, *Book of the Twelve Prophets*, New York, 1898; J. Wellhausen, *Israelitische und jüdische Geschichte*, Berlin, 1901; Francis Brown, *Contemporary History of the Old Testament*, New York, 1905; A. B. Davidson, *Theology of the Old Testament*, New York, 1906; Henry P. Smith, *Old Testament History*, New York, 1906; W. Robertson Smith, *The O.T. in the Jewish Church*, London, 1908; same author, *The Religion of the Semites*, London, 1914; R. H. Charles, *Eschatology, Hebrew, Jewish and Christian*, London, 1913; J. P. Peters, *The Religion of the Hebrews*, London, 1914; Harlan Creelman, *An Introduction to the O.T.*, New York, 1917; George A. Barton, *The Religion of Israel*, New York, 1918; A. C. Knudson, *The Religious History of the Old Testament*; S. R. Driver, *Introduction to the Literature of O.T.*, Edinburgh, 1913; John A. Rice, *The O.T. in the Life of To-day*, New York, 1921.

## CHAPTER XXIX

### *Judaism from the Christian Era*

THIS is a difficult chapter for the professed Christian to write and probably a painful one for either Jew or Christian to read. Even to the Jewish Christians of the first century it was the essence of "the seven-sealed" book of mystery, a draught bitter to the taste, to know that the Day of Yahweh had passed unrecognized. That the blood of all the sacrifices was, as it were, like water spilled upon the ground, that the *Four Horsemen* had ridden ruthlessly over the Holy Land, that the Holy City, which had once shaken her head at the foe, was now to be a desolation—all these things seemed like a blasphemy reflecting on the fidelity of God to His ancient covenant. Even to Christian apostles the realization that the Old Dispensation was as a mother who must die to give birth to her child was hard to understand.

Nevertheless, though from the time of the destruction of Jerusalem Judaism was left to wander shrineless and homeless, a Judaism without priest or sacrifice, a *Judæa capta* (as the coin proclaims her), yet she went forth into the world to continue her mission, as she understood it, and not without witness to the things she had learned through the travail of her soul. Like Jesus, she "went forth bearing the cross." Like Jesus, "outside the camp" she became a spectacle to the nations, that she might discover her power in martyrdom and her redemption through pain.

It is not necessary to dwell upon those last terrible days at Jerusalem with which the seven years' struggle against Rome terminated. Gessius Florus, worst of all the Roman procurators, did much to hasten the inevitable rebellion and the end was rendered the more certain by the fierce faction fights within and without the city. Nero, determined to subjugate once for all the most obstinate of rebels against

Rome, sent Vespasian to take charge, and sufficient progress was made in the pacification of the land for Josephus, the historian, first of all a general on the side of the patriots and then a captive, to announce to the Roman leader the greatness which was soon to be his. With Vespasian become emperor, the siege was pressed and brought to a bloody end by Titus in A.D. 70. The Arch of Titus is the monument of as grim a tragedy as may be read in the story of mankind.

For a time, as in the days of Ezekiel, the hope of Israel lay stunned in the dust. But presently, with all other parties discredited and disillusioned, the Pharisees began, under Johanan, son of Zaccai, the constructive work which that aged leader soon turned over to Gamaliel II. The need was to find a substitute for the Temple cult and much was done at the Council of Jamnia, in A.D. 90, first to stabilize the Canon of the Scriptures and next to organize the synagogue worship in all the towns and villages of the land. The Sanhedrin, too, was reorganized without interference by the Roman authorities at Cæsarea.

Trouble, however, was not long quiescent. In 95 Gamaliel, who had meanwhile been deposed and reinstated, went to Rome with a delegation to protest against the edict forbidding proselytism. Then in 132 came the so-called Second War, in the time of Trajan, encouraged by the rising of the Parthians. In the lull following the suppression of this pains were taken to supersede the use of the Septuagint with a Greek version less favourable to the Christian claims, or, better still, to suppress the study of Greek entirely. With the accession of Hadrian came the Third War, due in part to revolt against the prohibition of circumcision, in part to the patriotism of the famous Rabbi Akiba, who fixed his hopes on Simon of Koziba as the expected Messiah. But the would-be Messiah, known to ecclesiastical writers as Bar Kokba, was defeated, Jerusalem was almost completely demolished and turned into a heathen city, Aelia Capitolina. From this time it was forbidden for a Jew to enter the city, though many came as near as they could get to weep over and lament her desolation.

Hadrian's purpose had been to make a clean sweep of

everything Jewish, including circumcision, the observance of the Sabbath, and the study of the Law. But the policy called forth such an outburst of willing martyrdom (in which the Rabbi Akiba was one of the victims) that the attempt proved abortive. Many fled to Babylonia and the school at Jabneh was closed. But better times came with the accession of Antoninus Pius, 138–161, who suspended the most intolerant of the laws. Under the new Patriarch, or Nasi, Simon, son of Gamaliel, great devotion was shown to the Torah, which a little before had been in such imminent danger. Scholars like Rabbi Meir and Judah I. took in hand the codification of the *Mishnah*, or sum of traditional lore. Altogether, in the period between Hillel and Rabbi Judah, no fewer than 148 scholars were esteemed worthy of special mention. These are known as the Tannaim, or teachers of the *Mishnah*. During the long-continued wars between the Sasanids of Persia and Rome the possession of Palestine was several times in dispute, but the victory of Carus left it finally in Roman hands. Meanwhile, the headquarters of Hebrew learning had been moved to Tiberias, where scholarship still flourished, but no longer under control of the Patriarchs. The new type of instruction was known as *Talmud*, or dialectical exposition, and the foundations of what is known as the *Palestinian Talmud* were laid by Rabbi Johanan, who taught at Sepphoris and Tiberias, and died about A.D. 279.

Then, at the beginning of the fourth century, came a great change which affected all religions in the Empire alike. Constantine the Great, won the battle of the Milvian Bridge in 312 and the next year issued his famous *Edict of Toleration*. By this edict Judaism became a *religio licita*. Nevertheless, as interpreted, it speedily began to involve discriminations and restrictions against which the Jews protested in vain. For a brief period during the reign of Julian the Apostate who, out of his hatred for Christianity, favoured the Jews, and even promised them the rebuilding of their Temple, there was once again a real tolerance. Nor had the Jews much to complain of during the reigns of Theodosius I. and Theodosius II. But on the death of Gamaliel VI., in 425, the last-named Emperor abolished the Patriarchate and from that date Judaism, with its headquarters in Palestine, ceased to be.

The new centre of Judaism was Babylonia, where Jews had continued to form an important part of the population since the deportation under Nebuchadrezzar in 597 B.C. At this time (fifth century) the Jewish population numbered several millions and their settlements were not only in towns and cities like Nisibis, Pumbedita and Sura, but also in adjacent farm lands. In these communities life went on as it had done in Palestine, except that the head was no longer a Patriarch but an Exilarch (*Resh Galutha*), with whom the Persian authorities treated whenever necessary. The greatest of the early exilarchs was Rab, that is, the Master *par excellence*, who founded the illustrious school at Sura which, with some vicissitudes, endured nearly eight hundred years. "He found an open plain and fenced it." After the death of Rab in A.D. 247 the succession was continued by Samuel, who earned a reputation as physician, judge and liturgist. The Parthian, or Arsacid, rule, which had succumbed to the revolution under Ardashir in 226, had been generally tolerant of Judaism, but the Sasanids, who displaced them, were so zealous for the orthodox Magian faith that once again the Jews found themselves oppressed. The two chief schools of Pumbedita and Sura had therefore many trials to surmount, yet there were always scholars such as Rabbah, Nahmani and Ashi to carry on the tradition of learning. The most distinguished of them was Ashi, of the Sura school, who laid the foundation of the *Babylonian Talmud*, a gigantic encyclopædic work which involved the labours of a thousand scholars (known as the Amoraim) extending over wellnigh three hundred years. Some additions were made to this by the successors of the Amoraim, the Saboraim, or Ponderers, and to these succeeded the Geonim, or "Excellencies," under whom still further improvements were made.[1] By this time another revolutionary change was imminent. For several centuries the Roman and the Sasanid empires had bled one another white in mutual conflict and now that the Arab

[1] See article by I. Elbogen in *E.R.E.*, VIII. 99 f.; also article "Talmud," *Jewish Encyclopædia*, XII. 1 ff.

had risen to the appeal of Islam, there was nothing in the path of a conquest—at once political and religious—which was to stagger the world.

Muhammad had learned much from the Jews of Arabia long before he announced himself as the Apostle of Allah. He had been much influenced by the Scriptures and it was the Jewish element at Yathrib (afterwards Madinah) which was largely responsible for the invitation which preceded the *Hijra*, or Flight, from Mecca. But, once launched on his conquering career, the prophet was not over mindful of earlier engagements and, though the Jews remained always "a people of the book," they soon came under the heavy hand of the Prophet, who declared that two religions could not co-exist in the land. After Muhammad's death, in 632, efforts were made to expel the Jews from Arabia altogether, but this policy became impracticable as soon as Palestine and Egypt, not to speak of regions further to the west, yielded to Islam. Then a policy of accommodation became necessary and the Jews began to settle down under the rule of the Khalifs as they had done under other foreign rulers from the time of the Babylonian. The exilarchs once again resumed their oversight of the Euphrates Valley communities, the schools reopened and continued much of their literary activity, the results of which were felt westward as far as the settlements in Spain.

Not that the period of the Umayyad Khalifs, A.D. 661–753, and of the early Abbasids was without its troubles. Moved possibly by the Shiite expectation of "the hidden Imam," several would-be Messiahs sought to arouse the people and were put down by the Muhammadans with much bloodshed. Then arose trouble over the election of the exilarchs, and out of this schism—started by Anan and carried on by Benjamin of Nahawand—known as the "Scripturist," or Karaite, movement. Then, again, at the beginning of the tenth century, we have a Gaon of Sura, Saadiah, who was not only one of the greatest scholars of Judaism but also a born controversialist. At this time Palestinian Judaism had once again reared its head. The schools of Ramleh and Tiberias were once again active, the vowel system had been invented for the convenience of students of the Hebrew script, and a movement had been started to improve the Calendar from which the dates of the festivals were computed. It was this last which raised the fierce wrath of Saadiah, who kept the controversy unsleeping for seven years. It was not till 937 that the leaders were reconciled. But Saadiah deserved better to be known for his vast scholarship, his *Book of Creation*, his translation of the Scriptures into Arabic, his poems and, not least, for his *Grammar of the Hebrew Language*.

But the end of the great Babylonian schools was at hand. The school of Sura expired about the middle of the eleventh century and the Pumbedita, or Bagdad, school soon followed it to an honoured grave. For, though from this time the centre of gravity for Judaism passed from Babylonia to the West, the influence of the East was not dead. "In the halls of learning of Northern Africa and Europe reverberated the discussions of Rab and Samuel, of Rabbah and Joseph, of Abaye and Raba. The Geonim of Sura and Pumbedita had blazed the path and given direction to Jewish life for centuries to come." [1]

In some parts of Western Europe Jews had found a dwelling-place from the beginning of the Christian era and even earlier. Juvenal's reference to the Jew at the gates of Rome with his big basket (*kophinos*) and his wisp of straw is well known. In spite of occasional expulsions, as in the time of Claudius, and laws which became ever severer to the time of Justinian's *Code*, the Hebrew population continued to grow. The development of the Papacy did not at first have any effect on Jewish life in the Western Empire. Popes like Gregory the Great were tolerant, except in the matter of refusing Jews the ownership of Christian slaves. But, with the decline of Palestinian and Babylonian Judaism, the leaders of Israel began a westward movement which had the result of extending the faith in that direction and in a development of the communal spirit.

This extension presently embraced Spain, where the Jews were destined to "sit on thrones." Many had been in the Peninsula since A.D. 300, and under the Arian rulers

[1] Margolis and Marx, *A History of the Jewish People*, p. 276, Philadelphia, 1917.

of Spain had lived in amity. With the reascendency of Catholicism at the beginning of the seventh century, came a change for the worse. With occasional relaxation, the rule became one of severe restriction, especially when the Metropolitan Julian, himself the son of Jewish parents, came into power in 681. Judaism was now harried into discord and discontent, and only too ready to welcome the victory of Islam which came with the invasion of Tarik in 711.

Under the rule of the Muhammadans, and especially under that of the Western Umayyads, the Spanish Jews at once rose to positions of influence and power. Indeed, from the tenth to the thirteenth century they prospered exceedingly. Hasdai ibn Shaprut, prime minister under two khalifs, is representative of the Jew as the "middleman" of Oriental and Western learning. Poetry, in particular, with Hebrew verse accommodated to Arabic metres, now rose into eminence. Of the Jewish exponents of the "new poetry" it was said: "In the days of Hasdai they began to chirp."

Political conditions, however, did not continue stable. The Western Umayyads gave place to the Almoravides in 1085 and these to the Almohades in 1148. Toledo fell again to the Christians in 1085 and as time went on the Christian kingdoms in the north increased in number and in power. But through all vicissitudes Jews continued to prosper. Samuel-ha-Levi, known as Nagid, or Prince, became vizier, making a name for himself also as poet. Ibn Gabirol, known to the West as Avicebron, "the nightingale of piety," wrote the ever-beautiful *Royal Crown*.[1] Judah ha Levi, the singer "pure and faultlessly true," flourished, contemporary with Abraham Ibn Ezra, the master of Hebrew prose.

Then came evil times, and while some remained in Spain to pay lip service to Islam, others fled. One of the fugitives, in this case to Egypt, was Maimun, whose son, generally known as Maimonides, rose to become the greatest spiritual authority in Judaism of the age. He wrote three great

[1] See *Selected Religious Poems of Solomon Ibn Gabirol,* translated by Israel Zangwill. Philadelphia, 1923.

books, *The Sayings of the Fathers*, *The Second Torah*, and *A Guide to the Perplexed*. In the first of these he restates authoritatively the Creed of the Jew in thirteen articles. In these he proclaims the existence of God, His unity, incorporeality, immutability, eternity, pre-mundane existence, His worshipfulness, the inspiration of the prophets, the authority of Moses, the divine origin of the Torah, the doctrine of future retribution, the future advent of the Messiah, and the resurrection of the dead. When Maimonides died in 1204 the lament of an older generation was recalled: "The glory is departed from Israel; for the ark of God is taken," and men said: "From Moses to Moses there was none like Moses."

Judaism was now moving north. In France the Merovingians had imposed a number of vexatious regulations, but under the Carlovingians there was tolerance. Charlemagne even included a Jew in the embassage he sent to Harun al Rashid.[1, 2] Nevertheless, for various reasons, economic and religious, antagonism continued to develop. The Jews were blamed for the evils of the slave-trade; under the feudal system they could not own land, hence they were driven to commerce, and in this proved rather more successful than their competitors. Moreover, animosity was excited by certain cases of conversion to Judaism, and it was by no means appeased when permission was given to Christians, as at Bezieres, to throw staves at Jews in Holy Week, or, as at Toulouse, to smite the cheek of the Syndic on Good Friday. The Emperor Henry II. ordered the expulsion of all Jews from Mayence in 1012, and the forced baptisms which this act entailed did not make for sincerity or for peace.

Here and there was preserved some little oasis of quietness where some scholar like Rashi—born at Troyes in 1040—could pursue a great task, such as the writing of the commentary on the Scriptures and the Babylonian Talmud. But in general it was a bad time for Jews, especially when the end of the eleventh century brought about the First Crusade and undisciplined hordes of soldiery

[1] See article "Moses ben Maimon," *Jewish Ency.*, IX. 73 ff.
[2] Obviously because he was acquainted with the Arabic language.

were only too ready to include Jews with Saracens among the enemies of the Holy Sepulchre. Massacres, stormings of synagogues, assaults, wholesale suicides, forced baptisms —all these are elements in one of the ugliest chapters of religious history. Moreover, kings and barons were not slow to perceive a means of financing their campaigns in the Jews whose commercial genius had so obviously prospered, even though they showed no intention of returning the sums they borrowed.

What is true of the First Crusade applies equally to the Second and Third, with the addition that this time superstition and ignorance reared their heads together and raised the cry of ritual murder and of Christian blood mingled with the Passover bread. Hence savage reprisals on the part of the populace, heavy-handed injustice on the part of kings like Philip Augustus of France, and merciless severity on the part of Pope Innocent III. at the beginning of the thirteenth century. Yet amid all this carnival of crime individual scholars and mystics continued to brood, to write, and even to sing.

The thirteenth century carried on the tragic story, except for the influence of one remarkable man. This was the Emperor Frederick II. who, in Sicily and Provence, encouraged Arabic and Hebrew scholarship and was for his liberality adjudged a heretic. Elsewhere society was uniformly against the Jew, now compelled to wear a yellow badge of shame in order to distinguish him from his fellows and thereby invite insult and outrage. There was also a deliberate effort made by Pope Gregory IX. to destroy all Hebrew literature, and on one Sabbath eve, in or about 1242, twenty-four cartloads of books (which we would give much to-day to possess) were consigned to the flames at Paris. Even the general terror of the Mongol invasion, which conjured up all sorts of Messianic dreams, did not help matters, for many thought that the Jews were in league with the invaders, even if the Mongols themselves were not the "Lost Ten Tribes" reappearing for the devastation of Europe.

So far nothing has been said of Judaism in England, whither certain Jews came with William the Conqueror.

In spite of sporadic accusations of ritual murder, the Jews of England were in general protected by the kings, especially since as money-lenders they filled " a gap in the economic life " of the country. But the natural prejudices of debtors brought about an intense hatred for the lenders, a hatred which culminated in massacres such as that which marked the coronation of King Richard I. at Westminster, and the still more terrible massacre at York in March 1190. As a result of such incidents, English Jewry began of its own will to withdraw to the continent or to the Holy Land, even before the general expulsion proclaimed on July 18, 1290. As a result of this—the first general expulsion of Jews—about 16,000 men, women and children left for France and Flanders.

It was not long before France, too, adopted the policy of expulsion, first in 1306, when 100,000 Jews were turned adrift with little but the clothes upon their backs, secondly, after a brief period of recall, in 1394. It is interesting to note that during these periods, specially in Provence, which was outside the French jurisdiction, a great controversy was being waged between Maimunians and anti-Maimunians, that is, between liberals and orthodox. In this controversy the famous scholar, David Kimhi, played a memorable part.

It has been stated that, if Judaism had suffered eclipse in France, its sorrows were destined elsewhere to be all the more increased. In Germany where, as the serfs of the exchequer, the Jews could not well be expelled, they suffered terribly from the ignorance and superstition of the populace. Charges, such as could only be the spawn of the basest impulses of humanity, maddened the ignorant to outrages of the most heartrending kind. As a single instance we may take the case of Röttingen in 1298, where the whole Jewish community was burned at the stake. The Black Death only came to increase the anti-Jewish feeling, since the rumour prevailed that the Jews had poisoned the wells. Bands of fanatics roamed the land, recommending the killing of Jews as an act of piety, and though popes and emperors intervened when and where they could—the latter out of self-interest—little was done to cure the evil at its source.

Returning to Spain we find that the gradual reconquest of the Peninsula for Christianity boded in general no good to the Jew. In some of the Christian states there was tolerance and here and there scholars began to open schools and cultivate "the Jewish knowledge," with which was mingled a considerable element of neo-Platonism. At Gerona, Moses, son of Nahman (Nahmani), was a shining light, only, however, to be driven to an exile in the Holy Land when the Inquisition commenced operations in Aragon. Other scholars continued at work and the *Kabbala*[1] began to take shape. The controversy between Maimunists and anti-Maimunists also revived. Ibn Adret, the mystic, made a fantastic visit to Rome to convert Pope Nicholas III. to Judaism. Asher, son of Jehiel, established a school in Toledo. Under Ferdinand IV. and Alphonso XI. and, strangely enough, under Pedro the Cruel, there were even those who forecasted an era of religious peace.

From the time of Pedro, however, the wind of favour rapidly shifted to the opposite quarter. Bloody massacres throughout the Peninsula, involving not merely the professing Jews but the crypto-Jews who had accepted forced baptism and were known as Maranos, or *Accursed*, were frequent, and even the reading of the Talmud was prohibited. The persecution culminated, in 1483, in the setting up of the Inquisition under the infamous Torquemada. All these measures, moreover, after the surrender of the last Muhammadan stronghold of Granada, must be regarded as merely preparatory to the final expulsion of the Jews, by the edict of Their Most Catholic Majesties, Ferdinand and Isabella, on March 30, 1492. The result was untold suffering on the part of many thousands of fugitives, insincere conversion to Christianity of thousands more, and the flight of still more to the Ottoman Empire, where Sultan Bayazid II. gave them hearty welcome.

Though expelled from England, France and Spain, Judaism still found a dubious shelter in Italy, as might be suggested by the friendship of Dante with Immanuel of Rome. As the Renaissance dawned upon Western Europe, hope for the Jew increased, at any rate out of appreciation

[1] See article "Cabala," *Jewish Ency.*, III. 456 ff.

for his cultural life. Humanists like Pico della Mirandola found value as well as interest in the *Kabbala*. Later the same spirit penetrated Germany and Christian scholars like Reuchlin urged the study of Hebrew as well as tolerance for Hebrews. The invention of printing, too, came to make possible the printing of the Hebrew Bible and that of the Babylonian and Palestinian Talmud. For a time it seemed that the Reformation leaders might even become the champions of the Old Testament people, even as they made themselves responsible for the revival of Old Testament study. Unfortunately the expectation proved ill-founded, for even Luther, who in his early years had pleaded for tolerance, became rabidly anti-Jewish towards the end of his career.

Jews were now wanderers over the face of the earth, though in Italy, and not least in the Papal States, they found a welcome domicile, and were able to establish settlements in places like Amsterdam and Hamburg. Out of the former community arose that remarkable and "god-intoxicated" mystic, Baruch Spinoza, who, however, was not fortunate enough to square his pantheistic theories with Hebrew orthodoxy and was in consequence, in 1656, excommunicated. About the same time Oliver Cromwell, in England, out of self-interest, discovered that there was no legal barrier against the residence of Jews in England and thereupon sanctioned their return.

In the Ottoman Empire, meanwhile, Judaism was not only tolerated but flourishing. In Constantinople, the largest settlement, there were 30,000 Jews, while in Saloniki, the next largest colony, Jews outnumbered the rest of the population. Under such circumstances, Jews once again rose to power and eminence. Joseph Nasi became Duke of Naxos, under Selim II.; Solomon Ashkenazi became the same monarch's trusted ambassador to Poland and Venice. Also scholars like Joseph Karo and Isaac Luria conferred lustre on their age as well as on their race.

From the beginning of the Christian era there had been a continuous stream of Jews flowing into the territories now composing Poland, Lithuania and Russia. In the eighth century the conversion took place of an entire tribe on the Euro-Asiatic frontier known as the Khazars,[1] and from this community there went forth a deputation at the beginning of the eleventh century to urge the acceptance of Judaism by the Russian prince Vladimir. The prince, however, was not impressed by the appeal of a homeless race. In all these regions the Hebrew population increased rapidly, so that in Poland and Lithuania alone the Jews, who had numbered but 50,000 at the beginning of the sixteenth century, a century later numbered half a million. The zenith of prosperity was here reached during the first half of the seventeenth century, but Jews were not so fortunate in the Ukraine, where, after several hideous massacres, they were expelled and did not have the right to return restored till 1651. During the decade from 1648 to 1658 it has been estimated that at least 100,000 Jews were slaughtered.

It was about this time that a remarkable Messianic movement was inaugurated by a Smyrna Jew, Sabbatai Zevi, who in 1648 proclaimed the Ineffable Name, announced his mystic wedlock to the Torah, visited Jerusalem as Messiah, preached to frenzied multitudes, drew converts from every part of Europe, aroused the hopes of all Jewry and of many Christians, so that men wagered as to the time his coronation would take place in Jerusalem, and was after all this persuaded by Muhammad IV. to turn Moslem. As Mehemet Effendi, he died in 1676, but his followers were slow to abandon their expectancy. Similar impostures or illusions continued to appear for the rest of the century.

A movement of a different kind was that of the Hasidim, or Pietists, which arose partly out of the spirit of depression engendered by continued persecution, and partly out of a reaction against merely intellectual interest in religion. The leader of the movement was Israel Baal Shem Tob, 1700–1760, better known, from his initials, as Besht. He was a mystic and solitary of deep personal holiness but, on account of their apparent disparagement of learning, the

[1] The Khazar dynasty was converted in A.D. 740, the people following their rulers or not, as they pleased. See article "Khazars," *Ency. Brit.* (11th Edition), XV. 774 ff.

Hasidim were bitterly opposed and in some cases expelled from the synagogues.

Though the cup of suffering was as yet by no means fully drained, the dawn of better things for the Jew was not so far away as at the time seemed probable. The first signs of this dawn were discernible in Prussia, where the principles of the *Aufklârung* disposed men to liberalism, where "protected" Jews, like Moses Mendelsohn, were in themselves an augury of better things, where Lessing's *Nathan*, *der Weise*, was a notable tract in the interest of tolerance, and where Joseph II. marked a great advance from early days by the issuing of his *Patent of Tolerance* in 1782. The programme of "civic emancipation and fidelity to Judaism" was now clear to many besides Moses Mendelsohn.

The story of Jewish emancipation must be briefly summarized, with the omission of much that is important as well as interesting. We have said nothing of the story of the Jews in China (at Kai-fêng-fu), or in India, or in Africa; we have omitted all mention of the struggle between Reform Jews and Orthodox Jews; we have said nothing of the revival of learning in the nineteenth century.

What cannot be omitted is some reference to the great movement for emancipation which the conscience of mankind has backed during the past century and a half, the recognition of the equality of all religions under the American Constitution, the proclamation of that same equality in the French Revolution by the *Declaration of the Rights of Man*, the removal of all disabilities under which Jews had suffered in England for centuries, and by the free use of Jewish talent in the political history of Europe during the past two or three generations.

All this is the sign of a developing Christian conscience among the nations of the world. But the task of building up the practice of men to the level of their best ideals is but slowly being achieved. The nineteenth and twentieth centuries are by no means free from some of the blots which disfigure the story of the Middle Ages. We have to remember pogroms in Russia such as that of Kishinev in

1903; we cannot yet forget the Dreyfus case which for six long years drags its trail across the history of France; nor can we ignore the publication since the war of *The Jewish Peril* and *Protocols of the Elders of Zion*, as recently as 1920, or the rise of the Ku Klux Klan in the United States.[1] On the other hand, it is satisfactory to recall that other movements, less widely exploited, are in being for the inculcation of a kindlier spirit and for the removal of the traditional misunderstandings.

One movement stands by itself and cannot be ignored even in so brief a sketch as the present. This is Zionism, which has its roots both in the soil of economics and in that of religious idealism. No Jew for economic reasons alone would select Palestine as a national home, but in the soul of the Jew is an ancient *Heimweh* which has become a passion. There is also the conviction of many that " das ganz Land braucht Israel." Even movements as far back as those of David Reuben and Sabbatai Zevi witness to this. The Mendelsohnian movement of the eighteenth century diverted the hope into other channels, but the nineteenth century saw a renascence of the old longing for the Promised Land. In the mid-nineteenth century Sir Moses Montefiore, and towards the end Herzl and Pinsker, founded modern Zionism and no suggestion of settlement in East Africa for long superseded the desire to make Palestine the national home of Jewry. Then came the Great War and the *Balfour Declaration*, and following upon these the problems which it was hardly possible for statesmen to foresee. Much has been done to give Zionism " a local habitation " as well as a name. Jews have been planted on the soil and capital expended in making that soil productive. But the guarding of the rights of the non-Jewish part of the population and, indeed, the making of Palestine capable of supporting more than a very limited population, bristle with difficulties. Still the presence of 150,000 Jews in the Holy Land, the restored use of the Hebrew language, and the opening of the new Hebrew University on Mt. Scopus in 1925, are eloquent symbols of the new hope of Israel. Moreover, the Holy

[1] The year 1933 saw a recrudescence of anti-Semitism and the burning of Jewish books in Germany, under the rule of Chancellor Hitler.

Land itself, and its capital Jerusalem, are (as to the Christian world) but the outward symbol of that ideal fellowship of redeemed men, the city to which the tribes of men go up to appear before God, the cynosure of all faithful eyes, before us and not behind us. Through it, indeed, we see coming down out of heaven, " the Jerusalem which is above, the mother of us all."

The pilgrimage of Judaism towards this desired and desirable goal is not yet complete. It is still—and must be still—a *via dolorosa*, a way of pain. But in the pain itself is at work the victorious principle of sacrificial love, which the Jew could not reject even though he would. He has borne the cross for much of the way unflinchingly and found it to be his source of strength. As Miss Lazarus puts it:

> Daylong I brooded upon the Passion of Israel.
> I saw him bound to the wheel, nailed to the cross, cut off by the sword, burned at the stake, tossed into the seas.
> And always the same patient, resolute martyr face arose in silent rebuke and defiance.
> A Prophet with four eyes; wide gazed the orbs of the spirit above the sleeping eyelids of the senses.
> A Poet, who plucked from his bosom the quivering heart and fashioned it into a lyre.
> A placid-browed Sage, uplifted from earth in celestial meditation.
> These I saw, with prince and people in their train; the monumental dead and the standard-bearers of the future.
> And suddenly I heard a burst of mocking laughter; and, turning, I beheld the shuffling gait, the ignominious features, the sordid mask of the son of the Ghetto.
> Turn again, O daughter of Israel, my sister, and behold, with divinely awakened eyes the son of man, the man of sorrows and acquainted with grief.
> " Inasmuch as ye have done it unto one of the least of these my brethren, ye have done it unto Me." Who has ever spoken words so tender and close, so fulfilled of the brotherhood of man? " And I, if I be lifted up, will draw all men unto Me."
> Be ye then uplifted, ye who would uplift. You who come in His name and yet deny Him, with Christ on your lips but with hatred and scorn in your hearts, behold the suffering child of God, your brother; behold our divine humanity crushed beneath the burden of the flesh, the sins and sorrows of the world!
> Ye, who would bear witness to His spirit and His truth, to the Christ that is within you, look with the eyes of Christ, the heart of Christ;

pierce with illuminated vision the hollow mask; let the warm rays, the gentle touch of love, fall upon the dull clod of clay and awake the sleeping soul, the higher, the divine self, that slumbers in every child of earth, every one of God's creatures—the Christ that is to be, when all men know themselves as He knew, one with the Father and one with His fellow-men.[1, 2]

---

[1] Emma Lazarus, *Poems*.

[2] For the period of Jewish history covered in this chapter the reader is referred to the later volumes of H. Graetz, *History of the Jews from the Earliest Times to the Present Day*; Margolis and Marx, *A History of the Jewish People*, and the bibliography given as an " Appendix " to the last-named work.

## SECTION II

## CHRISTIANITY TO THE RISE OF ISLAM

# CHAPTER XXX

## *The Founder*

FROM the Christian point of view the last chapter must necessarily seem something of a digression, the continuance of an experience outside the direct line of religious evolution. If, according to the Christian view, all Jewish hope is " chaptered up " in Christ, it is inevitable that the story of Christ must be the apical point to which all previous religion converges and from which the religion of the future is to broaden out towards the fulfilment of the divine purpose. The first triangle, from the first stirrings of the religious instinct in the consciousness of man to the period represented by the Christian phrase " the fulness of time," has now been roughly covered. We have seen in primitive religion the yearnings—often expressed crudely, savagely, even obscenely—for the things upon which the heart's desire of the ancient world was set. We have seen, too, the religion of the Jew restated, refined, reinterpreted. We have seen, once again, the stream of Jewish witness reinforced by tributary waters which flowed into it from the religions of those nations which lived in contact with the Jew. We have seen it further enlarged out of emotions and experiences expressed in the faiths of lands at first remote. Now we have to take our stand at the point where Judaism, as the elect priest of humanity, is privileged to make the sacrifice of itself to the long-expected Messianic age, in order that the world's desire might be fulfilled.

As we face the story of nearly twenty centuries of Christian history it is easy to perceive the difficulty of approaching it objectively. In the middle of the eighteenth century, while a great scholar of the English Church was declining the Archbishopric of Canterbury because he thought it too " late to save a falling Church," another great English churchman was inaugurating the evangelistic movement which probably saved industrial England from rejecting religion altogether and became eventually a following of twenty-eight million souls—apart from all indirect results. Similar differences of temperament to-day will view Christian history from opposite points of view. Probably in America and Western Europe to-day there is not the open hostility to religion that existed in the eighteenth century. An occasional book appears like *The Twilight of Christianity*, in which the author is assured of the speedy demise of the religion and its ripeness for burial out of sight of men. But for one book of this type there are a dozen in which the history of the Christian Church is written so objectively as to miss altogether any element such as we may call divine. Of this sort of history three general criticisms seem to be invited. First, they are written in the popular style which is reminiscent of the journalism in which startling headlines and a " story " are of the first importance, with a murder as more significant than a million quiet and kindly acts, and a social scandal outweighing any number of lives lived in purity and piety. Secondly, they are written from the point of view which regards the entire field of history from start to finish spread before the author, so that he may neatly arrange his periods from the story of beginnings to the story of the halcyon days, thence to the breakdown, and then to the point where he stands sadly by the bedside of an invalid as to whose survival he is extremely sceptical. Anyone with a sense of humour, or who remembers the story of the *Ugly Duckling*, will perceive at once that, proportionately to the whole tale of man's development on earth, the two thousand years of Christian history are but a beginning, and that those who judge religion to have run its course because of present-day lapses and inadequacies might just as well take two thousand years out of the period when the great saurians flourished to demonstrate that God was unable to get beyond the creation of a brute.

Thirdly, and chiefly, books of the sort I have in mind leave out of the story of the Christian Church the presence of Christ as its living Lord. They try to describe the garden, but they do not recognize the gardener. To them Christ is nothing but a figure dimly seen at the back of a long tradition, to most men but a rapidly fading memory, and to those who are still mindful of Him only the dead teacher of a few beautiful maxims, a lovely example of a course of action such as brought Him to the cross.

In the following chapters I trust it may be remembered, even when I tell the story as objectively as I can, that these three errors, for the Christian, are fatal to any right understanding of Christian history. First of all, the main currents of the history flow softly, like the waters of Siloah. Beyond all the excitement of councils and controversies, religious warfare and religious persecution, corruption and worldliness, which make up so sadly large a part of the outward history of the Church, must be kept in mind the story of unrecorded struggle against temptation, humble endeavour to walk close to God, and the million-fold performance of inconspicuous duty through the grace received. Secondly, it will be kept in mind that God, who takes a summer to make a rose, requires ages to shape the spiritual plan through which by and by the animal inheritance of the race may be overpassed and man raise the cry: "Hallelujah to the Maker: Hallelujah, Man is made!" And, thirdly, it should be evident that Christianity is saved from failure, not by any *Back to Jesus* movement, but by realization of His promise: "Lo I am with you all the days, even to the end of the world."

In all religions, as we have seen, personality plays a great part, in fertilizing the age, stimulating the attention of men, and inspiring men to rise above their natural level. In Christianity this is true beyond any other case we may recall. While in other religions the teacher is subordinated to his teaching, we find in Christianity a religion not of a philosophy, or of a rule of life, but that of a Living Person actively engaged in distributing what we call grace. We do not go back to Christ as the Confucianist goes back to Confucius, or the Muhammadan to Muhammad, but we find Christ when we remember that " where two or three are gathered together in My name, there am I in the midst of them."

Hence, before attempting to offer any survey of the history of the system prepared for us as the means for securing this relation, it is necessary to ask, What do we know of this Person as an historical figure, before we accept the transcendent claims made for Him by the Christian Church?

Perhaps we are baffled at the outset by the very embarrassment of our wealth. Lives of Christ have appeared, particularly of late, with a profusion which is a curious comment on the assertion of a Professor of History at Columbia University that " all we have " upon which to rely for our knowledge of Jesus Christ " is the material for a three-line obituary." If this be so, the declaration of Dr. Robert Millikan that " when the life and teachings of Jesus became the basis of the religion of the whole Western world, an event of stupendous importance for the destinies of mankind had certainly taken place, for a new set of ideals had been definitely and officially adopted " would seem strangely baseless.

No doubt a great many theories have been presented to account for Jesus, an indication in itself of the imperious claim He makes upon human judgement. Some of these theories we can sift away from the others, as no longer having a right to stand in the light of sane and responsible scholarship. We may deal thus with the theory of Christ as myth, only now to be regarded as an eccentricity of hypothesis. We may also put aside definitely the theory of imposture, even when critics stumble over the self-consciousness and apparent " egoism " of Jesus in the setting forth of His claims. We may discard once for all the theory that Jesus was an impressionable visionary moved by the preaching of John the Baptist to imagine Himself the Messiah and so start the series of events which led to His condemnation and execution. If there are any conclusions to which all the evidence leads, these are, first, that Christ, so far from being " conformed " to the type of Messianism which was in the air, opposed it from beginning to end, choosing not to be Messiah by miraculous bread-making, or spectacular wonder-working, or to receive the world power as a gift from the Satanism of the time, but rather to win the kingdom slowly by the painful travail of the Cross. And, again, that from the very beginning He was conscious of the fate to which such a conception of Messiahship must bring Him, moving grandly on, and " measuring with calm presage the infinite descent."

With these theories discarded, what have we left? To my own mind none of the books which are most calculated to work serious mischief is an exposition of the theories mentioned above. They are rather those which exploit the subjective treatment of the Life and come from writers who, having discarded the Gospels as evidence, proceed to evolve a conception of Jesus out of their inner consciousness. Even here there are two things not wholly bad. For, in the first place, every man who handles with sincerity the subject finds in his own imagination something of the truth and at least touches the hem of the divine garment. And, secondly, in this sort of writing, criticism cancels criticism, so that he who accepts what any one writer admits will have the whole, while he who rejects what any one rejects will lose all.

The matter then settles down to be primarily a matter of sources, out of which we should be able to gather what the historical Jesus was like. This subject is simplified for us by the work of unbiased scholars outside the Christian fold, of whom we may take as a type the learned Rabbi Joseph Klausner of Jerusalem, whose *Jesus of Nazareth* [1] opens with a discussion of the sources. What a Jew of the highest scholarship regards as certain will not be suspected of Christian bias.

Dr. Klausner begins by setting forth the Jewish evidence available, all the more important because so commonly overlooked. He rehabilitates Josephus for Christian use, holding the historian to be only in certain phrases interpolated, to be saying just about as much as one given to hedging could be expected to say, and in what he does say proving as facts the preaching of John the Baptist, the

[1] Rabbi Joseph Klausner, *Jesus of Nazareth*, New York, 1929.

teaching and wonder-working of Jesus, and the suffering by Him of a cruel death under Pontius Pilate, with the connivance of the principal Jews. As to the *Talmud*, while the Rabbi points out that if we depended upon the *Talmud* for our information we should never have known of the existence of Judas Maccabæus, he shows that the Gospel stories were clearly known to the Talmudic authors, as is proved by the distortion of them rather than by silence or denial, and that under the name of *Balaam* (the destroyer) Jesus is several times alluded to, while the chief apostles are concealed under the names of *Doeg*, *Ahithophel* and *Gehazi*. Dr. Klausner also quotes the suggestion that the slanderous tale about Jesus as the illegitimate son of Mary by a man named Panthera is an echo of the description of Him as "Son of the Virgin" (*Parthenou*).[1] In the next place, the Rabbi deals with the Latin sources, scanty indeed, and ill informed, but no more so than we might expect from the superciliousness of Roman officials in regard to a *religio illicita*. Nevertheless, we learn from Tacitus that "Christ, from whom the Christians derive their name, was condemned to death in the reign of Tiberius by the Procurator, Pontius Pilate."[2] From Suetonius we learn that Claudius "banished from Rome the Jews who made great tumult because of Chrestus,"[3] thus confirming the statement of the Acts (xviii. 2) that ten years after the crucifixion Christianity was, at least, not unknown in the Imperial City. And from Pliny the Younger we learn that the Christians of Bithynia in Asia Minor, at the beginning of the second century, were already accustomed to sing "some sacred hymn in which they appeal to Christ as God."[4]

In the next place we have discussed the Scriptures of the New Testament. Now, of course, though no entire MSS. of these writings have survived from earlier than the fourth century, yet we could almost reconstruct the books from quotations made by earlier writers who use them as of authority, back indeed to the time of Clement of Rome.

[1] See also Rabbi Hyamson, *Jewish Quarterly Review*, October 1931.
[2] Tacitus, *Annales*, xv. 44—written about A.D. 115.
[3] Suetonius, *Claudius*, 25.
[4] Pliny the Younger, *Ep.*, x. 96–97.

Moreover, back of all the quotations thus made is the evidence of their use in the Christian communities. All of this Dr. Klausner candidly admits, speaking of the New Testament writings as "documents dated from the earliest days of Christianity." The Pauline Epistles, or at least the majority of them, he holds were written within a few years of Christ's ministry, and, of the Gospels, three were written prior to, or contemporaneous with, the Fall of Jerusalem, St. Mark between 66 and 68, St. Matthew about 70, and St. Luke not greatly later.[1]

Once again, apart from New Testament quotations, we have in writings of the sub-apostolic period much that belongs to the authentic tradition concerning Jesus. Dr. Klausner adduces in this category Polycarp, Ignatius, Clement of Rome, Papias and Justin Martyr, as well as the uncanonical writings of the first two Christian centuries. To all this (going beyond the Rabbi) we may add that we have in the Church, its creeds, its ministry, and its sacraments, avowedly recalling the teaching and commandments given by Christ Himself and founded on these as on a rock. The main facts of the Divine Life would still be validated by these, even had the New Testament books never been written.

Out of all this material only perversity can fail to reconstruct the picture that Browning gives:

> That one Face, far from vanish, rather grows,
> Or decomposes but to recompose,
> Becomes my universe that feels and knows.

Of course, men will continue to see that face through the coloured spectacles of their own personality. The Jesus who to the little child is "meek and gentle," or to the martyr "the Son of God" who "goes forth to war," or to the proud English queen "the man who hung 'twixt heaven and earth six mortal hours" and "spat out the anodyne and would not drink," will inevitably appeal to each in a different way. But to those who take the documents available as they are, and use them sincerely, He can at least never be myth, or impostor, or visionary, or weakling.

[1] Rabbi Enelow, in his still more recent book, *A Jewish View of Jesus*, even accepts, for certain incidents, the authority of St. John's Gospel.

Let us then, using these sources thus approved to us, see first of all what impression He made upon His own environment. That the people were in expectation of the coming of Messiah we have every proof, both from the canonical and apocalyptic literature of the time. The elect remnant of Israel, saints like Simeon and Anna, waited day and night in the temple courts. As the priests from the Temple platform watched for the first glint of the rising sun so that the silver trumpets might give the signal for the morning sacrifice, so, even beyond the confines of the Holy Land, an expectant humanity waited " upon the world's great altar-stairs " for the promised Redeemer. And when, heralded by the Baptist's cry, which in anticipation of the kingdom summoned the people to repentance, Jesus appeared " preaching the Gospel of the kingdom," what did the people see in Him?

First, unclouded by any variations of the Gospel records, we feel the impression He made as the unique Teacher who gathered up in exquisite parables all the wisdom of the sages in the closing period of Old Testament literature, and there so falteringly expressed. We see also the compassionate Healer, shrinking from the reputation of a wonder-worker, yet calling forth by His marvellous personality long-submerged powers in the weakened wills of those who came to Him for succour, reaching down into hitherto unfathomed depths to soothe bodily pain and restore peace to jangled nerves. Once again, we recognize the Prophet of the new era, proclaiming the approaching close of "*ha-'olam hazzeh*" (*the present age*) and the imminence of "*ha-'olam habbo'*" (*the coming age*)[1] which prophets and apocalyptists had predicted. He is seen, moreover, as the interpreter, in immortal words, of the difference between the passing era and the one about to dawn. He gives to men the new, positive and spiritual Law which is to supersede all outworn codes. Not with the Old Testament formula " Thus saith the Lord," but with His own authoritative " I say unto you," uttered without arrogance or conceit, He sets forth the spiritual principle behind the legal precept. That the people hailed Him as Messiah, Dr. Klausner,

[1] Phrases unfortunately rendered in A.V. as " this world," " the world to come."

speaking as a Jew, has no doubt. The term "Son of Man," used so commonly as a designation of Himself, made clear at the first, even as the declaration to the apostles and the oath taken at the High Priest's adjuration made plain at the last, that Jesus accepted the popular recognition, though He rejected the popular ideal.[1]

So much it was possible for the crowd to gather as to what Jesus was and what He claimed. But to the intimate friends whom He had gathered around Him and who companioned with Him daily He was infinitely more. It is said that no man is a hero to his *valet de chambre*, but the more the apostles knew of Jesus the more they stood in awe before the mystery of His being and His mission. First, they gained very distinct convictions concerning His Person. To Christ's question concerning Himself Peter replied: "Thou art the Christ, the Son of the Living God"; the doubts of Thomas vanished with the cry: "My Lord and my God!"; John, many years after, declared: "We beheld His glory, the glory of the only begotten of the Father, full of grace and truth"; and Paul, growing in knowledge as in zeal, with experience, could describe Him in no other terms than as "the fullness of Him that filleth all in all."

In the second place, they came step by step to appreciate the value of the method by which Jesus would overcome the world and open the kingdom of heaven to all believers. It was the method of the Cross, a method so startling and so incredible even (to those who saw power only in force), that for long generations to come that Cross was to be to the Jews a stumbling-block and to the Greeks foolishness. Yet with full confidence in it as the symbol of a sacrificial love stronger than anything the world had ever seen, Jesus went on unfaltering towards His goal.

Once again, the apostles lived to see and to proclaim the victory of that Cross which had at first seemed but the badge of shame. It was borne triumphantly through the grave and gate of death and in the Risen Christ they perceived that the method which at first only the robber crucified with Jesus recognized as valid was henceforth

[1] Of course the term "Son of Man" has been variously explained, but its general Messianic significance can hardly be questioned.

crowned with glory. "Of the reality of this conviction," writes Mr. J. Middleton Murry, "of the reality of the experience that created this conviction, we cannot doubt. The great Christian Church was not built on a lie, but on a truth. Nor can we doubt that the experience of Peter, like the later experience of Paul, was the experience of an objective presence. Peter was not the victim of an hallucination, nor Paul the dupe of an illusion. That our intellects cannot conceive the nature of an objective presence which is not physical, or that of 'a spiritual being' remains for our minds a contradiction in terms, is only evidence that our minds are still inadequate to reality."[1]

The proclamation of this victory of the Cross was not only the declaration that the life and character of Jesus stood secure from the corroding effects of time and the decay of death, but also the announcement of a new law for human life and a new revelation of the character of God. That God was all-powerful, all-wise and even all-loving was no news to the religious world, but that He was eternally pouring out His life "like the rush of a river" for the redemption of His creatures was something hitherto unrealized. Thus the supreme "epiphany," or manifestation, of God by Christ was not in His wise teaching or in His wonderful works, but rather in His revelation that "the being equal with God," so far from being "a grasping of things," was a "letting go of things," an emptying of Himself in love, even though it were the pouring out of life upon the Cross.

Lastly, the apostles came to see that the triumph of the Cross ensured a continuous and abundant supply of power for them to carry on the work committed to them. Never could the memory of what Christ had been empower them to fulfil this commission by itself. Only the sense of His ever-present grace, increasing their scant supply of human courage, deepening their devotion to the cause committed to them, and nerving them to hold out unto the end made of these Galilean fishermen and artisans the force which shook the world.

In the belief that the faith of the apostles is being vindicated in history I write these next chapters on the

[1] J. Middleton Murry, *Jesus, Man of Genius*, p. 371, London, 1926.

story of the Christian Church. We shall come upon many sins against that faith, on the part of imperfectly developed individuals as well as on the part of the official Church, itself often enough out of touch with the Master's guiding hand. We shall see corruption creeping in through the failure to renounce the depravities of the natural man. We shall see alliances with worldliness for the sake of securing the prestige which Christ repudiated when it was offered by Satan. We shall see men trying to extend the kingdom of God by means and methods totally opposed to the secret and method of the Cross. All this will furnish ample enough material for those who wish to pronounce Christianity a failure. It could scarcely be otherwise when we consider the slow process by which the spiritual man is fashioned by the operation of divine grace. Yet we shall also see that every departure from the faith brings inevitably its own Nemesis in humiliation and disaster, and at every disposition to turn in penitence to the pursuit of the old ideals there comes immediate resurrection as it were from the dead and new progress of the Church towards its distant goal. I hold it true that in no other way than by ever renewed possibility of living contact with a permanently accessible Christ may the story of the Church be other than a depressing record of gulfs ever widening between the ideals revealed of old in Palestine and the historic community which now represents these ideals to the world.

Hence no mere "Back to Christ" movement is to be considered consonant with fidelity to the plan of Jesus. Even if we could reproduce exactly for men of the twentieth century the conditions of life as it was lived in the first, we should not find the Living Christ under those old conditions. Much, of course, of that human life, the life "after the flesh," still remains valid for our imitation. As a great moral example, harmonizing in the white light of His perfection all the broken hues of virtue as we behold virtue exemplified in the best of all other men, the human life of Christ remains secure. It stands for ever "nearer than our own, by some space to us immeasurable, to that which is infinitely far."

Secure also is the Christian conviction that the life of

Christ as it was lived among men has been and will continue to be the mainspring of all social and religious reform in the history of mankind. To use the words of Baron Friedrich von Hügel: "A Person came and lived and loved and did and taught and died and rose again and lives on by His power and His spirit for ever within us and amongst us, so unspeakably rich and yet so simple, so sublime and yet so homely, so divinely above us in being so divinely near, that His character and teaching require, for an ever fuller and yet never complete understanding, the varying study and different experiments and applications, embodiments and unrollings, of all the races of men have not been able to conceive of a higher ideal or even to reach the heights thus realized." And Professor Le Conte says: "It is true that in many ways we have advanced and are still advancing by the use of partial ideals; but this use of partial and relative ideals is itself only a temporary stage of evolution. At a certain stage we catch glimpses of the absolute ideals. Then our gaze becomes fixed and we are thenceforward drawn upwards for ever. The human race has already reached a point where the absolute ideal of character is attractive. This divine ideal can never again be lost to humanity."[1]

To acknowledge all this, however, is still insufficient unless we hold that the Christ is not alone the interpreter of the past and the revealer of the path which still lies ahead for the pilgrimage of men, but is also the power (symbolized by the presence of *Beatrice* in the *Paradiso*) by which we mount from spiritual experience to spiritual experience, until we reach our rest in the Beatific Vision. The story of the ministry, which in the present chapter we have so briefly indicated, beautiful and eternally significant as it must continue to be, is but the earthly introduction to that eternal ministry which is carried on from the spiritual world. It was perhaps the good fortune of the apostle St. Paul that he was not permitted to companion with the Christ "after the flesh," since he was the sooner privileged to realize Him as his living, victorious Lord.

Thus in the history of religion, as the Christian under-

[1] Joseph Le Conte, *Evolution*, New York, 1897.

stands it, Christ can never be equated with the dead founders of other systems. He can never be the hero of a tradition such as Islam holds of Muhammad. He can never be compared with the Gautama whose attainment of Nirvana left him to be but a beautiful memory. He can never be likened to any Bodhisattva whom the disconsolate Mahayanist imagined as sharing the sorrows of humanity. He can never be thought of as a mere illusory *avatar* of the divine, like those of Vishnu, created to save the heart from breaking against the starkness of dependence upon an impersonal Brahm. We must insist, as already pointed out, upon setting Christ as the meeting-point of two evolutions, on the one hand, the revelation of transcendent deity, culminating in the Incarnation of the Son of God; on the other hand, the revelation of immanent deity, culminating in the birth of One who bears fitly the title of Son of Man.

So Christ is found to fulfil in His Person more than all the Confucianist hoped to behold in his " Superior Man "; more than all the Taoist dared to expect in the revelation of a Way by which he might gain immortal life; more than the Buddhist dreamed of aspiring to in the way of deliverance from the iron law of Karma; more than the Hindu longed to find in some downward manifestation of the divine such as might strengthen his will, enlighten his mind, and assuage his heart's unrest.

It should therefore be no presumptuous claim, but rather an appeal to the obvious facts of religious history, which finds but one place for Jesus in the long story of man's quest for God—which is, of course, also the story of God's quest for man. That place makes him unique and sets His name above every other name that may be named. To use the well-worn, but ever true, words of Browning, put upon the lips of the dying apostle, St. John:

> I say, the acknowledgement of God in Christ,
> Accepted by thy reason, solves for thee
> All questions in the earth and out of it,
> And has so far advanced thee to be wise.
> Wouldst thou unprove this to reprove the proved ?
> In life's mere minute, with power to use that proof,

Leave knowledge and revert to whence it sprung?
Thou hast it, use it, and forthwith, or die!
For I say, this is death and the sole death,
When a man's loss comes to him from his gain,
Darkness from light, from knowledge ignorance,
And lack of love from love made manifest.[1, 2]

---

[1] Robert Browning, *A Death in the Desert.*

[2] Out of the vast number of books dealing, more or less adequately, with the life and teachings of Jesus Christ, the following may be recommended: F. C. Burkitt, *The Gospel History and its Transmission* (3rd Ed.), 1911; B. H. Streeter, *The Four Gospels*, 1924; W. Sanday, *Life of Christ*, 1907; E. F. Scott, *The Kingdom and Messiah*, 1911; Charles Gore, *The Doctrine of Christ*, 1922; A. E. Rawlinson, *The New Testament Doctrine of the Christ*, 1926; H. R. Macintosh, *The Doctrine of the Person of Christ*, 1912; A. Schweitzer, *The Quest of the Historical Jesus* (2nd Ed.), 1911. See also the article "Jesus Christ" by C. A. Scott in *Ency. Brit.* (14th Ed.).

# CHAPTER XXXI

## *The Great Forty Years*

IN the last chapter I stressed the point that of two methods possible in writing a history of the Christian Church the professing Christian was necessarily restricted to the one which regarded Christ as a living, operative presence throughout, rather than a merely human originator. In the one case the Founder could only be regarded as a dead teacher whose memory must gradually dwindle to a legend and the Church could only be envisaged as an institution inevitably becoming the more feeble as it became the more venerable. In the other case the Founder is the victorious Lord who rules His Church from the eternal world and the Church is His Body increasing in power as it partakes of the power of its living Head. It is in this latter way alone that the Founder escapes the criticism of permanently wearing first-century clothes and therefore being inadequate to the problems of the present. It is in this way alone that the Church may be presented as a living and growing organism instead of being merely an interesting but archaic survival.

No more striking illustration of this conception of the Church can be conceived than is furnished by the story of what I have ventured to call the Great Forty Years. The period from the Resurrection of Christ to the Fall of Jerusalem, that is, from A.D. 30 to 70, is not only a period of forty years historically, but a period which lends itself readily to the suggestions of symbolism. *Forty* (4 × 10) is the number of world-wide development, as well as the number signifying a generation. It lends itself also nicely to the parallel to which attention is drawn in the third and fourth chapters of the *Epistle to the Hebrews*, where the forty years now in question is suggested by the forty years in the wilderness between the Exodus and the entrance into the land of Canaan. As in the Old Testament period God took the people of Israel, gave them His Law, trained them to become a nation ready to advance to the conquest of the land, so in the corresponding New Testament period the Spirit of God was preparing the Church to be launched upon the field of history, independently of Judaism, to begin its task of conquering the world. The writer of the epistle utters his solemn warning to the Jews of his time lest they should neglect the opportunity of entering into the rest of the kingdom, even as their fathers had neglected the opportunity offered by Moses, with the result that " their carcases fell in the wilderness." It was to him a tragical thought that a promise having been given to Israel that they should enter into this rest, any of them should seem to come short of it.[1]

Moreover, the writer of the epistle was but reaffirming what Christ Himself had declared in the last days of His ministry when by parable and discourse alike He solemnly warned that generation of His countrymen that, while people were seeking entrance to the kingdom from north, east, south and west, " the sons of the kingdom " were in danger of self-exile to the outer darkness. It has been a most unfortunate misinterpretation, as already remarked, of those wonderful twenty-fourth and twenty-fifth chapters of St. Matthew, first, that the phrase " the *age* to come " has been misrendered as " the *world* to come," thus suggesting some *post mortem* condition, and, secondly, that the substance of Christ's teaching on this occasion has been so split up by interpretation as suggesting that one part refers to the destruction of Jerusalem and another part to the ending of our planetary life by a kind of General Judgement. In consequence, many people, finding the expected end of the planet deferred beyond the point at which they fixed it, have decided that the apostles were deceived, without reflecting that, if so, Christ Himself had deceived them. It should be plain to every intelligent reader that in using the terms, " this age " and " the coming age," Christ was but employing familiar Jewish terminology descriptive of the anticipated transition from the pre-Messianic to the

[1] Hebrews iv. 6 ff.

Messianic eras. It was in the Messianic age, the age of the New Testament Church, that His "Coming" (literally "*Presence*") was assured and the promise fulfilled: "Lo, I am with you all the days, even to the end of the world."

Let me sketch very briefly the story of the great transition period from the point of view thus presented. It begins with the story of the Day of Pentecost as described in Acts ii. To the outsider this account must remain a great mystery. But we must judge the event by its fruits and these are so obvious that "he who runs may read." The men who had been stampeded by the tragedy on Calvary into a group of perplexed and panic-stricken fugitives become "a small transfigured band whom the world could not tame." Pentecost becomes the starting-point for a development unparalleled in human history. But the common habit of describing Pentecost as the birthday of the Christian Church is unwarranted. It would seem fitter to think of it as the day on which the material elements of which the Church was to be composed were quickened, while these were still parts of the body of the mother Church, that is, of Judaism. It was the divine operation by which the Church, to be born only by the death of the mother in A.D. 70, began that shaping which would by and by set it free to pursue its separate way through history and yet continue in history the inheritance of all the past. During this period the apostles were still Jews faithful to the obligations of the Old Testament Law. They went up to the Temple to pray at the accustomed hours; they kept the annual feasts; they remembered their responsibilities to the Hebrew poor. Even St. Paul, who by some of his brethren was regarded as a dangerous innovator, not only kept the feasts at Jerusalem but even took upon himself unnecessary vows to show that he was still obedient to the requirements of the Law.[1] Yet all the time something was going on in secret which would presently reveal the new order in all the power of its liberated life.

Let me describe this gestation period as a threefold shaping, a shaping which emerges upon the world of history as a complete fulfilment of the idea conveyed in the Buddhist

[1] Acts xxi. 23 ff.

Trinity of *Buddha*, *Dharma* and *Samgha*, namely, a conception of the *Person* of Christ which would take the place of merely reminiscent homage to a Jesus " after the flesh "; a conception of *teaching* and discipline to which Christians would hold through all the ages to come; and a conception of *society* in the Church which would be catholic and worldwide in its appeal to humanity.

First of all, let us consider the gradual shaping of doctrine, especially of doctrinal conceptions of the Person of Christ. Some people will misunderstand this idea of a developing doctrine, supposing that all truth had been revealed to the disciples by Christ at a flash and understood at a flash. These forget the saying: " I have many things to say unto you, but ye cannot bear them now." It will save us many a futile effort to gather fruit out of season if we remember that the apostles, who grew in spiritual power and in practical experience, grew also in understanding of the principles of the faith. Some of the first generation of Christian teachers were more rapid in their apprehension of this faith than others. James, the " brother" of Jesus, remained to the last attached to the old order and disposed to see in Jesus the Prophet of Galilee, the moralist of the *Sermon on the Mount*, the exponent of Divine Wisdom. Others, like the writer of the Fourth Gospel, were quick to attain the vision of the mystic, seeing in the historic the temporal illustration of the eternal fact. Others, again, like St. Paul, grew gradually from the one attitude to the other. Every student of the New Testament will naturally put the *Epistles* of the great Apostle to the Gentiles in their proper chronological sequence (an arrangement unfortunately lacking in our current versions) in order that he may watch the steady unfolding of the truth to the apostle's mind. From the earliest surviving letters written to the *Thessalonians* on matters of local concern, on through the Epistles to the *Corinthians*, *Galatians* and *Romans*, occupied with the then burning controversy as to the relation of Jews and Gentiles within the Church, and so on to the great Christological Epistles to the *Philippians*, *Colossians* and *Ephesians*, in which we learn his final views as to Christ and a Christocentric universe, we see consistent advance towards the ultimate Christian conviction as to the Personality of the Master. In all this there is no revolutionary change, nor any departure (such as some have fantastically imagined) from the mind of Christ Himself. It is a genuine unfolding of ideas germinal in the religious systems of Hebrew, Greek and Roman, yet "chaptered up" in Christ. And St. Paul—Jewish Rabbi, student of a Greek university, and Roman citizen—was peculiarly fitted to proclaim the ultimate synthesis.

In the second place, there is in these forty years the shaping of those organs which were necessary for the functioning of the Church's life as a living body. From the very first, as we have seen, the community as a spiritual fact needed the organs by which it came to be something more than a machine. We have seen these shaping in primitive religious societies and have watched their development into the organs of the Jewish Church. And it is from behind these, as the grain grows behind the husk, that we may note the development of the living organs of the Christian Church. The divine authority of ministry and sacraments does not depend upon their manifestation full-statured from the date of Pentecost, even though in certain cases we connect these with explicit commands given by Christ to His disciples. It depends rather upon the claim to take the place of all that had had the sanction of the earlier systems now on their way to obsolescence. The early Christians, together with the apostles, for the forty years of which we speak, lived (as already pointed out) as faithful sons of the Jewish law, keeping the obligations to which they had been trained. But within these ordinances were ripening for manifestation new growths which would presently burst their sheath and become obligations of a new and more permanent sort. Behind the covenant rite of circumcision, now becoming out of date, appeared the new rite of Christian baptism, with its implication of regeneration as well as cleansing. Behind the observance of the Passover there appeared the new obligation of the Christian Eucharist, not merely as a memorial feast but as the channel for transmission of divine strength and refreshment. Behind the old Aaronic priesthood, about to become (through the destruction of the Temple) a sinecure, was growing up the new priesthood whereby the ministry of Christ in heaven was to be everywhere made effective in the Church on earth. And behind the old Temple, with its services and its sacrifices, was growing up the new Temple, "not made with hands," which was to remain after the old shrine, "with the courts thereof," was given over to destruction. Moreover, every one of these new institutional elements must be understood as foreshadowed by the religious rites of the non-Hebrew world, from the earliest magic of the *shamans* to the sacramental initiation of the Greek mysteries. In other words, the sacramental system and the ministry of the Christian Church have their sanction, not merely in the authoritative words of Christ as their Institutor, but also in the need which runs through all religious history for just such a climax as Christ's words of institution express.

Thirdly, in the great forty years we have the shaping of a great and catholic plan of missionary work, through which the universal character of the Church to be is at once illustrated and in part realized. The conclusion has sometimes been drawn, by singling out certain isolated words of Christ and certain incidents of the ministry—as, for example, the story of the Syro-Phœnician woman—that Christ came consciously only to "the lost sheep of the house of Israel." No such conclusion can be legitimately entertained in the light of other incidents and in the light of the Great Commission given to the apostles (St. Matthew xxviii.19)[1]—certainly no misrepresentation of the purpose of Jesus, who had willed through the travail of His soul to draw all men unto Him.

Yet on more than one occasion Christ did declare that the whole of the Jewish people, scattered abroad throughout the Roman "world," must be given the opportunity of entering the kingdom before the end of the Old Dispensation came about through the Fall of Jerusalem. And it is one of the marvels of religious history that this diffusion of the Gospel over the cities of the Dispersion was actually realized prior to the fatal year A.D. 70. How it came about we are able to trace (though only in part) in the story of the *Acts*.

[1] Cf. e.g. Matthew xxiv. 14.

In this book we have described step by step the circumstances under which the apostles bore their message—"Jesus and the Resurrection"—from Jerusalem to Judæa, from Judæa to Samaria, from thence to Antioch in Syria, for the benefit of the Gentiles, and thence again, along the great Roman highways, from city to city, from land to land, till even Rome, within ten years of the Crucifixion, had its Christian colony. From this one narrative we might naturally conclude that a large part of this diffusion was due solely to the marvellous zeal and passionate courage of St. Paul. Yet it is, of course, certain that many others contributed to the result. Of this we have illustration in the famous letter of Pliny the Younger to Trajan, by which we learn that in Bithynia, the very place which St. Paul through illness was prevented from visiting, such a multitude of men and women had deserted the pagan temples for the meetings of the Christians that the Roman official was puzzled how to proceed. To such missionary work as this, doubtless, many agencies contributed. Tradesmen carried the "good news" from city to city as well as their wares; artisans in search of work, or, like Aquila and Priscilla, expelled from Rome by Claudius, were carriers of the evangel. Whenever Christians were scattered abroad "they went everywhere, preaching the word."

In this far-flung effort of missionary expansion, moreover, it is interesting to note that, as Christianity in its foundations was the heir of all that had been conveyed along the main channels of religious history, Hebrew, Greek and Latin, so for its propagation it was providentially destined to use the means which had been no less providentially prepared. What, for example, could these simple Galilean evangelists have done to find a starting-point for their proclamation had it not been that wherever they went throughout the Empire they were bound to discover communities of fellow-countrymen always ready to listen to any rabbi, however humble, who had a word for them from the old land reminding them of the hope of Israel? Wherever there were ten men of leisure there would be a synagogue and even where there were fewer Jews than this a *proseucha*, or prayer-place, by the riverside would be the gathering

point for the faithful on the Sabbath.[1] Co
Christian missionary would always have his p
which to preach the Master's message. The ru
"To the Jew first and also to the Gentile." Even i
apostolic address led to opposition and a riot, it was no
the less an inducement for others to come on succeeding Sabbaths, that they might hear whatever was to be said.

So, again, there had been providentially prepared for them the Greek "*koiné*" or vernacular, such as would everywhere make their speech intelligible. Even on the Day of Pentecost at Jerusalem the apostles had occasion to note the glad surprise of the multitude assembled at the Feast, when, instead of the pedantic speech of the Hebrew pandits, was heard the language of the Dispersion, the common Greek. "We do hear them speak," cried the motley throng from all the provinces of the Empire, "in our own tongue the wonderful works of God."[2] We must remember, of course, that this preparation had been begun two hundred years earlier when, for the convenience of Jews residing in Egypt, the Old Testament Scriptures had been translated into the language of Alexandria. The *Septuagint*, as this version is called, has been termed "the first apostle to the Gentiles," and with equal truth we may speak of it as the precursor of Pentecost.

Yet once again, we may see how providentially the first-century world had been prepared for the sowing abroad of the Christian message by the organization of the Roman Empire, the making of the Roman roads, and the imposition on the Western world of Roman law. The great Roman highways had much to do with the successful missionary strategy of St. Paul and his fellow-apostles. Travelling along these with an ease which was perhaps never again equalled until the era of railways, they journeyed from metropolis to metropolis, staying but a short time in the smaller towns, but making great cities like Ephesus the headquarters of operations in the entire countryside. In this way the news flew as though carried by the imperial couriers, and the disciples who were left behind to continue

[1] Cf. Acts xvi. 13.
[2] Is this an untenable interpretation of Acts ii. 5–8 ?

organizations such as made the
nanently fruitful. Nor was the
rly in the case of St. Paul—less to
an law. Three times the apostle
mob violence to his status as a
other occasions, too, we find him
of the Roman officials to whom his
[1] In after times, of course, when the
a policy of persecution, the situation
wa... that time the Gospel had been preached
throughout ... pire and the forty years of opportunity
were nearing their close.

The end of this significant period is coincident with the time of transition termed by the Jewish apocalyptists as "the pangs of the Messiah." The many who at this time were keeping watch for the coming of the promised kingdom knew that Judgement and Deliverance were the two hands on the clock of time and that salvation could not come except by the shaking of what had been their heaven and earth. For Christians who seek to understand the significance of this period, as it appeared to the generation then alive, there is no document so illuminating as the Apocalypse known as the *Revelation of St. John the Divine*, an apocalypse mystifying enough to those who would use it as a manual of soothsaying, but plain enough to those who knew it as an "unveiling" and not as a mystification, a book whose reading brought with it a special blessing, rather than an enigma whose key had been flung into the waters of the Ægean. The Jews who sought the aid of the Apocalypse were like those who suggested the writing of the *Epistle to the Hebrews*, patriots who in view of the menace and tyranny of the time were eagerly demanding, "Hath God cast away His people?" And the answer was to reveal the figure of the Messiah, Judge as well as Saviour, at the very door, moving indeed among the candlesticks of the Churches, and calling them to repentance. To those who judged of the universe and its forces solely through the outward eye things looked black indeed. The power behind all things was that old Dragon, symbol of the ancient Chaos which

[1] See Acts xviii. 14; xxii. 25; xxv. 10.

after all, they thought, had not been slain by Marduk, as in Babylonian myth, but was lord of all. Evidence of this undefeated power of darkness was plain enough in the Dragon's emissary and agent, that Wild Beast from the Sea, which was incarnate in the Roman Empire and its heads, the emperors whose armies encircled the walls of the Holy City, and whose brute force was being invoked to crush the infant Church of Christ. In addition, there was the Wild Beast from the Land, that spirit of pagan philosophy, speaking with glozing tongues of falsehood against truth as revealed in Jesus. What could the outcome be of a society founded on belief in this anti-Trinity of Hell but the Harlot City, defiant of God and worshipping the powers of Force and Falsehood? The majority of men at this time—possibly the majority still—believed that all this represented the world of reality. If not, why should truth be slain in the streets and the ungodly triumph?

But the Seer, entering in spirit into "the Day of the Lord" so long predicted by the prophets, saw reality in another guise. He gives us in two wonderful chapters (iv. and v.) "The Revelation of the Things that Are." He shows us first that Ancient of Days, the primal power of righteousness already victorious over Chaos, the eternally creative force which Christians describe as the Father. Then he bids us see that the agent of this Eternal Power is (not the Beast, but) "the Lamb, slain from the foundation of the world," the eternal principle of sacrificial love which Christians call the Son. Then, again, he shows us the Seven Spirits of God which, like the Amesha-spentas of Zoroastrianism, are the reflected personality of God in all the events of history, the immanence of God in the process of evolution. And the outcome of this is the Bride City, humanity redeemed and glorified, which is the Church coming down age by age out of the heaven which is the realm of the absolute, to realize itself in the earth which is the realm of becoming.

All this, moreover, is no dream of a visionary removed from the events of the time, but rather the philosophy of religion as that time made it plain. As in the great conflict of Marduk with Tiamât, victory may not be bought except through war in the spiritual realm. So we have unfolded before us a marvellously dramatic picture of the troubles of the age in three separate sevenfold sequences of Seals, Trumpets and Bowls. The Seven Seals of the Book of Mystery are one by one broken by the Lamb to show the inner meaning of the things from which the land of Palestine was suffering, from the horrors of invasion, war, famine, and death, to the fall of the great " silence " in which the Old Testament dispensation is to close. Then comes the sounding of the Seven Trumpets of War, which brings before us the incidents of the Roman campaign against Jerusalem, up to the day when the Temple was destroyed, with its courts, though the Holy of Holies (that is, the eternal values of the old order) remains to appear as the Foursquare City. Then, in the description of the outpoured Bowls of Judgement, we have depicted the trials which are to fall upon the infant Church, forced to flee into the wilderness from the fury of the Wild Beast.

But beyond all the tribulation of the time the Seer is able to describe the victorious issue. He sees the Dragon, the Wild Beast and the False Prophet slain and Death and Hell cast into the Lake of Fire. People, he foresees, will still go on worshipping the shadows of these things, ignorant of the fact that they are dethroned and dead. In consequence they will gnash their teeth in pain, suffering the results of their illusion.

Then, in the last chapters of his book, the apocalyptist unveils for us the descent from heaven of the Foursquare City, the city of redeemed humanity, perfect in its length and breadth and height, the fulfilment of the symbolism embodied in the Holy of Holies which survives from the Old Testament order. Within the walls of this city, with its twelve courses of vari-coloured precious stone—like the coloured courses of the Babylonian zikkurats—will be drawn the glory of all the nations streaming through the open gates which invite mankind from north and south and east and west. Here is to be realized the new Heaven and Earth, free at last from the Sea of Chaos which had been the raw material of their evolution. Here is the " continuing city " which men had sought ever since the time when they turned their backs upon companionship with the brute in Eden. Here is to be found the new Paradise, with its Tree of Life and Water of Life, from which the curse has been for ever excluded.

Two kinds of people have misunderstood the implications of this sublime vision and, in consequence, have started amiss with the story of the Christian Church on earth. On the one hand are those who put the realization of the whole in the celestial world at some infinite remove from our present-day experience. And on the other hand are those who claim to see the whole vision as realized with the first steps taken by the infant Church in its historic pilgrimage. Of course, neither of these views is the entire truth. What we do see is the working of a new force which has begun the process of changing the face of society, the first scene of a drama which is not to have its *dénouement* till the progressive devolution of God and the progressive evolution of man are alike complete. The victory ideally *has* been won. Ideally "the kingdoms of this world *are* become the kingdom of our Lord and of His Christ." Ideally, in the revelation of God through Christ, the Dragon, the Wild Beast and the False Prophet *are* dead, however much the deceived among men may continue to worship their shadows.[1] Shadow gods are shown up for what they are; the "genuine" God is made manifest. So, again, the City of God, which is also the City of Man, *is* coming down, and the union of God and Man *is* achieved in the bridal of Christ and His Church. All through the history to be surveyed, even in the darkest ages, we shall see glints and glimpses of the descending splendour. Nevertheless, the vision of our high moments is as yet far from being realized among men. The Seer knows that the battle will continue far beyond the time of Rome, on and on to the present, and through ages yet to come. Though before his eyes gleamed the walls of the eternal Camelot, most men would exclaim with Tennyson's hind, "Lord, there is no such city anywhere." As the woman told the painter Turner, that she had never seen such colour in a sunset, so the sceptics of all

[1] See Charles Kingsley, *The Roman and the Teuton* (London, edition of 1889), chap. iii.

ages will refuse to behold what was so plain to the eyes of St. John the Divine.

Yet it is a wonderful starting-point for the history of the Christian Church, freed from the trammels of the past, that a few at least, with little in the way of history to go upon, could look from the small and doubtful beginning to the triumph of the completed work. By anticipation they could sing:

> This hath He done and shall we not adore Him?
> This shall He do, and can we still despair?
> Come, let us quickly fling ourselves before Him,
> Cast at His feet the burden of our care.
> Flash from our eyes the joy of our thanksgiving,
> Glad and regretful, confident and calm,
> Then through all life and what is after living,
> Thrill to the music of Creation's psalm.

It may be retorted that this is not the proper attitude for the historian who aims at objectivity. The facts of history, it will be said, must be set forth dispassionately and the issue decided by the ultimate result. Yet I am sure we shall reach altogether wrong conclusions as to the significance of religious history, unless we keep in mind some vision of the glory which faith sees as the final goal. Christian history will be to us a sad record of futile hope, of misspent zeal, of wrongly directed enthusiasm, unless we see beyond the achievement of any age in the past. We shall have sickening records of cruelty, error, fanaticism, stupidity, foolishness, unless we can remember that the Golden Age of religion is still indefinitely ahead. If we employ our simile of the two triangles, one of the past, with its apical point in Christ as the heir of all the ages, and one with its apical point as the Christ from whom starts all the story of the future, we shall have to confess that, in comparison with the finished triangle of the past, the space in our second triangle, represented by but two thousand years, is a relatively insignificant segment of time, small even by comparison with the historical era embraced in the earlier half of our diagram. In a very striking illustration Sir James Jeans asks us to take a postage stamp and stick it on a penny, then put the penny, with the postage stamp uppermost, on a pillar like Cleopatra's Needle. The height of the whole structure will then represent the age of the earth; the thickness of the penny and the stamp together will represent the time man has been on earth; and the thickness of the stamp will represent approximately the time during which man has been "civilized." Then, he adds, keep on adding stamps to your pillar till it reaches the height of Mont Blanc and you will have represented the ages during which man may still survive upon this planet.

When we get depressed, as we often must, in our reading of history, over the littleness of our gains, let us remember this. It is in the courage afforded by such a thought that I shall endeavour in these succeeding chapters to give a rapid sketch of the progress, the lapses, the failures, and withal the achievements of the Christian religion.[1]

[1] Books to be consulted on the period will include: W. M. Ramsay, *St. Paul, the Traveller and the Roman Citizen*, London, 1895; the same author's *The Church in the Roman Empire*, 1898; F. W. Farrar, *The Life and Work of St. Paul*, 1872; the same author's *The Early Days of Christianity*, 1882; A. C. McGiffert, *History of Christianity in the Apostolic Age*, New York, 1906; G. P. Fisher, *History of the Christian Church*, New York, 1889, pp. 1-87; Salomon Reinach, *A Short History of Christianity* (Eng. trans.), London, 1922; Ernest Renan, *L'Antichrist*, Paris, 1873; Flavius Josephus, *The Wars of the Jews*.

## CHAPTER XXXII

### *Christ versus Cæsar*

JERUSALEM had not yet fallen when the Christians residing there, warned, as Eusebius says, "by a certain oracle given to their leaders by revelation," or, as Epiphanius declares, "by an angel," left the doomed city and took refuge in the little Perean town of Pella. They could not have been a large company, yet already the mustard-seed of the Church was developing into a tree and sending branches abroad throughout the Empire. If Cæsar was sitting in untroubled security on the Seven Hills, God, at any rate, "within the shadow," was "keeping watch above His own."

For the most part the members of the Christian Church, whether in Palestine, Asia Minor, Greece, Italy, Gaul, or Egypt, were drawn from the poorer strata of society. St. Paul tells us "not many rich, not many wise," so far as this world is concerned, were chosen. And, many years after, Celsus used the gibe that "any one who is a sinner, or foolish, or simple-minded—in short, any unfortunate, will be accepted by the kingdom of God." Yet, doubtless, a few wealthy, as had been the case in Jerusalem, and one or two connected with the imperial court, had found their way into the Church.

Organization followed evangelization very rapidly, and for this training in the system of the Roman Empire was to a considerable extent responsible. Yet the development of the threefold ministry was indebted also to the Old Testament order and, quite obviously, also to the teaching of Christ and His training of the apostles. The genuine epistles of St. Ignatius of Antioch bear eloquent witness to progress made in this direction.

Until the close of the ministry of St. Paul the policy of the Roman authorities had been, in respect to Christianity, tolerant and protective. To use the symbol of the Apocalypse, "the earth helped the woman." But under Nero, about A.D. 64, persecution broke out furiously at Rome, involving, in all probability, the death of two leading apostles (SS. Peter and Paul), and of a large number of others who on this occasion "passed through the great tribulation."

From the time of the Neronian persecution to the *Edict of Milan*, in 313, persecution of the Christians was the rule rather than the exception, though this was not often empire-wide, or due to the direct initiative of the emperors. In any case the statement as to the sequence of Ten General Persecutions is far from being correct. Christianity came under the definition of a *religio illicita* more or less permanently from the time of Vespasian, but the putting of the law into effect depended largely upon local circumstances and upon the attitude of the provincial governors. The letter of Pliny the Younger, when governor of Bithynia, about 117, together with the Emperor Trajan's response, illustrates very well the general procedure. Doubtless many Christians were punished solely because of their profession, but in most cases it was thought necessary to bring against them some specific charge, substantial or imaginary. Sometimes persecution arose because of the popular demand, sometimes a fit of panic at time of national catastrophe, earthquake or fire, sometimes the result of widely propagated slander, such as the existence of Thyestean banquets or the indulgence in unnatural vices, sometimes through mere prejudice, because Christians abstained from the gladiatorial sports and other occasions involving pagan rites. While the populace was carried away by unreasoning madness, the philosophers were hostile because of what seemed in the Christians to be narrowness, philistinism, or even lack of common humanity. As for the emperors, they encouraged or discouraged persecution according to their personal temperament, public policy, or to their agreement or disagreement with the popular mood. There can be but little doubt that Nero and Domitian were persecutors out of personal cruelty and dislike of the Christians. Trajan was a persecutor when it seemed necessary for the security of the state and when it seemed likely that the Christians were chargeable with crime. Yet in later times Trajan was so far forgiven that Dante admits him into the *Paradiso*. Hadrian, who occupied the imperial throne from 117 to 138, and in whose reign the *Apologies* began to appear, persecuted for much the same reasons, though he opposed the yielding of the officials to popular clamour. It was in this reign that the Jewish revolt under Bar Cochba ("*son of a star*") was suppressed and Jerusalem further destroyed and renamed Aelia Capitolina. The two Antonines, Antoninus Pius and Marcus Aurelius, were not naturally persecutors, but the latter as a philosopher had a rather hard contempt for the Christians as obstinate bigots. Commodus was infamously cruel, and Septimius Severus carried on persecution for reasons of state. Nothing good can be said of Caracalla and Heliogabalus, but of Alexander Severus we have the story that he reverenced a statue of Christ in his rather eclectic pantheon. In the time of Philip the Arabian, A.D. 248, the millennium of the foundation of Rome was celebrated with great éclat, but the outlook was viewed with misgiving on account of the breakdown of the old religious sanctions. Under Decius the first really general persecution was carried out with great severity, as a sincere effort to unify the Empire by enforcing the worship of the emperors. Valerian revived the persecution, but fell into the hands of the Persians and died an exile. Gallienus proved rather favourable to the faith than otherwise and it is not till the reign of Diocletian, in 283, that another concerted effort was made to crush out Christianity by the destruction of books and buildings as well as by the execution of Christians. This was the final endeavour on a large scale to suppress the faith by force, and after the civil war which followed the death of Diocletian we come to the accession of Constantine and the promulgation of the *Edict of Tolerance* at Milan in 313. Cæsarism was defeated and Christ had conquered. How far the victory was complete we shall have occasion presently to enquire.

There can be no certainty as to the actual number of those who died as martyrs during the entire period of persecution. On the one hand there were many who did not stand the test of the times, the *libellatici*, who took tickets (*libelli*) to show that they had conformed to the requirements of the officials, the *thurificati*, who, under pressure, consented to sprinkle incense upon the altars erected to the genius of the emperor, as well as, no doubt, many who recanted from sheer shrinking of the flesh. On the other hand, there were many who, in a fit of ecstasy, offered themselves needlessly to martyrdom, or those, like Origen, who had to be restrained by the hiding of their clothes. Taking all the localities together affected by the persecutions, Asia Minor, Italy, North Africa, Gaul and Britain, and putting together such accounts as have come down to us, "the noble army of martyrs" swells to a notable size, and the heroism with which timid men and weak women and tender children faced the flame, the sword and the wild beasts, is a wonderful testimony to the faith which had overcome the world.

> They climbed the steep ascent of heaven,
> Through peril, toil and pain.

There was Ignatius of Antioch, journeying to Rome as in a kind of triumphal procession, to be ground by the teeth of hungry lions to become "the fine wheat of God." There was the venerable Polycarp at Smyrna, confessing Christ through the roaring veil of flame. There was, again, Justin Martyr at Rome, in the reign of Marcus Aurelius, a philosopher suffering death at the edict of a philosopher. There were the martyrs Perpetua and Felicitas, who with their companions suffered by the beasts in North Africa. And in the churches of Lyons and Vienne there was the valiant company who endured a cruel death in 177. So the terrible story runs, till we come to the innumerable multitude of the age of Decius and on to the last flare of imperial desperation in the days of Diocletian. The words of the *Epistle to the Hebrews* are a fitting description: "They were stoned, they were sawn asunder, they were tempted, they were slain by the sword; they went about in sheepskins and goatskins; being destitute, afflicted, ill-treated (of whom the world was not worthy), wandering in deserts and mountains and caves, and the holes of the earth." [1]

[1] Hebrews xi. 27.

Among the great figures of the period we have some who were martyrs both in will and deed; others who were martyrs in will but not in deed. A few are notable as continuing the catena of witness from the days of the apostles in literary form. To the earliest of these we give the name of the *Apostolic Fathers*, as to men linked with the first generation of the Church. There is Clement of Rome, possibly the friend referred to by St. Paul in the *Epistle to the Philippians*.[1] His *Epistle to the Corinthians*, written about 96, is an effort on the part of the community at Rome to settle a dispute in the Corinthian Church. It is not a great work, but remarkable for its ready quotations from the New Testament books as already of authority. It adds to our knowledge of the apostles SS. Peter and Paul, mentioning the martyrdom of each and, in the case of St. Paul, stating that he had visited "the utmost bounds of the west."[2] It speaks also of the ministerial order of the Church and, in support of the doctrine of the Resurrection, uses the quaint Egyptian myth of the Phœnix. The letter was sent by the hands of trusted brethren to the elders of the church addressed.

Ignatius, Bishop of Antioch, A.D. 30–107, according to legend the child whom Christ had as an example taken in His arms (and therefore called *Theophoros*), wrote letters which have come down to us in two rescensions. The longer rescension, however, which consists of fifteen epistles, is not regarded as authentic, and only the shorter version, of seven letters, has been generally accepted. These letters are of great importance. When Trajan visited Antioch in 107 Ignatius, as Bishop of the local church, could hardly do otherwise than confess himself a Christian and was thereupon condemned to be devoured by wild beasts at Rome. On his journey thither he wrote the letters which have survived, to the *Ephesians*, *Magnesians*, *Trallians*, and *Romans*, from Smyrna and, from Troas, to the *Philadelphians*, *Smyrniotes*, and to his friend *Polycarp*. They have great human as well as doctrinal interest. Ignatius suffered not a little from his surly guards, whom he describes as "leopards," but he is in an ecstasy of expectation with regard to his imminent

[1] Written about A.D. 96.

[2] Possibly referring to Spain.

martyrdom and hopes that no intercession will rob him of the triumph. Doctrinally, the letters confirm the use made of the New Testament books as scripture, speak very definitely and dogmatically of the need of the threefold ministry, and bear witness to the Christian acceptance of the divinity of Christ and the virginity of Mary. From the literary point of view, also, the letters are notable for such terse expressions as " Find time to pray without ceasing "; " Every wound is not healed with the same remedy " ; " The times demand thee as the pilots the haven "; " Stand like a beaten anvil."

Polycarp, 65–155, Bishop of Smyrna, is traditionally the disciple of St. John and died by fire at Smyrna as the result of a popular uprising demanding a Christian victim at the hands of the officials. He has left us an *Epistle to the Philippians* which is a singularly beautiful testimony to one of the noblest of Christian confessors. It is full of New Testament quotations, reminds us not a little of St. Paul's letter to the same community, and warns against the rise of Docetism, a heresy which denied the reality of Christ's suffering upon the Cross.

Other writings of this class we must pass over in order to refer to a new type of Christian literature, the *Apologies*, written deliberately for the purpose of informing the emperors and officials as to the harmless and law-abiding character of the Christian religion. They appear first in the reign of Antoninus Pius, about 138, and include as authors the names of Quadratus, Aristides, Justin Martyr, Tatian, Athenagoras, Minucius Felix, and Melito of Sardis. The most illustrious of them all is Justin Martyr, a student of philosophy, born in Samaria and converted to Christ after experimenting with various other systems. He wrote his *Apologies* to Antoninus Pius and to Marcus Aurelius, and suffered martyrdom in the reign of the latter about 165. The *Apologies* are exceedingly valuable, not merely for their defence of the Christians against the usual charges, but for their constructive testimony as to things actually believed and practised. Much stress is laid upon Christ's fulfilment of Old Testament prophecy, but the most striking passages are those which deal with Baptism (Chapter. LXI.), the

Eucharist (LXVI.), and the weekly worship of the Christians (LXVII.). These are among the most illuminating pieces of literature which have come to us from the Second Century.

Not only pagan officials but Christians themselves needed information and instruction. While many sought to propound authoritatively the principles of the faith, others were beginning to ventilate strange opinions and speculations, which naturally invited refutation. The word *heresy* (Gk., *hairesis*, *choice*) was in its first meaning harmless enough, but " choice " became dangerous when it led to rebellion against the authorized teaching of the Church, or even to schism, that is, an actual rending of " the seamless robe of Christ." The first controversy of Christianity, over the relation of the New Testament Dispensation to Judaism, was now dead, though in the time of Marcion it was destined to be revived in an altered form. But other errors began to rear their heads and to find supporters among men, who, if they were eccentric, were also at the same time, for the most part, sincere. We have already mentioned Docetism, the teaching which maintained that the Incarnation was a mere " seeming," since the Christ could not be born as a babe nor as a man hang upon the Cross. Not unconnected with this theory was the dangerous heresy which came out of the East about the beginning of the second century and which for a time threatened to turn the Christian story into a myth. This was Gnosticism, a speculative system associated with many names, such as those of Valentinus, Basilides, Heracleon, Ptolemæus, Marcion and Bardesanes, but essentially one in its repudiation of the material universe as the work of the Supreme God, or as the sphere of redemption by Christ. It was a system founded on speculations as old as the dualism of Babylonian and Magian times, but subversive of the entire Christology expounded by St. Paul in the *Epistle to the Colossians*. Marcion carried the Gnostic position into a thorough-going opposition to the entire Jewish dispensation as the work of a *Demiurge*, or secondary God, wholly inimical to the doctrine of grace as revealed by Christ. To support his theory Marcion, who appeared in Rome about 140, made his own New Testament out of a bowdlerized Gospel of St. Luke and ten of the Pauline Epistles. About the same time Valentinus was preaching at Rome his doctrine of æons, emanating in pairs, male and female, from the High God dwelling in the Pleroma. All alike the Gnostic systems failed to recognize in Christ the one, all-sufficient revelation of the Eternal, redeemer of the whole universe, material as well as spiritual.

A movement of a different sort is Montanism, so called after a truly sincere and unworldly Phrygian, Montanus, who appeared at Pepuza about the middle of the second century. The early Montanists exhibited much of the disposition to extravagant ecstasy which was characteristic of Phrygian religion generally, but their main aim was to raise the standard of Christian living in the face of what appeared to be a growing disposition to worldliness on the part of bishops and clergy. They maintained also a stern, unbending attitude in withholding the Church's forgiveness from those who had lapsed under stress of persecution. They did not deny the possibility of forgiveness at the hand of God, but refused to permit the Church to be the instrument for extending leniency to sinners of this type. At a time when large numbers of Christians were being driven into apostasy by persecution there was some excuse for this severity but, as in the case of the later Novatian schism, the attitude became one of needless hardness, which became the more pronounced as it extended into Africa. It was here that "the fierce Tertullian," as Matthew Arnold calls him, became one of the champions of Montanism.

A few years later there came from Persia, then under the Sasanids, that curious eclecticism which was to prove a serious competitor with Christianity as far east as China, as far west as Britain, and particularly in North Africa and the Balkan peninsula. This was Manichæanism, so named from Mani, who began his teaching before Shapur I. in Seleucia-Ctesiphon in March 242. About thirty years later Mani was savagely executed and his skin stuffed with straw. But his doctrines gained wide sway and eventually a kind of papacy was established in Bulgaria from whence missionaries went forth over the empire and beyond. The youthful Augustine became a hearer of the Manichæans; the *Catechism* of the sect was taught in the capital of China; and, as late as the thirteenth century, the Albigenses are supposed to have represented the heresy in Europe. It taught a dualism, with the Lord of Light and Spirit inhabiting the Pleroma, and Satan, the Lord of Darkness and Matter dwelling in the Abyss. The frontier had been straightly drawn and it was Satan's raid across the border which led to the creation of the solar system, a machinery designed, like the buckets of a Persian water-wheel, to dredge up the particles of light taken captive by Satan, until once again the frontier could be established and the world destroyed by fire. As a dualism holding that matter was irredeemably evil, Manichæanism had opposite consequences in the realm of morals. While some sought to rid themselves of the material by asceticism, others maintained that the pure spirit could not be polluted by the flesh, and so plunged into extremes of license. The system was highly organized, with its five grades of believers, its sacred literature, and even its sacred language.[1]

Against all these forms of error the Church waged valiant warfare and Christian theology owes much, in insight and clarity, to the writers of the first three Christian centuries. Though in its organization Catholic, yet at this time the Church exhibited certain regional characteristics. It is therefore convenient to speak of the writers of the time as belonging to certain " schools."

In point of importance, if not in date, we must give first place to the school of Alexandria. This great city, the foundation of Alexander, had already played a rôle in the history of Judaism and was destined to play no less a part in the history of Christianity. Even in the lifetime of the apostles, it is said, a Catechetical school had been there established by the evangelist St. Mark, and in the middle of the second century Pantaenus, " the Sicilian bee," was keeping up the repute of the academy. To Pantaenus succeeded the more famous Clement of Alexandria, born

[1] Recent books on Manichæanism include : F. C. Burkitt, *Religion of the Manichees*, Cambridge, 1925 ; A. V. W. Jackson, *Researches in Manichæanism*, New York, 1932.

about 150, and bringing to the oversight of the school a well-trained Greek mind, a large knowledge of Greek literature, a clear appreciation of the doctrine of the Logos, and a sympathetic insight into the relations which must exist between Greek philosophy and the Christian revelation. In the *Stromata* Clement has given us a fine exposition, in Christian terms, and within the bounds of Christian theology, of what the Gnostic had been labouring to express.

A still more considerable figure in the Alexandrian school of the third century is Origen, appropriately enough surnamed *Adamantius*. He was the son of the martyr Leonidas, whose witness unto death the youthful Origen strove hard to share. Frustrated, however, in this, he took up the task of teaching and, by selling the manuscripts in his possession, endeavoured to make his instruction gratuitous. He soon acquired that mastery of the Greek text of the Scriptures which made him the first textual critic in the long story of Christian scholarship, and the compiler of the *Hexapla*, a version in the Hebrew, the Hebrew in Greek letters, and the four Greek texts of Aquila, Theodotion, Symmachus and Alexandria, arranged in parallel columns. Origen also found time for controversy and wrote a refutation of the attack on Christianity by Celsus. His controversial talents brought about a quarrel with the Alexandrian Bishop, Demetrius, and this led to an exile in Syria from which Origen never returned. It was in Syria that much of his critical work was done and the great scholar died in Tyre about 252 after intense sufferings incurred during the Decian persecution. Later theologians arose to impugn the orthodoxy of Origen, but he will nevertheless remain an heroic example of devotion to a cause for which he was ready to lay down his life as well as to consecrate to it the fullness of his extraordinary talent.

Earlier than Origen, as representative of the Church in Gaul, we have Irenæus, *c.* 130–202, who provides an important link between the churches of the West and those of Asia Minor. Irenæus was born in Asia Minor, where he held Polycarp in reverence as his master. In early manhood he visited Rome and, a few years later, about 177, succeeded the martyr Pothinus as Bishop of Lyons. He seems to have fallen a victim to the persecution of Septimius Severus about the beginning of the third century. Irenæus wrote a famous treatise *Against Heresies*, dealing mainly with the errors of the Gnostics. In his theology he represents a moderate orthodoxy such as specially recommends him as an interpreter of Christian belief at this time. The Gallican school, embodying, as it did, the Asiatic rather than the Roman tradition, was destined to have some influence in the shaping of belief and practice in the Church in Britain.

More important than the Gallican school in the third century, though later destined to witness the extinguishing of its candle, is the Church of North Africa, as represented by the two outstanding personalities of Tertullian and Cyprian. Tertullian was a Latin lawyer, with all the extreme logic of the profession, and with some strain also of the African hardness. He was born about 160 and, on attaining manhood, soon began the development of his unusual ability, not only in the defence of Christians against attack but also in carrying the war into the enemy's camp. He has been described as the "Carlyle" of his generation, though the comparison hardly does justice to the clearness of his thought and the relentless logic of his argument. He is a master of epigrammatic phrase, such as occasionally leads to misrepresentation. The phrases: "I believe because it is absurd," "the soul naturally Christian," "The blood of Christians is their seed," only in part convey Tertullian's meaning. In his later years fear of minimizing the moral standards of religion led to his joining the Montanists, but he never ceased to contend as the unflinching champion of orthodox doctrine and remains to-day one of the most stimulating and impressive of the Christian fathers. The Spanish "tertulia," a club or debating society, bears witness to some part of his reputation. A recent writer has described him as "the most human of the Fathers, keen, witty, sarcastic, argumentative, morally intense, intellectually extreme, capable of love and wrath and scorn, and in the midst of his strong assertions and high moral imperatives, a lowly man, conscious of his own sin and ashamed." [1]

[1] Robert Rainy, *The Ancient Catholic Church*, p. 189.

Inspired by the writings of Tertullian, but in most respects a man of different character, is Cyprian, one of the very greatest Christian names in the third century. Carthage at this time was the most important city in the western world, after Rome, and when Cyprian was chosen as its Bishop about 248, there was much surprise and some criticism, since the new Bishop had only come into the Church in mature years and had not long been baptized. But it was very soon perceived that he was the man for that difficult time. The fierce persecution of Decius brought into prominence many "certificated" apostates, with whom the Bishop of Carthage was disposed to deal severely. In Rome, on the other hand, great leniency was shown, with the result that Novatian, a rather gloomy Puritan, made a schism. Cyprian was severe on schismatics, whether at Rome or in Carthage. He was the author of the famous saying: "He has not God for his Father who has not the Church for his mother." He even denied the validity of baptism performed outside the organized Church and on this question had a dispute with Stephen, Bishop of Rome. But while Cyprian was doing much to strengthen the power of the episcopate, he was also, like the humblest of his flock, facing the perils of persecution. During the Decian persecution he felt that, in the interest of the diocese, he should go into hiding, but later on, during the persecution of Valerian, he felt it equally his duty to give himself up to the authorities. He was tried at Carthage, condemned to death, and perished by the sword, about 261, with the words, "Thanks be to God!" upon his lips. He had just previously issued a touching pastoral to the clergy and laity of the diocese of Carthage.

The *Edict of Milan*, promulgated in 313, by Constantine, the Augustus of the West, and Licinius, the Augustus of the East, is a turning point in world history. Constantine at this time probably knew little of Christ or Christianity, but twenty-five years after the battle of the Milvian Bridge he swore that he had seen, just before the battle, a vision of the Cross, with the motto below it, "By this sign thou shalt conquer." His victory confirmed him in the belief that only through Christianity could the Empire be unified.

It took Constantine ten years to make himself sole emperor, but when this was achieved in 323, he began at once to carry out his plan to make Christianity the established religion. Constantine was not baptized till some short time before his death and it cannot be alleged that his life as emperor was free from acts grievously at variance with a Christian profession. But there is much evidence that Constantine was in general worthy of the title "Great," and the New Rome which he built at Byzantium, and which was eventually called Constantinople, after himself, was the first city in the Roman Empire to be built without a pagan temple. Of certain achievements of this first Christian emperor we shall have to speak in the next chapter. It is only necessary now, in summing up the present chapter, to ask: What were the main results, good and bad, of the conversion of Constantine?

To speak of the good results first, we must recall that more than two centuries of official opposition to the faith had now come to an end, bringing a relief from strain which it is hard to over-estimate, and a freedom to pursue the normal Christian life in acts of worship and service unshadowed by the tyranny of a hostile world. There was, moreover, protection extended to the buildings hired or erected for Christian worship, so that no longer need Christians flee for refuge to caves and catacombs. There were grants also now available for the evangelization of districts where the Gospel had not hitherto been able to penetrate. And, instead of the treasured manuscripts of the Christian Scriptures being sought out for burning, imperial orders were given for fifty sumptuous copies of the Scriptures of both Testaments to be set up for reading in the larger Churches of the Empire.

Unfortunately, there is another side to the shield. After all, the Empire, so far as it represented the power of this world, could not be converted, and must still remain the throne of Antichrist. The persecuting power of the emperors had indeed been curbed and the imperial favour secured, but this was at a price. If there had before been danger from the power of the lion, the power of the serpent was no less a menace. If the *sacrificati*, *thurificati*, and *libellatici* had once been a weakness to the cause of Christ, there was a hundredfold greater danger through the fawning courtiers who had once been persecutors but were now patrons. The growth of worldliness stimulated the increase of insincerity. It was easy now for men to be nominally Christians who had never had in them the stuff to be martyrs. Though there were doubtless many thousands of Christians who carried into the new order the ardour which had never flagged beneath the assaults of paganism when that paganism was openly arrayed against them, there were also thousands who found it hard to resist the paganism which was sapping the life of the Church from within. The story of the *Donation of Constantine* is historically baseless, but the words of Dante are not without their sad fullness of truth:

> Ah, Constantine, to how much ill gave birth,
> Not thy conversion, but that plenteous dower
> Which the first wealthy Father gained from thee! [1]

It is plain that the City of God is not yet fully established on the earth—in the fourth century no more than in the first. Nor could the "converted" Empire be hailed as identical with the Church of redeemed humanity. The main lesson of the period is that men's eyes must still be turned towards the future. The Wild Beast and the False Prophet had indeed been slain, but their shadow was still generally worshipped. The fight must go on. Christians must learn to be "in the world, yet not of it." Some shirked the difficult task and went out to seek the descending City in the deserts; some all too easily succumbed to the lure of the world. But the "sinners who kept on trying" were witnesses to the faith as were the martyrs of the earlier generation, and among these were some of the Church's greatest saints, whose testimony was not in vain.[2]

[1] Dante, *Inferno* xix, 118-20.

[2] Other books to be consulted will include: *The Ante-Nicene Fathers* (Edited by Drs. Alexander Roberts and James Donaldson, American edition, 1896), Vols. I. to IV., containing the Apostolic Fathers, Justin Martyr, Irenæus, Clement of Alexandria, Tertullian and Origen; Williston Walker, *A History of the Christian Church*, New York, 1921; Louis Duchesne, *The Early History of the Christian Church*, 2 vols. (Eng. ed.), New York, 1909-12; H. M. Gwatkin, *Early Church History to A.D.* 313, 2 vols., London, 1909; Adolf von Harnack, *The Mission and Expansion of Christianity in the First Three Centuries* (2nd ed.), 2 vols., New York, 1908; F. W. Farrar, *Lives of the Fathers*, 2 vols., New York, 1889; H. B. Workman, *Persecution in the Early Church*, London, 1906.

# CHAPTER XXXIII

## *Controversies, Councils, Creeds*

SOME writers, including John Stuart Mill, have remarked on the strange circumstance that the first Christian emperor was such a one as Constantine rather than a Marcus Aurelius. Niebuhr, too, has declared that "when certain Oriental writers call him 'equal to the apostles' (*isapostolos*), they do not know what they are saying: and to speak of him as a saint is a profanation of the word." This is, of course, true, yet we must not transport Constantine out of his own age and environment. His acceptance of the Christian name was symbolic of the conquest of the pagan state by the Cross, a bowing of the imperial neck to the victorious Christ, the end of the age-long conflict between two opposed ideals. The acceptance, moreover, bore immediate fruit in a long series of reforms, beginning with the *Edict of Toleration*, and including the recognition of the weekly anniversary of the Resurrection as Sunday, the abolition of the gladiatorial sports in the East (to be followed later—after the self-immolation of Telemachus—in the West), the ban on infanticide and other pagan vices, and the blessing of the new city of Constantinople, of which the foundations were laid soon after the Nicene Council by the visiting bishops.

The period from the accession of Constantine to the invasions in the West of Alaric and Attila was, nevertheless, one of intense political and religious unrest. Politically three dynasties divided the epoch East and West, sometimes ruling the entire Empire in their own name and sometimes with emperors sharing their responsibility with sons or brothers. Constantine died in 337 and was succeeded by his three sons, Constantine II., Constantius and Constans, of whom Constans, in the West, favoured orthodoxy, and Constantius, in the East, the semi-Arian party. Then came a pagan reaction under Julian, called the Apostate, really an idealist who sought to bring in a religion which was neither Christian nor pagan. When Julian died in 363, in battle against the Persians, (according to a doubtful legend), with the cry, "Galilean, thou hast conquered," on his lips, he was succeeded for a year by the Christian soldier Jovian, and he in 364 by Valentinian I., founder of a second Christian dynasty. With his brother Valens in control of the East—until his defeat and death at Adrianople, in battle against the Goths—Valentinian ruled the West till 375, when he perished at the hands of Theodosius I., founder of the third dynasty. Theodosius died in 395 and from that time to the sack of Rome by Alaric in 410 and the invasion of Attila in 453, we have nothing but futile rulers unable to hold together what the strong rulers had consolidated and leaving little but a heritage of confusion.

Parallel with the vicissitudes of the political realm are those of the ecclesiastical, though out of the controversies of the time emerge convictions which were hammered, as it were, on the anvil and tempered to a strength such as proved capable of surviving the wreck of the Empire itself. Constantine was not a little disappointed to find that the religion he expected would be the means of unifying the Empire was itself torn by discord and party strife. Under the circumstances, of course, it was natural that, in a religion which had extended itself with remarkable rapidity and had been for so long occupied in defending itself against persecution, differences of theological opinion should have multiplied. The revelation, nevertheless, was bitter to the emperor and he immediately took steps to unify the Church, in order that it might the more effectively in turn unify the Empire. The result was the calling of the great Œcumenical or General Council of Nicæa in 325, to settle the points, both doctrinal and practical, which were at issue.

Of the Four General Councils of the Church—all of them held in the East—there is no question as to the supreme importance attaching to that of Nicæa. It was the only one which had any considerable representation from the Western Church, and the results—though supplemented by the acts of the later councils—were such as are plain to-day in the worship and beliefs of the Christian Church both East and West. Nothing more picturesque can be imagined than the assembling of the 318 bishops, with their attendants, at the little town of Nicæa, on the summons of the emperor. There were men from every grade of society, of every grade of culture, city men and men from the rural districts, men who had withstood the rigours of persecution and bore in their bodies "the marks of the Lord Jesus," as well as men from the court. The Council that followed, too, was marked by the presence of personality and in any other assembly it would have been impossible to overlook men like Eusebius of Cæsarea, Hosius of Cordova (representative of the Western Church), the Alexandrian Patriarch Alexander, together with his deacon, Athanasius, or that "strange, captivating moon-struck giant," Arius, who was to a large degree the cause of the assembly. No one, moreover, could overlook the significance of the emperor's presence and of the opening charge to the Council.[1]

It was plain to all that men had been called together from the ends of the Empire, and beyond, for no mere theological debate. The teachings of Arius at Alexandria—teachings which had been even popularized as songs—touched vital points in theology and Christology. In default of the knowledge that Christ is the meeting-point of a revelation of God—and so Son of God—with that of a revelation of Man—and so Son of Man—and therefore "divinest when He most is Man," it seemed at the time that the Divinity and the Humanity of Christ were at opposite poles and that therefore to guard the Humanity one must swing away from the Divinity, or *vice versa*. Arius had been specially concerned with the assertion of Christ's Humanity, but by teaching "there was when the Son of God was not" he was making Christ only the first and greatest of creatures rather than the Logos. His position is but one illustration out of many we find in this age of controversy that paradox rather than logic provides the solution of most of our difficulties, intellectual and practical, and that the logician almost invariably became the heretic. The argument on either side was bitterly waged

[1] See A. P. Stanley, *History of the Eastern Church* (London, 1883), Lectures I. to VI.

and language used such as happily is seldom employed in our most partisan assemblies to-day. St. Gregory of Nazianzus spoke later of some of these ecclesiastical councils as "assemblies of cranes and geese," but the truth remains, as even so undogmatic a thinker as Thomas Carlyle acknowledged, that had the Arian position been maintained, the Christian doctrine of Christ would have dwindled into a legend. In spite of all strong language, a very real unity prevailed and the legend-makers were not entirely wrong who asserted that the 318 Bishops always counted up as 319, since there was a presence there which added the divine to the human element. There was, therefore, secured for the Council a very substantial result in the adoption of the Nicene Creed, a formula by no means new at the time, and differing from the Nicene Creed of to-day mainly in the use of "We believe" instead of "I believe," in the addition of "Life of Life" to the epithets descriptive of the Son, and in the ending of the Creed with the words: "And we believe in the Holy Ghost." The formula ended with an *anathema* pronounced on those who refused to accept the Symbol of the Faith as thus promulgated throughout the Church.

There were, of course, many other acts of the Council which space compels us to ignore, but the authoritative decision as to the Arian controversy was the outstanding achievement. The Arian movement, however, was not immediately curbed by the action of the Council. The emperors patronized and persecuted Arians and Orthodox with consistent impartiality. Arian teachings were widely disseminated by missionaries like Ulfilas, the first evangelist among the Goths, with the result that most of the barbarian invaders, so far as they were Christians at all, were Arians. But the heresy was ultimately overcome, in no small degree through the dialectical skill and unflinching moral character of men like Athanasius. Three memorials exist to-day in our Christian liturgies in the West, first, the use of an Eastern Creed, the Nicene; secondly, the use in that Creed of the so-called *Filioque* clause, inserted as the result of a western council; and thirdly, in the use, after a Psalm, of the *Gloria Patri, et Filio, et Spiritu Sancto*. It was a great and memorable struggle, but it eventually left the Church the stronger for the conflict. Whatever crimes we may impute to Constantine, we need not begrudge him the title of *Great* when we consider how much he accomplished for the unity of the Church by calling together the Nicene Council.

Though, as we have seen, the decisions of Nicæa did not destroy Arianism, it is from that date we perceive the swing of the pendulum in an opposite direction. The swing is particularly associated with the teaching of Apollinarius, Bishop of Laodicæa, who illustrates the fact that a very acute mind may be pressed into an apparent heresy by over-emphasis of statement. In his eagerness to champion the cause of Christ's divinity, Apollinarius was led to ascribe to Him the possession of the Divine Logos instead of a human spirit (*pneuma*). So the complete humanity of Christ was apparently denied, a position which at once caught the attention of ecclesiastics with a flair for heresy. The teaching of Apollinarius, together with that of Macedonius and others, was condemned at a Council summoned by the Emperor Theodosius to meet in Constantinople. The Council of Constantinople, 381, is regarded as the Second General Council, but was not at the time thought of great importance. Only 150 bishops attended and, apart from the condemnation of Apollinarius, the main result was the acceptance of the Nicene Creed, with the additional articles (following on "We believe in the Holy Ghost") which had been meanwhile appended to the formula. It should, however, be remembered that these articles were not drawn up at the Council itself.[1]

Further stress was laid on the finality of the Nicene Creed by the Third General Council, which was called, under the authority of the Emperor Theodosius II., to meet in Ephesus in 431. The circumstances were as follows: A certain eloquent presbyter of Antioch, named Nestorius, had been raised to the Patriarchate of Constantinople. Here his preaching attracted great attention, but on one occasion he aroused the heresy-hunters by declaring that the term *Theotokos* (*the bearer of God*) should not properly be applied

[1] But see W. P. Du Bose, *The Œcumenical Councils*, p. 177 f.

to the Virgin Mary, since she was the bearer only of the human part of the Christ. This was, of course, a return swing to emphasis on Christ's Humanity, but to the critics of Nestorius it appeared that he was making a separation between the Divinity and the Humanity and was therefore teaching heresy. Hence the coming of the bishops to Ephesus, some of them in such haste that the unfortunate Patriarch was condemned and exiled before the arrival of the Syrian bishops who were favourable to the accused. The positive side of the Council's work lay in the affirmation that in Jesus Christ the Humanity and the Divinity were united inseparably. In his exile Nestorius probably achieved more—though apart from the official recognition of the Church—than he would have done had he retained his see. For as a missionary he created a movement which spread through Syria and Persia and eastward to China and is still represented in the Churches of the East.

A Fourth General Council was called by the widow of Theodosius II., Pulcheria (who had meanwhile married the soldier Marcian), to meet at Chalcedon in 451. This was the aftermath of a controversy which had arisen in Constantinople over the teaching of an aged monk, Eutyches, who had supposed he was simply expounding his opposition to Nestorius, and was rather amazed to find himself a heretic. He had undoubtedly entangled himself in his own logic and in his desire to be precise had seemed to imply that the human nature of Christ was not consubstantial with ours, thus swinging back to something like the position of Apollinarius. His condemnation was pronounced, first, by a synod of bishops who happened to be in Constantinople. This decision was protested by the friends of Eutyches and a council was assembled at Ephesus in 449, at which the monk was restored and some of his opponents deposed. It was this act of what is known as the "Robber" Council of Ephesus which led to the summoning of the important Council of Chalcedon—one largely attended and strongly influenced by Leo, Bishop of Rome. Here the orthodox doctrine of the two natures was put into its final form. Henceforth Christ is to be "owned in two natures, without confusion, without conversion, without division, without separation; the difference of the natures not being taken away by the union, but rather each nature being preserved by its propriety, and concurring to one person and to one hypostasis; not parted or divided into two persons, but one and the same Son, only begotten, God the Word, Lord Jesus Christ, as the prophets of old, and the Lord Jesus Christ Himself, have taught us, and the confession of the fathers has delivered to us."[1]

It would be impossible, within the limits of our space, even to summarize the story of other disputes—some on matters of doctrine and some on matters of practice—which fill these significant centuries. Some things were settled, such as the controversy over the time for keeping Easter. This is known as the Quartodeciman (fourteenth day) dispute, because, while some maintained that Easter should always be observed on the fourteenth day of the month Nisan, like the Jewish Passover, others held that the Sunday after that was the correct date. The latter opinion became the officially accepted one. Other controversies, from the Melitian, of the early fourth century, to the Donatist, of the fifth, turned on the degree of severity to be meted out to the lapsed who desired restoration. The African churches showed themselves particularly hard on these offenders.

Probably we can best get an idea of the significance of the period by reference to some of the more conspicuous personalities who played their part in the age of the Councils. Certainly the presence of Christ in the Church is witnessed as much in the transformed character of individual men as in the decisions of the Councils. Such personalities we can group under the general heading of East and West.

In the East we have a number of names, of which the following are examples:

*Eusebius* (260–340) is famous as Bishop of Cæsarea, the friend of the Emperor Constantine, a vigorous participant in the debates of the Nicene Council, with some leaning

[1] A good account of the Great Councils is given by W. P. Du Bose, *The Œcumenical Councils*, New York, 1896. The subject is treated more exhaustively by K. J. Hefele, *A History of the Christian Councils* (Eng. trans.) 5 vols. Edinburgh, 1871-96. Volume XIV. of the Nicene and Post-Nicene Fathers contains a full report of the *Seven Œcumenical Councils*.

towards a semi-Arian position, and specially as "the father of ecclesiastical history." [1]

*Athanasius* (300?–373) is "the royal-hearted Athanase," a figure almost as outstanding in legend and romance as in the records of sober history, even the reputed wizard of the mediæval poets. It is well said by Dean Stanley that "no fugitive Stuart in the Scottish Highlands could count more securely on the loyalty of his subjects than did Athanasius in his hiding-places in Egypt count upon the faithfulness and secrecy of his countrymen." Yet beyond all the stories which show us this extraordinary man in the rôle "of an adventurous and wandering prince, rather than of a persecuted theologian," from the time of his first appearance as a deacon at the Nicene Council, on through his five-times-repeated exile, we have the impression of the man of iron will and steadfast character who by his championship of orthodoxy against Arian and semi-Arian emperors gave justification for the phrase: "*Athanasius contra mundum.*" We have also the record of a subtle, if not highly intellectual, mind in the writings which made the name of Athanasius a synonym for orthodoxy for many generations yet to come.[2]

In the case of *Antony* (250–356) we have a reminder of the extent to which dissatisfaction with the court and the world was breeding the desire—already exemplified in the Oriental religions—for complete retirement from the world. Two forms of monasticism grew up in the Church from the third century onward. One, monasticism proper, or eremitism, in which men and women retired to complete solitude in the desert; the other, better described as coenobitism, in which they devoted themselves to a community life, separated from all secular cares. The latter type is represented by men like Pachomius, the Copt who established his community on an island in the Nile, in the middle of the third century. The other type is represented by the Copt, Antony, who, apart from his one visit to Alexandria to support the cause of Athanasius, lived out his

[1] The works of Eusebius, including the *Ecclesiastical History* and the *Life of Constantine,* are given in Vol. I. of the Nicene and Post-Nicene Fathers (Amer. ed.), New York, 1890.

[2] See A. P. Stanley, *History of the Eastern Church,* Lecture VII. Volume IV. of the *Nicene and Post-Nicene Fathers* contains the selected works of Athanasius.

life—not without strange experiences—in his self-chosen hermitage, to the neighbourhood of which flocked so great a multitude in pursuit of the same ascetic ideal.

Among the famous names of the fourth century bishops must be included the three Cappadocians, *Basil* (329–79), who after a career as advocate and rhetorician, became Bishop of Cæsarea, his brother *Gregory* (336–95), Bishop of Nyssa, and one of the most valiant foes of Arianism at the Nicene Council, and *Gregory* (326–90) *of Nazianzus*, esteemed as author and poet as well as ecclesiastic.[1]

Lastly (so far as the East is concerned), we have the great *John* (347–407), known as *Chrysostomos* ("*the golden-mouthed*") because of his eloquence. St. Chrysostom was born at Antioch and was there ordained to the priesthood. His repute as a pulpit orator at length brought him to the attention of the emperor, and in 398 he was elevated to the Patriarchate of Constantinople. But the austere ascetic had little in common with the gay life of the Imperial court and it was not long before violent antagonism was aroused in the breast of the Empress Eudoxia. In due course followed the Patriarch's exile, first to the solitary regions of the Taurus Mountains, and then to the desolate shores of the Black Sea, where death ended the weary way of the great preacher. Just before he died St. Chrysostom uttered his last word in the thanksgiving: "Praise be to God for all things."

No less an array of great names is to be found during these centuries in the Church of the West. Out of them we must select but four or five. First of all we may take two from the fourth-century history of the Church in Gaul, namely, *Hilary of Poictiers* and *Martin of Tours*. The former passed from "a refined and thoughtful paganism" to Christianity in mature manhood, was baptized about 350 and three years later was chosen by popular acclaim to be bishop of his native city. Though at a distance from the red-hot centre of Arianism, Hilary took his full share in the dispute and brought to the support of the orthodox position an acute mind and a judgement the more independent since the less affected by proximity to Constantinople. He was

[1] Some of the works of the three great Cappadocians are contained in Vols. V., VII. and VIII. of the *Nicene and Post-Nicene Fathers*.

not, however, so remote as to escape banishment, though he sensibly improved his exile by the writing of his two most considerable treatises. He returned to his see city in 362 and died four years later, famous not only for his championship of the Nicene faith, but also as a commentator and a hymnologist.[1]

Martin, elected Bishop of Tours in 371, was a disciple of Hilary. Originally from Pannonia and of pagan parentage —later on his mother was converted to Christianity— Martin became a catechumen while in the Roman army and the famous story of his charity bestowed upon a beggar and the vision of Christ arrayed in the half-cloak belongs to this period. After baptism, the neophyte made a visit to his native Pannonia, but returned to Poictiers where he set up a religious house. His election to the episcopate is the prelude to a long list of services for the Church, only terminated by his death in 397. St. Martin leaves on the mind of the student an impression of soldier-like courage, of singular charm, and of a humanity such as that which appealed to the emperor against his execution of the heretic Priscillian.

Passing to Italy we have before us the very distinguished figure of *Ambrose*, the great Bishop of Milan. Ambrose was born in 340, the son of a high Roman official at Milan. Apparently the family was Christian, but Ambrose himself was not baptized till his call to the episcopate. The story of this call is among the most familiar episodes of Church history. Auxentius, the Arian holder of the see, had just died, and the struggle was fierce between the orthodox and Arian parties to select a successor. All at once a child's voice was heard: "Ambrose for bishop!" and, in a way regarded as miraculous, the cry was taken up till the popular young governor of Liguria found himself stampeded into the sacred office, of course, after his baptism and his passing through the lower orders of the ministry. Ambrose ruled over Milan for twenty-three years, and indeed over much more than Milan, for his influence upon the politics of this distracted time was immense. To the young Emperor

[1] The works of Hilary of Poictiers are given in the *Nicene and Post-Nicene Fathers*, Vol. IX.

Gratian (till his murder in 383) he was guide, philosopher and friend. In the next reign he was in opposition, but eventually he won the favour of Justinian and later acted as intermediary between Valentinian and his general Maximus. One of the most dramatic events in Church history occurred in the following reign when the Emperor Theodosius I., after his massacre at Thessalonica, found himself barred from the cathedral services at Milan by the orders of Ambrose and was only admitted after an expression of penitence. The connection of Ambrose with the story of Augustine is familiar and must be referred to again. The great bishop was not only a voluminous writer but also pre-eminently an administrator and statesman who raised the prestige of the episcopate throughout the Empire. He was also, like Hilary, a hymnologist and a patron of church music. His stamp has remained upon the Church at Milan unto the present day.[1]

Italy has also much to do with the next great figure we have to name. This is *Jerome*, or Hieronymus (346–420). He was born at Stridon in Aquileia, but came to Rome at an early age, there commenced the studies which remained his passion to the end, and was there baptized. After a while, restless and quarrelsome, he wandered from monastery to monastery, visiting in his wanderings Gaul, Asia Minor, and Constantinople. An illness determined him to forsake his beloved Cicero for an ascetic devotion to Christ, and from this time his severity, towards himself and others, knew no bounds. Finding favour with Pope Damasua, Jerome devoted his scholarly leisure to a revised Latin Psalter and a revision of the Latin version of the New Testament. His austerity found scope in the spiritual direction of certain ladies who flocked around him. Notable among these was the wealthy Paula and her two daughters, the widowed Blesilla and the unmarried Eustochium. Under the regime which Jerome prescribed for Blesilla the lady died, and the incident called forth so much criticism that it was thought better for the little band of devotees to leave Italy for the East. After a brief stay in Egypt

[1] For the select works of Ambrose see *Nicene and Post-Nicene Fathers*, Vol. X.

and Mt. Sinai, Jerome, with his fellow-pilgrims, came to Bethlehem, where the wealth of Paula provided establishments which proved attractive to other ascetics. Here Jerome lived for thirty-five years, engaged at his main task of learning Hebrew and utilizing his learning for the gigantic work of a new translation of the Bible into Latin. This monumental edition was destined to become the *versio vulgata*, commonly known as the *Vulgate*, of the Roman Catholic Church. At intervals in the work of translation Jerome found opportunity to carry on a long correspondence with St. Augustine of Hippo, sundry rather quarrelsome controversies with a number of others, and the making of commentaries on various parts of the Scriptures. He had abundant energy and a general scholarship much in advance of his own time, but all Jerome's diligence could not make him a sagacious exegete. Of his work as translator, on the other hand, there is much to be said in the way of praise.[1]

The greatest of all the Western Fathers of the Church during this eventful period is undoubtedly *Augustine*, a man no less significant for the spiritual experience which lifted him from degradation and sin than for the vigour of his intellect and the dominance of his influence as a theologian upon the generations which followed. Augustine was born at Tagaste, in Numidia, in 354, the child of a rough, pagan father, Patricius, and of a Christian mother, Monica, who is rightly numbered among the great Christian mothers of history. The bright, high-spirited, mischievous boy was sent to school at Carthage, where he easily distinguished himself (except in Greek) among his fellows, but early fell into the lax ways of a great heathen city. As the result of an irregular union a child was born to him to whom was given the name of Adeodatus. But the mind of Augustine was still bent on finding the truth and we see him wandering through a tangle of strange philosophies. He was much attracted to Manichæanism—perhaps because of his admiration for a famous Manichæan orator—and for nine years he remained a " hearer " of this oriental dualism. For a while he taught at Rome and then, providentially,

[1] The select works and Letters of Jerome are given in the *Nicene and Post-Nicene Fathers*, Vol. VI.

went to Milan where he fell in love with the preaching of the great bishop, Ambrose. His mother, too, was now with him and the well-known story is told of her anxious visit to the bishop and of St. Ambrose's reply: "Go thy way, it cannot be that the child of so many prayers should perish." Monica's prayers were answered, for not long afterwards the event occurred so beautifully described in the *Confessions*, when Augustine, in the garden of Alypius, heard a child's voice, "*Tolle, lege*," and, taking up the Gospel read the words which almost instantly unsealed the long-accumulating flood of tears and sent him back to the house an exultant penitent. Augustine was baptized by St. Ambrose in 387 and the same year the devoted mother yielded up to God her grateful soul. It had been Augustine's wish to take his mother back to her native Africa, but Matthew Arnold interprets aright her real desire:

> Care not for that, but lay me where I fall,
> Everywhere heard will be God's judgment call,
> But at God's altar O remember me.[1]

The new convert himself returned to Africa, determined upon a life of retirement. But his ability soon called him to service in the Church and in 395 he was made bishop of the city of Hippo Regius, where he lived and laboured till his death from fever in 430.

Augustine's administration of his African see was in itself notable, but to future ages his importance derives rather from his voluminous writings—writings which make his career epoch-making in the history of the Western Church, for Roman and Protestant alike. Perhaps we may say that his thought became too dominant, to the obscuring of other elements of Christian theology which we find in Alexandrian rather than Western writings. Apart from the general mass of his theology, in which it is plain that the Manichæan cast of thought is not wholly expelled, we may divide the works of Augustine under three heads. There are, first, the controversial writings, as against the Pelagians and Manichæans, marked with all that hard and ruthless lucidity which is characteristic of the Latin lawyer at his

[1] Matthew Arnold, *Monica's Last Prayer*.

best. Then there are the *Confessions*, surely one of the most candid and beautiful of human documents, in which all the waywardness of a human soul is traced, through all "the labyrinthine ways" of its own ignorant impulse, until at last the sublime conclusion is reached: "Lord, Thou hast made us for Thyself, and our heart is restless till it rest in Thee." Lastly, there is the wonderful work, in twenty-two books, *De Civitate Dei*, which stands at the end of this period much as the *Apocalypse* stands at the end of the Great Forty Years.[1] In 410 Alaric was hammering at the gates of Rome and while the Bishop of Hippo lay dying in 430 the Vandals were besieging the city. In the first generation of the Christian Church the destruction of Rome as "Babylon the Great" had been looked upon as a foregone conclusion. The fall of Antichrist on his city of the seven hills had been envisaged as coincident with the triumph of the Christ. But, after a while, and particularly from the time of Constantine, it had appeared possible that Empire and Church might prosper in alliance—as later in the days of the so-called Holy Roman Empire. That dream was now about to be dissipated. Rome was doomed and men were asking in fear and trembling whether this might not also imply the downfall of the Kingdom of Christ. Would not the barbarian flood, just about to burst into the heritage of the Roman, bring about both the end of Roman civilization and the destruction of the Church? It was St. Augustine's special mission to stand, as St. John had stood at Patmos, to reveal beyond the falling of the stars from heaven the upbuilding of the great spirtual Empire in which both Jew and Gentile, Roman and Vandal, Greek and Goth, should have their place, under the kingship of Christ and bound together in the common service of humanity.

[1] There is a veritable library of works on St. Augustine of Hippo. His writings are contained in the great Benedictine edition of 1679, reprinted in 11 volumes in 1838. Poujoulat's *Histoire de S. Augustin*, 2 vols., Paris, 1843-52; P. Schaff's *Life and Labours of St. Augustine*, London, 1851; and A. Dorner's *Augustinus*, Berlin, 1873, are still to be recommended. For a brief but sympathetic sketch see Rainy, *The Ancient Catholic Church*, chap. xxviii.

## CHAPTER XXXIV

### *Christianity and the Barbarians*

THE religion of Christ, in the first century of its existence, had been called upon to make a great leap beyond the boundaries first recognized by the apostles, namely, from the world of the Jew to that of the Gentiles. Now, after several centuries of rapid progress, it was summoned to make a leap still more considerable, even from the Empire which had done so much to shape its system of administration, and to suggest the idea of catholicity, to that outside world of the barbarian, which to the apocalyptists was but a sea of anarchy and chaos whose waves beat eternally against the shores of the civilized earth. Yet it was now to be revealed that the organization of the Christian Church must transcend even the organization of Rome and that the catholicity of the Church must grow to include in its comprehension nations that "Cæsar never knew."

First of all, we must, of course, admit that much missionary work had been carried on among the barbarians who were, actually or theoretically, under the sway of the Imperial eagles. Some of it would seem to have been necessary for the protection of the Empire. For example, the *Goths* to whom Ulfilas, the great apostle to the Goths, ministered in the fourth century, had already been giving concern to the Wardens of the Marches in the eastern part of the Empire. It was inevitable that the boundary between the two dominions should be exceedingly elastic. Many Goths were serving in the Roman army and many Christian captives were in slavery north of the Danube. Some have supposed that Ulfilas himself was descended from these slaves. His name, at any rate, is good Gothic and he was born among the Goths about 311. Yet he was educated at Constantinople and, since the time was one of Arian ascendency, he went back to his native land in 341 at least a semi-Arian, though never one of the extreme and controversial sort. For forty years he laboured and taught and never did missionary see a more abundant harvest from his labours. For the Apostle to the Goths created through his work a Christian people, who in due course captured the city of Rome without plunging the imperial domain into the darkness of pagan barbarism. He became also the founder of Teutonic literature by his translation of the Scriptures into the language of the Goths, and by creating, to start with, a Gothic alphabet by means of which his translation might be made available for his fellow-countrymen. Certainly, when Ulfilas died in 380, he had accomplished work of immense significance for the future history of Europe. It may here be noted that all the barbarian conquerors of Rome, Visigoths, Ostrogoths, and Vandals, were Christians, though with Arian proclivities.[1]

But missionary work among the barbarians had begun even earlier than the time of Ulfilas. *Britain* was, of course, part of the Empire, but the Christianization of the Empire had in certain large areas chiefly concerned itself with city-dwellers or with communities evangelized from the city as a centre. The terms *pagani* (country-people) and *heathen* (heath-folk) still imply localities outside the Church. If such was the case in continental Europe, we may be sure it was still more so in outlying regions like Britain. As to how Christianity first reached Britain we have no certain knowledge. Legend has been busy with the story of Joseph of Arimathea landing, with eleven companions, and planting the Holy Thorn at Avalon, or Glastonbury. The reference by Clement of Rome to St. Paul's visit to "the utmost bound of the West" suggested to some a visit to Britain in the interval between the two Roman imprisonments. This is unlikely, though the great apostle may have come into contact with the British chief Caractacus, when the latter was a prisoner under Claudius. Linus, an early Bishop of Rome, referred to by St. Paul, is

[1] For the life and work of Ulfilas see Waitz, *Das Leben des Ulfilas*, 1840; H. M. Gwatkin, *Studies in Arianism*, 1900; C. A. Scott, *Ulfilas, Apostle of the Goths*, 1885.

said to have been the son of Caractacus. Other stories tell of Lucius, the British king in the second century, who sent an embassy to Bishop Eleutherius of Rome, asking for missionaries. None of these tales may have historical foundation, yet the testimony of Tertullian, Origen and Theodoret is clear to the effect that Christianity had arrived in Britain long before the çonversion of the Empire. The persecution of Diocletian, about 303, though lasting but two years, took heavy toll in Britain as elsewhere, and the names of Alban, Aaron and Julius are in the martyrologies of the time. Alban is often called the proto-martyr of Britain, and the city and cathedral bearing his name have given a local habitation to the story. When the conversion of the Empire came about it was a matter of pride to British Christians that the first Christian emperor had been born at York. In the Council of Arles, called in 314, to deal with the Donatist heresy, three British bishops attended, namely, those of York, London, and (probably) Caerleon on Usk. British bishops also were present at two other councils of the fourth century, that of Sardica in 347, and that of Rimini in 360. There must have existed considerable Christian communities in the British townships during the fourth and fifth centuries, and there was without doubt very close connection with the Church of Gaul. This is evidenced by the fact that the British Church followed the use of the East rather than that of Rome, in such matters as the date of keeping Easter, the method of administering Baptism, and the style of wearing the tonsure. There is no proof that British Christianity was affected in any large degree by the Arian controversy, but in the Pelagian movement the island church must have had a lively interest, since Pelagius (the Latinized form of *Morgan*) was himself a Briton. It was to counteract this heresy, which taught the sufficiency of human nature in itself to perform works acceptable to God, that two bishops, Germanus and Lupus, were sent over from the continent. During one of the two visits of Germanus, in 430, a memorable victory was won by Christian soldiers over an invading band of Picts and Scots. The battle was won on the " Field of German " and is known as the *Alleluia* victory, from the battle-cry of the victorious army, which alone was sufficient to send the raiders away in panic. But by this time the Roman protectors were already commencing to withdraw from the island, leaving the British a prey to the marauding bands of Angles, Jutes and Saxons harrying the eastern coast. From this date the British Church held its own only in the mountain regions of Wales and Cornwall.[1]

Only a step from Wales lay the island of *Ireland*, the one piece of Western Europe (unless we reckon the Scandinavian peninsula) outside the Roman dominion. Ireland was at this time a barbarous land, ruled by chiefs more or less constantly at war with one another, and in religious matters devoted to the worship of the old Keltic gods. The British Christians, perhaps naturally, considering what they had suffered from the Saxons, were not active in missionary work among the invaders, but they found both opportunity and inducement to propagate the faith among people of their own race across the Irish Channel. Of one such effort, that of Palladius, about 431, all we know is that it failed. Of another the fruits remain to the present day. This brings before us the famous St. Patrick, who has attracted to himself almost as much of the legendary as of the historical. Succoth, called *Patricius*, on account of his family's rank, was born about 389. As to his birthplace there are many surmises, but the balance of authority now suggests a place on British soil not far from the Severn, rather than the neighbourhood of Dumbarton in Scotland. Both his grandfather and his father, Calphurnius, seem to have been clergy, so that the boy had from the first the advantage of Christian nurture. But as a youth Succoth became the victim of a piratical raid which sent him into slavery in the island he was destined to evangelize. He escaped, but only to be recaptured a little later, and this time the *Vox Hiberionacum* sounded so appealingly that, after a second escape, Patrick made up his mind to become a missionary in the land of his exile. He was trained and ordained in Gaul and thence

[1] For the early history of the British Church, see W. Bright, *Early English Church History*, Oxford, 1878; A. H. Hore, *Eighteen Centuries of the Church in England*, Oxford, 1881; A. W. Haddan, *Apostolic Succession in the Church of England* (new edition), London, 1883.

returned to Ireland in 440, where he made without delay that attack, as courageous as it was well-timed, on the primitive idolatry. Made a bishop in 454, he founded the see of Armagh and established here the centre for a splendid and successful administration. Schools and monasteries were planted, hundreds of churches built, converts baptized by the thousand, and all strongly welded together by fifty years of devoted labour. Patrick died about 466, leaving behind him a church rooted to endure, and three interesting pieces of writing. The *Confession* throws much light on his methods for inculcating Christian truth. The *Letter to Coroticus* is one of the earliest protests of the Christian Church against the iniquities of the slave-trade. And the *Lorica*, or *Breastplate*, is a Christian hymn which is still repeated by the peasantry to ward off the evil influences of the night. It forms, moreover, in the beautiful version of Mrs. Alexander, one of our church hymns of the present day:

> I bind unto myself to-day
> The strong name of the Trinity.

There are many other characters—some of them much transformed by legend—in the early history of Christian Ireland. The work of these pioneer missionaries was such as to win for Erin the title of "The Isle of Saints." This missionary zeal, moreover, overflowed the limits of the land into the neighbouring domains of paganism.[1]

Notable among these pioneers is Columba, or Columskill (Dove of the Church), through whom was achieved the conversion of North Britain, or *Scotland*. Some work had already been carried on here among the Lowland Picts by Ninian, son of a British chief, but Columba's work was both more permanent and more extensive. The saint was born in Donegal in 521, and gave himself early to a life of piety and study in the school of St. Finnian. After his ordination Columba established the monastery near Derry—the place of his heart's love. But about 560 circumstances brought about change and exile. Through his love of learning Columba had been led to copy a certain *Psalter* belonging

[1] See Douglas Hyde, *A Literary History of Ireland*, London, 1903; J. B. Bury, *St Patrick and his Place in History*, London, 1903.

to St. Finnian, and the copy was subsequently declared by tribal law to belong to the owner of the book, on the principle, "To every cow its own calf." Columba's indignation led to a tribal war with considerable loss of life, and the angry scholar was condemned as "a man of blood" to go into exile in order to expiate his fault. So we see Columba, with his companions, in their coracles crossing the channel to settle in the rocky archipelago off the west coast of Scotland. Hy, or Iona, thus destined to become the cradle of Scottish Christianity, was soon made the centre for a work which was as practical and civilizing as it was inspired by faith. Slowly the influence of the Christian chief, with his athletic figure, his noble presence, and his winning method of instruction, spread to and across the mainland, till the rude Picts stooped, like their Irish kinsmen, to accept the yoke of Christ. For thirty years Columba worked to lay the foundations for Scottish Christianity and, well pleased to leave the further harvesting of his labours to others, passed to his rest on a June day of 597.[1]

This same year, 597, is for ever memorable in the religious history of the more southern portion of Great Britain. The ravages of the Saxons had not destroyed Christianity, but had driven it to find shelter among the mountains of Wales. In the south-east corner of the island was the kingdom of *Kent*, where the reigning chief, Ethelbert, had been permitted to marry Bertha, daughter of Caribert, King of Paris, on condition that the princess was allowed the practice of the Christian religion.

At this point it is convenient to interpolate a brief reference to the conversion of the *Franks*, at the close of the fifth century, without which the conversion of the Saxon tribes is scarcely conceivable. Towards the end of the fourth century a young Frankish hero, Clovis (Louis) by name, was hoisted upon the shields of his comrades and acclaimed king of the Salii. Down to his thirtieth year this Clovis was merely a pagan barbarian waging more or less successful war against the neighbouring tribes. But when

[1] See W. Reeves, *Life of St. Columba, written by Adamnan*, London, 1857; also Douglas Hyde, *A Literary History of Ireland*, chap. xv. The poems here given, however, are probably of later date.

he married the Christian princess Clothilde, from the Burgundians, Clovis became transformed. With fatherly tenderness he consented to the baptism of his child, and at a crisis in the battle of Tolbiac he promised in case of victory his own personal allegiance to the Christ. It was no mean struggle, and there are few incidents in history so dramatic as the challenge flung down before Clovis by the Bishop Remigius, or St. Remi. " Stoop, proud Sicambrian," cried the bishop, " thou must burn what thou hast hitherto adored, and worship what thou hast hitherto burned." The Sicambrian stooped and that day of baptism, in 496, was memorable not only for the Franks but for all Western Europe. The conversion, naturally, was but a superficial one and the wars of Clovis were not waged with the less relentlessness because of the king's new profession.[1] But Christ had been, nevertheless, recognized, and one of the consequences of the recognition was the journey of a Christian princess from Paris, with her chaplain, to find her home in the land of the Kentishmen.

Thus the old Roman church of St. Martin's at Canterbury was not wholly unused at the time when the monk Augustine arrived with his comrades as missionaries from the presence of Gregory the Great, Bishop of Rome. The story is familiar of Gregory's earlier sight of the Saxon slaves in the Roman slave-market, of his punning reference to the opportunity afforded to the Church of the time, and of the way in which his missionary intention was at the time thwarted by his election to the episcopate. But now Gregory was in the seat of authority, and the sending of Augustine was the result.[2] Once out of fear the missionaries turned back, but they soon recovered their courage and, passing through Gaul, arrived at the court of Ethelbert. The Kentish chief suspected witchcraft and refused to meet Augustine except in the open air. Here, however, the monk witnessed valiantly to the faith and made such an impression on his hearers that on Christmas Day Ethelbert, with some thousands of his subjects, submitted to baptism.

[1] The sources for the career of Clovis (to be used with caution) are to be found in Book II. of the *Historia Francorum* by Gregory of Tours.

[2] See F. H. Dudden, *Gregory the Great*, 2 vols., London, 1905.

The king furthermore made large and munificent gifts to the Church in his capital with the result that here in Canterbury arose the first English University, the monastery of SS. Peter and Paul, the first Cathedral, Christ Church, and the first school, King's School. So Canterbury became the cradle of *English* (as distinguished from *British*) Christianity, and the Metropolis of the English Church from that day to the present. Had Augustine been a greater man he might at once have established amicable relations with the remnant of the old British Church, but at the one meeting recorded as having taken place between the Archbishop—for Augustine had been consecrated archbishop by the bishops of the neighbouring Church of Gaul—and the British bishops, the pride of the Italian was resented by the representatives of the older order and it required some generations for the various elements of Christianity in England to come together under one central authority.

Even among the Saxons many missions from different sources co-operated in laying the foundations for the Church of England as we know it to-day. The work of St. Augustine and his successor St. Lawrence did not extend far beyond the kingdom of Kent, but in Northumbria, where Edwin was reigning, a missionary named Paulinus achieved a notable success by his preaching. This, together with an opportune victory, led to the conversion of the king and many of his people, and the establishment of the northern Archbishopric of York. It may be said that the baptism of Edwin in 627 was as epoch-making for the north as that of Ethelbert was for the south. Northumbria unfortunately suffered one relapse into paganism, but a new period of evangelism was opened with St. Aidan, a missionary from Iona, who succeeded Paulinus at York in 635. Soon after Aidan removed his headquarters to Lindisfarne, on the Northumbrian coast, a foundation which in a short time led to the foundation of the illustrious See of Durham, "half Church of God, half fortress against the Scot." Wilfrid, another distinguished ecclesiastic, returned later to York and still later became the evangelist of Sussex and founder of the See of Chichester. In East Anglia the Gospel was spread in the pagan kingdom of Redwald by a Burgundian,

Felix and by the Irish monk, Fursey. In Wessex, at the time sunk in the deepest paganism, the work of evangelization was carried on by Birinus, who founded the Bishopric of Dorchester. In Mercia another famous British missionary, St. Chad, established the See of Lichfield. So it came to pass that between 597 and 681 the whole of the island was drawn into the Christian fold and only the arrival of the seventh Archbishop of Canterbury, Theodore of Tarsus, in 669, was needed to weld the separate missions into one organic body under one head. Thus the Church of England was one long before there was a union of the kingdoms of the Heptarchy into one nation. Of Theodore it was said by the Venerable Bede: "Is primus erat in Archepiscopis cui omnis Anglorum ecclesia manus dare consentiret."[1]

And now, as Keltic Ireland had combined with missionaries from the Continent to Christianize the marauding Saxons, so English Christianity became responsible for heroic and successful efforts to extend the faith among the barbarians of Western and Northern Europe. Already some splendid work had been carried on by the British missionaries. St. Columban had crossed from Ireland to Gaul in 589 and founded three monasteries in the Vosges. Driven from the country in 610, he went first to Switzerland and thence to Italy, founding a new monastery in the Cottian Alps, where he died in 615. His companion, St. Gall, remained behind in Switzerland, established a famous monastery named after himself, and there died in 627. Kilian, with another band of Irish missionaries, laboured about the same time in Thuringia and there died a martyr to the faith.[2]

Now came the turn of the Saxon missionaries and we have the illustrious name of Winfrid, better known as St. Boniface, the Apostle of *Germany*. Winfrid was born at Crediton about 680 and, after ordination, proceeded to Utrecht to join the aged Willibrord. Visiting Rome in 723 he was consecrated, under the name of Boniface, as missionary bishop to Germany, and from that day to the date of his martyrdom in 754 his holy and laborious life witnessed

[1] For the whole of this period see Bede's *Ecclesiastical History*, translated by L. Gidley, Oxford, 1870.

[2] See G. F. Maclear, *Apostles of Mediæval Europe*, London, 1869.

marvellous fruition in Friesland and Germany. By this time the greatest catastrophe Christianity had yet known was taking place in the East through the onslaught of Islam. That we shall consider separately in the next chapter, but may meanwhile complete the story of the evangelizing of the northern barbarians, which went on comparatively undisturbed by the advance of Muhammadanism.

The word " comparatively " is used advisedly, for there was a time in the early eighth century when it seemed likely that, with Spain in the grip of the Muslim, Gaul also must rapidly succumb, and the recently converted barbarians go the way of the Eastern and North African Churches. But the staunchness of Charles Martel and his Franks saved the day, and the victory at Tours in 732 rolled back the tide of Islam, making possible the continuance of missionary work among the barbarians. Charlemagne, grandson of Charles Martel, made little difference between the methods to be used in subduing Islam and those lawful in the conversion of his Saxon subjects, and the latter exploit will always remain a discreditable episode in the ecclesiastical history of the West. But Charlemagne, with his assumption of the title, Emperor of Rome, touches a period as to which we must defer discussion; so, passing over much of the contemporary history, we must complete our summary within the limits already defined.

North of the dominions of Charlemagne lay a region which was at this time quite untouched by Christian influence. Nay, more, for the great Emperor at Narbonne had burst into tears at the sight of the viking ships, reflecting on the menace to civilization which his own power was unable to stem. The remedy, as in the earlier case of Rome menaced by the Goths, was, of course, in fresh missionary work, and in 826 the first mission to *Denmark* resulted in the baptism of Harold, King of Jutland, together with his wife, and a large number of his retainers. The event had a political complexion, since Harold thus became a feudatory of the Carlovingian crown, but out of it came another piece of missionary work of the most genuine and heroic quality. The missionary was Anskar, from the monastery of Corbey, who made his first headquarters in Schleswig, where he found bitter opposition and resentment over the baptism of Harold. In 831 Anskar, with a brother monk, went still farther north, to *Sweden*, where he received permission to preach and baptize, and was ultimately consecrated Archbishop of Hamburg. The time, however, was hardly ripe for successful work in Sweden and the entire mission at Hamburg was presently destroyed by an invasion of the Northmen. "The Lord gave, and the Lord hath taken away; blessed be the name of the Lord," exclaimed the gallant missionary, and he began all over again. Prospects brightened, Anskar won some measure of favour with Eric II. of Sweden, grants of land were made, and monasteries erected. One of the last events of Anskar's life was his interposition on behalf of the slaves kidnapped by the pagan chiefs. He succeeded in ransoming some and even obtaining the freedom, without ransom, of others. Anskar had hoped to win the martyr's crown; he certainly lived the martyr's life. He spent his last days in arranging the affairs of his vast diocese and passed quietly away on February 3, 865.

At this time *Norway* was divided into a number of small States, whence hordes of pirates swarmed forth to devastate the coasts of the western world. But, in the latter part of the ninth century, Harold, son of Halfdan, in order to make himself a fitter match for the Princess Gyda, vowed never to cut his hair until he had become a real monarch. Harold Lufa (" of the horrid hair "), as he was thenceforth called, achieved his ambition, married his beloved Gyda, and died in 938, leaving his kingdom to a son, Eric Blodoxe. But Eric's cruelties brought about a revolution in which the king was obliged to flee, while his younger brother, Hacon, came over from England and took the vacant crown. Now Hacon in the court of the English Athelstan had become a Christian and, once established in his new realm, he attempted the wholesale conversion and baptism of his subjects. The bonders bitterly opposed so tremendous an innovation and, when at a great festival the horse was sacrificed and the feast commenced, the reluctant king was forced to hold his mouth over the cauldron to inhale the steam, even though he refused to partake of the flesh. After this, naturally, Hacon's propaganda was rather lukewarm.

In any case, the kingdom was presently invaded by his nephews, the sons of Eric Blodoxe, and Hacon was mortally wounded in the battle which ensued. At the last he repented his slackness as an evangelist. Yet, curiously enough, the eldest son of Eric, who had also been baptized in England, continued the attempt to Christianize the land, though harried by foreign invasion and internal dissension till the coming in 995 of Olaf Tryggveson.

Olaf, who was welcomed as a deliverer, had been first attracted to Christianity through the militant Bishop Thangbrand, whose shield, bearing the figure of the Crucified, was henceforth highly prized by the chief. Journeying to England Olaf was confirmed in the faith by the famous Alphege, Bishop of Winchester. He then returned to Norway, resolved upon the extermination of paganism. The story of his journeys in the ship *Crane* and the strong measures he took to convert his subjects, high and low, make the substance of some famous sagas. Truth to tell, the missionary methods of Olaf Tryggveson smack too much of the pagan temper of the times to be admirable. Nor was their success really great. Much more was accomplished a few years later when a descendant of Harold Lufa, known as Olaf the Saint, came to the throne, and, attended by the famous Bishop Grimkil, made a systematic visitation of the realm to enforce the observance of Christianity. Not even St. Olaf's methods were free from blame, but the zeal of the kings began from this time to prevail and soon " the White Christ " was definitely enthroned in the land above the might of Odin and Thor. By the time of Canute, who was king both of England and Norway, the Christianization of Scandinavia, so far as extension is concerned, was complete.

Now we must turn back again several centuries in order to survey the victories of the Cross over the barbarians in an entirely different part of Europe. So far scarcely any impression had been made by Christianity upon the tribes on either side of the Danube, where there had been no Charlemagne to bring order out of chaos. At the end of the seventh century a people of Asiatic origin, whom we call *Bulgarians*, had been moving slowly southward into the

Balkan Peninsula. By the beginning of the ninth century their inroads had become so serious as to compel the attention of the Greek Emperors. In 811 the Emperor Nicephorus made an attack upon their capital, but the Bulgars took a terrible revenge and the skull of the slain Byzantine was fashioned by the barbarians into a drinking-cup. One good thing, however, came out of this conflict, for the captive Bulgarian princess, sister to Bogoris (Boris), learned in Constantinople the Christian faith, and her appeal in course of time led to the establishment of relations between Bogoris and the Patriarchate. In response to the prince's request a painter—the monk Methodius, who was later connected with the conversion of Moravia—was sent to decorate the palace of the barbarian and so luridly did the artist treat his subject, the *Last Judgement*, that the prince and many of his subjects were literally terrorized into the acceptance of Christianity. Missionary work in Bulgaria was considerably retarded and complicated by the competition of rival evangelists, Greek, Roman and Armenian, but there was, nevertheless, real fruit, and many reforms of a practical sort were carried into effect.

From Bulgaria the Gospel soon made its way into various parts of the Slavic world. In *Moravia*, particularly, largely through the interest of the Greek Emperor Michael, the two sons of Leon of Thessalonica, Methodius and Constantine (better known as Cyril), laboured with great devotion and success. The brothers had gone earlier to the Crimea, where they studied the Khazar language, but lack of success in this region suggested their coming to Moravia in 864. Cyril was the creator of the Slavonic alphabet which is still called after him, the *Cyrillic*. A considerable part of Holy Scripture was also translated and churches erected wherever possible. But the Moravian Church, like other parts of the East, suffered grievously from the invasion of the pagan Magyars. They suffered also from the rivalry of the German bishops, who maintained that since only Hebrew, Greek and Latin were used in the inscription on the Cross it must be heretical to translate the Holy Scriptures into any other tongues. Yet, spite of all opposition from within or without, the work prospered and before the death of Methodius in 885 foundations had been laid which were destined to endure.

We have long passed the period marked by the first onslaughts of Islam on the Churches of Christendom, but there is still one part of Europe to the story of whose conversion we must devote a paragraph. This is *Russia* where in 862 had arisen the kingdom of the Norman Ruric, in which, again, a woman's influence was the means chosen to prepare the way for the conquests of the Cross. This woman was the Princess Olga, who visited Constantinople in 955 and there received baptism. Legend indeed says that as far back as the time of the apostle St. Andrew, Christianity was proclaimed at the ancient capital of Russia, Kiev, then a city of the Scythians. But it was not really till the ninth century that the barbarian Russ came into contact with Christian civilization, and this by way of Constantinople. At the beginning of the century the Russians extended their raids so rapidly that in 865 they came under the very walls of Constantinople, greatly to the consternation of the inhabitants and of the Patriarch Photius. An opportune storm, regarded as a divine interposition, scattered the fleet of the marauders, but before many years the invaders returned under Oleg, who is said to have put his ships on wheels for use on dry land. It was shortly after this that the widowed Olga received baptism, under the name of Helena, and with the Emperor himself acting as godfather. But, on returning to Russia, Olga strove in vain to secure the conversion of her son Sviatoslav, who remained a barbarian to the last, using a human skull as a drinking-cup, and died in battle in 972. Olga's grandson, Vladimir, was more amenable, though he resisted renunciation of paganism for some years. About this time several religious deputations appear to have visited the Russian prince, asking for his favourable consideration. The Jews were rejected because they represented a people without a country; the Muhammadans because of their abstinence from wine; the Romans because Vladimir was unprepared to recognize the Pope. Only the Greek emissaries remained and the Russian prince would not at once commit himself. Instead he sent his own representatives to Constantinople to gain a first-hand impression. They returned amazed at the beauty of *Santa Sophia* and completely carried away by the splendour of the services. "We want no further proof," they had exclaimed, "send us home again." So Vladimir, confirmed by the opinion of the boyars, who reminded him of the faith of his grandmother Olga, determined to make Russia Christian and, in the spirit of the age, to suppress paganism by force. One other consideration comes into view, since Vladimir was desirous of marrying the Greek Emperor's sister, Anne, and could only do so as a Christian. So the great thunder-god Perun was dragged ignominiously down to the Dnieper, at a horse's tail, flogged on the way by those who had but recently paid him honour. And the next day, on peril of being declared enemies of the king, the whole population of Kiev swarmed down to the riverside to receive the lustral waters of baptism. On the site of the old temple of Perun arose the beautiful cathedral church dedicated to St. Basil. Schools and churches were erected throughout the land, the liturgy of Cyril and Methodius, written in the old Slavonic alphabet, introduced, and the splendid music and ceremonial of the Greek Church widely welcomed. The *Chronicle of Nestor* declares: "Thus did Christianity diffuse her light over Russia, like the rising sun, with progressively increasing splendour, and Vladimir rejoiced thereat, and was liberal towards the poor and afflicted, and distributed his gifts among all the people." [1]

Paganism still lingered in certain parts of Europe, such as Pomerania, Lithuania and Prussia, but the first great period of Christian extension was closed, with the first millennium of Christian history. We shall see in the next chapter that, while all this extension was proceeding, there were also large lapses taking place through the spread of Islam. Except, however, in Spain these made little change in the map of Christian Europe, at least for a long time to come.

Outside of Europe, moreover, there are certain gains to be recorded for Christianity which, notwithstanding the proper limits of the present chapter, we may refer to for the sake of convenience. The most important of these move-

[1] See W. F. Adeney, *The Greek and Eastern Churches*, pp. 355–70, New York, 1908; A. P. Stanley, *History of the Eastern Church*, Lecture IX.

ments is that connected with the missionary enterprise of Nestorius, the patriarch of Constantinople condemned by the Council of Ephesus in 431. Even before the time of Nestorius we find great monastic establishments at Edessa and in the Euphrates Valley generally. In 424 there were Christian bishops at Rai, Nishapur, Herat and Merv. Under the Sasanid dynasty of Persia Christianity was fairly strong, but bitterly persecuted for its supposed dependence on the hostile Empire of Rome. Later on the Nestorian headquarters were moved to Bagdad and from thence missionaries followed the trade routes into Central Asia and even into China. The most interesting reference to this is contained in the famous *Nestorian monument* at Si-an-fu, the capital of China under the T'angs, 618–905. This monument, erected in 781, and rediscovered in 1625, commemorates the arrival of the missionary Alopên (Olupun) from Ta-ch'in (the Roman Empire), his favourable reception by the T'ang Emperor, T'ai Tsung, and the consequent spread of the faith among the Chinese. The inscription is signed, both in Chinese and Syriac, by over fifty ecclesiastics, headed by one "Adam, priest and chorepiscopus, and pope of China." The inscription, headed with the figure of a cross, is described as: "Monument commemorating the propagation of the noble law of Ta-ch'in in the Middle Kingdom." From the self-felicitating terms of the inscription it is plain that Christianity had made great progress in China in the eighth century, and had doubtless done something towards the shaping of Buddhist doctrine. Other references to the Nestorian missions in China are contained in documents from the Tun-huang oasis and from edicts issued by the emperors in 638 (soon after the arrival of Alopên), 745 and 845. It was in the last-named year that Christianity, together with all the other "foreign religions," came under the imperial ban. Persecution became general, though Nestorianism lingered here and there and was not extinct in the time of Marco Polo, towards the close of the thirteenth century.[1]

[1] See K. S. Latourette, *A History of Christian Missions in China*, chap. iv., New York, 1929; P. Y. Saeki, *The Nestorian Monument in China*, London, 1916.

Now we must turn for a while from the story of Christian missions, alike in the West and in the East, to dwell upon the terrific catastrophe which drove a wedge between the two great mission fields and tore away some of the fairest provinces of the Christian Church.

Yet, before doing so, we may well sum up the significance of the period in a sentence or two. It is sadly easy to see that the age we have considered is no more an ideal one than that which preceded it. There was, it is true, a marvellous extension of the Christian name. But the methods used were wild, rough and ignorant; often they were quite at variance with the spirit of Christ. The extension was, after all, the ploughing of lands and the seeding of lands rather than the reaping of a harvest. But in the lives of thousands of individuals there was more than promise of the harvest to come. The path towards the ultimate victory was blazed. Kings and queens, like Clovis and Clothilde, Ethelbert and Bertha, Olaf of Norway and Olga of Russia, *did* become nursing fathers and nursing mothers of the Church. If still displaying the traits of the barbarian, they did, nevertheless, learn to become as little children that they might find entrance into the Kingdom. Moreover, ignorant as they often were, they rejoiced to bring the glory of the nations within the open gates of the City of God. And, amid all the tumult of the times, a new knighthood was being slowly formed out of the old pagan society whose battle-cry might be expressed in the words:

> Blow, trumpet, for the world is white with May;
> Blow, trumpet, the long night hath rolled away;
> Blow through the living world: Let the King reign! [1]

---

[1] For the general subject of this chapter the four volumes of Dr. G. F. Maclear, *The Conversion of the West*, London, 1878–79, will be found useful.

SECTION III

THE STORY OF ISLAM

# CHAPTER XXXV

## *Islam: I.—To the Abbasid Khalifate*

THE error of treating religions as self-contained and independent movements has no better exemplification than in the history of Islam. St. John of Damascus was right, as Dante was right several centuries later, in thinking of Muhammadanism as a Christian heresy.[1] To be more explicit we should say that it is a Judæo-Christian heresy, with a background of Semitic animism. By the sixth century A.D. Christianity had already been ravaged by many forms of doctrinal error, due sometimes to the swing back and forth of a pendulum which passed from one extreme of over-emphasis to the other, and partly due to conditions peculiar to particular localities. In Arabia, given all the conditions at this time prevailing, it would have been surprising if the misconceptions of Christianity there entertained had not avenged themselves in a disastrous fashion.

Again, in accounting for the rapid extension of Islam we have to take into account the political circumstances of the time and especially the fact that the "bleeding white" of the Eastern Empire and of the Sasanid Empire of Persia by centuries of warfare had left all Western Asia and Eastern Europe exposed to the assaults of a fanatical horde of Semites in a way which at an earlier period would justly have seemed impossible.

In any case it is not easy to overestimate the effect upon a hitherto victorious Christianity of the Muhammadan movement. The great Florentine who depicts the founder of Islam as in *Hell*, mangled as a schismatic, and his son-in-law Ali with face cleft from chin to forelock, was quick

[1] Dante, *Divina Commedia,* Inf., xxviii. 31 ff.

to realize the damage done to the chariot of Christ by Islam:

> Then it seemed
> That the earth opened, between either wheel;
> And I beheld a dragon issue thence,
> That through the chariot fixed his forked train;
> And like a wasp, that draggeth back the sting,
> So drawing forth his baleful train, he dragged
> Part of the bottom forth; and went his way
> Exulting.[1]

Yet, although Muhammadanism is in its origins so strangely compounded of such various elements, and in its extension so strangely indebted to political as well as to religious motives, there is probably no great religious movement whose actual history is so much in the open and therefore so easy to trace from stage to stage. We may add that there is no religion whose principles and practices are so definitely laid down. Indeed, it is out of the very definiteness and precision of the creed and cult of Islam that spring some of its most obvious limitations.

The story of the founder is one of the romances of history. In the province of the Arabian peninsula known, perhaps through an etymological misunderstanding, as *Arabia Felix*,[2] the principal market-town was Mecca, earlier known as Bacca. The city was at the same time a sacred shrine. The attraction to the religious was in the presence of the fetish known as the Black Stone, kept in a building called the Ka'aba (or Cube). Here was worshipped the chief god of "the days of ignorance," known as Hubal. Near by was the sacred spring, called Zem-zem.[3] The keepers of the shrine were drawn from the family of the Quraysh, of which Muhammad was a member. Here in A.D. 571 was born to Abdullah—destined never to see his illustrious son—the boy distinguished by the name of

[1] Dante, *Purg.*, xxxii. 130 ff.

[2] *Felix* is the Latin translation of *Yemen*, which means, first *south* (literally, *right hand*) and, next, *fortunate*. It is possible that the term was applied to the district because of its "temperate climate, reasonable rainfall, and good soil."

[3] Muhammad claimed that the Ka'aba was the original home of our first parents in Eden, shrunken and blackened by the sins of men, and that the Zem-zem was the spring miraculously created to save Ishmael from death by thirst, as narrated in Genesis xxi. 19.

Muhammad, "the Praised." The year of the prophet's birth came to be known as "the Year of the Elephant," because in this year an Abyssinian prince, Abraham, the Slit-nosed, raided the sacred city, and, in order to terrorize the unsophisticated Meccans, brought with him that hitherto unknown beast, an elephant. But, the legend declares, the animal refused to advance upon the Ka'aba, sinking to its knees. At the same time appeared a swarm of small birds, who dropped stones on the heads of the invaders with such fatal effect that only one returned to his prince to tell the tale. Later on, Muhammad included in the *Quran* a Sura known as the *Sura of the Elephant*, beginning: "Hast thou not seen what thy Lord did with the masters of the Elephant?"[1]

Abdullah, dying away from home, left his son only five camels, a flock of goats, and a slave-girl, but the young child was first of all adopted by his grandfather and, on the latter's death, by his uncle, Abu Talib, who had the custody of the shrine at Mecca. So, from A.D. 578 onward, the boy had ample opportunity to learn the traditions of the place and also to open his eyes on the outside world through contact with the numerous strangers who made their pilgrimage to Mecca. Occasionally also he went far afield with his uncle and came to know something of the religion of the Jews, who were strong at Yathrib, and that of the Christians, who, in small sectarian bodies, were scattered here and there, or as ascetics were to be found isolated in various parts of the desert.[2] He would also doubtless come across some of those earnest religionists known as Hanifs, who probably turned his attention in the direction his teaching was afterwards to take. But in addition to drinking in a certain amount of rather muddled information on the subject of religion, drawn alike from Arabian legends and bits of Jewish and Christian tradition, Muhammad also saw something of the fighting spirit of the Arab, and, we are told, loosed his first arrows against the foe. He entered thus early into one of the

[1] See *Quran*, Sura cv.

[2] Many Christian sects had taken refuge in Arabia in order to evade the imperial edicts against their particular tenets. This will explain in part the inadequate conception of Christianity the Prophet acquired.

traditions of Arab life, though Muhammad never developed personally into a very successful soldier.

Up to the age of twenty-five the young camel-driver of Mecca seemed unaware of the beckoning hand of destiny. It was through his marriage to the rich widow Khadijah, a woman already twice married and considerably older than her new husband, that there came to the future prophet that social prestige and that leisure which afforded him opportunity to indulge his brooding thoughts. For this latter purpose he retired frequently to Mt. Hira, not far from the city, and there his meditations shaped themselves into a growing sense of the unity of God, as opposed to the animism and polytheism of the Arab, together with a gathering abhorrence of the Arab practice of infanticide. Visions attended his prolonged reveries, due supposedly, in part, to certain epileptic tendencies, but, nevertheless, tremendously real to Muhammad, and destined to become immensely fruitful. In the voices which seemed to him the utterance of the archangel Gabriel, speaking the eternal decrees of Allah, we have the germ of the *Quran*, or *Recitation*, which, afterwards put together by the Prophet's successors, became the Bible of Islam. The first revelation is that which now forms Sura xcvi., commencing: " Read, in the name of thy Lord, who hath created all things; who hath created man of congealed blood." [1]

But when Muhammad lifted up his voice to preach, he found on the part of the Quraysh at Mecca nothing but hostility. Vested interests, together with the inertia of long-established tradition, proved too strong in the sacred city to be easily disturbed. For a while Khadijah was her husband's only convert, and as time flew by without more visible result, the Prophet experienced the reaction of profound discouragement. At one time he was even tempted to compromise, and issued a revelation permitting the worship of the old goddesses, such as Allat, Uzzat, and Manat. Then he repented and cancelled the unworthy permission.[2] While a few " companions," such as the

[1] An attempt has been made to put the revelations of the Quran in their proper chronological order by Stanley Lane-Poole in his *Speeches of Muhammad.*
[2] See *Quran,* liii. 19, 20.

freedman Zaid, Ali, his nephew, and, a little later, Abu Bekr and Umar, gradually rallied round him, their numbers were still so few that he was at one time disposed to shake the dust of Arabia from his feet and betake himself to Abyssinia. Circumstances became so difficult that the members of the Quraysh were only prevented from slaying their kinsman by the fact that the city was a sanctuary within which no execution could be suffered. When the Prophet sought refuge at Taif the plotting became open and unabashed and the experiment of preaching at this place resulted in hopeless failure.

Then, when the horizon was darkest, came the turning-point in Muhammad's fortunes. Two hundred miles north of Mecca was the city of Yathrib, where lived a considerable community of Jews, and where a kind of religious revival, somewhat along the lines of Muhammad's own teaching, had already found a welcome. One day in A.D. 621 there arrived at Mecca from Yathrib a deputation with the proposal that the Prophet should transfer his residence to that city, and that they should yield themselves to his religious direction. Some local rivalry probably lurked in the proposal, as well as genuine religious zeal, but the offer provided just the outlet Muhammad desired. So the *Pledge of Aqaba*, as the covenant came to be known, remains an agreement of epoch-making significance.[1] The immediate result was what is known as the *Hijra*, or "Flight," from Mecca to Yathrib, hereafter to be famous as Madinah, that is, "The City" (of the Prophet). The *Flight* was not without its perils, for the Quraysh got wind of the movement and attempted to slay the fugitives. One story (told, however, of other heroes in history)[2] describes the Prophet, with one of the "Companions," trapped in a cavern, from whence they only escaped their pursuers through the spider which had spun its web over the entrance and the dove which sat peacefully above its eggs. On such occasions

[1] Al Aqaba was a hill to the north of Mecca, where the oath was taken by the deputies from Yathrib to renounce idolatry, to refrain from fornication, infanticide and stealing, and to obey the Prophet in all things reasonable.

[2] As of David, in his flight from Saul, and other heroes in places as remote as China and Japan. The story is given by Sir Edwin Arnold in his *Pearls of the Faith*.

Muhammad was wont to impress on his followers the truth that where there seemed to be but two there were really three, with Allah himself the third. It is not strange that this year of the Hijra, A.D. 622, came to be the starting-point of Islamic chronology.[1]

Arrived at Madinah, the little company found unfolding itself before them a wonderful opportunity. The Meccans naturally were much displeased, since the northern city was in a position to intercept all the trade between the south and Syria. But, within the city, the "Helpers" became zealous in the cause of Muhammad, and the Jews likewise expected great things from the new movement. Unfortunately, the ten years of success which followed the Hijra were purchased at the cost of considerable moral decline. The preaching of Islam was now accompanied and confirmed by military demonstrations on a large scale, and the Arabs who had been left cold by the doctrine of the Unity waxed ever more enthusiastic before the opportunity of loot. The use of force by those who had but lately been its victims, turned out first to the disadvantage of the Jews, who soon found the teachings of Islam less sympathetic than they had at first surmised. Then came the expeditions against Mecca, resulting in 630 in the capture of the Holy City and the restoration of the Pilgrimage. The entry of Muhammad, riding on a camel, into the city which had cast him forth was a dramatic symbol of success. And coincidently with the effort to unify Arabia by the bearing down of all opposition to Islam came to Muhammad the idea of extending the faith into the contiguous territories. The letters which the Prophet despatched to rulers such as Heraclius of Rome and Khosru Parviz, the Sasanid, would have seemed amusing had the armies of Islam been eventually less successful. But while Muhammad was inditing letters, demanding submission to Islam, generals like Khalid were enforcing that submission with fire and sword.

The second evidence of moral decline is seen in the growing polygamy of the Prophet. In the lifetime of Khadijah Muhammad took no other wife, but two months after her death the Prophet married Sauda and espoused

[1] It is to be remembered, however, that the Muhammadan year is lunar.

Ayesha, then a child of ten years old. A little later he married Hana, somewhat later Zeinab and Um, and four others in rapid succession, without reckoning the concubine, Mary the Copt. Thus Muhammad soon overpassed the liberal limit he had imposed upon the believers. In this were the seeds of disaster and family disintegration, and out of it issued feuds which have divided the Muhammadan world down to the present day.

In A.D. 632 Muhammad made a memorable visit to Mecca on pilgrimage. Returning to Madinah he preached his last sermon in the mosque, though mortally ill at the time, and soon after reaching home expired on the lap of Ayesha, his favourite wife, with the words upon his lips: "Lord, grant me pardon; and join me to the blessed companionship on high."

Muhammad is doubtless one of the most faultily human of religious founders. He was neither the demon *Mahound* or the unscrupulous imposter of Crusading imagination on the one hand, nor was he the hero imagined by Carlyle and others of the early nineteenth century. His human weaknesses were many and he had probably in his original plan no exact idea beyond that of welding together the Arab tribes under the banner of a simple monotheistic creed. But he started something which no one person was able to control, and to-day to over two hundred millions of the faithful Muhammad is the latest and most authoritative word of the Most High, the founder of the dispensation which has superseded Christianity and must endure till the expected Mahdi prepares the way for the final Judgement.

As to the system itself, it is one admirably adapted to accommodate itself to the piety of the average man, neither too lofty nor too low for human nature's daily food. The term *Islam*, from a root *salama*, "to be at peace," signifies the attitude of submission to the divine decrees, and the follower of Islam is thence termed a *Muslim*. The religion has a very definite creed and a very definite set of obligations.[1] The Creed includes the acceptance of the five following

[1] The obligations of Islam are taught not only in the *Quran* but also in the *Hadith*, or traditional sayings of Muhammad, the *Ijmah*, or consensus of opinion, and the *Qujas*, or "analogy."

beliefs: (1) The Unity of God, that is, the belief that "God has no partners," a tenet aimed alike at the polytheism of the heathen and at the trinitarianism of the Christians. God, or *Allah* (a title, rather than a personal name, signifying "the Mighty One"), is conceived as a magnified sheikh, paternal but despotic, ordering all things according to his own fore-ordained and absolute will. Muhammadan theology stresses the transcendence of God, apart from his immanence. He "remains eternally apart upon a frosty throne; his voice is heard, but he cannot condescend." (2) The existence of spiritual beings, good and bad, all the way from the four supreme archangels, Jibrail (Gabriel), Rafail (Raphael), Azrail (Azrael), the angel of death, and Izrafil, the angel of the last Judgement, to evil beings like Shaitan (Satan), or Iblis, and the jinns and afrits of primitive Arab animism. (3) Heaven and Hell. Heaven is conceived after the manner of an Arabian oasis, with plenty of shade, rest, water, fruit, and pleasant company. Hell (Jahannum) is patterned after the infernal vortex of Irano-Judaic eschatology, with its seven circles for the sundry torments of the damned. (4) The Resurrection and the Last Judgement, expected to take place in the Valley of Jehoshaphat, at Jerusalem. After burial it was believed that a man was visited by the two angels of examination, Munkir and Nakir. If the inquisition was satisfactory, the dead man was permitted to rest in peace till the Judgement. Otherwise he was beaten with iron maces till his cries could be heard throughout the universe by all except men and jinns. Then the earth was pressed down and his body left to be torn by serpents and dragons. At the Day of Doom all were summoned to life by the threefold trumpet-blast of Izrafil and were compelled to cross the bridge Al-Sirat (the Chinvad bridge of Persia), which was supposed to be suspended between the Mount of Olives and the Golden Gate at Jerusalem. The Judge would be Isa (Jesus), as in the creed of the Christian. Preceding the general Judgement the Mahdi, or "Guide" was expected to appear, filling the earth with righteousness, but at the same time sealing the doom of the impious. (5) The Prophets were 224,000 in number, 313 of them apostles and five founders of dispensations. The five founders were

Adam, the Chosen of God; Noah, the Prophet of God; Abraham, the Friend of God; Jesus, the Spirit of God; and Muhammad, the Apostle of God. By adopting the word "*Paraklutos*" (Praised) as the reading in St. John xiv. 16 instead of "*Parakletos*" (Comforter), Muhammadans were led to believe that the dispensation of Islam had been foretold by Christ Himself.[1]

The practices of Muhammadanism were still more definitely prescribed than the articles of belief. These also were five in number, as follows: (1) The recitation of the *Kalimah* (Word), that is, the formula: "There is no God but Allah, and Muhammad is his Apostle."[2] (2) Prayer, to be performed at five stated times a day, namely, between dawn and sunrise, after the sun has begun to decline, midway between these two, shortly after sunset, and in the night. Prayer must be preceded by ablutions, which might be made in sand, provided (as was all too often the case) there was no water at hand. The attitude in prayer varied in different sects, but was generally that of standing, with the thumb touching the lobe of the ear, and the face turned towards the *qiblah*, which was Mecca. The hours of prayer were generally announced in the cities by the muezzin from the top of a minaret, with the formula added at morn: "Prayer is better than sleep." This was the form used by the Prophet's own crier Bila, at the establishment of the first mosque (*masjid*), or place of adoration (*sijdah*). The mosques are everywhere open for prayer, and on Fridays there is a special service with the giving of a homily. (3) Fasting. The great fast comes in the ninth month, Ramadan, when it is unlawful between sunrise and sunset to take even a drop of water on the lips. When Ramadan occurs in the hot season this is a rigorous piece of discipline, though dispensation is granted to the sick and infirm, and to soldiers on a campaign. The most solemn part of Ramadan is the tenth night, known as the *Night of Power*, kept in observance of the Prophet's famous Night Ride to

[1] Of course this identification was the work of a later and more sophisticated age than that of Muhammad himself.

[2] The term *apostle* (*rasul*) was used of Muhammad to distinguish him from Noah, who was specifically called "the *prophet* of Allah."

Heaven.[1] The legend states that, summoned by the angel Gabriel, Muhammad flew on his seraph steed, Al Borak, to Jerusalem, tethered the fleet courser at the temple entrance, and thence ascended through the planetary spheres to the empyrean where he beheld Allah. (4) Alms-giving, which includes a kind of poor-rate, known as *Zakat*, originally a contribution to the war-chest, to carry on the campaign against the unbelievers, but now a charity fund, consisting of one-fortieth of all such property as a man has had for a year; and *Sadaqah*, a special offering voluntarily made. Under the same head is mentioned the *Waqf*, a religious bequest or endowment. (5) The Haj is literally the "circuit," but includes a considerable number of complicated ceremonials, such as the putting on of the pilgrim garb, the sevenfold circling of the venerable fetishes, the kissing of the Black Stone, the stone-throwing to drive away the devil, the sacrifice, the visit to Madinah, and so on. On his return home the pilgrim takes to himself the name of *Haji*, and regards himself as having attained the earthly goal of piety.

Of course, there are other observances, such as the keeping of the birthday of Muhammad, and the like, and the various sects have special festivals of their own, but the above-mentioned obligations sum up the duties enjoined on the whole body of the faithful.

Something must here be said of the *Quran*, a book read, and often memorized, by many millions of people, to whom the book is support in life and consolation in death, the one great miracle of Muhammad, and the Khalif Umar's one necessary book. Islamic tradition speaks, indeed, of a hundred and four sacred writings, ten ascribed to Adam, fifty to Seth, thirty to Enoch, ten to Abraham, and besides these, the Pentateuch, the Psalms, the Gospels, and the Quran. Muhammad challenged the angels and the demons to produce the like of the *Quran* and, of course, they failed. It has already been remarked that the word *Quran* signifies merely the *Reading*, or rather the *Recitation*, since reading in

[1] The Night Ride is said to have taken place during the "year of waiting" on the proposals from Yathrib, in A.D. 621. Cf. *Quran*, xvii. 1: "Celebrated be the praises of Him who took His servant from the Sacred Mosque to the Remote Mosque, the precinct of which we have blessed to show him of our signs."

ancient times was always *ore rotundo*. Sometimes, however, the word *Kitab*, or *Writing*, is used, though we are ignorant as to the circumstances under which the Prophet's revelations were copied down. In all probability he himself could neither read nor write. Certainly not sufficiently to acquaint himself at first hand with the Hebrew and Christian Scriptures. At Muhammad's death the whole mass of inspired documents was but a miscellaneous collection of writing made by his amanuenses on parchment, palm-leaves, leather, shoulder-blades of sheep, and the like. It was impossible to put them into any accurate chronological order, so the plan was adopted—unfortunately on the precedent of the arrangement of our Old Testament prophets—of placing them in order of their length. One exception has been made, since the whole collection is prefaced by the *Fatiha*, or "opening" Sura, sometimes called the *Lord's Prayer* of Islam. As now arranged, the *Quran* consists of 114 suras, or chapters, each preceded by certain mysterious letters, such as ALM, which have been variously explained, but may be nothing less or more than labels attached to the various fragments.

The *Quran* owes its authority to the belief that it is taken from an eternal tablet in the heavens, from whence the revelation was brought in piecemeal form by Gabriel. But it owes much also to the fact that it is composed in a sonorous Arabic, in rhymed prose, and particularly impressive when declaimed to the multitude. No variation has been allowed in the text since the time when the Khalif Uthman, in 650, found his short and effective method of securing textual uniformity by the destruction of all variants. Yet, however impressive to the faithful, as recited in the original, it must be confessed that the *Quran* makes but a poor show in translation. (Many, however, will keep certain beautiful and impressive passages in reverent memory.) Its contents, moreover, are full of discrepancies, historical absurdities, and tiresome repetitions. Its main limitation is that it "stays at home," the work of one man, in one style, and applicable to but one type of society. In this it contrasts, much to its disadvantage, with the magnificent comprehensiveness of the Old Testament. Nevertheless, the *Quran* set for all time the standard of the Arabic language and literature, and when the book was passed on to other peoples, Berbers, Persians, Indians, and others, it became the means of winning among non-Arabic peoples an immense prestige for the original tongue. Nor must we minimize the importance of the faith which was sustained by the sublime assertions of the Divine unity in the *Quran*, or by the recitation twenty times a day of the opening sura, the *Fatiha*. We must remember again that the *Quran* is one principal source of Muhammadan jurisprudence, civil and ecclesiastical alike. Few books, indeed, in the history of religion have been so literally received and so implicitly followed as the Bible of Islam. Yet, to Christians, the words of Lord Houghton will recur:

> Muhammad's truth lay in a holy book,
> Christ's in a Sacred Life.
> So while the world rolls on from change to change,
> And realms of thought expand,
> The letter stands without expanse or range,
> Stiff as a dead man's hand.
> While, as the life-blood fills the glowing form,
> The Spirit Christ hath shed
> Flows through the ripening ages, fresh and warm,
> More felt than heard or read.[1]

It will be convenient here to continue our summary of the history of Islam, even though the summary must carry us far beyond the date we have already reached in the story of Christianity. As stated above, when Muhammad died there seems to have been but little foresight as to the future of the religion he had founded. Probably Ali, the husband of Muhammad's surviving daughter, Fatima, and likewise his nephew, was expected to succeed. But that strong-minded virago, Ayesha, had taken offence at some putative reflection upon her modesty by Ali, and was determined to thwart the young man's ambition. So Abu Bekr, one of the "Companions" and Ayesha's father, was designated as Khalif, that is, "Vicar," or representative. Thus was inaugurated the remarkable religio-political institution which, existing in various forms, and regarded with varying degrees of reverence, was only abolished after the

[1] Lord Houghton, *Palm Leaves*, 38.

inauguration of the Turkish Republic by Mustapha Kemal in March 1924.

Abu Bekr was already an old man on his accession and only held office for two years. He was the only one of the four Orthodox Khalifs to die a natural death. The Orthodox Khalifs are those who held the headship of Islam from 632 to 661, with their capital at Madinah, and preserved the original form of simple Arab theocracy propounded by Muhammad. At this time the future of the faith was by no means too secure, but the progress of foreign conquest soon gave an impetus which distracted the attention of Muhammadans from the situation in Arabia. These conquests became miraculously rapid and extensive in the days of the second Khalif, Umar, who took office on the nomination of the dying Abu Bekr. "I have no occasion for the office," protested Umar, but when Abu Bekr replied: "The place has occasion for you," he felt constrained to accept. Umar, 634–644, proved to be a great ruler, whose personal policy was to limit the extent of what was fast becoming a mighty empire, but whose armies were continually adding thereto. Damascus was captured in 635, and in the following year all Syria, with Jerusalem, fell to Islam. Egypt was overrun in 641, and in the same year the empire of the Sasanids in Persia was brought to an end through the battle of Nahawand. At home Umar's policy is illustrated by his famous dictum: "He that is weakest among you shall be in my sight as the strongest till I have vindicated his rights, and he that is strongest shall be as the weakest until he obeys the law." At the end of ten years of masterly rule Umar refused to will the Khalifate either to Ali or to his own son, but selected six electors to make a choice for the government of a still expanding realm after his own death. This event came, unfortunately, soon after his decision. Umar was stabbed in the mosque by a workman of Kufa who was disgruntled over the fiscal laws enacted by the Khalif. The succession now fell to one of Muhammad's sons-in-law, Uthman, who had been also the Prophet's secretary. He held sway over the faithful for twelve years, but was in most respects a weak ruler, guilty of nepotism and unable to provide troops for his own defence, while the armies of the faith were victorious almost to the ends of the earth. After a somewhat inglorious reign Uthman too was murdered, in his own house, with the *Quran* (for the compilation of which he was largely responsible) on his lap. His wife, Na'ila, vainly endeavoured to shield him and had her fingers cut off in the attempt to ward off the assassin's blow. Uthman was eighty years of age at the time of his death. Now at last was Ali's opportunity to come to his own. It was probably too late, though for five years the Prophet's nephew enjoyed (if the term does not seem ironical) the tardy reward of his patience or impatience. Ali was much loved by those who knew him, and highly reverenced by those who remembered his relationship to the Prophet. He was also personally respected for his great simplicity of life. His particular rival was the Syrian general Muawiya, who exhibited the severed fingers of Na'ila and the bloody garments of Uthman in the mosque at Damascus and thereby roused all Syria to a frenzy of revolt. A battle between the factions took place at Siffin, in which the tide was flowing strongly in behalf of Ali when the *Quran* was suddenly hoisted by the other party on a lance and a demand made for an appeal to the sacred volume. Thereupon a truce was made and for a while compromise was in the air. Nevertheless, shortly after a conspiracy was hatched by the extreme democratic wing of Islam, the Kharijites, who resented the retention of the Khalifate in the hands of the "Companions." The conspirators, in their eagerness to proclaim any Arab eligible for election to the Khalifate, determined to make a clean sweep of Ali, Muawiya and of Amru, the conqueror of Egypt. The plot succeeded only in the case of Ali, whose murder in 661 in his sixty-third year, brought the Orthodox Khalifate to an end and at the same time removed the control of Islam from Arabia and the Arabs.

The next period of the Khalifate, from 661 to 753, is known as that of the Umayyads, inaugurated by the above-named Muawiya, who like Uthman had once been one of the Prophet's secretaries. He was a born ruler, with splendid self-control, gifted also with mildness and magnanimity. During this reign many expeditions were made to the Mediterranean, in one of which the famous *Colossus of Rhodes* was broken up and sold to a Jew of Edessa. Constantinople itself was twice threatened and in one naval battle, known as the "Mast Fight," the Greek Emperor was utterly routed. Yet Muawiya was far from enjoying unanimous support at home, and the sack of Madinah, after a three months' siege, created much hostility. Under Muawiya's successors Yazid and Abd al Malik occurred the tragedy which made a permanent schism in Islam. The Umayyads were really a Syrian despotism, with its headquarters in Damascus, to which the older traditions of the faith were entirely alien. Hence there were many who clung to the belief that the family of Ali, as represented by his two sons, Hasan and Husayn, might yet recover the Khalifate. Hasan had been persuaded to abdicate his claims, but sufficient encouragement was given to Husayn to lead him into a fatal conflict on the plain of Kerbela. The result was a massacre rather than a battle, and from that time to the present day Islam has been divided between the Shiites who follow the *Shiah*, or faction, of Ali and his "martyred" sons and the Sunnites who follow the *Sunnah*, or tradition. The two sects differ mainly on the legitimacy of the first three Orthodox Khalifs. Sunnites acknowledge Abu Bekr and his successors, and the Shiites commence the Khalifate with Ali. But the Shiites differ among themselves as to the number of Ali's successors, the *Sect of the Twelve* holding the doctrine of the twelve Imams and the *Sect of the Seven* acknowledging but seven. In either case a "hidden" Imam is expected prior to the coming of the great Day of Judgement. In later centuries an extreme section of the Shiites provided the famous "assassins," or users of hashish, employed for political ends by Hasan ben Sabah, the original "Old Man of the Mountain" (Sheikh ul Jebel) of the Crusaders. The feud between Shiite and Sunnite is kept alive to-day by the annual performance of the *Passion Play*, commemorating the death of Hasan and Husayn, during the first ten days of the month Muharram, in Persia, India, and other lands where Shiites are to be found.

Abd al Malik was the most powerful of the Umayyad Khalifs, but he represents something of a pagan reaction.

"Lo, now there is separation between me and thee," he exclaimed to the *Quran* when informed of his election. This same reaction is manifested in the reign of Walid, during whose time took place the conquest of Spain. This notable event came about in part through the treachery of Count Julian, Governor of Ceuta, who out of animosity against Roderick, the last Gothic king of Spain, lent his aid to the Moor Witiza, and assisted Tariq, the Arab governor of Tangier, with ships, thus enabling him to cross the straits which have since borne the name, Gibraltar (Jebel Tariq). The invasion thus begun was not undone till the end of the fifteenth century. The best of the Umayyads is said to have been Umar II., of whom it was written: "Thou hast succeeded to the throne and didst not revile Ali, nor terrify the innocent man, nor follow the counsel of the evil-doer. Thou didst speak and confirm what thou didst say by what thou didst do, and every Muslim became well content." With Umar II. we come to the end of Islam's first century and the last days of Umayyad power. For there were several forces engaged in bringing about the termination of the Syrian dynasty. One was the hatred of the Syrians by the subject peoples, particularly in Persia. A second was the growth of Shiite sentiment due to horror at the cruel fate of the Prophet's grandsons. A third was the expectation of the Mahdi, who would announce the end of all things.

The collapse of the Umayyads came about in this manner. The family of Ali was still represented, namely, by Muhammad ben Ali, and to him was born a son, Abu'l Abbas (Abdullah ben Ali ben Abdullah). On the other hand was the last Umayyad Khalif, Marwan ben Muhammad ben Marwan, nicknamed the Ass. It had been prophesied that in the *Year of the Ass* 'A. ben 'A. ben 'A. was to slay M. ben M. ben M., and the poets chanted the song: "I see amid the embers the glow of fire and it wants but little to burst into a blaze." So it came to pass that in 747 the Black Standard of the Abbasids was raised and a call addressed to all the disaffected to rise in revolt, under the leader Abu Muslim. Marwan was defeated in 750 on the banks of the Zab; Damascus was taken; the tombs of the Umayyads sacked. One member of the Umayyad line escaped to Spain where, under the name of the Western Umayyads, Khalifs continued to claim authority with their capital at Cordova. Abbas now became the first Khalif of a new line, known as the Abbasid, with his capital at Bagdad. The great general, Abu Muslim, who had done most to secure victory, had his reward in 755, when he was cruelly murdered.

The chapter may fitly be closed with a quotation from Gibbon, eloquently summing up the achievements of the ill-fated Umayyads:

"At the end of the first century of the Hijra, the Khalifs were the most potent and absolute monarchs of the globe. Their prerogative was not circumscribed, either in right or in fact by the power of the nobles, the freedom of the commons, the privileges of the Church, the votes of a senate, or the memory of a free constitution. The authority of the companions of Muhammad expired with their lives; and the chiefs or emirs of the Arabian tribes left behind, in the desert, the spirit of equality and independence. The regal and sacerdotal characters were united in the successors of Muhammad; and if the *Quran* was the rule of their actions, they were the supreme judges and interpreters of that divine book. They reigned by the right of conquest over the nations of the East to whom the name of liberty was unknown and who were accustomed to applaud in their tyrants the acts of violence and severity that were exercised at their own expense. Under the last of the Umayyads, the Arabian Empire extended two hundred days' journey from east to west, from the confines of Tartary and India to the shores of the Atlantic Ocean. And if we retrench the sleeve of the robe, as it is styled by their writers, the long and narrow province of Africa, the solid and compact dominion from Fargana to Aden, from Tarsus to Surat, will spread on every side to the measure of four or five months of the march of a caravan. We should vainly seek the indissoluble union and easy obedience that pervaded the government of Augustus and the Antonines; but the progress of the Muhammadan religion diffused over his ample space a general resemblance of manners and opinions.

The language and laws of the *Quran* were studied with equal devotion at Samarcand and Seville; the Moor and the Indian embraced as countrymen and brother in the pilgrimage of Mecca; and the Arabian language was adopted as the popular idiom in all the provinces to the westward of the Tigris." [1]

[1] Gibbon, *Decline and Fall*, iv., 490.

# CHAPTER XXXVI

## *Islam: II.—From the Abbasids to the Present Day*

THE Abbasid Khalifate, with its capital at Bagdad, represents a decided decline of the Arabian influence upon Islam and a swing back politically to the earlier predominance of Persia. This swing of the pendulum is illustrated not merely by the choice of the capital, but also by the use of some of the old Sasanian machinery of government, and particularly in the employment of Persians in the office of Vizier. The rise of the Barmecide family—Barmak with his son Yahya and his grandson Jafar—is a special instance of this, until the massacre of the family in the reign of Harun-al-Rashid. The undivided Khalifate was no longer co-extensive with Islam, since the formation of the Western Umayyad Khalifate in Spain, but the first Abbasids were immensely powerful, particularly such men as Mansur, the founder of Bagdad, Harun-al-Rashid, who is said to have corresponded with Charlemagne, and Mamun, who reigned from 813 to 833.

It was in this last reign that we find that great enthusiasm for literature which was destined in time to influence so powerfully the Europe of the Middle Ages, by the way of Spain, Sicily and Provence, and even to affect the ideas of the Schoolmen. The Arabs did not quite maintain their early importance in the extension of the faith, but among the non-Arab peoples there was an immediate demand for grammars and dictionaries, since it was only permissible to study the *Quran* in the original. The wide diffusion of the faith also called forth books on geography and history, as well as translations from the Greek. Travelling developed into a craze. It was said: " Whosoever goeth forth to seek for learning is in the way of God until he returns home:

the angels blithely spread their wings over him and all creatures pray for him, even the fish in the water."

This interest took, among other forms, that of devotion to science, and medicine, astronomy and mathematics found many ardent votaries. Fiction also flourished, as may be noted in the case of the *Thousand and One Nights* of universal fame. The beast fables of India, too, became popular in the version of the Persian *Qalilah and Dimnah* made by Ibn'ul Muqaffa. Muhammadan law attracted many students, moreover, and eventually produced the four famous schools of law known as the Hanifite, founded by Hanif, the Malikite, founded by Malik ibn Anas, the Shafiite, founded by Shafi'k, and the Hanbalite, founded by Ibn Hanbal. Naturally, too, there was special interest in philosophy and theology, particularly as the Semitic dogmatism became more and more leavened with the Aryan spirit of enquiry. A rationalistic sect of great prominence at the time was that of the Mutazilites, whose doctrines were embraced by the Khalif Mamun. The Mutazilites denied the doctrines of the uncreated *Quran*, and tried hard to rid the conception of God of its cruder anthropomorphism, but these teachings were later declared heretical, largely through the influence of the theologian Al-Ashari (died 935), who went over from the Mutazilite to the traditional position.

The golden age of the Abbasids declined after the time of the Khalif Motasim, who did nothing to stay the decadence. At the beginning of the tenth century it was obvious that the ecclesiastical rulers of Bagdad were no longer capable of holding together the Muhammadan Empire of the East, not to mention the territories of Egypt and North Africa and the far western conquests in Spain. From the tenth century onward, while the Khalifs fretted themselves unavailingly in Bagdad, or became but pawns and puppets in the hands of men stronger than themselves, it was open to these latter to carve out on their own behalf kingdoms, small and great, to last just as long as their dynasty could hold itself together. Politically the power of the Khalifs sank almost to zero, however much their religious authority might be theoretically recognized. For the conquering rulers of lines such as Samanids, Saffarids, Ghaznavids, and the like, were still good Muslims and harried the lands they invaded in the name of Allah. In some few countries, as in China, peaceful penetration (rather than force), was used, at least to start with, but in most of the new Muhammadan territories entrance was won by militaristic methods. For example, as early as 664, the Muslim entered Afghanistan and captured Kabul. A little later, about 714, Scinde was conquered by Muhammad ibn Qasim, who presently advanced to Multan, making many converts and, at the same time, securing immense loot. At the beginning of the eleventh century the great Ghaznavid, Mahmud ("Allah-breathing lord"), made his seventeen invasions of India in the course of twenty-five years, and demolished the idols on a large scale, without attempting any permanent conquest. It was plain that Islam, in passing from one race to another, was by no means diminishing in vigour.

One remarkable development to be noted in Islam in its passage from the Semite to the Aryan and thence to the Mongol is to be found in the philosophical mysticism known as Sufism. The word *sufi*, from the Arabic *suf* (*wool*)—not from the Greek *sophos*—denoted primarily the follower of the simple life who preferred the coarse woollen garments of the ascetic to robes of linen or silk. Several theories as to its origin have been advanced. Some describe it as an esoteric doctrine preached by the Prophet himself. Others regard it as a reaction of the Aryan mind against the dogmatism of a Semitic religion. Others suppose it to be derived from what is known as neo-Platonism. Still others think it a product of Indian Vedantism. And, lastly, there are those who believe it to be of entirely independent origin. In any case, it represents that mystical, quietistic and pantheistic attitude which has had its votaries in most religions, from the Taoism of China to the mysticism of a Thomas à Kempis or a Tauler.

Sufism appears first about 777, in the teaching of Abu Hashim and finds a rather extreme expression in Al Hallaj, who insisted that one could perform the Haj in a private room quite as well as by undertaking the tedious journey to Mecca. The language of the Sufists, however, is frequently so extravagant that it is often impossible to take it literally. Sometimes, indeed, it is difficult to draw the line between what is spiritual and what is merely erotic. Three types of Sufism are generally recognized, namely, the *Theosophic*, in which the emphasis is laid on fellowship with God in His vision; the *Theopathic*, in which the believer is raised emotionally almost to identity with God (as is illustrated in the story of Bayazid);[1] and the Theurgic, in which the mystic claimed to be able to work miracles. Persia was the true home of Sufism and most of the great Persian poets, such as Sana'i, Faridu'din Attar, Jalalu'din Rumi, down to Jami, were Sufists. Later on, as a result of the Muhammadan invasions, India became powerfully influenced by this form of mysticism, and much of the religion represented by men like Kabir and Nanak, not to mention the great Bengali poets, was probably the result of this importation.

As the Arab had yielded the torch of Islam, in the west to the Moor, and in the east to the Persian, so—at least so far as the east is concerned—we find, from the twelfth century on, the Persian yielding the leading *rôle*, first to the Seljuk, and then to the Mongol. The Seljuks appear as early as the eleventh century and found the disintegrated Khalifate ripe for attack. "These rude nomads," says Stanley Lane-Poole, "unspoilt by town life and civilized indifference to religion, embraced Islam with all the fervour of their uncouth souls." From Seljuk and Tughril, on through the reigns of Alp Arslan and Malik Shah (who died in 1092), we have a succession of able leaders who were rigidly orthodox Muslims and therefore the foes of the Fatimid or Ismaili (the *Sect of the Seven*) Khalifs then ruling in Egypt. It was under Malik Shah that Hasan ibn Sabah lived and founded the order of the Assassins, and it was shortly after that the power of the Seljuks and their possession of the Holy Places in Palestine led to the appeal of Urban II. and the launching of the first Crusade. It was a Seljuk too, the famous Salahu'din (Saladin), who made himself master of Egypt through the removal of the Fatimid Khalif and

[1] A native of Khorasan whose self-identification with God led him to declare: "Verily, I am God, there is no God but me, so worship me. Glory to me! How great is my majesty!" See *E.R.E.* xii., p. 12.

became the most formidable foe of western chivalry. On their return the Crusaders took back with them many crude ideas as to Muhammad and his religion, but they at least learned to respect the courage and courtesy of Saladin, finding his ideals of knighthood in no way inferior to their own. But the last of the great Seljuks, Sanjar, fell before the invasion of the Khwarazmshahs, and a great Persian poem, *The Tears of Khorasan*, laments his fate.

The Kharazmshahs, or kings of Khiva, did not long retain power within the territories of the Khalifs. In 1162 was born that thunderbolt of war, Jenghiz Khan, and before his death, in 1227, the empire of the Khivans was shattered to pieces. His son Ogdai followed this up with an attack on the Khalifate and in 1258 Bagdad was taken and sacked, with the massacre of 800,000 people. The last of the Khalifs of Bagdad was beaten to death in a felt sack (to avoid bloodshed) and the survivors of his family escaped to Cairo which for the next two or three centuries was regarded as the capital of Islam.

The Mongols, in the course of their career probably "inflicted more suffering on the human race than any other event in the world's history of which records are preserved to us," [1] but on their first appearance in Western Asia, their arrival was taken to be the death-blow of Islam. Indeed, it was for a long while believed that they offered the means, so ardently desired by Christendom, for making headway against the conquering forces of the Turk. Jenghiz Khan, brought up in the principles of primitive shamanism, was minded to favour all religions equally while giving adherence to none. His grandson, Kublai Khan, while personally favouring a form of lamaistic Buddhism, was anxious for the Polos to secure Christian missionaries from Europe. Had this plan succeeded, the history of Asia might well have been completely changed. A few missionary envoys, like John de Plano Carpini and William de Rubruk, did their best, during the brief visits they paid to the Great Khans, and John de Monte Corvino, the Franciscan Archbishop of Peking, laboured with conspicuous success for many years. But eventually the attractions of Islam pre-

[1] E. G. Browne, *Literary History of Persia*, II. 427.

vailed with the Khans. Ghazan Khan, 1295–1304, was the first to embrace Muhammadanism, and a little later some of the Il-Khans of Persia, who had even been baptized in infancy, became fiercely attached to the religion of the Prophet. From this time on, the Mongols were as vehemently bent upon the spread of Islam as had been the Seljuks earlier.

As it was in Persia and in Central Asia, so it was in India. One Muhammadan dynasty after another carried fire and sword into the peninsula, together with the message of the *Quran*. The Slave Kings of Delhi began with Qutb-ud-din in 1206; then came the Khiljis, from 1290 to 1320, extending the propagation of the faith into South India. At last, at the beginning of the sixteenth century, came that redoubtable descendant of the Timurids, Babar, and laid the foundations of the Great Moghul Empire, the strongest and longest-lived of the Muhammadan dynasties. Babar and Humayun were devout, Akbar was eclectic, anxious to create a religion inclusive of the best points in Islam, Hinduism and Christianity, Jahangir and Shah Jahan were more orthodox, though sadly lax in the matter of wine-bibbing, Aurungzib, who reigned from 1658 till 1707, was a gloomy fanatic, who provided for his own funeral expenses by copying the *Quran*, and warred incessantly upon those who resisted his effort to Islamize the whole of India.

This is, of course, but one side of a great period of missionary zeal. To many doubtless Islam appeared to be propagated only by the sword, and the world was divided rigidly into the two realms, Dar ul Islam (the rule of Islam) and Dar ul Harb (the rule of war). Yet, in spite of all the forced conversions which have taken place in India—some of them as recently as 1921, in the course of the Moplah Rebellion—there has been a good deal of peaceful penetration, and some fine examples of missionary work by persuasion, as, for example, the work of Kwajah Mu'in ud Din Chishti (died 1236), who heard the voice of the Prophet commissioning him to convert Ajmir.

Outside of India great impetus was given to the military and political prestige of Islam by the rise of the Ottoman Turks. These were but a small horde of some three or four thousand warriors when they arrived in Asia Minor but the timely aid they rendered to the Seljuks in their struggle against the Mongols, won permission for them to settle in the neighbourhood of their present capital of Angora. Before the middle of the fourteenth century the Greek power was practically expelled from Asia Minor and a few years later the Sultan Murad I. captured the city of Adrianople and made it plain that the Turks had entered Europe to stay. There was a temporary set-back through the great victory of Timur Leng over Sultan Bayazid at Angora in 1402, but fifty years later, in 1453, Sultan Muhammad II. put an end to the Eastern Empire by the siege and capture of Constantinople. We here reach one of the chief landmarks of Muhammadan history, when the great city of the Eastern Cæsars became the capital of a triumphant Islam, and the Church of Santa Sophia was transformed into a mosque.

After the destruction of the Abbasid Khalifate at Bagdad the title Khalif came to be assumed by many independent sultans of various dynasties, more by way of political pretension than out of a desire to claim ecclesiastical authority. As early as 1362 the Ottoman Murad I. called himself Khalif, and from that time on the title was used by successive Turkish Sultans. The story that Selim I. bought the Khalifate in 1516 at Cairo from a descendant of the Abbasids is now generally discredited. But there is no doubt that the Ottoman Sultans made large use of the claim, for political purposes, down to the end of the nineteenth century. On this ground they assumed the titular headship of Islam, an honour precariously held till after the Great War, when Mustapha Kemal summarily "pricked the bubble" of the Khalifate by its abolition, only two years after the office had been bestowed upon Abdul Majid, cousin of the last Sultan, Muhammad VI.

The apogee of Muhammadan power, at any rate in the political and military sense, was reached in the sixteenth century, and that power did not begin to decline till the long-continued wars with Venice from 1646 to 1669. From this time onwards such extension as is gained by Islam comes rather through peaceful penetration than through warlike measures. Conversion to Muhammadanism in India was quite common, sometimes indeed merely to escape from the tyranny of caste. In Western China the advance of the faith was due in large part to immigration. In Eastern Africa the penetration had a sinister association with the slave trade and can hardly be regarded as peaceful.

In Arabia, towards the close of the eighteenth century, the long repose of the "silent peninsula" was interrupted by a movement of religious as well as of political importance, even down to the present day, known as Wahabism. The founder, Ibn Abd'ul Wahab, had grown up in serious distress over the increasing laxity of Muhammadan belief and practice. He noted the use of wine and tobacco, the worship of the Muhammadan saints, or *walis*, such as had developed into a kind of polytheism, and the growing disrespect for the "traditions." Thereupon he preached a great Puritan revival, and enforced his preaching by the slaughter of heretics and unbelievers. To every one of his soldiers he gave a passport to heaven, in case of death on the battlefield. Ibn Abd'ul Wahab died in 1791, but the movement was espoused by Muhammad Ibn Sa'ud, and in 1804 led to the capture and looting of Madinah. So seriously was the menace regarded that the famous Muhammad Ali, an Albanian soldier in Egypt, was called upon by the Turkish Government to crush the movement by force. This was accomplished, but the Wahabi State was reconstituted in 1824 and in 1836 was once more independent of foreign control. The line of descent from Ibn Sa'ud has been maintained to the present bearer of the name, and the Wahabi power is still supreme in certain parts of Arabia.

An important chapter in the history of Islam, to which but the barest allusion has so far been made, is that which concerns the Iberian Peninsula. The crossing of the Straits of Gibraltar by Tariq in 711, at the command of his general Musa, and through the treachery of Count Julian, speedily brought about the downfall of the Visigoth kingdom. Though Tariq was presently recalled, the mixed host of Berbers and Arabs flowed northward in an irresistible tide, in 718 crossed the Pyrenees, and was only brought to a standstill by the great victory of Charles Martel at Tours in 732. There followed a time of confusion and anarchy, but in 758 a representative of the Umayyad family, now fugitive from Syria, reached Spain and commenced a rule independent of Bagdad. This was Abd ur Rahman I., under whom Muslim Spain began its era of prosperity. Many years later, in 929, Abd ur Rahman III. promulgated an edict that from Friday, January 16 of that year, he was to be acclaimed as Khalif and Commander of the Faithful. This begins the Khalifate of the Western Umayyads in the official sense. It was a period during which Muslim culture reached its highest point in Spain and began to extend its influence thence into the rest of Europe. These were indeed halcyon days for Islam. Cordova took on the appearance of a great capital, with large libraries and impressive assemblies of learned men. With the help of Jews, who were only too glad to escape from Christian persecution by courting the followers of the Prophet, translations of many important works were made and circulated far beyond the Pyrenees. The greatest of Western Umayyad princes, whose navy disputed the mastery of the Mediterranean with the Fatimids of Egypt, and with whom the proudest of monarchs sought alliance, passed away in 961. His work was carried on by Al Hakam II., who possessed a library so large that forty volumes were required for its catalogue, and under Al Hakam's successors the great minister Al Mansur (Almanzor) for long kept up the prestige of Spanish Islam. When Almanzor died in 1002, on his tomb were engraved the words: "His history is written on the earth if thou hast eyes to read it. By Allah, the years will never produce his like, nor such another defender of our coasts."

After this there was swift disintegration and a series of shifting principalities took the place of the Western Umayyads. From A.D. 1100, for a few years, the Almoravides, a Berber dynasty with a considerable intermixture of other blood, held sway over Spain in the name of the King of Morocco. Then an even more bigoted line arose, the Almohades, or followers of the Mahdi. But the time was now ripening for a Christian reconquest. For a long while the kings of Leon and Aragon had been using every opportunity to attack and weaken the Muslim rule. Now, with an increasing disposition on the part of the Christian princes to unite against the foe, came ampler opportunity for driving them from stronghold to stronghold, southward to the dividing straits. The final blow came in 1492, in the reigns of Ferdinand and Isabella, through the reconquest of Granada. So once more Spain entered the Christian fold, though the strong impress made by five centuries of Muhammadan culture was never lost in the Peninsula and in the contiguous lands.[1]

Before presenting two or three general observations on the history of Islam, it remains for me in this chapter to mention several movements in the Muhammadan world which are of considerable present-day significance.

One of these is the Babist movement, genetically connected with the Shiite Sect of the Twelve, and with antecedents, moreover, which carry us far back into the curiously eclectic history of Persian Islam. The religion of the Bab, or *Gate*, was founded by Ali Muhammad, the son of a Shiraz tradesman. He was born in 1820 and, after a visit to the tombs of Hasan and Husayn at Kerbela, announced himself as the Bab in 1844. Later on he visited Mecca and subsequently commenced the sending of missionaries throughout Persia, even announcing himself to the Shah as the " Hidden Imam," the " Primal Point " of revelation, and other things which led not merely to controversy but also to an outbreak which had to be suppressed by military force. The Persian Government, deeming that the new prophet's teachings were dangerously subversive, executed him in a cruel way at Tabriz in 1850. Two years later an attempt on the life of the Shah led to the arrest and death of twenty-eight of the leading lights of the movement.

But now arose a disciple of the Bab, one Husayn, who assumed the title of Baha Allah, the *Splendour of God*, and proceeded to teach the old doctrine in a new form. Bagdad was the centre first chosen for what soon came to be known as Bahai, but the Turkish Government was persuaded by Persia to transport the two chief leaders first to Constantinople and then to Adrianople. In this last-named city Baha Allah formally announced himself as " Him whom

[1] See Reinhart Dozy, *Spanish Islam.*

God shall manifest" and a split was caused by the announcement. Baha Allah and his party were now transported to Acre in Palestine, where a propaganda was organized which has reached the United States as well as other parts of the civilized world. Bahaism claims to be not so much a form of Islam as a universal religion, with a revelation superseding both the *Quran* and the Gospel. The founder died in 1892 and his death led to still further schism in an already divided community. The number of those professing Bahai has been variously given, all the way from one or two hundred thousand to as many as three million.[1]

Another interesting offshoot of Islam is what is known as the Ahmadiya movement, started in India about 1889 by Mirza Ghulam Ahmad, who eventually claimed that he was not only the promised Mahdi, but also Christ in His second coming, and the predicted tenth avatar of Vishnu. He died at Lahore in 1908, but his work has been continued by disciples who have made the most of Ahmad's syncretistic teachings. Missionary stations have been established outside of India, including England, an *Islamic Review* has been published in England and a *Review of Religions* in India, while an edition of the *Quran*, in an English translation, has been made in the interest of the sect. The number of people professing the Ahmadiya doctrine has been set down by some authorities as about 50,000.[2]

Some reform movements in Indian Islam are along more orthodox lines, though doubtless much influenced by contact with Christianity. One is that associated with the *tabligh* (propaganda) carried on by Kwajah Hasan Nizami, of Delhi, a Sufi of the Chishti order, who gives the objects of the Tablighi Mission as follows: "(1) To strengthen Muslims through religious teaching. (2) To assist Muslims to improve their economic condition. (3) To inspire Muslims with missionary zeal. (4) To propagate Islam among non-Muslims."[3]

Undoubtedly, western influence has sufficiently leavened Muhammadanism in India so as to diminish intolerance, at

[1] Dr. E. G. Browne gives us much interesting information on the origins of this movement in his fascinating, *A Year Amongst the Persians*.
[2] See H. A. Walter, *The Ahmadiya Movement*, Oxford, 1918.
[3] Murray T. Titus, *Indian Islam*, p. 51, Oxford, 1930.

least in certain quarters, and to dispose some to see the good in other systems. A few have even insisted that "there is no inherent antagonism between Christianity and Islam." [1] But this attitude is not common in Islam as a whole. For example, we have, outside of India, a quite militant movement known under the name of Sanusi (or Senusi). This, which is in part an outcome of Wahabism, is so named after a North African reformer, born about the end of the eighteenth century, who visited Mecca and there obtained the support of the Prince of Wadai, Muhammad Sherif. Anticipating his death Sanusi called his two sons and ordered them to jump from the top of a palm-tree. The younger son jumped first and was thereupon designated as his father's successor. Under this Sanusi el Mahdi the sect has spread widely throughout North Africa, and from the Sahara to Somaliland. The Sanusi were troublesome to the Allies during the Great War, but profess to be less interested in politics than in religious reform. Their tenets are puritanical as well as mystical. The drinking of wine and coffee is forbidden, as well as the use of tobacco. Missionary agents travel extensively and are often persons of wealth and importance.[2]

Other reform movements in modern Islam might be mentioned, but for the most part they are of slight importance. It will be sufficient to note the attempt to adjust Islam to modern scientific knowledge made in recent years by the Egyptian reformer and patriot, Muhammad Abdu, whose exposition of the Muslim religion from this new point of view has been translated into French.[3]

Muhammadanism, while mainly a "religion of the heat belt," is professed over a large part of the earth's surface. There are in the world about 233,000,000 Muslims, of whom 169,000,000 are in Asia. In China they number about 16,000,000, largely as the result of immigration since the day when the Khalif Mansur, in 755, sent 400 men to assist the T'ang Emperor to suppress the rebellion of An Lu-shan. In Turkey there are 10,000,000, mostly now in their homeland of Asia Minor. In India there are

[1] Titus, *Indian Islam*, p. 209. [2] See article "Sanusi," *E.R.E.*, xi. 194 f.
[3] *Rissalat al Tawhid*, Paris, 1925.

77,000,000, distributed among many races. All Persia is Muhammadan, largely of the Shiite sect. Most of North Africa, including Egypt, is under the banner of the Prophet. In Central Asia there are even Soviet Republics which are Muhammadan in religion. Java, into which Muhammadan missionaries entered in 1419, is now predominantly Islamic; in the Dutch East Indies as a whole there are 25,000,000 Muhammadans. Even in the Philippines, among the Moros (Moors) there are some 300,000 of the faith.

All these populations constitute a vast brotherhood, but Islam has no longer a living head. Following upon the Great War and the drawing up of the *Treaty of Sèvres*, great excitement prevailed in Islam over the belief that the Sultan of Turkey, representative of the leadership of Islam, was to be deposed. The result was the raising of the Khalifate, or *Khilafat*, question in every Muhammadan land from Morocco to the Philippines. In consequence of the agitation the Allies scrapped the *Treaty of Sèvres* and negotiated the *Treaty of Lausanne*, which was signed by Turkey. The new treaty avoided the thorny question of the Khalifate, but, almost immediately after, the new Turkish leader, Mustapha Kemal, himself deposed the Sultan and shortly afterwards abolished the Khalifate. Very little protest seems to have been made and to-day, though there are potential claimants to the office here and there, the question seems to be dead. Muhammadanism is to-day a religion of brotherhood, but with no overlordship or directing priesthood.

Of Islam we may say in conclusion that, as shown by its history, it is a religion with many obvious defects, apart from its general lack of idealism and its catering to the standards of the average man. In its morals Islam is proverbially static and unprogressive. A low position has been commonly assigned to woman, and slavery has been generally condoned, even though slavery has been abolished in some Muhammadan lands.

In addition to its congenital defects, Muhammadanism has retained no small amount of pre-Islamic animism, while many corruptions have crept into beliefs and practices which were originally blameless. The worship of saints, for example, has served to create even a species of polytheism, and the reverence for dervishes has made up for the lack of an organized priesthood.

Where political reform has been introduced into Muhammadan countries the result has frequently been seen in the breaking down of religious faith and in the neglect of religious obligations. In Istanbul, for example, to-day the mosques are wellnigh empty, even on festival occasions, and the edict abolishing the fez has made it difficult for men to make the customary prostrations in prayer, with head covered and forehead touching the ground.

On the whole, while Islam has not been without its beneficial influence on peoples of a low degree of culture, and while we must certainly not forget the great boon that Muhammadan learning rendered to mediæval scholarship in Europe, Islam has been a religion of stagnation, an instrument only too well fitted for the use of tyrannical and oppressive governments. Sir William Muir concludes his *History of the Khalifate*, first published in 1888, with the words:

"The political ascendancy of the faith is doomed. Every year witnesses a sensible degree of subsidence. In the close connection of the spiritual with the civil power, this cannot but affect the prestige of the religion itself; but, nevertheless, the religion maintains, and will no doubt long continue to maintain, its hold upon the people singularly unimpaired by the decline of its political supremacy. As regards the spiritual, social and dogmatic aspect of Islam, there has been neither progress nor material change. Such as we found it in the days of the Khalifs, such is it also at the present day. Christian nations advance in civilization, freedom and morality, in philosophy, science and the arts, but Islam stands still. And thus stationary, so far as the lessons of history avail, it will remain." [1]

The political and social renaissance witnessed in recent years in Turkey, Persia and Egypt has not greatly served to modify this view in the minds of most. What the future has in store for Islam is, of course, unpredictable. In a

[1] Sir William Muir, *The Caliphate, Rise, Fall and Decline*, p. 603. Reprint of 1924 (Edinburgh).

recent *Survey of International Affairs*, by Mr. Arnold J. Toynbee, the statement is made: "In 1929 it was hardly possible, after all, to answer the question whether there was still an Islamic World in the spiritual sense. In the eyes of certain Western observers, Islam was then *in articulo mortis*; in the eyes of certain Wahabi fanatics, who recognized no true believers among contemporary mankind outside the ranks of the Ikhwan, Islam in 1929 stood again where it stood in 633, when the tribes of Arabia, fused together by the Faith, were straining at the leash as they awaited the signal to go forth conquering and to conquer far and wide beyond the bounds of the Peninsula." The writer adds that whether the observer's analysis or the fanatic's intuition comes nearer to the mark only the future may reveal. But he suggests a third possibility, namely, that Islam may yet adapt herself to the environment of a Westernized World, whatever this environment may become.

## SECTION IV

## THE SECOND MILLENNIUM OF THE CHRISTIAN CHURCH

# CHAPTER XXXVII

## *Christianity in the Middle Ages*

IT is unfortunate that, looking at the story of Christianity from the point of view of our own time—to some a time of failure and decadence, to others a time of realized perfection—we should put ourselves at the mercy of terms such as that of "the Middle Ages." It matters little whether we view the period as one of darkness, or whether (as a recent writer has done) we speak of it as "the halcyon years" which enable us to describe the following era as the time of "breaking down." In the story of a religion which we can only worthily judge as coincident with the whole range of human history, future as well as past, we cannot fix a middle point. Nor can we speak of an ideal age in any century of the past any more than we can brand any other century as one of breaking down. Christianity in history has often seemed to flag and fail, through the frailty and ignorance of those who profess it, but it always rose again to pursue its course when it resought the power of the promised Spirit to fulfil its mission.

Looked at from the outside, the failures of any age are more obvious than its triumphs. It was so with the period we are now concerned with. To those who see only the imperfections of the time against the splendours of the envisioned City of God the age from A.D. 800 to 1300 may well be the Dark Ages, gathering up towards a fitting *dénouement* in the end of the world. But it is equally an error for men to-day, looking back as to an era of undimmed faith and unquestioning acceptance of the Church's authority, to talk of the Middle Ages as "the halcyon days."

The Middle Ages (so-called) had their failures and their

successes, but from neither the one point of view nor the other were they aught but a single stage in the age-long march of the Church of God on earth. As a stage, and not a stopping-place, as a challenge from both the past and the future, rather than as a station in which to rest, they must always be envisaged in the light of the propulsive force which gave them being and in the light of the goal which beckoned them.

A great period of extension had come to an end, as a result of which the larger part of Europe had been superficially evangelized. It was now time to commence that new work of intension, which would require for its completion who shall say how many generations—generations during which the incompleteness of the stages would be all too sadly evident? In the religious history of the individual and of the nation alike the "ugly duckling" phases must frequently enough be more than exasperating to those who expected miraculous transformation. The misunderstanding of this is the source of the common criticism of "first generation Christians" in heathen lands to-day. But, in justice to the work of extension in the first millennium of Christian Europe, we may recollect the production of saintly lives like that of Alfred among the kings, or Nicholas I. among the Popes, or many an "ignotus" in the cloister.

It cannot really be wondered at that, almost coincidently with the end of this millennium, there should be great misgiving as to the future of mankind on earth, even to the oft-expressed expectation of the general Day of Judgement. Though for the present Rome had beaten off the Saracen through the valour of Pope Leo, and Constantinople had repelled Islam through Leo the Emperor, men's hearts were failing them with fear of what was to come. Of the five patriarchates three—Jerusalem, Antioch and Alexandria—had fallen to the Muslim, and many were trembling as to the ability of the remaining two capitals of Christendom to survive. Society, too, though nominally Christian, was pagan in heart and conduct. Many indeed were wondering whether any refuge for virtue remained outside the monastery. Yet, though the Church, East and West, was menaced by the arms of the unbeliever, there seemed a superabundance of time and energy to spend upon inter-patriarchal controversies. For this the responsibility is to be shared alike by Constantinople and Rome.

It is, of course, to the credit of Constantinople that for several centuries after the rise of Islam in her eastern territories she continued her missionary work—in Bulgaria, Moravia, Bohemia and Russia. But it was most unfortunate—not merely for herself, but also for the Western Church—that the occasion was now found for a controversy which issued at last in open schism. There were several reasons for this controversy, racial, political, as well as religious. The ideals of Eastern Christendom were far removed from those of the West, which followed in the main the political pattern of the Roman Empire. There were also the conflicting personalities of the Pope and the Patriarch Photius. There was, again, the insertion of the so-called "*Filioque* clause"—"Proceeding from the Father *and the Son*"—in the Nicene Creed, by the synod of Toledo in 589. And there were trivial questions as to the keeping of Saturday as a fast, as to the marriage of priests before ordination, as to the right of priests to administer confirmation, and the like. But the immediate cause of conflict is to be found in the dispute over the use of *icons*, or sacred pictures. In the Iconoclastic controversy, as it is called, we may perceive the indirect influence of Islam in the general condemnation of pictures and statues. Leo III, the Isaurian, in the first stage of this controversy, 716, was genuinely anxious to propitiate Jews and Muslims by the repudiation of anything that savoured of idolatry. He had, however, against him the full power of the monks, and, fifty years after his death, his policy was repudiated by the Second Council of Nicæa, 787. A few years later, in the days of Leo, the Armenian, 815, it broke out again, but this time the Empress Theodora arose as a champion of the *icons*, and their use has continued in the devotions of the Eastern Church ever since.

Irritation over this question, and others mentioned by Photius in a famous encyclical of 867, brought about an open quarrel between Rome and Constantinople which was continued into the next two centuries. Excommunications were hurled at one another by the ecclesiastical heads of either patriarchate, and at last, in the patriarchate of Caerularius and the papacy of Leo IX., on July 16, 1054, a formal bull of excommunication was laid by the papal legates before the high altar of the Church of Santa Sophia. Its language is sufficiently drastic: "Let them be Anathema Maranatha, with Simoniacs, Valerians, Arians, Donatists, Nicolaitans, Severians, Pneumatomachi, Manichees and Nazarenes, and with all heretics; yea, with the devil and his angels. Amen. Amen. Amen." Henceforth, in the eyes of the Roman Church, the Orthodox Church of the East was to be regarded as excommunicate, heretical and schismatic. For nearly a thousand years this unhappy breach—to the great loss of both communions—has remained unclosed.[1]

The Great Schism, together with the weakening of the Eastern Church through the impact of Islam, played miraculously into the hands of the Papacy, which from this time forward, at least for some centuries, now assumed control of all Western Christendom. For this control there were many reasons, apart altogether from the doctrinal arguments based on Christ's commission to St. Peter, and apart also, in the other direction, from the use of fraudulent means of support such as the so-called *Donation of Constantine* and the forged *Decretals of St. Isidore*. Rome was the one great apostolic see of the West and, moreover, was advantaged by the withdrawal of the Emperors to Byzantium, the prominent part taken by the Bishops of Rome in the repression of heresy, and the important part taken also by the Popes in resistance to the barbarian invasions. Even more important was now the use made by the Roman pontiffs of political conditions, whereby the Emperors of Germany, blessed by the Popes, and in open alliance with them, were to take the place of the rulers (hostile to Rome) at Byzantium. The Holy Roman Empire, as this alliance came to be called, has been criticized as neither *Holy*, nor *Roman*, nor yet an *Empire*, but it must never be forgotten that, given the unsettled conditions of the time, it did render service to the religion and civilization of Europe. It

[1] W. F. Adeney, *The Greek and Eastern Churches*, chaps. iii.-vi.

embodied a grandiose ideal of unity, secular and ecclesiastical such as surrounds even its failure with a sort of halo. Like other idealistic schemes since, it failed largely because of the corruption and frailty of human nature.[1]

When Charlemagne, grandson of the great Mayor of the Palace, Charles Martel, the victor of Tours, became King of the Franks in 768, it was not without foresight that the Pope looked to him for some solution of the problems of the age. Charles the Great was not unworthy of his name, in spite of his cruel wars and forced conversions. He was, according to the light of his time, a sincere Christian, with some pretension to scholarship, and a true patron of learning through his employment of scholars like the Anglo-Saxon, Alcuin. He was also, unlike the Eastern Emperor, on good terms with the Abbasid Khalif of Bagdad, Harun al-Rashid, and had received from him (according to tradition) three unique presents in the shape of an elephant, a clock, and the keys of the Holy Sepulchre. Hence, when, on Christmas Day, 800, Pope Leo III. placed a crown on the Carlovingian's head, and proclaimed him Roman Emperor, as well as King of Germany, a relation was established which, in theory, was destined to a thousand years of life. At the time, too, there seemed some likelihood of the theory being translated into fact. For all Western Christendom to be under a government, which was at once the heir of St. Peter and of the Cæsars, was to ensure a unity which would abolish the civil and religious anarchy of the time. The whole world would be illuminated by the greater light of the Church which rules the day and the lesser light of the Empire which rules the night. Alas, after a while nothing but the theory remained, often nothing but a fitful phantom of the theory. As a fact, the Holy Roman Empire perished, and its unquiet ghost troubled the peace of Europe—a Europe it was unable to unify. Yet, though the ghost of empire passed, from Carlovingian to Franconian, and from Franconian to Hohenstaufen, the ecclesiastical side of the dazzling vision survived and even for long continued to increase in might.

As the political influence of Rome declined, her social

[1] See James Bryce, *The Holy Roman Empire* (new edition), London, 1904.

and religious position grew in significance as a symbol of authority and unity. The power of the old Roman Emperors revived in the persons of the Popes, who even took the title of *Pontifex Maximus* which the Emperors had used. Clothed in " the decent rigidity of the Latin language " the Papal Bulls thundered with the same authority as that once wielded by the Imperial edicts. As a modern Roman Catholic historian puts it: " The majority (of the Popes) were wisely content to increase their power slowly and cautiously."[1] But from time to time personalities arose who shaped the occasion to the interest of the Roman See. One of these is the great Hildebrand—one of the most impressive figures of the period—who, after exerting powerful influence in the court of several of his papal predecessors, came to the Chair of St. Peter in 1073 as Gregory VII. Like Charlemagne, Hildebrand had fashioned dreams out of the reading of St. Augustine's *City of God*, and, like the great Carlovingian, he proceeded to translate these dreams into reality. The papacy of Gregory VII. was a brief one, for all the work that he was able to accomplish. He imposed celibacy upon the clergy; he battled with the civil rulers of the time for the abolition of lay investiture; and he carried out to the bitter end the struggle with Henry IV., which culminated in the Emperor's submission at Canossa in 1077. There is hardly an episode in mediæval history at once more dramatic and more pitiful than the grovelling of the erstwhile proud and arrogant monarch at the feet of the peasant-born ex-Cluniac who had risen to the supreme place in Christendom. The ruthlessness of Gregory VII. had its triumph, but later on the Emperor had his revenge in the setting up of Guibert as anti-Pope. Gregory had presently to flee, and the great Pope died with the words on his lips: " I have loved righteousness and hated iniquity; therefore I die in exile."[2]

The Papacy regained its lost prestige shortly after through the alertness of another Cluniac monk, raised to

[1] Gilbert Bagnani, *Rome and the Papacy*, New York, 1930.

[2] See M. R. Vincent, *The Age of Hildebrand*, New York, 1906; also *The Correspondence of Gregory VII.*, translated by Ephraim Emerton, New York, 1932.

the Popedom, to take the tide of fortune at the flood. His adroitness, moreover, meant not merely great consequences for the Papacy, ultimately bad as well as good, but also great consequences for all Western civilization. This was the Frenchman Urban II., chosen by the College of Cardinals to oppose the usurping anti-Pope. The excommunication of the Emperor Henry IV. by Gregory VII., and the consequent choice of Guibert to be Pope, had put the Papal authorities into something of a quandary. Guibert held the fort at Rome, backed by Henry and his Council, and when Urban was elected by the College of Cardinals he seemed to be little more than "an apostolic wanderer." It was a deadlock between Emperor and Pope, when the idea came to Urban of a way open by which he might become leader of all Christendom in a cause to which, if the right note were struck, the better part of Europe would rally.

The occasion was supplied by the stories which had been filtering into Europe of outrageous treatment of the Christian pilgrims in the Holy Land. In the golden days of the Abbasid Khalifs Christians were protected from maltreatment by treaty. But in 1077 the brother of Malik Shah, the Seljuk ruler now in possession of the territories of the Khalifate, conquered Syria and captured Jerusalem, accompanying his conquest with terrible barbarities inflicted upon the pilgrims. A certain Peter the Hermit had, it is said, been already bent upon stirring up Europe to the situation, but with small success. In any case, it was Urban's initiative which created the great movement of the Crusades, whose successive waves were destined for two centuries to dash against the western frontiers of Islam. Urban's address at Clermont, in Auvergne, delivered in the vernacular Romance tongue, made an instant impression. "Dieu lo vult," cried the excited throng, and almost at once the wind was taken out of the sails of Guibert, while a great multitude of men and women, quite ignorant of the difficulties, or even of the geography, of the situation, prepared to rescue the Holy Sepulchre from the infidel. The enthusiasm of the enlisted crusaders outran Urban's organization, and long before the real army, led by seasoned warriors, was able to start, there were dust-covered crowds pressing on towards Constantinople and the lands beyond. It was a mere mob which first reached the Byzantine capital, and the Emperor, Alexius Comnenus, only half anxious to be delivered by such allies, gladly shunted them across the Bosphorus to Nicæa, there to be massacred wholesale by the Saracens. It was already becoming almost a tragi-comedy, when the real Crusading force under men like Godfrey of Bouillon, his brother Baldwin, Robert of Normandy, Bohemund and Tancred, reached Byzantium. They also had their troubles with Alexius, and before they could be speeded onwards had to pledge him their conquests in Asia Minor and Syria. This they did with much mental reserve and then, repelling the Turks at Nicæa, marched on to the taking of Antioch. Here Bohemund, wanting only a conquest of his own, prepared to stay, but the other knights continued their advance and, with great emotion, found themselves beneath the walls of Jerusalem. The Holy City was taken on July 15, 1099, the capture sullied by a massacre which Godfrey and Tancred did their best to halt. Godfrey was then made King of Jerusalem, but refused to wear a crown where Christ had worn a diadem of thorns. The other leaders were suitably recompensed, orders of knighthood, like the Knight Templars and Knights Hospitallers, were founded, and the Pope expressed his satisfaction by the establishment of a Latin Patriarchate. Two weeks later Urban died and on his tomb the words were inscribed: "Urbanus Secundus, Auctor Expeditionis in Infideles."

The kingdom of Jerusalem lasted eighty-eight years, but was in difficulties almost from the first. Godfrey died in 1100 and was succeeded by his brother Baldwin. After this the Latin rulers of Jerusalem were weaklings and for the most part unworthy of their charge. The little Frank principality had again to look to Europe for recruitments and in 1147 St. Bernard preached the Second Crusade. This time no English joined, because of the war then raging between England and Scotland, but Louis VII. of France and Conrad III. of Germany led a host which had as its objective the restoration of Edessa rather than the giving of aid to Jerusalem. It failed completely; Conrad returned after an unsuccessful siege of Damascus, and Louis a year later. St. Bernard tried to rally Europe to another effort, but he, too, failed and died in 1153.

In 1187 came the loss of Jerusalem through the new Saracen troops from Kurdistan and their brilliant leader Salah-ud-din (*Prosperity of the Faith*), or Saladin. He had become Sultan of Egypt, had routed the Crusading force in a great battle near the Horns of Hattin, not far from Tiberias, and soon thereafter took Jerusalem, purifying the mosques afresh with four camel-loads of rose-water brought from Damascus.

The loss of Jerusalem stirred Europe to its depths and a new Crusade—the Third—was preached by William, Archbishop of Tyre, who gathered together a great array of princes, knights and common folk. The princes included King Philip Augustus of France, Richard Coeur de Lion of England, and Leopold of Austria. Had these been of one mind, they might have done great things. But they disagreed from the first. Richard went off on a private expedition to Cyprus, and when he arrived before Acre a little later, even his renowned valour could not compensate for the offence he gave to Leopold and the King of France. The city was taken, but Philip Augustus went home in high dudgeon and Richard was left to continue alone the march to Jerusalem. It was in sight of the city that, harassed by fever, and still more by the knowledge of treachery behind him in England, that the Lion-hearted reluctantly made a truce for three years, three months, three weeks, three days, three hours, three minutes, three seconds with his brave antagonist Saladin. Richard had hardly sailed when the knights he left behind broke the truce. Moreover, Saladin died in 1193, sending his shroud around the city the day before his decease to show men how little so great a warrior could take with him.

The end of the twelfth and beginning of the thirteenth century were of ill omen for the crusaders defending their scattered posts in Palestine. But Pope Innocent III., one of the greatest of all the Popes, was now occupying St. Peter's chair, and big with ideas for the aggrandisement of his office. Fulk, *curé* of Neuilly, preached on the Pontiff's behalf a new Crusade, with promises of salvation to those who should give themselves and their wealth. But this time the crusaders decided to go to Palestine by sea, and for transport hired the fleet of the Venetians, who, with their old blind Doge, Dandolo, had their own ideas as to the outcome. For, first of all, Dandolo insisted on the crusaders recapturing the city of Zara, of which the Hungarians had robbed the Republic. This done, they insisted further on the need of restoring Isaac Angelus to the throne of Byzantium. These tasks were entirely foreign to the object of the Crusade, but they were accomplished and the expedition thereupon proceeded to compel the allegiance of Byzantium to the Popes. Thus the result of the Fourth Crusade was to establish a Latin kingdom in Constantinople rather than in Jerusalem, and to force Baldwin, Count of Flanders, upon the Byzantines as king. The knights of the West held their Eastern principality for over fifty years, but the spirit of the Crusades was gone. Innocent III., moreover, having once used the armed forces of the West against his fellow-Christians was not minded to stop there. To quote Mr. Harold Lamb: "From the years 1206 to 1213 Innocent availed himself of the crusade power to further his own policy from Constantinople to Granada. For the first time, in the south of France, he had drawn the papal sword to exterminate heretics. But it was not to be the last time. For more than five blood-stained centuries other popes and monarchs would follow his example." [1]

But the attempt to regain the Holy Land was by no means over. In the Easter of 1212 that pathetic tragedy took place known as the Children's Crusade, a miracle of faith and fanaticism, but ending in one long horror of misery, starvation and slavery. Perhaps something in this shamed the grown-up folk, for at the Council of the Lateran in 1215 once more Innocent appealed for men to take the Cross. One army went to Damietta in Egypt, and with it St. Francis of Assisi, anxious to convert the infidel or win the crown of martyrdom. Meanwhile, too, the famous

[1] Harold Lamb, *The Crusades,* II. 275, New York, 1930–31. See also Dr. Ernest Barker's article, "Crusades," in *Ency. Brit.* (14th Ed.), with its Bibliography.

Frederick II. of Germany and Sicily promised, on falling heir to the Imperial Crown, to lead a Crusade. He collected a fleet and sailed in 1227, but soon returned, having been delayed by a storm. His dilatoriness brought an edict of excommunication from Pope Gregory IX. and, still under the ban, Frederick sailed the following spring and marched from Acre to Jerusalem. Here he obtained rights for all but the Mosque of Umar from Malik el Kamal, but found all the monks and Knights Hospitallers against him, so that he had to put the crown on his head with his own hands. All Frederick's efforts at reconciliation with the Papacy failed and when he died in 1250 he was still excommunicate and under suspicion of heresy.

By this time the Seventh Crusade had been launched, with St. Louis of France as its leader. The saintly king had made the vow on his recovery from a dangerous illness and sailed from Marseilles for Damietta in 1248. Louis IX, however, was no great soldier and allowed his army to be surrounded at Mansurah. Sick almost to death he was captured and with great difficulty ransomed. Then, recovered from his fever, he sailed for Acre, but was soon after recalled to France by the death of his mother, Blanche of Castile.

We must only summarize the rest. The Greeks recovered Constantinople in 1261, under Michael Palaeologos, and another attempt at reconciling the Eastern and Western Churches was made, only to fail, in 1274. The last Crusade took place in 1270, when St. Louis once again took the field, followed by Prince Edward (afterwards Edward I.) of England. Louis IX. went to Tunis only to die, with the words, "O Jerusalem, Jerusalem" upon his lips. Prince Edward went to Acre, recovered Nazareth, wellnigh lost his life through an attack by "assassins," and was soon thereafter obliged to return to England. He had set his mind on returning to Palestine, but this was not to be. The Crusades were over. They had entailed the misery and death of countless thousands and had failed in their main object. But they had done something through the sacrifices made, though something quite different from what they had purposed. "They drained the cup of devotion, and if they tasted the dregs of shame, they knew also the exaltation of victory. They reached the summit of daring. And the memory of that will endure long after our own workaday lives are ended." [1]

Even before the final failure of the Crusades doubt had begun to insinuate itself into the minds of many as to the validity of the method, apart altogether from failure or success. Was the military method congruous with the way of the Cross? Was success possible through the ideals of the "iron men"? We have already noted the visit of St. Francis to the Muslim lines, based on the desire to witness for Christ by preaching or by martyrdom. The incident is symptomatic of a great change. Already men had retired in multitudes from an unconverted world to save their souls from impending doom. Now men began to conceive of the ascetic way as a method by which the world around them might be saved. Surely this way, neglected throughout the Crusading period, was worth the trying.

The beginning of monasticism in the Eastern Church has already been described. Simple eremitism developed, as we have seen, quite naturally into cœnobitism. Moreover, in the East the regulation of monasteries had been accepted by many according to the rule of St. Basil. Western monasticism was a little slower in development, but in 480 was born the great organizer St. Benedict who, moved by the prevailing anarchy, drew up in 529 the famous "Rule" which was soon widely accepted. Benedict of Nursia created no new order, but regulated the life of the western monks, making each monastery a self-contained and self-supporting "house," within which dwelt men who were bound by lifelong vows and attached permanently to their own establishments. The life of the monk was to be devoted to the chief religious duties of prayer, study, labour and self-denial, and the three vows of poverty, chastity and obedience had to be rigidly observed. It was not long before houses following the Benedictine Rule were scattered all the way from Monte Cassino to Rome and to the coast. In Gaul especially men like St. Martin, Cassian and Cæsarius

[1] Harold Lamb, *The Crusades*, II. 467. See also J. M. Ludlow, *The Age of the Crusades*, New York, 1896.

of Arles devoted themselves enthusiastically to the propagation of the Benedictine Rule.

Yet the time came when this, like other human institutions, corrupted itself, and the rules became more honoured in the breach than in the observance. Even though personal poverty was maintained, the monastic corporations became enormously rich. Also, though the obligation of clerical celibacy was insisted on, the concubinage and unchastity of the ecclesiastics, including the monks, became notorious. Nor could superiors always depend on the obedience of those in the ranks. Hence such reform movements as that which established the monastery at Cluny, from which many of the Benedictine houses, including even the mother house at Monte Cassino, adopted reforms. All the new orders from the beginning of the eleventh century, Carmelites, Carthusians, and the rest, originated in the fervour of reform. The Cistercian order was founded in 1098, but its great influence dates from the arrival of St. Bernard in 1121, and Clairvaux soon eclipsed Citeaux when Bernard became abbot a little later. In 1130 the Cistercian order possessed only thirty houses, but before St. Bernard's death, in 1153, there were 288.[1]

The twelfth century, however, is remarkable for an ascetic movement which took lines entirely different from those adopted by the monastic orders—a movement which for a time proved singularly fruitful, though in the end it too yielded in many respects to the influence of the world around it. The movement which we may describe as that of Preaching Friars, unconnected with any house and free to wander wherever opportunity led them, includes the work of two great mediæval Christians, St. Francis of Assisi, founder of the order of Friars Minor, or Franciscans, and St. Dominic, founder of the order of Dominicans.

St. Francis (Pietro Bernardone) was born at Assisi in 1182. At the age of twenty-four, after a somewhat gay and thoughtless youth, he was converted to a desire to give himself wholly to the service of Christ. Cast off by his father on account of such "eccentric" acts as changing

[1] See article "Monasticism" in *Ency. Brit.* (14th Ed.); and article "Monasticism" (III. "Christian Monasticism"), in *E.R.E.*, VIII. 783 ff.

clothes with a beggar, he renounced his property and in 1209, at the Chapel of the Portiuncula, vowed himself to religious poverty. Having thus found his vocation and gathered around him a few like-minded souls, he obtained permission from the Pope to organize the Friars Minor, whom he began to send abroad, first throughout Umbria and then farther afield. The characteristics of St. Francis himself were striking and appealing. He accepted poverty as a bride, showed his appreciation of Nature in true poetry, as well as in his preaching to birds and fishes and the wolf of Gubbio, while the joyousness with which he carried on his work gained for him and his comrades the title of "Troubadors of God." His visit to the Muslim camp has already been mentioned and Giotto's picture "Before the Soldan" commemorates the incident. At home St. Francis organized, in addition to the Friars, the order of St. Claire for women, and the Tertiary order for lay-folk. In his sufferings he is said to have received the *stigmata* on his hands and feet and side. He died in 1226, leaving a name for sanctity not approached by that of any other in the Middle Ages.[1] Not long after his death Franciscans were at work almost all over the world. Raymond Lull laboured to introduce the study of Arabic into the Universities, as a means for converting the Muslim, and was stoned to death June 30, 1315.[2] Men like John de Plano Carpini and William de Rubruk went as ambassadors of Christian Europe to the court of the Great Khans. John de Monte Corvino laboured for forty years in China and became the first Archbishop of Peking.[3] Roger Bacon, in England, laid the foundation of modern science. The list might be indefinitely extended.

St. Dominic, born in Castile, in 1170, at first joined the Augustinian order, in 1204, but was presently awakened by the spread of the heresy of the Cathari to organize a body of preaching friars whose business it should be to

[1] See Paul Sabatier, *Life of St. Francis of Assisi*, New York, 1894.

[2] Lull was regarded by his fellow-countrymen as a martyr, but his death at Bugia was in fact the consequence of his own fanaticism. For a full account of Lull and "Lullism" see W. T. A. Barber, *Raymond Lull, the Illuminated Doctor*, London, 1903.

[3] K. S. Latourette, *History of Christian Missions in China*, chap. v.

combat heresy in all its forms. The order spread rapidly and in 1215 Dominic begged the approval of Innocent III. This was not forthcoming, as the Pope deemed that the existing orders were sufficient for the task. A year later, however, the new Pope, Honorius III., gave the movement his blessing and the "Domini canes," or "watch-dogs of the Lord," soon became well known throughout Europe. Unfortunately, their flair for heresy was unduly developed, and out of the Dominican zeal arose the Inquisition, with its unexampled horrors.[1] Yet Dominic was sincere enough in his desire to exterminate what he believed perilous beyond the pain of every earthly torment and, of course, by handing over the culprits to the secular arm for punishment, the Church believed she was keeping her own skirts clear. An illustration of the dangerous course to which the Church was committing herself, after the failure to overcome the Muslim, is in the suppression of the Albigenses in Provence. Pope Calixtus II. prepared the way in the Council of Toulouse in 1119 when, going beyond the previous policy of excommunicating heretics, he invited the secular arm to use force for their extermination. The Albigensians doubtless held a doctrine similar to that of the Manichæans—one generally held to be subversive of political as well as of ecclesiastical orthodoxy. But the purity of their life made Raymond of Toulouse unwilling to drive them from his territories, and there was but the slenderest right on the side of Innocent III. when he moved the princes of Europe against these Provençal sectaries as though they had been infidels. The so-called Crusade of Simon de Montfort developed into a racial as well as a religious war, and the destruction of the Albigenses involved much more than the heresy of which they had been adjudged guilty. It was a bad precedent which was only too frequently followed in succeeding generations.

This is all the more to be deplored seeing that at this time a certain tolerance as to matters of thought was beginning to find place among the ecclesiastics of Europe. This was in part the result of the larger learning introduced into Europe by Islam, and especially into such territories

[1] There is no need to associate Dominic himself with the persecuting zeal of his successors.

as Spain, Sicily and Provence. Of course, western learning of the classical sort had never been completely eradicated. The Irish monasteries had done much to preserve it and to circulate it, and men like Alcuin at the court of Charlemagne had done much to impress their age with the love of literature and scholarship. Nevertheless, the Church and the Universities of Europe owed an immense debt to the Islam they had sought to destroy, both in the matter of the books translated from Greek into Arabic and thence into Latin, and in the matter of the spirit of learning itself. It was largely through Islam that Aristotle once again became " the master of them that know," and the spirit of logical reasoning, out of which grew what we call Scholasticism, was largely due to the fact that Aristotle had found a secure place in the cloister as well as in the academy.[1]

The most obvious expression of this new thirst for learning is seen towards the end of the twelfth century in the establishment of Universities, of which the earliest types are the Universities of Paris and Bologna. In each case the initiative came from certain famous teachers who attracted students to their lectures from all parts of Europe. In Paris the Episcopal school had already gained some repute under the directorship of William of Champeaux, but when Abelard arrived about 1115 and commenced his lectures in the " Isle," and later opened the school on Mont St. Geneviève, students flocked to him in incredible numbers. Other teachers followed Abelard's example and the result was the organization of a corporation, or *Universitas*, to protect the interests of students and teachers. The students were divided into " nations," according to their respective provenance, and lived in extreme indigence. Dante's reference to " the street of straw," of which he had personal experience, will be recalled. But " colleges " were formed in course of time, to supply food and lodging, and the curriculum gradually broadened to embrace not only the *trivium* and *quadrivium*,[2] but also law, medicine and theology. The University of Bologna originated about

[1] See *The Legacy of Islam*, edited by Thomas Arnold and Alfred Guillaume, Oxford, 1931.

[2] The *trivium* included the subjects of grammar, rhetoric and logic, and the *quadrivium* those of astronomy, arithmetic, geometry and music.

the same time, largely through the influence of the foreign students, and the success of the establishment—or rather the two establishments, one for the Ultramontanes, or students from beyond the Alps, the other for the Citramontanes, or students south of the Alps—led speedily to the foundation of others. Thus came into being the Universities of Padua, Oxford and Salerno, and in the fourteenth century there were in all Europe as many as forty-five.[1]

As we have noted, the fame of the Universities was from the first associated with the reputation of the individual teachers, and much of the teaching took the form of a philosophical statement of the traditional theology. This is known to us as *Scholasticism*. Much of it was arid and, from our point of view, profitless, dealing by the methods of logic with subjects largely beyond its province. But the schoolmen were by no means engaged in what a modern writer calls "a perverse crucifying of the mind." They were in general the possessors of a keen and subtle mentality which did much to strip away many of the misinterpretations of theology then current. Given the limitations of the mediæval knowledge, many of their arguments had value beyond the limits of their own age in the formulation of Christian dogma. Scholasticism drew from many sources, alike from Scripture and from Aristotle, using freely the methods of dialectic and exposition.

In the eleventh and twelfth centuries the chief schoolmen were Anselm, Archbishop of Canterbury in 1070, whose famous treatise on the Incarnation, *Cur Deus Homo?* (to quote Dr. G. F. Moore) "gave a new orientation to the theological mind" and "accustomed it to translate dogmas into rational concepts connected with one another by more or less vigorous bonds," and Abelard, the popular teacher at the University of Paris, whose *Sic et Non* is "the first great theological synthesis," a work setting over against one another all the contradictory opinions held by the ecclesiastical authorities on the various doctrines of the Christian faith.

In the thirteenth and fourteenth centuries we have a

[1] See J. B. Mullinger, article "Universities," *Ency. Brit.* (14th Ed.).

number of great schoolmen whose lustre has been dimmed without being destroyed by subsequent ages. St. Thomas Aquinas, born in 1225 at the village of Aquino, in the territory of Naples, of royal descent, is the great systematizer of Christian doctrine. His *Summa Theologiæ* assembled all the knowledge of his time, and it is not fair to say that it has been wholly buried "in the grave dug for it by the friends of experimental research since the time of Roger Bacon." Fifty years after his death Thomas Aquinas was canonized by the action of Pope John II. Alexander of Hales, who joined the Franciscan order and died about 1245, is the putative author of an earlier *Summa Theologiæ*. Albertus Magnus, like St. Thomas Aquinas, whom he outlived but six years, was a Dominican. He was born in Bavaria in 1206, joined his order in 1223, taught both at Cologne and Paris, and wrote commentaries on Aristotle and the *Sentences* of Peter Lombard. Bonaventura was born in Tuscany in 1221, became a Franciscan in 1243, taught at Paris, and later became both Bishop and Cardinal. He also wrote a commentary on the *Sentences*, and a mystical work, *Itinerarium mentis ad Deum*. Duns Scotus, of Scottish or Irish descent, was likewise a Franciscan and taught at Oxford, Paris and Cologne. He too wrote a commentary on the *Sentences*. The last of the great schoolmen was William of Occam, in the county of Surrey. He found himself in opposition to the Pope and was in consequence imprisoned at Avignon. Escaping thence he became a partisan of Louis of Bavaria, and dwelt at Munich, where he taught and wrote. Later on he again fell into the hands of the Pope and died, probably excommunicate, in 1349. He marks the turn from the rationalism of Anselm to the dogmatism of the next century.[1]

At the same time that scholasticism was blazing the way towards a completer freedom of theological thought,

[1] Occam himself was very much of a rationalist. Mr. Williston Walker writes : "His system was a far more vigorous and destructive nominalism than that of Roscelin. Yet actual knowledge of things in themselves men do not have, only of mental concepts. This denial led him to the conclusion that no theological doctrines are philosophically provable. They are to be accepted—and he accepted them—simply on authority." (*A History of the Christian Church*, p. 279 )

the like end was being served by a religious movement of a quite different character. The *mysticism* which appears in European Christianity in the thirteenth and fourteenth centuries, notably in Germany and in Holland, had much to do with preparing for the reformation which was to follow. St. Bernard in the twelfth century was a mystic, so were others of the French and Italian school. But the new endeavour to bring the soul into direct and ecstatic communion with God is especially associated with men like Eckhart, Tauler and Nicolas of Basle, or, in Holland, with the Brethren of the Common Life, an order founded by Gerhardt Groot, under the influence of Ruysbroek, and including among its members Thomas à Kempis, author of the famous *De Imitatione Christi*. It is well known that Luther was powerfully influenced by these writings, and more particularly by the *Theologia Germanica*, which he esteemed as almost on the level of Holy Scripture.

The chapter is already threatening a disproportionate length, but I must just allude to other aspects of the late Middle Ages which, in view of the future, have their significance. The great awakening of *art*, with its realization of the religious value of colour, as in the pictures of Cimabue and Giotto, is characteristic of a new attitude and a new enthusiasm. Similarly, whatever the motives which inspired them, we see in the *Cathedral builders* of the time an expression of faith and devotion as well as the desire to purchase mansions in heaven by erecting mansions for God upon earth. It was a movement in which lay-folk were as enthusiastic as the monkish communities, as we note in Florence, for example, where, while Dominicans laboured at building Santa Maria Novella and Franciscans worked on the Santa Croce, the citizens rejoiced in rearing the fabric of the Duomo.

Lastly, we have in literature the *Divina Commedia* which is to the close of the Middle Ages what the *Apocalypse* of St. John was to the Apostolic period and St. Augustine's *City of God* was at the time when Rome was menaced by the barbarians. It is characteristic of Christianity, in its earthly course, to set terrestrial goals which fade away as they are about to be reached, and to dream of institutions, as realizing the Christian ideal, which break down as they are approached. Dante had dreamed often enough of the glorious *dénouement* when all the world should live in peace under the two great earthly vicars of Christ, Pope and Emperor. His disillusionment did but lift his eyes to the vision of a vaster fulfilment in the spiritual world. The breaking down of the theory of the Holy Roman Empire served only to reveal the spiritual realm in which God's inexorable love was operating on the infinite and eternal scale. The will that revolted against the eternal law was seen to be suffering, not for sinning, but by sinning, until it learned the lesson that only through following the divine plan was peace possible. This stage is life's *Inferno*. The will that repents its wilfulness, but still suffers from the weakness which the habit of sin has left behind, was seen aided and sustained till the weakness is outgrown. This is *Purgatorio*. And, thirdly, the will that, without other compulsion than that of love, has learned the law of its own being (which is also the will of its creator), was seen entering into that fullness of joy which is essentially nearness to the Throne of God. This is *Paradiso*. However impermanent the material out of which the poet fashioned the framework of his poem, we here behold a vision only to be realized after the breaking down of temporal hopes. It is but one illustration among many in the history of religion that crusts form only to be burst asunder by the insurgence of life beneath, and that all earthly failures save us from dependence on the transitory and consequent loss of the perfection yet ahead. All the failures of the Middle Ages are of small account in view of the emerging triumph presented to us by Dante, until "vision fails the towering fantasy." It was the triumph of Creation, beheld as the fruit of the toil of endless æons, the victory of Love's infinite patience, the revelation of *Rosa mystica*, with each petal perfect in its individual beauty, and all blended into the perfection of God's realized idea.[1]

[1] For the subjects touched upon in this chapter the following works, among others, may be consulted: *The Cambridge Mediæval History*, Vol. II., New York, 1913; Wilhelm Moeller, *History of the Christian Church*, Vol. II., *The Middle Ages* (Eng. trans.), London, 1893.

## CHAPTER XXXVIII

## *The Reformation Movement*

THE Reformation movement which came to a head in the sixteenth century has been described as a revolution rather than a reformation. There is some ground for the statement. In that shaking of all things which was involved in the Reformation crisis many good things were imperilled and some (at least temporarily) lost. The unity of the Church, which had already been shattered by the schism of East and West in 1054, and which subsequent efforts, down as late as 1437, failed to heal, was once again broken by the separation of important sections of the Church from the Western Patriarchate. The unity hitherto prevailing had, of course, been largely the result of pressure from outside, but now that the pendulum started to swing in the opposite direction, the result was for a time a veritable riot of irresponsible individualism.

Much has been said as to the slowness with which the Reformation movement gathered, though we have to note also the suddenness with which it broke. It is due to the fact that many forces, *moral*, *intellectual*, *social* and *political*, were all working coincidently towards the climax. I shall devote a few words to these forces before essaying the briefest summary of the period covered.

First, we must consider the revulsion slowly gathering against the moral corruption in the Church of the Middle Ages and its rulers. In this revulsion the entire Papal system was involved. There were Popes like Boniface VIII. who, according to the supposed prediction of Pope Celestine, "intrabit ut vulpis, regnabit ut leo, morietur ut canis," like Innocent III., and like Alexander VI., the Borgia.[1]

[1] See Ranke, *History of the Popes* (Eng. trans.), 1840; Mandell Creighton, *History of the Papacy*, 6 vols., London, 1907.

It is charitable to call these merely "sullied souls." And with them we must associate plenty of cardinals, bishops, monks, and lay-folk of every degree. Yet the moral ideal of Christianity was not dead, and indeed was vigorous to protest against the travesty in high places. The rise of pietism at this time is a striking illustration of the way in which individual souls turned from dependence upon external authority to find security in personal communion with God. It is therefore by no means strange to find a general loss of respect for a Papacy entangled in political intrigue, playing off Empire against France and France against Empire. A Pope exiled in Avignon, as the creature of France, lost face just because he was not in Rome. The seventy years of "Babylonish Captivity," ending after the Council of Constance with the deposition of three Popes, had much to do with preparing men's minds for a final break with Rome.

Secondly, we must keep under consideration the revival of learning, in all its many phases. Scholasticism, by its championship of rationalism, and its use of the dialectic of Aristotle, had already gone far towards undermining the unintelligent acceptance of ecclesiastical pronouncements as to doctrine. Now we have to note the beginnings of an *éclaircissement* due, first of all, to the invention of printing in the West, and the consequent multiplication of books, including, of course, the Scriptures in the Latin or in European vernaculars. Coincidently, there developed a humanism which profited by the Fall of Constantinople in 1453. When the splendid Eastern capital fell from the hands of John Palæologos into the arms of Muhammad II., there resulted a great scattering of scholars and a wide diffusion of books and manuscripts which were eagerly fought for by the awakening West.[1] A new and unexampled enthusiasm took possession of men like Reuchlin, Erasmus, Pico della Mirandola, John Colet, and scores of others. The Popes, not foreseeing the ultimate result to their own disadvantage, became the patrons of a Renaissance, which if not frankly pagan, was in many of its aspects non-Christian. In some countries, such as Germany, where the spirit of the Italian Renaissance found small response, the

[1] See E. Pears, *Fall of Constantinople*, London, 1890.

enthusiasm for learning showed itself in the study and translation of the Bible, and many private—and often erratic—interpretations of the Scriptures did much to prepare for the rejection of ecclesiastical authority as hitherto understood.

Thirdly, there were causes which were purely social and economic. The invention of gunpowder had proved almost a death-blow to the chivalry of mediæval times. The common man was now, with his new weapons, a match for his master. The submissive serfs of feudal times began to awaken to a consciousness of their own manhood. "We are men formed in Christ's likeness and we are kept like beasts," they cried—and rose in revolt. Hence movements like the Jacquerie in France, the Peasant Rebellion in England, the Peasant War of 1525 in Germany. The conscience of the common man was from henceforth to determine the acceptability of dogmas and duties which had so far been forced upon him by his liege lord as well as by the authorities of the Church.

In the fourth place, many political considerations enter into the situation. The rise of many new nationalisms out of the wreckage of the Empire was fatal to the theory of the Holy Roman Empire. These new nationalities resented such interferences as appeared in Innocent III.'s *Interdict* in France and England, in the insistence upon *Investiture*, such as bred so many disputes between popes and kings, or even in the flooding of a land with clergy of alien nationality. This resentment was particularly strong in England, where the independence of the Church had been continually insisted upon from the time of the Conqueror. William I. refused to accede to the demands of Gregory VII. and William Rufus quarrelled with the Pope over Anselm and in the matter of investiture. The feud was continued through the reigns of Henry I. and Henry II. The despicable John defied the Pope till brought to his knees by the *Interdict* of Innocent III., but then became servile in his submission. To save English pride Archbishop Langton and the barons brought about the signing of the *Magna Carta* on June 15, 1215, and laid down the principle, "This Church of England shall be free and maintain all its rights and privileges inviolate." Succeeding kings took the same position and scarcely a reign passed without some enactment designed to protect the realm from encroachments on the part of the Papal See. So we proceed till we come to the final breach in the time of Henry VIII. In this long-drawn-out contention English bishops as well as English monarchs played their part, as witness the story of Bishop Grostête of Lincoln and his defiance of Innocent IV.[1]

In the fourteenth century we find several Reformation movements coming to a head. The first is that associated with John Wiclif, who was born in 1324, educated at Queen's and Merton College, Oxford, and presently came into prominence at the University by his denunciation of the corruption of the Mendicant orders. In 1374 Wiclif was included in a mission, headed by John of Gaunt, to Bruges, to discuss with the Papal Nuncio the intrusion of foreign clergy into English benefices. On his return he was made Rector of Lutterworth, and from this countryside pulpit inveighed against the evils of the Papacy and the friars. The effect of this was such that in 1377 Pope Gregory XI. began to issue bulls to Archbishop Courtenay calling for the reformer's suppression. Wiclif was haled into the Archbishop's court, but was saved—somewhat at the expense of the dignity of the occasion—by the intervention of his friend, John of Gaunt. Support was also vouchsafed in a letter from the young king Richard's mother and in the sympathy of the mob rather menacingly displayed. Wiclif, nevertheless, was brought by worry wellnigh to death's door and the friars improved the occasion by paying a visit to the sick bed. But the fiery reformer raised himself from his pillow to exclaim: "I shall not die but live and declare the works of the friars." He did recover and proceeded from the attack on the morals of the friars to an attack upon the doctrines of the Church, notably upon the doctrine of Transubstantiation. Steps were again taken to silence him and but for the Papal schism might have proved successful. As it was, Wiclif retired to Lutterworth, went on with his Latin writing and

[1] See R. W. Stephens, *The English Church from the Norman Conquest to the accession of Edward I.*, London, 1901 ; W. W. Capes, *The English Church in the 14th and 15th centuries*, London, 1900.

his despatch of "poor priests" to propagate his teachings throughout the country, and then died in his bed in 1384. Later on, in 1415, the Council of Constance decided to take vengeance on his bones, but the sentence was not carried out till 1428, when Wiclif's ashes were cast into the Swift, whence they were carried to the Avon, thence into the Severn, and thence into the ocean. "Which things," it has been remarked, "are an allegory."[1]

It is not fair to attribute to Wiclif all the excesses of his followers, the so-called Lollards. Nevertheless, we may be glad that the English Reformation was not carried out along the lines he favoured. There was much in his opinions which was revolutionary rather than reformatory, politically as well as ecclesiastically. Some of his teachings were without doubt socially subversive. Yet one great legacy Wiclif left to England in the Bible which he translated, with the help of Nicholas Hereford and John Purvey, from the Vulgate. Beyond this, too, was the influence he exerted, in England by the preaching of his "poor priests," and on the Continent by such writings as his *De Ecclesia*, *De Potestate Papae*, and *De Sufficientia legis Christi*. It is certain that Luther was much influenced by these.

The most direct effect of Wiclif's teaching, however, was felt rather far afield, namely, in Bohemia. This will appear strange till we recall that Richard II. had married a Bohemian princess, "the good Queen Anne." After the queen's death many of her ladies returned to Bohemia, carrying with them a number of Wiclif's tracts. Hundreds of these were burned, but some fell into the hands of a young man, John Huss, who was already moved by the prevalent nationalism against the Papacy. Huss was no heretic, in the proper sense of the word, but it was determined to bring him to book. At this time the Western Church was in a sufficiently critical situation. Islam was steadily advancing westward; the Eastern Church was getting desperate; Lollardism was in several lands thriving on the popular discontent. The summoning of the Council

[1] See G. M. Trevelyan, *England in the Time of Wiclif*, London, 1909; E. L. Cutts, *Parish Priests and their People in the Middle Ages in England*, London, 1898.

of Constance, 1414–1418, by Pope John XXIII. furnished an opportunity for real reform, but the evil genius of the Council was the Emperor Sigismund, who was far from equal to playing the *rôle* of a Constantine at Nicæa. Sigismund has earned undying infamy by granting a safe conduct to John Huss and then betraying him immediately on his arrival. "The blush of Sigismund" has become proverbial. Huss was imprisoned, condemned to death, and consigned to the flames, his ashes being cast into the Rhine.[1] A few months later his friend Jerome of Prague met a like fate. The Council of Constance did nothing to promote peace. In England, where from fear of an impending Lollard revolt, Sir John Oldcastle and others were executed, the policy of repression was continued. In Bohemia Ziska revolted, demanding that the laity be permitted the use of the chalice in the Eucharist. But Ziska died in 1424 and the last Hussite "Crusade" was quenched in blood by 1431.

Some effort was made by Pope Eugenius IV. to meet the appeal of the Greek Church—now in despair because of the Muslim advance. But this came to nothing. The Council of Florence in 1437 ended in useless compromise. In 1453 the walls of Constantinople fell before the assault of Sultan Muhammad II. Even in Italy there were many who, moved by the weakness and corruption of the age, had become inspired with the desire for ecclesiastical reform. The most important of these was the fervent Dominican monk, Girolamo Savonarola, who, as prophet, politician, reformer and preacher, occupies the stage in Florence during the second half of the fifteenth century. Savonarola's immediate concern was with public and private morals, and such was the preacher's eloquence on this subject that the conscience-stricken Florentines came together with their *Bonfire of Vanities* as a symbol of their penitence. Savonarola was also a politician, strong for the upholding of the rights and liberties of the Florentine citizens, and insisting that Christ was their only king. Yet he was at the same time a reformer in matters doctrinal and practical within the Church and was demanding the calling of a General Council

[1] See David S. Schaff, *John Huss, His Life, Teachings and Death*, New York, 1915.

to initiate the needed reforms. All this was naturally distasteful to the Borgian Pope, Alexander VI., and to his sons. These were not slow to denounce the prophet-preacher as a heretic. Savonarola's excommunication followed, while he appealed from the decision of the Church Militant to that of the Church Triumphant. After the failure of the projected ordeal, and after enduring the rigours of imprisonment, Savonarola, with two other friars, was brought out into the Piazza for degradation from the priestly office and for death at the stake. The martyrdom took place in the month of May, 1498. So perished yet another who might have aided the reform of the Western Church without the danger of further schism.[1]

Thus we hasten on from movements which have been described as "abortive reformations" to the great explosion of the sixteenth century. By the end of the fifteenth century combustible materials had so far accumulated as almost to make certain a spontaneous conflagration. One added source of discontent with things ecclesiastical is to be found in the enlarged use made of the Inquisition which followed the union of the Crowns of Christian Spain under Ferdinand and Isabella. Isabella had many virtues, but few can fail to associate her unfavourably with the work of her Dominican confessor, Tomas de Torquemada. Against the unfortunate Jews and against wretched heretics of every description the fires of the Inquisition were lighted and, by a kind of irony, the horrors which received the sanction of Pope Sixtus IV. in 1478 and commenced in Spain with the Epiphany of 1479 were known as *autos da fé*, or "acts of faith."[2] Another fact to be taken into consideration is that of the consolidation of temporal power in the hands of Pope Julius II., to which must be added the sale of *Indulgences* authorized in order to meet the expense of building the great church of St. Peter's at Rome. It was this trafficking in pardons, with the abuses springing out of the traffic, and with the particular horror aroused by the salesmanship methods of the Dominican monk, Tetzel, which precipitated

[1] See P. Villari, *Life and Times of Girolamo Savonarola*, 2 vols. (Eng. trans.), New York, 1888.

[2] See H. C. Lea, *A History of the Inquisition in the Middle Ages*, New York, 1887; F. Vacandard, *The Inquisition* (Eng. trans.), London, 1908.

the storm which had so long been brewing. The man destined to be the protagonist of the Reformation movement, at least in Germany, was now awaiting his call to the task.

Martin Luther was born in 1483 at the village of Eisleben in Saxony. He was the son of a poor miner and spent his childhood in a hard and sordid environment, redeemed, however, by the genuine piety of a Christian family life, and early instructed in the Creed, Lord's Prayer, and Commandments. The practice of witchcraft and sorcery was all about him, but to combat this Luther had from the first the buckler of sincerest faith in the Church's teaching and practice. He attended school first at Mansfeld, then with the Brethren of the Common Life at Magdeberg, and then at Eisenach. In 1501 he entered the University of Erfurt for the study of Law, but he occupied himself so largely with the study of the Bible as to incur the rebuke of his superiors. Suddenly, about 1505, he joined the order of Augustinians at Erfurt, probably because of doubts as to spiritual matters. Here he lived a hard and ascetic life and only found peace several years later, while reading the *Epistle to the Romans*. Shortly after he was sent to the newly established University of Wittenberg, where he greatly distinguished himself. In 1511 he was sent on business to Rome and the journey proved a turning-point in his career, since, while climbing (so it is said) the Scala Santa at Rome, he was suddenly taken with a thorough-going detestation of the corruptions he had witnessed in the Papal city and of the distance separating the life there led from a life looking for justification by faith. He went back to Wittenberg, but as a changed man, feeling a breach gradually widening between his own views and those of the official Church. The long-gathering cloud-burst came with the arrival of John Tetzel, preaching the *Indulgence* which Pope Leo X. had so recently authorized. On All Saints' Day Luther nailed his *Ninety-five Theses* on the door of the church at Wittenberg and awaited the consequences. These were not long in coming. To attack *Indulgences* was not only to diminish their sale but to impeach the authority of the Pope. The bold monk was summoned to Rome, but the summons was cancelled through the intervention of the Elector Frederick. Nationalism in Germany supported the cause of Luther and further support came after the famous "disputation" with Eck at Leipzig, and especially after the publication of Luther's three great Reformation treatises. These at once drew the lightnings of the Papacy in the form of a Bull of Excommunication—a Bull which was burned by Luther in 1520. So great was the consternation at Rome that an appeal was made to the Emperor, Charles V., and Luther was summoned to appear before the Diet at Worms in 1521. Here the reformer made his defence, but could not avoid being placed under the ban of the Empire. He resided for a while in the castle of the Wartburg, but presently returned to Wittenberg where he continued to carry on a brisk campaign. So large a national support was given him that it was impossible to enforce the ban. In 1524 came the Peasants' Revolt, an unfortunate illustration of the influence which the breaking away from authority was exercising on the popular mind. In this matter Luther was on the side of the princes and against the people, thus occasioning a good deal of bitter controversy. Controversy also arose within the ranks of the reformers between Luther and the Swiss reformer Zwingli over the doctrine of the Eucharist. The result was an estrangement between the several groups of reformers. Luther had already parted company with Erasmus and the Humanists. But the German was to the last a fighter, though it would serve no good purpose to detail the disputes of his later years. The important work of his declining years was the revision of his German Old Testament and his translation of the New Testament, an epoch-making contribution to European literature as well as to the cause which the reformers had at heart. Luther died in 1546 in his native town, steadfast to the last in the doctrines he had taught. He had all the faults of a strong character, but probably without these faults he would have gone less far. Possibly, too, we must place some of his extreme views and acts to the credit of those who so ruthlessly opposed him.[1]

[1] See A. C. M'Giffert, *Martin Luther, the Man and His Work*, New York, 1911; H. Boehmer, *Martin Luther in the Light of Recent Research* (Eng. trans.), New York, 1916.

From this time the German Reformation went on its own way and there was no real attempt to heal the breach which had been made. The princes of Germany were by no means unanimous in proclaiming their legal right to establish territorial churches. What was resolved at the first Diet of Augsburg in 1526 was rejected at the Diet of Speyer in 1529. It was this which drew forth the protest of 1529—a political rather than a religious pronunciamento—from which the name *Protestant* came into use. As to the doctrinal aspect of things, this was presented in the Augsburg Confession of 1530. The quarrel over this—which, however, did not concern the Swiss reformers or the Reformed, or Calvinistic, Church—led to the Emperor's efforts to crush the Reformation. The war broke out in 1546, but was terminated by a compromise, known as the Religious Peace of Augsburg. From this time the German Reformation was carried out on conservative lines, and organized itself after the manner familiar to us to-day.[1]

It is plain that a large part of the history of the Reformation concerns itself with countries beyond the German states, Switzerland, France, Scotland, England, the Netherlands, Bohemia, Hungary, not to speak of Italy and Spain, all felt the tension of the time. For a small country, *Switzerland* had rather more than its fair share of reform movements. The thirteen cantons were independent, but presented generally a united front against foreign interference, though Swiss soldiers were in the employ of both France and the Papacy. Ulrich Zwingli himself was in receipt of a Papal pension for many years. This remarkable man was born in 1484, the son of the headman of the commune and nephew of the parish priest. He was educated at Berne and Vienna and was a Humanist before he became a Reformer. It was the influence of his friend Thomas Wyttenbach which led to his detestation of *Indulgences* and other abuses of the time. Wyttenbach also gave him his enthusiasm for the study of the Scriptures. In 1506 Zwingli became parish priest of Glarus, whence he accompanied his parishioners, as chaplain, to the campaigns in Italy. Gaining increased reputation as a preacher,

[1] See T. M. Lindsay, *A History of the Reformation*, Vol. I., New York, 1906.

he was appointed people's priest at Zurich, the city with which he was henceforth to be identified. He now became known as an out and out reformer, taking part in public disputations, spreading his doctrines by letters (drafting the famous *Ten Theses*), casting down the gauntlet to the Papacy, on the one hand, while coincidently he was maintaining quarrels with his fellow-reformers (including Luther) over Eucharistic doctrine. Zwingli's contention was that the Sacrament of the Altar was a commemoration and nothing more. In 1531 he went out to war with his fellow-citizens of Zurich to oppose the invasion of the Forest Cantons, which were Romanist. A battle was fought at Kappell in which Zwingli was slain. A great boulder marks to-day the spot where he fell. The Peace of Kappell followed and the Swiss Reformation proceeded under other direction. For a brief period Henry Bullinger held sway and then the leadership passed from Bullinger to Calvin and from Zurich to Geneva.[1]

The career of John Calvin brings us into immediate contact with the Reformed movement in France. As related to Humanism the French Reformation doubtless owed much to Marguerite d'Angouleme, sister of King Francis I. The more religious side of the movement is likewise indebted to Jacques Lefevre d'Etaples. But it was Calvin who gave it its main direction. John, or Jean, Calvin (Cauvin) was born in 1509, the son of a lawyer belonging to the ecclesiastical court of Noyon, the boy studied first at Paris, where he narrowly escaped being a fellow-student with Ignatius Loyola. Then he was sent to study law at Orleans, but on his father's death returned to Paris to take up more congenial subjects. About 1533 he experienced a kind of sudden conversion and embraced the principles of the reformers. Obliged on this account to flee from France he took up his abode in Switzerland, where he entered enthusiastically into the reform campaign. At Basle he wrote his epoch-making treatise, *Christianæ Religionis Institutio*, generally known as the *Institutes*. This was dedicated to the King of France and was destined to exert great influence upon the course

[1] See S. M. Jackson, *Heroes of the Reformation*, London, 1901.

of the Reformation. Soon after this Calvin went to Geneva, and, largely through the influence of William Farel, plunged into the task of making Geneva a city with room in its streets for the soul. His zeal brought about expulsion, but in 1541 he returned and, according to John Knox, made Geneva "the most perfect school of Christ that ever was on the earth since the days of the Apostles." In the light of what happened to Servetus and other heretics this may be regarded as an exaggeration. Undoubtedly, in turning Geneva into a theocracy, Calvin did reorganize the life of the community pretty thoroughly. He refused to regard the State as subject to the Church, as did the Romanists, or the Church as subject to the State, as did the Lutherans, or, with the Anabaptists, the Church and State as distinct, the one from the other. To Calvin the Church was the State, as with the people of Israel in the wilderness. In doctrine Calvin taught a very rigid system of Predestination, by which every man's fate was determined by the absolute foreknowledge and decree of Almighty God. This doctrine, it has been said, made for democracy, but it certainly is at some removes from the teaching of the Gospels. Yet even Renan says of Calvin that he was "the most Christian man of his generation." [1]

In *France*, where the New Learning had taken hold among the aristocracy largely, as stated above, through the influence of Marguerite d'Angouleme, the Reformation, as a religious movement, suffered many vicissitudes. It prospered greatly in the early years and was then persecuted through the agency of Henry II.'s Fiery Chamber in 1547. Yet the churches continued to multiply and, in the latter part of the sixteenth century, Coligny estimated their number as over two thousand. Then came the unfortunate trend towards politics and warlike preparation, which culminated in 1572, on St. Bartholomew's Eve, in one of the most hideous massacres in religious history. The Huguenots, as the French Protestants were now called, never rallied from this brutal attack, which was justified on religious as well as on political grounds. Henry of Navarre,

[1] See Williston Walker, *John Calvin*, New York, 1906; H. Y. Reyburn, *John Calvin, His Life, Letters, and Work*, London, 1914.

of whom the Huguenots expected much, failed the cause, deeming Paris "well worth a mass." He believed, possibly with sincerity, that only by making the religion of France Roman Catholic could he secure the unity of his realm. From this time on, the French Protestants, though unsubdued in spirit, were fitly enough described as "the Church in the Wilderness." In 1598, indeed, the Edict of Nantes restored to the Huguenots their rights as citizens, but it could never restore the numbers who had perished or the prestige of an earlier day.[1]

In the *Low Countries* some preparation for the Reform movement may be discerned among the Brethren of the Common Life, but the main sources of Dutch Protestantism are Lutheran. The first martyrs, also, Henry Voes and John Esch, were Lutherans. But the persecution was even more severe against the Anabaptists, who in 1532 had a price set upon their heads. Persons who harboured them were adjudged equally guilty. This severity had the effect of driving the Anabaptists to every extreme of fanaticism, and even to the taking up of arms against the Emperor. The Lutherans loved the Anabaptists as little as they loved the Papacy, but stood side by side with them in the battle for national liberty. It may be said that the struggle waged with Charles V. was as much a national as a religious movement, and that the Emperor introduced the Inquisition in 1522 as much to quell the patriots as to extirpate the heretics. When Charles abdicated in 1555, his successor Philip II. was no milder in his methods. It is said of him that he "was not much liked by Italians, was thoroughly disliked by the Flemings, and was hated by the Germans." His general, the Duke of Alva, raised the opposition to fever point. The establishment of the Bloody Tribunal and the execution of Counts Egmont and Hoorn had their repercussions as far as Japan, where the Dutchmen were glad to vent their hatred on the missionary friars who represented the Peninsula Empire. During these years the Lutheran character of Protestantism in the Netherlands gradually yielded to Calvinism, and when the Belgic *Confession* was adopted at the Synod of Emden in 1571 this

[1] See T. M. Lindsay, *History of the Reformation*, Vol. II., pp. 136–221.

character was confirmed. The struggle against the Duke of Alva and the Empire brought out a great hero in William of Orange, who became a Calvinist in 1573 and fought on behalf of religious and national freedom until his assassination in 1584. It is remarkable that during these terrible years the Dutch love of learning, which had been conspicuous from the time of the great humanist Erasmus, did not wane. The establishment of the University of Leyden, as a thankoffering for the deliverance of that city, and subsequently of the Universities of Groningen and Utrecht is evidence of this fact. Among the great Dutch theologians of the time is Arminius, whose teaching conflicted somewhat fundamentally with that of Calvin. But Calvinism triumphed at the Synod of Dort in 1618. To-day it is said that the Reformed Church in the Netherlands has a membership of over a million.[1]

The more or less continuous contact of the Low Countries and France with *Scotland* made it inevitable that the latter country should speedily be reached by the Reformation. Scotland had even before this been affected by the speculations of scholasticism and by the preaching of Wiclif's "poor priests." Patrick Hamilton, the first victim in the persecution of Protestantism, in 1528, was a Lutheran. George Wishart, who was executed in 1546, was a Scottish Calvinist. To Wishart succeeded the famous John Knox, who was born in 1505, and grew up as a loyal son of the Church till about 1547. Then it was said of him that, while others merely shed the branches of Papistry, he had chosen to strike at the roots. Labouring for a while in England, he found his way to Geneva, visited Calvin, prepared the *Book of Common Order* and the *Metrical Psalms* for the Scots reformers, and returned to Scotland in 1559. In the next year the Reformed Church of Scotland was organized, the Confession of Faith drawn up, and the First Book of Discipline put forth. There followed a dramatic struggle between Knox and Mary Queen of Scots, but by 1567 the victory for Scottish Protestantism had been definitely won. Knox died in 1572, having left the proud

[1] See P. J. Blok, *History of the People of the Netherlands* (Eng. trans.), 5 vols., New York, 1898–1912.

testimony: "None have I corrupted; none have I depraved; merchandise I have not made of the glorious evangel of Jesus Christ." After Knox, under the influence of Andrew Melville, the Reformed Church of Scotland was definitely shaped on Presbyterian lines. In 1592 by Act of Parliament it was declared that Church government was by General Assembly, Synods, Presbyteries and Kirk Sessions. To this system Scotland has remained generally faithful to the present day.[1]

The Reformation in *England* took an entirely different course from that in Germany, or Switzerland, neither going to the revolutionary extremes of the continental reformers, nor seeking to maintain what were deemed accretions in the Papal system. It drew from the several sources of humanism, nationalism, and protest against ecclesiastical corruption, but the force of the movement in each of these aspects had been long gathering to a head. National disapproval of the Papal Supremacy, indeed, had been sporadically displayed from the time of the Conquest and only now reached the final explosion. It has often been stated that the breach with the Papacy was the result of the moral depravity of that much-married man, Henry VIII. This is a serious misrepresentation of the matter. The original marriage of Henry with Katharine of Aragon was at the time regarded as of doubtful validity, and when the question of the divorce came up the opposition of the Popes (who had given such dispensations before) was not so much moral as political, due to the pressure of Katharine's relative, the Emperor. Pope Clement even made the suggestion that Henry might take a second wife without the formality of divorcing Katharine. Moreover, it should be remembered that Cranmer, who has been vilified as a mere time-server, appealed to the canonists of Europe and was upheld not only by the Universities of England but also by those of France and Italy. Henry was certainly of no estimable character, but he was probably sincere in his desire for a marriage which would yield male issue and so make the succession secure. Whatever the immediate occasion for

[1] See P. Hume Brown, *History of Scotland*, 3 vols., Cambridge, 1902–1909; D. Hay Fleming, *The Scottish Reformation*, London, 1910.

the breach, it was clearly in line with the expressed will of Church and people, and was regarded as no separation from the historic Church. There was, again, to start with, very little controversy on doctrinal subjects, though Lollardism had been prevalent in England since the time of Wiclif. Nor was there anything essentially new in Henry's claim in 1531 to be "so far as the law of Christ permits, the Supreme Head of the English Church and clergy." It was an appeal to the *Statute of Præmunire*. In 1534 the Acts of Parliament which confirmed the action taken earlier by Convocation forbade the payment of *annates* and of Peter's Pence to Rome, affirmed the validity of the King's marriage to Anne Boleyn and the legitimacy of her issue, and solemnly reaffirmed the declaration that "the Roman Pontiff had no greater jurisdiction bestowed on him by God in the Holy Scriptures than any other foreign Bishop." [1]

Yet though the Reformation in England at first placed little stress on doctrinal issues, these were bound, sooner or later, to come to the front, because of the then existing relations between England and the Continent. The *Ten Articles* put forth by Henry in 1536 varied little doctrinally from the older formulas. They were such, it has been said, that "a pliant Lutheran and a pliant Romanist might agree upon." A much more important step was taken when it was agreed to offer the English people a Bible in their own tongue. The first real translation of the Bible into English from the original languages was that of William Tyndale, a great scholar, whose language still survives in much of our modern versions. Tyndale had to work abroad and his Bible was burned at St. Paul's Cross in 1530. The translator himself suffered the like fate on the Continent. But after the Bible of Miles Coverdale—made from the Vulgate—had been licensed in 1536, Archbishop Cranmer himself recommended the adoption of a version which, signed by the fictitious name of one Matthews, was really a work edited by John Rogers and made up largely of the translations of Tyndale and Coverdale. When licensed, it was

[1] See R. W. Dixon, *History of the Church of England from the Abolition of the Roman Jurisdiction*, 5 vols., London, 1878–1892; A. F. Pollard, *Henry VIII.*, London, 1905; same author, *Thomas Cranmer*, New York, 1904.

known as the Great Bible, or, on account of the Archbishop's preface, Cranmer's Bible.

One of the most significant incidents of the English Reformation is the dissolution of the monasteries, due in the first place to the transfer of these establishments from Pope to Crown, and secondly to the visitation by Thomas Cromwell. Though this attack on the monasteries was in large part carried out as it was through the rapacity and avarice of the king, we must remember that Wolsey had already sequestrated some of the emoluments of the monastic houses in the interest of education. There is no doubt also that many of the monasteries had outlived their usefulness and were the homes of idle if not dissolute monks. But Cromwell's "visitation" was carried out with entire lack of scruple and a very large part of the loot went to other interests than those of education and the establishment of new bishoprics. Altogether 376 houses were suppressed and their revenues handed over to the king, after the several thousands of the expelled monks had been placated with a small pension. The general feeling of the people against this act of spoliation was shown in the several insurrectionary movements which broke out, notably in Yorkshire, where the revolt was known as the Pilgrimage of Grace. The insurgents were appeased by promises which the king had no intention of keeping. Indeed, later on, in 1545, a third statute of confiscation was passed, whereby more colleges, chantries, chapels and hospitals were closed. Only six new bishoprics and some colleges were established from the proceeds; the rest went to the king and his friends.

Altogether the reign of Henry VIII. contributed little to the English Reformation beyond the breach with the Papacy, the dissolution of the monasteries, the licensing of the English Bible, and the setting forth of the *Litany* which still remains part of the Prayer Book. In some respects Henry was even reactionary, winning the title of *Fidei Defensor* from the Pope for his book against Luther. Fisher and More were put to death for disputing the king's supremacy, but more persons were executed for the teaching of heresy.

In the next reign, however, that of Edward VI., Protestantism gained a temporary ascendancy. New counsels prevailed, and Edward reigned entirely under the thumb of that ardent Protestant, Somerset, Lord Protector. There were now three parties in the Church, moderate reformers, who wanted only to maintain the independence of the historic English Church as against Papal aggression, reformers who leaned towards the principles of the German Reformation, and reformers who favoured the extreme Puritanism which had taken hold in Switzerland. In addition there were swarms of Anabaptists, regarded by all the rest much as we regard Bolshevists at the present day. Happily, while the Protector favoured the extremer type of reform and even appointed commissioners to make a still cleaner sweep of the old ecclesiastical establishments, his downfall in 1549 and the good sense of the general body of Convocation frustrated too radical a departure from the old lines. Some things of great value were achieved in Edward's short reign, notably the setting forth of the Prayer Book of 1549, which has been described as "the noblest monument of piety and learning which the sixteenth century has produced." It was, however, not satisfactory to the ultra-Protestants and a revision was undertaken which resulted in the Second Prayer Book of Edward VI., of 1552, considerably more Protestant in tone. The same year witnessed the publication of the *Forty-two Articles*, a formulation of doctrine which was later transformed into the *Thirty-nine Articles*, still bound up with the Prayer Book largely as a matter of historical interest.

Edward died in 1553 and was succeeded by his sister Mary, whose reign was reactionary from beginning to end. There was no disposition on the part of the Papacy to deny the continuity of the English Church but, while Mary continued to use the title of Head of the Church, the authority of the Popes was restored by Act of Parliament in 1554. The statutes against heresy also were revived and a large number of Protestant recalcitrants suffered the extreme penalty in this reign. Mary was certainly a bigot, but she was sincere, and the execution of heretics was quite in accordance with the intolerant spirit of the age. Mary rendered herself hateful to her subjects, however, not merely through her religious views, but also because of her marriage to the foreigner, Philip of Spain, and, not least of all, because of her loss of Calais. She died after a brief reign of five years, a gloomy and disappointed woman.

The reign of Elizabeth, 1558–1603, shows a return to equilibrium and the inauguration of an era marked by the complete victory over the menace of Spain, as well as the definite rejection by the English Church of the Papal Supremacy. Elizabeth and her counsellors, especially Cecil, desired the Church to be equally removed from Romanism and Puritanism. By a new Act the Queen was declared to be Supreme Governor rather than Supreme Head, and the title was explained as a declaration that, under God, she was sovereign over all persons in the realm, whether ecclesiastical or civil. A new revision of the Prayer Book was set forth, which Pope Pius IV. was not indisposed to consider, provided the Queen would acknowledge the supremacy. Elizabeth's refusal led to her excommunication and, in 1570, to the creation of a schism which has ever since separated the Roman and the Anglican Churches. The new Jesuit order opened seminaries on the Continent for the training of missionaries for the reconversion of England. When this happened the Romanists were already settling down to the worship of the English Church, but the intrusion of agents who regarded Elizabeth excommunicate and therefore dethroned led to the execution of many, considered as traitors, or martyrs, according to the point of view. This severity seemed at the time to be successful, for when Elizabeth died there were but few Romanists in the land, and these in hiding. Calm reigned during Elizabeth's last years, but Puritanism, of the continental type, was by no means extinct. Indeed, in the closing years of the reign it was becoming a menace both to Church and State and continued so until it found its inevitable climax in revolution. The story of the triumph of Puritanism we must, however, reserve for another chapter.[1]

[1] On the general subject covered by this chapter see Williston Walker, *The Reformation*, New York, 1900; T. M. Lindsay, *History of the Reformation*; Wilhelm Moeller, *History of the Christian Church*, Vol. III., *The Reformation and Counter-Reformation*, *The Cambridge Modern History*, Vol. II.

## CHAPTER XXXIX

## *From the "Counter-Reformation" to the End of the Seventeenth Century*

IT is a very common error to limit the term "Reformation" to those religious movements which concern only northern and western Europe, such as the Protestantizing of Germany in 1525, of Sweden in 1523, of Denmark in the same year, and to the separation of the English Church from the Roman obedience in 1534. In this use of the term the Churches yielding allegiance to Rome are regarded as untouched by the reforming spirit. While it may be true that the Churches of Protestant and Anglican complexion, in breaking away from the Papacy, found themselves freer to adopt changes of a thoroughgoing character, we must not ignore the fact that the desire for reform was not all on the Protestant side. Emperors like Charles V., Popes like Adrian VI., and Cardinals like Ximines, were probably as sincere in their desire to see the Augean stable of the Church cleansed from its abominations as anyone in Germany or in Switzerland.

From this point of view the term "Counter-Reformation," which seems to imply a movement inaugurated merely to recover from losses inflicted on the Church by the Reformation, is not a particularly happy one. In carrying on the Christian story through the present chapter, it must be kept in mind that reform movements occurred in Italy and Spain as well as in Germany and that these were not less significant for the future than those we associate with the names of Calvin and Luther.

First, we may speak of movements in the direction of reform in Italy. Here in the main the echoes of the Lutheran controversy which crossed the Alps suggested first the removal from the institution of the Papacy of the things which had caused men to stumble rather than any revolutionary change. This impulse was felt in the formation of new societies and in the revival of others. For example, we have the new Oratory of Divine Love, founded specially for the deepening of spiritual religion. Associated with this we have reformers of the type of Cardinals Contarini and Caraffa. There was also a host of devout individuals, many of them women, like Vittoria Colonna, who engaged in correspondence with one another in the ardent endeavour to bring about reformation, within and outside the Peninsula, without the risk of revolution. The monastic establishments themselves caught the fire of this desire and so we get the revival of the great Benedictine order and the founding of the order of Capucins. Paul III., who assumed the tiara in 1534, was himself a reformer and appointed a commission to formulate a programme. Cardinal Contarini was deputed by both Pope and Emperor to visit Germany and find means for the ending of the Lutheran schism. The effort, unfortunately, came too late by two decades. Nevertheless, the effort was made and the Regensburg Conference of 1541 was the result. It failed and henceforth Contarini's influence was gone.

Outside of Italy the most important part of Latin Christendom which demanded reform was Spain, which had once before made its contribution towards the purifying of the Church in the founding of the Dominican order. The Iberian Peninsula, by the expulsion of the Moors and the union of the crowns of Castile and Aragon under Ferdinand and Isabella was now politically one and so naturally in a favourable position for advance towards religious reform. In the attempt to realize this aim several great personalities were engaged. One of the most conspicuous was Cardinal Ximines, whose interest lay particularly in purifying the morals and enlightening the ignorance of the Spanish clergy. The attitude of Luther, to begin with, had in Spain a host of admirers, though these gradually fell away as the German Reformer's methods led to open schism. The zeal for reformation in Spain then took the form of a passionate yearning to cleanse the ship of the Church of all those barnacles of corrupt accretion which were impeding its voyage. Men already saw opportunities, not only in Europe, but even in those new lands across the Atlantic, to repair the ravages made by all the foes of the Church alike, pagan humanists, sensualists, hypocrites, heretics, schismatics, and the rest.[1]

To this great task one man was particularly called—Ignatius Loyola, one of the greatest figures in all ecclesiastical history. Ignatius was a Basque, born about 1493, who began his active career as a soldier. In 1521, while defending Pampeluna against the French, he was badly wounded and, with great agony, had to accept the fact that his soldiering days were done. In distress of soul he passed through an experience out of which he arose determined to consecrate his life to God and to turn all his militant ambitions towards the Cross. The parallel between the conversion of Ignatius and that of Luther has frequently been pointed out. But the sequel in either case is strangely different. Ignatius went for a while the way of the mystics, like Sta. Teresa and other Spaniards, and out of his devotion grew that remarkable manual, the *Spiritual Exercises*, destined to have such important results. Life was not easy just now and twice Ignatius fell into the hands of the Inquisition, escaping with difficulty. In 1528, after wanderings in other lands, he went to Paris, where he began to discern his life's work, and gathered together the little band of nine disciples—among them a fellow-Basque, the future St. Francis Xavier—who, in 1534, in the Church of St. Mary at Montmartre, became the first Company of Jesus. They met again in 1537, at Venice, and thence journeyed to Rome to seek the favour of the Pope. They settled the Constitution of the Order, stressed the fact that they were enrolled to be the Pope's own militia, but were obliged to wait until 1540 for the issue of the Bull which gave definite substance to the Company. Ignatius, somewhat against his will, was elected as the first General, and soon made the new organization felt throughout Europe. It was an organization, like its founder, "at once sternly practical and wildly visionary." Its members were under an iron discipline, with the significant motto, "Perinde ac cadaver."

[1] See W. T. Walsh, *Isabella of Spain*, New York, 1930.

They were fashioned as a polished weapon wherewith to fight all the enemies of the Pope everywhere and by all means. The Company of Jesus had great and almost immediate success in Europe, winning Portugal at once, Spain and France more slowly, and soon carrying the Gospel message and the organization of the Roman Church into the countries of the Far East, as well as to the newly discovered Americas. Of these great missionary adventures we shall speak later in the chapter. Suffice it to say here that, though the Company suffered some lowering of ideals under a few of Loyola's successors, the Jesuits as a body, by their splendid training, their broad-minded knowledge of human nature, and by their extraordinary personal devotion, did much to win for the Roman Churches territory far larger in area than those which had been lost through the Protestant Reformation.[1]

The general desire for reform within the Church of the Roman obedience, which was shared by the Emperor, the national episcopates, and such Popes as Paul III., Paul IV. and Pius IV., and greatly stimulated by the nephew of the last named, the famous Cardinal Borromeo, led to the holding of the Council of Trent. This important assembly was convoked by Paul III. in 1546, later on removed to Bologna, then reassembled at Trent by Pope Julius III., and brought finally to a close in 1563. Altogether the Council covered eighteen years, but these included an intermission of nearly a decade. The delegates represented three parties, distinguished by their attitude towards the Reformation. The objects they had mainly in view were the healing of the Lutheran schism, and the reforming of the ecclesiastical abuses which had been its immediate cause. Many different subjects, however, came up for discussion, including the sources of revelation, the Catholic doctrine as to original sin and justification, the means of grace, the veneration of saints, and the source and limits of ecclesiastical authority. As the Council proceeded, the hope of restoring the broken unity of the Church through an arrangement with the Reformers

[1] See article, "Jesuits," by H. Thurston, in *E.R.E.*, Vol. VII.; also article, "Society of Jesus," in the *Catholic Encyclopædia*.

gradually diminished, and from 1555, the date of the Peace of Augsburg, fell out of the programme. But the results, apart from this, were quite sufficient to justify the assembly. A systematic exposition of doctrine did much to dispel uncertainty as to Roman Catholic teaching, the Bible (inclusive of the Apocrypha, as in the Septuagint) was set forth, important steps were taken for the stricter education of the clergy, abuses in the way of pluralities and non-residence were abolished, and reforms introduced into the Curia. The results of the Council, in these directions, are plainly to be noted in the lives of the successive Popes in this era, and in the many saintly characters which appeared shining like stars in the firmament, even when all around them was dark. In this connection one has only to mention such men as Carlo Borromeo, 1538–1584, nephew of Paul IV., statesman at the age of twenty-two, Archbishop of Milan, founder of the order of Oblates, and canonized in 1610; Philip Neri, 1515–1595, founder in 1575 of the Congregation of the Oratory, a man whose labours among the sick poor won him the title of "apostle of Rome" and canonization in 1622; Francis de Sales, 1567–1622, Bishop of Geneva, founder of the order of the Visitation, canonized in 1665; and Vincent de Paul, 1576–1660, worker among the galley-slaves, for whom he established a hospital at Marseilles, founder of the order of Lazarites, and canonized in 1737.[1]

Unfortunately, neither the reforms initiated by the Council of Trent nor the lives of the devout Churchmen of the period brought peace to Europe. Out of the very zeal for reform which animated so many leaders of the Church came the horrors of the Inquisition and the injustices of the *Index*. The Papal Inquisition itself dates back to the time of Innocent III., in the early days of the thirteenth century, when the Pope sought to go over the heads of the diocesan authorities for the suppression of heresy. It was revived in Spain (where zeal against heresy survived from the time of St. Dominic) at the close of the fifteenth century. The revival is associated with the sinister

[1] See J. A. Froude, *Lectures on the Council of Trent*, London, 1905; and article, "Council of Trent," *E.R.E.*, Vol. IV.

fame of Tomas de Torquemada, the confessor of Queen Isabella, and took the form of obtaining papal permission for the Spanish sovereigns to control the inquisitorial machinery. The Papal Bull to this effect was issued in 1478, and in 1480 the first *auto da fé* was carried out. The hideous system included the use of spies, informers, and every extreme of torture. It is said that in the first century and a half of the Spanish Inquisition there were 3,000,000 persons who suffered from it in one way or another. In the eighteen years of Torquemada's presidency over ten thousand persons were burned alive in Spain and nearly a hundred thousand consigned to perpetual imprisonment. The system spread to the Netherlands and Italy; it brought about the death of Giordano Bruno at Rome in 1600, and the condemnation of Galileo in 1623—the saying " e pur si muove," however, was the invention of a wit more than a century later. But nowhere was the machinery of the Inquisition so relentlessly employed as in Spain, and in this country the institution was not abolished till 1834.[1]

The *Index Librorum Prohibitorum*, designed to do for heretical writings what the Inquisition sought to accomplish for heretical men and women, was finally published in 1564, after the adjournment of the Council of Trent, whence it is known as the *Tridentine Index*. It had small effect north of the Alps, but to learning in the south it brought disastrous consequences, especially in Italy.[2]

Notwithstanding all these efforts, some of them, in intention at least, conciliatory, and some of them relying on the use of force, neither unity nor accord came to Christian Europe. Already the Reformation movement had become so entangled with political aims and methods that war rather than peace was the result. Zwingli had died in the Battle of Kappell, Luther had consented to the formation of the League of Smalcald, Calvin had lent aid to the fighting Huguenots, and William of Orange had warred (both for country and for conscience) against the Spanish generals in the Netherlands. But, just a century after Luther had nailed up his

[1] See H. C. Lea, *History of the Inquisition of Spain*, 5 vols., London, 1905–8.
[2] See article, " Index," by J. Hilgers, in the *Catholic Encyclopædia*.

*Theses* at Wittenberg, there broke out a conflict bitterer than any of the preceding, known because of its duration as the Thirty Years' War. It started in 1618 at Prague with the throwing of the Hapsburg agents out of the castle windows, an incident honoured with the high-sounding name of the Defenestration of Prague. There were three phases of the struggle, one ending in 1629 with the all but complete defeat of the Protestants, a second, in which the great Gustavus Adolphus of Sweden came to the front as a hero, and in which the Romanists were beaten, and a third, following the death of Gustavus Adolphus at the Battle of Lutzen, which ended in the Treaty of Westphalia in 1638. The story of the war is one long record of grim and inhuman wastefulness, with whole territories devastated and depopulated. Schiller well says that "history has no speech and poetry no pen" to describe its horrors. The Peace of Westphalia was intended to guarantee "a peace Christian, universal and perpetual, and a friendship true and sincere." But it did nothing more than assure to an outwearied Europe the continuance of a *status quo* in which Germany remained largely Lutheran, Switzerland Calvinist, and southern Europe faithful to the Papacy. The most beneficent result was that from this time on some measure of tolerance took the place of futile efforts to bring about a return to uniformity. This approach to religious liberty had been dearly purchased, but it was something European Christianity had long awaited in vain.

Two or three other incidents in seventeenth-century religious history on the Continent may here be mentioned. The most serious, perhaps, concerns the quarrel between Jansenists and Jesuits which arose from the publication of a ponderous work by Cornelius Jansen, Bishop of Ypres. The work savoured of what the Jesuits described as "a bungled Calvinism" and was accordingly opposed. The condemnation of the book in 1641, however, rallied support for its teachings from a little group known as the Port Royalists, who included the Arnaulds and the more famous Blaise Pascal. The latter's *Provincial Letters*, by their biting irony, created a great sensation, but eventually the Jesuits procured Papal action against their adversaries and the breaking up of the community of Port Royal. The nuns were expelled and vengeance did not stop with cruelty towards the living. Jansenism, nevertheless, died down very slowly in France and still survives in Holland.[1]

Another incident is the revival of Gallicanism about 1682. This for a while promised to put Louis XIV. of France in the *rôle* of Henry VIII. of England. But the interest of Louis in the restoration of national rights was rather sordidly limited to the desire to reclaim for himself certain ecclesiastical revenues. This was resisted by Innocent XI. with such firmness that in 1689, through the refusal of Bulls of appointment, twenty-nine French bishoprics lay vacant. After this, interest in the matter waned and the "four articles" drawn up by the French clergy were abrogated.

In England the stabilizing of the religious situation was long delayed and required at last a resort to arms. When James I. succeeded Elizabeth in 1603 there was an expectation on the part of his Puritan subjects that he would favour the extremer reformers, and the Millenary Petition was presented by professedly Church of England clergy requesting this support. But James proved loyal to the National Church and, to bring about a common understanding, he summoned the Hampton Court Conference in 1604. Out of this came a very few alterations in the Prayer Book, but a very great achievement in the appointment of a commission to undertake a fresh revision of the translation of the Bible. After seven years the result of this work was published and is generally known as the *Authorized Version*, or the *King James Version* of 1611. It has since been improved, so far as text and accuracy of translation are concerned, but will ever remain a precious monument of Elizabethan English and a means of grace to millions within and without the Christian Church. James did not otherwise contribute to the religious settlement of Europe, though he sent delegates to the Synod of Dort in 1618 to accept a reconciliation between Arminians and Calvinists. When he died in 1625 the gulf had been considerably widened between the Church and the Puritans,

[1] See article, "Jansenism," by St. Cyres, in *E.R.E.*, Vol. VII.

while the famous Gunpowder Plot of 1605 illustrates the attitude of the Roman Catholics.[1]

Under Charles I. the struggle continued, aggravated by the popular resentment against the despotic habit of the Stuarts, who were thoroughgoing believers in the divine right of kings. It was no doubt due to political as much as to religious causes that this disaffection at length broke out into open warfare. Charles was in some respects the victim of circumstances, but his tactlessness and vacillation contributed largely to the defeat of his own cause. Moreover, Charles dragged down with him better men than himself, including Archbishop Laud, who was reluctantly the king's adviser, and for this reason, rather than for his religious views, came at last to the Tower and, in 1645, to the block. The attempt to foist episcopacy upon the Scottish people was particularly ill-timed and such incidents as the "casting of the stools," the signing of the Solemn League and Covenant, and the calling of the Westminster Assembly showed clearly enough the temper of the people in North Britain. The situation was complicated by the Protestant division into Presbyterians and Independents, and when the English Parliament fell into the hands of the latter and of their leader, Oliver Cromwell, the end was to be foreseen. Charles was beaten in battle, in spite of the rallying to his side of the most gallant Cavaliers of the realm, and after his delivery into the hands of his enemies by the Scots the end came quickly in his trial, condemnation, and execution at Whitehall on January 30, 1649.[2]

The Commonwealth under Cromwell lasted from 1649 to 1660 and placed the English Church under a tyrannical and unjust ban. Much of value was destroyed in the cathedrals and churches of the land, the use of the Prayer Book and of the feasts and fasts of the Church was proscribed, and a gloomy, if conscientious, Puritanism became

[1] See W. H. Frere, *The English Church in the Reigns of Elizabeth and James*, London, 1904.

[2] See W. H. Hutton, *The English Church from the Accession of Charles I. to Anne*, London, 1905; S. R. Gardiner, *History of the Great Civil War*, London, 1893; G. M. Trevelyan, *England under the Stuarts*, London, 1906.

temporarily supreme. The Cromwellian regime, in fact, worked its own undoing, so that when the Restoration of Charles II. came about in 1660 the king was welcomed with an enthusiasm he by no means personally deserved. The general rejoicing, however, was not without its tragedies. There was another Black Bartholomew's Day, in 1662, when the Presbyterian and Independent ministers who had been placed over English parishes were ejected, though we must remember that they owed their place to the earlier eviction of the Church of England clergy during the Commonwealth. Nevertheless, the general desire for a settlement led to the holding of the Savoy Conference, which resulted in nothing more important than the setting forth of the revised Prayer Book of 1662, the last revision until modern times. It was an era of plots and counter-plots and of rumours as mischievous as the plots themselves. Yet, despite the wickedness of the court and the unrest of the people, it was also a "golden age" of English divinity. The Caroline divines hold a deservedly high place among the Fathers of Anglicanism. But with the death of Charles and the accession of James II., who went over to the Romanists, a new era of confusion, both political and ecclesiastical, arrived. The king made a deliberate attempt to undo the work of the English Reformation and was probably surprised at the strength of the resistance his arbitrary actions called forth. The opposition of the Seven Bishops, including such men as Sancroft, Compton, Lake and Ken, and their triumphal acquittal by the Judges, will always remain one of the high points in the story of the development of English liberty. After this rebuff to his policy, James had no option but flight, and William, Prince of Orange, who had married the king's sister, Mary, was called in to receive the crown which James, it was held, had forfeited. The success of the Revolution, as it is called, ushered in a period of comprehensiveness and toleration. Some of the Bishops, it is true, regarded their oath to James as precluding them from swearing allegiance to the new regime, and these remained as the Non-juring Bishops. Apart from such incidents as this, the Church of England settled down to pursue the even tenor of its way and to minister as best it was able to the needs of the nation.[1]

The brightest aspect of Christianity in the period we are considering is not to be found in the controversies between reformers and traditionalists, but rather in the great outburst of missionary activity which characterized the Roman Church, and to a much lesser extent a few of the Reformed Communions. Several facts account for this renewed evangelical ardour. In part it was due to the new geographical discoveries which opened fresh territories to the Gospel message, in part to the new intellectual movement which stimulated curiosity as to the manners, customs and religious beliefs of peoples beyond the sea, in part also to the emergence of new nationalities bent upon expansion and the reproduction of their own culture, and in part, once again, to the new religious fervour kindled by the rise of the Jesuit and other orders. If the question be asked why it so happened that the missionary work of the sixteenth and seventeenth centuries was so largely in the hands of Roman Catholics, the answer is, first, that the great powers earliest to seek dominion beyond the seas were Spain and Portugal, the most devoted to the Roman obedience, and but recently emerging from their triumphant expulsion of the Muslim from the Peninsula—powers, moreover, whose position on the high seas had been guaranteed to them by the famous Bull of Pope Alexander IV. Secondly, we must remember that the Protestant powers were still in the throes of the formative period, both religiously and politically. We must still, however, admit that Protestantism was slow in awaking to a sense of missionary responsibility. Some, like the Dutch, smarting under the operation of the Inquisition, deemed it their duty to hinder the work of the Peninsula missionaries in the Far East as much as was possible. Some Protestant theologians even insisted that the Christianity of their own day had no missionary responsibility so far as the heathen were concerned. Be this as it may, the missionary history of the sixteenth and a large part of the seventeenth century is the history of

[1] See T. Lathbury, *History of the Nonjurors*, London, 1845; J. H. Overton, *The Nonjurors*, London, 1902.

Roman Catholic missions in the Americas, the Philippines, in India, Japan and China—a work at first almost entirely under the patronage of the sovereigns of Spain and Portugal, but later carried on by hosts of Frenchmen, with a smaller sprinkling of priests drawn from Italy, Germany, Austria and Belgium. All the work was, of course, gradually centralized in the Curia at Rome. There was, quite naturally, a large intermingling of political and commercial motive in all this, but the religious motive in many places, and in the majority of individual cases, was maintained as the predominant one. In our disapproval of some of the methods used and in our criticism of some of the results secured, it is only too easy to blind ourselves to the enormous mass of consecrated heroism which fills the story of this great missionary revival.[1]

The story begins with the evangelization of the Americas, following upon the voyage of Columbus in 1492. The Spaniards seem to have made but little effort to convert the Caribs of the West Indies, but in Central America a splendidly successful work, albeit not enthusiastically supported by the conquerors, was carried on by the great missionary, Las Casas. Las Casas sailed with Columbus in 1498 and by his labours in Haiti, Cuba, Nicaragua, and Guatemala won for himself the title, "Protector of the Indians." He was the first priest ordained in the West Indies; in 1522 he became a Dominican monk, and many years later, after his return to Spain, we find him, at the age of ninety-two, still pleading before His Catholic Majesty of Spain the Indian cause.

Ponce de Leon, sailing for Florida in 1520, brought to the natives the Spanish king's command to submit themselves to the Cross of Christ and the Crown of Spain under penalty of the sword. The expedition was deservedly repulsed, but eventually Dominicans, Franciscans and Jesuits arrived, and soon the converts were to be counted by their thousands. When, however, Florida passed to Great Britain in 1763, the fabric reared at the cost of so much devotion seemed to collapse. Similar failure was the

[1] See C. H. Robinson, *History of Christian Missions*, New York, 1915.

ultimate outcome of the work in New Mexico, where the population had been evangelized by Franciscans from 1598 onwards. Texas in 1717 and California as late as 1769 became fields for the missionary energy of the Franciscans and here the results were more satisfactory. Farther north, where the territory was under French control, French Jesuits were the missionary agents and no one should forget the heroic and successful labour of Père Marquette who, from 1674 on, converted a large part of the Illinois nation. In what is now Canada the earliest of many famous missionaries was Father Fleché, who joined Champlain's expedition on the shores of the Bay of Fundy. In 1633 we find Jesuit missionaries working among the Indian tribes of Quebec, and among the many stories of exalted heroism and willing martyrdom (among native converts as well as foreign priests) we must not omit that of Father René, who, after unexampled sufferings among the Ottawas, won the martyr's crown sometime later than 1660.[1]

When Cortés came to Mexico in 1521 he was avowedly engaged in a crusade on behalf of the Christian religion. In 1524 twelve Franciscan friars arrived to undertake the work of conversion in the newly conquered land. So successful was their work—though we may not condone the violence by which many of the Spanish conversions were achieved—that, nine years later, nine million converts were claimed, a number in excess of the whole population at the time. The Spanish policy was to make a clean sweep of the old Aztec religion, and to this end not only were temples cast down and idols destroyed, but many valuable pieces of literature were ruthlessly burned, to the great regret of modern scholars. At the present time, while the population of Mexico is nominally Roman Catholic, much of the old superstition, and probably many of the old pagan practices, survive.[2]

In South America the missionary work in Brazil was carried on by Portuguese Jesuits, who, by the Bull of Pope Alexander, claimed this as their sphere of influence. The

[1] See Thomas Hughes, *History of the Society of Jesus in North America*, 2 vols., London, 1908.

[2] See Francis Parkman, *The Jesuits in North America*, New York, 1909.

first missionary band was sent by King John in 1549, and many hundreds—most of them men of devotion—followed. One of the greatest was Joseph Anchieta, who laboured from 1553 to 1597 with great success. For the most part the Jesuits supported the cause of the Indians against the cruelty of the military. Consequently they became very unpopular with the government and were deported, for this and other reasons, in 1760. It must be acknowledged, however, that as time went on the morals and manners of the missionaries suffered deterioration, with ill results in the case of their flocks. A Roman Catholic bishop is quoted as saying: "Brazil has no longer any faith. Religion is almost extinct here"—a statement, one hopes, greatly exaggerated. In the rest of South America most of the missionary work was inaugurated and carried on by the Spaniards. In Peru the conquest of the Incas by Pizarro in 1532 left behind the rankling memory of much cruelty, but the missionaries did their best to heal the wounds made. One great name stands out from the rest, that of St. Francis Solano, 1589–1610, a man greatly beloved whose converts were numbered by the thousand. Spanish priests also accompanied Valdivia in the conquest of Chili in 1540, while the Jesuits established a mission in Bolivia in 1577. In Paraguay there was a great Jesuit missionary in the person of Manuel de Ortega, who died in 1622, while scarcely less famous was Christoval de Mendoza.

The missionary work of the Spaniards was not confined to the Americas. In 1521 the Philippine Islands were discovered by Magellan and a few years later, in 1565, the work of conquest and conversion was simultaneously commenced. On the whole the conquest was carried out with less cruelty than had been employed on the Western Continent. The pioneer missionary was an Augustinian friar, Urdaneta, but others followed rapidly. After the Augustinians came the Franciscans in 1577, the Jesuits in 1581, and the Dominicans in 1587. All gained and used a considerable amount of political as well as ecclesiastical authority, and all orders alike seem to have lost their original zeal through encroaching ease and wealth. It was for this reason, among others, that the Jesuits were expelled in 1767, not to be readmitted till 1852.[1]

Now we may turn to the work of the Portuguese missionaries who followed in the wake of Vasco da Gama to the Malabar coast of India in 1498. It was natural that the Portuguese should blend their interest in commerce with an intense zeal for proselytism, since the great pioneer of Portuguese discovery, Prince Henry of Portugal, had been Grand Master of the Order of Christ. Portuguese Dominicans reached Goa in 1510, and a few years later, in 1542, arrived the great "Apostle of the Indies," Francis Xavier, Papal Nuncio and head of the Jesuits in the East. We may well pause a moment to view more closely this illustrious missionary.

Francisco de Xavier,[2] born 1506 in his mother's castle of Xavier at the foot of the Pyrenees, was of a noble Navarrese family. At the University of Paris he came under the compelling influence of Ignatius and became one of the original Company of Jesus in 1534. In 1541 he sailed from Lisbon for the Portuguese Indies and spent many months of self-denying labour at Goa and Travancore. Xavier was not a linguist and did all his preaching by interpreter, a fact which makes the more remarkable his great personal influence, though reflecting also on the thoroughness of the work accomplished. The poet Whittier describes the missionary as ringing a bell in the streets of Goa to attract the crowd. There were many conversions, especially among the low-caste pearl-divers, or Paravas. Xavier left India in 1549 and from that date there was a change of policy. Forced conversions were frequent from 1567 and when the Italian, Robert de Nobili, arrived in 1605, we may even suspect an element of fraud, since the production of a new *Veda*, confirmatory of the Christian position, may hardly be designated by any other name. The missionaries accepted, too, the caste system, and work on these lines was continued for the rest of the century.

[1] See John Foreman, *The Philippine Islands*, chaps. iv., v. and xii., New York, 1906.

[2] See E. A. Stewart, *A Life of St. Francis Xavier*, London, 1917; Otis Carey, *A History of Christianity in Japan*, 2 vols., 1909.

Xavier had gone on to Malacca, where he met a Japanese, Anjiro (or Yajiro), whom he baptized as Paul. Then with his new convert, and with Father Fernandez, Xavier sailed for Japan, which had been first reached by the Portuguese in 1542. They landed at Kagoshima and for twenty-seven months worked indefatigably in a field which seemed ripe for the harvesting. At Yamaguchi, on the Inland Sea, Xavier built the first Christian church in Japan, calling it "The Temple of the Great Way." He says of the people here: "In all my life I never tasted so much consolation as at Yamaguchi." Thousands of converts were made here and elsewhere, but in accounting for the success we must allow not only for the attraction of Xavier's personality and the sincere desire of the people, but also for the commercial advantage of being friendly with the Portuguese and also for the hostility of the dictator Nobunaga (a little later) to the Buddhists. Xavier left Japan in 1551, because he realized that it was wiser to start the work in China, the mother land of Japanese culture. His work was continued by Fathers Torres and Fernandez and by native converts. It was not only continued but flourished; Nagasaki was built up as a Christian city, with wellnigh 30,000 inhabitants. Within thirty years of Xavier's departure there were seventy-five Jesuits at work in the Empire and the converts were estimated to be not less in number than 300,000. Then came trouble, partly from the accession of Hideyoshi, less favourably inclined to the Christians than was Nobunaga, partly from bigotry on the part of some missionaries in their relation with the Buddhists, partly from the intrusion of Franciscan and Dominican monks from the Philippines, and partly from the suspicion of the rulers (encouraged by the Dutch) that conversion to Christianity was but the preliminary to conquest by Spain or Portugal. Hence, though Hideyoshi used a Christian general, Konishi Yukinaga, in his war with Korea, in 1587 he promulgated an edict expelling the missionaries and in the same year took place "The Crucifixion of the Twenty-six," by which six Spanish Franciscans, three Japanese Jesuits, and seventeen Japanese laymen bore witness to Christ by their death.[1] Hideyoshi died in 1598 and in 1600 the Tokugawa Shogunate was founded by Iyeyasu, who initiated (for political reasons) a thorough-going system of persecution which was not relaxed until 1865. All Christian books and symbols were prohibited, the notice-boards offered rewards for the betrayal of Christians, the ceremony of the "trampling on the cross" was made a regular obligation, and many thousands of victims perished in what was practically a war to the death against the religion of Christ. The historian Lecky adduces the persecution as one instance of a complete and successful suppression, yet when, in 1865, the edicts against Christianity were abolished something over 2000 persons were found in the neighbourhood of Nagasaki who for more than two hundred years had in secrecy kept the faith. "The Discovery of the Christians" is observed as a festival of the Roman Catholic Church in Japan on March 17. But in the seventeenth century the Christian cause seemed hopeless. Edicts followed one another in 1624, 1633, 1634 and 1637. In 1638 came the terrible Shimabara massacre, in which 33,000 persons (including 13,000 women and children) perished. In this affair the Dutch assisted the Japanese authorities with ships and guns. It was thought that the *coup de grâce* had been given to "the evil faith."[2]

The first stage of missionary enterprise in China on the part of the Roman Catholic missionaries was almost entirely in the hands of the Portuguese. Later on, the adjustment of the Portuguese political sovereignty over the missionaries with the authority of the Papacy was not the least of the difficulties encountered in the Middle Kingdom. Portuguese reached China first in 1516 and, after having suffered expulsion from ports such as Ningpo, settled down in the little island of Shang-ch'uan, off Canton, and about 1550 built the city of Macao which is still a Portuguese possession. We have spoken of Xavier's desire to visit China which led him to leave Japan in 1551. He sailed first to Goa and returned eastward in April 1552. With some opposition

[1] See *Transactions of the Asiatic Society of Japan*, Vol. XLIV., Part I., Tokyo, 1916.

[2] See H. H. Gowen, *An Outline History of Japan*, pp. 249 ff., New York, 1927.

he left Malacca for Shang-ch'uan and was there landed, only to die in a lonely hut, attended by one faithful Chinese. He had sought to purchase with his life an entrance to the Chinese Empire. Several attempts followed, of which that of Valignani in 1573 is the best known. The despairing words of Valignani: "O Rock, Rock, when wilt thou open?" are familiar. No real touch was gained with continental China till the time of the great missionary Mateo Ricci, who reached Goa in 1578, proceeded to Macao in 1582, and thence planned the career for which he stands almost supreme among missionaries to China. For awhile he worked at Nanking and about this time gained the conversion of Paul Hsü and his daughter Candida, from whom came the princely bequest on which the Roman Catholic establishment of Zikawei now stands at Shanghai. In 1601 Ricci reached Peking and inaugurated that policy which has sometimes been described as "egregious concession," but which may more fittingly be regarded as a wise and sympathetic discernment as to what was fundamental in Christianity and what Chinese practices might safely be tolerated. Ricci died in 1610 leaving, as he said, with his last breath, "a door open to great merits, but not without trouble and danger."

Soon after Franciscans and Dominicans began to arrive from the Philippines—not too welcome, because of the reports of massacres of Chinese in the Islands by the Europeans. They were also unwelcome to the Jesuits. In 1616 and 1622 persecution began to raise its head, but this was followed by a period of success in which converts were won from the royal house of the Mings. The heir of the last Ming Emperor, with his wife and mother, were Christians, named by the Jesuits Constantine, Anne and Mary respectively. The Manchu conquest of 1644 changed the whole situation, but many Jesuits, including the famous Adam Schall, recommended themselves to the Manchu Emperors through their superior skill as calendar makers. Yet from this time the Jesuits in Peking had a difficult task, beset on the one hand by rivals among the native astronomers and on the other hand by Dominican and Franciscan friars who strongly criticized, and reported to the Pope, the concessions made to Chinese practice. Strained relations also existed between the Portuguese missionaries who still acknowledged the royal authority and the other missionaries, particularly those sent out by the French Societé des Missions Etrangères, who worked directly under a Vicar-Apostolic from Rome. In 1664, during the minority of the Emperor K'ang Hsi, a new persecution broke out, but the danger passed for a while when the Emperor assumed control. At this time many Jesuits, French, Italian, German and Belgian, were contributing to the scientific knowledge and skill of the Chinese. Among these was Verbiest, who was responsible for some of the famous astronomical instruments on the walls of Peking. At the close of the century there were in all China 75 priests, 38 of them Jesuits, 9 Spanish Dominicans, 5 Spanish Augustinians, 7 French missionaries of the Societé, 12 Spanish Franciscans, and 4 Italian Franciscans. While missionary hopes were still high, there broke out the unfortunate Controversy of the Rites, the Dominicans and others objecting to the use by the Jesuits of the old Chinese name for God, *Shang Ti*, instead of the term *T'ien Chu* (Heaven-Lord), which they themselves favoured. The matter, greatly to the Emperor's indignation, was referred to the Pope and ultimately decided against the Jesuits. Browning refers to the case in *The Ring and the Book*, though mistakenly writing " To-kien " for " Fu-kien ":

> Five years since in the Province of To-kien,
> Which is in China, as some people know,
> Maigrot, my Vicar-Apostolic, there,
> Having a great qualm, issues a decree.
> Alack, the converts use as God's name, not
> Tien-chu, but plain Tien or else Shang-ti,
> As Jesuits please to fancy politic,
> While say Dominicans, it calls down fire,—
> For Tien means Heaven, and Shang-ti, supreme prince,
> While Tien-chu means the Lord of Heaven.[1]

The decision was unfortunate in more ways than one. It superseded a good term for God by a bad one, now generally discredited; it angered the Emperor to see a matter appealed

[1] R. Browning, *The Ring and the Book,* X. *The Pope.*

to an authority outside the realm; and it revealed a bitter antagonism between representatives of the different orders. The question is an open one as to whether the Papal decision was not the ruin of the Roman Catholic missions in China for the time being. There is no question at all as to the severe damage inflicted by the dispute on the Christian cause in the Empire.[1]

Outside the Roman Catholic Church the amount of missionary work undertaken before the end of the seventeenth century is not large. Among Protestant bodies we may recall that the Pilgrim Fathers who sailed for Massachusetts in the *Mayflower* in 1620 did not altogether forget their duty to the Indians, though it was not a propitious time for conversions. "Oh, that you had converted some before you had killed any!" wrote John Robinson. Appeals, however, were made on behalf of missionary work and the charter of King Charles I. to the colony said that the principal end of the plantation was to "win and invite the natives of the country to the knowledge of the only true God and Saviour of mankind and the Christian faith." A little later we have the inspiring career of John Eliot, "Apostle of the Indians," who in 1632, when pastor of Roxbury near Boston, commenced his missionary work among the tribes. In course of time the fourteen "praying Indian villages," with some 3600 Christians, was the result. In addition Eliot made translations of both the Old and New Testaments into the Mohican tongue and put forth Indian grammars, primers, and other manuals. He died in 1690, after witnessing the ruin of much of his work through war.[2]

Dutch colonization and conquest here and there paid tribute to the importance of missionary work, as in Ceylon after the expulsion of the Portuguese, and in South Africa, where the efforts of Van Riebeek were extended on behalf of slaves and Hottentots as well as settlers.

Anglican missions were at first wellnigh confined to the care of English subjects, as in India, where eighteen chaplains were employed by the East India Company between

[1] See K. S. Latourette, *History of Christian Missions in China*, chap. vii.
[2] See L. W. Bacon, *A History of American Christianity*, New York, 1901.

1667 and 1700, though even here we read of the conversion of a certain Indian known as "Peter Papa," taken home by Captain Best in 1614. In the charters given to the adventurers of the sixteenth and seventeenth centuries, however, there was generally some reminder of religious duty, as in that given to Sir Humphrey Gilbert in 1583, where in speaking of the "poor infidels" it was added that it seemed "probable that God hath reserved these Gentiles to be introduced into Christian civility by the English nation."

Having now strayed over the world field in our survey of the missionary activities of the sixteenth and seventeenth centuries, we must return to Europe to pursue the story of Christianity through another interesting and significant epoch.[1]

[1] See article, "Missions" (with its Bibliography), by W. Paton, in *Ency. Brit.* (14th Ed.); also C. H. Robinson, *History of Christian Missions*.

# CHAPTER XL

## *Christianity in the Eighteenth Century*

AT the close of the last chapter I spoke of the eighteenth century as interesting and significant. Others have set it down as dull and decadent. It may be described in either way—a Janus-faced era, on the one hand, depressing in its evidence of failure in faith and morals and, on the other hand, manifesting even out of deadness and corruption signs of vitality which meant much for the religion of the future. It is an illustration of the ever-present truth that, however much religion may seem to die down in the heart of man, the germ of life still remains and will presently revive. In the present chapter our survey must necessarily be both brief and general. We shall touch on parts of the Christian story in many different parts of the world, but seeking rather a total impression than an account of the history in detail.

Glancing first at the Eastern Church, which had suffered most in the earlier centuries from the ravages of Islam, we see very distinct indications of recovery from the tyranny of Saracen and Mongol and Turk. They begin with the great victory of John Sobieski at the gates of Vienna in 1683 and the new freedom becomes fairly assured with the Treaty of Carlowitz in 1699, by which Hungary and Transylvania were restored to Christendom. Following upon this, we note a very vigorous effort on the part of the Church in Constantinople to regain its hegemony over the Eastern Churches. But, as a matter of fact, the centre of orthodoxy turned out to be in Russia rather than Byzantium. Up to the time of Peter the Great the Russian Czars took an enthusiastic interest in the restoration of the faith which had been trampled underfoot through so many generations. As for Peter, as was natural with a man of his antecedents, he sometimes flirted with the Lutherans of Germany, then seemed inclined to seek union with the Church of England, and at times even showed interest in the Church of Rome. When he suppressed the Patriarchate, it was made clear that he meant to use the Church as a tool for the furthering of his political plans. Yet it is to be observed that during this very period the Russian Church was more active in missionary work than any other of the Eastern communions. The pioneering adventures of Yermak the Cossack, by which Siberia was won for Russia, opened up a way for missionaries of the Russian Church as far as to China.[1]

The Roman Catholic Church in the eighteenth century was not quite living up to the promise of the century before. In England Roman Catholics were still struggling against heavy disabilities and found it difficult to obtain the ministration of the sacraments. In 1789 they found it advisable to draw up a *Protestation* affirming their sincere loyalty to the Crown and their innocence of the plots in which participation was suspected. Toleration, nevertheless, made very slow progress through the eighteenth century, though a path was being prepared for the abolition of the *Test Act*, in 1828, and the *Emancipation Act* of the following year. On the Continent there was a fairly general attack by the various national governments on the Jesuits, and soon after the middle of the century the order was expelled from France, Portugal and Spain. A certain type of revival in the Church came about through the consecrated zeal of St. Alphonsus Liguori, who has been termed "the father of modern Roman Catholicism." Alphonsus, who was canonized in 1839, did a great deal to arouse the laity to a more devout attitude. The cult of the Heart of Jesus and the increased place given to the worship of the Virgin Mary are characteristic of the directions taken by his pious zeal. In spite of the revival, however, the power of the Papacy was much diminished during the century. Frederick the Great told Voltaire that he would live to see the end of the Roman Church. The swing of the age seemed to be away from the centralized power of the Papacy and in the direction of the National Churches. In France Gallicanism seemed to be

[1] W. F. Adeney, *The Greek and Eastern Churches*, Division III., chap. iv.; A. P. Stanley, *History of the Eastern Church*, Lectures IX.–XII.

in the ascendancy. In Germany a similar attitude took the name of Febronianism, from Febronius, the pseudonym of Bishop Nicolas von Hontheim. In Austria we have coincidently what was termed Josephism, in reference to the support given by the Emperor Joseph II. to the *Toleration Act* of 1781. Among the Protestant Churches Calvinism had now won an equal place with Lutheranism. But in both these communions there was a depressing sense of deadness, except where pietism still lingered to warm the hearts of men. To this point we shall presently return.[1]

To all Europe there came a great shaking, of the living hearts of men as well as of the dry bones of decaying faiths, in the outbreak of the French Revolution. This world-shaking cataclysm discharged its wrath on Church as well as Throne and it is impossible to contend that a time-serving and corrupt clergy, in alliance with a still more corrupt political system, had not been in large part responsible for the storm which burst upon them. Within a year from the time that a French mob stormed the Bastille on July 14, 1789, the Church was despoiled of all her vast material wealth, bishoprics were abolished, hundreds of priests slain, and the Goddess of Reason enthroned on the high altar of the Church of Notre Dame. In 1793 all religion was declared abolished and the worship of Reason alone permitted. But this proved too radical a step for the Deist leaders of the Revolution, who had had Christianity mainly in mind in following the Voltairean injunction, "Écrasons l'infame." Presently a kind of religion known as Theophilanthropy, or "the love of God and Man" was set up, and in 1797 there were eighteen Theophilanthropist churches in Paris. Religious freedom was granted to the French people two years earlier than this date, and ere long there was a revival of the old French attitude towards religion called Gallicanism. It was made clear that while the Pope's spiritual authority was admitted, the Church of France was henceforth to be regarded as outside his jurisdiction. This attitude lasted only till the establishment of the *Concordat* between Napoleon Buonaparte and the Papacy in 1801. On Buonaparte's visit to Rome in 1797 Pius VI.

[1] See article, "Toleration (Christian)," by W. F. Adeney, *E.R.E.*, Vol. XII,

was forced to sign a humiliating treaty by which he sacrificed a third of the territory included in the Papal States. The Pope was also compelled to come to France, where he died in 1799. After this episode Napoleon was willing enough to come to terms, recognizing the support that the Papacy could impart to his usurpation of power in France. He therefore admitted that "the Catholic, Apostolic and Roman religion is the religion of the great body of French citizens." The French Church established by the *Concordat* was in many respects a new creation and thirteen bishops who declined to recognize it were excommunicated, and thereupon founded a religious body known as *La Petite Eglise*, which lasted for about a hundred years.[1]

It is now necessary to go back a few years to follow the fortunes of the Church of England after the accession of William III. William, who was a Dutch Calvinist, and is reputed to have worn his hat during divine service, had no particular love for the English Church, but he perceived that the people were, for the most part, greatly attached to the Prayer Book and to the principle of episcopacy. So he had at least to appear sympathetic, even if his actual preference was for the Puritans. In favour of these the *Toleration Act* was passed in 1689, a welcome move towards religious freedom, though no *civil* disabilities were removed from any dissenters and no disabilities of any sort from Roman Catholics, Unitarians and Jews. During the whole of this reign and for long after the schism caused by the Non-juring bishops, who had refused to swear allegiance to William, persisted, though the bishops and clergy—some 400 in number—made no other protest than that implied in the resignation of their offices in the Church. In Scotland Episcopacy was abolished by Parliament and both north and south of the Tweed there was still the old fear of Roman Catholicism which had been fanned anew by James II. in the *Declaration of Indulgence*.

When Queen Anne succeeded William and Mary the Church entered on better days. Anne was a dull woman herself, but the Church of her day flourished. The reign

[1] See article, "France, The Revolution," in *Ency. Brit.* (14th Ed.), IX., pp. 635 ff.

is particularly noted for the *Societies* which sprang up and which have for the most part continued to the present day. The famous Dr. Bray, Rector of Sheldon, who had failed to get a bishop consecrated for the North American colonists, succeeded in several other important endeavours. He founded libraries, eighty of them in England and thirty-nine in North America; he started in 1698 the English *Society for Promoting Christian Knowledge*, which has grown to such vast proportions in our own day; having visited the American Colonies as the commissary of the Bishop of London, he returned to found the missionary Society for the *Propagation of the Gospel in Foreign Parts* (more familiarly known as S.P.G.). On the Queen's birthday in 1704 she performed a great and generous act of belated restitution in assigning the *Annates* which had been seized by Henry VIII. for the use of the Crown to a Fund for augmenting the stipends of the poorer clergy. This Fund, known as *Queen Anne's Bounty*, has continued to be of service in promoting the Church's work. It may be added that many of the churches which had been destroyed in the Great Fire of London were now rebuilt. Sir Christopher Wren was responsible not only for the rebuilding of St. Paul's Cathedral, but also for fifty-three parish churches in the same city.

It was in the reign of Queen Anne that the distinction began to be made between the particular type of Churchmanship known as Low Church and the more ritually ornate type known as High Church. The former, which leaned to Protestantism, found its chief supporters among the Whigs; the latter, which stressed the Catholic character of the Church, was in large part the party of the Tories. The controversy between the two came in this reign to a head in the trial of Dr. Sacheverell, who had preached before the Lord Mayor of London, and subsequently published, a sermon which was much resented by the Whigs. The Lords convicted him and ordered two of his sermons to be burned, but the populace regarded it as a virtual acquittal and a wave of High Churchism took possession of the Church. Altogether Churchmen were in a curiously restless mood, objecting strongly to the establishment of Presbyterianism in Scotland by the *Act of Union* in 1707 and looking askance at the *Act of Toleration* of 1712.[1]

But another wave was about to pass over the land in the form of Deism, that is, a belief in God which so stresses his transcendence as to afford little room for the doctrine of the Incarnation. In England the father of Deism is generally set down as Lord Herbert of Cherbury, but the philosophy of Locke had much to do with extending its influence. The most famous Deists in England during this period were, in addition to those just named, Toland, Shaftesbury, Collins, Woolston, Tindal and Bolingbroke. They did not have things all their own way, for valiant defenders of the Christian tradition appeared in men like Bishop Berkeley, the idealist, Coneybeare, and Warburton. But the influence of Deism spread far beyond England and even had something to do with preparing for and shaping the course of the French Revolution. In Germany it was largely responsible for the movement known as the *Aufklärung*, or *Enlightenment*, of which Goethe was a distinguished representative. Kant, Fichte, Schelling and Hegel were also sharers in and contributors to the *Aufklärung*. It produced, it has been said, " a Christianity without Christ and a Protestantism which was Protestant without being Christian."[2]

Nevertheless, though Deism exerted a kind of deadening influence on the fervid Protestantism of earlier times, German Pietism was not dead. It began to rally even while Deism seemed in the ascendant and the signs of its renewed vitality are nowhere better seen than in the awakened zeal for foreign missions. One of the great figures in this connection was Nicolaus von Zinzendorf, 1700–1760, who had been a pupil of Francke. Zinzendorf, after a remarkable spiritual experience, joined a little community of German-speaking Moravians at Herrnhut. Here was revived, in 1727, the Moravian Church, or *Unitas Fratrum*, resembling closely one of those *collegia pietatis* which had earlier played their part on German soil. In a few years the movement

[1] See A. H. Hore, *Eighteen Centuries of the Church in England*, Part VI., chap. i.

[2] See J. A. Dorner, *History of Protestant Theology, Particularly in Germany* (Eng. trans.), 2 vols., Edinburgh, 1871.

spread to America where, on Christmas Day 1741, a settlement was made at Bethlehem, in the present State of Pennsylvania. From this and other similar settlements missionary work among the Indians was carried on. A notable example is in the life of David Zeisberger, who laboured for the almost unprecedented term of sixty-three years among the North American Indians.[1]

It is curious to note that just as English Deism had passed over to Germany to produce the *Aufklärung*, so German Pietism should have been brought into contact with the evangelicalism of the Church of England to produce one of the most far-reaching revivals of religion in modern times. One can hardly describe the Methodist movement, with its present membership of some thirty million souls, in any lower terms. The Hanoverian line had now succeeded to the throne vacated by the last of the Stuarts and the outlook for the Church under a German Lutheran was scarcely more promising than it had been a generation earlier under a Dutch Calvinist. As already noted, the Church of England at the time was not lacking in able champions against the prevailing Deism, but most of these made their appeal to the intellect rather than to the heart. Even Bishop Butler, whose *Analogy* was destined to be a text-book of Christian Evidences for many years to come, was not enthusiastic as to the future of the Church. He wrote: "It has come, I know not how, to be taken for granted, by many persons, that Christianity is not so much a subject for enquiry; but that it is, now at length, discovered to be fictitious." Where the giants had lost heart, it is not surprising that the rank and file stayed in the tents rather than take the field against the foe. Happily no time is so dark but that men are raised up to redeem the time. This was now the case in the appearance of the Wesleys and their associates.

John and Charles Wesley were the sons of a clergyman of the Church, Rector of Epworth, in the diocese of Lincoln. John in his childhood was rescued with difficulty from the

[1] See Williston Walker, *History of the Christian Church*, pp. 501–507; A. G. Spangenberg, *Life of Nicholas, Count Zinzendorf* (Eng. trans.), London, 1838; A. C. Thompson, *Moravian Missions*, New York, 1895.

burning of the rectory and ever after regarded himself as a brand plucked from the burning. Taking life with corresponding seriousness, he passed through Lincoln College, Oxford, was ordained in 1725, and soon after elected Fellow of his College. For two years he assisted his father in the work of the parish and then returned to Oxford. Here he found that his brother Charles had gathered around him a little band of earnest men who, on account of the devotion which they showed in keeping the fasts and other obligations of the Church had been nicknamed *Methodists*. In addition to the rigid studies they had prescribed for themselves they spent much time in visiting the sick and prisoners at the Castle. One of the young men who attached themselves to the little band was a poor servitor named George Whitefield, afterwards a preacher of almost equal fame with John Wesley himself.

In 1736 John went out to the colony of Georgia as a missionary under the S.P.G. and it was on this voyage he formed the acquaintance of a band of Moravians with whose piety he was much impressed. Wesley's work in Georgia was not an unqualified success and he soon returned to England. Then, in 1738, he had the spiritual experience which his Moravian friends persuaded him he had hitherto lacked and, after a brief visit to the Moravian settlement at Herrnhut, he returned to England to commence that marvellous career of preaching and evangelizing which turned the country upside down with religious emotion. The time, with its industrial revolution, was ripe for the work, which, though it had in it much that bordered on the hysterical, gave new direction to the lives of many thousands of the common people. It was unfortunate that many bishops and most of the parish clergy received Wesley with less than his proper meed of sympathy, but we must remember that he himself was not over-scrupulous as to intruding into the vineyards which to him appeared to be neglected by their authorized guardians. A more serious failure was the impatience which led him to go eventually against his own conviction in the recognition of Dr. Coke as a bishop, and the ordination of two others, to act as superintendents for the work growing with great rapidity in America. John Wesley had appealed to his lay-workers: "Be Church of England men still; do not cast away the peculiar glory which God hath put upon you." But circumstances were too strong for him. He endeavoured to persuade the Greek Bishop, Erasmus of Arcadia, to ordain preachers for his work, and on a repulse from this quarter felt that, with old age creeping on him, and much work still to be done, he might be pardoned for the transgression of ecclesiastical regularity. In 1784 Wesley executed the *Deed of Declaration* by which a hundred of his preachers were designated as the Methodist Conference to care for the societies after their founder's death. For seven years longer the great evangelist continued his indefatigable labours and passed peacefully away in 1791. After this a *Plan of Pacification*, framed in 1795, gave permission to the preachers to administer the sacraments. Thus a movement which commenced within the Church became separate from the Church—left weakened by the loss of many who could ill be spared.[1]

But the loss, serious as it was, was not without compensation, in stirring up a new spirit of evangelicalism, such as in a few years issued in a definite movement, this time retained in communion with the Church of England. The author of this movement was George Whitefield, whom we have already mentioned as an early associate of Methodism at Oxford. Whitefield was ordained at the unusual age of twenty-one and had soon after commenced that career of itinerant preaching which made him famous. Whitefield's views were Calvinistic where Wesley's were Arminian, so the two revivalists by no means saw eye to eye. The two types of Methodism were promulgated coincidently but, though some of Whitefield's work crystallized in the denomination known as Lady Huntingdon's Connection, a great deal of its results flowed back into the Church of England and inaugurated an evangelical movement notable for many saintly lives. Men like Fletcher of Madeley, Venn of Huddersfield, Newton, Cowper, Simeon, Williams and Wilberforce did much to prevent the salt of the Church

[1] The standard Life of Wesley is by J. S. Simons, *John Wesley, The Master Builder*, London, 1927; see also W. H. Hutton, *John Wesley*, London, 1927.

from losing its savour. Some of them did evangelistic work on the lines of Wesley and Whitefield; some of them cultivated piety in the circle of their own parishes and families; Wilberforce became an earnest worker for the emancipation of the slaves; Robert Raikes in 1781 commenced the work at Bristol which gained him his title of *Father of Sunday Schools*. And, in line with the development of the *Unitas Fratrum*, a new-born zeal for the conversion of the heathen brought about, in 1800, the foundation of the *Church Missionary Society* of the Church of England.

This will be a convenient point at which to give some general sketch of the development of Christianity in the North American continent, even at the risk of touching again on several points referred to in earlier chapters. The whole of the continent had so far, as we have already seen, been strongly coloured by the religious faith and practice of the first Spanish conquerors and this remained in large part the background against which the later work proceeded. As the Spanish hegemony weakened, its place was taken first of all by the French who continued the same religious tradition. But already the Anglo-Saxon was entering into the heritage of the Latin, with the immediate result of a religious confusion accentuated by the various types of Christianity represented among the new-comers. As early as the latter part of the sixteenth century some Anglo-Saxons had looked enviously upon the religious propaganda being carried on by their Spanish rivals. In 1584 Richard Hakluyt had contrasted the Iberian zeal for the conversion of the pagan world with the lukewarmness of his own countrymen. And John Davis, the explorer of the north-west passage, had written: "Sith it is appointed that there shall be one Shepherd and one Flock, what hinderth us of England not to attempt that which God hath appointed to be performed?" [1]

The real movement of Europeans of Anglo-Saxon stock towards the American shores came with the seventeenth century and as a result of the twofold dissatisfaction felt by lovers of liberty with the prevailing conditions in Church

[1] See Mrs. Ashley Carus-Wilson, *The Expansion of Christendom*, London, 1910.

and State in the other countries. Thus from the first there was among the colonists an element of unrest, though naturally less so in the case of members of the Church of England than elsewhere. As a matter of fact, the first service according to the English Prayer Book was that held by Sir Francis Drake's chaplain on the shores of San Francisco Bay, where now stands the impressive Prayer Book Cross. But English settlements on the Atlantic coast began with the founding of Jamestown in Virginia, where the Rev. Robert Hunt was the minister of the Church of England, in 1607.

Meanwhile, the Puritans were beginning to arrive from various parts of Western Europe. The most celebrated of all the arrivals was that of the "Pilgrim Fathers" in the *Mayflower* in November 1620. The story is a familiar one. A little band of impoverished separatists had left England under the leadership of John Robinson and settled at Leyden, in Holland, in 1607. After some years of continental exile, they set out in their famous ship and landed near Cape Cod on the coast of Massachusetts. They had not, it would appear, originally planned to leave the Mother Church. Indeed, their farewell to England declared: "We do not go to New England as separatists from the Church of England, though we cannot but separate from the corruption in it." Presently, however, separation, as was more or less inevitable, became a fact. A little theocracy was established which in that form lasted for about fifty years. Soon circumstances shaped the religious life of the community into a fixed polity and larger numbers of immigrants kept arriving, of like views, to swell the New England Puritan communities.[1]

Meanwhile, others came of far different ecclesiastical antecedents. For instance, in 1634 came Lord Baltimore, who was the means of establishing his little company of Roman Catholics in Maryland, especially in the city called after his name. Another religious element, again, gave a special character to the beginnings of the city of New York. As early as 1609 Henry Hudson had arrived off Albany in the *Half-Moon*. He thought he was entering the harbour

[1] See Williston Walker, *Ten New England Leaders*, Boston, 1901.

of Canton in China, but concluded that he had discovered an excellent site for the Dutch settlers who were demanding a home in the New World. The territory was not colonized till 1626 and it was not till 1628 that an authorized minister was introduced to cater to the spiritual needs of the Dutch Calvinists who formed New York's first church-going population. In 1647 came the illustrious Peter Stuyvesant, just in time to save the colony from ruin. It is said that at this time there were in Manhattan eighteen different languages spoken and the varieties of religion represented included, in addition to the Calvinists, Roman Catholics, English Puritans, Lutherans, and Anabaptists (Mennonites).

Even as early as this, the ranks of the New England Puritans were beginning to exhibit signs of cleavage. A notable example is the case of Roger Williams, who not only insisted on separating from the Church of England but also from other Puritans who held different views from his own. So he passed over to the Baptists and succeeded in founding a strong Baptist community in Rhode Island. Acrimonious controversy came to be the prevalent atmosphere of the time and the life of Ann Hutchinson is an example of the difficulty many genuinely good people found to be pleasant as well. Even the Quakers of the time are described as "a fierce, aggressive type."

These latter had come over in 1677, when the town of Burlington was established by a community of Friends. By 1681 1400 Quakers had arrived and "the Burlington Yearly Meeting" became a regular event. The great success of Quakerism, however, is associated with the coming of William Penn, who had turned from being "the petted favourite at the shameful court of the last two Stuarts" to engage in "the Holy Experiment" in his new city of Philadelphia. In August 1683 "the City of Brotherly Love" consisted of but three or four cottages. Two years later there were six hundred houses. And by the end of the century the city had a population of 20,000, about equally divided between Quakers, German Lutherans and Moravians, and people of miscellaneous affiliation.

The general character of American Protestantism was at this time sufficiently apparent. There was a much larger sympathy with Old Testament theology, legislation and social ideals than with the system inaugurated with the New Testament in the establishment of the Christian Church. The resemblance of the Puritans to the people of the Old Testament has often been pointed out. "Born of the wrong race," says Dow, "Aryan when they should have been Semitic, the Puritans aspired to the sublimity of the old Hebrews." "The Puritans," says Fiske drew from the Old Testament "the same ethical impulse which animates the glowing pages of the Hebrew poets and prophets." The language of the Puritans is redolent of the Old Testament. England is "the land of Egypt," James I. is "Pharaoh," the Atlantic is "the Red Sea," America is "the Promised Land." The Puritan names are from the Old rather than from the New Testament, even to *Shear-jashub* and *Maharshalalhashbaz*. The Mosaic Code was the foundation of the *Pilgrim Code* of 1636 and of its revision in 1656. More than one legislator demanded the incorporation of the entire Mosaic legislation in the law of the land. Even as it was, the eight causes for capital punishment in the Pentateuch were also accepted in New England. Spengler says: "The grand Old Testament exaltation of Parliament and the camps of Independency . . . dominated also the emigration to America which began with the Pilgrim Fathers of 1620. It formed that which may be called the American religion of to-day."[1] Well might Lecky say: "The Hebraic mortar cemented the foundations of American democracy."

Into all this, about the middle of the eighteenth century, came a wave of emotionalism which did much to break down some of the scholasticism of the earlier Protestantism and to fuse elements which had hitherto preserved themselves apart. This is known as the *Great Awakening*, which swept over many parts of the country about 1740. It is generally associated with the life and work of Jonathan Edwards, perhaps the most illustrious of America's Protestant divines. He was at Yale when, in 1722, a serious defection from Protestantism took place in the conversion of Dr. Timothy

[1] See Oswald Spengler, *The Decline of the West*, II., p. 305, New York, 1929; see also L. W. Bacon, *History of American Christianity*.

Cutler, the Rector, Tutor Brown (these constituting the entire faculty), and five prominent pastors in the Connecticut churches to the principles of Episcopacy. Five years after this, Jonathan Edwards was ordained and started out on his wonderful career.[1] In 1733 there were signs of the coming "time of refreshing" and ere long the new warmth, like that of a spiritual springtide, had spread over all the Connecticut Valley, till John Wesley, in England, was moved to write in his journal: "Surely this is the Lord's doing and it is marvellous in our eyes." Soon afterwards the great evangelist George Whitefield came on the scene and the revival spread still further. Not all people approved, since of excesses there were enough and to spare. Presbyterians generally watched the movement coldly, Episcopalians held aloof, and many others were more than a little doubtful. But for Methodists, among some other bodies, the type of evangelism was fixed for many years to come. The Baptists, too, benefited by the use of revival methods, especially in the South.

It should be noted that while movements of this kind were infusing warmth into the rather censorious sectarianism of the earlier days, new bodies were arriving to make their contribution to the religious life of the Colonies. Immigration was responsible for a large influx of German Lutherans, who remained for the most part shepherdless until the arrival of Henry Melchior Muhlenberg in 1742, and of Michael Schlatter, who brought about the establishment of the Lutheran Synod in 1748. The Lutheran Church in America to-day is largely a monument to the sagacity and zeal of these men.

Methodism also was beginning to assume the character of an organization separate from the communion which had given it birth. It was in 1766 that some of the American Methodist groups began to organize on their own lines. The work was carried on successfully by Philip Embury, but in 1769 John Wesley himself sent over a commission for the organization to proceed. Francis Asbury was chosen as director in 1771 and the choice ratified by Wesley in the following year. During the Revolutionary War Methodists

[1] A. V. G. Allen, *Jonathan Edwards*, Boston, 1889.

were under some suspicion as British sympathizers but, having weathered this test, they continued to thrive apace. In 1779 came the self-ordination of three of the preachers, contrary to the advice of Wesley and Asbury, but in 1784 Wesley himself yielded in the matter of the consecration of Dr. Coke, and soon after Asbury too was made a bishop. Thus the Methodist Episcopal Church of the United States was founded and started on its vigorous career.[1]

The coming of Presbyterianism was due largely to the great influx of immigrants of Scots-Irish race who arrived about the beginning of the eighteenth century. Their first minister was Francis Makemie, who got into trouble with Lord Cornbury and was for a time imprisoned for preaching without a licence. Presbyterianism at the time of the Revolution found itself much in accord with the national feeling and prospered accordingly.[2]

Naturally the religious community which suffered most through the Revolution was the Episcopal Church, which was still part of the Church of England and under the jurisdiction of the Bishop of London. This anomalous situation had come about through the steady opposition, on both sides of the Atlantic, to the consecration of bishops who should be able to give complete organization to American Episcopalianism. As far back as the time of Archbishop Laud, in 1638, the proposition had been made to consecrate a bishop for the colonies. In 1700 it was still being discussed, and opposed largely because the Puritans regarded bishops as officers of the State on which they had turned their backs. Some of the Puritan separatists opposed the introduction of the Episcopate none the less vigorously that they themselves were freed from episcopal control. At the time of the Revolution it was obvious that baptized members of the Church could not go back to England for Confirmation, nor could candidates for the ministry go back for ordination. So at last, in 1784, came the consecration of Samuel Seabury of Connecticut at the

[1] See Abel Stevens, *History of the Methodist Episcopal Church*, 4 vols., New York, 1864–67.

[2] C. A. Briggs, *American Presbyterianism, Its Origin and Early History*, New York, 1885.

hands of three non-juring bishops in Scotland, and in 1787 the consecration of Bishops White and Provoost by the Archbishop of Canterbury. With three bishops lawfully consecrated, the American Episcopate was now self-perpetuating, and in 1788 Seabury, White and Provoost united in the consecration of Bishop Maddison. By this time the ecclesiastical authorities in England had awakened to the duty of caring for the Church's children overseas, and in 1787 Bishop Inglis was consecrated as Bishop of Nova Scotia. Six years later a bishop was set apart for Quebec, and from that date the Colonial Episcopate multiplied rapidly. In 1679 there was no Episcopal Church in all New England; in 1700, with the exception of Trinity Church, New York, founded in 1697, there was no Church of England organization in all Long Island or New York Province. From 1702 to 1740, through the efforts of S.P.G., there were nine missionaries of the Church at work in North Carolina and thirty-five in South Carolina. But progress was not remarkable till after the granting of the Episcopate and the holding of the First General Convention at Philadelphia. Even then the outlook was not otherwise than gloomy, and Bishop Provoost prophesied the extinction of the Church with the dying out of the old Colonial families.[1]

The period of reconstruction which followed the Revolutionary War showed the following bodies at work within the territories of the United States: Episcopalians, Reformed Dutch, Congregationalists, Roman Catholics, Friends, Baptists, Presbyterians, Methodists, German Reformed Church, Lutherans and Moravians. In 1800 came the "United Brethren," an offshoot from Methodism; a few years earlier the followers of Emmanuel Swedenborg, known as the Church of the New Jerusalem. The first Universalist Church was founded by a Mr. Murray in 1779 and Unitarianism with the beginning of the new century found its way into the theological school at Harvard. All these were regarded as free and equal before the law by Jefferson's *Act of Religious Liberty* which was at first thought to be aimed against religion.

[1] See S. D. McConnell, *History of the American Episcopal Church*, New York, 1890.

Another "Great Awakening" came about in 1792, rather badly needed when one considers the deadness and scepticism of the time, but manifesting itself in a variety of extravagances. At the end of the eighteenth century American religion, so far as most of the Protestant denominations are concerned, had attained a character shaped as much by the new environment as by inheritance. The very freedom which the air of the continent was supposed to favour was an inducement to run riot in sectarianism. Early difficulties, too, in the way of securing an educated ministry, particularly as the population commenced its westward trek, made conditions tolerant of personal eccentricity in the preaching of the Word. With careers, ecclesiastical as well as political, open to all talents, or to no talent at all, no absurdity was debarred from shining success. So the field was prepared for Shakerism, Mormonism, and many vagaries of a similar sort. It was not even too absurd to found a sect on objection to High Schools because of the injunction: "Mind not high things." With sectarianism came naturally the spirit of competition, which in religion well matched the cut-throat policies which at this time seemed to be the normal thing in business. When eventually it was forced upon the logical mind of the American that religious competition was undesirable it was not on the ground of its conflicting with the mind of Christ, but because it was demonstrably wasteful and inefficient.

That there were certain gains through the American inheritance and the American environment may be taken for granted. The Puritan conscience was an inheritance of which more use might reasonably have been expected to-day. Freedom from historical prejudice was again something which promised great things. But the weakness of American religion at this stage, through historical conditions, is none the less obvious. It was bound to lend itself to such forms of caricature as Sinclair Lewis' *Elmer Gantry*, which unfortunately is not all a caricature. The religion which, by the very nature of its dependence on what the world calls success for its existence, is bound to lay emphasis on such qualities as smartness, management, and the ability to be a good "joiner" and a good "mixer." Not only scholarship but even piety of the old-fashioned sort is apt to be regarded as a handicap, or to be discarded as " highbrow stuff," which fails to " get across " with the public.

Eighteenth-century American Protestantism, moreover, was not only emotional—sometimes even hysterical—but also largely negative, making religion to consist mainly in a number of things prohibited rather than in positive Christian virtues. When the vigour of the nation began to express itself in accomplishment, then religion, too, became busy manward rather than godward. American churches were erected for the comfort of man rather than for the glory of God. Cushions were commoner than crucifixes. Greetings at the church doors were more in vogue than reverence before the altar. The practice of the presence of God was less the aim of the churches than the organizing of " mixers," bazaars and church suppers. The love of one's fellow-man may well, of course, earn the approval of the recording angel for what it is in itself. Some years ago Dr. David Starr Jordan put this as well as it could be put in his *Religion of the Sensible American*: " The religion of the sensible American is not one of creed, or ceremony, or emotion, not one primarily of the intellect, but a religion of faith, and love, and action—a confidence that the universe of matter and of spirit is a reality, that its functions are in wise hands, for the time being our own hands as well as the hands of God, and our part is to help our brother organisms to more abundant life."

Nevertheless, Mr. Chesterton is well advised in directing American attention to the other side of our responsibility in the poem commencing:

> Abou Ben Adhem (may his tribe decrease
> By cautious birth-control, and die in peace !)
> Mellow with learning, lightly took the word
> That marked him not with them that loved the Lord.[1]

[1] Gilbert K. Chesterton, *Poems, The Philanthropist.*

## CHAPTER XLI

### *Christianity in the Nineteenth Century*

THE common habit of depreciating that which is immediately older than ourselves, and which led nineteenth-century people to despise the eighteenth, has made it fashionable for moderns to express themselves disdainfully with regard to the nineteenth. As a matter of fact, a sane survey will convince fair-minded people that the nineteenth century is one of the most significant in human history. It does not seem fanciful to see in the centuries of our history a certain rhythm, with crests and hollows recurring every third hundred years. The first Christian century gives us the story of the Founder; the fourth witnesses the conversion of the Empire; the seventh the conversion of the Western barbarians; the tenth the conversion of the Eastern Slavs; the thirteenth marks the culmination of the Middle Ages and prepares for the modern era; the sixteenth is the age of the Reformation; and the nineteenth can scarcely be deemed less important than any previous climacteric.

It is impossible here to give more than the briefest summary of religious movements which have been world-wide in a sense with which no previous movements may compare. Commencing our survey in the east of Europe we find in Russia in the early part of the century a recrudescence of intolerance due, strangely enough, to reaction from the policy of Alexander I., who showed some sympathy with outside forms of Christianity and gave permission for the establishment of a Bible Society. In 1815 the Jesuits were expelled from St. Petersburg and four years later from the whole of Russia. The proclamation of the Holy Alliance led to a persecution of the unorthodox sects, especially of the so-called Doukhobors, or "spirit-wrestlers," who had first come into existence about 1740 through the erratic teachings of a Prussian Quaker. In 1861 the Metropolitan of Moscow, Philaret, became responsible for drafting the edict by which 23,000,000 serfs were emancipated. Unfortunately, these unhappy beings, long unused to self-support, found themselves worse off than before, and it was out of the discontent thus engendered that much of the Nihilistic agitation sprang which continued to accumulate force until the storm broke in 1917. After the murder of Alexander II. in 1881, we have another period of reaction under Alexander III. The Procurator of the Holy Synod, the notorious Pobiedonostseff, gained an unenviable reputation through the repressive measures he brought into operation against dissenters, such as Jews and Stundists, and the growth of disaffection towards both Church and Throne continued to the end of the century and beyond. The suppression of the Stundists, who had revived the old opposition to image-worship, was particularly savage. It is not pleasant to accuse the clergy of the Russian Church in the nineteenth century of bringing down on their heads a fate they themselves had earned, but it is clear that, in spite of the mystic piety of many, the clergy as a whole were at this time an ignorant body who discredited in their persons the creed they professed.[1]

Elsewhere in the Eastern Church the story is of gradually won freedom from the Turkish yoke. In Serbia freedom was won as early as 1830 in matters of religion, and after a time the Metropolitan of Belgrade was recognized as the head of an autonomous church. Greece freed herself from the Muslim in 1827, and in 1833, after the abolition of many superfluous monasteries, the Church was placed in the hands of a Holy Synod. Rumania was declared free from the authority of any foreign bishop as late as 1864. In 1860 the Bulgarian Church was released from the authority of the Œcumenical Patriarch and placed under an Exarch. As for other Eastern Churches, the pitiful story of the Armenian Christians and of the horrible massacres in 1894 and 1896 by the orders of Sultan Abdul Hamid II., will be too readily recalled. In Egypt the Monophysite

[1] See W. F. Adeney, *History of the Greek and Eastern Churches*, Division III., chaps. vi. and vii.

Christians, forming the Coptic Church, secured freedom to worship according to their consciences and their ancient rites in 1882, after the British victory at Tel el Kebir. The old Assyrian, or Nestorian, Church, which had suffered from the Turks almost as much as their brothers in tribulation, the Armenians, was assisted by a Mission of Help sent by the Archbishop of Canterbury. This had great effect in dispelling the ignorance of the priesthood and in raising the standard of life and teaching.[1]

During the nineteenth century the progress made by the Roman Catholic Church has been remarkable, though the century seemed to open badly. The secularization of the German archiepiscopal electorates and the use of the territory thus made available, to rehabilitate the princes who had been Napoleon's victims, seriously impaired the secular power of the Church, especially when the Diet ratified the spoliation in 1803. Then in 1806 came the surrender by Francis II. of the title of Holy Roman Emperor, a surrender which swept away the phantom of a dream vastly attractive to the idealists of the Middle Ages. The coronation of Napoleon by himself, while Pope Pius VII. merely bestowed upon the Emperor the unction and the blessing, was followed by the seizure of the Pope's person and the annexation of the papal estates. But with the passing of the Napoleonic era in 1815 the Papacy rapidly revived and many European rulers looked hopefully to the Church for support. In 1814 the ban on the Jesuits had been rescinded and the members flocked back to exercise even greater influence than before. It is due largely to the Jesuit order that the new type of Roman Catholicism we call Ultramontanism gained supremacy. The Pope was encouraged to issue edicts denouncing such Protestant institutions as the newly founded Bible Societies (1816) and a few years later (1824) to issue a further fulmination against the errors of Rationalism. Later still, in the Papacy of Pius IX., the papal authorities decided to deal strongly with dogma, and in 1854 was promulgated the dogma of the Immaculate

[1] See W. F. Adeney, *History of the Greek and Eastern Churches*, Division IV.

Conception of the Virgin Mary, a belief which had long been held as a private opinion but was now raised to the rank of official doctrine. The publication of the *Syllabus of Errors* in 1864 was a further attack on Liberalism and Protestantism. Then, in 1870, was held the famous Vatican Council in which the dogma of Papal Infallibility was set forth in the following words: "The Roman Pontiff, when he speaks *ex cathedra*, that is, when in the discharge of the office of pastor and doctor of all Christians, by virtue of his supreme apostolic authority, he defines a doctrine regarding faith or morals to be held by the universal Church; by the divine assistance promised to him in blessed Peter, is possessed of that infallibility with which the divine Redeemer willed that His Church should be endowed." This dogma was not put forth without creating a schism. Though only two votes were cast against Infallibility in the Council, there was much searching of heart among Roman Catholics all over the world. The chief opponent, Dr. von Döllinger, of Munich, was excommunicated, while others of like mind organized the Old Catholic Church, to which the apostolic succession was secured through the Jansenist Bishop of Utrecht. Pope Leo XIII., who succeeded Pius IX. was one of the ablest in the long line of able men who have occupied the Papal Chair. He maintained his hostility to the Government of Italy, which he considered had, on the accession of Victor Emmanuel, deprived him of temporal power. But his generally sympathetic attitude to other questions, and his skilful diplomacy, did much to create better feeling towards the Papacy in France and Germany. At the same time, he showed himself hostile to the movement initiated to secure the recognition of Anglican orders.

Pius X., who came next, was neither so wise nor so successful as his predecessor. France broke off relations with the Vatican and passed the *Loi de la Separation*, and the Italian Government was affronted by the Papal protest against the visit of the French President to the King of Italy. Coincidently, trouble was stirred up by the Pope's unsympathetic attitude towards Modernism, as exemplified by the ban placed upon the works of the Abbé Loisy and the author's excommunication in 1907.[1]

Outside continental Europe Roman Catholic influence increased rapidly, in England through the *Act of Emancipation* which came in 1829, and in the United States through the immigration of people from Ireland and Southern Europe. The establishment of the Papal hierarchy in England in 1850, soon after the conversion of Newman, was much resented by Anglicans and Protestants, but Cardinal Wiseman, as Archbishop of Westminster, undoubtedly gained prestige for his communion, as did Cardinal Manning after him.

In the Church of England at the beginning of the nineteenth century, and indeed up to the passing of the Reform Bill of 1832, the condition of the Church was deplorable. Though the Methodist revival had stimulated piety within the Church in creating what is called the Evangelical movement, to which reference has been made, in other directions it drained the Church of much of its fervour, and indeed produced a kind of repulsion away from what were deemed the extravagances of revivalism. In 1812 a bill had to be passed compelling the non-resident clergy either to stay in their parishes or at least to provide a curate who should be responsible for the services. When Bishop Blomfield was consecrated Bishop of London in 1828 he found the most meagre provision for the spiritual care of his vast diocese. In one parish of 40,000 souls there was only one clergyman. From 1787 to 1808 not a single new church had been built in the capital city. Bishops were wont to owe their preferment to family interest or political services. The examination of candidates for the ministry had become in many cases a farce, one man being examined while the examiner was shaving and another being let off with the construing of a couple of words. Many of the parish churches were in a ruinous condition or cluttered up with huge monuments in the worst taste. There were no hymn-books except metrical versions of the Psalter, such as

[1] See article "Ultramontanism," *E.R.E.* XII., by F. F. Urquhart; F. Neilsen, *History of the Papacy in the 19th Century* (Eng. trans.), 2 vols., London, 1906; article "Modernism," *E.R.E.* VIII.; M. Petre, *Autobiography and Life of George Tyrrell*, London, 1912.

that of Tate and Brady, while the accompaniment was provided by a fiddle and a bass violin. On Easter Day, 1800, there were only six communicants at the services at St. Paul's Cathedral.

It was this condition of neglect and decay to which the Church was stormily awakened by the *Tractarian* movement. In 1833 John Keble, who in 1827 had published the beautiful collection of religious poetry known as *The Christian Year*, preached at St. Mary's Oxford his famous Assize Sermon on National Apostasy. It was just the spark needed to divert men's minds from an individualistic pietism and to rekindle an appraisal of their heritage in the historic Church. That same month was held the meeting of a few kindred souls which resulted in the writing and publication of *Tracts for the Times*, from which the term *Tractarian* is derived. Popularly it was known as Puseyite, on account of the prominence therein of Dr. E. B. Pusey, Regius Professor of Hebrew at Oxford, though Dr. Pusey was not associated with the movement till 1835. One of the most famous of the early Tractarians was Dr. John Henry Newman, Vicar of St. Mary's, whose sermons during these eventful years had the most profound influence on the University and the country. The Tractarians bent their energies not only on the restoration of primitive Catholic practice in the Church, but also on opposition to Erastianism in the Establishment. The appointment of Dr. Hampden, whose *Bampton Lectures* had been accused of unorthodoxy, by Lord Melbourne to be Regius Professor of Divinity, was the occasion for an outspoken protest. At the same time, the expression in the *Tracts* of beliefs unfamiliar to the churchmanship of the period evoked storms of disapproval from the rank and file of churchmen. It was a situation with which the timid episcopate of the time was unprepared to cope. In 1841 the *Tracts* had to be discontinued, and thereafter there were signs of impatience and loss of heart among some of the Tractarians. A few of these found refuge in the bosom of the Roman Church. The most outstanding of these was Dr. Newman who, in addition to his general disquietude, had been seriously disturbed by the scheme to create a Bishopric of Jerusalem in alliance with the Prussian Protestants. Newman was received into the Roman Church in 1845, but, while his change of faith caused great perturbation in the hearts of his friends and a disposition to identify Tractarianism with a Romeward tendency, it did but serve to steady the devotion of men like Keble and Pusey. The movement thus inaugurated had before it a long period of popular misunderstanding, even expressing itself in riots and persecutions; it received scant sympathy from the majority of the bishops; in Parliament it was attacked by the forces of Erastianism—an attack culminating in the *Public Worship Regulation Act* of 1874. But, as time went on, it was clear that much of value had been accomplished. The so-called "Six points"—Eastward position, Vestments, Lights, Mixed Chalice, Unleavened Bread, and Incense—were by no means in general use. Nevertheless, their right to a place in the Eucharistic ritual was confirmed, and there were few churches which did not witness a steady (if slow) improvement in the order, decency and beauty of the Church services, in the quickened devotion of the clergy to the care of souls committed to them, and in a broader appreciation of the Church as something more than a department of the State.[1]

Apart, too, from all interest in history and tradition, or in dignity of worship, a stimulated interest in the general mission of the Church resulted. New bishoprics were established, the first since the Reformation, in England, to take care of the new centres of population which the industrial revolution had created. To note only the earliest, such were the sees of Manchester and Ripon. Interest, too, began to be more practically expressed in the spiritual condition of the English populations overseas and, in addition to the sees of Nova Scotia and Quebec, bishoprics were established in Calcutta, Jamaica, Barbadoes, and elsewhere. Hitherto all overseas Churchmen were supposed to be under the pastoral care of the Bishop of London. In the one year 1842 no fewer than five additional bishops were consecrated at one service. A further and very concrete expression of interest in the world-wide mission of Anglican

[1] See R. W. Church, *The Oxford Movement*, London, 1891; J. H. Overton, *The Anglican Revival*, London, 1897.

Christianity was afforded by the summoning of the first *Lambeth Conference* by Archbishop Longley, at the suggestion (it is said) of the then Bishop of Ontario. Only seventy-six bishops attended, from the Churches of Great Britain and Ireland, the Colonies, and the United States, and the proceedings were far from harmonious. Dean Stanley refused Westminster Abbey for the closing service of the Conference. But a beginning had been made which was destined to grow to great things, as may be realized by a comparison of the Conference of 1867 with that of 1930. One of the burning questions was the status of Bishop Colenso, of Natal, whose views as to the accuracy of certain Old Testament statements were so far beyond the official opinion of the Church of his time as to warrant his deposition for heresy. The days of unfettered Biblical criticism, for the general body of the clergy, were still far in the future. But that the educational standards of the clergy were not unregarded is seen in the establishment at this time of Theological Colleges. Some of them, like Wycliffe Hall and Ridley Hall, were founded to ensure the preservation of evangelical tenets, and others, like the Colleges at Cuddesdon, Ely, Lichfield and Salisbury, were representative of the views of the Tractarians. In addition, from 1841 onward, we have the revival of Sisterhoods in the English Church, and for men devoted to service under special vows the order of the Cowley Fathers was formed in 1866. Convocation, though still subject to the will of the Crown, was restored in 1851.[1]

From the middle of the nineteenth century, and on to the end, without expressing itself in anything which could be described as a "Movement," we may mark the rise of what is called the Broad Church school. The term was intended to denote a liberal attitude towards the many ecclesiastical, scientific and critical questions which at this time excited the attention of men. Individuals like F. D. Maurice, Thomas Arnold, Charles Kingsley, Thomas Hughes, Benjamin Jowett, suggest themselves rather than societies and organizations, but the influence of these individuals was

[1] See A. H. Hore, *Eighteen Centuries of the Church in England,* Part VII., chap. iv.

strong enough to demand notice and to bridge over some of the chasms which had opened before men's feet. The appearance of Darwin's *Origin of Species* had shaken the older hypothesis of separate creative acts, and the new sciences, with the advance of knowledge through historical, archæological and philological research, had thrown an entirely new light on the composition and contents of the Old and New Testament Scriptures. Adjustment to the implications of all this raised many a fierce storm in ecclesiastical waters, from the publication of *Essays and Reviews* in 1860 to that of *Lux Mundi* at the end of the century. Old traditions were only slowly abandoned and there were many to whom the shattering of an obsolete opinion seemed to evoke the cry, "They have taken away my Lord, and I know not where they have laid Him." Others, happily, recognized in the new light the Divine command, "Take away her battlements, for they are not the Lord's."[1]

Coincidently with the struggle for order in worship and for such restatement of the symbols of faith as the "New Learning" made inevitable, we have at this time, and continuously therefrom, a remarkable revival in the interest taken in the poor and the social problems connected with the life of the poor both in the cities and the rural districts. The work of men like Canon Barnett was the inauguration of much that in course of time developed such experiments as Toynbee Hall and the University Settlements. Whatever were the fears of churchmen as to the intellectual tendencies of the time, it is plain that the Church of England was getting into touch with the life of the nation as never before.

At the same time we must recognize that in these years she was in part paying the price of earlier neglect and at the same time bowing to the new spirit of the age by yielding, often reluctantly and ungraciously, some of the privileges she had inherited from days when the Church had actually provided the pattern for the State. Thus we have the *Tithe Commutation Act* of 1836, the abolition of Church

[1] A long list of books might be given to show the modern adjustment which has taken place between Science and Religion. Many of these are included in the Bibliography to *An Outline of Christianity*, Vol. IV., Book I., New York, 1926.

Rates in 1868, the *Education Act* of 1870, by which a system of School Boards came into competition with the National Schools supported by the Church, the abandonment of Tests at the Universities in 1871, and the amendment of the Burial Laws in 1880, by which permission was given to Nonconformist ministers to officiate in the burial grounds. In addition, we have the Disestablishment of the Irish Church in 1871, following on the recognition of the fact that the ancient endowments of the Church were in the hands of a small minority of the population. The movement for the disestablishment of the Church of England and Wales was also kept alive, though the agitation only succeeded in the case of the Welsh Dioceses, and that not until the second decade of the twentieth century.

In spite of the rapidity with which the Church was readjusting itself to the new needs of the nation, during the greater part of the nineteenth century Dissent was widespread and militant. In addition to the numerical growth of the older sects, particularly Methodism, new denominations were continually appearing. Some of these present special features. For example, we have the "*Catholic Apostolic Church*," commonly known as Irvingite. It was founded by Edward Irving, a Scots Presbyterian minister who, coming to London, commenced there a series of apocalyptic lectures which led to the separation of the movement from the Church of Scotland in 1832. It rested itself largely on the belief that the spiritual "gifts" of apostolic times had been revived in Irving's own case and also on the expectation of an imminent reappearance of Christ. Irving repudiated the creation of a new sect but, after his death in 1834, six additional "apostles" felt themselves called upon to complete the number of the twelve, and these maintained supreme authority. Each congregation, moreover, was presided over by an "angel," under whom were twenty-four priests, besides "sub-deacons, acolytes, singers and doorkeepers." [1]

More widely diffused was the influence of *Plymouth Brethrenism*, or Darbyism, so called from the Rev. J. N.

[1] See Mrs. Oliphant, *Life of Edward Irving*, 2 vols., London, 1862; Thomas Carlyle, *Reminiscences*, Vol. I., London, 1881.

Darby who left the Anglican Church to start the new organization about 1830. Progress was rapid and the movement spread from England to Switzerland, France, Sweden, Germany and North America. Division soon overtook the sect and by 1885 two rival churches had been formed, agreed in regarding the baptism of infants as an open question, but repudiating the ordination of ministers as a denial of the spiritual priesthood of all believers. In addition to a somewhat vague membership in England and on the continent of Europe, there are said to be about 10,000 Plymouth Brethren in the United States. But an accurate estimate is difficult, since Plymouth Brethrenism may leaven the opinions of men without leading them to separate from the body to which they are already affiliated.[1]

Still more generally diffused, and of vast practical significance to nineteenth-century Protestantism, is the *Salvation Army*, founded by William Booth, a Methodist revivalist who was casting about for ways to carry the appeal of the Gospel more effectively to the impoverished masses of East London. It was in 1878 that Mr. Booth reorganized his London mission on military lines, and two years later he gave the movement the name it has since borne, together with the uniform and general methods of evangelization which have been distinctive. The theology of the Salvation Army was along popular evangelical lines. Little attention was paid to the sacramental side of religion, but much stress was laid on preaching, prayer, singing, and the use of instrumental music. The lives of members were strictly regulated and marked by abstinence from alcohol, tobacco, and luxurious clothing. From the first, service for others was emphasized. The poor, the "down and out," fallen women, and other victims of the social system became the special care of the Army. Under the tremendous driving power of the General, branches of the Army were created in many lands, including Canada, Australia, New Zealand, the United States, India, Japan, and most of the countries of continental Europe. The publication in 1891 of *Darkest London and the Way Out*

[1] See W. B. Neatby, *A History of the Plymouth Brethren*, second edition, London, 1902.

made a great appeal to the British public and £100,000 came into the treasury of the Army for its social programme. On General Booth's death the organization came into the hands of his son, William Bramwell Booth, who held it to the year before his death, when, in the interest of the Army, it was decided to appoint a High Council with power to elect the General. The present head is General E. J. Higgins, formerly chief of staff.[1]

Protestantism in Scotland was strongly Presbyterian throughout the century. In the early years there was much interest taken both in education and in missions, and the famous Dr. Alexander Duff, the first missionary of the Church of Scotland to be sent abroad, went out to India. Later on troubles of a sectarian kind began to multiply. In 1820 came the secession of the body known as the United Presbyterian Church, and controversies continued in the Church of Scotland till the Disruption of 1843, when 450 ministers out of 1200, together with many of their flocks, went over to the *Free Church*. The Church of Scotland was badly hit, but rallied to its task with courage. At length (to continue the story into the twentieth century) the United Church and the Free Church came together in 1904 and, finally, after many tentative negotiations, the Church of Scotland and the United Free Church healed their long schism on October 2, 1929, in the Cathedral of St. Giles.[2]

The revival movements which in England had done so much for the extension of the Protestant evangelical sects had their counterparts on the continent, especially in Switzerland, Germany and Scandinavia. There was a reawakening of German *Pietism*, of which signs have been noted in the philosophy of Kant. Schleiermacher, 1768-1834, taught a kind of religious romanticism, declaring that "religion should float about human life like a sweet and pleasant melody, a vague but beneficent presentiment of a life of dreams in which the human soul can find felicity." In France a somewhat similar position was held by Alexandre

[1] See William Booth, *In Darkest England and the Way Out*, London, 1890; Harold Begbie, *Life of William Booth*, London, 1920.

[2] See article, "Free Church of Scotland," *Ency. Brit.*. IX., pp. 729 f. (14th Ed.).

Vinet, 1797-1847, who "preached a pacific Christ, reconciled to modern civilization, and still living in the conscience of humanity."[1] Much of the new energy of continental Protestantism was directed into practical channels, such as the building of churches, the formation of Bible societies, and the organisation of work by colporteurs, lay-preachers, and workers among seamen, in prisons, and hospitals, and those engaged in rescue work.

In the United States the "Awakening" of 1792 was continued into the new century, with a remarkable revival in Kentucky and Tennessee commencing in 1800. The camp-meeting of this period has been thus explained: "A population *perfervido ingenio*, of a temper peculiarly susceptible of intense excitement, transplanted into a wild country, under little control either of conventionality or law, deeply engrained from many generations with the religious sentiment, but broken loose from the control of it and living consciously in reckless disregard of the law of God, is suddenly aroused to a sense of its apostasy and wickedness." But the emotionalism of the time did not save religion from fresh schisms. *Unitarianism* had taken possession of King's Chapel at Boston, and from among the Congregationalists no fewer than 126 churches turned their backs on the Trinitarian doctrine. Harvard became a strong citadel of Unitarianism and many distinguished men, including Channing, Emerson, Longfellow, and Holmes, gave it their adhesion. In 1837 came a schism between the New and Old School among the Presbyterians and in 1844 the Methodist Church divided into North and South. Meanwhile, denominations hitherto unknown were multiplying. From among the Baptists came the body known as *Disciples of Christ*, originating about 1809 from the preaching of Thomas Campbell and his more famous son Alexander. Separate existence was achieved at length under the rather too inclusive title of "Churches of Christ". One very remarkable movement came from the following of Joseph

[1] Solomon Reinach, *A Short History of Christianity*, p. 197; see also W. B. Selbie, *Schleiermacher, A Critical and Historical Study*, New York, 1913; F. A. Lichtenberger, *German Theology in the 19th Century* (Eng. trans.), Edinburgh, 1889.

Smith, who in 1827 claimed the discovery of the Book of Mormon and founded on his translation of this the Church of Latter Day Saints, generally known as *Mormons*. The first organization was at Fayette, N.Y., in 1830; thence the sect moved to Nauvoo, Ill., where Smith was brutally murdered, out of popular hostility to the recently announced sanction given to polygamy. The Mormons thereupon found a new and able leader in Brigham Young, who led his followers westward to the present site of Salt Lake City in Utah. Here a Temple was built and, as the Mormons showed themselves to be capable pioneers alike in agriculture and business, the settlement prospered and was readily recruited from European countries where missionary agents carried on an extensive propaganda. Eventually, in 1890, the practice of polygamy was abandoned and the Mormons settled down to a religion not greatly differing from that of the evangelical sects.[1] Contemporary with Mormonism, we have the rise of *Adventism*, founded by William Miller about 1831. Miller was obsessed with fantastic ideas as to the near approach of the end of the world. He first announced the event as due in 1843, but subsequently proclaimed a revised date, October 22, 1844. Adventists, distinguished by their observance of the seventh day Sabbath rather than the Christian Sunday, are now divided into about five bodies and have spread far beyond the borders of the United States. Still another movement which has obtained widespread influence, not merely in the upbuilding of a new denomination but also in the leavening of thought generally among members of the older organizations, is that known as *Christian Science*. It was founded in 1876 by Mary Baker Eddy and is now represented in practically every considerable American community, as well as in Europe. The kernel of the teaching is that God is Spirit and that all creation is derived from Him. Sin, sickness, evil and death have therefore no reality and belief in them is a disease of the mortal mind. The general practice is to renounce the use of medical aid in the treatment of disease, relying wholly on prayer and faith. Many

[1] See James H. Snowden, *The Truth about Mormonism*, New York, 1926.

varieties of this attitude towards sickness and evil generally have sprung up all over the United States.[1]

North of the United States the population is largely representative of the religions of the old countries whence it was derived. The Roman Catholic religion is dominant among the French of the Province of Quebec, the Church of England is strong in the larger cities and in the smaller communities near the Atlantic and Pacific coasts, while Presbyterianism and Methodism are particularly strong in the central provinces. The first Methodist society reached Montreal in 1803 and, much increased by emigration in the intervening years, Methodists organized the Methodist Episcopal Church of Canada in 1828. After the Act of Union of 1867 the title became Methodist Church of Canada. Since the beginning of the twentieth century efforts were made for the union of all Methodists, Congregationalists and Presbyterians in one body. This was finally effected in 1925, when the United Church of Canada came into existence, with two and a half million members.[2]

Outside of Protestantism we find notable expansion both in the United States and Canada during the nineteenth century. In the United States the Roman Catholic Church had grown consistently, especially during the years of the great rush of immigration from Ireland and Southern Europe. Many communicants are said to have lapsed in the course of their westward movement across the continent and during the process of settlement, but it has been estimated that in 1893, out of a population of 70,000,000, there were 9,000,000 Roman Catholics in the United States, while to-day the total is not far short of 15,000,000. The Roman Church has been particularly active in the large cities, in which splendid churches, parochial schools, and hospitals have been erected, while the clergy and laity have taken a conspicuous part in the social service work of the communities.

[1] A comprehensive but by no means sympathetic study of a large number of the cults at present in vogue in the United States is given by C. W. Ferguson, *The Confusion of Tongues*, New York, 1929. The Bibliography will be found particularly useful.

[2] Not all Presbyterians joined the United Church. There is a flourishing body of "continuing Presbyterians."

The Anglican Church, known by its cumbrous legal title of the Protestant Episcopal Church in the United States of America, has also grown steadily, and from four bishoprics in 1792 has increased to considerably more than a hundred in the early years of the twentieth century. Moreover, the Church's influence has been far more widespread than its communicant list of over a million might suggest. Similarly in Canada the small beginnings of the episcopate made in the closing years of the eighteenth century have borne fruit in the creation of some thirty episcopal sees between the Atlantic and the Pacific.

One feature of religious work which is characteristic of the nineteenth century, and which is not confined to any one Church or any one land is that of work among young men and girls. Of these particular organizations we may mention the Y.M.C.A., founded in England in 1844, by George Williams, a draper's assistant, who came from Somersetshire in 1841 and started meetings in his bedroom. The movement thus initiated spread across the Atlantic and associations were formed in Montreal and Boston in 1851. In 1876 Mr. Williams (afterwards Sir George Williams) crossed the Atlantic himself to oversee developments. The Y.M.C.A. is now familiar all the world over and Japanese Buddhists have done the Association the compliment of organizing the Y.M.B.A. (Young Men's Buddhist Association) on the model. In 1884 the Y.W.C.A. was started, also in England, by Miss Roberts, and has since seen phenomenal growth. The present membership is over a million, scattered over forty-six countries, and engaged in an extraordinary variety of social and religious enterprises. Of a more specialized type is the Student Christian Movement, originated by the famous "Cambridge Seven" in 1885, just before they sailed for China. It was stimulated by the adhesion of men like Henry Drummond, John R. Mott, Robert Wilder and Sherwood Eddy, and has had remarkable success in recruiting young men for missionary work in foreign lands. Beside the above-mentioned organizations we may recall the Epworth League, a young people's movement fostered by the Methodists, the Brotherhood of St. Andrew, a society for men in the Episcopal

Church, and the Knights of Columbus, a powerful organization of men in the Roman Catholic Church.

Of all the evidences which may be adduced as proving the vitality of Christianity during the nineteenth century none is so convincing as the extraordinary development of *Foreign Missions*. To give even a summary of this development would occupy more space than we have available. It is almost sufficient to say that for the first time in human history we have the entire world open for the proclamation of the Gospel. In India that "heaven-sent genius," William Carey, sent out by the Baptists from England, associated himself with two other members of the Serampore Brotherhood, Marshman and Ward, and achieved marvellous success as evangelist and translator. Henry Martyn landed in Calcutta in 1806 and spent his short life in fruitful service in India and Persia. His one convert, Abdul Masih, was one of the first natives of India ordained to the Anglican priesthood. Other English missionaries entered into the labours of the great Danish evangelist, Christian Schwartz. Bishop Middleton was consecrated the first Bishop of Calcutta in 1814 and from that time on new sees were constantly created, till at last, in 1912, the first Indian Bishop was set apart for work in South India in the person of Dr. Azariah. Many Societies had entered into this promising field, including the C.M.S., the S.P.G., the Cambridge Mission to Delhi, and the Oxford Mission to Calcutta. The Church of Scotland had sent out Alexander Duff in 1830 and by 1857 this great educator had laid the foundation of a magnificent future. American Protestant Missions — Congregationalist, Presbyterian, Baptist and Methodist—had also claimed a share in the work. Meanwhile, the Roman Catholic missions had flourished, till, by the end of the century, there were 8 archbishops, and over 2600 bishops and priests. The Christian population of India since the end of the nineteenth century has grown even more rapidly and now numbers something like five million souls.

In China the Roman Catholic missions which had struggled through the persecutions of the eighteenth century continued their heroic witness. Bishops like Dufresne (1815) and Boric, tied to a stake and cut slowly into little bits, together with hundreds of their priests and laity, died as martyrs. But the roll of living adherents grew till, at the end of the century, it included at least a million and a half baptized members. The great revival began as early as 1830. Outside the Roman Catholic Church in 1842 there were but six native Christians in China, but by 1877 these had increased to over 13,000. Robert Morrison, of the London Missionary Society, had come, by way of America, in 1807; in 1835 the American Episcopal Church sent Dr. Boone, who became bishop in 1845. The Church of England began its work in 1844 and George Smith was the first Bishop of Victoria (Hongkong) in 1850. By this date a dozen Anglican and Protestant Societies were vigorously at work, with some missionaries of outstanding fame. The China Inland Mission was founded in 1865, and since then every province of the Middle Kingdom has been occupied by men who have held on through good report and ill report, not always successful, or even wise in their methods, but braving death and persecution unflinchingly and, after every period of discouragement, returning to the field with added zeal.[1]

The story of Christian missions in Japan during the nineteenth century is not less inspiring. No sooner was the Empire reopened to the foreigner than missionaries of many Societies began to enter for the work. To the surprise of the outside world, it was found that 1500 people in the neighbourhood where St. Francis Xavier laboured came forward in 1865 as a proof that the faith had never been completely exterminated by the two centuries of persecution. The day of the "discovery of the Christians" is still observed on March 17. American Protestant and Anglican missionaries were active from the time of the Treaty of 1858 and their work has produced direct results in the creation of strong native churches and a more significant indirect result in the leavening of Japan with Christian ideals.[2]

In Africa, from the time when, in 1846, 50,000 liberated

[1] See K. S. Latourette, *History of Christian Missions in China,* from chap. xvii.. onward.

[2] See Otis Carey, *History of Christianity in China,* 2 vols. The work of Sei Kokwai (Anglican) is now represented by eleven bishops.

slaves were gathered together in Sierra Leone, marvellous results have been achieved. Samuel Crowther, the ex-slave, became a bishop in 1864. In Central Africa the Universities Mission was established in 1858 as a result of the appeal of David Livingstone; in 1873 a cathedral was built on the site of the slave-market at Zanzibar; in 1875 the C.M.S. established its mission in Uganda, as a result of the impression produced by the discoveries of Stanley. Watered by the blood of the martyred Bishop Hannington, this mission grew to wonderful proportions after 1894. In South Africa Robert Moffatt, of the L.M.S., laboured for fifty years in Bechuanaland; in 1847 Bishop Gray was consecrated Bishop of Capetown; and from this date the work spread over the whole of that vast territory among whites and natives alike.

In Australasia and Oceanica—isles which even John Wesley believed beyond the possibility of evangelization—Christianity has become generally supreme, though here and there, as in Tasmania, the native population died out before missionary work had begun. In Australia, while a large part of the organized work of the churches aimed at providing spiritual care for the colonists, missionary work among the aborigines goes back to the time of Marsden's arrival at the beginning of the century. In the Church of England work was begun in 1823 by S.P.G. and in 1830 by C.M.S. The L.M.S. started a mission in 1825 and since then work has been undertaken by Presbyterians, Methodists and Moravians. An interesting Roman Catholic mission was inaugurated near Perth, where Bishop Salvado laboured for more than fifty years of his episcopate, dying in 1900. Samuel Marsden's appeal, about 1809, led to the first recruiting of missionaries for New Zealand and Marsden himself arrived in 1814. The Williams brothers came in 1822 and 1825 and one of them became the first Bishop of Waiapu. But the work was slow till the annexation of the group by Great Britain in 1840. In 1842 Bishop Selwyn was able to announce: "We see here a whole nation of pagans converted to the faith." Later on considerable losses were experienced through the rise of a strange fanaticism known as the Hau-hau. In addition to the

Anglican work among Maoris and whites, much has been done by Wesleyans and even by Mormons. About 5000 Maoris belong to the Roman Catholic Church. The Hawaiian Islands were first evangelized by missionaries of the A.B.C.F.M. beginning with 1820, the year after the abolition of the tabus by Kamehameha II. In fifty years paganism was almost entirely destroyed. After considerable opposition, the Roman Catholic Church commenced work in 1839 and in 1861 the Church of England sent its first Bishop of Honolulu, as the result of Kamehameha IV.'s appeal to Queen Victoria. Since the annexation of the group by the United States this work has been taken over by the American Episcopal Church. The religious work of the Hawaiian Islands has been made specially significant and interesting through the numbers of Chinese, Japanese and Koreans who are accessible away from their former pagan environment. To describe the work of evangelization in the separate Pacific groups is impossible. It must suffice to say that some of the very greatest names in missionary annals have a place among the evangelists of the Pacific. Such are Bishop Patteson, murdered in the Santa Cruz group in 1871, James Chalmers, martyred in New Guinea in 1877, John Williams, martyred in the New Hebrides, and, in the same group, J. G. Paton gave twenty-four years of devoted labour and lived to see 20,000 natives brought into the fold.

In the Muhammadan world Christian missions have been hitherto less successful, but here too there are names which will shine for ever, such as those of Henry Martyn, missionary in India and Persia, Ian Keith Falconer, who died prematurely at Aden in 1887, and Bishop Thomas Valpy French, who died at Muscat in 1891.[1]

It is not a little significant that by the end of the nineteenth century, as already noted, the religion which at the Cross on Calvary was represented only by a dying robber and a few heart-broken disciples now found the whole world, with a few insignificant exceptions, open to its appeal.[2]

[1] See C. H. Robinson, *History of Christian Missions*.

[2] On the whole period Vols. IV. and V. of *An Outline History of Christianity* (New York, 1926), will be found useful, together with the bibliographies provided.

## CHAPTER XLII

### *On the Threshold of the Future*

A THIRD of the twentieth century has gone by and perhaps the majority of those who welcomed its dawn with hope survey its achievements up to date with disappointment. The expected millennium has not arrived, in spite of all the boasted mechanism which has speeded up our civilization and added to life's material facilities. Yet it is at least equally certain that, whatever be our misgivings, hope still "springs eternal in the human breast" and it is not impossible in gathering up our experience of the past to look to the future with some measure of courage and faith.

Let us grant at once that many people are convinced, as some have been convinced in every generation for the last two thousand years, that religion is now on its last legs. The discredited pessimists of earlier ages have said the same thing, but to-day's sceptics say it a little more blatantly and confidently. And, of course, it would be idle to deny that, as in previous times, there is plenty of human faithlessness and failure to support their argument. It is enough to recall some of the anti-religious movements of the age. In China, according to some, religion is "an out-of-date problem," and the systems of Confucius, Lao-tzu and the Buddha are put in the same condemned cell with that of the Christ. In other Buddhist countries, with the possible exception of Siam and Japan (where Buddhism has been fertilized with western ideas), the faith of Gautama is manifestly decadent and corrupt. In most large Muhammadan centres, notably in Istambul, Islam has lost its hold over even the outward habit of many and flourishes only where, as in Palestine and India, it is stimulated by fanatical hostility to another faith. Nor is Christianity anywhere immune from attack, even though the western writers who regard it as moribund express their wish rather than their thought. Yet even here is material at hand. The denunciation of the *Concordat* with the Papacy by France in 1905 was hailed as the apostasy of "the eldest daughter of the Church." The *Vatican Edict* against Modernism in 1907, whereby the Roman Church sacrificed such sons as Loisy and Tyrrell, was set down as the final break with the "New Learning." The Russian Revolution of 1917, with its bloody sequels, was plain evidence to the critic that a death-blow had been inflicted on the venerable Churches of the East and that godlessness was established in the new order of the Soviets. The rejection of the traditional authority of the Roman Church in Mexico and some of the South American Republics, followed by the overthrow of the ecclesiastical supremacy in Spain, was but fresh evidence tending towards the same conclusion. Protestantism, weakened by the loss of much of its historical *raison d'être*, and struggling to maintain itself by all kinds of popularity-seeking devices, was, to the same observers, in no better state. In certain cases, success seemed only attainable by the adoption of eccentricities allied to the professional tricks of the mountebank. Even the staid Churches of the Anglican Communion seemed deadlocked with dispute over trivialities, as was illustrated by the frustration of Prayer Book reform through the intervention of a Parliament representative of all creeds and of none. Outside organized Christianity, moreover, in lands still professing Christian ideals, there was conspicuous the spectacle of shaken ethical standards, of weakened discipline, of lowered sense of obligation, and even of communities delivered over to the tyranny of gangsters and outlaws.

It is a gloomy enough picture, in all conscience, yet not the whole. All along our story we have been watching the gradual descent of the City of God against a background of Babylonish shadows in which the majority of men have continued to put their trust. And when we watch the slow evolution of religious consciousness with eyes open to the glints and gleams of the descending City rather than to the dark features of the background we find no more need for discouragement than had Christians of the first, or fourth, or sixteenth centuries. Even the lapses and set-backs we have been forced to note may have, in the eternal process, no more significance than a landslip on the side of a mountain or an eddy by the bank of a flowing stream. Indeed, set-backs may in the long run be seen as incidents in the story of a general progress, the "reculer à mieux sauter" of which religious history has so many examples. Sometimes it is the nemesis of overstress on some one-sided apprehension of truth, an overstress which demands readjustment in what seems to be an opposite direction. Not infrequently it is the due punishment of a mistaken method or the discipline needed to make possible a more effective witness. Progress seldom moves along with even front, but often by reaction against movements projected beyond the proper line of advance. The student of religious history needs often to recall the words of Arthur Hugh Clough:

> Say not, the struggle nought availeth,
> The labour and the wounds are vain,
> The enemy faints not nor faileth,
> And as things have been they remain. . . .
> For while the tired waves, vainly breaking,
> Seem here no painful inch to gain,
> Far back, through creeks and inlets making,
> Comes silent, flooding in, the main.

That we may see how, through "Eastern windows" and "Western" alike, the light does grow upon the world, let us give attention to the following considerations:

1. As remarked in our last chapter, the world is open as never before to the message of the Gospel. No fewer than 500,000,000 souls are nominally within the Christian fold. If we be disposed to depreciate the quality of the religion thus professed, let us remember that the gulf between profession and practice has always been wide and deep, in former ages as much as in our own. Yet, even so, the number of "sinners who keep on trying," and are therefore the potential saints, is probably larger to-day than ever. Certainly, as judged by the amount of religious literature produced and read, earnestness in religious matters is extraordinarily widespread. Moreover, the indirect influence of religions on one another, and

especially of Christianity on them all, has had a stimulating effect in extending the power of Christian ideals, while the new science of Comparative Religion has revealed to men the omnipresence of the Divine Spirit, moving as in a garden, even though men may not recognize the Gardener. Even in Russia, where the "godless" seem for the moment in control, in the revolt of ignorance against an ancient tyranny may be detected an idealism with its martyrs, its servants and its worshippers—an idealism which is the rejection of a super-Czar rather than the conscious turning of the back upon a Father in the heavens. Of all religions in the world to-day it may be said that subjection to the fierce test of historical and social criticism tends only to the removal of the things which may be shaken and may be depended upon ultimately to "leave free from mist the permanent stars behind."

When we look at movements rather than at isolated events, our judgement on the outlook for religion need not be other than reassuring, and our failures themselves point the way from error towards a resplendent success. This is particularly true of the Mission Field, where nationalistic and sectarian methods have deserved the set-backs which they invited. A Christianity which in the past history of India or China seeks for the leading of the Holy Spirit, which finds in the ancient scriptures of these peoples an Old Testament to which the religion of Christ supplies the New, which learns to employ the terminology of the people, and finds use for Indian or Chinese ideals in modes of worship or type of ministry, is not likely to fail.

2. We feel in the air, like the prediction of a spiritual springtide, the unmistakable desire for religious unity. Intolerance, it is true, is by no means dead, and religious discord, as in Palestine between Jew and Arab, or in India between Hindu and Muslim, has by no means disappeared. Race-feeling, too, even in so-called Christian lands, still rears its ugly visage and takes its toll in rioting and lynching. Yet in the presence of such manifestations men in cool blood are no longer unashamed. The old competitive spirit, again, in which men gloried—as a legitimate stimulus to zeal—a generation ago, is no longer in vogue, if only for

reasons of economy. Efforts are now more frequently made to synthesize opposite views than to exaggerate them. Indeed, even principles are occasionally neglected in order to make the more display of tolerance. Be this as it may, the longing for unity is achieving results. It is seen in the formation of the United Church of Canada, alluded to in our last chapter, and in the movement towards unity in South India. It is seen in the larger tolerance of parties, or schools of thought, for one another within the same communion, notably in such gatherings as the General Convention of the American Episcopal Church and in the decennial meetings of the Lambeth Conference. It is reported of the last Lambeth Conference, held in 1930, that almost every resolution was passed with practical unanimity. It taxed the ingenuity of the sensational press to invent discords where there were none to be discovered. Still more impressive to many is the evidence of a striving after unity manifested in the assembling of Conferences between different religious bodies to find some basis for common practice and belief. Among these will be recalled the Stockholm Conference of 1925 and (more significant still) the Lausanne Conference on Faith and Order of 1927, participated in by representatives of the Eastern Churches as well as by those of the Protestant and Anglican communions. Indeed, the recent movement of the Eastern Orthodox Churches towards fellowship with the various branches of the Anglican Communion is one of the happiest omens of the coming time when schisms shall be healed and all become members of one flock under one Shepherd.[1]

The securing of the Church's visible unity must, of course, require a larger patience than some of its enthusiastic advocates may realize. There are many schemes for achieving unity, but the adoption of most of these would be fatal to the object sought. With some the belief prevails that unity is to be secured by blending all varieties of Christianity into a homogeneous and boneless system by finding the lowest common denominator of all the Churches.

[1] See Charles H. Brent (Editor), *Can the Churches Unite ?*, New York, 1927 ; Edw. S. Woods, *Lausanne*, New York, 1927 ; James Marchant (Editor), *The Reunion of Christendom*, New York, 1929 ; T. A. Lacey, *The One Body and the One Spirit*, New York, 1926.

By such a plan all distinctive truths which, while they have separated men into denominations, have yet their saving virtue, become nebulous and undistinguishable. What was intended to be a body becomes a jelly. Others have sought a basis for unity through the subjugation by one of all the others, by compelling all divergent forms of belief and practice to yield themselves to the dominance of the stronger. It is a theory more generally held than might be suspected, since the tyranny which demands unity by way of subjection may be as characteristic of the tiniest sect as of the Holy Roman Empire itself. The dogmatism of an individual is even more distasteful than the dogmatism of a Council. Still another favoured theory is that of federation, whereby denominations remain content with their own segmentary creeds and methods of worship, while allowing themselves to be bound together by a tenuous thread of tolerance such as makes creed and cult of relatively small account. Fortunately, by no one of these paths is unity realizable, for a unity brought about through mistaken premises must in the long-run prove a mischievous failure. In true unity there is no losing of oneself but the finding of the full self meet for communion with God. In the obedience required by loyalty there is no servile subjection to the divine will but rather the free co-operation of sons. We may be very sure that the shattering of ecclesiastical unity which resulted from the attempt to impose on the Church a system in which the individual possessed no rights was but the legitimate step towards the recovery of the liberty of the sons of God. Equally true is it that the riot of individualism which marked the return swing of the pendulum cannot be regarded otherwise than as a call to the enfranchised mind and spirit in the Church to learn unity once again by voluntary submission to the Church's Lord. The synthesis of the two movements is the harmonious unity so wonderfully described by St. Paul in the *Epistle to the Ephesians* (iv. 15, 16) as the growing up of the Church "in all things unto Him who is the Head, even Christ, from whom all the Body fitly framed together, through that which every joint supplieth, according to the working in due measure of every several part, making the increase of the body unto the building up of itself in love." To attain this would be even beyond that unity suggested in Kipling's tale of *The Ship that Found Herself*. First, we see the ship *Dimbula*, newly and strongly built, capable in each of its several parts, yet straining and complaining because no part is self-adjusted to its neighbour. So rivets and deck-beams, stringers and ribs, capstan and everything else, groan and whine and murmur, till one would have supposed the whole vessel about to go to pieces. Yet at last, after weathering a tremendous storm, there comes to the ship a strange lull, out of which emerges the voice: "I am the *Dimbula*, of course, and I've never been anything else but that—and a fool!"

3. We may also feel in the religious world increasing concern with the great question of world peace. Many, it is true, have expected peace too soon and too easily. It is often forgotten that peace is the last, crowning gift of God rather than the first. Love is the foundation, joy the fruit of love, peace the reward of love. The textual change in the angelic song: "Peace on earth to men of goodwill," made to read: "Peace on earth, goodwill to men," has blinded men to the fact that "the fruit of peace is sown to them that love peace." The cultivation of goodwill, social, national, and international, is the prerequisite for any possible attainment of peace. And how slowly has even the desire for certain kinds of goodwill been formed! International morals are hardly as yet apparent in the world as a whole, even the Christian world. Hence the presence of Christ in the world has first to banish the ignorance which separates men into potentially hostile camps; then to banish the suspicion which is the result of ignorance; and then to banish the fear which is the consequence of suspicion and which sooner or later makes war inevitable. Only with these things banished can we develop the international mind which in course of time will become an international conscience, and in due course bring about the possibility of international co-operation.[1]

The promotion of all this is definitely Christian work

[1] See W. E. Orchard, *Christianity and World Problems*, New York, 1925; J. T Shotwell, *War as an Instrument of National Policy*, New York, 1929.

and all the mechanism by which international co-operation may be made more effective is a definite application of Christian principles to human life. Efforts such as are embodied in the *Hague Court*, the *Kellogg Pact*, the *League of Nations*, and in the various Conferences called to promote reciprocal disarmament, may all fail as final solutions; but only as they fail to be supported by that goodwill on which the world must ultimately rely for the maintenance of peace. Just at present perhaps there is most apparent the preliminary need of repressing the hysteria which excites misunderstanding and hatred and the baser journalism which battens upon international discord. Till some curb is put upon the licence of a sensational press, voluntarily through our national sense of responsibility, no instrument of international government is likely to prove effective.

4. We may sense, in the fourth place, a gradually improved relation between the acknowledged representatives of science and the acknowledged representatives of the Christian faith. The old fight, waged during the second half of the nineteenth century, was largely a conflict between those on the side of science who went beyond their science to draw deductions fatal to the claims of religion and those on the side of religion who insisted on attaching to the faith cosmogonic and historical theories which they fondly supposed to have been supernaturally revealed. It is clear to-day that the long drawn-out conflict between science and religion was, like some other wars, absolutely needless. Each had its own field and its own lawful claim as being a revelation of the truth. Science has certainly in many respects added to the interest of life. To quote from the Lambeth *Encyclical* of 1930: "We recognize in the modern discoveries of science—whereby the boundaries of knowledge are extended, the needs of men are satisfied, and their sufferings alleviated—veritable gifts of God, to be used with thankfulness to Him and with that sense of responsibility which such a thankfulness must create." Unfortunately, for a time, many men of science felt that their discoveries supported a mechanistic theory of the universe and so denied or ignored the God to whom gratitude was due, with consequences to men's sense of obligation such as were

inevitable. Happily the turn of the tide has come, even though (to use the simile of Dr. Rufus Jones), like the raging of a battle on some remote front after the signing of an armistice, many of the underlings in science are not yet aware of the turn. Sir James Jeans makes the statement: "To-day there is wide-spread agreement, which on the physical side of science amounts almost to unanimity, that the stream of knowledge is heading towards a non-mechanical reality. The universe begins to look more like a great thought than like a great machine." Similarly, the President of the British Association for the Advancement of Science, in 1931, affirmed: "Materialism has practically disappeared. The ancient spiritual goods and heirlooms of our race need not be ruthlessly scrapped." From the International Congress of Philosophy at Oxford in 1930 comes the word: "The materialist front is broken up and scientists are no longer dominated by the notion that to be real is to be like a piece of matter and to work like a machine." And once again, on my own side of the Atlantic, Dr. Robert Millikan writes: "It is a sublime conception of God which is furnished by science and one wholly consonant with the highest ideals of religion, when it represents Him as revealing Himself through countless ages in the development of the earth as an abode for man, and in the age-long inbreathing of life into its constituent matter, culminating in man with his spiritual nature and all his God-like powers." [1]

Naturally, as already hinted, there are here and there "pockets" of obscurantism, reflecting the influence of ill-educated men of science and of ill-educated clergy. The Scoopes' trial in Tennessee is an even darker blot on twentieth century Christianity than was that of Galileo on that of the seventeenth. But the light is spreading and this is the result not only of the labours of biologists, astronomers, and physicists, but also of philologists, archæologists, historians and professors of literary criticism—all aided by the receptivity and insight of a more enlightened clergy and

[1] See *Science and Religion, A Symposium*, with Foreword by Michael Pupin, New York, 1931 ; Sir James Jeans, *The Mysterious Universe*, Cambridge, 1931 ; Charles A. Dinsmore, *Religious Certitude in an Age of Science*, North Carolina Press, 1924 ; J. W. Oman, *The Natural and the Supernatural*, New York, 1931 ; A. E. Baker, *The Gospel and Modernism*, Milwaukee, 1929. See also Bishop Barnes' recent *Scientific Theory and Religion*, Cambridge, 1933.

laity than in any previous age of the Church. It is now seen that whereas a little science disposed men to atheism, a larger knowledge is bringing men back to God. "No one knows better," it has been said, "than the man who works in science how soon we get beyond the boundaries of the known." To which Professor Munsterburg has added: "Science is not, and cannot be, and never ought to try to be, an expression of ultimate reality." I cannot more fitly sum up the subject than in a further quotation from Dr. Millikan to the effect that "the first fact which seems to me altogether obvious and undisputed by thoughtful men is that there is actually no conflict between science and religion when each is correctly understood."

5. Fifthly, we see signs of a more vigorous functioning of Christian activity in all that bears upon the regeneration of human society. To quote the words of Washington Gladden, Christ, in His Church, has "planted a social standard on the further side of twenty centuries which bids kings, law givers, prophets and statesmen march on with all their hosts till they attain it." And the Church is slowly proceeding towards this attainment. Not only do we see within the organized Christianity of our time a keener corporate interest in the education of the young, the establishment of guilds, the organization of conferences and retreats, the training of the clergy, the building of churches and cathedrals, and the provision of worship of a worthier and more dignified sort, but we find the Churches leavening the community with the sense of obligation in similar directions. It is now the conscience of the community, educated up to the Christian standard, which supplies schools and hospitals, gymnasia and recreation grounds, organizations for the poor, Red Cross and anti-tuberculosis societies, and a hundred other community projects which were once either the monopoly of religious establishments or neglected altogether.[1]

[1] See A. D. Lindsay, and others, *Christianity and the Present Moral Unrest*, Oxford, 1927; G. A. Studdert Kennedy, *The Warrior, the Woman and the Christ*, New York, 1929; Frederick C. Grant, *The Economic Background of the Gospels*, Oxford, 1926; Spencer Miller and J. F. Fletcher, *The Church and Industry*, New York, 1931; Shailer Mathews, *Jesus on Social Institutions*, New York, 1928.

So we face the future, not proud, but confident of the finality of Christ as the one Power of Life through whom all the bitter waters of the world must eventually be sweetened. To quote once again from the Lambeth *Encyclical* of 1930: "The Revelation of Christ was presented to the world under the forms of Jewish life and thought. It has found fuller expression, not without some admixture of misunderstanding, through the thought of Greece and Rome, and the sentiment of the Teutonic and Slavonic races. We anticipate that when this same revelation possess the minds of the Asiatic and African races, these nations will still further enrich the Church of Christ by characteristic statements of the permanent Gospel and by characteristic examples of Christian virtue and types of Christian worship."

Such a Catholicity is perhaps yet far in the future. For we need not merely a Christianity universally diffused and universally accepted, but one which has lost no element of the full witness made possible by the presence of the divine Spirit among men. We are even now, in some respects, more catholic than our controversies might lead the world to suppose, yet, alas, the majority of Christians still make more of their differences than of their agreements and regard getting to the eternal shore "on broken pieces of the ship" as the normal way of salvation. What a spectacle it is, as compared with what might be, this fleet of rudely constructed and ludicrously navigated rafts and tubs and hen-coops, proudly marked with sectarian badges, holding their precarious way upon the sea of life, rather than come grandly into port together! It is not, however, sufficient to be shamed into repentance for our discords; we ought also to be ashamed for the treacherous elimination of truths which seem to us discordant only because we have permitted them to remain unharmonized. It is to our credit to-day that sectarian banners are commonly raised only over neglected truths, though, alas, these truths are often distorted into errors for lack of correlation or by reason of misplaced emphasis. For segmentary truths may be exceedingly mischievous, not for what they state, but for the things unstated which they seem to deny. The cure for sectarianism is not in a spineless religion without theological affirmation or organized order, but in a real catholicity, worthy of the name because expressive of the fact—no exploitation of solitary elements, but the realization in principle and practice of "the whole counsel of God." Only thus may we attain the Christianity which provides for the world "the desirable things" of all the nations.

In addition to catholicity the religion of the future must reveal a genuinely spiritual quality. There may be less in the way of "wheels," but "the spirit within the wheels" must be assured. Since the Great War there has been a tendency to secure efficiency by an intensive and complicated mechanization of religious life. This machinery has had to be operated by technically trained men and women who keep things going by methods startlingly foreign to the spirit of Christ. Dean Inge has remarked that whereas Christ promised that "where two or three were gathered together" there was He in their midst, nowadays the first disposition of the "two or three" is to elect a chairman, a secretary and a treasurer. The craze for up-to-date organization, with societies to enlist the energies of men, women and children, ramifying from the congregation over the nation, claiming the attention of bureaus of secretaries and business agents, turning the pastor into a bewildered director of an administrative system, perpetually engaged in inaugurating, sustaining, reviving and galvanizing into the appearance of life a multiplicity of societies, while it has undoubtedly stimulated the physical activity of the Churches, has done little to increase their moral influence in the community. Not a little of the world's disbelief to-day comes from the consciousness of a Church which, in its lust for competitive organization, in its foolish habit of depending on statisticalized greatness, in its employment of methods which are more ingenious than religious, must surely be regarded by the devout as an obstacle in the way of the Kingdom rather than an instrument for the hastening of its coming.

When the Churches turn the whole force of their ministries and the loyalty of their congregations into the task of spiritualizing the atmosphere of the communities within which they function, men will not be backward in savouring the quality of their witness. They will discover that to withdraw from the noisier world into the secret place where power is generated for the whole world's use is by no means to relinquish the service of the active life, but rather to manifest that new and higher type of activity which is not the less real for being primarily spiritual. Growing up to the conception of Christian witness, as the mountain lifts itself to catch the dew wafted from the height of Hermon to fall upon the hill of Zion, the Church will be recognized as rising from the dwelling-place of humanity into that divine mystery whence grace is distilled for the helping and healing of all mankind.

The ages of the future, like those of the past, must be trusted to be agencies of the indwelling Spirit. In spite of all human lapse and apostasy, through ignorance and perversity, God "is working His purpose out." Institutions will often betray the very divine element through which they were embodied, yet, as of old, men will see the glint of the descending City of God through the ruin of what is temporal. Individuals will often enough betray the grace through which they were meant to grow up to the measure of the stature of the fullness of Christ, yet the failure of the Christian will not obscure the fact that, to those who seek Him, Christ is an ever-present source of strength. A nominally Christian society may still, through wars and lynchings, and all other forms of social injustice, betray the ideals which hold forth the promise of a redeemed humanity, yet the failures will but stimulate to fresh effort through shame and penitence. The religion which is found hard, and so remains untried, will insist on being tried before being condemned. Men who have built on false foundations or with untempered mortar, when they have seen their error, will begin again, and learn to build aright. All through, moreover, those whose eyes are open will discern the abiding presence and take courage from the slow march of men towards "the bounds of the waste." "Even now," says Dr. R. A. Holland, "the streets of the City of God turn to gold under errands of duty, and its meanest hovels shine like celestial mansions when the heavenly Father's children are greeted in their doorways; and its works, and cares, and sympathies—the farm, the shop, the mill, the wharf, hospitals, and schools, and hustings, and council chambers, and halls of justice—all have tints and lustres that fit them for foundation gems in the City of God. Immortality has begun."

Faithful and fearless, gratefully mindful of the past, yet ever confident as to the future, pandering to no man or movement, or age or race, yet bearing in her hands unfailing consolation for all, patient with the frailties of men and with the mysterious providences of God, firm to maintain and free ever to restate, the Church need never heed the cry of the panic-mongers that "the foundations are being cast down" and that we must therefore "flee as a bird unto their hill." The vision of the New Jerusalem is in our hearts, and the power to build up on earth according to the pattern revealed from heaven is in our hands. It is ours to resolve, and to work, until the resolve be realized:

> Bring me my bow of burning gold;
> Bring me my arrows of desire;
> Bring me my spear; O clouds, unfold,
> Bring me my chariot of fire!
> I will not cease from mental fight,
> Nor shall my sword sleep in my hands,
> Till I have built Jerusalem
> (Within this) green and pleasant land.[1, 2]

---

[1] William Blake, *From the Prophetic Book "Milton."*

[2] The following books will be found useful on the general subject of this chapter: J. W. C. Wand, *A History of the Modern Church*, New York, 1929; Rufus M. Jones, *Pathways to the Reality of God*, New York, 1931; same author, *A Preface to Christian Faith in a New Age*, New York, 1932; Joseph Fort Newton (Editor), *My Idea of God*, Boston, 1926; W. E. Orchard, *The Present Crisis in Religion*, New York, 1929; Charles L. Slattery (Editor), *Christ in the World To-day*, New York, 1927; Charles Fiske, *Christ and Christianity*, Milwaukee, 1930; Harry Emerson Fosdick, *Adventurous Religion*, New York, 1926; B. H. Streeter, *The Buddha and the Christ*, New York, 1933; P. T. R. Kirk, *The Movement Christwards*, Milwaukee, 1931; Shailer Mathews, *The Growth of the Idea of God*, New York, 1931.

# EPILOGUE

## CHAPTER XLIII

## *Beyond the Veil*

THE history of religion started, as we have seen, beyond the veil which hangs over the first awakening of creation into consciousness. It is but natural, therefore, that the story should pass again behind the veil which for the present conceals creation's future. The entire process of creation, like the soul of man itself, goes " from the great deep to the great deep."

The physicists tell us that there is still reasonable prospect of much extended experience of humanity upon this planet. Barring accidents, we are told, man's life here on earth so far, by comparison with what may still lie ahead, is but as the thickness of a postage-stamp measured against the height of some Alpine peak. Such a forecast, of course, implies room for much in the way of foolishness, for all manner of experiments in vice and godlessness. Yet, if we bear in mind the general line of human evolution, it gives also much ground for hope. Human nature is not likely to change radically as to its demands in the way of spiritual satisfaction, and the opportunity of coming nearer to the realization of its ideals is thus immeasurably enhanced. In view of the progress seen to be possible, our failures and lapses will cease to be impressive. What now seem to be mountainous illustrations of loss and defeat will have dwindled to the proportion of mole-hills. The race still has its chance to make " a new and a better world," on a scale which would seem incredible to modern reformers in a hurry.

This is, of course, as it should be. Religion has, at least for the present, a definitely terrestrial interest. It is surely, under present circumstances, the concern of religion to promote better business, better politics, better social conditions, better education, in short a wider distribution of happiness and of health. The effort to transform the world will be itself transforming.

Yet the humanizing and Christianizing of a merely terrestrial civilization will remain a quite inadequate object for religion. When Emerson was asked if he realized that the end of the world was imminent he responded, "I can get along very well without it." We shall all have to learn to get along without this present world. Be the end near or distant, our solar system, according to a law of thermodynamics, is "running down." Therefore, under such limitations, to speak of progress is only to adopt a new kind of geocentric philosophy in place of the old one. All we may ever be able to boast of in the way of progress, be that progress physical, intellectual or spiritual, must be ultimately waste effort, if Nature, which began by being our mother, is at last to prove our undertaker. However great our courage, we can scarcely fail to be haunted by the proffered spectacle of final failure, when the cooling sun shall have removed the last possibility of continued life on this planet. In the light of hopes excited, enterprises essayed, struggles to carry on through pain and sacrifice, how ironical must be the conclusion if, to the Divinity who made possible so much frustrated faith, and hope, and love, we have to say at last: "This one began to build and was not able to finish!" Or must we postulate of Nature the indifference, worse than powerlessness, which cries: "I care for nothing; all shall go"? In either case, what becomes of all the edifices, material and moral alike, which have been reared through æons of struggle? In the prospect of so tragic an end, has the effort to carry on the development of character something beyond the savage level been worth the while? If the victory towards which we have been fighting our way be but illusion, "why urge the long, unequal fight?"

Thus it becomes plain that, unless we desire to connive at our own delusion, we must look beyond the fate of this planet to find sufficient stimulus for the doing of the things we feel instinctively are worth the doing. Hence, the query, Is there an ascending stream of energy, of a spiritual character, to which we belong more than to that descending stream of material energy to which we are attached in time and space? The possibilities of life beyond this planet are certainly important for the individual and for society alike. Let us first ask as to the possibilities of personal survival for the individual.

To begin with, the question will occur, Is it desirable? We can hardly accept the statement of Eucken that as the Beyond has retired more and more into the background, we have needed it less and less and that the doctrine of immortality has lost its roots in the soul of the modern man. Huxley, on the other hand, was wont to say that the older he got the less he relished the idea of extinction. It is, of course, true that human life must find its meaning "through work in time and the experience of time," but this life in time must be rooted in an order which exists beyond time. It is a wrong conception of life as well as a wrong conception of immortality which is responsible for the sad lines of Robert Buchanan:

> Perchance He will not wake us up, but when
> He sees us look so happy in our rest,
> Will murmur, Poor dead women and dead men,
> Dire was their doom and weary was their quest—
> Wherefore awake them unto life again?
> Let them sleep on untroubled, it is best.

or the still gloomier and more rebellious words of James Thomson:

> We do not ask a longer term of strife,
> Weakness, and weariness, and nameless woes;
> We do not claim renewed and endless life,
> When this which is our torment here shall close,
> An everlasting, conscious inanition!
> We yearn for speedy death in full fruition,
> Dateless oblivion and divine repose.

When the present life is of such a quality as to make us crave for "dateless oblivion," there is little more to be said. One must find meaning in the life which now is, before we can aspire to have more of the same. Dr. Rufus Jones well says: "The appraisal of life as something worthy of immortality is the first step toward the discovery of solid grounds for the faith that it will be immortal." Christ especially stressed the need of knowing "eternal life" here and now, in order that men might embrace "the glory of going on," and Harnack is faithful to that teaching when he asserts: "Christianity is one simple and sublime thing. It is eternal life in the midst of time." We may most of us have been repelled by the crudeness of the symbols men have accepted or invented to bring home to themselves the character of the future life. But all who feel a real zest for life, whether on its intellectual or its moral side, are able to rise above the symbols to the thing symbolized with instinctive faith that the belief in personal survival, which has been man's oldest and most continuous conviction from prehistoric times, will outlast all assaults of doubt.

But another question raises its head: Desirable or not, is personal survival likely? Some have maintained the existence of reasonable evidence, apart from that accepted by Christians on the ground of the resurrection of Christ. Huge masses of literature, of more or less value, have been compiled by Societies of Psychical Research, and evidence has been proffered by Spiritualists as to the return of many a traveller from beyond the bourne of death. Such evidence must be allowed its due weight, and sceptics are not entitled to more than specific disproofs or the expression of their own agnosticism. To most minds the evidence hitherto adduced falls short of constituting proof. We may never be able to demonstrate scientifically the continuance of personal existence beyond the grave. Yet of recent years not a few men, distinguished in science and philosophy, have expressed themselves hopefully as to the scientific reasonableness of such a doctrine. For example, we have the words of Bergson to the effect that survival is not only possible but probable: "In its passage through the matter which it finds here, consciousness is tempering itself like steel, and preparing itself for a more efficient action, for an intenser life." According to Höffding, "The whole course of evolution is to increase and intensify values and it does so by bringing out that which was potential or latent, so as to make it actual or real." Or, to quote Professor William McDougall of Harvard, "The predominance of mind in the later stages of the evolutionary process, the indications of purposive striving at even the lowest levels, the combination of marvellous persistency of type with indefinite plasticity" are all predictive of a destiny beyond the material universe. If we dare say no more, we may at least affirm that the theory of personal survival is so reasonable and so in accord with the demands and intuitions of our nature, that the shaping of the present life on any other hypothesis must inevitably limit the character of our ideals and so the range of our experience. In any case, the denial, in the name of science, of the possibility of persisting personality is gratuitous. As Mr. H. G. Wells points out in the early part of his *Outline of History*, there was a point in the evolution of life when that life was associated with water, as its home, its medium, and its fundamental necessity. It seemed demonstrable that life must perish as soon as living things climbed above the water-line, just as jelly-fish dry up and perish on the sea-beaches. Yet some instinct in the climbing organism proved victorious over the menace of death. Life did climb and succeeded in adjusting itself to other conditions. It is at least as reasonable to believe that this will prove true of the life which has become valuable enough to the cosmic purpose to pass beyond the conditions of its present physical organism. As Dr. J. A. Hadfield puts it: "The mind may henceforth become indifferent to the disasters which, in course of nature, are bound to overtake the body, and may hope to survive its destruction and decay —and perhaps thereafter to find or create for itself a 'spiritual body' adapted to a different sphere of existence and to other modes of life."

Of course, no amount of probability so far constitutes what the scientist can be asked to accept as demonstration. The doctrine of the future life is, for the Christian, based on faith, not on sight. This is as it should be. It were not well, in the interest of the present, to be too sure about the future. Two modern poets have dealt with the return of Lazarus from the grave, as recorded in the Gospel, and each has stressed the fact that the *revenant* did not help the living with any revelation as to the condition of the dead. Tennyson says: "He told it not, or something sealed the lips of that evangelist," while Browning goes further and shows how the earthly life of Lazarus himself was put out of focus by his experience beyond the gates of death. For the Christian, I repeat, both the fact of the future life and its conditions are left to faith. And the experience of the "*Dark Chamber*," with faith as handmaid, is in every way salutary. For faith ultimately rests on love. "We love His stars too well to fear the night." For the present it is enough that man, the most unfinished of created beings, should feel the urge of life beyond this mortal experience, that he should be able to confess with "*Cleon*":

> We know this, which we had not else perceived,
> That there's a world of capability
> For joy, spread round about us, meant for us,
> Inviting us, and still the soul craves all,
> And still the flesh replies, Take no jot more
> Than ere thou climbest the tower to look abroad.

Feeling this, he is content to die in the faith that at the end of this life's volume the words are written: "*To be continued in our next*."

As to the *where* and *what* of the future life religion has been content to teach men in parables. Sometimes, unfortunately, the parable has been mistaken for the fact, the symbol for the reality. Insistence on the retention of outworn symbols suggestive of the life to come is responsible for the distaste or even disgust with which men have viewed the future. Possibly as many have been bored with popular conceptions of the Christian heaven as have been terrified by conceptions of the Christian hell. The request of the little child, trained in the hard school of sabbatarian piety, "Mother, if I'm good, do you think I shall be allowed to leave heaven on Saturday afternoons to play in hell?" reflects the natural result of such conceptions. The entire story of religion ought to teach us to escape from misconceived finalities in ideas as to the future life, on and ever onward to the grasping of more adequate symbols. In the advance from primitive religion men won a higher hope for the dead than that of a mere gathering in the subterranean dwelling-place of the ancestral shades. It was again a great advance to envisage those happy fields where to hunt and fight constituted man's main activity, even though there was pleasure in quaffing mead from the skulls of fallen foes. It was a still greater advance when heaven became a series of spheres nicely graded to reward men for certain kinds and degrees of primitive virtue. So men passed to the grasping of other symbols of bliss, to exchange these in course of time for others still. In the first Christian centuries these symbols were still sufficiently crude. There were holdovers from various stages of Hebrew eschatology, intrusions from the mythologies of Greece and Rome, millennial dreams from the Far East. Some views were as material as the one described by Papias, in which the Kingdom is depicted as a gigantic vine with a thousand branches, each branch with a thousand bunches of grapes, and each grape bursting with a superabundance of delicious wine. There is little to choose between a heaven of this pattern and that of Muhammad which so well recommended itself to the Arabs. And we are still so close to these ideas that many—not to speak of the negro children in "*The Green Pastures*" who find in heaven a celestial "fish-fry"—are content with the literalism which demands of God reward eternal in the shape of actual harps and crowns and palms and streets of gold.

Nevertheless, the presence of "the eternal primitive" is not without the suggestion of an inspiration vouchsafed according to our several needs, a means of grace, provided we do not mistake our metaphors for realities. To one, heaven is essentially rest after toil, the folding of quiet hands after a life of cark and care and drudgery. To another it is the promise of fuller activity, after a life of restraint and frustrated effort. To another it is the possibility of fuller knowledge, after years of vain beating against the closed portals of enticing mystery. To another, hampered and fettered by the clogging weight of a besetting sin, it is the proffer of freedom, advance in moral strength and holiness. To another it is greater amplitude of life; to another larger capacity and experience of joy; to still another larger opportunity for fellowship. No symbol, however faulty, may completely disguise the essential validity of these aspirations after life, since all are yearning for more abundance of life, and since for all Christians the flying goal of life is the prayer that we may " be filled with the fullness of Him who filleth all in all." It is thus that religion stimulates the desire and quest for fullness and at the same time both furnishes and spiritualizes the terms in which we express the heart's desire.

Yet are we justified in finding in the doctrine of immortality something more than the fulfilment of human yearning. Immortality is the consummation of that hope which runs through the whole story of religion, from the primitive man's first " sense of the numinous " to the full manifestation of God in Jesus Christ, the faith, namely, that human life is to be lifted up to fellowship with the divine, even as the divine life has reached down to contact with the human. If the infinite God can so project Himself into the experience of the creature, there need be no longer fear lest a jealous God should keep to Himself the overbrimming chalice of immortal life. A divine fullness has become our right, since God has established His own right to immanence in creation. It is on this ground of the Incarnation that the best thought of the day has insisted so passionately that life's enlargement is assured beyond the power of death to arrest it. Love must necessarily fulfil itself because of its likeness to the love of God. It is no longer blasphemy to say, " O thou soul of my soul, I shall clasp thee again." Knowledge must necessarily have its full fruition, so that here below, without distrust or impatience, we may do our work—even underground work, never to be revealed to or rewarded by man, work " aiming at a million," even though it may seem to miss its unit. Work, again, of every worthy sort, is made possible, because it is in line with what God asks of His partners. The artist in John Masefield's poem, *Dauber*, who, striving to paint the sea-scape aright, works as a common sailor and falls from the slippery mast, expresses but the truth when he cries: " It shall go on "—

> The eager faces glowered red like coal;
> They glowed, the great sea glowed, the sails, the mast.
> " It will go on," he cried aloud, and passed.

Even unfulfilled hopes, and our very failures, have promise of fulfilment in the hope that

> All we have willed, or hoped, or dreamed of good shall exist;
> Not its semblance, but itself; no beauty, nor good, nor power,
> Whose voice has gone forth, but each survives for the melodist,
> When eternity affirms the conception of an hour.
> The high that proved too high, the heroic for earth too hard,
> The passion that left the earth to lose itself in the sky,
> Are music sent up to God by the lover and the bard;
> Enough that he heard it once: we shall hear it by and by.

But we may go further than the thought of the fulfilment of the individual life. Many have perhaps failed to give complete expression to the Christian doctrine of immortality because too limited in their concern with the implications of the Incarnation as they bear upon the individual. The Creed contains the doctrine of the Communion of Saints as well as that of the Resurrection of the Body. The desire for reunion with a loved one, or the desire to fill one's cup to overflowing with knowledge, must not be placed out of relation with the fulfilment of an eternal purpose of which the perfecting of the individual is but a part. The faith which looks to heaven as merely the opportunity to secure personal ends, however exalted, is as defective as the Buddhism which makes nothing at all of these individual perfections. The purpose which goes on is cosmic, and we go along with it, because the cosmos cannot be complete without its parts, particularly those parts which represent the supreme gains of the evolutionary process.

Here is the triumphant issue the envisaging of which, and the attainment of which, constitute the ultimate aim of religion. It has had as yet no embodiment on earth, nor ever can have, though millions have lived in the light of the vision, seeing that which is invisible and beholding as present that which is still far off. The several stages of religious history catch glimpses of the issue, but only to betray it, and where men rest content with the form of their betrayal there Christ becomes Antichrist and their Church the "harlot" rather than the "Bride." Fortunately, however, the Church has seldom lacked its seers to recall men's hearts from the travesties of the time to the substance of the eternal vision—the eternally ideal which is also the only real. To one of these we may turn, in conclusion, as to the stimulus of a prophetic eye, in order that this faulty survey of the faith of men from the beginning of time may close upon a note not all unworthy of the theme.

For it is Dante, and Dante alone, who with wings divinely strong, beyond the power of any Icarus to emulate him, soars into the upper regions of religious philosophy that he may suggest for us something of the comprehensive sweep of the Christian faith as it bears upon the world of reality. In the *Divina Commedia* I find the dramatization of the whole process I have sought to keep in mind and to describe. The poet's theme is nothing less than that of the infinite energy of the divine Will, fulfilling the purpose of divine Wisdom, sustained by the inexorable might of divine Love: "the love that moves the sun in heaven and all the stars."

All this, which is the expression of the very nature and character of Almighty God, is seen as operant on the cosmic material—a material which, however refractory, has affinity with the will, and reason, and heart of God. But the creature's will is as yet weak and errant; the creature's reason gropes uncertainly with unopened eyes; the creature's love is as yet self-centred and perverse. If Creation, to fulfil the Creator's plan, is to be taken up into partnership, that the universe may become indeed a cosmos, one harmonious and perfected whole, then God must lift up His handiwork to the level of Himself. How may this be effected? To lower the divine standard in order to make the creature inheritor of a heaven less splendid than the dwelling-place of God, is to do violence to the fidelity of the Creator to His plan and to contradict the optimism of Almighty Love. To crush the creature into servile compliance with the Supreme Will is to do violence to the freedom which is part of man's essential endowment. What other course is conceivably open except the process of divine education which employs judgement as the means of maintaining before the eyes of men the standards of divine holiness and trains men to aspire to and love these standards through the patience and love and faith which represent the method of the Cross?

Hence the ultimate destiny of each and all must be viewed in relation to the creature's attitude in the presence of the Creator's untiring love. The will that revolts against the eternal law, imagining that persistence in revolt will leave man free to sin or immune from suffering for sin, must learn the lesson that we are by our very nature bound to suffer, not merely *for* sinning but *by* sinning. The rebel soul thus finds hell to be the reaction of his own attitude to the Will which is alone his peace. Then, secondly, the will which repents its wilfulness, but suffers still from the weakness which the habit of sin has left behind, must be sustained, as well as disciplined, until the weakness is outgrown. Thirdly, the will which, without other compulsion than that of love, has learned the peace which flows from obedience to law (the law of its own nature as well as the law of God) enters into the fullness of joy in a Paradise which is essentially nearness to the Throne of God.

Two things in all this are held to be fundamental. The first is that God evermore respects the freedom of His creatures' being, even as He must respect His own. The gains of evolution are in this respect absolute, not wantonly to be tossed aside out of indifference or despair. God does not create, as was imagined did Brahma, worlds which are outbreathed in sport and again inbreathed as things no more substantial than a mirage. In the lowest depths of hell, as well as in the spheres of Paradise, the optimism of divine Love holds fast that which the far-seeingness of divine Faith first launched into being. God is indeed "*the Hound of Heaven*," who through all the æons follows after the soul which seeks to evade pursuit. The soul at last is fain to confess:

> Halts by me that footfall:
> Is my gloom after all
> Shade of His hand outstretched caressingly?
> Ah, fondest, blindest, weakest,
> I am He whom thou seekest!
> Thou dravest love from thee, who dravest Me.

Thus the immortality of man, which secures the infinite spaciousness needful to achieve his ultimate perfection, is not merely the answer vouchsafed to man's own lust for life, but springs out of God's fidelity to His own primal purpose, regard for "His own Name's sake," as well as regard for the satisfaction of His children.

The second point is that—a point already stressed—God's regard for personal values must always be considered in close relation to His regard for the entire cosmic plan. Individual perfection is conditioned by its fitting into the whole scheme. It is only thus that we can round off our conception of the universal fellowship we have tried all along to keep in mind. Individual evolution and social evolution reach their consummation at one single point. So the pains of the *Inferno* are pains resulting from man's selfish disregard of the social rights violated by his sin. In proportion as he sins against society he sinks to the lowest vortex of self-abasement. The miserly and the spendthrift lose their very names, the things which most of all mark man's individuality; thieves lose the confidence which even thieves crave on the part of their fellows; liars lose that faith in the word of man which even liars know to be the necessary foundation of society. And at the awful focus of the horrible funnel, in the thick-ribbed ice, is Lucifer, the last embodiment of self, the supreme traitor against the divine plan, alone but for the three typical traitors he macerates in his infernal jaws, Cassius, Brutus and Judas, betrayers of the purpose which would have had all men under one rule of Church and State. Then, as we survey the paths which encircle the Mount of Purgatory, we see men climbing, and learning as they climb, the corrective of their former sins in the discipline of healing fellowship. The proud lean on one another's shoulders, who once chose to walk alone; the envious through purged eyes learn to look in love upon their fellows. And so on, till all the weakness of sin, which once kept men separate, is done away, and entry is permitted into the beauties of the terrestrial Paradise. Then, once again, we see in the *Paradiso* men discovering their true joy in ever closer fellowship as they mount from planetary sphere to planetary sphere, and so on towards the Beatific Vision. In every sphere some form of celestial fellowship is related to some special symbol of fellowship. The theologians who formed factions in the lower life are here to be seen hand in hand, making truth's perfect circle, a circle which revolves so quickly that every single truth is blended into a great wheel of stainless light. Martyrs in the heaven of Mars form themselves into the glorious Cross of Paradise, the cross which is the eternal symbol of redeeming love. Rulers in Jupiter spell out together the motto: "Love righteousness, ye that are judges of the earth," and form the symbolic figure of the imperial eagle. Mystics, again, in Saturn, make, through the fellowship of their ecstasy, the celestial ladder on which angels ascend and descend between heaven and earth. So from sphere to sphere men's spirits are borne from one glory of communion to another, till at the last the goal of all desire is reached, where all souls are knit together into the great White Rose of Bliss, which opens to the light streaming upon it from the face of God, and sends up into that face the fragrance of a perfected human devotion.

What a vision of the cosmic plan is here presented, fruit of all the toil of endless æons, victory of Infinite Love's eternal patience, *Rosa mystica*, with every petal, perfect in its individual beauty, blended into the one perfection of the universal. This is indeed the flower of which the poet sings, in answer to the question, "What does it take to make a rose?"—

> The God that died to make it knows,
> It takes the world's eternal wars,
> It takes the sun and all the stars,
> It takes the might of heaven and hell,
> And the everlasting love as well.

It is the making of this which constitutes the plot of that cosmic epic of which, from point to point, we have been trying to follow the development. Vision may well "fail the towering fantasy," however we view the stupendous theme, whether we look back to beginnings, or forward to their consummation. Yet, fail as we may or falter, we are

inevitably heartened when we turn our eyes i
little and local to gain even the faintest glimps
which embraces all " from life's minute beginni
the glory of Creation and Creator at one. We ar
to discover that all the tremendous reaches of t
the universe must have seemed, not only lifeless
but aimless, were nevertheless not outside the range of the operation of the divine Spirit; that all those countless æons when life was slowly climbing out of the water and the mire to inherit the dry land and the upper air, were not left to the dominion of the dragons which " tare one another in the primeval slime," but were already instinct with purpose; that God was not leaving Himself without witness even in the days when the first appearance of man, for millennium after millennium, seemed to produce nothing better than the Cro-Magnon; that, in all the ages since, our impatience is rebuked when we measure the changes our own scant history has been able to record of the upward way. Even to think on these things is to find faith in the forward movement of ages still to come. Are we not therefore justified in declaring that the ultimate summing-up of the epic must correspond worthily with the opening verse of Genesis which declares: " In the beginning God created the heavens and the earth "?

Looking expectantly ahead towards the infinite goal, with all creation represented as the Four Living Ones around the Throne, with all the religious movements of past, present and to come, represented by the Four and twenty Elders, and with all the angelic host, to the outmost rim of infinity, representative of all that lies beyond our tiny but most significant planet, even though we now see but through a glass darkly, and not face to face, we may surely even now join in the great " Amen chorus " of creation, and confess: " Worthy is the Lamb that hath been slain to receive the power and riches and wisdom and might and honour and glory and blessing." To share in that song is not only to discover the vindication of man's religious instinct in the eternal issue, but to pay reverence to that instinct as it has existed from the beginning—the germ of all the values which it has been the mission of story to produce and to conserve. It is to recognize the sanctity of the primitive man's first "sense of the numinous"; it is to triumph in the perfected work:

> Hallelujah to the Maker !
> Hallelujah, man is made !

THE END

# INDEX

B

D

I

N

## Q



## R

T